RUDY!

An Investigative Biography of Rudolph Giuliani

WAYNE BARRETT
Assisted by Adam Fifield

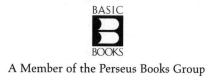

BASIC BOOKS

A Member of the Perseus Books Group

ISBN 0-465-00523-3
A CIP catalog record for this book is available from the Library of Congress.

Design by Elizabeth Lahey
Set in 10 point Aldus
FIRST EDITION

00 01 02 03 / 10 9 8 7 6 5 4 3 2 1

*For Lawrence G. Barrett, whose life of character and courage ended
halfway through this project
but who won the distribution rights in heaven*

C O N T E N T S

Preface   ix

1   Millennial Man   1

2   "Aggressive Traits" and "Haphazard Associations"   13

3   All in the Family: Crooks, Cops and a Junkie   43

4   Launching a Legend   67

5   A Star Rises on the Potomac   91

6   Heat Stroke: Delusions About Duvalier   115

7   Mr. Untouchable   133

8   The War Against Greed   157

9   Looking for Love: The Ed Koch Investigation   175

10 In John Lindsay's Footsteps   189

11 Blood Feud: The Fight with the Fonz   201

12 Political Possession of Stolen Property   221

13 A Season of Compromise: Preparing for 1993   241

14 Seizing City Hall   265

15   Metamorphosis of a Mayoralty   289

16   Brutal Blindside: No Benefits, No Doubts   313

17   These Statistics Are a Crime   341

18   Soap Opera Schools   367

19   Sex and the City   395

20   More Sex and the City   419

21   Soiling Mr. Clean   445

Notes   469

Acknowledgments   471

Index   475

P R E F A C E

I FIRST MET RUDY GIULIANI IN 1979 WHILE REPORTING A *NEW YORK* magazine cover story critical of the public corruption record of the U.S. Attorney's Office in the Southern District of New York. Rudy was a baby-faced, thirty-five-year-old partner at Patterson Belknap, and Tom Puccio, the Abscam prosecutor from the competing Eastern District office across the river, steered me to him to get the SDNY's best defense. I wasn't disappointed. Not surprisingly, all the examples of effective corruption prosecutions Giuliani described over the prior decade involved the same young former assistant—the one apparently born with a comb-over.

Puccio was also responsible for our second meeting more than three years later, when Giuliani returned to New York from a second stint in Washington, where he was associate attorney general. I had written a series of stories that led to a grand jury probe of then-congressman Chuck Schumer. The U.S. attorney in the Eastern District and several high-level Justice Department officials had approved his indictment based on an arguable interpretation of the mail fraud statutes. Giuliani helped kill it. So Puccio arranged a clear-the-air lunch with my *Village Voice* colleague Jack Newfield and myself.

I got to know Rudy well during his five-and-a-half-year term as U.S. attorney. We had periodic dinners and countless conversations. When he tried the municipal corruption case against Democratic powerhouse Stanley Friedman and several other defendants in 1986—a trial moved to New Haven, Connecticut, in search of an untainted jury—I saw him every day for ten weeks. Puccio, Friedman's lawyer, was responsible once again: It was his change of venue motion that created the closed-colony effect of the trial.

Giuliani was the hero of my first book, *City for Sale*, the 1989 chronicle of the corruption scandals of Mayor Ed Koch's administration, which I co-authored with Newfield. He celebrated with us at the book party.

When he left law enforcement for politics, our relationship changed. I never had another meal with him. We still talked often—mostly by phone—though

I went to his law offices and campaign headquarters for periodic head-to-heads. In 1989, I was the first reporter on the Inner City Broadcasting story—a scandal involving stock owned by Rudy's opponent in the New York City mayor's race—that helped him close an eighteen-point gap. He wound up losing by the closest margin in modern city history.

We stayed in frequent contact through the next four years, during which he functioned as a kind of mayor-in-exile and I lifted one rock after another, exposing the administration he hoped to topple. When I banged him hard as well, though, in the 1993 campaign, our relationship changed again. After he won, he told me in a whisper that "Donna thinks you betrayed us"—a reference to his wife, Donna Hanover, the professional journalist in the family. We had a few conversations and interviews in 1994, his first year as mayor, but he was suspicious and highly circumspect. I would never see again the open side of him—which I had seen so often before, a side he turns off and on with an inner, early-alert switch.

When he took a sharp rightward turn with the times in 1995, I wrote plaintive stories appealing to the Rudy I once knew. From then on, as the policies and ethics of his administration disappointed, I became more and more critical. He refused, of course, to talk to me for this book. City commissioners like Henry Stern, whom I have known for almost twenty-five years, told me he asked them not to, and that they were abiding by his rule. His best friend and former deputy, Peter Powers, as decent a public servant as I have known in decades of reporting, talked with me several times about sitting down but finally passed. I kept making it clear that these sources could restrict themselves to telling me only the good news about him, yet they wouldn't meet.

It got so bad that Sunny Mindel, the mayor's press secretary, refused to give me press releases. She twice told me to put the request in writing, then ignored two letters. She earns six figures a year as the top public information officer in city government. She knew a lawsuit would never get resolved before the book would be published.

The book, no doubt, suffers from this recent stonewall. I have never met a thoughtful subject who couldn't change my mind about some element of a story. So could his friends. But for every one who wouldn't talk, many did. Six of Rudy's relatives sat down, one for eighteen hours. Associates from every phase of his pre-mayoral life did. And so much about any government, no matter how secretive, is by definition available that efforts like Mindel's are silly. (I got most of the releases elsewhere anyway.)

People who are or were inside his government—with courageous exceptions like Lilliam Paoli—talked to me off the record, but in Rudyland that is common.

In 1999, the Sunday *New York Times Magazine* published a favorable profile of Giuliani called "Introducing Mr. Nice Guy" that set an all-time *Times* record for blind quotes. People who were praising him insisted on being quoted anonymously, apparently fearful he might be upset that they'd talked at all, to say nothing of what might happen if they got a nuance wrong. Only Rudy's concern about boosting the 6 percent rise in the murder rate in 1999 could have kept them safe.

There is, in any event, just one anonymous source who plays a large role in two chapters—the fly on the wall in Harold Giuliani's bar. His reasons for anonymity lie in the life of criminality he described. I did not decide to use any quotes from him until we verified an extraordinary list of pivotal facts he first told us, ranging from the criminal records of Giuliani family members to the names of their partners, in-laws and lawyers. He even correctly identified what prisons they'd gone to, as well as locations of crimes and other vital events later confirmed by court and property records. As unfailingly accurate as this source was, I chose not to use his most shocking information about Harold and the Brooklyn bar.

The book clearly has a point of view. I lived for fifteen years in Ocean Hill–Brownsville, perhaps the city's poorest neighborhood, a white man in a black world. When Rudy ran for re-election in 1997 against a little-known white woman, he got 14 percent of the vote in my old Brownsville district, a record of rejection unparalleled by any incumbent mayor in identifiable history, including other Republicans. With four years and extraordinary resources to make a friend here or there, exit polls said more than eight out of ten black voters citywide voted for Anybody But Rudy.

Though I left Brownsville many years ago, the experience still frames much of how I see New York politics and government. Through that lens, race is at the heart of Rudy's story; references to it can be found inside almost every chapter. It has also been one of the prime themes of my nearly twenty-three years of *Voice* work.

The other theme has always been public integrity. It is what drew me to Rudy in the first place. My investigative work knows no ideological or partisan limitations—every major Democrat on my beat has taken a hit on my keyboard. Particularly in the 1989 mayoral election, the choice between Rudy and his black opponent, David Dinkins, was a choice between these two motivating values of my journalism and my life. It was the only time I drew the curtain behind me in a voting booth still undecided about which lever to pull.

I identified with Rudy in so many ways in the '80s. He is only a year older than I am, so we shared the same eras. We are both products of sixteen years of Catholic school, and both of us have spent our adult lives in an uneasy truce with the church, never turning our backs on it but keeping our distance. Partly because of that background, no doubt, we shared a strong sense of good and evil, and for a time we chased the same bad guys.

Bill Bastone, who until recently occupied an office with me at the *Voice*, installed a red phone on the wall above my desk in the '80s with a sign that said: "The Rudy Hotline." I imagined myself always on it. My wife, Fran—whose sainthood-qualifying miracle will be her patience during this last mad year—used to scowl at me in my Rudy heyday, always a few senses ahead of me in recognizing the self-serving.

I was seen in liberal circles, where Giuliani became anathema long before he was mayor, as a Rudy man—so much so that to this day when I make appearances before such audiences and talk about him, a questioner will invariably blame me for helping to create him.

I did not know, when I started this book, if I'd misjudged him in the early days or if he had changed. Having learned more about him in the last year than I did in the first twenty years I knew him, I've concluded it's a bit of both. I willfully ignored the stories that surfaced in 1989 about his 1982 war against the Haitians, though I see them now as a predictor of his mayoralty. On the other hand, this book suggests that as mayor he may have lost the moral compass that guided him as a prosecutor. In a *Hoop Dreams*–like metamorphosis, the game of politics has diminished him.

Of course, by the time I finished the book, he was no longer morphing on any level. Changes were coming at a gallop. In each of the four weeks before this book closed, he shocked the city, state and nation with one rapid-fire revelation after another. "The Wonder Bread son of the '50s" suddenly was unraveling as if he were on some kind of speed. Keeping up with him was a psychedelic experience. The *New York Post* even published a piece—on its cover no less—quoting unnamed City Hall sources as saying that he'd decided to go public about his new significant "other," Judi Nathan, because he thought she would appear in these pages. If so, the book had bizarrely become a slice of its own story line, evoking events it could barely keep up with.

The last biography I wrote was of Donald Trump, and the king of the hill nearly went broke, got divorced, hid Marla Maples like a fugitive and became something of a joke in the year and a half I was on the reporting trail. My friend Nick Von Hoffman now greets me on the phone with his motto: "Only Do Dead Men."

With this hex record, I advise my next living subject to pay me not to write.

There are a few items of business the reader should be aware of before getting started:

Throughout the book there are references to a "vulnerability study." It is explained in detail two-thirds of the way through when, at Rudy's insistence, it is destroyed. This five-inch-thick opus was commissioned by Giuliani during the 1993 campaign to assess the weaknesses in his life and record, suggesting responses to every possible blot. I was handed a copy of it in the dead of night on a state turnpike last fall. I was told Rudy had the other copies deep-sixed, even the computer files.

The early chapters contain references to quotes from unpublished interviews that took place in 1988 and 1989. Virtually all these quotes—from Rudy, Helen Giuliani, Alan Placa, Peter Powers, Lloyd MacMahon, Donna Hanover, Regina Peruggi, Kathy Livermore and Joe Jaffe—are on tape; a handful appeared in transcribed form, but the tapes were lost. At first, the quotes are identified as coming from these unpublished interviews. Then, to avoid repeating the phrase, they appear just as quotes, without referring to their "unpublished" origin.

I have detailed the many people indispensable to this book in the acknowledgements at the end, but one person must be named here, just as he is on the cover. Adam Fifield actually wrote drafts of several chapters in this book, influencing Chapters 2 and 3 particularly. He was also a superb research assistant, again especially with those two chapters. His writing and reporting efforts were certainly not limited to those chapters—he also made a major contribution to Chapters 4, 5, 7 and 8. It would be impossible to find a single chapter that he didn't help make better.

This is not said to make him in any way accountable for the sometimes-controversial contents of the early chapters. The buck starts and stops here, and every chapter eventually passed through my computer.

At twenty-eight, Adam is a gifted journalist and a caring friend who was once my *Voice* intern, but from whom I now often take lessons myself—professional and personal. Completing a full biography of a complicated figure like Rudy in a year would have been impossible without Adam. I will always be thankful to him for helping me meet what turned out to be the most demanding challenge of my life.

One

Millennial Man

WITH TWENTY-EIGHT TELEVISION NETWORKS BEAMING LIVE TO AN estimated billion viewers in the world's two dozen time zones, the fifty-five-year-old grandson of Italian immigrants stood center stage at Times Square a minute before midnight, his finger on the trigger of a new millennium.

Rudy Giuliani, the 107th mayor of New York and the first to put himself at the helm of its New Year's ritual, was literally, for the single moment that the Time Ball took its seventy-seven-foot fall, at the Crossroads of the World. In the midst of an historic run for the U.S. Senate against First Lady Hillary Rodham Clinton—a race that could catapult him to Washington stardom—Giuliani was also at the crossroads of his life. Though no one would have believed it that night, just four months into the new millennium, the private world of this steely, moralist would detonate in four successive, pyrotechnic, press conferences, blowing apart, at least temporarily, a career of meticulously mythic measure.

After six years as mayor and five as U.S. Attorney, he'd become a municipal superhero without a cape, a media avenger who embodied the will to vanquish wrongs ranging from the greed of Wall Street to the infamy of common criminality.

He was the best-known law enforcement figure in America since J. Edgar Hoover, and his federal cases were epic: "Fat Tony" Salerno and the heads of the five mob families; Drexel Burnham and its colossus Michael Milken; the Philippines' Imelda Marcos, hotel queen Leona Helmsley and former Miss America Bess Myerson; the Democratic potentate of New York Stanley Friedman; and even the closest advisor to his own boss at the time, Attorney General Ed Meese. He became the model for the network television series, *Michael Hayes,* the story of a big-city U.S. Attorney, and the series star David Caruso came to New York to study him close-up.

The best-known mayor in America since the first Richard Daley, he'd taken aim at the blameless and the notorious: squeegees, the "fake homeless," pan-

1

handlers, sex shop purveyors, cabbies, jaywalkers, street vendors, cop-bashers, un-reconstructed liberals, black radicals, black moderates, anti-Catholic art exhibitors, drunk drivers, methadone users, graffiti artists, public school bureaucrats and, of course, welfare freeloaders. Even as crime plummeted almost everywhere across the nation, he'd managed to make himself the country's top cop, a legend whose zero tolerance stopped criminals in their tracks and tamed the toughest tribal streets. Booming Times Square itself, with glut replacing smut, was a symbol of the New York he'd re-created, an electric urban theme park as safe and, some said, sterile as a suburban mall.

America's mayor was atop the giant, thirty-five-foot-high "Temple of Time" riser in the middle of Broadway that night, his face alight with giddy joy, rubbing his hands together again and again in anticipation of hitting the one-foot crystal button, dancing to the pounding music and hugging his three handpicked companions.

With him were Ron Silver, the actor who'd hosted so many of his campaign fundraisers and now chaired the mayor's NYC 2000 Committee; Dr. Mary Ann Hopkins,, the millennial honoree whose war-zone work with Doctors Without Borders won the Nobel Prize; and Brendan Sexton, the president of the Times Square Business Improvement District (BID), the city-supported sponsor of the ninety-four-year-old ball-drop spectacle. Hopkins was a stand-in for Giuliani's first choice, Elian González, the six-year-old Cuban posterboy of the right.

When midnight struck, three tons of multicolored confetti was fired from thirteen buildings around the square by crews with hand-held cannons. A computer-generated fifty-piece symphony orchestra blasted through eighteen speakers attached to eighteen buildings. Seven minutes of fireworks lit up the sky. Sixty-one spotlights panned the scene, alive with seven giant Astrovision screens and seven-foot-tall numerals bursting into view atop One Times Square. The thousand-pound, six-foot-tall ball of Waterford Crystal, with 786 lights and mirrors, hit ground zero. Eight thousand cops barricaded off the fifty blocks of midtown filled with 700,000 penned-up celebrants, magically transformed into two million by a mayor who regularly breaks records by statistical fiat.

As soon as the climactic instant passed, Giuliani, his chiseled teeth flashing, rushed off the platform to the camera crews below, while his three companions remained. He had known the joy of two electoral wins and two inaugurals, two weddings and the birth of two children, two swearing-ins for powerful Justice Department posts and two for junior, career-building jobs. But this was the golden moment of his life and still he knew it was all prelude.

He had sensed since he was a boy at a Brooklyn high school that he was destined for greatness, maybe even the presidency. He rebuffed reporters now who asked him whether he would serve out his six-year Senate term should he beat Hillary. He did it because he believed that if George W. Bush lost in 2000, he could run and win in 2004. The millennial stage—with him coolly handling both the terrorist and the tipsy—offered a giant but fleeting box office, a chance to briefly insinuate himself into the subconscious of tens of millions of Americans.

Within twenty minutes of the celebration, Giuliani was on the phone with Jerry Hauer, the director of his Office of Emergency Management. The steadiest crisis hand in Rudy's administration, Hauer was already in the midst of a press conference at the city's downtown command center. Hauer and Deputy Mayor Joe Lhota, two Giuliani managers widely respected by the press corps, had agreed to appear for a post-midnight briefing with the seventy-five reporters and cameras waiting in the room right off the newly constructed emergency center. They were in the middle of describing an uneventful evening when an aide interrupted to tell Hauer: "The mayor wants to talk to you." While Hauer listened on a cell, Lhota smiled and said: "I hope this is a sanctioned press conference." Apparently it wasn't. In mid-sentence, the two left the press room and retreated to the command facility.

Giuliani shared face time on camera with no one. He ran an administration of media midgets and statues; when a camera was on, the most they could be was part of the set. Though Rudy would not get back to the command center until nearly 2 A.M., he wanted to have the final word on the successful management of a night that had actually managed itself. It was one of the warmer January nights, so the city's medical stations were underused. There were far fewer arrests than on a typical night, and no serious crime. Bomb threats went up slightly—one of Rudy's first, personally delivered, bulletins—but they were all bogus.

The biggest daylight story was a steam leak on the West Side that reporters in the command center heard about from their editorial desks. When they tried to get confirmation and details, no one at the emergency center would answer their questions. Mary Gaye Taylor, a usually staid radio reporter, had to call outside the compound to find out what had happened and went on the air reporting that there was only one person in this administration who could answer a question. And the mayor had not shown up yet.

In fact, the assembled press horde could not even see into the command center until Giuliani arrived, since a white screen was drawn over the large soundproof window that separated the press room from the center. Just before Rudy entered the room to handshakes and applause early in the evening, the curtain was lifted. That way there was nothing to shoot unless he was in the picture. Asked about the closed screen at his 5:30 press briefing, he attributed it with characteristic humor to the comfort of the staff: "Who knows what they might want to scratch?" he said of the mostly male emergency crew. When he left, a stooped, six-foot bundle of intensity and command shuffling face down in the direction of his next performance, the screen was dropped again, to the grumbles of reporters.

U.S. Senator Chuck Schumer, a Democrat whose wife was a deputy commissioner in her third successive city administration, appeared at the command center with their children shortly before midnight. His wife had to be there, so he joined her. Reporters lured him into the press room for a brief conference shortly after midnight. The screen was momentarily up. He was asked how the mayor had handled the night's events and he delivered one laudatory quote after another. "Excellently" was the starter. Suddenly the screen was drawn and reporters discovered that the mayor's staff had apparently pulled the plug on the senator's audio feed, unaware of what he was saying but sure that Rudy wanted no one speaking from his podium but himself.

Reporters didn't ask Giuliani where his wife of fifteen years, television personality Donna Hanover, and two children, ten-year-old Caroline and thirteen-year-old Andrew, were that night, though the kids would certainly have enjoyed the Times Square extravaganza, if not the high-tech emergency center. Donna had come with him for the 1994 ball-drop. She'd come again in 1995, though this time in a separate car. That was her last appearance at his side at Times Square—inside or outside the camera lens. The press had become so used to Donna's absence at this and other major events, and his annoyance with any question about it, that it had stopped asking. Photos of the kids were half-expected to appear on milk cartons any day now, they'd been missing so long.

As big as the night was, his forgotten family did not attract a sentence of ink, though Giuliani had just positioned himself in national fundraising letters as a champion of school prayer, the posting of the Ten Commandments in schools and more religious "faith" in American public life. Unbeknownst to the press, Donna and the kids had actually gone to a party she hosted for a dozen or more friends in the 20-something floor of the new Condé Nast building on 42nd Street, right next to the descending ball. The children could look down on their father's balding head, watch his stiff and mechanical waves and see him on a giant screen just as they often saw him on smaller ones at home in Gracie Mansion.

His family crisis, rumbling just beneath the surface for half a decade, was one of the earthquakes that would erupt a few months into the new millennium.

Another was the woman who shuttled back and forth with him all night—from command center to Times Square. Judi Nathan, just turned forty-five but looking much younger, had become his constant companion. The glacial barriers that divided his home sent him looking for warmth elsewhere, he rationalized, though it was looking for warmth elsewhere that had prompted the barriers in the first place.

He loved living on the edge and even as he plunged into the hottest Senate race in modern history, he dared the media to expose him. When he walked into the Times Square facility to flashbulbs that night, she was two steps behind him, looking down and away, bejeweled and decked out in a low-cut dark dress and a brocade-trimmed coat, a gold necklace, locket and pendant framing a beaming face. The mayor hosted his own party—minus Donna—at the All Star Café and Nathan was there, sparkling. His secret life on display gave him a personal power surge to complement the 225 million watts of power flowing through the square that night.

A third woman made a stunningly brief appearance at the Broadway press island underneath the platform. Cristyne Lategano, only seven months after stepping down as the second most powerful person in Rudy's government, had to call the Times Square BID to get access passes. Though appointed two years earlier to the four-member executive committee of Giuliani's NYC 2000 apparatus, she apparently could not get any kind of committee or NYPD pass. The new president of the Convention and Visitors Bureau, an independent but city-supported tourism booster, Lategano said she had to do a couple of interviews at the event.

Only a year earlier she'd run the 1999 ball-drop press arrangements. She was then a special woman in Rudy's life, the subject of scandalous surmise for so long that her presence with the mayor was as much an assumption as Donna's absence. She, too, at thirty-three, about to marry a golf writer she'd just met, was a time bomb set to rock Rudy's ambitions.

Around him that night were not just reminders of his personal disarray. *Ragtime*, the big musical that had opened a new theater on revived 42nd Street, was headlined by Alton Fitzgerald White, a black actor playing a victim of official misconduct at the turn of the century who was suing the NYPD for the real thing in 1999. On his way out of his Harlem apartment building to do a matinee performance that July, White was grabbed by cops looking for an Hispanic man, strip-searched and incarcerated for five hours.

If Giuliani was to bask in the glory of the city's plummeting crime rate, he also had to live with the sting of nationally spotlighted cases of NYPD brutality and rising indexes of cop misconduct. Other major cities—like San Diego and Boston—showed that it was possible to get one without the other.

The new $13 million command center the mayor visited twice that night was freely referred to in the *Times*'s January 1 coverage as a "bunker," a symbol of Giuliani's weakness for gadgetry, secrecy and militarist overkill. Located on the twenty-third floor of the World Trade Center and equipped with a video conferencing/hotline hookup to the White House, the facility had displaced an existing, state-of-the-art, emergency center.

Combined with the deployment of an astonishingly excessive 37,000 cops city-wide that night, the bunker was emblematic of an administration that had unconstitutionally closed City Hall Park to all but mayorally sanctioned public spectacle, blockaded bridges to kill a cab protest, barricaded midtown crosswalks to regulate pedestrians and yanked the homeless out of shelter beds on the coldest night of the year to enforce ancient bench warrants for open beer can violations.

"Freedom," said the mayor who put snipers on the roof of City Hall for an AIDS demonstration, "is the willingness of every single human being to cede to lawful authority a great deal of discretion about what you do and how you do it." He had a new rule a day for everyone in New York—blocking thousands more than necessary from a view of the ball that night, for example—but defied the most basic social precepts himself.

Times Square itself was a metaphor for Rudy's government—brash, self-serving claims of transforming achievement with little or no substance. As often as he cited the comeback of this seedy midtown core as one of the prime accomplishments of his administration, no one outside his hype office could cite a single development decision jump-started by his team.

He grabbed credit for Disney's pivotal determination to rebuild an old 42nd Street theater by announcing it at a grandiose City Hall press conference with Governor Mario Cuomo. The announcement came a month into his first year. In fact, Disney, the state and the administration of the previous mayor, David Dinkins, had signed the memo of understanding (MOU) celebrated at that press conference on December 31, 1993, the final day of David Dinkins's term.

Barry Sullivan, a Dinkins deputy mayor, signed the memo and three other agreements with Disney on a metal detector at City Hall as he was leaving the building for the last time. Dinkins, who'd lost to Giuliani a month earlier in a nasty rerun of their 1989 mayoral campaign, wanted to announce the Disney deal, but the savvy Michael Eisner, CEO of the globe's master myth-making monopoly, preferred to wait. He wanted the new mayor to make the deal his own by letting him announce it. So while Disney signed the December memo, it also insisted on a confidentiality agreement.

The side-letter explicitly stated that the parties would not "issue any press release, hold any press conference or make any other public statement" regarding the MOU. In the event of press inquiries, the parties pledged to respond: "There are still some open issues; no further comment at this time" or "no comment."

Though Eisner had been lured to New York by an architectural consultant retained by the Dinkins and Cuomo administrations, Robert A. M. Stern, and by a member of the *New York Times*'s Sulzberger family, Marian Heiskell, he did not announce the decision until February 2, 1994, when he could do it at Giuliani's side. The confidentiality agreement never became public. The press release for the announcement said the parties "have entered into an MOU" without saying when they did or mentioning the role of Dinkins, already the Invisible Mayor.

As crucial as Disney's arrival was, the Square's rebound was rooted in other events that had long preceded it. Cuomo and Mayor Ed Koch approved the creation of a development project for the area a decade before Giuliani took office, targeting unique tax abatements for redevelopers of the strip and authorizing massive condemnation of the porn palaces and other marginal operators that dominated it. Turning over control of the thirteen-acre site to a developer, George Klein, and Prudential, the city and state traded the abatements for Prudential's willingness to spend hundreds of millions of dollars to acquire and clear it. The Dinkins administration threw in an extra $35 million from its capital budget for additional condemnation in 1993.

Encouraged no doubt by this unprecedented public and private undertaking, Bertelsmann, Viacom and Morgan Stanley made major investments in the area just off 42nd Street before Rudy took office. Viacom signed its first lease at 1515 Broadway in 1990 and gradually took over twenty-six floors in the building at 45th Street, moving much of its MTV operations there. Aided by an $11 million incentive package from the Dinkins administration, Bertelsmann bought 1540 Broadway in 1992 for its Bantam Doubleday Dell Publishing Group and RCA Records divisions. Morgan Stanley acquired 1585 Broadway for its own use in 1993, and later closed on a second building in the area (750 Seventh Avenue), bolstered by $100 million in city and state incentives.

Bertelsmann and Morgan bought vacant, bankrupt buildings and added thousands of upscale pedestrians to Times Square streets. Bertelsmann also began negotiating with Virgin Records in 1993 to open the largest music store in the world on the commercial floors of its new tower.

Another turning point was the redesign of the Times Square plan completed by Yale's Robert Stern in 1993, replacing the Rockefeller Center vision of George Klein with what critics called "the honky-tonk diversity" of a "jumbled, kinetic, dazzling and loud" street featuring entertainment and retail uses. With tourist traps, hip outlets, amusements, theaters, a rooftop billboard park, garish signage and name-brand superstores, the Stern plan recognized the area's "genius," said a

Times critic, and encouraged it "to shine." Prudential vowed to invest an immediate $20 million to make it happen.

Shortly after the release of the Stern plan and two weeks before Giuliani was elected, New 42nd Street, a not-for-profit founded by the city and state to develop new theaters, announced an $11 million renovation of the Victory Theater, paid for by Prudential. Chaired by Marian Heiskell, New 42nd Street was another *Times*-connected effort to spur development in the area around its 43rd Street flagship property.

Arthur Sulzberger Jr., the current *Times* publisher, also founded and chaired the Times Square BID, which began operations in January 1992. Funded primarily through special tax assessments approved by the Dinkins administration, the BID brought together major business interests in the area and added an annual average of $7 million to the sanitation, security and other services already provided by the city. The BID was another pre-Giuliani building block re-energizing the area, opening a visitor center in January 1993 and launching a $1.4 million sidewalk lighting project.

Madame Tussaud's and American Multi Cinema did not actually close Times Square deals until the summer of 1995, but both began looking at the square in the Dinkins era. Dinkins deputies went to London to lure Tussaud's, but two early near-deals fell apart. The wax museum and AMC's massive twenty-six-screen theater were part of a 335,000-square-foot complex built by developer Bruce Ratner. But the Giuliani administration resisted state efforts to push the project until Ratner, Mayor Giuliani's top campaign fundraiser, was chosen to develop it without the usual competitive bidding process. Also forcing the city to end its recalcitrance was Disney, which retained a right to withdraw from the project if two other major entertainment companies didn't commit to it by that July.

Similarly, the other post-1994 linchpin to the Square's resurgence was developer Douglas Durst's decision to finally build one of the four office towers long planned for the strip. Durst, too, faced city resistance to okaying Prudential's sale of the site: "To our surprise the administration was initially cold to our attempt to build a new building." Charles Millard, the head of the city's economic development corporation, said the administration wanted stores, not a skyscraper, at the key corner of Broadway and 42nd Street. John Dyson, another deputy mayor, demanded Durst instantly produce a signed term sheet with a major tenant even though Durst, one of the city's most prominent developers, was willing to build at least a retail center if he couldn't get office tenants.

So Durst met Dyson's deadline—signing up Condé Nast, a major media company. The day before a planned three-party press conference announcing the $1.5

billion tower, City Hall leaked the story, taking credit for producing a deal that had started with state officials.

Other skyscrapers followed Durst—with the Rudin family developing an office tower for Reuters and *Daily News* owner Mort Zuckerman building one for Ernst & Young. A Canadian firm, Livent, built the Ford Center for the Performing Arts, and the Tishman Urban Development Corporation was designated to develop a hotel/entertainment center with a thirteen-screen SONY theater. The All Star Café moved into the Bertelsmann building, Warner Brothers opened a major store and ABC opened a studio for their morning show over the street. By then, the market needed no assistance from government to get developments off the ground.

As little as the Giuliani administration had to do with rebuilding the Square, it was always the first at the scene when a new development was celebrated. Its leak of the Condé Nast deal sabotaged the Durst press conference but put Rudy in the project's driver's seat. In the spirit of the Disney announcement, he was center stage at the opening of the New Victory Theatre in 1995, as irrelevant as he was to its restoration. When Governor George Pataki was late for the announcement of the Bruce Ratner complex with Madame Tussaud's and AMC, Giuliani's staff tried to start the press conference without him. Rudy dominated the announcement of the Reuters tower deal just days before his re-election, using it as campaign grist. His annual ball-drop appearance and simultaneous interviews merged him and the revival in the public mind.

Rudy was so concerned about maintaining that illusion that when a *Times* story in January 2000 noted that Dinkins "made the deal with Disney that led to the new Times Square," Giuliani, choking on his own mythology, denounced the simple statement of fact. "The deal that was made to bring Disney to Times Square was made in my office and announced by me," he declared. The *Times* assertion, he said, was the product of "either incompetence or political ideology." Giuliani berated top *Times* brass in phone calls but never made his reasoning clear. It was true that Disney did not sign a final contract with the city and state until 1995, though its essential terms were virtually identical to the Dinkins MOU. Giuliani apparently believed that any deal he didn't blow belonged on his scorecard.

In fact, the only arguable contribution that the Giuliani administration might have made to the Square's renaissance was the local effect of its general crime and sanitation service improvements, and the anti-porn zoning legislation the mayor steered through the City Council. But the BID reported that crime fell in the area 23 percent from January 1993 to January 1994—the year before Giuliani took office. That was a bigger drop than in any Giuliani year except 1994, when it fell 24 percent.

Sidewalk cleanliness soared from a 54.8 percent rating in the city's sanitation scorecard in 1991 to 93.3 percent in Dinkins's last year. Porn dropped from a peak of 140 outlets to twenty-one in 1998 before Giuliani's new law went into effect, with most of the shops eliminated in condemnation. In fact, Giuliani's law was a response to the growing number of porn palaces in residential Queens and was spearheaded not by him, but by a Queens city councilman.

Crime in the area continued to drop slightly, it got marginally cleaner and porn shops fell to seventeen by the end of 1999. The BID's sanitation and security crews clearly contributed to these improvements. In fact, the BID objected when Giuliani actually tried in his initial budget to cut sanitation services to all BID-covered neighborhoods, an illegal redirection of citywide resources.

Instead of Times Square savior, he was its beneficiary, the almost accidental heir to the glory of a booming new street, propelled by two mayors he maligned and a governor who shared the Disney catalyst with him. Its misappropriated saga was a familiar story in Rudy Giuliani's life.

There is little question but that New York City has become a better place to live on Rudy Giuliani's watch. It recovered all the private-sector jobs lost in the most recent national recession. It got dramatically safer and cleaner. The tax load dipped and the budget surplus soared. The fraudulent were forced off welfare. Medical coverage for gay city workers was extended to their domestic partners. There is also little doubt but that the Giuliani administration had something to do with these improvements, but "something" isn't enough for Rudy.

What says it better than Giuliani's rage about a playful ad planted on the side of city buses by *New York* magazine shortly after his re-election in 1997? The magazine described itself as: "Possibly the only good thing in New York Rudy hasn't taken credit for." Rudy forced the Transit Authority to remove the ad. The magazine sued and won. Rudy appealed. He lost again, and even a third time when the Supreme Court refused to hear it. The public cost of defending his ego skyrocketed.

Giuliani mythology doesn't permit recognition of any possible cause other than himself of the city's good fortune. Just as the recession, for example, decimated the city's economy under Dinkins, the national recovery belatedly restored it. The biggest boom in Wall Street history spurred the city's job growth. These are axioms everywhere but City Hall. He points endlessly to the upsurge in the hotel industry and credits it to his minuscule cut in the city hotel tax. The state cut in the same tax, announced before his, was far greater. Who thinks that the millions of international tourists who have flooded New York in recent years came because they saved a tax buck a night on room costs that skyrocketed anyway?

Giuliani mythology also permits no admission of downsides. The soaring budget surpluses, for example, were not used by the mayor to lower the city's awesome debt burden, as practically every fiscal overseer urged. Instead, while posing as a fiscal conservative, Giuliani dumped one year's surplus into the next year's budget, hiking expenditures and deepening the budget gaps projected for the years after he left office.

The city did get cleaner under Giuliani because he was the first mayor to appoint a commissioner who had once hauled garbage himself. The still-obscure John Doherty was Giuliani's finest appointee and the mayor showed the good sense to leave him alone. In Rudy's first year, Randy Levine, the labor commissioner, negotiated the only real productivity improvements achieved with a municipal union and the contract caused the cost of collections to drop from $121 per ton in 1994 to $108 a ton in 1997, in sharp contrast with rising costs in other major cities. But when Doherty left, Giuliani bowed to political pressure from his Staten Island GOP ally, Borough President Guy Molinari, and put a cop from the island on top of the agency. The new commissioner, who was criticized once because he campaigned for Molinari while still a top cop, brought in another ex-police executive. Led by patronage appointees, the place started stinking worse than the garbage.

Staten Island had to control the department to make sure it shut down the giant city dump located there. Giuliani was closing the landfill years before it was necessary to satisfy the borough that gave him his margin of victory in 1993 and would be key to a 2000 Senate race. It did not matter that an anti-recycling and anti-incinerator administration had nowhere else to get rid of the waste. He's now locked the city into spending hundreds of millions a year trucking the garbage to New Jersey, Virginia and anywhere else that will take it.

Similarly, his celebrated welfare cutbacks have harmed tens of thousands of the legitimate poor in a feverish hunt for the illegitimate. His police department has frisked and embittered a generation of minority youth.

Rudy the Mayor could be no better than Rudy the Man, whose life was a mesh of half-truths, double agendas and secrets, wins that had to be transformed into records, losses that had to be imagined as wins, flaws that were depicted as misunderstood strengths, opponents who could only be explained as evil. His rigid will had put him on the millennial stage, made him a national political force on every

Sunday morning news show and every major national cover. It was a daunting determination with him since childhood, a blessing of birth.

He had caravaned in the open back of a school bus across the city for ninety-six hours, almost without sleep, before his re-election victory in 1997 though polls showed him leading by eighteen points, scratching in the dead of night for the votes that would help him exceed Fiorello La Guardia's record margin. He missed, and actually ran up the lowest winning total vote in a two-person mayoral race in seventy-four years. He got 172,000 fewer votes than he had four years earlier, a 22 percent drop. The other two citywide officials, Comptroller Alan Hevesi and Public Advocate Mark Green, got 70,000 more votes apiece than he did. One in ten New Yorkers voted to give him a second term. But he declared it a landslide and the media agreed.

Hoarse and exhausted, he waited to give his victory speech that night while a couple thousand supporters in the Hilton ballroom watched the debut of a five-minute video with him. It depicted the city he claimed he'd resurrected. A majestic soundtrack accompanied scenes of glittering Gotham, shot mostly from a hovering helicopter. New towers reached for the sky. Children beamed on spotless sidewalks. Parks flowered. The campaign camera rushed past images of every slice of the city—except its vast neighborhoods of pain. The only recurrent face was Giuliani's. Without a syllable of voiceover, the pulsating message was nonetheless clear: Rudy is the rising city, the rising city is Rudy.

When it was done, he told his almost all-white crowd of donors and bureaucrats, that he would, in his second term, "reach out" to the very people left out of the video, the ballroom and the first term. Then he launched a thank-you tour the next morning.

In the city that never slept, he was omnipresent for years, at the hospital beds of cops and firemen, at sewer main breaks in the early hours of the morning, dispatching trucks from a morning command post at the first sign of an inch of snow.

Try to keep up with me, he sneered at the ordinary.

I am going places no one will believe, he smiled at those who smiled with him.

Boldness was his birthright, destiny his dream.

T w o

"Aggressive Traits" and "Haphazard Associations"

HAROLD GIULIANI AND HELEN D'AVANZO MET AT A PARTY IN 1929 or 1930. The roaring twenties had tapered to a whisper, the Great Depression had recently cast its vast and wretched shadow and Prohibition had long ago confined much of the American social scene to speakeasies. It was not an auspicious time for romance, and Harold and Helen's dating life was typically austere: picnics in the park, moonlight strolls, home-based dance parties and get-togethers. Occasionally, they would splurge on a movie at Times Square—tickets were only 35 cents, if you bought them before 5:30 P.M.

At 5'11", with a solid frame and big-knuckled hands, Harold was a thickset ruffian, who squinted at the world through cumbersome, Coke-bottle–thick glasses. He had been trained as a part-time plumber's assistant but had remained financially dependent on his parents into early adulthood. Much of his childhood had been spent on the streets of East Harlem, staving off boredom with stickball and other games. At age fifteen, he dropped out of high school and was soon arrested for burglary and sentenced to probation in New York City Children's' Court. Emboldened by regular beatings from his father, he took up boxing, and through a demonstration of sheer feral aggression, persuaded a local trainer to condition him for a professional career. But due to poor vision, Harold was kept out of the ring. Instead, he took his pugilistic prowess to the streets, engaging in countless scuffles. Blinking behind his half-inch–thick lenses, he would fling a flurry of punches, landing them anywhere and everywhere, mercilessly hammering his opponent into submission. The vision problem only compounded his volcanic temper, mixed in with it, to create a sort of unalloyed, inexorable ferocity. Taunting Harold with a typical teenage gibe like "four eyes" would guarantee an immediate pummeling.

Shy and proper, Helen was the perfect antidote to Harold. She was an excellent student, who skipped two grades and graduated from high school at the

13

age of sixteen. A dark-featured Southern Italian, she would often bleach her blond hair for social occasions and loved dancing the Charleston.

Throughout their seven-year courtship, Harold was a persistent suitor and Helen a hesitant target. Most of her five brothers, at first, turned their noses at her inelegant beau, regarding him as a poor match for their little sister. Helen harbored doubts of her own, she later admitted, particularly when it came to Harold's "terrible temper." She recalled one such incident early in their courtship. "It was about six months after we met and we were walking up 123rd Street," she said. "He had his arm around me and when a car passed by, somebody in it yelled, 'Ain't love grand!' The car stopped for a light and Harold ran to the corner, pulled the guy out of the car and boom! I yelled, 'Harold, what are you doing, you savage?'"

But it was not just Helen's honor he was protecting. If Harold overheard a man on the street utter what he perceived to be a disparaging remark about a woman, "Harold would smack the guy," Helen said. These incidents became so common that Harold would affectionately sign all his love letters with the sobriquet "your savage."

At least four years after they began dating, Harold truly earned his nickname. In the spring of 1934, just a week after his twenty-sixth birthday, jobless and restless, he resorted to desperate measures.

On April 5, the "savage" was arraigned on armed robbery and assault charges in the Magistrates Court for the City of New York and ordered held on $5,000 bail. Before Magistrate Alfred Lindau, Harold Giuliani lied about his age and address, claiming he was twenty-four and lived on East 84th Street. He also lied about his occupation, saying that he was an electrician. When asked to identify himself, he told the court that his name was Joseph Starrett.

On that day, Harold Giuliani (aka Joseph Starrett) pled not guilty.

On April 12, in the case of the *People* v. *Harold Giuliani indicted as Joseph Starrett*, Giuliani was charged with four felonies: robbery in the first degree, assault in the first degree, grand larceny in the second degree, and criminally receiving stolen property.

The crime occurred on April 2, 1934 at 12:05 P.M. in the unlit first-floor corridor of a ten-family residential building at 130 East 96th Street in Manhattan. Shortly before noon, Harold Giuliani and an accomplice positioned themselves in shadowy recesses near the stairwell. Within ten or fifteen minutes Harold Hall, a milkman for Borden's Farms, entered the building to make routine payment collections. As he began to make his way up the stairs, Giuliani emerged from the shadows and, according to the indictment, pressed the muzzle of a pistol against Hall's stomach. "You know what it is," he reportedly said. He forced the man into a nook behind the stairwell, where his counterpart was waiting. The other man plunged his hand into Hall's pants pocket and fished out $128.82 in cash.

As Giuliani's accomplice frantically stuffed the money into his own pockets, either he or Giuliani—or both—commanded Hall to "pull down your pants."

Hall refused.

Giuliani grabbed Hall's pants and yanked them down to his ankles. He told Hall to sit down. He grabbed the man's hands, pulled them behind his back and bound them with cord. Squatting, his back to the wall, Giuliani leaned over his victim, and began tying his feet together. Before he was finished, a police officer, Edward Schmitt, burst in the front door of the building.

"Throw them up!" yelled Schmitt. Giuliani obeyed.

His accomplice, who, at this point, had the gun and the money, fled down the stairs to the basement and escaped onto the street.

Schmitt collared Giuliani and took him to the 23rd Precinct. The officer later told the judge assigned to that case that he had been "tipped off by a citizen that a couple of fellows were hanging around 130 East 96th Street for about half an hour, and he finally saw them going into the hallway. After they went in, a milkman went in, and the citizen suspected that there was something wrong and he called me and told me about it."

Although Giuliani's family didn't have the means to help him, he had friends with resources. Three days after he was arrested, a man named Valentine Spielman put up $5,000 to bail him out. Spielman listed his address as 351 East 60th in Manhattan.

On April 19, a week after the indictment was filed, Hall changed his statement, telling a markedly different story. This time, he said, it was Giuliani's accomplice who pressed the gun to his stomach and said: "You know what it is."

During a hearing on May 23, Louis Capozzoli, an assistant district attorney, told the judge that Hall only altered his story after he was threatened. "This milkman tried to change his statement," noted Capozzoli, "after he was visited at about four o'clock that morning by several people who threatened him. Then he said he thought this fellow [Giuliani] ought to get a break."

Hall's coerced reversal may have been effective in reducing his assailant's prison time. On May 9, before Judge Owen Bohan in the Court of General Sessions, Giuliani switched his plea to guilty. He was allowed, in light of Hall's altered statement, to plead to one count of armed robbery in the third degree. While still a serious felony conviction, armed robbery drew less prison time than a guilty plea on any one of the original charges.

At Giuliani's sentencing hearing, his attorney, Robert J. Fitzsimmons appealed for leniency. "I believe this is the case that warrants extreme clemency," said Fitzsimmons, who later explained: "The defendant realizes his mistake. His home life has been of the finest and he comes from a wonderful family."

Judge Bohan firmly replied: "I am a very sympathetic judge, but I have no sympathy for robbers with guns."

Fitzsimmons, yielding, acknowledged that his client "should get some punishment to make him realize the seriousness of his act."

The judge then addressed Giuliani, bluntly asking: "Who is the other man that was in this thing with you?"

Officer Schmitt spoke up, telling the judge that Giuliani "gave a fictitious name and address" and "refused to give us the name and address of the other man."

Suddenly, Fitzsimmons announced the name of Giuliani's supposed accomplice—Joseph Podemo. (No one named Joseph Podemo, however, was charged in connection with this, or any other, crime between 1929 and 1935.)

The judge was suspicious of Fitzsimmons's remark. He wanted a name from Giuliani. "I will commit this defendant," he said. "If he wants to help himself, let him tell us the name of the man who had the gun."

On May 29, less than a week later, Judge Bohan sentenced Harold Giuliani to two to five years at Sing Sing State Prison.

According to Giuliani's "Receiving Blotter," obtained from Sing Sing Prison, he started serving his time on May 31. The blotter form requires answers to standard questions, such as height, weight and address. His address is listed as 313 E. 123rd Street, across the street from his parents' building at 354 East 123rd. The criminal act for which Giuliani was sentenced is described as follows: "Held up man, hallway, daytime, gun, money." The form indicates that his "habits" are "temperate" and include "tobacco." He speaks "good" English, the interviewer observed, and is also semi-fluent in Italian. His religion is noted as Catholic and his church attendance is described as "occasional." His alias is listed as Joseph Starrett.

When asked by the interviewer to what he "attributed" his criminal acts, Giuliani's answer was "unemployment." He listed two employers under his "Employment Record." The first mentioned was Koch Plumbing, where he earned a weekly wage of $30 as a "plumber's helper." But his 1934 employment at Koch only lasted two weeks. The second employer, John N. Kapp, also a plumber, hired Giuliani at a weekly wage of $24 and kept him on from 1929—around the time he met Helen—until 1932. Giuliani describes no other employment.

Two weeks before he was committed to Sing Sing, Giuliani underwent a psychiatric exam. Benjamin Apfelberg, a psychiatrist with the city's Department of

Hospitals, sent his report to Judge Bohan on May 18. Although Apfelberg found that Giuliani was "not mentally defective" and displayed "no psychotic symptoms at the present time," the report painted a troubling portrait.

"A study of this individual's makeup," wrote Apfelberg, "reveals that he is a personality deviate of the aggressive, egocentric type. This aggressivity is pathological in nature and has shown itself from time to time even as far back as his childhood. He is egocentric to an extent where he has failed to consider the feelings and rights of others."

Noting Harold's "nearsightedness," Apfelberg continued:

As a result of this physical handicap, especially because of taunts in his boyhood years, he has developed a sense of inferiority which, in recent years, has become accentuated on account of his prolonged idleness and dependence on his parents. . . . His school life was marked by retardation on account of the mischievous and unruly conduct. Due to his aggressive traits and through his excessive aimless idleness, he has been attracted to haphazard associations which apparently were the direct precipitating factors in bringing about the present offense. He is anxious about his predicament on account of a feeling of guilt. He rationalizes the motives of his offense in a self-pitying way in order to obtain sympathy.

Apfelberg concluded his report with this recommendation and caveat: "From a purely and strictly psychiatric standpoint, without considering the social, environmental and other factors in this case, the findings indicate that the social rehabilitation possibilities are favorable for eventual readjustment but are rather dubious as to the prognosis in regard to improvement in personality."

After a year and four months at Sing Sing State Prison, Harold Giuliani was released on September 24, 1935. A year later, while on parole, he married his longcourted sweetheart, Helen D'Avanzo, at St. Francis of Assisi Church in Brooklyn. On May 5, 1939, more than two years after he and his new wife had moved into a house they shared with her mother, he completed his parole.

Harold Giuliani's father Rodolfo, a tailor, was seventeen years old when he emigrated to New York in the 1880s from Montecatini, a village in Italy's Tuscany region northwest of Florence. In New York, he married a dressmaker, Evangelina, whose surname, Giuliani, happened, conveniently, to be the same as his own. The young couple moved into a six-room apartment on the third floor of a wooden building on East 123rd Street in Italian-American Harlem. There they raised five children, Harold, Charles, Marie, Olga and Rudolph.

Shown in a photo provided by his future daughter-in-law, Evelyn Giuliani, Rodolfo sits erect in a high-backed leather-upholstered chair, sternly regarding the camera. He is wearing a stiff suit. An ample mustache divides his handsome face into two angular, vaguely scowling halves. Evangelina stands behind him, propping herself on his shoulder, holding a flower. Wearing an ornate dress with a belt and long lacy gloves, she is soft-featured, pretty, serious—although she was reputed, say some relatives, to have had a wide smile and dazzling teeth.

A seamstress working grueling shifts in a garment industry sweatshop, Evangelina didn't spend much time at home. Because Rodolfo worked at home, stitching custom-made suits for a cadre of wealthy customers, he largely raised their children. He often sent his eldest, Harold, to deliver a finished suit. But the boy was easily distracted, often stopping en route to play ball. When Rodolfo learned from neighbors of his son's dallying, young Harold got a stern beating.

A passionate man and an ardent lover of opera, Rodolfo would play his records at top volume, singing along with the recitatives and arias. But he was also a stubborn man. When he found out he had cancer, according to his son's future sister-in-law, Anna D'Avanzo, he "turned his bed against the wall and wouldn't speak to anyone until he died." The day of Rodolfo's death, February 8, 1946, was three and half months before his grandson Rudy's second birthday.

Rudy's maternal grandmother Adelina Stanchi came to America with her family from Naples in 1884 when she was two years old. Her mother died young, when she was thirteen, leaving her with the responsibility of raising her younger brother and sister, Andrew and Louise. Her father, Vincenzo Stanchi, who would eventually remarry, was a cigar manufacturer in Brooklyn. A tall, husky man, who favored pipes over cigars, Vincenzo owned the building at 206 Skillman Street where his family lived. He also owned a bar in the basement, as well as a stable in the backyard that housed ten horses, which he rented out to coach drivers.

In 1903, when she was twenty-one, Adelina married Luigi (Louis) D'Avanzo, a barber who had emigrated from Avellino, a town outside of Naples. Adelina, who was "built like an Amazon," according to her half brother, Ralph Stanchi, dwarfed her short, cherubic husband. The young couple lived together at 181 Jackson Street in Brooklyn, a two-family frame house Luigi had bought, where they raised seven children, Vincent, Fanny, William, Helen, Leo, Edward and Roberto.

Although 206 Skillman was only two blocks from the Church of St. Francis of Paola, the D'Avanzo children were not baptized until they were much older than customary. Vincent was four when he was baptized, and Roberto was nine. Helen,

Leo and Edward were all baptized on the same day, April 2, 1921, when their mother brought them en masse to St. Francis of Paola; they were eleven, nine and six, respectively.

When the family went to Sunday Mass, Luigi did so begrudgingly. He had harbored a contempt for priests ever since he discovered that his uncle, a bishop in Italy, had secretly fathered three children with a hidden wife. "He had no use for priests," Helen would later say. "He used to say, 'They're all a bunch of fakers.'"

When Luigi died in June 1925, Adelina was a "pauper," according to her future daughter-in-law, Anna D'Avanzo. Forty-three years old, she was once again shouldered with the responsibility of caring for young children largely by herself. Vincent, her eldest son who was twenty at the time, shared part of the burden, becoming a father figure to his younger siblings. Luigi's estate totaled $4,814.79 in cash left in his bank account. After funeral and related expenses, that amount had been whittled to a fixed sum of $2,795.21. Adelina and her seven children continued living at 181 Jackson Street, surviving off the dwindling remainder of Luigi's estate. The $60 per month in rent collected from the occupants of the other half of the house just barely covered taxes, insurance, repairs and the interest on the mortgage. Fortunately, Luigi's friends, who still owed him money, honored their debt by paying Adelina. As commanded by Luigi's will, each of his children received a portion of his estate—money that had been put in Adelina's trust—on their twenty-first birthdays.

The Italy from which the D'Avanzos and Giulianis had emigrated was even then fractured by an ancient cultural and economic fault line separating the north and south. Northerners, many of whom identified culturally with Germany and Switzerland, were lighter-skinned, often blue-eyed, while southerners were darker-skinned, with thick shocks of black hair and deep brown eyes. Comparatively impoverished, southerners were looked down on and branded with racially laden stereotypes. Southern Italy, referred to in some circles as the Africa of Italy, was populated, some Northerners would have told you, with dirty peasants, boisterous drunks and conniving criminals. This divide even ran along culinary lines, with northerners eschewing red-sauced southern cuisine in favor of their cream-and-butter–based dishes.

Italy's cultural chasm, immortalized in Carlo Levi's *Christ Stopped at Eboli*, was bridged by some families who married across it. The D'Avanzos, from the Naples area, and the Giulianis, from Tuscany, were two such families, their lineages braided together by two marriages, not just one. Given almost Nordic-sounding names by their northern parents, Harold Giuliani and his sister, Olga, both married members of the southern D'Avanzo clan. In fact, Olga and William met at Harold and Helen's wedding in 1936.

It took the Giulianis six years and one miscarriage to have a baby. "Helen had the miscarriage early in the marriage," recalled Anna D'Avanzo. "The next time I saw her, she was crying. Harold always looked at the good side—'We'll have another one.'" Eventually, Harold was right. On Sunday May 28, 1944, Helen, age thirty-five, gave birth to her long-awaited and only child, Rudolph William Louis Giuliani. After receiving the news, Harold frantically ran up and down the steps of every building on his block, handing out cigars. Named after his grandfather Rodolfo, little Rudy (then spelled Rudi) was considered by his verging-on-middle-age parents to be a blessing from God, an answer to countless prayers.

The Giulianis smothered their son with attention. Helen stayed home to raise Rudy and, on many afternoons, would read out loud to him from biographies and history books. Years later, she would put off buying a dining room set, so her son could have a $400 tape recorder to record Saturday afternoon opera broadcasts from the Metropolitan Opera in Manhattan. Harold tried to teach his son how to box. When Rudy was just two, his father gave him a pair of boxing gloves and later hung a punching bag for him in the basement. To toughen his chubby toddler, Harold ordered Rudy to try to punch him in the face, to hit him as hard as he could.

It was Helen's mother, Adelina D'Avanzo, who spent the most time with "the little prince," as some relatives referred to him. Known to Rudy as Nana, Adelina never refrained from issuing her opinions in a flurry of gesticulation and embracing those she loved with forceful affection. She cooked voluminous four- and five-course dinners and, at night, kept an eye on her restless grandson, who had a tic in one eye and often remained awake throughout the night. "She practically brought him up," said Anna D'Avanzo.

Adelina was not only the Giulianis' emotional bedrock; she was also the family's financial foundation. She owned 419 Hawthorne Street, the building in East Flatbush, Brooklyn to which Harold and Helen had returned that Sunday with their newborn. A modest, two-family red and tan brick house, 419 was indistinguishable from all the others in the unbroken, block-long row of fused-together buildings between New York and Brooklyn Avenues. Like most other houses on the block, it featured a cozy brick archway under which the front door was set, a rippled-roofed awning shading the stoop and a low iron gate out front.

Harold, Helen, Adelina and Rudy lived on the second floor, in a narrow, six-room apartment with parquet floors, decorative moldings in the plaster walls and high ceilings. There were three bedrooms, a dining room, kitchen and bathroom.

The close-quartered living room was anchored by an overstuffed blue sofa, flanked by three armchairs and a few mahogany end tables. A Philco radio stood snugly in a corner.

The downstairs apartment at 419 Hawthorne was occupied by the other Giuliani-D'Avanzo marital link, William and Olga D'Avanzo. William was Rudy's godfather and then wore the badge of the New York City Police Department. A detective sharing the 67th Precinct on Snyder Avenue with his older brother Vincent and younger brother Roberto, William was thick-jawed, quiet and given to taking long, solitary walks in a nearby park. His wife, Olga, was a full-figured and big-lipped woman and drew stares when she sauntered down the street.

William and Olga's daughters, Evangeline and Joan Ellen, were like older sisters to toddler Rudy, playing with him and looking after him. "Rudy and Joan were very close," recalled their aunt Anna. "They grew up together." A shy, pretty girl who smiled brightly for the camera, Joan Ellen was forced to wear gauze bandages on her arms, from shoulder to wrist, because of severe eczema. "She always wanted to scratch her arms," said Anna. "And they wouldn't let her scratch her arms. She was very hard to manage."

Three doors down from 419 Hawthorne was Helen's sister Fanny, who rented an apartment with her husband John Visconti and their children, Assunta and Frederick. "I changed Rudy's first diaper," recalled Assunta, his cousin, who was fourteen years older. "Helen was putting the fold in the back, and I said, 'No, Aunt Helen, the fold always goes in the front.'"

At the time of Rudy's birth, World War II had lasted more than four and a half years. D-Day was just nine days away. The only member of either the Giuliani or D'Avanzo families who served in the war was Harold's brother Charles, stationed in New Guinea for four years until 1948. Harold's younger brother, Rudolph, born on December 13, 1926, was too young to be drafted. Four of Helen's brothers were excused from service because they were cops; her youngest brother, Roberto, entered the police force on November 21, 1942, in the middle of the war.

Harold told relatives and friends that he wasn't drafted because of his poor eyesight and ulcers. What, in truth, protected him from military service, however, was his criminal record. The record was almost impossible to find—then and now—because it is filed in the name of Joseph Starrett, his alias. Harold apparently helped the local draft board locate it.

On April 18, 1941, Morris S. Ganchrow, secretary of the Selective Service System's Local Board #217 in Brooklyn, wrote a letter to the Court of General Sessions, inquiring into Harold's criminal background. The letter read:

Dear Gentlemen:

We understand that Harold Angelo Giuliani, using the alias "Joseph Starrett," a registrant in this Board, was convicted of Attempted Robbery, 3rd degree, on April 24, 1934.

In order that he may be properly classified by members of this Board, will you please give us the details of his Court Record, as to the charge—whether a misdemeanor or a felony, and if sentenced, the period he was confined.

Enclosed is self-addressed envelope for reply.

The charge was, of course, a felony, and anyone guilty of a felony was barred from wartime service.

The D'Avanzos and Giulianis still discussed the Allies' great campaign over dinner. The fact that their homeland was an Axis country did not diminish Helen Giuliani's sense of patriotism. "Helen was a little sticking up for the Italians, a little on the Italian side," recalled Anna. "She liked Mussolini and things like that."

On July 2, 1944, just a few days over a month old, Rudy was baptized at St. Francis of Assisi Church on the corner of Lincoln and Nostrand Avenues, just six blocks away from his home. Sturdy, utilitarian, built of tan bricks, St. Francis of Assisi, at first glance, might have looked more like a fortress than a church. The tallest structure in sight, it was enclosed by a tall iron gate and abutted a shady yard with a small flower garden growing up around a statue of the Virgin Mary.

Although Rudy's father was reputed to pray every night before a small altar on the dresser top in his room, his wife and mother-in-law were not as enthusiastic or routine about their worship. On Sunday mornings, Helen would escort Rudy to Mass—but allegedly only on Harold's orders. Adelina and her daughter, perhaps still taking cues from the embittered, late Luigi, were tepid about their faith. "I don't remember Nanny ever going to church," remarked Anna D'Avanzo. Harold's sister-in-law Evelyn Giuliani recalled that Helen was "not very religious."

At five years old, Rudy was nonetheless enrolled in kindergarten at St. Francis of Assisi Catholic elementary, if not solely for the religion, then for a generous dose of discipline. Founded in 1909, the school served children of the parish, providing stern, regimented instruction from kindergarten through eighth grade. Wrist rappings and ear boxings were as commonplace then as detentions and demerits. When Rudy enrolled, the student population was 1,400 and the teachers were both priests and lay educators.

The most fabled story of Rudy's Brooklyn boyhood, one its protagonist has shared on many occasions, involves baseball. It was the height of the Brooklyn Dodgers' era, and the Giulianis lived only a ten-minute walk from Dodgers

Central, Ebbets Field. The Dodgers' star player—and the breaker of racial barriers—was Jackie Robinson, who had joined the team in 1947 and would remain until 1956. From his bedroom window, Rudy could see the lights of Ebbets Field beaming into the Brooklyn night. He could even hear the impassioned cheering of Dodgers' fans. But the Giulianis, as per Harlem Harold, remained stubbornly devoted Yankee fans. Rudy's famous boyhood baseball story has Harold dressing his young son, who was playing Little League on a local team, in a mini-Yankees outfit. The gruff, uncompromising man then sent Rudy into the streets, into the heart of Dodger country. "The first thing they did was throw me in the mud," Rudy recounted during a 1993 campaign commercial. Then the bloodthirsty Dodgers fans were reported to have looped a makeshift noose around toddler Rudy's neck. Adelina, hurtling out of the house screaming, as the story was told, drove the little terrors away, back into the enveloping environs of Ebbets Field. "I kept telling them, 'I'm a Yankee fan,'" Rudy said. "'I'm gonna stay a Yankee fan.' To my father it was a joke. Put a Yankee uniform on the kid, and it'll irritate all my friends and relatives and it'll be fun. But to me it was like being a martyr. I'm not gonna give up my religion. You're not going to change me."

Rudy's aunt Anna recalled the story a little differently. "Harold just put a Yankees hat on Rudy," she said.

Rudy may have inherited his storytelling abilities from his grandmother, who was an animated yarn spinner, regaling anyone who would listen with tales of the past. She plied her grandson with stories of the American Civil War she had heard decades after the war from families of veterans. Nana also told little Rudy about an insidious, real-life monster called the Mafia. Rudy learned about the terrifying time his maternal great-grandfather, Vincenzo Stanchi, received a note from the Black Hand signed with the ominous coal-smeared handprint demanding money or tribute. His grandmother impressed upon him how these stealthy extortionists blended into the community, living by their own law.

Another story handed down to the family by Adelina involved her late husband Luigi's relative, a baker who was also shaken down by the Mafia. His family had been threatened. After deciding he couldn't pay what they were asking, he took his own life.

One afternoon in 1948 as cab driver Leo (aka Tullio) D'Avanzo coasted down Kingston Avenue in Brooklyn in his taxi, hunting for customers, he noticed that an old neighborhood bar on the corner of Kingston and Rutland had been closed. He talked to the owner of the building, Philomena Mandelino, and within a few months, made a bold new career move: He bought the bar and re-opened it. The deed to the property wasn't filed in his name; it was listed under his wife's, Veronica "Betty" D'Avanzo. The business license wasn't in his name either; that was conveniently registered under the name of his brother Vincent D'Avanzo, who happened to be a patrolman in the 67th Precinct and after whom the reincarnated watering hole was named. Nothing was ever in Leo's name.

With ornate tin ceilings and a commodious dining area that stretched nearly half a block, Vincent's Restaurant could accommodate upwards of 150 revelers. A twelve-block walk from Ebbets Field, it was located in what was known in the '30s as "pig town," a densely populated area in which many poor Italian immi-grants raised pigs in the yards of their often ramshackle, makeshift homes. Convenient and familiar, Vincent's soon became a neighborhood social hub, a place to eat dinner and play a few songs on the jukebox on Friday night. It drew a hearty clientele of firemen, fishermen, bookies, sanitation workers and others. The bar was also a roost for a roster of wizened regulars, sardonic old Italian and Irish guys who drank rye whisky with rock candy and had nicknames like Ippy and Stumpy.

Most importantly, Vincent's Restaurant became the headquarters of Leo's loan-sharking and gambling operations, ventures he ran with a partner, Jimmy Dano, who was a made man. Dano had once worked as a runner for the powerful num-bers-racket operator and narcotics distributor James (Jimmy the Clam) Eppolito. Dano and Leo had a secret wire room tucked in the back of Vincent's and em-ployed a small army of as many as fifteen runners. "There was a lot of booking and numbers and all that nonsense," said Leo's former mistress of nearly thirty years, Elizabeth Mandelino, who was the daughter of the prior owner, Philomena. (The Mandelinos were related by marriage to the Eppolitos.) "That's how they survived."

And in East Flatbush, Brooklyn, it was Leo's show. If you needed money, you went to Leo. If you wanted to place a bet on a horse, he was the man to see. "Everybody in Flatbush knew Leo," said Mandelino, who had lived in an apart-ment above Vincent's with her mother and would later move into a nearby eight-family apartment building Leo bought on Beverly Road.

Tall and thin with fingernails as white as piano keys, Leo D'Avanzo was an im-maculate dresser, hair never out of place, shoes always freshly shined. Often tak-ing drags on a cigarette—he smoked a pack a day easily—he would tell his mistress about his loan-sharking business and extorting people and having to "break their legs." But he'd never kill anyone, he assured the woman sixteen years his junior. He'd never kill for money.

In family circles, Uncle Leo was the shadowy black sheep. "Everybody in the family said, 'Don't be like Leo,'" recalled Rudy's second cousin, Gina Gialoreta. "Leo was Mafia, bad, bad. . . . Uncle Leo lived by his wits—that's what my grandmother used to say."

On August 17, 1951, at age thirty-eight, Leo was arraigned in Brooklyn Criminal Court on felony "criminal receiving" charges, but the case was eventually dismissed. Seven years later, in April 1958, he appeared in Brooklyn Gambler's Court, arraigned on bets and book-making charges; he put up a $500 bond and was discharged by Judge Anthony Livoti. Even Leo's cop brother, Vincent, found himself on the receiving end of an arrest on a few occasions. On October 15, 1954, he was arraigned in Gambler's Court on minor charges related to the Alcohol Beverage Control Act, but was discharged. On February 14, 1961, Vincent was arrested with twelve other defendants by an officer from his brother Roberto's precinct, the 71st, for a violation of the New York City Administrative Code that appeared to be related to gambling; given a choice in district court between one day in jail and a $2 fine, Vincent paid the fine. Since New York State criminal records before 1970 are not computerized and, therefore, are either unavailable or extremely hard to locate, these incidents may not represent the totality of Leo D'Avanzo's criminal career.

Behind the mahogany bar at Vincent's Restaurant, puffing on a cigar while he drew pints and fixed cocktails, was Harold Giuliani. The forty-year-old father of a four-year-old son had a patchwork employment history of a few on-again, off-again jobs. When Rudy was born, his father was working at the Brooklyn Navy Yard as a plumber's assistant, the trade he had learned before prison. Nearly two years after prison, in July of 1937, at the age of twenty-nine, Harold had applied for a Social Security number, listing his job status as "unemployed." At some point in the late 1930s or early 1940s, he tried his hand at door-to-door sales, hawking tablecloths and bedspreads. Now what Harold needed most was security and a weekly paycheck. The one man who could provide both was his brother-in-law, whose illegal operations were fronted by his other brother-in-law, the cop. "My father-in-law [Leo] was kind of close with Harold," noted Lois D'Avanzo, who would later marry Leo's infamous son Lewis.

Like his brothers-in-law, Harold was a snappy dresser, usually attired in a starched shirt, tie and hat. Relatives described him as an affectionate man, who hugged as tight as a vise and kissed old ladies and children. Due to his stomach ulcers, the gray-eyed, bespectacled bartender often drank milk while his customers knocked back scotch. In case anyone got too rowdy, he kept a baseball bat behind the bar and a .38 caliber pistol next to the cash register. An opinionated and voluble Yankees fan in Dodgers land, a man who reputedly hated most politicians, Harold would engage in heated arguments with his customers, his voice booming sometimes out into the street. If there was a bar fight, it was Harold who broke it up. If a customer had let his tab go for too long, it was Harold who went with his baseball bat to collect.

But bar tabs weren't the only debts Harold collected. He had come a long way since the spring day more than fourteen years ago when he mugged a milkman. Now, the crimes he committed were part of an organized criminal enterprise. Known as the "muscle" behind the loan-sharking operation, Harold was Leo's collection agent, recouping money that had been loaned out and was now overdue.

Most debtors would pay at the bar, slipping an envelope to Harold across the counter. In the mid to late '50s, Harold collected as much as $15,000 a week, tapping dozens of debtors. The "vig" usually began at a stifling 150 percent and rose with the passing of each week. Many people borrowed money to pay rent or foot a business expense and would pay back four or five times the amount they borrowed. There were no excuses for being late.

One afternoon, a man reluctantly entered the bar to apologize to Harold that he didn't have the money—could he have just one more week? Frowning, Harold reached under the bar and, out of sight, gripped his baseball bat. As the man before him continued pleading for an extension, Harold swung the bat, cracking him flat across the face, sending him back a few feet, according to an eyewitness. "Don't be late again," Harold said.

That was the gist of Harold's job: Enforce Leo's law through threats or violence. He shoved people against walls, broke legs, smashed kneecaps, crunched noses. He gave nearby Kings County Hospital a lot of business.

"People in the neighborhood were terrified of him," said a frequent customer at Vincent's, who was one of Leo's son Lewis's best friends and whose family borrowed money from Leo.

He remembers what happened early one Saturday morning after his own father failed to make a payment. "When I was a kid, my father borrowed money from Leo," he said. "He couldn't pay, so Harold came to collect. He knocked on the door and yelled, 'I want the money now, or I'm going to break both your arms!'"

After Harold calmed down, an agreement was worked out. "They talked to Leo and straightened it out," he said.

While in high school, Lewis's friend did occasional chores around the bar, and his brother took a job in the wire room, charting bets on the numbers boards. Many years later, after opening his own business, Lewis's friend borrowed $90,000 from Leo and paid back $160,000—a fairly modest repayment total. "It would only take me four to five weeks to pay him back," he says, adding that his brother once borrowed $5,000 and ended up paying back $20,000.

Gambling, loan-sharking and booze weren't the only sources of income at Vincent's. A black man who worked in the payroll office at a local hospital would stop by the bar every week or so to give Harold several dozen fake paychecks. The checks were made to out to a host of fictitious employees and were drawn on the hospital's bank account. "Harold would cash them in the bar," said Lewis's friend. "There would be several thousand dollars worth of checks every week. Harold would get half, and the black guy would get the other half."

V incent's Restaurant was frequented, from time to time, by a few prizefighters, and Harold grew friendly with several. By some accounts, Harold even managed a fighter or two. He once "bought fifty-fifty" into a boxer, according to Gina Gialoreta. Robert D'Avanzo's son Steven recalled that "Harold managed several fighters over the years." Elizabeth Mandelino also remembered Leo in a managerial role. "Leo was going to help some guy who was going into training," said Mandelino. But that venture never worked out.

Leo wasn't the only "connected" guy in Harold Giuliani's life who had a hand in the boxing business. The burly bartender's lifelong best friend from his East Harlem days, Louis Carbonetti, was a cutman for fighters—one of whom was Italian boxer Vic Dellicurti. A middleweight fighter who went to the mat with Sugar Ray Robinson four times, Dellicurti was widely known as a human punching bag, a magnet for blows. Living on the third floor of Carbonetti's building at 325 East 108th Street, the thick-skulled palooka likely landed more blows on his wife than on any opponent in the ring. "He would beat the shit out of her," recalled Carbonetti's son, Lou Carbonetti Jr.

Dellicurti was controlled by Jimmy White, a notorious mob manager with an impressive arrest record. Charged, at various times, with murder, robbery, larceny and white slavery, White did a healthy dose of time and broke out of prison twice.

Carbonetti, whose tentacles extended into several spheres of influence, was also the personal secretary to State Supreme Court Judge Thomas Aurelio, the most notorious mob-tied judge on the bench in Manhattan. Aurelio's name hit the headlines when his voice was picked up on one of the first wiretaps, placed on the phone of the city's most famous mobster, Frank Costello, known as the Prime Minister of the Underworld. Clad in custom-made suits, chomping on English Oval cigars, Costello engineered Aurelio's 1943 nomination to the Supreme Court. When Aurelio called Costello at home to thank him, Costello offered his congratulations and then added: "When I tell you something is in the bag, you can rest assured." District Attorney Frank Hogan made the tape public—an extraordinary revelation at the time of how thoroughly mob influence had penetrated the judiciary.

Carbonetti was Aurelio's top aide—from the moment he took office—though not a lawyer himself. A Democratic district leader from East Harlem, Carbonetti was also a top supporter, in the early '50s, of Mayor Vincent Impelliteri, whose administration was swamped with mob and scandal allegations.

Lou Carbonetti Jr. recalls that Harold would usually swing by the Carbonetti residence for a beer and a weekend card game at the kitchen table. When Rudy was older, his father would take him to meet Lou Sr. and Jr. for a Yankees game. Lou Jr., not a baseball fan, often protested. "I hated it," he said. "But my father would say, 'You have to go. Harold's coming all the way from Brooklyn.'"

In the late '50s, Carbonetti remembered waiting with his father and Harold Giuliani outside a police precinct in Harlem late one night for Harold's younger brother Rudolph to get off duty. Rudolph had just started at the precinct, and the two were there to make sure he was OK.

Harold remained a close friend of Carbonetti's for most of his life. In 1952, more than fifteen years after he had left Harlem, Harold bought an ad in Carbonetti's clubhouse journal congratulating his buddy Lou on a good year. While most ads in the journal were a quarter or half page, Harold's was a full page and listed at the bottom not only his own name, but also Helen's and Rudy's.

In the early '50s, young white Brooklynites began flocking east to take part in the subdividing of the Long Island frontier. A nascent demographic shift, blacks moving into certain areas of Brooklyn, like Flatbush, spurred the migration. In August 1951, sixty-nine-year-old Adelina sold 419 Hawthorne, enabling her daughter, Harold and seven-year-old Rudy to live in a place of their own—far away from changing Brooklyn. With Adelina's money, the family bought a quaint two-bedroom Cape Cod house on Euston Road South, a somnolent, leafy street in Garden City, Long Island. The title was listed in Helen's name alone, though Adelina moved in with the Giulianis.

Rudy's new street was a changeless chain of nearly identical, squat, brick Cape Cods, each with a maple tree spaced two feet to the right of the driveway. In the summer the maples arched over the road, forming a lush canopy under which the neighborhood children played stickball. The road surface was not made of asphalt but rather of loose blue stone pebbles in which footprints and tire tracks were always visible.

When the town of Garden City was founded in 1869, *Harper's Weekly* predicted that it would become "the most beautiful suburb in the vicinity of New York." More than eighty years later, in 1951, Garden City, cozily nestled in the middle of Nassau County, had arguably earned that honor. A model "planned community," with both quiet, tree-shaded streets and a gauntlet of ritzy city department stores lining its main thoroughfare, it was a carefully manicured suburban Shangri-La, the residential jewel in Long Island's crown. What Garden City had also earned was a reputation for being one of the most elitist, homogeneous and exclusive villages in all of Long Island. It was a Caucasian Christian cocoon, with white Anglo-Saxon Protestants and Roman Catholics accounting for virtually its entire population. As late as 1968, there was not a single black family. Jews accounted for less than one percent of the population. The only two black students in the school system at that time were both imported from the South via the Urban League's Student Transfer Education Program—and, initially, the school board refused to accept them, citing overcrowding problems. At the village's three country clubs, there were no black or Jewish members. In 1970 when the Garden City Unitarian Universalist Church proposed starting a day-care center for poor minority children from neighboring areas, it was met with a fierce, visceral resistance by area residents, including legal challenges.

The Giulianis made one immediate change when they left Brooklyn. On the advice of his old East Harlem buddy, Lou Carbonetti, Harold and his wife switched their voter registration from Democratic to Republican. "Harold had a friend in Harlem who was a Democratic district leader," Helen said. "He told us that we'd better become Republicans if we were moving to Nassau County."

Now sheltered from the diversity of Brooklyn, young Rudy's world view was inevitably shaped by the uniformity of his new surroundings.

Unlike 419 Hawthorne, the Giulianis' new house had a basement in which Harold installed a Ping-Pong table and model train set and strung up a canvas punching bag filled with sand. In the living room, a new mahogany cabinet housed an RCA television set. There were only two bedrooms; Helen and Harold took one, and Rudy and Adelina shared the other. Soon after they moved in, Helen decided that Rudy needed his own room, and Adelina, whose largesse had made the purchase of this new house possible, was forced to sleep on the living room sofa.

The neighbors were friendly but kept to themselves. That was the unspoken code of Euston Road: Smile, say hello, mind your own business. Most Saturdays, the men of the neighborhood would nod to each other across their fences as they mowed their lawns or barbecued dinner.

From where the Giulianis lived, it was a convenient commute to Manhattan or Brooklyn. The LIRR station was only six blocks away, as was the bus station. But Harold, still tending bar at Vincent's, usually drove to work. Helen and her mother stayed home, cleaning the house, looking after Rudy.

Halfway through second grade, Rudy enrolled at a nearby Catholic school, St. Anne's, run by the nuns of the Order of the Sacred Heart of Mary. Built in 1950 to accommodate Long Island's recent influx of Catholic families, St. Anne's was a brand-new, utilitarian brick building with a statue of its saint displayed prominently out front. The student population was primarily Italian, Irish and German, kids from lower-middle- and upper-middle-class families. Everyone was required to wear uniforms, navy blue pants, a white shirt and blue tie. Each day began with a prayer and the Pledge of Allegiance. The Cold War was on, and the nuns instructed their pupils that Communists were godless and led them in prayers for the capitalist and democratic conversion of Russia. The neophytes also learned bible stories, studied the lives of the saints and memorized the ten commandments.

It was before Vatican II, and that meant meatless Fridays and Mass delivered in Latin. Goodness required diligence and discipline. From the catechism, Rudy learned a stark and unbending system that delineated venial sins and mortal sins, sanctifying grace and actual grace. There were several types of prayers to memorize; one could lessen your stay in Purgatory by five years, another, only by three. Rudy and his classmates once studied a sketch of three milk bottles meant to help convey the different levels of sin. The all-white bottle represented a soul free of sin and ready for heaven. The bottle mottled with black spots symbolized a soul blemished with venial sins and on the route to purgatory. Lastly, there was the bottle the color of black ink, which flagged a soul damned to eternal damnation.

Joan Lipp, Rudy's former classmate and neighbor, recalled him as charismatic and friendly, if a tad mischievous. "He was chubby and jolly," she said. "I remember the nuns saying 'Mr. Giuliani,' so he must have done something wrong, for them to say that."

Rudy's newspaper route had taught him many of the roads in and around Garden City. That business venture, however, was a financial disaster—Rudy apparently routinely failed to collect his payments—and he eventually gave it up. Without an encumbering stack of newspapers, the young teenager was now free to peddle on his three-speed Schwinn bicycle wherever his fancy took him. One such place was Klein's department store. Fourteen years old, Rudy parked his bicycle outside one afternoon and ventured in. He thumbed through the 45 rpm singles, through records by groups like the Platters and Bill Haley and the Comets. Out of the corner of his eye, a sign proclaiming "SALE" beckoned him.

"I saw a Julius Caesar album for 98 cents," recalled Rudy. Claiming that he thought it was Shakespeare—he had begun studying Shakespeare in school—he picked it up. He ended up buying George Frideric Handel's opera *Julius Caesar* and Peter Ilyich Tchaikovsky's *The 1812 Overture*. He peddled home with his new records and played them in his room. "I followed the opera by reading the libretto printed on the back of the album jacket," Rudy said. "I fell in love with the record. It was like a revelation."

Within a few days, he had bought Giuseppe Verdi's *Rigoletto*. An opera fan was born. Since his father eschewed opera in favor of baseball and boxing, young Rudy would usually sequester himself in his room and, like his grandfather Rodolfo, listen to his opera records alone.

In 1953, the building in which Vincent's was located—together with other parcels on the block—was condemned by court order and slated for demolition. Planning to build a high school on the site, the city bought up all the property. Real estate documents indicate that Leo's wife Veronica was paid $4,900 by the city for the property and his brother Vincent got $3,250 for the "fixtures." Leo's bar was relocated five blocks to the corner of Nostrand and Hawthorne, at 1203 Nostrand, just a block and half from 419 Hawthorne. The property, still in Vincent's name, was on the first floor of a three-story brick building that featured an incongruous Greek cornice trim above the door. The bar remained a front for Leo's gambling and loan-sharking.

By the mid and late '50s, Harold had become irritable and distracted, according to a few patrons at Vincent's. Sometimes, as a row of drinkers collected at the bar, the stooped, brooding bartender would be absently wiping down the counter while staring vacantly into the middle distance. When someone interrupted his daydreaming to ask for a refill, Harold might snap at the drunken nuisance and order him out of the bar.

Harold told his confidant, Brother Jack O'Leary, that one reason he left Brooklyn in 1951 was "to get away from my in-laws." He didn't want his son exposed to what went on at the bar, he explained. Rudy was at an impressionable age, when one begins to observe and emulate. Harold wanted him far away from the poisonous vicinity of Vincent's. He vowed that his boy would not end up like Lewis, Leo's boy, who hung around the bar, around the numbers charts, and lived with his family in the apartment above the new bar.

Sometime in the late '50s, Harold stopped tending bar full-time at Vincent's. On January 12, 1959, two and half months shy of his fifty-first birthday and shortly before Rudy's fifteenth, Harold Giuliani got an on-the-books, legit job. He was hired for $3,300 per year as a groundskeeper for Lynbrook Public High School in Lynbrook, Long Island, where Helen's younger brother Edward lived with his wife Anna and their three children.

Perhaps in connection with that job, Harold requested information about the cloud that had hung over him since 1934. A notation in the General Sessions Court file indicates he sought copies of the "complaint and certification" of the criminal case against Joseph Starrett. The notation lists Giuliani at his Garden City address, indicating that copies of the key documents were sent to him there.

As a member of the buildings and grounds crew for the Lynbrook district, Harold's day was spent maintaining sports equipment, buffing the terrazzo marble floors, grooming athletic fields and, in the winter, salting parking lots and driveways. Wearing his pants high over his hips, Harold would often tour the hallways looking for gum, which he would scrape up with a putty knife stowed in his back pocket. Michael Ortado, whose grandfather Bartolo Ortado worked with Harold and used to bring young Michael to work with him on Saturdays, remembered Harold as "huggy, very giving," adding, "just don't do something wrong. If you put the can down in the wrong place, [Harold would say] 'It belongs over here.'"

During lunch, Harold and his fellow custodians would engage in apple-peeling contests with their pen knives. Whoever could maintain the longest coil of peel won. They would often argue which apples were better, Macintosh or Golden Delicious, although, according to Ortado, Harold preferred tangerines. Often eating a sardine sandwich, Harold would regale the guys with stories about the bar, about the drunks who had poured their hearts out to him.

In October 1959, the Giulianis migrated once again. Harold, after only ten months on the job at Lynbrook High School, took out a $162-per-month mortgage on a new, comparably capacious split-level ranch house in North Bellmore, closer to Lynbrook. Fixed in a tidy row of similar houses on a short block called Pine Court, the Giuliani's new home, replete with a deck and a two-car garage, was Harold's castle. The new house also had a bay window and a façade of large cedar shingles. Birches and silver maples lined the street out front, shimmering in the fall breeze. Vine-covered trellises and cleanly cut hedges separated one yard from another. The Giulianis had moved from a lower-middle class neighborhood to an upper-middle-class town. Harold and Helen, always eager to conform, switched their voter registrations back to the Democratic Party, because, in Helen's words, "Bellmore was more of a Jewish area, and Democrats were more prevalent."

Helen had recently taken a job as a doctor's receptionist in Garden City, the town from which she had just moved. Prior to this job, which she would only keep for about a year and a half, Helen had stayed at home with Rudy, even though

Adelina was there. Helen had always wanted to be a teacher. Asthma, pneumonia, pleurisy and a hoarse voice were the various reasons offered by relatives and friends for her failure to realize that ambition. Over the prior fifteen years, her only other job known to a half dozen relatives was a brief, part-time hitch at a Brooklyn candle factory owned and run by the uncle of her sister Fanny's husband, Sylvester Visconti. Part of National Candle's staff of about thirty people, including her niece, Assunta, Helen had worked on the office side, typing up order forms and filing expenses. "She typed beautifully," recalled Assunta.

B uilt in 1933, Bishop Loughlin Memorial High School is a beige brick monolith, rising up from Clermont Avenue in Fort Greene, Brooklyn like a four-story monument to unnamed war heroes. Run by the De La Salle Christian Brothers, it was the Exeter or Andover for working-class Catholic kids from Brooklyn, Queens and Long Island. Through competitive entrance exams, each parish from the two boroughs and the island selected its top two students to attend the elite school tuition-free. In the '50s and '60s, Bishop Loughlin was a gateway for the children of largely immigrant families to college and the middle class.

Life at Loughlin was firmly regimented, governed by a set of nonnegotiable rules: Always wear a suit coat and necktie, but no loud ties and no loosening of ties either; stand when your instructor enters the room; no ducktail haircuts; no pegged pants; no smoking within two blocks of the school; no reading of newspapers other than the *New York Times;* no lateness. The academic requirements were rigorous, unforgiving. If a student failed more than two subjects, he was expelled. There were forty-one teachers, all Christian Brothers attired in long black robes, who moved from classroom to classroom throughout the day. Students remained in the same room all day, except for lunch and gym, wedged into hard wooden desks that were bolted to the floor. Every class commenced with the teacher reminding his students "that we are in the holy presence of God." The bareness of the classroom walls was interrupted only by a crucifix and an American flag. At lunchtime, students would file down to the cafeteria, a basement room lined with wall-to-wall lockers, and eat standing up at abdomen-high tables.

Freshmen at the prestigious school were continually, paradoxically, reminded to humbly submit themselves to the will of Almighty God and also to strive for personal excellence, to compete full-tilt against their peers in sports and academics. Loughlin's wide corridors, walled with tiles, featured intimidating display cases packed with trophies and congratulatory plaques. Displayed prominently was a photo of the school's nationally renowned track team, which had appeared on the cover of *Life* magazine in 1945.

When Rudy enrolled in 1957, the school's student population was 1,500, the average class size, forty-five. The students were overwhelmingly Italian, Irish and Polish. In Rudy's class of 378, there were only four black students and one Hispanic.

"I remember Rudy as a very personable young man," said Peter Bonventri, a guidance counselor at Bishop Loughlin, who in Rudy's day, was the assistant principal. "There was nothing absolutely outstanding about him, though. . . . He was serious, but he enjoyed life."

Rudy would wake up before 6 A.M. every weekday morning and commute on the LIRR with stockbrokers bound for Wall Street. He would get off at Atlantic Avenue, walk eight blocks up a hill in Fort Greene and report for homeroom. His relatives recall him as a hardworking student, never unwilling to do his homework. Rudy himself would later state that one of his teachers had told his father that "my grades were very good—I was one of the brightest kids in the class . . ." That teacher, Jack O'Leary, has a more accurate memory. "I don't recall Rudy being on the honor roll," said O'Leary. "I would not think of him as in the top ten percent of that school."

After seven semesters at Bishop Loughlin, Rudy's grade average of 84.8 earned him a ranking of 130, putting him in the class's second quintile. His report cards for those years show columns of mostly B's and C's, a few A's and one D. He scored a 65 in chemistry, a 74 in Latin and a 92 in American history. His combined College Board scores, 569 in verbal and 504 in math, were twenty-seven points shy of 1100, and quite ordinary.

Mr. Giuliani, as his teachers called him, might have been one of those extra-curricular activities junkies whose attention was dispersed in too many directions. During his freshman year, Rudy, just thirteen years old, was chosen as homeroom president. He also signed up that year for the baseball team, after-school intramurals and the LaSalle Club, which raised money for students who desired to become Christian Brothers. He had the top batting average on the intramural team his sophomore year. Junior year, he joined the weightlifting team and prom committee and founded an opera appreciation club. His activities accumulating each year, he was appointed senior year to the sixty-member student council. That year he also joined the catechism club, spurred by what he claims was an interest in becoming a priest, and visited schools in poor neighborhoods to give religious instruction. In a role he would later boast about in a major speech Rudy was given a badge and anointed as a hall monitor in his senior year, supervising students standing on line for the cafeteria and handing out student court summonses to misbehavers. In his first taste of electoral politics, Rudy was the round-the-clock campaign manager for classmate George Schneider in his run for senior class president. In his yearbook, the *'61 Loughlinite*, Rudy's mug shows a serious, slightly chubby and eerily inscrutable young man.

Uncle Leo's gregarious son Lewis was a junior during Rudy's freshman year. But, since Harold had urged Rudy to avoid his older cousin, the two had little, if any, contact. Rather, Rudy began to assemble a coterie of loyal pals who shared his sense of morality and righteousness. Alan Placa, now a Catholic priest on Long Island, and Peter Powers, who would become Rudy's deputy mayor, were his two closest buddies. He spent hours with both in their parents' living rooms, discussing philosophy, religion and politics, sometimes until five in the morning.

Placa and Powers were early recruits to Rudy's opera club. The boys lured other members by inviting them to performances at the Metropolitan Opera in Manhattan and at the Brooklyn Academy of Music right down the street. For only $1.50, they were allowed to stand in the balcony. The club members went to see Verdi's *La Traviata* and Giacomo Puccini's *La Bohème* and *Turandot*.

The young opera aficionado was torn, he would later claim, between entering the religious life and becoming a doctor. Through all four years of high school, he vacillated between the two altruistic career options. He visited several prospective seminaries, including the Diocesan, Jesuit and Franciscan. Senior year was when his adolescent desire to become a priest allegedly hardened into adult intention. "I decided very firmly that I wanted to go into seminary," Rudy later said. "I don't remember what it was in the last year of high school that said to me, listen, I really want to do this. I am gonna do it. I'm going into the seminary."

On an application form for a scholarship from Italian Charities of America, Inc., dated February 1, 1961—the beginning of his second semester senior year—Rudy's self-described passion for the priesthood, however, was nowhere evident. After the question, "Why do you desire a higher education?" Rudy wrote: "To study law or medicine."

(Italian Charities of America, Inc. eventually awarded the earnest young man a $100 scholarship. The President of Italian Charities, to whom Rudy addressed his cover letter, was Judge Anthony Livoti—the same judge who had discharged his uncle Leo from Brooklyn Gambler's Court three years earlier.)

When asked in an unpublished 1988 interview if, while considering the priesthood, he had ever chosen a favorite saint, Rudy, after a long pause and a laugh, replied, "No. No, I don't think I did." But the former scholarship recipient had no problems naming a favorite politician. When questioned about his "outlook on life," it became quite clear that this young man was obsessed, not with the religious oath nor the Hippocratic, but rather with a calling of a different color. "I followed the 1960 election very, very thoroughly," said Rudy. "I used to travel on the train, the Long Island Rail Road, and I can remember every morning getting two or three newspapers and reading about the primary campaigns. . . . I can remember the West Virginia primary, the questioning of [Hubert] Humphrey's war record, and that was the key, the key primary that Kennedy had to win, because [of] the absence of a Catholic vote in West Virginia and the predominance of a Protestant vote, and if you could win that it would be a real test, that he could be nominated as president. And I, I thought he was terrific. I thought Jack Kennedy was terrific."

During his senior year, Rudy convinced a few friends to skip class and sneak out of school to see JFK speak at a rally in the Garment district. The young fan shouldered his way to the front of the crowd so he could shake Jack Kennedy's hand. That fall, Loughlin held mock political conventions, and Rudy gave the nominating speech for Kennedy.

The Kennedy-Nixon debates were what motivated the Loughlin students to create their own electoral contest between the Purple, Gold and White parties. In the days preceding the school election, Rudy campaigned vociferously as the official manager and spokesman for White Party candidate George Schneider. The two drove around together in a station wagon with a hand-scrawled sign affixed to the back exhorting fellow students to "Jump on the White Wagon!" As the car coasted by the school grounds, Rudy pumped his fist out the window, shouting Schneider's name.

A few days later, all three candidates, Schneider, Anthony Shanley of the Gold Party and Joe Centrella of the Purple Party, gathered together on the stage of the school auditorium to give speeches. After the speeches, hands went up with questions for the nervous, neatly attired candidates sweating in their wool sports jackets.

In the back a student called out: "A question for Mr. Shanley."

Rising from a squeaky wooden seat, he asked Shanley why he had attacked his opponents with the claim that they were too busy with extracurricular activities to be senior class president. Wasn't Shanley himself busy with his own extracurricular activities, such as theater?

Shanley peered into the audience to see that his questioner was none other than his opponent's campaign manager, Rudy Giuliani. "I said to myself, 'Hey this is the other guy's mouthpiece,'" Shanley told the *Daily News*'s Paul Schwartzman years later. "I was had. He put me on the spot." In the '61 *Loughlinite*, while other students earned designations such as "Most Handsome" and "Most Popular," Rudy was awarded the distinction of being "Class Politician."

The class politician had, by his own estimation, maybe a half dozen dates in all of high school. "I had two or three crushes," Rudy admitted. "But [it was] really kind of retarded, certainly by modern standards."

When Jack O'Leary got a phone call at home one evening in the early spring of 1960 from one of his students' parents, he thought nothing of it. Harold A. Giuliani frequently phoned the twenty-five- year-old Christian Brother for progress reports on his son Rudy, who was known to act up in O'Leary's homeroom at Loughlin. Sometimes, though, the coarse but courteous man, who was more than twice O'Leary's age, wanted to talk about other things, to seek counsel on matters in his own life.

This time Harold was calling about Rudy's cousin, Lewis Vincent D'Avanzo, who, although better behaved than Rudy, had not been a typical student at the somber Brooklyn boys' school. Plump, garrulous and jocular, Lewis would amble through the halls, showily thumbing through wads of cash, slapping other students on the back, extending his hand with bravado for his teachers to shake.

Harold asked O'Leary, then known as Brother Kevin, if it was okay if he came by the Brothers' House with Lewis's father, Leo D'Avanzo, to talk.

"What's wrong?" O'Leary asked.

"Lewis is in trouble," Harold Giuliani said.

O'Leary knew very little about Harold's brother-in-law Leo. But Harold was his friend, and O'Leary was not the kind of man to refuse a favor to a friend.

The three men met in the parlor of the Brothers' House, a large, spare room with chairs lining the walls and a wooden table in the center. On the wall hung stern portraits of Brooklyn bishops. O'Leary, a soft-spoken, prematurely balding man with a kindly smile framed by deep parentheses, shut and locked the door and then invited Harold and his anxious brother-in-law to sit down.

Stooped with humility, Harold Giuliani smiled and immediately lowered himself into one of the chairs O'Leary had arranged around the table. But Leo would not sit down. Shrouded in a camel hair coat with the collar turned up, wearing a fedora with both front and back brims turned down, forty-eight-year-old Leo D'Avanzo paced to and fro as his brother-in-law relayed his son's quandary.

After dropping out of St. John's University, Harold explained, Lewis signed up with the draft board to go Vietnam, but was rejected because of obesity (at his portliest, Lewis reportedly weighed well over 300 pounds). Looking for action, the restless young man decided to steal a car parked on a street in Brooklyn, said

Harold. He then sold it to the first person he saw, a woman who happened to live on that very street. He had also stolen some New York State Department of Motor Vehicles license-making equipment out of a warehouse in Suffolk County, Harold said. Now the eighteen- year-old was facing grand larceny changes, his fate at the mercy of the unforgiving criminal justice system.

Striding about the room, Leo interjected that the cops had tortured his son. They had tried to extract a confession, he alleged, by plucking pubic hairs out of Lewis's groin.

Embarrassed by Leo's remark, Harold quickly asked O'Leary if he wouldn't mind speaking to the judge on Lewis's behalf.

Jack O'Leary took a minute to consider this. He had only known Lewis as Rudy's cousin and Harold's nephew. But Lewis was, after all, just a kid—in fact, only six years younger than O'Leary himself. And looking at the boy's father—a tall, lean man whose ominous bearing made the Catholic brother uncomfortable— O'Leary decided that Lewis probably wasn't to blame. And, again, he reminded himself, it was his friend Harold Giuliani who was asking the favor.

So Jack O'Leary agreed.

In few days, O'Leary sat down in the judge's spacious Brooklyn chambers. But before he could say anything, the judge, a diminutive Irishman dwarfed by his ample desk, pre-empted his appeal. "Don't bother telling me, Brother," the judge said. "I know what you're going to say. You're going to say Lewis was a good boy, and he did well in school, and he was good to his teachers and so on."

The judge then described Lewis's father as a "petty mafioso" whose main criminal venture was loan-sharking. As for Lewis—"I know how he grew up," the judge said. "He hardly had a chance."

So the judge promised O'Leary that he would suspend Lewis's sentence. Then he asked the young Christian Brother not to tell Harold Giuliani and Leo D'Avanzo, who were both standing out in the hall, what he had agreed to do, "because it would look like I was acting under undue influence," O'Leary recalls the judge saying.

A day after Lewis's trial, Harold Giuliani phoned O'Leary to thank him.

"You did it!" Harold said excitedly. "You did it!"

O'Leary, keeping his promise to the judge, laughed nervously. Then he modestly demurred: "Oh, right. I didn't do anything."

The staff at Loughlin were strict and exacting, but most of them also cared about these boys and were devoted to their education. Some brothers had been or would go on to become missionaries in third world countries as well as human rights activists. Brother Jack O'Leary, who would work as a missionary in Kenya after leaving Loughlin in 1963, was a deeply conscientious man whose belief in a thorough education even got him into trouble a couple of times. Bound by the strict Catholic curriculum, O'Leary taught the sanctioned English syllabus, which included Shakespeare and classic texts such as George Eliot's *Silas Marner*. Occasionally, though, he would weave, if only peripherally, other books into his class, books outside the Catholic canon. He once mentioned *The Catcher in the Rye* because J. D. Salinger's name kept popping up on the State Regents exam. That night one of his students' parents called, irate. "Boy, did I get in trouble for that," O'Leary recalled with a laugh. The ambitious teacher also organized a school-wide book fair, at which students could buy steeply discounted paperbacks like *Lust for Life*, Irving Stone's popular biography of Vincent van Gogh. Solely because that one title contained the word "lust," O'Leary was later rebuked by a senior brother, who publicly accused him during a staff meeting of leading the students astray.

Although open-minded and mild-mannered, Jack O'Leary was no softie when it came to discipline. When Rudy made a wisecrack in the middle of an afternoon lecture, his homeroom teacher marched over to the lisping upstart and cuffed him on the side of the head. In October 1959, the beginning of Rudy's junior year, at a Bishop Loughlin open house, O'Leary was surprised when Harold and Helen Giuliani tentatively approached him and thanked him for smacking their irreverent son. "They asked me if I remembered the time I punished Rudy. I said yes. They said, 'We want to thank you, because he became a much better student after that.'"

From that encounter, a relationship blossomed. Since Rudy and his friend Alan Placa were, in their earlier years, misbehaving to the detriment of other students, O'Leary "would report to my father on my conduct every week," Rudy said. This weekly check-in system soon evolved into a friendship with the Giuliani family. The young Christian Brother would join Rudy, his parents and his grandmother for spaghetti dinners at their split-level in North Bellmore. "There wasn't much furniture on the main floor," O'Leary recalled. "I think much of their resources had gone into buying the house. It was a nice house in a nice neighborhood."

With O'Leary, Rudy finally had an opera listening partner. Many nights after dinner, the two would retire to the basement and listen to Rudy's records, discussing their agreed-upon favorites, such as Verdi's *Otello*. It was O'Leary who helped Rudy found his opera club and served as its advisor. He also instilled in his emerging erudite pupil an appreciation for Shakespeare and poetry. The devoted, twenty-five-year-old Christian Brother would become one of the most important influences in Rudy's early life. "He was terrific," Rudy said. "He spent a lot of time with me, developing interests that I had that I wasn't comfortable about. Like reading and opera, things that I wouldn't talk to my friends about, because they would think I was a sissy."

Some evenings after dinner at the Giulianis, Harold, O' Leary and Rudy would excuse themselves and take a stroll in a nearby park. They would discuss news, politics, matters of religion. Rudy might prattle on about Jack Kennedy or jaw with his father and teacher about the Yankees. Sometimes the high school senior would tread a few paces ahead or lag a few paces behind, and when he was out of earshot, Harold might breach other, more serious, matters with O'Leary. In the spring of 1960, during one of these walks, while Rudy tagged behind them, Harold made a sudden, cryptic confession to his confidant.

"I've done things in the past that I've paid for," Rudy's father said.

The men continued walking, wordlessly, the sounds of their feet on the path suddenly loud in the wake of Harold's comment. Keeping silent, O'Leary waited. He would let Harold offer an explanation, pour his heart out if needed. And O'Leary was ready for whatever this hard, vexed man had to tell him.

But Harold Giuliani said nothing more. As dusk fell, Harold shunted the conversation back to generalities, and Rudy caught up with them and the three sauntered together through the dark back to the house.

The following winter, Harold Giuliani received a letter from Richard P. McLean, the assistant superintendent of the Lynbrook Public Schools. Dated December 7, 1961, the letter read:

"We have heard no word from you concerning your return to work in the Lynbrook Public Schools. The custodial staff is presently shorthanded one man. May I ask that we resolve this issue as soon as possible. . . . Your immediate response to this letter will be appreciated."

McLean was writing Harold because he hadn't been to work in months. Nearly two weeks after the first letter, the assistant superintendent sent the fifty-three-year-old AWOL custodian a second letter:

"As yet I have received no response to my letter of December 7th. As explained in that letter our custodian staff is shorthanded one laborer.

"Please accept this as official notification of the termination of your employment in the Lynbrook Public Schools.

"May we take this opportunity to wish you good luck in the future."

Harold lost his job just as Rudy was finishing up his first semester at Manhattan College. Asked a few months earlier—in his February 1961 application for a scholarship from Italian American Charities—what he planned to do in the case that financial assistance was not granted, Rudy had written: "My father will, of course, help to pay towards my college education as much as he can. Then I expect to work this summer. However, this will not be enough. I must, of necessity, have some outside aid in order to complete my education." He had listed his father's job as a custodian.

With scorching ulcers and the beginnings of a heart problem, Harold Giuliani was no longer the swaggering, hearty man readily disposed to put the knuckles on someone for looking at his wife the wrong way. But the reason he had failed to report to work since the previous spring was not a physical one. "Harold had something of a nervous breakdown," explained his confidant Jack O'Leary. "He wasn't working at the time."

Harold told friends that one of the events that triggered his breakdown was an incident in a Long Island state park in the spring of 1961. For the first time in many years, he was arrested—a chilling, jolting experience that abruptly exhumed old memories. The offense was trivial but embarrassing. Harold had long suffered from severe constipation. One afternoon, while strolling in the park, he suddenly felt the need to go. When he found a public rest room, he pulled his pants down and began doing deep knee bends outside the stalls to expedite the process. A police officer happened to walk in right then. Harold was arrested for "loitering" and hauled down to the local police station. The charges were eventually dismissed, but the experience haunted the fifty-three-year-old.

"The last time I saw Harold," recalled O'Leary, "he was practically bed-ridden. He was sitting out on a lawn chair in the backyard all pale and terrible-looking."

Three

All in the Family
Crooks, Cops and a Junkie

R UDY'S GRANDMOTHERS WERE BOTH ROTUND, ENGULFING ITALIAN Mamas who had lost their husbands at an early age and had thereby assumed the mantle of matriarch. His paternal grandmother, however, was not as pronounced a presence in his life as the affable Adelina. Evangelina Giuliani, whose disarming smile revealed the same kind of bold, bright teeth that Rudy now occasionally, robotically, flashes for stilted photo ops, was a kindly, quiet woman who lived with her daughter and son-in-law, Marie and Frank Scuderi, in Queens.

A seamstress schooled in the sweatshops of the Garment District, Evangelina was a one-woman dress factory. She prolifically stitched beautiful, elaborate dresses for all the women and girls in the Giuliani family, including bridal gowns for her daughters and daughters-in-law. "Eva made all our wedding dresses," recalled her daughter-in-law Evelyn Giuliani. "Every time we had an affair, we all had a dress."

Evangelina Giuliani's greatest gift to her large family was the small white wooden bungalow she rented each summer in Sound Beach, overlooking Long Island Sound. Starting in the late fifties, from early June to Labor Day, the cliffside cottage with the long set of ninety-seven steps down to the sand became the Giuliani clan's idyllic, ready bivouac away from the din of the city. Each family would stay at Sound Beach for two weeks at a time, but, on the weekends, everyone flocked out and nested en masse at the seaside house. "Sound Beach was heavenly," said Evelyn Giuliani. "It was a gift for all of us."

The weekends were cozy and communal. For the big evening feast, the formal mahogany table was dragged out to the driveway, ready to accommodate upwards of twenty-five diners. Over heaping pasta dishes, their tongues loosened by scotch and waters and Tom Collinses, the adults bantered about politics. In his later teens, young Rudy Giuliani would join the fray, usually squaring off with his incurably conservative uncle Rudolph. They argued over civil rights, how the Russians should be dealt with, what kind of a president John F. Kennedy would make.

After dinner, the festivities migrated to the garage for a theme night party. There was Roman night, when everyone would dress up in togas. On Hawaiian night, the revelers were attired in Hawaiian shirts and festooned with homemade floral wreaths. At bedtime, most everyone sprawled out across the floor, some on mattresses, others on box springs. It was all part of the fun.

Most of all, Sound Beach was a time for all the Giuliani cousins to reacquaint themselves. (The D'Avanzos, with the exception of William and Olga's family— who were also Giulianis—did not go to Sound Beach.) The usual crew, in addition to Rudy himself, was comprised of Uncle Rudolph's kids, Debby and Rudolph Jr.; William and Olga's girls, Joan Ellen and Evangeline; Marie's son Robert and Charles's son Charles Jr. Often Rudy's second cousin Regina Peruggi, whose family had rented a summer house just up the road, would join in the festivities along with her brother and sister, Richard and Rita Marie. Regina's father, Salvatore, an executive at RCA Victor Records, was Harold's first cousin—Harold's father and Salvatore's mother had been brother and sister. Sal, as he was called, had been taking his family to their Sound Beach summer retreat years before the Giulianis ever went out there; Evangelina had, in fact, selected her cottage primarily because the Peruggis were already ensconced nearby. Regina, a shy, pretty plump girl who had then volunteered as a summer camp counselor at Wading River, once taught her cousins how to dance the funky chicken at one of the Saturday night theme parties.

Kathy Livermore, a college girlfriend Rudy brought out to Sound Beach remembers a romantic spark between Rudy and Regina. "I think she had a crush on Rudy," remarked Kathy. "I knew she had a crush on him. Isn't that funny?"

Rudy's uncle Charles, the organizer of many a theme night, was a Sound Beach staple. The only member of the Giuliani or D'Avanzo families to serve in World War II, he was a tall, neat man with a finely trimmed mustache and an incongruously gregarious disposition. Like his nephew Rudy, Charles had inherited Rodolfo's love of opera and had even once mustered the mettle to audition for an opera company in New York. He was also an artist who transformed the basement of his house into a rec room for his kids by covering the cinderblock walls with cartoonish paintings of musical notes floating out of guitars and jukeboxes. With just a high school education, he logged twenty years at Queens County Savings Bank, starting as a teller and eventually ascending to assistant vice president in the mortgage department. After retiring from the bank, he bought and ran a gas station in Long Island City with his brother-in-law Frank Scuderi, who had married his sister Marie.

Uncle Rudolph, a patrolman in the New York City Police Department's Building and Repair Bureau, was a tall, lumbering man who would lead the kids on clamming expeditions amidst the tidal pools and jagged stretches of rock along the shore. "He was like a hero for me," Rudy would later say of the uncle with whom he had frequently engaged in political sparring matches. "Because he was very strong, very big man. He used to, when we would spend summers together, he would take all the kids swimming and put us on his shoulders. He was about 6'3" . . . gigantic shoulders."

Rudy and his parents did not spend as much time at Sound Beach as the other families, according to Evelyn Giuliani. Unlike his brothers, Harold would rarely, if ever, go down to the beach. "Most of the time I saw him, he was in a [business] suit," said Evelyn. "I never saw him in shorts."

If uncle Rudolph Giuliani had an equivalent on the D'Avanzo side of the family, it was probably Helen's brother Edward. He was, by everyone's lights, the picture of a stand-up guy and would assume a major role in Harold's, Helen's and Rudy's lives. A ruggedly built man with slightly stooped shoulders, Edward, like three of his brothers, had started his working life as a police officer. In 1942, at age twenty-seven, he shunted his career to an arguably less taxing, but no less dangerous, track of civic service. After taking the admission test for the New York City Fire Department, he started in September with Ladder Company #103 on Sheffield Avenue in Brooklyn. Dutiful and driven, Edward was seriously injured in the line of duty several times; once he was thrown from a hook and ladder when a car hit the fire truck and spent six months in the hospital with broken ankles. After putting in more than thirty years of service with the department, he was promoted to captain in 1974 with an annual salary of $22,051.

Edward had married at the age of twenty-three, in 1938. A thin, polite blonde of German and Scottish extraction, his wife Anna was initially shunned by the D'Avanzo clan because she had a son from a previous marriage, was not Catholic and, most importantly, was not Italian. What also irked some members of the family was that for a period of time before her marriage to Edward, while they were dating, Anna was not yet legally divorced from her previous husband.

Nobody from Edward's family came to his and Anna's wedding, and Edward's mother, the obstinate Adelina, wouldn't speak to Anna for two full years. When the two were finally on speaking terms, Anna once phoned Adelina to apologize for missing a few bridge games, and Adelina replied dismissively that it was okay, her son was the one she wanted to see.

Anna and Edward lived in East New York on 284 Conklin Avenue, until their daughter Lois came home crying that a black girl had shoved her on the subway platform. This solitary incident prompted the family to precipitously pack up and move in December of 1953—shortly after Harold and Helen's departure for the suburbs—to the homogeneous safety of Lynbrook, Long Island.

In the early 1960s, Leo D'Avanzo was mulling a move upstate. His partner and brother, the eponymous Vincent, who had been as frequent a customer as any at his own bar, had succumbed to ill health and would soon be diagnosed with cirrhosis of the liver. But there was another factor nudging Leo northward.

As Leo's loan-sharking operation expanded, radiating into environs outside Flatbush, a conflict surfaced with the head of another loan-sharking and betting outfit based in Coney Island. Lewis D'Avanzo's friend remembers one summer evening in 1962 when Leo drove out to Coney Island to settle the dispute. Harold was with him. After suffering a breakdown and losing his Lynbrook job, Harold was back at Leo's side on a daily basis, once again a captive of Vincent's world. They traveled in Leo's new 1962 convertible Chevy, and Lewis and his friend tailed in another car.

They drove slowly down an avenue in Brighton Beach that was darkened by a raised subway platform. Mickey "Scans," the mobster who ran the Coney Island operation, was standing outside a restaurant smoking a cigarette. Leo parked across the street. Twenty-one-year-old Lewis and his friend had been instructed to park their car a half a block away and remain inside it. They watched the scene from behind the windshield.

Harold and Leo got out of the car. As they ambled across the shadowy avenue, Harold brusquely shouted something at "Scans." With almost mechanical nonchalance, "Scans" pulled a gun out of his coat and began firing. Staggering back, Leo and Harold drew their guns and returned fire. A car parked outside the restaurant apparently provided some cover. "Harold and Leo were standing there in the middle of the street, shooting at this guy," recalls Lewis's friend. "The guy stood there in front of the restaurant and kept shooting."

Finally, Harold and Leo bolted, fleeing back to Leo's Chevy. "Scans just walked back into the restaurant." Lewis and his friend followed Leo and Harold as they sped away.

Leo was later sanctioned by mob bosses for shooting at a made guy and venturing beyond his territory. He was threatened, frozen out of Coney Island and informed that he "would never be a made man." He eventually decided it was time to pick up and resettle far from Brooklyn.

In October 1964, the D'Avanzo duo, Leo and Vincent, sold the bar to their above-board younger brother Edward. When the transaction was completed, Edward had bought not only the bar, but the building that contained it. Vincent's Restaurant was reincarnated once again, this time into an ostensibly honest operation with no bets or back rooms.

Edward's hold-over brother-in-law, Harold Giuliani, without making any investment, became his business partner. Since he was fired by Lynbrook High School three years ago, Harold had had no other known employment. In interviews with six members of the family, no one could site a single job he had held in that time. Working "very little," according to Anna, Harold would show up around 1 P.M. to open Vincent's. Edward, after working all day as a lieutenant in the fire department, would get off duty at 5 or 6 P.M. and come in to relieve Harold. After closing up shop late in the evening, Edward would be left with the responsibility of cleaning up, mopping, sweeping, washing the tables. On some days Harold wouldn't show at all, claiming he was under the weather. "Harold was always getting sick with something," Anna recalled. "He always had something wrong with him. I think he was a hypochondriac." Edward would often gripe to his wife about how little Harold worked, how he obstinately refused to do menial tasks, like cleaning the floors. "Edward complained about it lots of times."

The new Vincent's, stripped of gambling and loan-sharking revenues, was not as profitable as before. Edward borrowed a batch of loans to pay for the place, to try to inject new life into it. While Harold drew a salary, primarily from the loaned money, Edward did not. The loans carried steep interest rates and would put Edward's family into debt for more than twenty years. Even after Edward's death in 1988, his wife Anna was still paying off the loans that had paid Harold Giuliani's salary.

Rudy would later describe his father as an ardent champion of hard work. In the 1997 campaign, in stumping on welfare reform, he regularly invoked Harold Giuliani's advice that there is no such thing as a menial job if it supports one's family. In August 1999, the mayor wistfully declared how happy he was in filing his tax return because his father "used to say it's small price to pay for the freedom that you have in America, and that people should stop complaining about that." But in the mid-sixties at Vincent's Restaurant in Brooklyn, what the allegedly proud promoter of principle had become was a burden on his brother-in-law's back.

Donald Slater, Anna's son from a previous marriage who worked in the bar for a brief period in the mid-sixties, remembers contentious conversations between his mother and Edward over Harold. "I heard my mother yelling at my stepfather, 'Why are you giving him money all the time?'" Edward employed Harold partly out of a charitable impulse, partly because his mother and sister lived with the indolent man and, perhaps, partly even as a favor to his older brothers, Vincent and Leo. The full-time fire lieutenant with a business on the side even helped Harold with his mortgage payments. "He helped him with everything," said Slater.

Slater, who relieved Harold on a few occasions, described him as jittery and nervous. "He had some problems, I don't know what they were," he said. "He was the kind of guy, if an incident happened, it would affect him more than it would other people. . . . He was a born worrier—'What will happen if I do this or do that?' He worried all the time."

Harold and Edward had frequent quarrels. But as the years limped by, that wasn't the only problem. The price of beer was increasing. Loans were piling up. The tenants upstairs weren't paying rent. The gas burners were on the fritz. The plate-glass window out front had been smashed twice. As the neighborhood evolved—devolved in the eyes of some—from Italian to black, the clientele grew rougher, according to Anna. "We were getting a lot of low-class people," she said. "There were fights—it wasn't like it used to be."

And so in December 1971, Edward D'Avanzo decided it was time to sell Vincent's Restaurant as well as the building that housed it. Now, finally, the exhausted fire lieutenant could sit back on his porch on Saturday afternoons, overlooking the tranquil, tree-lined corridor of Lynbrook Avenue, instead of mopping beer-stained floors and repairing busted windows and trying to reason with his progressively unreasonable brother-in-law.

After the bar was taken over by its new owners, "it became a bucket of blood," according to Matthew Barrett, who owned a funeral home across the street. "We used to call it the Boom Boom Club. Shootings, fights, you name it."

In the fall of 1961, Rudy Giuliani, seventeen years old, was commuting from his parents' house in North Bellmore, Long Island to Manhattan College in the Riverdale section of the Bronx. The Long Island Rail Road took the serious young man, often sheathed in a formal suit, to Penn Station. There, he caught the No. 1 subway. His stop was the last on the line, 242nd Street. When he walked off the train, the raised station platform afforded him a sweeping view of Manhattan's hillside campus studded with red-brick Georgian-style buildings.

The atmosphere at all-male Manhattan, run, like Loughlin, by the Christian Brothers, was familiar in the rigidity of its routines. There was a mandatory dress code, and minor infractions, such as tardiness, were treated harshly—being late to class six times amounted to a failing grade in the course. Liquor was banned from campus and women were not allowed in the dormitories. Each class began with the same prayer as at Loughlin: "Let us remember that we are in the holy presence of God."

What must also have felt familiar to Rudy was the cultural insularity of Manhattan's campus. Of the 744 students in his class, three were black and four were Hispanic. The overwhelming majority of the student population at that time were Italian and Irish, usually the first in their families to attend college. Dozens of Rudy's classmates were fellow Bishop Loughlin graduates.

Manhattan students, civilized while on campus, occasionally submitted to their baser instincts off campus, especially when loosened by alcohol. At a 1962 basketball game at the old Madison Square Garden, drunken Manhattan fans clashed with the fans of the opposition, New York University, throwing whisky bottles and beer cans. As the melee escalated, Manhattan fans shouted anti-Semitic slurs at the NYU team, whose star player, Barry Kramer, was Jewish.

The academic challenge at Manhattan was rigorous, with a hefty 148 credits necessary to obtain the bachelor of arts degree. A political philosophy major, Rudy slogged through the required literature, history and fine arts courses.

"I was a crammer in college," Rudy admitted. "I read very fast. This was during the era of President Kennedy's speed reading course, the Evelyn Wood speed reading course. I got all this material about the course, and it did increase my reading speed."

Neighbors in North Bellmore recall seeing the light in Rudy's room, which sat over the garage, remain on until 1 or 2 A.M. most weeknights throughout his college career. In the mornings at 5 A.M., other neighbors would see earnest occupant of that room, marching with certitude out of the house on the way to the bus that would take him to the train that would take him to Manhattan. "Rudy was always very intense," his mother said. "It used to annoy me. Everything to him was real. It wasn't for fun. He wouldn't do anything lightly. I used to say, 'Loosen up!'"

Cramming with the help of Evelyn Wood apparently paid off. Rudy's freshman year grades showed a marked improvement over his high school marks. In his first semester, Rudy earned four A's, three B's and one C. His A's were heavily concentrated in subjects relating to ancient Greece. The one subject for which he earned the C, however, was "Art in the Ancient Orient and in Greece." The B's were obtained in theology, French and biology. His second semester freshman grades, not as strong, were one A, seven Bs and one C. The A was in philosophy, the C in calculus. One of his Bs was awarded in "Dogmatic Theology."

As is his nostalgic tendency, Rudy later hyperbolized the level of his academic achievement at Manhattan, claiming to have graduated magna cum laude; records indicate that he only graduated with honors.

Unlike many of his peers, Rudy did not have a part-time job through most of his school years at Manhattan. His father had lost his custodial job the second semester of Rudy's freshman year. With mediocre high school grades, he did win a small scholarship, $100, from Italian American Charities. Additional, but probably not significant, sources of financial aid might have been the two other organizations to which Rudy applied for scholarships: the New York State Board of Regents and the Knights of Columbus. Neither organization keeps records dating back to Rudy's day. His average score on Regents exams, according to his high school transcript, was 79.25, certainly not a surefire snare for a monetary award. Rudy also joined the Air Force Reserve Officers Training Corps (AFROTC) in his freshman year, which paid a small stipend. But he got out of AFROTC in 1963 due to a "minor hearing problem." Though he did work summers, his known sources of financing didn't come close to paying the $990-per-year tuition bill.

Rudy immersed himself in extra curricular activities, testing Manhattan's political waters. In the spring of his freshman year, Rudy and his loyal sidekick Peter Powers, who had followed him from Bishop Loughlin, mounted a joint electoral bid for leadership of their sophomore class. Rudy would run for President; Powers, a business major, would contend for Treasurer.

Although they shared starkly different political views—Powers was a Goldwater Republican, Rudy a Kennedy Democrat—the two stood outside classrooms, pumping hands and passing out political pin-on buttons. They hatched their own party, the Eagle Party, assembling a slate of candidates from Manhattan's four schools, Liberal Arts, Science, Engineering and Business.

The duo's determination paid off. For the first time in his life, Rudy Giuliani won an electoral contest. He overcame his challenger by eighty-one votes; Powers won by fifty-six.

Galvanized by his victory, Rudy entered another, arguably more arduous, contest. He pledged at Alpha Sigma Beta, a fraternity brimming with jocks and other big men on campus. For several weeks in the fall of 1962, along with twelve other underclassmen, Rudy submitted himself to the mercy of the brothers at ASB. They carried shoeshine kits to buff their elders' shoes. They ate raw eggs and bowls of garlic. They dropped their drawers and allowed themselves to be struck with a large wooden paddle. On top of all this, they gladly tolerated a barrage of verbal insults.

But Rudy Giuliani didn't make the cut. He was blackballed in the first vote, held three weeks after the pledging began. Humiliated but defiant, Rudy responded by pledging at a near-defunct fraternity called Phi Rho Pi and taking over as its president or "praetor." With his ever-loyal buddies, Peter Powers and Alan Placa, Rudy's recruiting efforts reportedly swelled Phi Ro Pi's membership from less than half a dozen to as many as thirty.

In addition to running his class and his fraternity, Rudy wrote a weekly political column for Manhattan's student newspaper, the *Quadrangle*. His columns showcased the arguments and prognostications of an emerging and penetrating political intellect that was at times idealistic, at times pragmatic, but almost always decidedly progressive. In the October 9, 1964 installment of "Ars Politica," Rudy criticized Republican Senator Kenneth Keating for branding his out-of-state challenger, Robert F. Kennedy, as a carpetbagger. "The carpetbagger issue," Rudy wrote, "which is so far the only issue Sen. Keating has gotten any response on, is a truly ridiculous reason for not voting for a man in the year 1964." He went on to issue the following challenge to New York voters: "Let us hope that cosmopolitan New Yorkers can rise above the ridiculous, time-worn provincial attitude that has so disunified our nation. A Kennedy victory will bring about the assertion of a most valuable precedent; that a representative from a particular state must be able to think and vote in the light of national needs and not to be tied only to local and sectional pressures."

In another column, he condemned the John Birch Society, stating, "This is an organization whose fear of Communism has grown to such proportion that all become suspect and all that is needed to convict is allegation, not trial by jury." He described the writings of a John Birch Society extremist as the "disgusting, neurotic fantasy of a mind warped by fear and bigotry." In other installments, Rudy praised President Johnson's "war on poverty" and characterized Barry Goldwater as an "incompetent, confused and idiotic man."

During Rudy's sophomore year, his father bought him a used Plymouth Valiant, and he and a few of his frat brothers would squeeze into his car with their dates and drive to My Father's Mustache or the Village Gate. Rudy's girl, Kathy Livermore, was a tall, shapely and highly coveted blonde from Massapequa, Long Island, who, according to one of his former frat brothers, was "very sexy." They had met over the summer at a savings bank in Freeport, where Rudy had been a summer assistant and Kathy a clerk.

The portly young man with a pronounced lisp was perhaps a tad self-conscious about dating such an attractive girl. He was possessive and easily provoked to jealousy. On at least one occasion, taking cues from his palooka pop, Rudy dealt a blow to protect Kathy's honor. "I think we were going to a dance," recalled Kathy Livermore. "We were in the city. The guy either said something, or made a remark, or whistled and Rudy just turned right around and punched him. His friends pulled him off the guy. They said, 'Don't do that, what's the matter with you?'"

Kathy's beau also harbored an occasional tendency to become pedantic. "I remember one time, he was taken with Sartre and he used to quote Sartre a lot," said Livermore. "He loved to teach, he loved to explain things, and he'd really get—it would be almost like a lecture, like he was teaching a class, you only needed to be one person."

Livermore remembers going with Rudy up to his room in his parents' North Bellmore house and watching him deliver mock speeches as he sat behind an oversized walnut desk. He would try out different hand gestures as he spoke, asking her how it looked, and would even rehearse pounding his fist on the desk for dramatic effect. Rudy discussed with his girlfriend the possible strategies for ascending the political ladder. In one conversation, he admitted that his allegedly die-hard devotion to the Democratic Party and the ideals of JFK might become a liability for him in the long run. The single-minded, square-jawed young man explained offhandedly that the Democratic Party was weighed down with an overabundance of other young men like himself. "The Republican Party had a lot less young men," Livermore recalls Rudy saying. "More stodgy and there might be more room to get farther that way. He discussed that with me."

He also described to his girlfriend the kind of wife he would need to become a successful politician. If possible, Rudy insisted, she should be a clone of Jackie Kennedy. "She was the perfect person for that position," Livermore remembers Rudy explaining to her. "She really never expressed strongly any opinions about anything. She stayed in the shadows, and that was the kind of ideal type of wife. She had the babies, she did things like redecorate the White House."

The aspiring politician also confided in his girlfriend his single greatest ambition—to be the first Italian Catholic President of the United States.

At New York University Law School in the fall of 1965, Rudy Giuliani sat quietly, attentively, in the back of the lecture hall, his eyes slowly rising and falling, moving between his notepad and the distant form of a gesturing instructor, his tensed fingers shimmying his pencil across the page.

"The thing about Rudy," said former classmate Stephen Gillers, now an NYU professor, "is that he was not prominent in the class. If you came into our class in 1968 and said 'I can see into the future and one of you will be mayor of New York—who do you think it would be? Write down the ten most likely candidates.' I don't think Rudy's name would have appeared on any lists." He was known, however, as a disciplined worker bee.

Although hardly, if ever, speaking up in class, Rudy did distinguish himself by making law review in his first year. "It was the highest honor for the first year of law school," recalls Steve Hoffman, Rudy's former roommate, who also made law review.

Before rooming with Steve, Rudy still lived with his parents in their North Bellmore house. The walls of his room were covered with law books that had been donated by Harold's friend from East Harlem, Louis Carbonetti. The books, which Carbonetti removed from the Supreme Court building in Manhattan and carted all the way to the Giulianis' house in Long Island, had expired. "Rather than tossing them," said Carbonetti's son, Lou Jr., "he passed them onto Rudy."

When Rudy left the house his second year, he and Steve were assigned a large room in Hayden Hall. They slept on Murphy beds that swung down from recesses in the wall and shared a refrigerator that was situated in an alcove off the main room. The roomies quickly became friends. Hoffman introduced Rudy to *The Free Wheelin' Bob Dylan*. Rudy, in turn, played opera records for his new pal.

During their third year, Rudy and Steve moved together into an L-shaped studio in the West Village. Decorating the walls were a Ronald Reagan movie poster and a dartboard with a photo of Richard Nixon's face affixed to it.

It was at the outset of Rudy's senior year at Manhattan that his uncle Edward had taken over Vincent's from Leo. Soon after, Rudy himself served behind the counter with his dad, pulling pints and mixing drinks. "One day Harold asked Rudy to serve at the bar," said Edward's wife, Anna D'Avanzo. "He did it for one day, then he would never do it again. He didn't want anything to do with it."

During his law school days, however, Rudy would spend a lot of time at another bar. After an exam at NYU, regardless of the time of day or night, he and his bleary-eyed buddies would ritually gather at Mc Sorley's Old Ale House, a dark, smoky Irish pub on 7th Street in the East Village with sawdust-covered floors, for some celebratory pints. "If anyone talked about exams, he had to buy everybody a round," recalled Hoffman. "One morning at 10 A.M., after Rudy and I had handed in a take-home exam, we banged on Mc Sorley's until they let us in."

Another Mc Sorley's regular, Chris McKenna, who edited the law review, remembers that Rudy was "very arrogant, the same as he is now," and a "real RFK democrat, a liberal, except on law and order."

Nonetheless, while Rudy pored over his law books in the NYU library, outside in the streets of Greenwich Village, the sixties raged. But the earnest law review student with the conscientious comb-over was not the type to join a march or a sit-in, according to his roommate. "We both wanted to become lawyers," Hoffman said. "And we both didn't want to get arrested."

The Kennedys' number one fan did, however, ally himself with the activists and protesters on two key issues of the time: civil rights and the Vietnam war. "It was the wrong war in the wrong place," said Rudy of Vietnam. "It was something I used to analyze morally. Vietnam didn't meet the conditions of what Catholics call a just war. It wasn't right to be sacrificing all these lives."

Toward the end of law school, Rudy's romantic life rekindled when he began dating a woman he'd known all his life. His second cousin Regina Peruggi was a cute, quiet young woman, and like Rudy, an ardent Kennedy supporter. The cousins had gone on one date years earlier, when Rudy took Regina to his high school junior prom. They were chaperoned by both their fathers, who jointly drove them to the dance. "I remember wearing a black and white dress, and Rudy brought me a baby orchid," Regina recalled. "Afterward, our two fathers picked us up and drove us to a Brooklyn restaurant. Quite a family affair!"

Now, as Rudy finished up law school and Regina worked as a counselor in a drug rehabilitation clinic, the nature of their relationship grew far more serious. And Helen Giuliani was none too pleased. Her objection was not that the two were cousins, but, rather, that their personalities were incompatible. "I think they were in love with the thought of being in love," Helen said. "My son is very affectionate, he's always hugging and kissing. Gina is lovely, but she is very quiet and shy. Sometimes you would try to hug her and she would pull away."

In late spring of 1968, despite his mother's opposition, Rudy proposed to Regina. His cousin accepted.

One night a week or so later, the newly engaged twenty-four- year-old was roused by his father. "You won't believe what happened," Harold whispered.

And, at first, Rudy didn't.

Harold had just seen it on the news—Rudy's hero, Bobby Kennedy, had been shot. He died the next day, and the day after, in a state of shock, Rudy and Regina joined 120,000 other mourners who filed slowly past St. Patrick's Cathedral to view the mahogany casket that contained a man Rudy had once unequivocally described in his college column as "great and brilliant."

Rudy deeply admired Bobby Kennedy for pursuing the mob-infested Teamsters union as attorney general. But the depth of his affinity was far greater than that or his religious identity with the Catholic Democrat. "I thought Robert Kennedy's presence in national politics was irreplaceable," said Rudy. "He had the support of the minority community in a way no other white politician did, and he had the ability to communicate with the white middle class. There was no one else with a foot in both camps."

The chameleonic Leo D'Avanzo, now in his early fifties, had once again reinvented his career. The former taxi driver cum bar owner cum loan shark was now a contractor. He and his wife Betty and their two daughters, Lee Ann and Helen, had nestled in the bucolic environs of Binghamton, in Broome County, New York, not far from the famously mob-saturated town of Apalachin.

An old, loyal associate from Brooklyn, Nicholas "Doc" Somma, who had run a demolition business in Flatbush, followed Leo to Binghamton. As did his longtime mistress, Elizabeth Mandelino. She moved into an apartment that Leo found for her and took a factory job at Kroehler, a furniture manufacturer.

D'Avanzo Contracting, a demolition company, was Leo's principal business venture in Broome County, founded soon after his arrival. A November 18, 1967, article in the Binghamton *Press & Sun Bulletin* reported that D'Avanzo Contracting had asked the town of Union for permission to use the DiAngelo gravel pit as a dumping site for the debris of demolished homes. The pit in question had been the scene of two tragic accidents: one child had drowned there and another had been asphyxiated after a bank of earth had collapsed. Somma, the treasurer of D'Avanzo Contracting, wrote the town: "We believe the filling of this area will be of mutual benefit to all parties concerned."

But the memory of two dead children and the debris from demolished homes may not have been the only things buried in that gravel pit.

Gina Gialoreta, the daughter of Leo's niece, Assunta, had lived in Binghamton with her family long before Leo settled there. She remembers watching one day as her uncle Leo and a few other men rolled several brand new Cadillacs into a pit. "They just drove them into the dirt," she said. "And covered them. . . . They had to be hot."

In September of 1970, after he had founded his own contracting firm, Somma was arrested on felony charges of criminal possession of twenty stolen dump trucks and other construction equipment. Some of the stolen trucks had also been used by D'Avanzo Contracting. Lewis D'Avanzo's friend from the bar said the trucks were stolen from the city and driven up to Binghamton on Leo's orders and that Somma "took the heat for it." Somma pled guilty and got five years' probation.

Leo's son Lewis didn't go to Binghamton with him. An instantly likable, contagiously easy-going fellow with a coarse charm, the Bishop Loughlin Memorial High School graduate and St. John's University drop-out had always been "book smart." Neighbors on Rockland Avenue in Staten Island remember a hulking man, who would always trot out to the ice cream truck when it stopped on his block and lumber back to the house carefully carrying a cluster of ice cream cones for his four kids. He was a doting father and husband, and, although some "associates" occasionally came over for dinner, he tried to separate his home and "work" life. "He treated my first children like they were his," recalled Lois D'Avanzo, who married Lewis with two kids from a previous marriage.

When not playing the part of suburban family man, Lewis D'Avanzo, however, was "Steve the Blond," a ruthless and widely feared mob associate in charge of a massive stolen car ring. Listed repeatedly on FBI bulletins as "armed and dangerous," D'Avanzo was characterized by a bureau informant in a November 1977 report as a "brutal individual who fancied guns." Suspected of taking part in several murders, the thug was also "known to be a very intelligent and versatile 'mover' in hoodlum circles and a real money maker," according to the FBI memo.

During their childhoods, Lewis and Rudy were not allowed to spend much time together, despite the fact that Rudy's father worked for Lewis's father. The two cousins grew up, however, in close proximity, attending the same elementary school and high school. Lewis enrolled at St. Francis of Assisi Roman Catholic Parochial School in July of 1947, two years before Rudy started there. A model student, Lewis maintained a 92 percent grade average at St. Francis of Assisi and earned an "A" in conduct. At Bishop Loughlin, he earned an 86 percent grade average. Rudy's academic performance at Loughlin was similar, with a slightly lower average of 84.8. But the future mayor's classroom behavior paled in comparison with his gangster cousin's: Lewis was rewarded at Loughlin for "good" conduct, while Rudy was routinely punished for acting out.

Despite Brother Jack O'Leary's attempt to help Lewis after his initial arrest for auto theft in 1960, the enterprising young man followed in his father's wayward footsteps. Two years later in January 1962, he was arrested again, this time for armed robbery, forgery and grand larceny; he pled guilty and got one and a half to three years' probation. In the mid to late '60s, as he ricocheted from one job to another, his crimes became increasingly more serious and calculated.

A brunette bombshell from Bensonhurst, Lois met Lewis in 1966 at her sister's wedding. The groom, a friend of Lewis's, introduced them. "He was very intelligent," said Lois, her voice softening with nostalgia. "Very quiet . . . he was very romantic." Within a few months, they moved into an apartment on East 52nd Street in Brooklyn. A year later, in a strip-side chapel in Las Vegas, they were married.

In 1968, Lewis and his wife accepted an invitation to Rudy's wedding to Regina Peruggi. The twenty-seven-year-old felon walked up to his aspiring law-man cousin at his wedding reception and congratulated him. Lewis then introduced Rudy to his petite, polite wife Lois. That was the first and last time Lois D'Avanzo met Rudy Giuliani. "I think he stood away from Lewis because of their different lifestyles," she offered.

The D'Avanzos soon moved out of Brooklyn, taking out a mortgage in May of 1969 on a $38,000 two-story house with a garage on Rockland Avenue in Staten Island. Lewis landed a job at nearby Caton's Scrap Metal on Richmond Terrace, making $175 per week as a non-ferrous metals sorter. He woke early and got home early, around 4:30 P.M., to spend a little time with his kids. Later, in the evening, he often left to meet with "associates."

Lewis D'Avanzo's criminal career crystallized just one month after he and wife had moved into their new house. In June of 1969 at the age of twenty-eight, he was arrested for taking part in the armed hijacking of a truck containing $240,000 worth of mercury. On December 4, Lewis was sentenced to ten years at the federal penitentiary in Lewisburg, Pennsylvania, to be followed by five years' parole.

While serving his sentence for the hijacking, he was in indicted in March of 1972 on charges of running a document-forging operation that had furnished the paperwork to cover up the theft of $250 million in stolen luxury cars in New York City in 1971—roughly 60 percent of the 96,000 cars stolen that year. Brooklyn District Attorney Eugene Gold stated that the ring had also purloined $8 million in luxury cars, selling them for $1,500 each. Gold then identified Lewis D'Avanzo as the mastermind behind the operation.

Lewis's document forging and stolen car ring was a "big earner," according to Doug Levien, the detective in Gold's office who worked the case. Levien, who has also kept a file on Lewis's father, Leo, said the ring furnished clients with cars and fake licenses and registrations "all over the world," including the Middle East. When the state police raided the operation, they found a "mini motor vehicle department," said Levien. "It was like a license and registration shop." The "shop" included, among other things, a Vehicle Identification Number (VIN)-making machine and Department of Motor Vehicle typing balls that enabled the outfit to make documents indistinguishable from the real thing.

FBI head William Webster wrote a memo on the D'Avanzo crew: "Five ring members were murdered 'gangland style.' Informant information corroborated the murders." Webster also noted that the "sources" of many of the ring's counterfeit registration titles "were various organized crime associates and a Capo in the Luchese La Cosa Nostra Family."

The capo was later identified as Anthony Tortorello. The ring was also involved with Colombo crime family capo and FBI informant Greg Scarpa, according to Levien.

Lewis's partner, John Quinn, was a chop shop operator and car thief who delivered the ring's Cadillacs and Lincolns to the Gambino family's notorious number-one butcher, crew chief Roy DeMeo. A September 9, 1977 FBI report described Quinn and D'Avanzo as "the principal operators of a commercialized auto theft ring operating out of Brooklyn."

DeMeo's crew—the bloodiest in city history—was later convicted of executing Quinn and his nineteen-year-old mistress, Cherie Golden, with whom he had shared sensitive details of the ring's operation. A November 1977 FBI report notes that "D'Avanzo was rumored to have been behind the murders."

On August 30, 1977, Lewis's father Leo, sixty-five years-old, died of emphysema at Binghamton General Hospital. Leo D'Avanzo was lowered into a grave marked by a small brass name plate. His on-the-books estate, worth $202,403.56, was left to his wife Betty.

On October 31, almost exactly two months after his father's death, Lewis D'Avanzo was observed by FBI agents barreling through Brooklyn in a late-model luxury car, with two associates, brothers Ralph and Joseph Esposito. Lewis and the Esposito brothers were wanted on warrants accusing them of interstate transportation of 100 stolen late-model luxury cars. His FBI "armed and dangerous" profile had also been upgraded since the early 1970s. A 1977 FBI "administrative" report noted that "in addition to the Quinn and Golden murders, stories have been in circulation for years that D'Avanzo had knocked off a number of individuals he was associated with."

At the corner of 65th Street and Twelfth Avenue, adjacent to the Regina Pacis Church and Elementary School, agents watched the car, driven by one of the Esposito brothers, slow to a stop. Lewis got out and sank into another car, a 1975 green Ford Maverick. One agent drove his car behind the Maverick, blocking an escape. The other agents walked toward Lewis's car, shouting that he was under arrest and ordering him to get out of the car. Flustered, Lewis mumbled, "Okay, okay," but remained in the car.

Throwing the Maverick into reverse, Lewis backed up abruptly, smashing into the agent's car. Then, according to the FBI's report, he gunned his engine, accelerating forward, and tried to run down agent Richie Mika. Two other agents drew their guns, a .57 Magnum and a 12-gauge shotgun, and fired into the Maverick, shattering the windshield. As Lewis's car slowed to a stop and his ample body slumped over the driving wheel, the agents hauled the Esposito brothers out of their car and took them into custody. A half hour later, Lewis D'Avanzo, thirty-six, was dead on arrival at Maimonides Hospital.

Agents found three envelopes containing over $8,000 in cash on Lewis. In the glove compartment of the 1975 Maverick was an envelope with the car's registration and insurance, listed under the name, not of Lewis, but of his late father, Leo "Tullio" D'Avanzo.

Lewis's wake was held in a funeral home on Richmond Road in Staten Island. Harold Giuliani, who made it his credo to never miss a wake, missed this one. So did Helen and Rudy.

Elizabeth Mandelino, Leo's former mistress, was living in Binghamton when she found out about Lewis's death in a phone conversation with her brother Michael. As Elizabeth wept, Michael interrupted her. "Mona," he said to his sister. "Don't cry for Lewis. He had a hit on me."

Five months later, Michael Mandelino was ambushed outside his body shop by members of the DeMeo crew. Suspecting him of tipping off thieves who had robbed an associate of DeMeo's, the crew members shot Mandelino and a friend in the head, stuffed them into the trunk of a car parked in the lot and then set Mandelino's body shop on fire.

"We had Cambodia right here in Brooklyn," said Elizabeth. "The killing fields."

Ralph Stanchi Jr., another Rudy cousin, was the moral opposite of Lewis Vincent D'Avanzo. A patrolman for the 32nd Precinct in Harlem, he was a slight, soft-spoken, by-the-book cop, who, according to his former fellow officers, eschewed force in favor of talking things out. He had served two tours in Vietnam and won the Bronze Star with silver clusters. In his four years at the 32nd Precinct, he won four citations for outstanding work.

On Sunday, June 17, 1973, Stanchi and a fellow officer, Richard Chiappa, received a report that an armed man was terrorizing customers at the Capri Bar on Lenox Avenue and 135th Street in Harlem. Joined by a third officer, Carmine Morra, Stanchi and Chiappa arrived at the bar a little after 9:30 P.M. The bartender's son, lingering outside, warned them that the gunman was standing to the right inside the door. Stanchi entered first, stepping gingerly across the threshold. The bar was packed with fifty people, revelers at a Father's Day party.

"I hear Ralph say, 'Drop the gun!'" recalled Chiappa. "Then I see the guy in front of us, the gun pointing down. Ralph says, 'Drop the gun!' again. The guy comes straight for us. I said, 'Drop the fucking gun!'"

When the gunman, fifty-six-year-old Boyce Russell, was within an arm's length of Stanchi, the conscientious cop finally drew his weapon. Russell then raised his .38 caliber revolver and fired almost point-blank into Stanchi's abdomen.

"Then my gun and Ralph's were going off," said Chiappa. "I shot him twice. Ralph shot him twice. He shot at me. I looked down, and said 'How could he miss me?' Then I shot him four times."

Officer Morra finally killed Russell but not before the gunman's bullets had taken their toll. The bartender was dead and seven people were wounded, including Chiappa, who staggered over to Stanchi, now gasping on the floor. "Ralph was down," said Chiappa, holding back tears. "Eyes open, blood coming out of his mouth, blood coming out of his ears."

Stanchi was immediately rushed to Harlem Hospital. He died in the emergency room.

On June 21, just a few days after Father's Day, Ralph Stanchi Jr., the twenty-nine-year-old father of two young children, received a full inspector's funeral with sixty-four official pallbearers at Our Lady of the Snow Roman Catholic Church in Floral Park, Queens. In attendance were more than a thousand police officers, the seven borough commanders, the Police Commissioner and Mayor John Lindsay. Stanchi's father, Ralph Stanchi Sr., shook a lot of hands that day. He greeted William and Robert D'Avanzo as well as Harold and Helen Giuliani. He does not remember Rudy coming. Neither does Stanchi's widow Florence.

Several of Rudy's former friends and associates, many of whom were extremely close to him at the time of Ralph Stanchi's death in 1973, say the prosecutor never mentioned his hero cop cousin. Jeff Harris, who was Rudy's deputy at the U.S. Attorney's Office for the Southern District at the time, and a close personal friend, says Rudy never spoke about a cousin killed in the line of duty. "It doesn't ring a bell," said Harris. Ken Feinberg, who socialized with him often at the time, also never heard him mention Ralph Stanchi, Jr. Neither did undercover informant Bob Leuci, who spoke with Rudy on an almost daily basis in the summer of 1973, nor federal investigator Carl Bogan, who was Rudy's driver at that time. "Rudy and I were pretty good friends in those days," said Leuci. "I never heard that." Harris,

Leuci, Bogan and Feinberg worked with him on police corruption cases, making his failure to say anything about Stanchi puzzling.

Rudy did mention his cousin on July 30, 1992 in a campaign appearance at the Institute for Puerto Rican Policy that was not covered by the press. Buttressing his attack on David Dinkins's police policies, Rudy proclaimed: "The assault that the Mayor is presently conducting on the New York City Police Department is counter productive. . . . And I say that as somebody who comes from a background in which I have four uncles who were police officers, and two cousins, one of whom lost his life in the line of duty." (He actually has four cousins who were cops—Ralph and Edward Stanchi, Robert Scuderi and Robert D'Avanzo Jr.). Candidate Giuliani assailed Dinkins once for missing a cop's funeral, and was slammed himself by a group of police widows for campaigning "on the gravestones of our husbands" when he did a press conference endorsement at a ceremony honoring fallen officers.

When asked about Rudy's treatment of cops as mayor, Ralph Stanchi Sr., a retired airport stock clerk whose other son is still on the force, was blunt. "Koch, he was good to the cops," said Ralph Sr. "Rudy, he doesn't give the cops a hell of a lot of money. His gave himself a raise; he gave all his asshole buddies a raise."

Neither Ralph Stanchi Sr. nor his daughter-in-law Florence Vidicksis received any condolences, written or otherwise, from Rudy after the funeral. Florence said she didn't even know her late husband and Rudy were related until she read about it years after the funeral in a police magazine. Rudy and Ralph Jr. had known each other as boys, according to Ralph Sr., but drifted apart as they got older. "When Rudy went to college," said Ralph Sr., "Ralph Junior naturally didn't see him anymore." Regardless of whether or not he went to the funeral, Rudy was so distant from the Stanchi family that Ralph Sr. has only seen him in person once in the last thirty years.

That one occasion was the mayoral inaugural in 1998. It took the eighty-one-year-old veteran three hours to get there from his home in Long Island, taking a car, bus and train. After the ceremonies, he found his niece, and Rudy's mother, Helen Giuliani. His famous nephew strode over at one point, hugged his uncle and left.

Ralph Sr. fished out of his pocket a 100-year-old rosary bead necklace that used to belong to Adelina D'Avanzo, his half-sister and Helen's mother. He explained to Helen that Adelina had brought the beads from Italy and that they had been passed down through the family to him. And now, he said, as he strung the bead necklace around Helen's neck, I'm giving them to you, so you can pass them on to Rudy. After all, said Stanchi, he was, at that time, Rudy's only surviving uncle on his mother's side of the family. "I'm the only blood relative," he said. "The only uncle he has." After the inauguration, Ralph Stanchi Sr. took the same long, cold, three-hour commute home.

Rudy has never spoken publicly about Joan Ellen D'Avanzo, a cousin far closer to him than either Ralph Stanchi or Lewis D'Avanzo. A couple of years older than Rudy, she and he lived in the same home until Adelina sold 419 Hawthorne when Rudy was seven. Many relatives described Joan—the daughter of William D'Avanzo and Olga Giuliani—as Rudy's surrogate sister.

In the summers, the two cousins vacationed together at the Giuliani clan's cottage in Sound Beach, Long Island. Helen was Joan Ellen's godmother. As with Stanchi, however, Rudy grew apart from Joan with age, and in adulthood, the two cousins took starkly divergent paths.

Rudy became chief of the U.S. Attorney's narcotics division, while Joan was a junkie, addicted since her late teens. Disappearing from her parents' Rego Park apartment for days at a time, Joan Ellen fed her addiction with "a smattering of everything," according to Gina Gialoreta, Joan Ellen and Rudy's second cousin. "Everyone knew Joan Ellen had a drug problem," recalled Gina. "She would stiff my grandmother with cab bills." Several other relatives confirmed Gina's account of Joan's life.

On September 28, 1973, just three months after Ralph Stanchi was gunned down, Joan Ellen D'Avanzo was found by police. "Joan was beaten in an alleyway," said Gina. "She probably owed someone money for drugs." Upon admission to Bellevue Hospital, Joan underwent a craniotomy that revealed a "purulent brain abscess of [the] cerebral hemisphere." In a coma for the next six months, she remained motionless in her hospital bed, until on April 22, 1974, just thirty-four years old, Joan Ellen D'Avanzo died.

Though the medical examiner had catalogued the cause of Joan Ellen's death as "undetermined," three family members said she was murdered—some of whom insisted on talking about it only if they weren't quoted, though they'd freely discussed much of the rest of the family history. The proper and polite Evelyn Giuliani produced the prayer card with her niece's date of death, but refused to speak about the circumstances of her death. When asked if she knew how Joan Ellen had died, Evelyn refused to say if she had been murdered.

The relationship between Harold Giuliani and Edward D'Avanzo wasn't the only family tie that unraveled. In the early 1970s, Adelina complained to her

daughter-in-law, Anna D'Avanzo, that life with Harold Giuliani was becoming un-
bearable. The ailing octogenarian told Anna, to whom she had grown exceptionally close in her waning years, of her irascible son-in-law's increasingly
uncontrollable temper. He had once excoriated Adelina after she had accidentally
set a fire in the kitchen at 2654 Pine Court.

Adelina, who had enabled Harold and Helen to buy their first house, compen-
sated Harold for the damage caused by the fire. Anna said that since Rudy no
longer lived in the house, Adelina hadn't been able to tell her grandson what a
"bastard" his father had become. The desperate old woman was increasingly re-
liant on her new confidant; Anna even cut her toe nails when no one else would.
At one point, Adelina said that "she couldn't stand Harold anymore" and asked
her sympathetic daughter-in-law—to whom, many years ago, she had once refused to speak—if she could live with her and Edward in Lynbrook. "She was very
serious," recalled Anna.

Explaining that Edward had just been diagnosed with cancer, Anna told her
mother-in-law that she was sorry, but that that would be impossible. In November
1976, Adelina, ninety-four years old, died of leukemia at Mercy Hospital.

Two years later, his prostate cancer advancing, Harold was making frequent visits
to the hospital himself. In October 1978, he and Helen sold their split-level house in
Bellmore for $52,000 and rented a three-bedroom apartment in Bayside, Queens for
$600 per month. A sedate middle-class neighborhood, their section of Bayside was
populated with clusters of retired Italians, Irish and Germans. The Giulianis' apartment building on the corner of 218th Street and Horace Harding Parkway would
have been just as peaceful and quiet as Pine Court if not for the relentless roar of the
Long Island Expressway less than fifty feet from the front door.

A friendly Italian couple, Joe and Lina Merli, owned the building, living in the
first-floor apartment. The Giulianis, who lived upstairs, would often join the
Merlis for dinner, bantering in Italian over Lina's sprawling pasta feasts.

"Harold, he was so funny man, a very familiar person," recalled Lina, an eighty-
two-year-old retired hotel housekeeper, who still struggles at times with her
English. On Saturday afternoons, Lina and Harold would often share stories,
lolling in lawn chairs on her small garden patio, just a chain-link fence and a few
lilac bushes away from the drone of the LIE. Harold proudly predicted that his
lawyer son Rudy would go on one day to become President of the United States
and, perhaps as evidence, carried with him a photo of Rudy standing next to
President Ronald Reagan. He once told Lina how happy he would be if Rudy married her beautiful daughter, Luchana.

On one of these afternoons, Harold also shared with his new landlord his views on race. "Giuliani's father," recalls Lina, "was disturbed by colored people." The polite woman listened as Harold expounded on the differences between whites and blacks. "Harold say, 'God separate the colored and the white.' He say, 'Because all the world is white, except Africa.'" Harold's explanation for why blacks are black? "God said the colored were not mature," Lina remembers Harold telling her. "So God put them in the oven to make them mature. But God, he forget to take them out, so colored people came out black."

Because of his progressing prostate cancer, Harold had to urinate frequently, and often while out in the garden with Lina, he would stagger into a corner, unzip his pants and moan with relief as he pissed into the weeds.

Rudy, then a full-time partner at Patterson, Belknap, earning $160,000 per year, frequently visited his parents in Bayside and even had his own room in their apartment. Lina remembers that the third bedroom in Harold and Helen's apartment had been made up for Rudy, who would occasionally stay for as long as a week at a time.

At seventy years old, Harold was commuting by bus to a part-time custodial job at the Gotham Building Maintenance Corporation on 28th Street in Manhattan. A man whose sporadic fifty-year work history was composed of largely off-the-books jobs, was back on the books again, part of a 300-man fleet that, among other things, waxed floors, shampooed carpets and washed windows in city buildings.

Lina's husband, Joe, a decorated World War II veteran, was the cousin of legendary old-time Democratic district leader, John Merli, who ruled a swath of East Harlem adjacent to Lou Carbonetti's old district. Soon after Harold and Helen moved into his building in Bayside, Joe Merli became a close friend. "Helen say, 'Joseph Merli, he is not a landlord—he is my brother,'" recalled Lina.

Helen and Lina spent a lot of time together in the kitchen. In lamenting her age, Helen would joke to Lina how her mother "used to make the pots burn," adding, "now, I make the pots burn."

On the weekends and on Harold's off-days, he and Joe would usually walk three blocks down the Horace Harding to the Bayside Senior Citizens' Center, a flat, maroon-brick building where they would spend the afternoon playing pool and poker with the grumbling, ill-tempered old-timers. It was a familiar setting for Harold, its fluorescent lighting, dull salmon-colored linoleum floor tiles and bright multicolored plastic chairs reminiscent of a high school cafeteria. It was a place to hang out, chew the fat, get away from the house. Everybody had chores, though, and Harold and Joe would usually end up washing dishes. As they sponged plates one afternoon, Harold suggested to Joe that if they only did a so-so job washing these dishes, maybe they could escape dish duty in the future.

It was more than a year since they had moved to Bayside, and the pain from Harold's prostate cancer was becoming so severe that he had trouble walking. He quit Gotham Maintenance. His routine checkups became more frequent. Lina remembered Harold telling her about his doctor's warnings. "The doctor, he tell him—you have to be operated on," she recalled. But when it came to surgery, the proud man was obstinate. "Nobody is going to touch my balls!" Harold declared to Lina one afternoon in the garden.

On some nights, wracked with pain, Harold would roll out of bed and fall onto the floor, helpless, unable to move. Helen would rush downstairs and rouse Joe Merli, who would help hoist the stubborn, tortured old man back into bed.

Three cousins killed within five years. A mob uncle and cousin. A cop uncle protecting the mob uncle. A family junkie. A father broken by a nervous breakdown, unable to hold a regular job, dependent on relatives. How did New York's champion of chastity manage to so deftly emboss his past, to sweep such a broad, wholesome stroke across it all? And how did these circumstances and events shape this man, this supposedly self-sculpted Goliath? Did they carve further flutes into his pillar of righteousness? Or snake cracks deep into its center? Or is he himself so buoyed by denial that it has all receded into a fog of dreams?

In 1989, Dan Collins, who was working on Giuliani's biography with the cooperation of the legendary prosecutor, was given Jack O'Leary's telephone number in California. Rudy suggested he call O'Leary, a longtime close friend of the family. O'Leary remembers getting several Collins messages on his machine. Even though Collins claimed Guiliani had suggested they talk, O'Leary decided not to call back. Next O'Leary heard Rudy's voice on the phone for the first time in years. The then mayoral candidate told O'Leary that Collins said O'Leary wasn't returning messages and urged the ex-brother to call Collins back. O'Leary expressed concern about how to handle questions about Harold.

"Do you remember the time your cousin Lewis stole a car?" O'Leary asked.

"Yes," Rudy answered.

"Do you remember when you came with me and your father and your uncle Leo to a Brooklyn courthouse?"

"I wasn't there," Rudy interrupted, correcting O'Leary.

"Oh," O'Leary said. "Well, anyway, your father had asked me to speak to a judge—"

"I don't want to know," Rudy snapped. "I don't want to hear it."

"Okay," Jack O'Leary said.

"And don't tell Collins," Rudy instructed his former teacher.

Four

Launching a Legend

IN THE SUMMER OF 1968, WHILE MANY MEMBERS OF HIS GENERATION worshipped the Rolling Stones and the Beatles, Rudy Giuliani was starstruck with a markedly more sober band of idols: the prosecutors in the office of the United States Attorney for the Southern District of New York. The young, driven legal talents who put away dope dealers, wise guys and corrupt public officials were, in Rudy's eyes, the equivalent of glamorous rock stars bathed in light on an elevated stage.

But the twenty-four-year-old aspiring lawman with an Italian afro and a little extra baby fat knew that he couldn't just walk into a job at the Southern District fresh out of law school. First he had to pay his dues, and his law school evidence professor, Irving Younger, had once advised him on how best to rack up real-world legal experience. "It was because of what he told me that I thought clerking for a federal judge would be a very good way to learn about being a trial lawyer," Rudy said.

Clerking for a judge in the Southern District, Rudy understood, would also improve his chances of landing a coveted job at the U.S. Attorney's Office. But the competition for clerkships was formidable. Rudy, who had to contend with applicants from Ivy League law schools like Harvard, Yale and Columbia, interviewed with several judges.

One of them was Lloyd F. MacMahon, chief judge of the Southern District of New York. Appointed by President Eisenhower in 1959, MacMahon was an irascible Republican warhorse with a magisterial bearing, who, when it came to selecting law clerks, valued street smarts and intuition over Ivy League pedigree. "Rudy was very intelligent and he had a great sense of humor," said MacMahon. "He hadn't come up with a silver spoon in his mouth. His parents were working-class people. I prefer well-rounded people."

In September 1968, Rudy made the cut and was clerking for MacMahon in his Manhattan chambers for an annual stipend of $7,000. He researched and wrote drafts of legal opinions and acted as an intermediary between MacMahon and lawyers. When MacMahon traveled upstate to try cases, Rudy often accompanied him. The judge encouraged his protégé, with whom he soon grew close, to observe some of the country's best trial lawyers in action arguing cases at the courthouse in Foley Square—as long as Rudy returned to the chambers in the evening to research legal opinions and take care of other matters.

While this young RFK Democrat would cultivate relationships with many older, connected Republicans, none would influence his career like MacMahon. His first boss and most important mentor, MacMahon would open doors for Rudy, not only to the U.S. Attorney's Office, but to a top job on the national stage in Washington.

"Judge MacMahon, as a teacher, was one of the four or five people who had the biggest impact on my life," Rudy said. "He would sit down and patiently explain to me the mistakes that were being made by lawyers who appeared before him. It was practical advice you could never get in law school."

The surly judge, whose clerkship applicants had mostly graduated from second- and third-tier law schools, displayed a clear penchant for helping young Catholic lawyers. MacMahon had made Tom Cahill, an Irish Catholic like himself, acting U.S. Attorney in November 1975. William Tendy, another Irish Catholic, also would receive MacMahon's help in becoming acting U.S. Attorney in March 1980.

But Lloyd MacMahon went even further with his clerk from Brooklyn. The gruff, stocky man developed an avuncular, if not fatherly, disposition toward Rudy and became a dominant force in his early life. After Harold Giuliani, it was the hoary MacMahon who molded young Rudy's view of the world. The judge even made an appearance at a party in Rudy's Queens apartment, slinging his arm snugly around his protégé's shoulder. Like O'Leary, MacMahon developed a relationship with Rudy's father. Harold frequently phoned the judge to check up on his son's performance: "His parents would come to me like some parents would go to a kindergarten teacher," MacMahon recalled.

MacMahon was a federal judge for more than twenty years. On the bench, he was armed with a ready scowl, off the bench, with a guffaw and full-toothed grin. Before being made a federal judge, he was an assistant attorney for the U.S. Attorney for the Southern District whose reputation as a crackerjack prosecutor was, over the years, woven into the fabric of New York trial lore. In 1955, when he briefly served as the acting U.S. Attorney, he successfully prosecuted monolithic mob boss Frank Costello for tax evasion. Before Costello, he had won a case against Communist Party Secretary Robert Thompson, sending him to prison for four years for contempt and fleeing a court order. As part of the later stages of the Rosenberg espionage case, MacMahon successfully prosecuted Columbia University professor William Perl for perjury.

MacMahon's judicial record, however, was by no measure a uniformly illustrious one. His two greatest liabilities were his trip-wire temper and his knee-jerk belligerence toward trial lawyers. A former assistant who worked with Rudy and knew MacMahon described the judge as a "lunatic" who would "fly off the handle." The cantankerous chief judge, easily provoked to animated bursts of derision and vituperation from the bench, would call trial lawyers "stupid," "morons" and "boobs" and was known to throw memos back at lawyers in fits of disgust. He once told a defense attorney to "call your next liar." In a narcotics case, he referred to the assistant U.S. Attorney, who was black, as a "creampuff" and said to his court clerk—although loud enough for everyone else to hear—"this is how not to try a case." Court transcripts, however, were frequently found to be free of the invective, lawyers clearly remembered.

Trial delays enraged the impatient MacMahon to the extent that he sometimes picked juries himself, rather than wait a half hour for counsel to show up. He was also known to force parties to rest a case if they could not produce a crucial witness within hours. Occasionally he would announce that he was scheduling a trial within twenty-four hours' notice. To save time during trials, he often reduced every motion and piece of testimony to its barest minimum.

In July 1980, he was named one of the nation's "worst" judges in a survey conducted by the *American Lawyer* of a group of lawyers, professors, reporters, prosecutors and Court of Appeals judges. Every judge occasionally gets reversed, but young Rudy's favorite judge often got blasted by the U.S. Court of Appeals. For example, MacMahon's reversed rulings on a drug case were characterized by the appeals court as "arbitrary" and "capricious," and his refusal to grant an adjournment to a defense attorney was described as "a gross abuse of discretion." The Second Circuit also overruled MacMahon on his handling of a malicious prosecution case, stating in its opinion that the case was "an example of a trial court's permitting its zeal for clearing its calendar to overcome the right of a party to a full trial on the merits."

MacMahon was best known, however, for a case in which he was not reversed but acted so forcefully he earned a timeless reputation as an iron-fisted demagogue. The 1962 narcotics case involved the Bonanno crime family's Carmine Galante and crew, who were accused of running an international, multimillion-dollar heroin ring. The two-and-half-month trial devolved at times into a madhouse. One defendant, Carmine Pancio, called MacMahon a "bastard" and "a lousy bum." His brother, Salvatore, climbed into the jury box and walked along the front rail, shoving jurors in the first row as he screamed at them. Another defendant, Anthony Mirra (aka Tony Bruno), as he was being cross-examined, hurled a fifteen-pound wooden chair from the witness stand at the prosecutor, John Rosner, who was trying the case with MacMahon protégé William Tendy. The chair hit the jury box and landed a few feet away, convincing court officials to bolt all witness chairs in the Southern District to the floor ever since.

The FBI provided MacMahon with around-the-clock protection, guarding him in court as well as at his home in Westchester. Despite the constant guard, a severed dog's head was discovered one evening on the judge's porch.

MacMahon, whose heavy-handed handling of the case may have contributed to the circuslike atmosphere, ordered three of the defendants shackled and gagged with gauze and tape. The rattling of chains was as common a sound in the courtroom as the clearing of throats. Thirty deputy U.S. marshals were stationed in the courthouse, four flanking the jury box and two standing attentively on each side of MacMahon. The perimeter of the courtroom was lined with wall-to-wall marshals. The first two rows of seats were roped off and left empty. The defendants all sat behind an L-shaped desk, Mirra and the Pancio brother, of course, chained to their chairs. MacMahon also levied plenty of contempt sentences for the obstreperous bunch, including a year for the chair-throwing Tony Mirra. When one of the defense attorneys, Al Krieger, moved for a mistrial, MacMahon replied: "Your motion for a mistrial is denied, Mr. Krieger. It is obviously a put-up job."

In July 1962, thirteen of the fourteen defendants were convicted. MacMahon gave John (Big John) Ormento, who ran the drug ring, a stiff forty-year sentence and called the 240-pound thug "an incurable cancer on society." Carmine Galante got twenty years, as did six other defendants. Nine of the thirteen convictions, including Ormento's and Galante's, were upheld on appeal.

The curmudgeonly courtroom colossus, who crushed Communists and mobsters, who favored the hard line over fine line, became the chief legal and life role model for his young Catholic clerk from Brooklyn. MacMahon was, in Rudy's eyes, an in-the-flesh incarnation of success, a man whose take-no-prisoners style would serve as a template for his own.

Clerking for MacMahon also afforded some practical perks, particularly when it came to a war in which Rudy wanted no part. After he had graduated from NYU law school in June 1968, the educational deferments that had kept Rudy out of the Vietnam War were no longer valid. He was classified 1A, available for service. But Rudy was morally opposed to the war, believing it did not meet the muster of what Catholics considered a "just war." More than 14,500 American servicemen were killed that year in Vietnam, and America was aflame with protest.

Rudy applied to a draft board for a deferment but was promptly turned down. Deferments were usually only granted to students and those holding jobs deemed essential, such as police officers and public officials, like assistant U.S. Attorneys. Rudy appealed the decision. But it was only after MacMahon, himself a World War II veteran, wrote a letter to the draft board that Rudy won the coveted deferment.

In May 1970, Rudy was reclassified as 1A but picked a high number in the draft lottery and again escaped service in Vietnam. The MacMahon draft deferment, however, would dog him years later when he ran for mayor in 1989. Paul Crotty, the campaign manager for the incumbent in that race, Ed Koch, had clerked for Judge MacMahon alongside Rudy and knew about the unusual draft deferment letter. Stories about it were leaked by the Koch campaign to newspapers.

The consultants who wrote Rudy's 1993 "vulnerability study" anticipated that Giuliani could face what they called "draft-dodger" charges. The study said Rudy could be accused of "receiving special treatment from a friendly judge to avoid military service during the Vietnam War when thousands of less fortunate people were dying." The only argument offered in the study to rebut the charge was that Rudy had "joined the Air Force ROTC program," while a student at Manhattan College, "but was processed out because of an ear problem." The study insisted that this AFROTC service meant that he "did not avoid military service" during Vietnam. In fact, Rudy signed up for ROTC in 1961—before American troops were fighting in Vietnam. He got out of the officer training program in 1963, when thousands of American advisors were stationed in Vietnam and the budding war was starting to attract attention at home. He used an ear defect, which he later characterized as "a minor hearing problem," to cut short his four-year ROTC commitment. Had he remained in the ROTC, he would have been required to do several years of Air Force service during the war.

Rudy and Regina were married in October of 1968, a month after Rudy began clerking for MacMahon, at Gina's home parish, the majestic St. Philip Neri Roman Catholic Church on the Grand Concourse in the Bedford section of the Bronx. It was a traditional, Catholic wedding that drew a large crowd from the Giuliani and Peruggi families as well as friends.

The newlywed cousins rented a cramped apartment on East 58th Street in Manhattan for $500 per month. The place was so small that Regina could touch both walls in the kitchen by simply extending her arms. After the bed and dresser had been moved into the closet-sized bedroom, there was nowhere left to walk. With what space remained in the rest of the apartment, they installed hand-me-down furniture donated by both their families.

After a year of close-quartered coziness, the Giulianis migrated east in October 1969 to Woodside, Queens. Their new one-bedroom apartment, located on the fourth floor of a large seven-story, red-brick building in a residential neighborhood was larger than their Manhattan grotto but by no means capacious. The apartment had dark hardwood floors and a large central room and bedroom. The bedroom window looked onto 41st Avenue, a small, bare, mostly treeless block.

Drowsy and antiseptic, the Woodside of the late '60s and early '70s was an overwhelmingly white neighborhood, peopled primarily with Irish working-class families, whose breadwinners were often doormen and chambermaids. With its hedge-lined streets, small neighborhood delis and absence of blaring horns and screeching bus brakes, it was a respite from the frenzy of Manhattan. When Rudy and Regina took up residence there, however, the neighborhood's sleepy serenity was steadily being corroded by the draft drain of the Vietnam War. What had increasingly enraged neighborhood residents, who had initially supported the war, was the disproportionate number of their sons, brothers and husbands returning home in body bags. According to its current city councilman, John Sabini, the neighborhood demarcated by the Woodside zip code, in fact, suffered more casualties, among its young male residents sucked into Vietnam, than any other zip code in the United States. "It got to the point," said Sabini, "where they lost so many of their boys, they decided they had enough."

For the Giulianis, however, Woodside was a quiet backdrop to the novelty of a fledgling marriage and the challenge of new careers. While her husband pored over legal briefs, Gina struggled with a demanding job as a narcotics counselor in a state jail, working with female drug addicts—an occupation she would later describe as "no picnic for someone from a middle-class home."

Rudy's long hours with MacMahon soon began to tax his relationship with his new wife. When she came home from work in the evening, Regina liked to make dinner. Often, though, she would be left to eat it alone.

On a hot August day in 1970, the dream that had burned like a pilot light inside Rudy Giuliani's head, the dream that had fueled his white-hot ambition, was realized: He was sworn in as an assistant U.S. Attorney by Whitney North Seymour, the U.S. Attorney for the Southern District of New York. In the conference room adjacent to Seymour's office, all eighty assistant U.S. Attorneys (or AUSAs) gathered to watch the new guy inducted into their ranks. Standing between his wife and his father, twenty-six-year-old Rudy, wearing a seersucker suit and an ample mustache, listened as his new boss told a story.

Seymour, a tall, stately man, told Rudy about his own days as assistant working for none other than Lloyd MacMahon when he was prosecuting mob boss Frank Costello. The hours were onerous, and the assistants were so rarely home that their wives often packed lunches for them. On the day Costello was convicted, the women, to celebrate the victory, all gave their husbands lunch pails embossed with a gold American eagle.

The fact that Rudy had worked for MacMahon, noted Seymour, meant he knew what hard work was all about. MacMahon, who had recommended Rudy for the job, simply remarked: "Mike Seymour and I were good friends."

Refusing to be intimidated by the abundance of Ivy League degrees among his new colleagues, Rudy flourished at the Southern District, reveling in the generous mix of hard work, camaraderie and competition. The office was then headquartered on the third and fourth floors of the federal courthouse in Foley Square. The driven neophyte was given a modest interior office on the fourth floor, the walls of which he adorned with photos of the Kennedys and one of Judge MacMahon. Also affixed to the wall was a chart on which Rudy kept a daily log of the fluctuations in his weight.

Judging by what Rudy ate for lunch on most days, that chart must have, at first anyway, showed a steady incline. Often joining a few colleagues for lunch at a hamburger joint off Foley Square, Rudy would usually order the "sizzler," a giant, grease-oozing hamburger served on a metal platter. The "sizzler" would come with a complimentary napkin draped over it to soak up all the grease. Rudy would often wolf down two of them or more on his lunch break. With a perpetually pallid complexion and a tendency to dress like a math teacher on a date, Rudy was once told by a judge in open court that he "looked like shit" and was then advised to "sit at Coney Island and get some color."

The "short trials" unit, in which new prosecutors accrued experience by trying minor cases, was where Rudy got his start. Taking Judge MacMahon's advice to accumulate as many trials as possible, he actively hoarded cases others didn't want, collecting them the way a teacher's pet seeks extra credit assignments. "I enjoyed trying cases so much," said Rudy, "I would go out and take cases of my own. I mean, I would go ask other people. . . . I used to go around asking people for trials because I really enjoyed doing it."

In Rudy's first year at the Southern District, there was another chart to which he perhaps paid even more attention than the one in his own office. It was pinned to the wall of Seymour's office, and like a vast scroll, extended from the ceiling to the carpet. On the chart was a staggering list of backlog cases Seymour had inherited from his predecessor, Robert Morgenthau. On top of new cases, the assistants were saddled with a hefty share of backlog.

"When you disposed of an old case," recalled Rudy, "you'd go into Seymour's office, he'd shake your hand, and you'd cross the case off the chart."

Rudy crossed off more cases, he claims, than anyone else in the office. With his combination of backlog and short trials and extra cases he had begged for, Rudy worked long, punishing hours, often preparing trials up until midnight.

The very first case Rudy argued before a jury concerned a stabbing on a boat. The case landed in federal court, because the incident occurred on the "high seas," as Rudy put it, where no other court had jurisdiction. Rudy won a conviction.

Another early case, involving an illegal still in Harlem, was more memorable if only because, at one point, both the judge and defense attorney fell asleep at the same time. Rudy, not yet entirely familiar with trial procedure, was about to introduce a document into evidence when he realized that his counterparts were dozing. "I didn't know what to do," he said. "I had been trained by Judge MacMahon to do a lot of things, but I didn't quite know what to do. So I decided the thing to do was to get very close to the defense lawyer and just yell that I wanted to put it in evidence. And I did. I yelled. I startled him. He awakened. The jury laughed. He then said, ah, I don't care, I don't object." Rudy won the case.

In his five years at the Southern District, Rudy claimed to have tried thirty-two cases, both new and backlog, and to have won all but two. One of those two was a fraud case, *U.S.* v. *U.S. Telephone & Paul A. Brown*, that resulted in a hung jury. Rudy told his colleagues he lost because the jury didn't like his mustache. So he got rid of it. Cleanly shaved, he retried the case and won. The other was a small piece of the largest puzzle in Rudy's prosecutorial career.

Rudy's arrival at the Southern District coincided with a confluence of events that would point up one overriding social ill infecting government and ravaging public morale: police corruption. The magnitude of the problem was first revealed when Frank Serpico, an honest cop, came forward in late 1968 to disclose widespread graft within the police force. In the spring of 1970, spurred by Serpico's revelations, Mayor John V. Lindsay established the Knapp Commission, which conducted an investigation into the spreading cancer of crooked cops. The commission's public hearings in October 1971—held a year after Rudy started at the Southern District—uncovered an astonishing amount of crimes committed by the men in blue. Cops would pilfer cash off a corpse, take bribes, sell drugs. The notorious French Connection case—in which three hundred pounds of heroin had been stolen from the police property room—followed the Knapp Commission hearings, ripping into headlines in December 1972. It cast a citywide pall of public distrust over the NYPD.

The Knapp Commission's lead witness was a corrupt cop named William Phillips, who had been nabbed taking money and agreed to work undercover to escape prosecution. As criminal cases were prepared against the officers Phillips had exposed, it was Rudy's job to ready Phillips for trial. After eleven months of slogging through short trials and backlog cases, Rudy's moral meter was finally being put to good use: Seymour had offered him a spot in the Southern District's public corruption unit.

Phillips would admit to Rudy that he had followed in the footsteps of his father, a corrupt police detective. The wayward cop told the serious young prosecutor about police officers who were crooked the minute they graduated from the academy, men who had entered the force expressly to reap the unspoken fringe benefits. That's why Phillips had joined the department. That's why his father had joined. Phillips admitted to Rudy that he had even taken payoffs from a prominent East Harlem wise guy named "Fat Tony" Salerno, who ran a gambling operation and would later become head of the Genovese crime family.

"You had to do more than turn your back on gambling," said Rudy. "Every now and then a body would turn up, and you couldn't very well lean on a man who was paying you $25,000 a month. The mob wasn't paying that kind of money just to protect its gambling operations. They owned a piece of the cops."

Despite his family history, Rudy insisted his sheltered life had left him utterly unprepared for the likes of William Phillips, who was at one point convicted of killing a prostitute. "I had this youthful conviction that all human beings were basically good," said Rudy years later. "If you just turned on the right switch, goodness and rationality would flow forth." With William Phillips, Rudy claims to have experienced a significant epiphany, a tectonic shift in his view of humanity. "I came to realize that rationality does not necessarily rule and that some people were simply evil," Rudy concluded. "There was very little you could do to change them, and if you entertained the romantic notion that they could be changed, you would wind up endangering innocent people."

His first case with the corruption unit involved George Burkert, a twenty-three-year-old tow-truck driver, who testified to standing ovations at the Knapp Commission hearings that vindictive cops had slapped him and another tow-truck driver with a slew of fourteen traffic tickets after they refused to make payoffs to the cops. Burkert told the Commission how the officers had, astonishingly enough, alleged that all fourteen violations had occurred within a span of twenty minutes. The officers, Charles Edmonds and Matthew Carr, who quickly became targets of a grand jury investigation, insisted that Burkert had led them on a high-speed chase and that all fourteen tickets were legitimate. No one believed the officers. The public had decided: Burkert was good, and the cops were bad. And at first, Rudy agreed.

Then two witnesses came forward backing up the cops. Aided by the FBI, Rudy initiated an investigation of the two officers and found not a single hint of corruption. Then he joined forces with a tough, legendary investigator named Carl Bogan, whose career would inspire the television series *Kojak*. At the age of fifty-eight, Bogan had moved onto the feds after a career as an NYPD detective assigned to the Manhattan District Attorney's Office. He took Rudy under his fatherly wing. The two men spent three hours one afternoon interviewing people in the neighborhood where the high speed chase was alleged to have occurred. Several witnesses recalled just such a chase, police cars tailing a tow truck, and corroborated the police officers' account.

The officers were cleared and Burkert was indicted for lying to a federal grand jury. But with the jurors voting ten to two for acquittal, the Burkert trial ended in August of 1972, as Paul Brown case had, with a hung jury.

Rudy vowed to retry the case. On January 12, 1973, in the midst of the French Connection scandal—when credibility of police officers was at an all-time low—Rudy won a conviction against Burkert. The accomplishment was not insignificant.

The enterprising Bogan aided Rudy on several other cases, including a celebrated 1972 investigation of the Model Cities Administration, a federally funded antipoverty agency. Bogan learned from one of his informants that Model Cities officials were being bribed in exchange for giving out lucrative summer camp contracts and leases. He procured an incriminating undercover tape recording of the assistant director of Model Cities, Pedro Morales. That's where Rudy came in. Bogan played the tape for Rudy, and, in September 1972, Rudy drafted an arrest warrant for Morales. After his arrest, Morales sat with Rudy and Bogan and listened to the tape. The two men then asked the stunned Morales to cooperate with the government by going undercover and making tapes like the one they had just played for him. He told them he would think about it.

Bogan suggested that they let Morales go home and stew on the matter, let him steep in the guilt of facing his wife and kids. Rudy agreed, and Morales returned to Staten Island. "He seemed like a very decent guy," Rudy would later say, "after having been through all the police cases."

The next morning, a Saturday, Rudy got a call at 5:30 A.M. from Bogan, who proposed that the two men travel to Staten Island. With a laugh, Rudy recalled the conversation, which he says was the prelude to the best lesson he ever had on how to flip a witness. "He said, 'We're going to go have breakfast with Pedro.' I said, 'Are you crazy?' He said, 'No, no. We're gonna go have breakfast with Pedro'."

Bogan's car idled outside Rudy's apartment an hour later at 6:30 A.M. Rudy opened the passenger door, but there were two large packages stacked on the shotgun seat. Bogan told Rudy to put them in the back seat, and Rudy asked what was in them. Doughnuts, for the wife, Bogan replied. The other package? Rudy asked. Toys for the kids, Bogan said.

The two arrived at Morales's house at 7:15 A.M. and were welcomed warmly. They spent most of the day there, talking about the decision Morales would have to make. "We'd play with the kids," recalled Rudy. "And then Pete would say, well, what does it mean to cooperate. And it taught me a whole way of approaching people and dealing with people. The end result is, Pedro still wanted to think it out. He said, I'll come in on Monday and I'll tell you yes or no. He came in Monday. He said yes. He then became an undercover agent."

Bogan remembers the Staten Island visit but says it was neither he nor Rudy who finally persuaded Morales to cooperate. "Morvillo flipped Morales," Bogan insists, referring to Bob Morvillo, then head of the Southern District's criminal division and Rudy's boss.

Morales became an excellent undercover. He tape-recorded fifteen people, all of whom were convicted. He testified at three trials, including the trial of William Del Toro, the head of an East Harlem anti-poverty organization and brother of the local state assemblyman.

Later, Morales got a suspended sentence, and Rudy helped him land a job as an investigator in the special state prosecutor's office, as well as getting one for his daughter in the Southern District.

In his five years at the Southern District, Rudy would work for two influential U.S. Attorneys—Whitney North Seymour and Paul Curran—and serve as the head of two important units, narcotics and corruption. He would eventually earn the rank of executive assistant U.S. attorney, the third–highest-ranking attorney in the office. And all the while he would obsessively cultivate his reputation.

The case that shaped that reputation for years after Rudy left the Southern District revolved around another cop caught in the Knapp Commission storm, Bob Leuci. Involving himself in Leuci's Kafkaesque life was the best public relations move Rudy Giuliani ever made. The Leuci investigation cast Rudy in the limelight of a 1978 best-seller by Robert Daley called *Prince of the City*. It even put a fictionalized version of Rudy in his first movie, the 1981 screen version of the book, directed by Sidney Lumet. A heroic figure, particularly in the movie, Rudy truly became larger than life, immortalized in celluloid at the age of thirty-seven.

A charming, boyish detective, Leuci was a member of the NYPD's Special Investigating Unit (SIU), a cadre of about sixty detectives who worked major narcotics cases with virtually no supervision. Once labeled "princes of the city" by a judge, the coroneted cops had been selected for the elite unit because of distinguished investigative careers. The "princes" had one other thing in common: Nearly every single one of them was corrupt. They stole cash from dope dealers, provided informants with seized heroin, used illegal wiretaps and routinely committed perjury.

In February 1971, Leuci was summoned to the offices of the Knapp Commission to meet with Nicholas Scoppetta, one of the commission's lawyers. A former assistant district attorney, the thirty-eight-year-old, gravel-voiced Scoppetta, an Italian-American like Leuci, asked if Leuci knew anything about corrupt cops in the SIU. Leuci said he didn't. That night, over a few steaks in Scoppetta's West Side Manhattan apartment, the lawyer, who had no clear evidence of Leuci wrongdoing, pushed him nonetheless to reincarnate himself, to separate from his SIU friends and to wear a wire for the government. Bob Leuci said he would think about it.

He eventually agreed, taking his undercover venture into the deadly world of mob fixers, crooked lawyers and compromised law enforcement officials. Scoppetta convinced the federal government to make him a special assistant U.S. Attorney and foot the bill for the project, which would be run independently of the Knapp Commission.

Leuci, whose SIU nickname name had been "Babyface," quickly embarked on his new clandestine career. Always wired, the Southern District's secret star ventured out to these meetings long after rumors percolated throughout the police department that he was a rat. He reportedly came very close to death at least once.

Finally in June 1972, two years after the operation started, the New York *Daily News* broke the story, identifying Leuci as a federal operative and printing his photo. He and his family were moved to a house in the secluded Virginia woods and placed under the guard of federal marshals. The operation was over, the indictments were coming in, Scoppetta was leaving and Leuci was preparing to testify.

Bob Morvillo and an assistant named Elliot Sagor were scheduled to try the first case that was dependent on Leuci's tapes—a bribery charge against Edmund

Rosner, a crooked defense lawyer. As Morvillo prepared Leuci for cross-examination, he pressed the cop to detail the crimes he had committed himself. Leuci told him the same thing he had told Scoppetta in the beginning: His criminal résumé was negligible, consisting of only three minor incidents of misconduct.

Leuci was an adept liar. Before he had signed up with Scoppetta, he had habitually committed perjury in drug cases. Now, he insisted, he was telling the truth. Scoppetta first, and then Morvillo, believed him.

Morvillo put Leuci on the stand, and Edmund Rosner was found guilty on five of seven counts.

At the beginning of 1973, Morvillo and Sagor left the office, and Leuci was passed along to another prosecutor, Richard Ben Veniste. Ben Veniste, too, moved on quickly, and Leuci wound up in the hands of Rudolph W. Giuliani, the new twenty-nine year-old chief of the corruption unit.

Rudy and Leuci have different recollections of when and where they first met. Rudy has told reporters over the years that he became part of Bob Leuci's world at a late-night emergency meeting at the Southern District offices, right after the undercover surfaced in the *Daily News*. Leuci says, however, that he first met Rudy earlier in the case, during a meeting in the Brooklyn apartment of a former SDNY chief. Leuci remembers a young rookie in a rumpled suit, sitting in a corner, watching him. "He looked like he just stepped out of law school," said Leuci. "He kept staring at me, listening. Staring. I wasn't talking to him. He was sitting off on the side. He wasn't at the table. I got nervous."

After the meeting was over, Rudy introduced himself. "He told me he was U.S. attorney working on big drug cases," recalled Leuci. "He was an Italian guy who sounded like a WASP."

Rudy's first case with Leuci also involved a mob lawyer who offered the detective a bribe in a drug case, Benjamin Caiola. Rudy developed an immediate affinity for Leuci, though he was concerned about his credibility by his own account. "He identified with me," said Leuci.

Jeff Harris, a member of the corruption unit who was very close to Rudy, remembered the prosecutor's "soft spot" for the turned detective. "Leuci is a very charming guy," said Harris, "and Rudy was charmed by Leuci."

Before Rudy got the chance to put the great charmer on the stand, Caiola pled guilty. He was sentenced to three years in jail.

In the movie, Leuci's character was played by Treat Williams. As the indictments added up, suspicions arose that Leuci was himself always playing a part, not only during his taping performances, but with the very people who oversaw his investigation.

Assistant U.S. Attorney Joe Jaffe, who was a close friend of Rudy's, never believed Bob Leuci was telling the truth about his criminal past. "The first time I heard Leuci testify I was convinced beyond a doubt that he wasn't telling the truth," Jaffe said in an unpublished interview. "I never met a cop who worked in junk who could get up and say he never did anything wrong or, if he did, it was only three things."

Whispers of doubt soon grew into a chorus of angry accusations. A notorious drug dealer nicknamed The Baron came forward with an affidavit providing detailed deals he and Leuci had done together. Another corrupt SIU detective named Carl Aguiluz was indicted and agreed to cooperate. He confessed to a lengthy series of crimes and then told the prosecutors interviewing them that Bob Leuci had a history at least as illustrious as his own. He ridiculed them for letting their darling detective play them for fools.

As these charges engulfed him, Leuci drew closer and closer to Rudy. While prosecutors in and out of the Southern District were debriefing Leuci and using his tapes, the one who controlled him as a witness was Rudy Giuliani. Rudy would not tamper with his office's star. The Baron was forced to take a lie detector test, but the man who could have compelled Leuci to take one chose not to do so.

Thomas Puccio, chief of the criminal division for the U.S. Attorney for the Eastern District in Brooklyn, believed Aguiluz. He thought Leuci was a con man. There were two versions of what happened next: Puccio's description and the one depicted in the book and movie. The *Prince of the City* scenario was a byproduct of the Leuci and Giuliani bond. Puccio got two Drug Enforcement Administration agents to threaten Leuci, insisting that if he didn't divulge everything he knew, Puccio would indict him by five o'clock that afternoon. Leuci stormed out and drove down to Rudy's office. "I was a wreck," recalled Leuci. "I screamed at him."

Rudy calmed Leuci, called Puccio on the phone and after a brief conversation, hung up. He told Leuci that there would be no indictment today. "Rudy said don't worry about this guy [Puccio]," said Leuci. "And then I went back to Virginia," where his wife and children still lived in a "safe house."

Leuci phoned Rudy the next day, a Saturday, and talked openly about a threat of suicide, which one SIU detective caught in this web had already committed. Accompanied by Joe Jaffe, Rudy took the next available shuttle to Washington, where Leuci met him at the airport. Rudy tried to persuade Leuci to come clean all the way this time. No way, Leuci said, I can't turn in my partners. Rudy replied that Leuci couldn't do this thing halfway, he'd have to pick sides. This went on for hours, with Leuci at times, it seemed, closer than he had ever had been to a full confession. Leuci now remembers that Rudy, staring him dead in the eye, promised: "If you tell me, I'll never leave you. . . . I'm your partner now. We have a friendship." At four A.M., Leuci unwilling to talk further, showed Rudy and Jaffe beds in one of the kids' rooms. They slept for a few furtive hours. In the morning, Rudy pressed Leuci again, and finally at the airport, just before Rudy and Jaffe were about to board the plane, Leuci muttered that he would do it.

Rudy wanted to help Leuci, he said years later, but he also wanted to get him to talk. Carl Aguiluz's allegation had burrowed deep into Rudy's blind faith in the detective. "I realized that Aguiluz had to be absolutely right," said Rudy. "I now knew that Bob had a lot more to tell us, and that he had committed perjury in the Rosner case. We tried to figure out the best way to get him to talk."

Puccio's own memoir, *In the Name of the Law*, published seventeen years after Daley's book, counters this version. He claims that he and Rudy were playing good cop, bad cop all along. Puccio called Leuci into his office one Friday after another. Knowing Leuci was itching to catch the next shuttle to his family in Virginia, he locked him into long, meandering conversations, dropping hints of impending doom. Rudy then let the rattled man cry on his shoulder, while winking across the East River in Puccio's direction. Rudy's supposed deep concern for Leuci—projected in the book and movie—was, Puccio contends, an act.

Puccio also says that Leuci's decision to tell all was a lot less dramatic than its portrayal in *The Prince of the City* . Several days after Puccio's indictment threat, Leuci "called early in the morning, from his mother's house in Brooklyn," begging to see the prosecutor. After, at first, refusing, Puccio finally said he would see him at five o'clock. What ensued was one last round of good cop/bad cop, in which Rudy, in Leuci's presence, called Puccio. "You've played with this guy's mind for weeks," Rudy is alleged to have said. "And you've turned him into a total basket case!" This jointly coordinated ruse, claims Puccio, finally pushed Leuci to spill his guts.

"If that's true," says Bob Leuci, referring to the Puccio-Giuliani tag team, "Rudy Giuliani is a prick. I was within an inch of suicide. He knew that. If they had indicted me, I would have killed myself."

But the ex-cop, who has since become a best-selling crime novelist, still believes Rudy "was concerned for me personally."

Puccio writes: "I guess for once the star manipulator got manipulated himself."

Whether it was Giuliani's coaxing or Puccio's threats that flipped the switch inside Bob Leuci, or a combination of both, he finally opened up. Jaffe and Rudy listened for hours as Leuci confessed to an eighty-four-page list of crimes, including supplying informants with dime bags of heroin and shakedowns of drug dealers for large sums of money. In all, Leuci estimated, he had illegally squirreled away between $20,000 and $30,000 dollars during his SIU years. He had concealed this long litany of lawbreaking, he explained, to protect his former colleagues.

But, now, he had fingered them. As the roundup began, one of them, Dave Cody shot himself in the head.

In the movie version of *The Prince of the City*, Rudy's character, named Mario Vincente, is a sympathetic, mild-mannered prosecutor, with an almost ascetic bearing. His character is the one, ultimately, who saves Bob Leuci's life and soul. The movie even has the saintly Giuliani character threatening his resignation in the event of a Leuci indictment.

The book and movie spawned the legend of the converted cop and the caped-crusader lawman bringing down a legion of on-the-take police.

In reality, Rudy never prosecuted a single cop case Leuci brought in, and he never put Leuci on the witness stand. The only time he ever prepared him for the witness stand was the Caiola case, which ended in a plea. In July 1973, when Rudy took over the Southern District's corruption unit, many of Leuci's cases, like Rosner, had either been tried or led to pleas. Others were later transferred to the special state prosecutor, who, Leuci said, "put a lot more cops away than Giuliani."

Rudy has often boasted of convicting hordes of corrupt cops—forty-three is the number he cites. The total number of convicted cops listed in the Southern District's "Report of Activities" for the period Rudy ran the corruption unit—June 1973 to September 1975—is ten. The cases stemmed from the work not of Leuci but of other undercover detectives like Aguiluz.

Rudy tried the most celebrated one himself, the trial of Joe Novoa and Peter Daly. Working with Aguiluz, the two were involved in the seizure of 105 kilograms of heroin and cocaine, but they only turned in 100 kilograms. The rest was sold by the three cops and went back out on the streets. Novoa and Daly were both eventually sentenced to ten years in prison.

While Rudy and Leuci never teamed up to prosecute crooked cops, they did spend a lot of time together. They worked on the Caiola case. Rudy helped Leuci prepare for the important hearing that had been called into the Baron's affidavit, which could affect the conviction of Rosner. They also worked together on some of the cases sent to the state special prosecutor.

The two men, both products of working-class Italian families, became friends. As their relationship bled into the social, they were each afforded bay-window views into the tumult of the other's personal lives. They would remain close for many years. Leuci would visit Rudy at his apartment in Washington and attend his wedding to Donna Hanover in 1984. Leuci's own wife, when she wanted a divorce from him years later, approached Rudy for legal advice; Rudy sent her to his lawyer friend Mike Mukasey and then broke the news of the possible divorce to Leuci himself. As recently as March 2000, when Rudy was on a fundraising trip in Rhode Island, where Leuci currently lives, the two men met for drinks.

During the Leuci investigations, the two men often talked intimately late into the night. Leuci detected in Rudy a surprising capacity for empathy. When speaking about the families of drug dealers he had flipped while working in the narcotics unit, the young prosecutor was often overcome with emotion. "He'd talk to me," recalled Leuci, "and have tears in his eyes."

As he had with Peter Powers in high school, Rudy engaged his detective friend in long philosophical conversations about government, crime and law enforcement. The enterprising young prosecutor would tell the attentive, sometimes sycophantic detective that, in his mind, a great distinction existed between police misconduct and police corruption. "Police misconduct, he'd understand that," said Leuci. Rudy, he explained, could understand a cop telling a white lie to make an arrest work—but the prosecutor was intolerant, insists Leuci, when it came to cops who lied to cover up corruption.

Leuci learned that Rudy could be a good friend and a terrible enemy. "Either you were on his side or you weren't on his side," he said. "If you weren't, he'd come after you with both guns."

As Rudy adjusted to the rigors of his job and his new $12,000-a-year-salary—nearly twice what he made with Judge MacMahon—he and Regina tired of Woodside, and in 1973 moved west again into a two-bedroom apartment on Manhattan's well-heeled West End Avenue, at 83rd Street. Not that Rudy had much time to enjoy his new home. While the ceaseless job demands at the Southern District fed his voracious appetite for work, they would also—he himself later suggested—smother his personal life and badly impair his marriage.

"I became an assistant in August 1970," Rudy said. "And I can remember waking up the day after my birthday the following May—it was the first weekend I had been home."

During the Leuci cases, the nights grew even longer. On some nights, Rudy would crash on the couches of close colleagues like Ken Feinberg, who lived in Greenwich Village and with whom Rudy shared an affinity for opera. "Rudy stayed with me a half dozen times," said Feinberg.

As it became clearer than ever that Rudy's number-one priority was not his wife, Regina withdrew further into her cocoon of reticence. When Rudy did come home, stumbling in late, often a buddy or two from the office would be with him.

They would huddle around the kitchen table, rehashing cases, sometimes sharing leftovers from the meal Regina had prepared hours earlier.

Rudy's herculean Southern District hours, however, weren't only work-related.

Bob Leuci, who was afforded an intimate view of the workaholic's crumbling marriage and active social life, saw a side of Rudy revealed to a privileged few. "Rudy Giuliani preferred WASPy women, blondes," said Leuci. "He hit on everybody. He hit on everybody, hit on them all, all the time. He bounced around the Village. He was pretty wild."

Regina's maid of honor, Pat Rufino, told two reporters in separate interviews years later that Rudy dated other women during his marriage. Rufino claimed that Regina had once discovered another woman's jewelry in their bedroom.

Even Carl Bogan, the detective who was once Rudy's driver and now sings his praises, when asked to describe the prosecutor's greatest weakness, remarked: "So what if he bounces around?"

In early 1974, the cousins separated. Rudy moved in with his Southern District pal John Gross, according to Feinberg. "He was closer to Gross than me," said Feinberg, who then remarked that "the marriage was rocky but survivable—I didn't think they would get a divorce."

Feinberg recalls that during what he thought was the separation, Rudy dated a Southern District law clerk named Nancy Friedman. "I think Rudy saw her a couple of times or had a relationship with her for a while," said Feinberg. "I remember going out with her and Rudy a couple times."

Years later, Rudy was still dating Nancy Friedman. On September 12, 1981, the two appeared together at the Manhattan wedding of Nancy's friends Sarah and Jim Moss, both Southern District veterans. Serving in a key Justice Department post at the time, Rudy traveled up from Washington to attend the wedding with Friedman, who was then an SDNY assistant. "Nancy was our invitee," recalled Jim Moss, "and Rudy was her escort."

Another woman, a young legal assistant, confided in a colleague at the U.S. Attorney's office that Rudy used to pay her visits in the "middle of the night." Surprising her late one night, Rudy "rang her bell and asked if he could come up," said the colleague. The legal assistant buzzed him in. He returned again and again, usually without calling beforehand, and established a relationship that both embarrassed and pleased the woman.

Rudy and Regina were eventually reunited after this initial separation, but an unbridgeable distance yawned between them. Their marriage was a translucent formality, their intimacy a fading vestige. "Things just gradually deteriorated," was Rudy's benign summation. He then remarked that his wife was "very shy and private," adding that "I'm much more outgoing."

Rudy's marital malaise didn't diminish his perpetual Southern District high, and the majority of his social life involved fellow assistants from the office. They would congregate in bars and restaurants around the courthouse and jaw about trials. As he had in high school, Rudy organized an opera appreciation club; a half dozen Southern District assistants and their wives would meet monthly in one of their apartments to listen to and discuss Rudy's assigned pieces. Rudy joined fellow assistant Bart Schwartz in occasional upstate horse-racing excursions at the racetrack in Saratoga.

Congressman Bertram Podell's file landed on Rudy Giuliani's desk in 1972. The Brooklyn Democrat was under investigation by the FBI, which suspected that he had illegally accepted financial compensation from a small airline in return for trying to help it secure a lucrative flight route from Miami to the Bahamas. The FBI was considering closing the case, unable to substantiate the claims. Rudy was asked to look over the file one last time before the matter was finally dropped.

Rudy dissected the file. He found an ostensible pattern: Payments to Podell seemed to coincide with steps he had taken to help the airline. The young prosecutor also identified several witnesses the FBI had neglected to interview. As he reviewed the file's contents, Rudy Giuliani felt a strong jolt of possibility: This was his case, this was his chance to take down a connected crook. The conduct offended him, and the opportunity enticed him.

The U.S. Ambassador to Nicaragua at the time, a man named Shelton Turner, had formerly headed the U.S. mission in the Bahamas and had reportedly exercised his influence, at Podell's behest, to help the airline. One weekend, Rudy flew down to Nicaragua to interview Shelton.

The senior, aristocratic Turner was, at first, a hospitable host. He sent a car to the airport to pick up Rudy, arranged for him to stay at the embassy compound and invited him to dinner. But when the two sat down to chat, pleasantries evaporated fast. Turner refused to discuss Podell. Rudy, young enough to be Turner's son, pressed him. The ambassador was obstinate.

So Rudy handed him a grand jury subpoena and told him brusquely: "See you in New York on Monday."

The ambassador, after conferring with an on-site FBI agent, agreed to give Rudy a statement as long as he didn't have to travel to New York to do it. Rudy wrote up an affidavit by hand and, in the ambassador's residence on a hill overlooking Managua, he took a statement from Turner under oath.

Rudy lost his room at the embassy that night and his dinner invitation, but he had what he wanted: a statement under oath that was damaging to Podell.

Many years later, Rudy would admit that in issuing Turner the subpoena, he had "probably violated five rules of the Justice Department." He explained further: "I certainly had authority to subpoena him. . . . I was on American property. . . . But, as I subsequently learned, being in the Justice Department, there are all sorts of rules about how you coordinate getting officials from the State Department before a grand jury. I had coordinated none of that. Absolutely none of that. But, the principle was right."

The grand jury that took Turner's statement was impaneled in the spring of 1973. The specific allegations were that in 1968 and 1969, the Brooklyn congressman, who was also a lawyer, represented Florida Atlantic Airlines before the Civil Aeronautics Board in violation of a federal law barring members of Congress from representing clients before government agencies. Podell received $12,350 in "legal fees" and a $29,000 "campaign contribution" from the president of the airline's parent company. When the *Wall Street Journal* revealed the conflict two years before Rudy started taking testimony, Podell admitted he had "made a boo-boo."

In July 1973, Podell was indicted for accepting bribes to wield his influence with federal agencies and the Bahamian government to obtain the airline's coveted Caribbean route. The indictment also charged that he had hidden part of the bribe by channeling $12,350 in "legal fees" to a fake law firm.

The Watergate scandal was then engulfing Washington, and the Democratic congressman exploited it to the hilt. "I am the first," claimed Podell, "and, for sure, not the last congressman whose career is threatened by the corrupters, burglars, wiretappers, bagmen and psychopaths in and about the White House."

It only took two weeks for Rudy to present a government case that relied primarily on documents, agents and a description of accounting maneuvers. When the government rested, the defense started with character witness, including House Speaker Tip O'Neill and a freshmen congressman named Edward I. Koch. Though the government rarely cross-examines character witnesses, Giuliani even went after a monsignor who appeared.

Koch told the jury that he had known Podell for ten years and said his reputation for honesty was "excellent."

On cross-examination, Rudy began by saying, "I don't mean to be disrespectful." He then asked Koch whether or not he had provided the "same kind" of testimony for Congressman Frank Brasco, who had recently been convicted in another SDNY bribery case.

"I have," Koch replied.

"And in this case as in that case you didn't know the underlying facts, the testimony of the witnesses, the exhibits, the facts that were presented to the jury?" Rudy asked.

"Absolutely correct," Koch said. "I knew nothing about the facts in either case."

In their first of many encounters, Rudy Giuliani had ambushed Edward I. Koch.

The climax of the trial was when Podell took the stand. Rudy's cross-examination was a defining moment under the stage lights, and although two of the defense attorneys recalled his cross as "unremarkable," Rudy's performance in the courtroom that day, over the years, accrued healthy dollops of drama. The supposedly searing, surgical interrogation of Bertram Podell, in fact, became one of the most invoked stories of Rudy's take-no-prisoners tack toward those who had abused their power.

"The cross-examination was something trial lawyers have fantasies about," Rudy proudly claimed. His boast was the opening salvo in what would become a lifelong pattern of inflating accomplishments into legends. But Podell's guilty plea in the middle of the cross had little to do with any Perry Mason–like performance by Giuliani.

The exchange was, no doubt, contentious.

Rudy, at one point, asked Podell if he had written in the name "Citizens Committee for B. L. Podell" as payee on the $29,000 check from Martin Miller, the president of Florida Atlantic's parent company.

After examining the check, Podell replied: "It looks like my handwriting."

"It sure does," Rudy snapped.

Rudy then asked whether the $29,000 was a de facto payment for Podell's work on behalf of Florida Atlantic Airlines.

"That's a lie!" Podell shouted.

"Who's telling the lie, Congressman?" the fiery assistant U.S. attorney shot back.

"You are, sir," Podell retorted. "You are."

Rudy recounted in countless subsequent interviews what he regarded as a high point of the cross-examination, a moment when Podell either dropped his glasses or poked his finger through a lens—depending upon which version Rudy relayed to a variety of reporters. Podell's lawyer, Gerald Shargel, who has no recollection of his client doing anything notable with his glasses, suggests that if the incident did, in fact, occur, Rudy might be exaggerating the import of it. "I don't think

Podell was particularly rattled by Rudy," he said. A veteran trial attorney, Shargel said that every defendant who takes the witness stand is nervous, regardless of the effectiveness of the cross-examination.

Another supposed Hollywood moment came when the testimony concerned payments to a phony law firm Podell had invented to hide the money. To showcase the transparency of Podell's ploy, Rudy resorted to a prop. After fellow prosecutor Joseph Jaffe handed him an enormous volume of Martindale Hubbell, a directory of lawyers and law firms, Rudy slammed it suddenly down on the witness stand before the stunned congressman. He told Podell to look up his so-called firm.

"I object to slamming the book on the desk," defense attorney James La Rossa interjected.

Agreeing with La Rossa, Judge Robert Carter warned: "No dramatics, Mr. Giuliani."

Dramatics or no, Podell could not find the law firm. It was perhaps the most effective moment in Rudy's questioning of the wayward lawmaker.

On the whole, however, the legendarily withering nature of Rudy's cross-examination and Podell's alleged unraveling on the stand are both apocryphal, likely more spin than substance. The *New York Times* described Podell as "composed" during testimony and the New York *Daily News* noted that he "seemed to lose his composure only once yesterday while he described his former hope of running for the U.S. Senate."

Both of the congressman's attorneys, Gerald Shargel and La Rossa, say now that before Rudy's alleged evisceration even began they had told the government of Podell's willingness to plead guilty to two counts. At the start of the trial, the lawyers contend, they told Rudy that Podell would admit his guilt to conflict of interest and conspiracy but not to bribery. The ruined politician's primary concern was losing his license to practice law. These two of the ten counts in the indictment, explained La Rossa, were federal felonies, but misdemeanors under state law. Consequently, conviction on these counts would not necessarily result in his disbarment. Podell only testified, La Rossa and Shargel explained, because they were waiting for approval from Washington for a plea to these counts.

"The pleas had been in motion and had been agreed to in principle before Podell took the stand," said Shargel. "Giuliani just told us he needed permission from Washington. This was just another staged Giuliani event. Even then he was a politician."

La Rossa recalled that "Rudy's cross-examination had nothing to do with [Podell's plea]." He added: "It wasn't that Podell was on his knees. Podell didn't say, 'This guy is killing me, let's do a deal.' There was great opposition in the

Podell camp to taking the plea. Bert recognized the cross wasn't going any-where. . . . We were attempting to settle the case before we put him on the stand."

The transcript implicitly supports this contention, with La Rossa informing the judge that he'd gone to see U.S. Attorney Paul Curran after the government rested. La Rossa says the purpose of that meeting was to push acceptance of the plea.

Rudy's fellow prosecutor, Joe Jaffe, confirmed Podell's plea efforts in an unusual post-trial hearing. On the stand in a pre-sentencing hearing as a sworn witness, and questioned by Rudy himself, Jaffe was asked if there had been "prior discus-sions" about Podell pleading guilty. "Yes," Jaffe replied. "Those discussions ex-tended over the history of the case."

One close friend of Giuliani's from his Southern District days recalls that the Justice Department in Washington actually approved the plea before the cross-examination started, but Giuliani told no one until the lunch recess. That would make the entire cross an act. This extraordinary version of events is, however, un-supported by any corroborating references on the record.

In any event, during the afternoon break on October 1, 1974, Shargel recalls Giuliani approaching him and Podell in the stairwell off the main corridor to tell them that he had received permission from D.C. to accept the congressman's plea. The government would allow Podell to plead to the lesser non-bribery counts. Everyone sat down in a conference room and hammered out the details of the agreement.

Rudy promised La Rossa that if Podell pled guilty, the government would not rec-ommend a prison sentence for him and that Rudy himself would testify, in the event of a disbarment proceeding, that Podell's offenses did not involve bribery or reflect "corrupt and criminal intent." Then they appeared before U.S. District Court Judge Robert Carter, and he accepted the deal, setting a sentencing date in January.

Shortly before sentencing, on January 2, 1975, Rudy's office sent a letter to the judge noting that "Podell pleaded guilty to conspiracy to defraud the United States and a substantive violation of conflict of interest statutes," adding that "both of these are serious violations of Federal Law and should be treated seriously at the time of sentence." The letter also urges that Podell's "history of lying is one the Court is fully entitled to consider in imposing punishment."

Outraged, Podell moved to withdraw his guilty plea—contending that his deci-sion was based on the promises Rudy made to him. Judge Carter ordered a full hearing on Podell's motion, and everyone, including Rudy and Jaffe, testified un-der oath. In the end, Carter told Rudy directly that "this letter is a letter which does indicate that you are attempting to persuade the Court to a point of view," adding, "it seems to me you ought to admit that and be honest about it, that that is what you are doing." Rudy insisted it wasn't, and the judge firmly rebuked him: "I view the letter, in essence, as a violation of the spirit, if not the letter of the agreement." Carter ruled, however, that Podell was not allowed to withdraw his plea. He reasoned that the congressman had accepted the plea, not due to the government's position on prison time, but rather in hopes of avoiding disbarment.

On January 10, Carter told the crest-fallen congressman that he had been "trying in my own mind to justify not sending you to prison." But in a direct reference to Watergate, Carter said that there was "too much corruption in Government at the present time and Government officials who engage in corruption must at least be symbolically punished." Podell was sentenced to two years, all but six months suspended, and fined $5,000.

Rudy apparently thought it wasn't enough. Years later at a private dinner for twenty people honoring a federal judge, Rudy and his pal John Gross were seated next to a lawyer with a long and prestigious résumé, Jack Bonomi.

A former assistant district attorney who prosecuted many early mob cases, Bonomi served in 1960 as the special counsel to the seminal U.S. Senate subcommittee, headed by Estes Kefauver, that conducted the first televised hearings investigating the influence of organized crime. One mob skell Bonomi uncovered in his probe of boxing was Jimmy White, the manager for Vic Dellicurti, the fighter so closely tied to Harold Giuliani's old friend Lou Carbonetti. From 1963 to 1976, he served as chief counsel to the Grievance Committee of the Association of the Bar of New York. In that capacity he brought cases that resulted in the disbarment of a number of powerful lawyers, including former President Richard Nixon and his attorney general, John Mitchell. In private practice in the late 1970s, Bonomi represented many lawyers before the committee he had once served as chief counsel. One of those lawyers was Bertram Podell.

After his guilty plea in 1974, Podell had been temporarily disbarred from practicing law. But Bonomi, arguing before the Grievance Committee, managed to get the disbarment permanently reversed.

Somehow at the dinner, Podell's name popped up. Bonomi mentioned offhand how he had represented the former Congressman and had won back his law license. Upon hearing this, Rudy's eyes narrowed and all the lines in his face were marshaled into a sharp scowl. Despite his pledge to aid Podell in his efforts to avoid disbarment, Rudy took this white linen opportunity to cross-examine the congressman one last time.

"Rudy Giuliani started in on me," said Bonomi. "He said, 'You should never have taken the case!' I told him to screw off."

Five

A Star Rises on the Potomac

As he spoke to a group of federal prosecutors at the dedication of a new Manhattan prison one afternoon in the spring of 1975, Deputy Attorney General Harold "Ace" Tyler noticed a pasty-faced young man sitting front-row center, "watching me like a hawk." Tyler found himself glancing again and again, as he spoke, at those fixed, coal-colored eyes. The man seemed to be processing Tyler's every movement, taking in his every word—and the second most powerful man in Gerald Ford's Justice Department thought to himself: This must be Rudy Giuliani.

"I asked Paul Curran who he was," said Tyler. "And it was Rudy. He was a vacuum cleaner in his ability to absorb everything that might help him." His calculated stare was also his own brand of introduction.

A distinguished New York Republican, Tyler had resigned a few months earlier from the Southern District bench to become Attorney General Edward Levi's top deputy. He was looking to bring a young legal dynamo with him to Washington as his aide, and the U.S. Attorney's office in Manhattan was a hive of candidates.

Rudy applied for the job with the backing of his old mentor, Lloyd MacMahon. "MacMahon always raved about Rudy," said Tyler. "He kept telling me to bring him to Washington."

Tyler dallied, but MacMahon's calls kept coming. Soon after meeting Giuliani at the dedication, Tyler took MacMahon's advice. He hired Rudy as an associate deputy attorney general, a position that paid $38,000 a year. It was a great job, putting Rudy at the center of power, where he would help Tyler run the criminal wing of the U.S. Justice Department. But Rudy also viewed the appointment as a stepping stone to even bigger, better jobs. "It was a terrific opportunity," he said. "I thought it would be a seminar on how government works."

Bald, soft-spoken and possessed of a cool equanimity antithetical to the likes of MacMahon, the six-foot-two-inch Tyler had earned his "Ace" nickname in his youth by scoring fifteen points in a prep school basketball game. This was not his first stint in Washington, and he was not unfamiliar with its mercurial currents and undertows. In 1959, President Eisenhower had appointed Tyler the first head of the Justice Department's Civil Rights Division. He was named U.S. District Court Judge by President Kennedy three years later in 1962. Now, in September 1975, when Rudy joined him, Tyler's job was to oversee the day-to-day operations of Justice, a task made all the more onerous by Watergate. Sapped of its morale, the department's criminal division was so sluggish Tyler billed it a "fudge factory with 680 lawyers."

"Tyler was very good under pressure," Rudy said. "I learned from him that in a pressure situation, the best thing to do was remain calmer than everybody else. I also learned that it was good to become angry and upset when everybody else is calm and complacent. It helps to motivate them."

A few other promising young lawyers had clambered their way onto Tyler's staff, including Antonin Scalia and Robert Bork—two conservative icons who would eventually be nominated, one successfully, to the U.S. Supreme Court. "Nino Scalia was a bouncing Italian," says Tyler. "He played the piano. Rudy and he got along pretty well."

Rudy did not get along so well with another member of Tyler's staff, a young black lawyer named Togo West, who handled the deputy attorney general's civil matters. A tension blossomed between Rudy and West, according to Tyler. "Rudy was always difficult with West," said Tyler. "Rudy didn't think he was savvy." Tyler thought West, who had clerked for him, was just too subtle for the head-strong Rudy. "Togo was a master at the indirect," Tyler noted, a fact that seemed to completely escape Rudy's notice. "Scalia really liked Togo," said Tyler. "Even Bork liked him." Only Rudy went to war with him. West went on to a distinguished career in the Clinton administration as secretary of the army and, later, secretary of veterans' affairs.

Also detecting a deeply rooted contempt within Rudy for members of Congress, Tyler thought it wise to steer his aggressive aide away from Capitol Hill. "If you don't suffer fools gladly," he explained, "you better not try to sell them anything."

One of Rudy's primary tasks was to "keep an eye" on the FBI and U.S. Marshals Service. The FBI "considered Rudy their man," said Tyler. The thirty-one-year-old associate deputy joined his boss at meetings with FBI head Clarence Kelly and other top law enforcement officials, including the then director of operations for the Marshals Service, Howard Safir, who would eventually become Rudy's police commissioner.

The "white collar crime committee"— founded by Attorney General Levi in October 1975 and placed under Harold Tyler's supervision—became Rudy's responsibility. Charged with critically examining the Department's performance on white-collar crime and recommending improvements, the committee was established in response to a group letter sent to Levi that August. The letter was signed by a number of legislators and consumer advocates, including Ralph Nader and future New York Public Advocate—and Giuliani nemesis—Mark Green.

When Togo West resigned to return to private practice, Rudy inherited his responsibilities and was suddenly Tyler's point man on both the criminal and civil fronts. He became a de facto chief of staff.

In June 1976, Rudy sat in on a meeting Tyler held with Philadelphia's mayor, Frank Rizzo, the rough-edged former chief cop of the City of Brotherly Love. Worried that the upcoming July 4th bicentennial celebration to be held in Philadelphia would become the target of terrorists, Rizzo asked Tyler to order that 15,000 federal troops be assigned to the city. As Rizzo and Tyler spoke, Rudy sat in quiet awe of the crude Italian-American politician, mesmerized by him.

Rizzo was notorious for his blunt, bigoted remarks. During his first campaign for mayor, he boasted: "I'm going to make Attila the Hun look like a faggot after this election's over." An unequivocal racist, Rizzo told an acquaintance during his second run for mayor: "Forget about the niggers, I don't need 'em." He called Governor Milton Shapp "that Jew in Harrisburg" and referred to City Councilman Pete Camiel as "that Polack."

A six-foot two-inch Navy veteran, who had earned nicknames such as "The Cisco Kid" and "Super Cop," Rizzo was also famous for his Stalinist approach to policing. He had made headlines in 1970, when, in the wake of the shooting of a cop, he ordered a raid of the Philadelphia Black Panther offices. With no evidence against them, fourteen Panthers were arrested and stripped naked in the street. It turned out another group was responsible for the police killing. In 1973, Rizzo was caught running a secret thirty-four-man special police unit formed expressly to dig up dirt and spy on his political enemies.

At the sit-down with Tyler, Rizzo told Tyler that he was especially concerned about two activist organizations, even though both had already obtained permits to protest the day's activities. Without troops, Rizzo insisted, chaos would surely erupt.

Tyler recalls Rizzo's request as excessive, if not slightly maniacal. "He wanted to move the Eighty-second Airborne into combat position!" says Tyler, incredulously. "He was saying, 'We're gonna be attacked!'"

During the discussion, Rudy's attention remained fixed on Rizzo. "Rudy was fascinated," said Tyler. "He was staring at Frank like he had stared at me. I was thinking that he kind of likes this guy's approach."

After watching Rizzo bluster his way through a press conference on the bicentennial terrorist threat, Rudy told Tyler he thought the Philadelphia mayor was "masterful." Tyler guessed that the press conference "maybe influenced Rudy."

Ultimately, Rizzo's request was denied. As for what happened in Philadelphia on the 4th of July, 1976? "Nothing," said Harold Tyler. "Nothing happened."

Rudy's lifestyle changed in Washington. After he had decided on a rather modest apartment and returned to New York to pack, resourceful Regina discovered a comparably priced palace. Rudy heard her description over the phone and instantly agreed.

Looming high above the Iwo Jima memorial, stolidly stationed on top of a steep ridge in Arlington, Virginia, Prospect House looked more like a modern fortress than a high-rise luxury apartment building. Angular and aerodynamic, it was shaped like a shallow "W" vaguely reminiscent of a stealth bomber, as if the building might roar thunderously into the sky. The 268-unit, eleven-story building featured such amenities as a swimming pool, in-house gourmet restaurant, private garden, underground valet parking, grocery store and dry cleaning service. The view from this elite residential bunker was spectacular: a panoramic vista of the entire D.C. skyline, with the monuments and federal buildings laid out below like a sparkling miniature city.

Their neighbors at Prospect House included a host of congressmen and other Washington luminaries, like Larry King. The Giulianis were thrilled with their new $550-per-month, fifth-floor duplex, replete with a sunken living room, thirteen-foot-high ceilings, a giant bay window and balcony overlooking the splendor of the nation's capital. The couple entertained many visitors at their new pad, often hosting parties on their broad balcony. "The building was so crowded that when you looked up and down the terrace," said Regina, "you were almost afraid the building was going to fall over because the whole place had parties." On the night of July 4th, 1976—the 200th anniversary of the United States of America, the auspicious day that had had Frank Rizzo so desperately worried—Rudy and Regina hosted a bicentennial bash for a swath of friends and acquaintances. As the daylight dwindled, everyone gathered on the balcony to watch the fireworks. "There were dozens of Justice Department people," Regina recalled. Among them were former FBI director William Gray and future Attorney General Richard Thornburgh, then chief of the Department of Justice's criminal division. Rudy Giuliani was making some very powerful friends.

With the brisk change of scene, the new apartment, and the parties, Rudy and

Regina's marriage was being molded into more conventional shape. Regina, whose presence was much more evident in Rudy's life here than it had been in New York, was giving the relationship a second try.

In accompanying Rudy to Washington, however, his wife was also pulling up fresh but firm roots in New York, leaving a brand-new job she liked almost as much as Prospect House. On April 1, 1974, she had been appointed a higher education assistant at the City University of New York's York College in Queens. Earning a salary of $15,280, she served as the program coordinator for York's Continuing Education Department, which was run by an affable CUNY professor named James C. Hall. York was a new college that targeted Queens's growing African-American community and had drawn a number of black educators. Hall was one of many black professional colleagues who would become a close friend of Regina's, nudging her politics in a liberal direction, just as Rudy's moved rightward, surrounded by his new Republican friends.

After a long job hunt in Washington, Regina was hired as the coordinator of the Center for Continuing Education and Mental Health, an affiliate of the Psychiatric Institute of Washington, a local hospital. Her primary responsibilities were organizing seminars and other programs for the hospital's employees and overseeing continuing education programs for psychiatrists who needed to renew their licenses.

Tyler met Regina on a handful of occasions, most memorably at two Justice Department parties in Virginia and Maryland. His wife and children also met her at the Virginia party, said Tyler, and "thought she was terrific." He added, "So did I."

Rudy's wife, however, was curiously timid. "She was withdrawn," said Tyler. "She wouldn't react. She was extraordinarily quiet, pushing everyone away."

After a year and a half at Justice, Rudy suddenly had to look for work. Gerald Ford had lost his re-election bid to Jimmy Carter and the musical-chairs flurry of fresh political appointments was about to beset Justice. The most seductive voice whispering in his ear was Harold Tyler's. Rudy's mentor suggested that they present themselves as part of a five-lawyer package deal to high-powered New York law firms. Also part of the package was another Tyler protégé, a black attorney named Richard Parsons. In early 1977, Tyler signed on with the old-money, Republican firm of Patterson, Belknap & Webb; his name was quickly appended to the firm's already lofty, but somewhat stale, triumvirate of names. Rudy was initially offered an associate position, but after persistent protestations and a little pouting—no partnership for Rudy and Rudy walks—the firm relented. Rudy even got a stake of less than 1 percent of Patterson's profits.

From offices in Rockefeller Center, Patterson's attorneys, most of whom had Ivy League degrees, represented a roster of corporate clients and worked on estates, trusts and taxes. It was an unequivocally stodgy outfit where few cases went to court.

Tyler was brought in as a rainmaker, a big-name attorney who could lure clients with deep pockets. At first, Rudy found himself replicating his Justice Department role. "Essentially, I served as Tyler's chief of staff," said Rudy. "He'd bring in the business and I'd work on the cases."

Emboldened by the hubris of Washington, Rudy soon came to be viewed as an iconoclast of sorts at the staid, buttoned-down Patterson. Renee Syzbala, who had joined the firm shortly before Rudy, said the new partner would often flout the office's rigid code of conduct. "No one could know what anyone else was making," said Syzbala. "Rudy would tell you who was fighting with who, what so-and-so was making. Rudy would take people out on the firm. . . . I wasn't happy until Rudy got there. When Rudy came, the place got to be fun."

Rudy's mild insubordinations earned him the loyalty of a group of associates, including Syzbala, who worked and played with him. Known as "Rudy and the Rudettes," the upstart clique would regularly meet after work for a few rounds of scotch. The social outings often became late-night affairs that might start at a bar or restaurant and end up at a disco joint in the early hours of the morning. On some occasions the Rudettes stayed out so late that they would eat breakfast together. "Rudy was a cigar smoker, a heavy drinker," said Renee Syzbala. "Completely un-health conscious."

Spurred by a spontaneity seldom seen in his later public life, Rudy was famous among the crew for his hijinks. After one night of reveling, he climbed into the public water fountain in front of the Seagram Building and splashed around, daring his colleagues to join him. And so they did, wading in the fountain, splashing each other.

When Syzbala first met Rudy in January of 1977, she said he led her to believe that he and his wife had already been separated for a period of several years and that he was a free man. Rudy even went on a few dates with Syzbala's cousin, whom he had met at Renee's wedding. Syzbala said years later that she thought her night-clubbing pal was single all of the four years he was at Patterson. Jeff Harris, Rudy's friend from the U.S. Attorney's Office, said of the marriage that "it was clear by the time he was at Patterson Belknap that they were not together."

Harold Tyler, who knew Regina from Washington, said he never saw her again after Rudy joined Patterson. "I knew something was going on," he said. "But that was more intuition."

In fact, Rudy was not only still married; he lived with Regina for all of the first three years at Patterson.

The fun-loving fountain jumper once staged a practical joke on Syzbala that revolved around the perception of him as a wild man. One morning Syzbala heard a knock at her door. It was a partner, Mike Mukasey, who was also a friend of Rudy's. Mukasey was worried. He told Syzbala that Rudy hadn't come into work and wasn't at home. Then he blurted out that their friend had been arrested by an undercover police agent the night before for soliciting a prostitute. Mukasey convinced Syzbala that the two of them would have to break the news to Tyler. "Mike pushed me in front of him," said Syzbala. "I knocked on Judge Tyler's door." When she opened it, Rudy was sitting in the office, laughing. "I didn't truly believe Mike, . . . but it was believable that it could happen."

The bulk of Rudy's work at Patterson involved contracts, real estate and libel suits. Since two of his and Tyler's major clients were the Tribune Company, which owned the *Daily News,* and Dow Jones, which owned the *Wall Street Journal,* much of Rudy's early litigation experience involved First Amendment work. Though he had earned a reputation as a capable trial attorney in the SDNY, he tried very few cases at Patterson, none of them criminal.

One of his handful of civil trials involved Dow Jones. The company was being sued in March 1977 by Robert Nemeroff, a Manhattan dentist, who alleged that one of its publications, *Barron's National Business & Financial Weekly,* had used its columns to depress the price of a listed stock he owned. In the spring of 1978, after a round of motions, counter-motions and other legal maneuvers, Nemeroff dropped the charges. But the settlement allowed Rudy to pursue Nemeroff for Dow's costs and expenses and he did. He submitted a fifty-one-page memo of law, calling Nemeroff's suit "an attempt to silence the press" and "circumvent the First Amendment." Dubbing Nemeroff's action a malicious lawsuit that had been "filed either with the knowledge that counsel had no adequate basis to sustain the allegations or in reckless disregard of the fact that proof of the charges was not available," the judge ruled in Rudy's favor. He ordered that Nemeroff and his attorneys reimburse Dow Jones for $50,000 in legal fees incurred in fighting these "unsupported" charges.

Rudy made the claim, many years after his stint at Patterson, that, as a private attorney, he was exceptionally picky about his clients—rejecting anyone with a sleazy profile. Definitely no mob guys, he had decided. Anyone Rudy Giuliani represented would have to be a "legitimate" individual, he said, who had "redeeming social value."

A reasonable definition of "redeeming social value," however, would have to be drawn and quartered to apply to Albert Terranova, the frumpy head of a New Jersey job training program called National Training Systems Corp. In 1977, Terranova, his staff assistant and his company were all indicted by the U.S. Attorney in Newark on thirty-five counts of bilking the government by filing false records. Two years later, after hiring Giuliani as his personal attorney, Terranova entered a guilty plea to a misdemeanor charge of "knowingly and willfully" stealing federal funds. His company pled guilty to felony charges of conspiring with Terranova and his assistant to defraud the U.S. government. The judge said that the only thing keeping Rudy's client out of jail was the fact that his wife was gravely ill.

Five months later, Terranova and his wife acquired a Brooklyn vocational school and renamed it Adelphi Institute. Rudy helped Terranova draft the incorporation papers for Adelphi and notarized his application for a New York vocational school license. The school was dependent on the same sort of vocational school funding Terranova had already stolen in New Jersey. But loyal Rudy went even further for his convicted client—in August of 1980, he wrote a letter to state officials on Terranova's behalf, stating that "Adelphi's management is experienced, dedicated and responsible." The letter did not mention that Terranova was currently serving probation—in a deal Rudy had worked out himself.

Rudy would later insist that "there was nothing else I could do as a lawyer," adding, "I would have had to want to gratuitously hurt my client to have added facts concerning his misdemeanor conviction."

Adelphi Institute secured its license and, over the next eight years, harvested more than $80 million in federal vocational funds. In the summer of 1986, the Terranovas bought a $1.9 million house in a suburb of Phoenix, Arizona. A year later, Adelphi went bankrupt. In July 1989, Terranova was arraigned on charges that he stole more than $63,000 in tuition funds from Adelphi students as part of a nation-wide multimillion-dollar fraud scheme. In September 1989, the incorrigible thief pled guilty. He got a $150,000 fine and was later forced to pay a $1.3 million settlement.

Terranova, who still lives in Arizona, has remained friendly with Rudy over the years. When Rudy remarried in 1984, and when his son was born in 1986, Terranova sent gifts.

The Terranova matter, like the draft deferment issue, also made it into the "vulnerability" study that Rudy's campaign commissioned when he ran for mayor in 1993. The study's authors warned that Giuliani could be accused of "being sneaky and hypocritical" when he wrote the Terranova letter. The study's "rebuttal strategy" recommends: "If asked about Terranova, Giuliani should rebuke him in harsh terms for breaking the law. Beyond, that, the best answer to this rather frivolous charge might be 'no comment.'" The authors also noted that in the 1989 campaign, Giuliani "made the mistake of discussing the particulars of the case which forced him to claim he could not remember facts and prevaricate." This, they cautioned, "is a bad strategy."

Terranova wasn't Rudy's only conspicuous client at placid Patterson. Elliot Cuker, an eccentric, bow-tie–wearing proprietor of a Greenwich Village Rolls Royce limousine service, hired Rudy to represent him in the late 1970s in a tax investigation stemming from an IRS audit of his business. After coaxing his client into paying back taxes and interest, according to Cuker, the resourceful Rudy even helped him set up a computerized accounting system.

Cuker, who would forge an enduring friendship with Giuliani, was a savvy businessman with a tendency toward the garish. A late 1970s billboard advertisement for his limo service showed Cuker in a chauffeur's outfit, leaning nonchalantly against an old Rolls-Royce, a glass of champagne glinting in his hand. Below his photo, as one friend recalls it, was the smug slogan: "Poverty Sucks."

After graduating from the American Academy of Dramatic Arts in New York, Cuker struggled through the 1960s—mostly unsuccessfully—to find work as an actor. He purchased a pair of 1954 Bentleys, though, and began renting himself out in the mid-1970s as a driver. Affecting a British accent, Cuker told his clients: "Your chauffeur's name is Elliot. Please make sure you give him the proper gratuity." Within three years, he was running a limo service with a fleet of thirteen cars. By the time Rudy met him, Cuker's business had grown into a highly successful luxury classic car dealership.

When he settled the tax probe, Cuker sold or gave Rudy a vintage white Porsche. It was one of four cars the quirky entrepreneur would convey to Rudy over the years, all of which Rudy would wind up returning. Of Cuker, who eventually became one his closest personal advisors, Rudy would say in 1998: "I really love him."

Rudy's biggest case at Patterson landed squarely in his lap, courtesy, not of "Ace" Tyler, but, rather, of that crusty old U.S. District Court judge with the bushy eyebrows: Lloyd MacMahon. Aminex Resources Corp., a coal-mining company in Kentucky had been plunged into bankruptcy due to the looting of more than $1 million by two executives, and in March of 1978, MacMahon appointed Rudy as its legal receiver.

MacMahon had to wrest jurisdiction away from another federal court to deliver this prime patronage cut to his protégé—who had never been a receiver and had no background in bankruptcy cases. "Rudy didn't have any experience," said Tyler. "MacMahon knew Rudy didn't know anything about this."

Further stretching the legitimacy of MacMahon's decision to appoint Rudy was a simple matter of geography: The Aminex mines were located in the forlorn backwoods of Kentucky and Patterson was situated in an antiseptic honeycomb of offices at Rockefeller Center in New York City. A Kentucky firm certainly would have commanded a more intimate understanding of the local issues affecting Aminex and its employees.

Nonetheless, Rudy went south. For three years, he, fellow Patterson partner Joel Carr and a team of six other attorneys kept Aminex above water and finally managed to right it back to its feet. For a period of nine months, Rudy claims he spent an average of three days per week in Kentucky, overseeing efforts to ensure Aminex's prompt coal deliveries to an Ohio utility. By Rudy's account, his time was split between the company's offices in Lexington and its mines in a remote town called Hazard—although, years later, two Aminex executives told Newsday that they couldn't remember Rudy making many visits to Hazard.

Kentucky, as the antithesis of New York, had an exotic appeal for Rudy: the beautiful though sometimes desolate landscape, the Southern twangs, the giant mounds of coal, the ubiquity of shotguns and chewing tobacco, the rugged, unadorned texture of everyday life. It was also a place which perhaps reminded the young attorney of his freshly well-heeled status, a place that captured his curiosity the way an inner-city slum initially entrances a kid from the suburbs. He was also quite taken with the local racetrack and spent many weekends there with a colleague or two from Patterson. "Rudy got a big kick out of going to Kentucky," said Tyler, who added that the Aminex case was "one of the best parts of his life."

In 1981, in an arrangement Giuliani and Carr negotiated, Aminex was sold for $15.1 million, and creditors were repaid 100 cents on the dollar. Patterson drew $2.4 million in legal fees and sought an additional $500,000 bonus for "spectacular results" in salvaging Aminex. Attorneys for the company's new owners opposed the bonus on the grounds that "Giuliani and his firm [have] already been rewarded for their excellent legal services." Bankruptcy Court Judge Joel Lewittes concurred in part, approving only a $200,000 bonus.

Rudy's self-described single-handed bailout of the Kentucky coal-mining company—frequently cited as evidence of his "CEO" prowess in both his 1989 and 1993 mayoral campaigns—was another example of his penchant for hyperbole.

Joel Carr, who was portrayed by some newspapers as Rudy's loyal sidekick, "was really running the show," said Harold Tyler.

The *Newsday* piece also cast doubt on Rudy's rescue role by reviewing his work days in Kentucky and discovering that he was a "distant manager who did not run the day-to-day affairs of the mining operation, preferring to delegate most of the work to subordinates." When Rudy resigned as Aminex receiver in March of 1981 to leave Patterson for a new Washington post, MacMahon named fellow mentor Tyler as the replacement receiver. Tyler stayed on as receiver until the pre-negotiated sale of the company was completed later that year.

While Rudy enjoyed his man-about-town days during the Patterson, Belknap years, Regina found a new life on the York College campus, where she returned to work after their Washington stay. She and Rudy continued to live together in the five-and-a-half-room apartment they jointly owned on the fourth floor of their sixteen-story West End Avenue building, but it was an increasingly chilly home, with distant partners sharing the same refrigerator. With two bedrooms and attached baths, the apartment seemed designed for people who walked through its French doors in the foyer and went in different directions.

The garrulous Jim Hall, twelve years older than Regina and the dean of the adult and continuing education department, was becoming a more and more important figure in her life. Tall and stocky with a mustache, ex-marine Hall was a commanding figure when he entered a room. He talked endlessly, slipping often into philosophical tangents. While getting his graduate degree at NYU, he co-authored a book published by Vantage, a vanity press, called *Damn Reading! (A Case Against Literacy)*, which railed against the teaching of reading as a socioeconomic "screening process" and a cause of psychological distress. He saw literacy as a stigmatizing weapon used against black youth and called for "discarding literacy, as we know it, from our educational system." A leader of black students and faculty at York, Hall was a thorn in the side of York's white administrators and attempted, at one point, to mount a campaign to become president himself.

Regina shared a small office with Hall and wrote the proposals that kept the adult program percolating. One of her biggest—in the early '80s—won federal funding for a project targeting the thousands of new Haitians arriving in New York, refugees from the Duvalier tyranny. Hall was part of a City University–wide underground railroad of black professionals—especially those running adult education departments—and Regina became part of that network as well. Hall's *Damn Reading!* co-author Jim Gibson was the assistant director of the York department. Gibson, Hall, Regina and another woman in the small unit began hitting after-work bars in Manhattan together. Hall was already in the middle of his second divorce, leaving his wife and Staten Island home by the summer of 1979, and moving into Manhattan.

In February of 1980—according to divorce papers filed more than two years later—Regina left Rudy and began a twelve-year relationship with Hall. It's unclear exactly when she moved in with him. Property records indicate that she lived with him at 75 Livingston Street in Brooklyn—a new co-op building that he moved into soon after it opened in 1982. Records also show they bought a house together in 1985 on Lincoln Road—near the D'Avanzos' old Hawthorne Street home in what had become an almost entirely black section of Brooklyn. Finally, in 1989, after their Lincoln Road home was burglarized, they moved into a large apartment building with a capped doorman, overlooking Grand Army Plaza and Prospect Park.

Hall's connections helped Regina become the top aide to Augusta Kappner, who ran the adult programs on all twenty-one City University campuses, and move into the university's central office by 1984. A few years later, she replaced Kappner, who became a college president, and became Hall's boss, directing the citywide program. In 1990, Kappner was vice chair of the board at Marymount Manhattan College, when Regina was named its president. But two years later, Hall, at the age of sixty, dropped dead while he and Regina vacationed in Maine.

Hall's close friend Solomon Goodrich, the executor of his will, said the main reason the two were never married was because "Jim was scared of Rudy." Goodrich recalled: "I said, 'Why don't you marry the woman?' He said the whole Rudy factor was one of the impediments to that. Jim didn't think Rudy liked him being black." Of course, Rudy was in two powerful law enforcement posts during most of Hall's years with Regina—associate attorney general and U.S. Attorney.

Rudy had never been much of a presence in Regina's York life during the years they were together. Secretaries remember that as late as 1979, Helen Giuliani phoned more often than Rudy. Colleagues recall Rudy coming to the wedding of one York friend of Regina's, but otherwise, Hall and Regina were usually together at campus events. Regina made the final decision to leave their apartment in 1980—a decision Rudy would not make. With Harold Giuliani already seriously ill, neither Rudy nor Regina made a move to turn their latest separation into a divorce. Harold was now Regina's champion. "Being Catholic, divorce is not supposed to happen," Giuliani said in an unpublished interview in the late 1980s. "But when you separate for the second time, the handwriting is on the wall. It just wasn't working out."

In November of 1980, Ronald Reagan defeated Jimmy Carter, making the White House once again an elephant's fortress. A month later, on December 8, 1980, Rudy Giuliani, the once outspoken Kennedy fan, switched his voter registration to Republican. His political metamorphosis was now complete. Rudy's switch coincided with the handing out of new political appointments by the Reagan administration. And Rudy, whose former Patterson colleague, Richard Parsons, was on the Reagan transition team, knew he had a shot at one.

Rudy's mother confirmed that her son's registration switch was designed to snare a Reagan job. "He only became a Republican after he began to get all these jobs from them," said Helen Giuliani in an unpublished 1988 interview. "He's definitely not a conservative Republican. He thinks he is, but he isn't. He still feels very sorry for the poor." In a simultaneous interview, Regina recalled that when she split with Rudy in early 1980, she had still considered him to be liberal Democrat. "He generally won't do things unless he believes them," said Regina, adding, "but he's not a saint, and he will do things that serve his interests."

While Regina was always a Democrat, Helen Giuliani was herself no stranger to party hopping. Twenty-four years earlier, she and her husband had bolted the Democratic Party when the family relocated to conservative Garden City, Long Island. They later switched back when they moved to moderately liberal North Bellmore. As far as his voter registration records indicate, Harold remained a Democrat at least until his late sixties. Helen, however, would switch again back to the Republican Party by October 1988.

Unlike his parents' party hopscotching, Rudy's political journey had been a slow, steady trek from left to right. He parted with the Democratic Party years before becoming a Republican, registering independent by designating his partly affiliation box as blank. He claimed in subsequent interviews to have registered as an independent in 1973 while at the U.S. Attorney's office. He said he did so to avoid any perception that his public corruption prosecutions were politically motivated. The earliest voting records available at the New York City Board of Elections, however, indicate he registered as an independent in 1977, when he returned from Washington.

Harold Tyler recalls Rudy's registering as an independent—perhaps from his Virginia address—during his first stint at the Department of Justice in 1975. "When Rudy was with me, he registered as an independent," said Tyler. "He changed his registration."

In early 1981, a month after his party switch to Republican, Rudy was to be appointed the No. 3 man in the Reagan Justice Department, the associate deputy attorney general under Attorney General William French Smith and Deputy

Attorney General Edward Schmults. Since neither Smith nor Schmults had any background in criminal law, they both wanted an experienced criminal prosecutor at their side.

But it was more than Rudy's criminal experience or the fact that he knew someone on the Reagan transition team that opened the door at Justice: The old mentor network had revved back into action. Harold Tyler had spoken with both Smith and Schmults and "told them Rudy was a very good man."

The nomination was a crowning achievement for Rudy. Casting a shadow, however, over the sweetness of the moment was the rapid deterioration of his father's health. Prostate cancer had spread mercilessly throughout much of Harold Giuliani's body, guaranteeing constant pain. A pacemaker had also been installed to keep his troubled heart beating. Since moving to Bayside, Queens in 1978, the stubborn champion of toughness had worn down into a groaning, crumpled form under hospital blankets. Now Rudy was forced to confront his hero father, confined to a bed, robbed of all his hubris, his mortality as bare and fragile as his body.

As his father's condition worsened, Rudy had moved him from Northshore Hospital in Queens to Memorial Sloan Kettering Cancer Center in Manhattan. With his Senate confirmation looming, it was a busy time, and the rising Republican star made frequent trips between New York and Washington, trying to fit hospital visits in between.

Further crowding the clock was a matter from Rudy's days as Tyler's assistant in the 1970s that had stubbornly clawed its way into the present. In March 1976, the Justice Department's Office of Professional Responsibility had asked Giuliani to assign "a lawyer under your supervision" to review allegations brought by a Pennsylvania building contractor named Jack A. Nard. Nard charged that several Justice Department officials, including Rudy's friend Richard Thornburgh, had covered up their failure to prosecute officials of an Iowa-based meat-packing company, Armour & Co., for committing perjury in two civil suits in the late 1960s. As a result of the suits, Nard and his partners had been ordered to pay Armour more than $800,000. Nard produced a footlocker of documents for review, and Rudy assigned his subordinate, Mary Wagner, to examine the materials. On July 26, 1976, Wagner wrote Nard a letter informing him that, due to a lack of evidence, his case was being dropped.

Four years later, in late 1980, Rudy became one of several targets of a Senate Judiciary Committee investigation into the Justice Department's alleged submarining of politically sensitive public corruption cases, including the Nard probe. Republican Senator Orrin Hatch from Utah, who had formerly represented Nard as a client, and Democratic Senator Dennis DeConcini from Arizona, began pushing for an investigation of the department's handling of Nard's allegations.

In April 1981, while Rudy worked as a Justice Department consultant pending his Senate confirmation, he admitted in the *Federal Times* that when the Nard case was under review, "I had a close working relationship with Thornburgh" and considered him a "personal friend." His primary involvement in the case, he said, was advising Wagner on routine questions such as whether to issue subpoenas. He also said that Wagner's review of the Nard case took "several weeks."

Congressional investigator Peter Stockton, who reviewed the Nard documents for the Senate Judiciary Committee in the fall of 1980, claimed, however, that Wagner had admitted she only spent one day looking into Nard's allegations. In his report, Stockton wrote that he had found evidence of an "inefficient and possibly corrupt operation by the Justice Department." He described the Wagner investigation as "no investigation at all."

"The Nard case was a major priority before and during the time that Rudy's confirmation was pending," said Robert McConnell, then assistant attorney general for legislative affairs and the Justice's point man for all its nominees facing confirmation.

McConnell was ordered to conduct an investigation into Rudy's relationship with the case. Without formally interrogating Rudy, McConnell concluded that a review of the records found no proof Rudy was involved in the decision to spike the probe, nor any evidence that he wasn't. "I then told Hatch that it would impossible for me to prove a negative," McConnell says.

In March 1982, McConnell wrote what he now refers to as a "stop this" letter that cleared Giuliani. A close friend of Rudy's, McConnell would sit on the dais of Rudy's 1993 inaugural, visit the mansion and ask Rudy to be his daughter's godfather.

The Nard investigations ultimately resulted in a three-month delay in Rudy's Senate confirmation. When he testified on the matter before the Senate Judiciary Committee, the crackerjack trial attorney widely reputed to have a steel-trap memory, insisted that he had "virtually no recollection" of the case. McConnell said with a laugh that Rudy was "absolutely worthless" as a witness. "He couldn't remember a thing."

What was most surprising about Rudy's confirmation and background review for this pivotal position was that no information about his family's criminal past surfaced. While Rudy may not have known about his father's 1934 armed robbery conviction, he had to be aware of the Leo/Lewis mob wing of his family. His aunts and cousins certainly knew about it when interviewed years later. Rudy also knew that his father worked for the man who ran the mob wing, and that a cousin tied to the mob had done time in federal prison before being gunned down by the FBI.

Yet, despite two probing background checks performed in 1975, when Rudy first went to the Justice Department, and 1981, nothing about Harold, Leo or

Lewis appears to have been discovered. Rudy filled out exhaustive questionnaires and submitted to extensive interviews by FBI agents, but the family's secrets remained intact.

"I never heard of any such fact—if it were a fact—that he had a cousin or any other relative that was charged with having a criminal history of some sort," said Harold Tyler. "I would be surprised to hear that there was something developed at that time, because I think I would have heard about it from the FBI, but I did not. I never heard of anything like that."

Asked if knew about any criminality in Rudy's family history, Jeff Harris, Rudy's friend from the Southern District who accompanied him to Washington to serve as his deputy in 1981, said, "I know of no such problem." Harris is convinced that if Rudy knew, "I would have known."

Former Justice Department Inspector General Michael Brombwich had to undergo a background check similar to Rudy's and remembers being asked by FBI agents to volunteer any potentially scandalous information about his own or his family's history. "I pretty clearly recall that I was asked that—is there anything about your background or anything about your associations that might prove embarrassing if it were publicly disclosed?"

The onus, Brombwich explained, was squarely placed upon the candidate. "It's up to the discretion of the person, the judgment of the person," he said. "[That way], if you're the person doing the background, you can't be accused of engaging in a witch hunt. You're basically asking them to provide you with the information that they think is relevant and that they think may be germane."

If FBI agents had independently unearthed the criminal histories of Lewis and Leo D'Avanzo and Harold Giuliani, they would have surely informed Rudy, according to an ex-FBI agent familiar with background check procedure.

The "sad footnote" to Rudy's confirmation delay, said McConnell, was that Harold Giuliani never got to see his son sworn in as associate attorney general. In late April of 1981, Rudy's father died at the age of seventy-three at Memorial Sloan Kettering hospital in Manhattan.

Jeff Harris recalled the day Rudy got an emergency call summoning him to New York. "We were in the office, he got a call in the morning sometime, saying his father was fading," said Harris. "He dropped whatever he was doing and headed for the shuttle to New York."

Harris was one of a throng of friends and colleagues, including, of course, Lloyd MacMahon, who attended Harold Giuliani's wake on the north shore of Long Island. It was at his father's wake when Rudy got a call from one of his aides in Washington: the confirmation had gone through.

"My father gave me such a great gift," Rudy said years later. "He gave me an internal sense of how to find a positive way to deal with whatever life has in store for you. But I lost a great source of strength when he died."

On May 15, 1981, less than a month after his father's death, Rudy Giuliani was sworn in as the youngest associate attorney general in history.

One of the very first matters Rudy handled as Reagan's new no. 3 man at Justice involved a criminal case against the McDonnell Douglas Corporation, a St. Louis-based airplane manufacturer. The mammoth company and four of its executives had been charged with authorizing $1.6 million in secret payments to Pakistani officials between 1972 and 1977 to push the sale of four $80 million DC-10 jetliners for Pakistan's national airline. The payoffs were merely tacked on to the listed price of the aircraft. The company was also accused of making false statements to hide payments of $6 million to airline personnel and government officials in South Korea, the Philippines, Venezuela and Zaire.

Michael Lubin and George Mendelson, the department prosecutors handling the case, had secured the indictments against the company and its executives in November 1979, when President Jimmy Carter was still in office. Now, with the pro-business Reagan administration in power, they were both concerned about the fate of the case—concerns that would soon prove well founded. As chronicled in James Stewart's *The Prosecutors*, the story of the McDonnell Douglas investigation became an almost Orwellian nightmare.

The two prosecutors were stunned to learn from defense lawyers that the new associate attorney general, Rudy Giuliani, had, without their knowledge, met McDonnell Douglas counsel John Sant to discuss the indictment. The meeting, which also included Giuliani's aide, Ken Caruso, had occurred on May 14, 1981, the day before Giuliani was sworn in. Sit-downs between attorneys for indicted defendants and top government brass were certainly not standard operating procedure, especially without informing the prosecutors handling the case. Fearing a fix in the works, Lubin and Mendelson penned a harsh letter to Giuliani expressing their "shock" and "dismay" at learning of the meeting and arguing that it could seriously undermine the prosecution's case. Figuring it best that some select people be made aware of the incident, they cc'd copies of the letter to several colleagues.

One of the last paragraphs of the letter read: "It is sadly ironic that a corporation that has been charged by a grand jury in connection with the purchase of improper influence and under-the-table dealings in foreign countries should be permitted by the Department of Justice to engage in back door approaches, presumably in an effort to dispose of the case. We would ask you to think back to your years as a federal prosecutor and contemplate your own reactions had former Congressman Podell or his lawyers lobbied senior Department of Justice officials without your knowledge while the case was awaiting trial."

Within a few days, Lubin and Mendelson were summoned to Giuliani's office. After they waited a considerable time out front, the secretary told them to enter. They walked in, noticed the dour Giuliani sitting silently behind his desk. Beside him was his assistant, Ken Caruso, also silent. Without shaking hands or saying hello, Lubin and Mendelson sat down.

Then Rudy Giuliani exploded.

"As far as I'm concerned, we were watching a madman," Lubin told Stewart. "It would have made a great videotape. I've never seen or heard anything like it, even in the movies. He ranted and raved for a full twenty minutes. He just went nuts. I've never seen a public official behave like this."

Later that night, Lubin got a call at home from a United Press International reporter. A few days earlier, other reporters had obtained copies of his and Mendelson's letter from someone they had cc'd. Lubin learned from the UPI reporter that Giuliani, in an attempt at damage control, had crafted a response to their letter that was leaked to the press. Among his many sharp-tongued counter-lashes, Rudy wrote that "Messrs. Lubin and Mendelson displayed a disrespect for the facts and an immature petulance."

Rudy then told the *Washington Post* that he didn't know the purpose of the meeting beforehand and, in fact, had not even known that McDonnell Douglas was under indictment—a dubious assertion, since the case had already attracted more press attention than any criminal fraud matter in the department. Rudy insisted that he had done nothing wrong and said he would continue to meet with defense attorneys without line prosecutors present.

On June 24, 1981, Republican Senator John C. Danforth of Missouri, who had set up the meeting with Sant, offered a version of events in direct conflict with Rudy's. Danforth told the *Washington Post* that he had explained to Rudy that the company's attorney wanted to meet with him expressly to discuss complaints about treatment by the Justice Department. "I certainly imagined he [Rudy] knew what it was about," Danforth said.

During his earlier blow-torch session with Lubin and Mendelson, Rudy claimed that he had notified the criminal division chief, D. Lowell Jensen, of the meeting and had requested the file on the case from him. A memo written by Caruso, and addressed to Jensen proved he had done this, said Rudy. But Jensen, when questioned by Lubin, would not confirm that any such memo had ever been sent. Lubin submitted a Freedom of Information Act request years later for Caruso's memo, and the department informed him they could locate no such document. Lubin suspected all along that it had never existed.

Fred Wertheimer, president of Common Cause, asked for a review of Giuliani's conduct. The Office of Professional Responsibility, headed Mike Shaheen, responded by conducting an investigation into the propriety of Rudy's meeting with Sant but ultimately determined that it was "a permissible exercise of his discretion."

Wertheimer told reporters in July, after the Giuliani review results were announced: "His conduct may have been permissible, but it would be disastrous for the system it if became a regular activity."

The dispirited Lubin and Mendelson were somewhat buoyed by a June 9, 1981 letter announcing that they had both been chosen to receive the Special Commendation Award, one of the Justice Department's highest honors. But three weeks later they got another letter saying their awards were being held "in abeyance pending resolution of issues arising from your letter of June 19, 1981, to Associate Attorney General Giuliani with respect to the McDonnell Douglas prosecution."

They had already seen the programs for the awards ceremony with their names listed in them, but they soon discovered that every one of those programs had been destroyed. "This kind of retaliation was almost unbelievably petty," Lubin said.

Rudy insisted that Lubin and Mendelson didn't deserve the awards. "They are jerks," Rudy said. "They had no perspective or judgment." The two prosecutors, Rudy claimed, exemplified what he would later describe as the Carter administration's "McCarthyism" in pursuing white-collar criminals.

On September 9, 1981, Rudy announced that the criminal charges against the four McDonnell Douglas executives would be dropped. More than three years of Lubin and Mendelson's work was summarily erased. The case concluded with a plea bargain Giuliani approved, in which the corporation alone pled guilty to fraud and making false statements and paid $1.25 million in penalties.

Philip Heyman, the department's criminal division chief under Carter who had initially approved the criminal charges against the McDonnell Douglas executives, told the *Washington Post* shortly after Rudy's announcement: "I would have been extremely reluctant to drop any charges brought after very careful consideration by a previous administration."

Rudy, in rationalizing his decision, remarked: "Do the innocent ever get convicted? That is the nightmare of being a prosecutor. There are enough cases of clear criminality that we shouldn't waste a moment on a case when the individual might be innocent." Rudy then conceded: "I did think the conduct was wrong. But when they committed the misconduct, it wasn't clear what they did was illegal. A foreign bribe was not a clear violation of U.S. law."

Those same arguments, Stewart points out, had been used by the McDonnell Douglas defense and had been soundly rejected by both the trial court and the Court of Appeals.

Months after Lubin and Mendelson left the government and started their own law firm in Washington, they received a box in the mail from Jensen's office. Inside were their Special Commendation Awards.

In late 1981 and early 1982, the new associate attorney general began making frequent trips to Miami. Two items of business drew him there: thousands of Haitian boat people who were overwhelming the Florida coast and an anti-cocaine initiative led by Vice President George Bush. In early February of 1982, however, he discovered a third reason to visit: a pretty, blond, 32-year-old TV anchorwoman named Donna Hanover.

Donna had the bubbly bearing of a 1950s high school cheerleader. Often attired in tight pants and low cut dresses, she was enviably dishy and readily disposed to play the part of trophy. With green eyes offset by crinkly crow's feet, she flashed a disarming smile and emanated a facile charm, able and quite willing to create the illusion of immediate intimacy. She was perfect for Rudy.

Shortly after arriving at NBC affiliate WCKT in Miami in 1980, Donna didn't waste any time investigating her romantic possibilities. "She wanted to know where a lot of lawyers hung out," said David Choate, her news director. "It was one of the first things she asked me." Choate added that soon thereafter she started auditing a law course at the University of Miami. That meant she didn't show up at the station some days until 2:30 P.M.

After getting a degree from Columbia University Graduate School of Journalism in 1973, Donna's first journalism job was as a radio newscaster in Danbury, Connecticut, at WLAD-AM. Late that year, she took her first TV job at WKTV in Utica, New York, where she also was an associate instructor in broadcast journalism at nearby Syracuse University. In 1975, she accepted an on-air position in Columbus, Ohio, and in 1977, moved on to Pittsburgh, Pennsylvania, where she co-hosted the *Evening Magazine*, a feature production of the news department. In this role, she earned the reputation of an indefatigable and entertaining spot reporter, who, among other things, rode a dolphin, piloted a blimp, drove a racecar and scaled an icy mountain.

Art Greenwald, Donna's producer, characterized *Evening Magazine* as "TV boot camp." Hanover, whom he called a "combination of smarts and talent," once stayed up all night editing a story, and in the morning, after a few furtive hours of sleep on the office couch, was roused by Greenwald, put in a van and driven to the banks of the ice-cold Youghiogheny River in Pennsylvania. They hopped into the water, and Donna went white water rafting. Since the camera sustained water damage, they had to return several days later to get more footage. "We got a good story," says Greenwald.

Like Rudy, the bright-eyed broadcaster had struggled through a difficult marriage marred by separation. Now, two years past the landmark age of thirty, her biological clock was ticking rapidly. Her marriage to a Harvard-educated intellectual named Stanley Hanover was, in some respects, even more mysterious than Rudy's and Regina's.

In 1968, Donna Anne Kofnovec, the sunny daughter of a Navy lieutenant commander, met Hanover on a tennis court at Stanford University. A wise, soft-spoken erudite three years Donna's senior, Stanley made an instant impression on the nineteen-year-old freshman. In 1972, after Donna's graduation, the two were married and moved east to New York City.

"We had a church wedding, somewhere not in California," Stanley told a reporter in one of the few instances he's answered any questions about their life together. "It wasn't a big deal."

Stanley, who was described in a 1997 *Dallas Morning News* story as a lawyer and writer, followed his new wife as she jaunted from job to job around the country. Despite his Ivy League English degree, it wasn't clear if Hanover worked while his young wife put in long hours in front of a camera. In 1973, when the Hanovers lived in Utica, the first signs of marital tension surfaced. A former colleague of Donna's at Utica's WKTV told *New York* magazine in 1994 about a conversation he had had with Donna about Stanley years earlier. "Stanley was home all the time," the colleague said. "And she was earning the dollars." The colleague recalled asking Donna what her husband did for a living. "He's a 'quote unquote writer'," she said. "I asked what he wrote, and she gave me a stare that could kill. 'The great American novel' she said."

By the time Donna arrived in Pittsburgh in 1977, Stanley Hanover seems to have dropped out of her life. Greenwald says he never met Stanley Hanover. "He did not live with her," Greenwald said. Bruce Kaplan, another Pittsburgh colleague, who says he socialized often with Donna, also never met her husband.

Yet when Donna moved to Miami in 1980, Stanley Hanover reappeared—at least on legal documents. On October 17 the two Hanovers bought a $60,000 condominium together at 8035 South West 107th Avenue. They listed themselves as "husband and wife" on the deed, and both of them signed it. Florida's Homestead Law requires that marital partners be listed on the title of any residential property, but Stanley's name also appears, with Donna's, on the mortgage documents. Donna kept the condominium for a decade after she left Florida, reporting rental income of about $6,000 per year, apparently from a sublet. A January 5, 1992 "Quitclaim" deed indicated that the property was transferred from Donna K. Hanover and Stanley I. Hanover exclusively to Donna. Donna sold the property to a new owner the same day. That deed bears a new signature accompanying Donna's—Rudy Giuliani's.

The Hanovers have declined in numerous interviews to say where and when they divorced, and Stanley, who still lives near Columbus, Ohio, continues to refuse. It's clear, however, from the Florida records that they were married and presumably separated—much like Rudy and Regina—until at least shortly before Donna and Rudy met.

"It seems to me," said Rudy's friend and colleague Jeff Harris, "that by the time [Rudy] met her, she was in the final throes of her divorce or had it."

Donna's first marriage isn't the only arena in her life where curious inconsistencies have cropped up. Two different versions of how she and Rudy first met have floated freely throughout newspaper and magazine accounts. The first and most common begins with the Justice Department colleague who cleared Rudy in the McDonnell Douglas case—Michael Shaheen—attending a wedding in Memphis. Donna was a bridesmaid at the same wedding. Shaheen told her he knew someone who visited Miami often and asked if she would be interested in a blind date. When she said yes, Shaheen added that his friend would make a great interview as well.

Rudy had his secretary, Kathy Smith, make the call. According to several Giuliani friends, and one published account, Rudy had been dating Smith for some time, and had brought her from Patterson, Belknap to Justice. All Smith, a short, cute woman with a blondish, page-boy hair cut, said to Donna was that "Mr. Giuliani" would be in Miami and understood that Donna had expressed interest in an interview. Annoyed, Donna said she thought he would be more interested in arranging a dinner date.

"Rudy called me the next day, and he didn't seem to know about my conservation with his secretary," Donna recalled. "I told him he ought to get his personal relations and press relations straight."

Rudy recalled the conservation as more of an interrogation. "She asked me what I was all about and why she should go out with me," he said. "I said, 'Do you want my resume?' She said, 'O.K.' I thought that was very cute. I told her I liked New York, baseball and opera. She said she liked warm weather, football and country and western music."

Despite the stilted exchange, the two met for dinner on February 7, 1982 at Joe's Stone Crab in Miami Beach. The evening was pleasant—except for Donna's persistent political questions. She wanted to find out just how conservative this top Reagan official was. She inquired if he was pro-choice; he said yes. She asked if he thought anyone who smoked marijuana should automatically go to prison. He said, of course not. Donna says she interviewed him live the next day.

Three weeks and a few dates later, Donna got a call late at night in her Miami apartment. "Rudy tells me he loves me," Donna recalled. "I thought, 'What makes him so sure I'm here alone?' I didn't know what to say because, while I liked him very much, I really wasn't sure about my feelings toward him. So when he told me he loved me, I said, 'Ah, well, gee, that's very nice.'"

Donna's reluctance quickly thawed, and in another three weeks, at a prosecutor's convention at Disney World, Rudy proposed marriage. She made him repeat the question. When he did, she giddily nodded, yes, yes, yes.

Version number two of Rudy and Donna's romantic debut, which appeared in a 1993 Fort Lauderdale story in the *Sun Sentinel*, has the plucky anchorwoman receiving a tough afternoon assignment: interview Vice President Bush's point man in the war on drugs, a Justice Department bulldog named Rudy Giuliani.

"I thought I was pretty tough on him," Donna said of the interview.

By this account, Rudy then asked this cute, spunky TV reporter for a date. That's where the two versions merge.

On May 28, 1982, Rudy's thirty-eighth birthday and three and a half months after first meeting him, Donna quit her job at WCKT, left Miami and joined Rudy at his Capitol Hill apartment on Maryland Avenue in Washington. Tucked into the back of a quaint, four-story, red-brick townhouse, the apartment was roomy and lightly furnished. Separated from the building by a dainty flower garden, Maryland Avenue was a shady, hedge-lined, upper-middle-class corridor of tasteful townhouses and brownstones. The Supreme Court and the Capitol were only a five-minute walk. The neighborhood was just what Rudy wanted: tranquil, anonymous and quietly oozing power.

Enchanted by her new home—the cherry blossoms, the museums and the marble halls of power—Donna did not find a job in Washington. "I had worked very hard for many years, and it was nice to be in Washington," she said later. "I would go and listen to Senate hearings about various issues. I heard part of the Hinckley trial. It was a wonderful environment for a journalist, because you go to these hearings, and you didn't have the responsibility of writing stories afterward."

Rudy had a conspicuously dangling loose end to tie up before his new life with Donna could officially begin. On June 2, 1982, right around the time Donna moved in with Rudy in Washington, a financial agreement between Rudy and Regina, "disposing of all rights and obligations as exist among and between them," was finalized. Their apartment at 470 West End was sold in the same time period, with the new owner moving in that July. Two months after the legal separation, in August, Rudy applied for a civil divorce, and on October 14, 1982, it was granted in the Superior Court of the District of Columbia. They acknowledged in court papers that they had separated in February 1980.

Donna has never disclosed whether she did the same with Stanlet Hanover. Instead she has deliberately shrouded the marriage in mystery—saying it occurred in a civil ceremony, while he has said it happened in a church. The same trail of inconsistency occasionally clouds her career description. She redacted from her résumé her idle year in Washington when she told the reporter for the *Sun Sentinel* that she left her job in Florida in order to take one in New York. In several sassy profiles of her, references pop up proclaiming she had worked as a reporter in Los Angeles—something she never did.

What neither Donna nor Rudy has ever mentioned in the many cheery interviews they have given on their whirlwind courtship was that Rudy was in Miami so often primarily to oversee the detention of thousands of Haitian immigrants. Harris, Rudy's deputy on Haiti, who often traveled with him, produced calendars showing that in April 1982, Rudy visited Miami three weekends in a row, arriving each time on a Thursday or Friday. Rudy himself estimated he was spending more time on Haitian matters than any other single issue during this period.

Ironically, the leader of Miami's Haitian community, the Reverend Jean Juste, a Catholic priest who chaired the Haitian Refugee Center, remembered years later that Donna, while at WCKT, had broadcast a particularly distasteful piece about the refugee center. Located in front of the center's building was a small green donation box inscribed with the words: "Give what little bit you can." Donna's story, according to Juste, focused on his failure to renew his permit for the donation box.

Roger Biambi, another Haitian community leader in Miami, also remembers seeing the broadcast. Several former colleagues of Donna's could not remember whether she did such a story, though none denied it.

"How could she find this story?" Juste wonders now. Rudy's conflict with Juste and the center would become one of the most troubling episodes of his young life.

Eighty-four-year-old Helen Giuliani, the teacher in Rudy's life, at his mayoral inaugural in January 1994. (Photo by Richard B. Levine)

Rudy's yearbook photo from Bishop Loughlin Memorial High School, Class of 1961—already a politician with a yen for the operatic. (Photo by Catherine Smith)

Staged embraces were a staple of the early Rudy and Donna fantasy marriage. This one was at the Columbus Day Parade during the 1993 campaign. By 1996, it was impossible to get them inside the same camera frame. (© Frances M. Roberts)

Regina Peruggi, a.k.a. Regina Giuliani, was "offended" when Rudy annulled their fourteen-year marriage "with *what her brother called* a lie"

(Courtesy of *The Daily News*)

Lilliam Paoli, the Mexican-American welfare commissioner in the Giuliani era who was deemed unfit for draconian duty.

(© Frances M. Roberts)

Rudy's smash performances at the Inner Circle annual revue—a fundraiser thrown by the city press corps—ranged from his portrayal in 2000 of pelvis-swiveling Tony Manero in a parody of *Saturday Night Fever* (Left), to his 1998 Rudy-the-Beast from *Beauty and the Beast* (Below), to his 1997 version of a pink-chiffoned Marilyn Monroe (Opposite page). He and Hillary Clinton shook hands at the 2000 extravaganza, while still-secret girlfriend Judi Nathan sat next to him at his ballroom table. (© Joe DiMaria)

"Gentleman" Dave Dinkins greets Giuliani at City Hall right after Rudy's 1993 triumph. Their two campaigns were a blood war, with Giuliani probing Dinkins like he was a grand jury target. (© Fred W. McDarrah)

After a bus ride through the city that lasted ninety-six virtually unbroken hours, a hoarse and exhausted Giuliani delivered a 1997 re-election victory speech that announced his determination to reach out to minorities who felt left out. He did not return to that theme until he got prostate cancer in 2000. (© Frances M. Roberts)

Mario Cuomo and Ed Koch were two pivotal figures in his public career—his endorsement of Cuomo in 1994 damaged him with the GOP for years and Koch's endorsement of him in 1993 put him over the top (© Fred W. McDarrah)

Six

Heat Stroke

Delusions About Duvalier

O{N HIS WAY INTO THE PRESIDENTIAL PALACE IN PORT-AU-PRINCE,}
Haiti, on March 16, 1982, thirty-seven-year-old Rudy Giuliani was pat-
ted down. The offending hands were those of the Léopards, the elite personal
guard of Jean-Claude "Baby Doc" Duvalier. When his father, François "Papa
Doc" Duvalier, died in 1971, eighteen-year-old Jean-Claude had become the
youngest president-for-life anywhere since Rome's Caesar Augustus.

Only twenty-nine when he met Giuliani at 11:30 that sunny morning,
Duvalier was used to looking over his rather large shoulder. Just two months
earlier, twenty Léopards had lost a mountain gun battle with eight revolutionaries from Miami who had seaplaned to the beautiful Haitian island of La
Tortue in hopes of stirring an uprising. The regular army had to take over,
killing five and delivering the surviving three to the palace, where the president emerged from his hermetically sealed living quarters to question them
and order their instant torture and execution. Interior Minister Edouard
Berrouet had then issued a communiqué officially informing the Haitian public that all eight had died in the island gun battle.

Three dead Haitians and the truth, however, were hardly the only casualties
of the white-pillared, Mediterranean-style palace. Its two Duvaliers, who ruled
for three decades before Baby Doc finally fled in 1986, gouged the hemisphere's poorest country of a provable half billion dollars, some of it American
aid diverted into Swiss accounts. They also killed at least 60,000, a per capita
body count that put them among a bloody century's bloodiest tyrants.

Giuliani had arrived in Haiti two days earlier, on a Sunday 2:40 P.M. flight,
accompanied by Jeffrey Harris and Renee Syzbala, his two old friends who had
become top assistants at Justice. Georges Léger, the Haitian ambassador to the
United States who had invited Giuliani four months earlier, met the trio, plus
Harris's wife, at Duvalier International Airport. They went immediately to the

American embassy, guests of Ambassador Ernest Preeg, who'd first met Giuliani in Washington in June, shortly before beginning his Haiti assignment.

Preeg's early contacts with Giuliani were an indication of just how single-minded the Reagan administration's Haitian policy was. All that mattered was stanching the flow of "boat people," who had been washing ashore in Florida at a rate of 1,500 a month aboard crammed and leaky freighters and sailboats. Rudy, whose expansive Justice portfolio included the Immigration and Naturalization Service, was, in Preeg's terms, the Reagan "point man" on Haitian issues.

His first visits to the White House, beginning in the spring of 1981, were as working staff for a cabinet-level task force on immigration chaired by Rudy's boss, Attorney General William French Smith. With the president championing the cause of the 125,000 Cubans dumped by Fidel Castro's government, mostly also in Florida, the Haitians had quickly become the administration's substitute bogeymen. Though far outnumbered by the Cubans, they were both black and fleeing a government backed by the White House. In the Reagan era, that made them convenient targets in a politically turbulent sea otherwise bereft of scapegoats.

Giuliani had already helped negotiate a September agreement with Léger that allowed Coast Guard cutters to effectively blockade Haiti, interdicting the ships whose only cargo was human misery and sending them back to Haiti. The deal was cut in Washington talks with Giuliani and the State Department—the first time American force had ever been deployed to keep a troubled people home.

That spring he'd also launched Reagan's new detention policies, ending a preference for paroling illegals to families and churches that had been in place since 1954 and putting them instead in camps and federal prisons. By the time of Giuliani's visit, 2,000 Haitians were in a jailed limbo awaiting hearings, mostly at Krome, a converted missile base at the edge of the Everglades. Giuliani had even traveled with Syzbala to San Juan in mid-1981, convincing Puerto Rico's governor to accept 800 of the Haitians at Fort Allen, a military facility closed on environmental grounds by a federal court order.

The Puerto Rico agreement, personally signed by Giuliani, moved half the Krome population to Fort Allen, where they lived in stifling canvas tents behind twelve-foot-high wire fences embedded with giant fishhooks. Allen was a treeless, grassless, sun-soaked sinkhole—similar to the fifteen-acre Krome, which had been housing as much as three times its ordinary capacity of 530. The punitive conditions in both large camps, as well as at a dozen other prisons where smaller numbers of Haitians were jailed, were transparently designed to prod Haitians to voluntarily surrender their right to a hearing and return home. Hundreds did.

If Rudy was devising wily ways of encouraging repatriation, Duvalier had come up with his own scheme to discourage the departures in the first place. The police fired at one boatload as it left Cap Haïtien, killing twenty and sparking the stoning of the police chief's car at the mass funeral. Then, when the corpses of twenty-three who drowned off Fort Lauderdale were shipped back in November 1981, Baby Doc personally ordered the funeral home opened to the public. Large crowds streamed past the bodies Duvalier had turned into object lessons.

Though Giuliani refused to acknowledge it, the timing of his Haiti trip was inextricably linked to a lawsuit filed in Miami by the Haitian Refugee Center against the detention policies he'd implemented. He had done a private deposition in the case on March 5, and would testify April 1. As he, Preeg, Harris and Syzbala sat in a row of wooden chairs in Duvalier's austere office, opposite the awkward, obese boy-king, lawyers for the Haitians were calling their opening witnesses in a federal courtroom in Miami. Rudy was in Haiti preparing to become the government's key witness in the two-month-long trial, taking a crash course that would soon qualify him as Justice's Haiti expert.

Duvalier played with a chain-link bracelet on his bulky wrist, sitting behind a paperless desk, underneath a large ceiling fan. Thick, boot-shaped sideburns framed a vacuous, smirking face. A translator stood beside him, repeating Rudy's words in French. Oddly, Duvalier would listen to the translation and respond in English. His two-piece, short-sleeved khaki leisure suit, with matching pants, gave the meeting a military air, as did the office itself, which had no furniture or wall decorations other than a potted plant and photos of his mother, Simone, and wife, Michele. Giuliani would later testify that the meeting lasted an hour and fifteen minutes, suggesting that a substantive discussion had occurred. Harris remembered it as a "ceremonial ten- to twenty-minute courtesy visit."

"You are the highest-ranking U.S. government official to ever come to Haiti," Duvalier announced. "I would be favorably disposed to an invitation to come to the U.S."

Giuliani said he would report that to the State Department, but his subsequent, seven-page memo on the trip, sent to Undersecretary of State Lawrence Eagleburger on April 14, made no mention of the unrealistic request. Photo-ops of Reagan and Baby Doc were hardly on the White House agenda.

Giuliani's memo did say that Duvalier's "main concern" was the Caribbean Basin Initiative, a new Reagan program of foreign aid that was less generous to Haiti than virtually any other nation in the region. "I explained that this was not within my area of responsibility," Giuliani wrote, adding that he had also stated that "the Justice Department would make its own concerns about aid to Haiti and those of the Government of Haiti known to the Department of State."

Giuliani also reported that Duvalier argued that "the problem of illegal migration" would not "be solved without the development" of his country. He said, according to Rudy's memo, that "his government was a good friend of the U.S. (one of the few remaining in the area) and ought to be treated as such." This and other parts of the Giuliani memo read like a brief for more aid to Haiti. His regurgitation of the Duvalier bailout line at the meeting, however, ignored the abundant evidence that Baby Doc's government was a kleptocracy, as a Canadian government report had just branded it.

An International Monetary Fund review had also found that $20 million of a $22 million IMF crisis supplement to Haiti, made in late 1980, had disappeared within weeks. The IMF revealed that $16 million wound up in various personal accounts of the president's family and $4 million with the Tontons Macoutes, the notorious civilian secret police who embodied decades of Duvalier terrorism. A milder U.S. General Accounting Office report, issued just a month before Giuliani's visit, attributed the "failure" of aid programs to the "poor performance" of the Haiti regime, corruption and the "frequent and capricious changes of key Haitian development personnel for allegedly political reasons."

In fact, Giuliani and Harris had actually seen a group of vendors the day before selling grain in bags marked "Food for Peace: A Gift from the People of the United States" on the side of a dirt country road. The two old friends shook their heads at each other as they passed the vendors, who were hawking the grain from open bags.

They had also already heard the sordid aid pitch they were now getting from Duvalier. The night before, Rudy and his Washington companions had driven up the mountain overlooking Port-au-Prince for a lavish 8 P.M. dinner hosted by the chief minister, Henri Bayard, and attended by the entire cabinet. The view of Haiti from the restaurant, the Belvedere, created an illusion: for an evening, Haiti did not appear to be a destitute nation. The valley below was lush with shimmering lights and treetop green. But the festivities ended with a media ambush, well planned by Bayard, who'd taken on such a fatherly air with the young Duvalier that Jean-Claude freely called him "Père."

Foreign Minister Jean-Bertrand Estime, the son of a president prior to Duvalier, had assured Preeg that there would be no press. But when the dinner conversation died down, the klieg lights went up. Bayard rose, standing at the far end of the long table covered by a gold cloth, and delivered a toast that was really a screed for more aid. He added nationalist protests over the detention of Haitians for the camera, even though no one in the regime, including Duvalier himself the next day, would utter a word of protest about the policies.

"It seems unthinkable," Bayard declared, "that in a corner of the U.S., the land of liberty, justice and the Fatherland of Abraham Lincoln, that human beings, whatever their race, find themselves in conditions strangely reminiscent of the concentration camps, the memory of which is a shameful page in the history of the last war. We thus ask for our brothers in Krome, the application of those humanitarian principles which the U.S. brandishes like torches in its unceasing struggle for human dignity." Léger, the gray-haired, erect ambassador with a talent for mediation borne from his family's legal service to the Haitian government since 1804, tried to soften this attack in translation. But what the television crews recorded was what appeared in the subsequent State Department cables.

Preeg was worried by the rhetoric since he had not briefed Giuliani for the event, trusting Estime's promise that it would be an informal celebration. But an unfazed Rudy rushed to his feet as soon as Bayard paused.

In a dark suit, dark tie and white shirt, unaided by the microphone Bayard kept in his own hand, Rudy made the case for detention without ever addressing Bayard's invocation of the Holocaust. He blamed American lawyers representing the detainees for the year-long stays they were suffering in prison, saying that the attorneys were now arguing that detainees are "political refugees fleeing persecution." Based on "my own observations," as well as other reports he'd reviewed, Giuliani said he knew that was untrue. By stating the refugee claims were "casting something of a false light on this question," Giuliani planted the notion that he was on the side of the Haitian government in challenging the concocted charges of the detainee lawyers.

The Haitian press, of course, reported Bayard's statements and omitted Giuliani's.

Duvalier's transparent shakedown at the meeting the next day was merely a muted echo of Bayard's, linking cooperation on the interdiction/detention front with a louder clang of the government's tin cup. And just as Giuliani had waited for Bayard to finish his predictable posturing, he waited for Duvalier to finish. Then Giuliani got to the concealed point of his visit. He wanted a promise he could use like a weapon in the courtroom where the fate of thousands of Haitians would shortly be decided. "At my request, the President gave me his personal assurances," Giuliani's memo proclaimed, "that Haitians that returned to Haiti are not, and will not be, persecuted." Duvalier also insisted that there was no political repression in Haiti—of returnees or anyone else. His pledge and claim would become the centerpieces of Giuliani's Miami testimony, though Harris recalled that Giuliani left the meeting describing the no-repression contention as so "preposterous" it was "laughable."

"Did Duvalier sound sincere?" asked Harris years later. "Yes. Did I believe him? Not for a second. He was just mouthing the words."

As soon as Rudy's meeting with Duvalier was over, he hurried back to the embassy for a 12:30 luncheon with a half dozen prominent guests, where he pressed the same two questions. The setting, however, was hardly conducive to candor. Victor Laroche, head of the government-tied Haitian Red Cross (unaffiliated with the International Red Cross) and soon to be a Duvalier minister, was prominently placed at the table. Laroche's brother-in-law commanded the presidential guards.

Yet Giuliani would report in his memo that "all present stated that the allegations concerning political persecution of returnees" were "absolutely untrue" and that they had seen "no evidence of persecution." He said that Papal Nuncio Luigi Conti "was particularly adamant on this point." In Rudy's subsequent Miami testimony, he'd turn each of the luncheon guests into unwitting witnesses for the detention and repatriation programs, creating the impression that he'd talked to them individually.

He'd been trying to collect evidence to support this predisposition since he'd arrived in Haiti. In fact, during his first meeting with State Department staff that Sunday, he'd pressed them about the treatment of interdicted or detained returnees. Several had gone to some length to make it clear "that tracking such people" was "an extremely difficult and time-consuming job." Towns, they explained, "are often loosely knit rural areas covering miles," where "addresses are frequently of little use" and "roads are poor or nonexistent." The best they could offer, according to Giuliani's own memo, was the assurance that the embassy would "continue in this effort" and obtain "the information required."

Yet Giuliani's testimony, only days after this embassy briefing, was that "a huge amount of material both written and oral" had "documented the fact" that repatriated Haitians had "been returned to their villages" and had not been arrested or persecuted.

The Haitian lawyers in Miami countered with affidavits—like the one from a woman whose weather-battered boat had returned to Haiti and who'd wound up at the Cassernes Dessalines, a notorious prison where she watched ten men from her boat stripped and "beaten with sticks as big as my arm." Another affidavit recounted the imprisonment of fifteen refugees who'd returned from Fort Allen, pointing out that it was a crime to leave Haiti without an exit visa.

Years later, the United Nations High Commissioner for Refugees revealed that they and the U.S. Government had documentary evidence that dozens of returnees had been harassed, beaten, tortured and in some cases, even murdered. But in 1982, the evidence was impressionistic, largely because the INS refused to release the names and addresses of voluntary returnees. When the lawyers did manage to get the addresses of five and tried to visit them, none could be found. The only hard number Giuliani cited involved just sixteen returnees. The American mission, Giuliani told a congressional committee, tracked this handful unmolested to their homes. Their safe passage became the shaky foundation of the policy Giuliani celebrated on his Haiti tour.

T he day before the meeting with Duvalier, Giuliani, Harris and Syzbala helicoptered to the Coast Guard cutter *Westwind*, anchored just outside the harbor of Port-de-Paix, the longtime launching pad for boat people. Insulated for ice cap forays, the *Westwind* boiled in the Haitian sun. The mere presence of this and other 210- to 378-foot armed ships, supported by Dolphin helicopters, Falcon jets and Hercules long-range surveillance aircraft, had clearly, as the captain and crew argued, deterred Haitians from attempting the 700-mile voyage.

The INS staff aboard the *Westwind* told Giuliani that all the required questions—necessary under law and international treaties to determine if any passenger might have a legitimate claim for entry—were asked of those on the first of the two vessels so far interdicted. But that "somewhat fewer questions were asked during the interdiction" of the second boat, because it had already turned around and was heading back to Haiti.

Despite the INS admission of incomplete compliance, Giuliani would testify in Miami that everyone on both boats was asked the brief battery of questions and that none had offered answers that would "give rise" to an asylum claim. He did not disclose that when he had made the same claim at a House hearing two months earlier, he had been vigorously challenged by a congressman. The House committee's staff director had witnessed the debriefing of the boat people aboard the second vessel. His report indicated that a mandated question "was not asked in any of the instances observed by staff." The unasked question was the $64 one: "Do you fear return to Haiti?" The only question that really mattered to the INS was why an interdictee was going to America. As soon as he said he wanted a job, he'd get a return ticket as an "economic refugee." During the nearly two years that Rudy ran Haitian policy, only five Haitians were granted asylum as political refugees, the highest record of rejection in modern immigration history.

In addition to the *Westwind* visit, the Giuliani team toured two of the sixteen boats that made up the Haitian navy, which, with American fuel subsidies, had joined the interdiction force. A Coast Guard officer working with the navy said that it was now patrolling the coast for boats 200 hours a month, whereas it didn't patrol at all before the interdiction subsidies. The navy commander asked Rudy to keep the gas money coming and his memo echoed the request.

Incredibly, 68,696 returnees would be intercepted over the thirteen-year life of the interdiction agreement. The annual average was 2,215 through 1990, when the turmoil surrounding the election and overthrow of Jean-Bertrand Aristide caused a sudden and dramatic upswing. Not only did Giuliani testify that he "had a role in negotiating" the deal, Preeg says that from the moment he met Rudy in mid-1981, "it was clear to me that he was really in control" of the interdiction talks. The "floating Berlin Wall," as it was called, would remain intact until Aristide, the first democratically elected Haitian president in decades, ended it in 1995.

Haitians who had been turned around at sea and their American advocates could never get standing to sue in a U.S. court, just as a pre-policy memo to Giuliani from the Office of Legal Counsel at Justice had predicted. The memo acknowledged that there was "no precedent for such an operation" but doubted that "anyone would be able to challenge it." Ultimately, appeals courts reversed three different restraining orders against the interdictions, finding that intercepted Haitians had no right to sue because they were outside U.S. territory. The rulings led one frustrated judge to remark in his dissent: "Haitians, unlike other aliens from anywhere in the world, are PREVENTED from reaching the continental U.S."

Another department memo acknowledged that the interdiction strategy flew in the face of the United Nations Protocol and Convention, which required governments to "adjudicate refugee claims prior to returning a claimant to his homeland." Instead of placing U.N. representatives aboard the interdiction ships, as the memo suggested, Haitian Navy officials were often on the Coast Guard cutters, further cowing intercepted boat people into compliant answers to the questions when asked.

Duvalier's acquiescence to interdiction was so important that one of Giuliani's final stops on his Haiti tour—right before his palace visit—was designed to reward him for it. He went to the Foreign Ministry that morning and met with

Estime, Berrouet and Léger to spell out what Justice would do about the Florida-based Haitian insurgents who were constantly planning invasions to overthrow Duvalier. As he put it in the State Department memo, "we explained in some depth" the prosecution of Bernard Sansaricq, an exile who owned a gas station in Fort Lauderdale and had put together the attack in January led by the eight revolutionaries whose deaths were falsely described in Berrouet's communiqué.

Sansaricq and thirty other men had tried, aboard a motorized sailboat, to join the eight, but they were caught by a Coast Guard cutter. The Coast Guard brought Sansaricq and his group back to Florida, confiscating their thirty-three guns, twenty-two pipe bombs and 5,320 rounds of ammunition, charging them with violations of the Neutrality Act.

Estime and the rest of Duvalier's ministers were, Giuliani wrote, "extremely interested in this case." Estime offered to turn over to the U.S. Government the weapons they'd seized from the eight who'd been killed or captured at La Tortue. "We arranged for an FBI agent or prosecutor involved in the case to travel to Haiti to continue this discussion," Giuliani concluded. Harris recalled that the ministers were "very concerned that the U.S. would allow these things to occur" and that Rudy was "strong and definitive" in his assurances that he would "look into it and investigate it."

Fifteen members of Sansaricq's family, including a two-year-old child and a crippled woman, had been slaughtered by Papa Doc's Tontons in 1964. "Don't cry, I'll dry your eyes for you," the Tontons lieutenant supervising the killing told a four-year-old boy, before pushing a lit cigarette into his eyes. Another Macoute tossed the boy into the air and stuck a knife into his belly as he fell. The legend of the Sansaricq slayings haunted the Presidential Palace. After Giuliani's visit, Reagan's Justice Department prosecuted the Sansaricq rebels, only to be frustrated by a judge who sentenced them to probation.

The only other noteworthy stops on Giuliani's Haiti tour were a visit to a casino, where Rudy and the rest gambled briefly, and a cocktail party at the home of the general manager of the Rawlings baseball factory, which at that time was manufacturing the balls the major leagues used. Haiti produced 90 percent of the world's hardballs, and Rawlings employed almost a thousand piecework seamstresses. With a needle in each hand, the women stitched the balls, 104 swooping butterfly strokes a ball. Each ball took ten minutes for a fast, young seamstress and earned her ten cents. Yet Rawlings's little white factory in a grimy industrial suburb of Port-au-Prince was in a tax-free enterprise zone.

As Harris recalled it, Rudy was only interested in the ball itself. Grandson of a seamstress, he did not ask a single question about the pay or working conditions of the women. Instead he grilled the general manager about the so-called "pill," the red golfball-sized pellet at the core of the ball. He wanted to know how tightly wrapped it was, and what went into the cork and rubber mix that made it hard.

He wasn't interested in prison conditions either. In fact, Syzbala, who was so moved by her three days in Haiti that she sent money to a family there for the next nineteen years, remembers walking past a prison on a dirt road with Rudy and saying she wanted to see inside. "Go look," he said and kept on walking. She stopped and looked in, and afterward he expressed no interest in what she saw.

They rode through the countryside near the tawdry port town where the *Westwind* anchored but, by Rudy's own account, never stopped to talk to the people.

They did not speak to any of the on-site monitors or advocates that were independent of both the Haitian and U.S. governments. Nor did they meet a single returnee.

They did listen to Bach, almost nightly. Preeg's other guests at the embassy during Giuliani's stay were Sam and Ellie Thaivu. Concertmaster with the Pittsburgh Symphony Orchestra, Sam was spending two weeks teaching at the Trinity School Orchestra in Port-au-Prince. At Rudy's urging, he played violin at the mansion each night. The Thaivus, who had vacated the downstairs wing of the mansion when Giuliani's party arrived, never talked politics. Instead Rudy recounted his old days as an usher at the Met, and the three shared their mutual love of music. When the help disappeared one night, the Thaivus and the Giuliani gang whipped up a spaghetti dinner together. Ensconced in this manicured, antique-filled estate on a hill, complete with swimming pool and servants, the Giuliani group could pretend, with Sam Thaivu's masterful sounds floating through the house, that they were in a tropical paradise.

Indeed, pretense was in such substantial supply that Rudy closed his State Department memo with a final bit of fancy: "Throughout this trip, we were shown great hospitality and all our questions were candidly answered." A younger Rudy was so incensed at Bert Podell's prevarications he'd wanted the convicted congressman stripped of the right to practice law. He'd traveled to Virginia to get the "Prince of the City" to finally come clean. He'd enrolled in a seminary in search of a life of integrity. No less than Carl "Kojak" Bogan had taught him how to recognize falsehood in the eyes of a culprit. And now, having risen to the forefront of American law enforcement, he was saluting the self-serving declarations of a despot and his interchangeable minions. The exigencies of power had eclipsed the urgency of truth.

Ten days after Rudy left Haiti, DEA agents arrested Franz Bennett, the twenty-eight-year-old brother of Baby Doc's wife, Michele, on cocaine-smuggling charges in Puerto Rico. Bennett had offered undercover agents "safe-passage for a drug-laden aircraft through Port-au-Prince for $60,000," according to a DEA memo.

Bennett also agreed to handle monthly shipments of fifty-five kilos of cocaine, worth $2 million each, steering them through Haiti without police interference. He even offered to guarantee passage for heroin. When the agents asked him in tape-recorded conversations if Duvalier knew about his activities, Bennett replied with surprise: Of course he knew.

Another agency like the INS that reported directly to Giuliani, the DEA saw the Bennett sting in the context of an elaborate, Haiti-based drug operation. According to the agency, shortly after Bennett's arrest:

> Reportedly, several large narcotic trafficking organizations based in Haiti utilized Bennett's fuel concession at Duvalier International Airport in Port-au-Prince to refuel private aircraft while smuggling cocaine and marihuana from Columbia [sic] to the U.S. Haiti is used as a storage depot and transshipment point for narcotics destined for the U.S. It is alleged that military personnel guard the storage depot and that Bennett was insulated from arrest in Haiti since his sister is married to President Duvalier. Bennett has also been smuggling approximately 40 kilograms of high quality cocaine per shipment in false bottom suitcases aboard an air taxi service from Port-au-Prince to Miami via Nassau.

The bust was the first public look at the drug scandal inside the presidential family. Michele's father, Ernest, was, according to Haiti bureau chief for Reuters Elizabeth Abbott, "Haiti's most important link in the Colombia-Haiti-U.S. cocaine traffic, soon winning the title 'The Godfather.'" Determined to protect her brother from jail and to keep a lid on the family business, Michele thought anything could be fixed. Ernest Bennett visited Preeg at the embassy to see if he would intervene.

A few days after the arrest, Jean-Claude and Michele were at a routine dinner party at Bayard's home and the avuncular Bayard decided to take the president aside, in an upstairs room. He said he'd just talked to Léger, who was being hounded by American reporters about the Franz Bennett case. Léger had consulted with top American lawyers, Bayard said, and everyone advised that the Haitian government should stay away from the case. He told Duvalier that Berrouet, another minister and two top police officials had listened to the DEA tape of Franz's conversation and that, under the circumstances, "silence would be golden." Duvalier went downstairs and told his wife what Bayard had said. She stormed out of the house, her husband trailing behind her.

Bayard, Berrouet, Léger and the police officials who had listened to the tape were fired, with everyone ousted by May 6. A month and a half after Giuliani's departure, the entire upper echelon of the government he'd just met was gone, dismissed because they wouldn't rally around a cocaine dealer. Bennett had to plead guilty anyway, getting a four-year jail sentence in August.

Duvalier even dumped the well-connected Washington law firm that had set up Rudy's Haiti tour in the first place, Anderson, Hibey, Nauheim & Blair. Stanton Anderson, the lead partner in the firm, had signed up with Duvalier in January 1981. Counsel to the Reagan-Bush campaign in 1980 and a director of the presidential transition, Anderson was as wired into the Reagan White House as a lobbyist could get.

The first foreign government Anderson registered for was Duvalier's, filing a February lobbying contract for $37,500 per quarter, plus $5,000 in expenses with the Justice Department. The firm's filings indicate that they lobbied Giuliani, Harris and Syzbala throughout the period of October 1981 through February 1982. They submitted an expense voucher for February 2 for a lunch with Harris "to discuss Justice Department delegation to Haiti." As Harris recalls, "we had been talking to Bob Davis," an associate in the Anderson firm, "and he suggested that someone from the U.S. should come down and talk about the refugee problem." Davis actually joined the Giuliani group in Haiti, sitting in on the key meeting at the Foreign Ministry and the dinner at the Belvedere.

Anderson's post-trip filing took full credit for producing Giuliani. "Registrant coordinated an official visit by Giuliani, Harris and Syzbala," the firm's disclosure statement read, "accompanied them to Haiti, and assisted in communicating the concerns of the Government of Haiti." Elsewhere in the filings, the firm cites some of the specific issues they discussed with Giuliani et al. before the visit, indicating that they "provided liaison between U.S. officials during Sansaricq invasions of Haiti and criminal investigations of the same." They also billed $176.33 for a dinner with Giuliani in early April, right after his testimony in Miami and right before he wrote the April 7 memo about the trip that he later sent to the State Department. Léger and the Anderson firm were forced out at the end of April.

On April 1, while these key allies were still hanging on, Rudy walked into a Miami courtroom to defend the Duvalier regime. Asked at the end of his cross-examination if he was aware that Haiti had "an authoritarian government," Giuliani initially replied: "I really don't think it is appropriate for me to characterize the government." Pressed a second time, he said it "probably does have" one. Asked if he knew "what constitutes political oppression in Haiti," he said he "didn't understand the question." When the question was repeated, he jousted: "What do you mean by that?" Asked if there was any political opposition to Duvalier, he said he thought it was a one-party system, but added: "I am not absolutely sure of that."

Pressed about the secret police, he testified: "I don't know if the Tontons Macoutes exist or don't exist," suggesting that they'd only "existed under François Duvalier." In fact, Harris recalled his wife Joyce seeing Macoutes in their distinctive black sunglasses and a Peugeot while sightseeing, and embassy officials debriefed Rudy on their continued role in Haiti, as his own memo indicated.

In addition to these evasions, Giuliani insisted that "political repression does not exist, at least in general, in Haiti." He repeated this claim again and again over the course of his day of testimony, basing it on "my own trip to Haiti." He cited his conversations with "the people who ran the Peace Corps, AID, and CARE." He invoked the hopelessly compromised administrator of the Red Cross. He stressed his talk with Papal Nuncio Conti. "Every single person that I spoke to," he said, "agreed that it was not a problem of political repression, that by and large, people were not leaving because they feared intimidation by the government." This assertion was the heart of Giuliani's testimony, refuting any possible political asylum claim and making the detainees excludable.

But Larry Holzman, the CARE director at the embassy lunch, says now: "I never said that. He misquoted me." A retired, sometime-consultant to CARE, Holzman recalled how impressed he was with the way Giuliani handled himself at the lunch, but said: "I don't think anyone would have said there wasn't any repression. I think we were pretty frank as to what we thought was the misuse of American aid."

Harlan Hobgood, a career USAID official with a Yale divinity degree assigned by the Reagan administration to take over the Haiti program in July 1981, said he never spoke to Giuliani and neither did his deputy. "I could not have concurred with any such statement," said Hobgood. "I find it totally unbelievable. The political climate was one of state political repression. Elements in the military and the pseudo-military through the Tontons Macoutes maintained a firm grip on security. Repression would be used whenever suitable to the regime." Hobgood even contended that it was "a delusion on the part of U.S. policymakers—one of self-induced proportions—to say the motivations for refugees were purely economic. They were as much political as economic."

Ernest Preeg said there was no Peace Corps in Haiti until July 1982, well after Giuliani's trip. "I was pushing for it to come in for over a year," says Preeg. "I just don't understand how Rudy could say that. He may have talked to someone who had Peace Corps experience."

Michael Hooper, a lawyer with the International Lawyers Committee on Human Rights, testified in Miami as a rebuttal witness, insisting that Conti told him "that he would never comment on the existence or nonexistence of political conditions, because, as the Vatican representative, that would compromise his position." In a later interview, Hooper said that Conti told him he was "extremely concerned" about Giuliani's testimony and "wanted to clarify that he had made no such statements." Hooper also worked for Church World Services, another organization Giuliani erroneously listed in his memo as attending the embassy lunch and joining in the no-repression claim.

The irony is that nine months after Giuliani's visit, Pope John Paul II visited Haiti and publicly reproached the Duvaliers, refusing to dine with them and demanding that "things have got to change here." The January 1983 papal visit makes Giuliani's invocation of the Nuncio—whom Rudy cited under oath in Miami a half dozen times—all the more absurd.

Rudy had, in fact, been told by embassy staff about the November 1980 mass expulsion of opposition press and party leaders—a rout described in a 1982 State Department report. What prompted that sweep was the Duvalier "happy-times-are-here-again" anticipation of the Reagan years, welcomed by a champagne party at the palace. One of the few leaders not expelled was Silvio Claude, who was in prison when Rudy visited. He had been tortured twice, once with electric shocks, on September 28 and October 14, 1981, at the very time that Giuliani was negotiating the interdiction treaty.

Hooper's human-rights committee published a list of nineteen incommunicado prisoners in the National Penitentiary as of the day of Giuliani's meeting with Duvalier. This list did not include dozens more who had been charged on political counts but never tried, though jailed, often for years. Hooper testified that "you can't understand anything" by "looking at what occurred in Haiti in the last 3 or 4 months." Very little is happening in terms of recent arrests, he said, "because there is no one left."

In mid-June, U.S. District Court Judge Eugene Spellman overturned the detention program, ordering the release of all the Haitians at Krome, Fort Allen and elsewhere. He rejected the plaintiffs' charge that the policy had intentionally discriminated against Haitians while agreeing that it disproportionately impacted on them. Spellman threw the policy out because the Reagan administration "never seriously undertook the difficult task of drafting a set of guidelines" spelling out "who would be placed in detention." INS made "a conscious decision not to promulgate a rule" about this new policy, leaving no one with any notice that it was in effect.

"Those who would assert the omnipotent power of the government" have to recognize that "they are never above the rule of law," Spellman said. "The Court cannot think of any administrative action that would have a greater impact on a regulated group of people than a change in policy which results in their indefinite incarceration where, under the previous policy they would have been free." A moderate Democrat, Spellman and his law clerk, Jeffrey Fisher, had retreated to Key West to write the fifty-five-page decision, debating it one night in a bar until the early hours of the morning, outlining it on a napkin while consuming a bottle of Stolichnaya. Death threats and hate mail from the Floridians who wanted the Haitians gone descended on Spellman after he ruled.

"Because we did not give the world advance notice that our immigration laws were to be respected," Giuliani charged, "we have been told they must be ignored." Even though he had played a last-minute card to try to forestall the ruling—offering a plan to parole some of the Haitians two days before it—Rudy now tried to get an injunction barring its implementation. His brief bellowed that the release of the Haitians could pose a threat to national security. He lost again. The same three-judge Circuit Court panel that rejected the injunction would now hear the appeal on an expedited basis. Giuliani decided to argue it himself.

By then, he and the administration were swimming in bad ink. Back on March 10, right before Rudy's Haiti trip, a *New York Times* editorial saluted a finding by a New York judge, Robert Carter, the same judge who'd presided at the Podell trial, that the eleven-month detention of eighty-six Haitians in Brooklyn was discriminatory. Another *Times* editorial in April charged the detention of Haitians had "started to smell: like the detention of Japanese-Americans in World War II; like racism, like cruelty." A July editorial recounted how thirty detainees had tried to kill themselves—"some swallow shards of glass, try hanging themselves with trousers or cut their wrists." Opposing any judicial stay, the *Times*: "What is it about those 1910 pitiful Haitian migrants that makes otherwise reasonable

Reagan administration officials so relentless?" Even a Dade County grand jury in Florida issued a report blasting the detention camps as "discriminatory and racist."

By the time the Circuit Court heard the appeal in September, half the Haitians had already been released. Still Rudy fought on, hoping at this point for legal vindication since all the detainees would surely be free before the appeals court ruled. In April 1983—as Rudy prepared to leave Washington for New York—the panel not only ruled unanimously against him on Spellman's notice findings, they also reversed Spellman's decision on equal protection, finding the detention discriminatory.

The panel juxtaposed "the plaintiffs' statistical evidence" disclosing "a stark pattern of discrimination" against the testimony of Giuliani and two subordinates, which it characterized as "inconsistent" and "self serving affirmations of good faith." The panel said the three "contradicted one another several times, and did not agree on the substance of the policy," indicating "the disarray with which the administration" acted. It was clear, the court concluded, that "no one knew exactly what the policy was, and no one in authority attempted to supervise the exercise of discretion under the policy." While these findings were an unmistakable blast at the architect of the policies, Giuliani was named only a handful of times, accused at one point of utterly misrepresenting the applicable parole statutes.

This panel would be effectively reversed in 1984, when the full twelve-judge appeals court, with five judges dissenting, found that migrants like the Haitians have no constitutional rights, meaning they were not entitled to equal protection. The U.S. Supreme Court would also hear the case. Their opinion questioned whether the Circuit Court had to go so far as to rule on the question of the constitutional rights of aliens. Neither of these two decisions altered the heart of the Spellman or panel factual findings. Rudy lost the notice war 4-to-0 and discrimination war 3-to-1. Ringing in the ears of anyone who read the decisions was a Supreme Court opinion from years earlier, upholding the parole policies for illegal immigrants that had lasted for three decades prior to Rudy's 1981 changes. The Court found that releasing refugees exhibited the "humane qualities of an enlightened civilization."

R udy described himself on the witness stand, in answer to a question raised by Judge Spellman, as "the singular individual" responsible for immigration policy. He conceded he'd never taken an immigration law course or sat in on an immigration hearing, even while admitting that he'd written instructions to the immigration administrative judges handling the Haitian exclusion cases. He said he'd worked closely in drafting the president's immigration policy with William French Smith's chief of staff, Kenneth Starr, but that he had carried it out virtually alone. At times, he testified, it "felt like" he was spending 100 percent of his time on it.

He had convinced himself from the start that the policies had a rationale: protecting the country's borders. He had contempt for the vacillation of the Carter administration, claiming repeatedly that more immigrants entered the United States in 1980 than at any time in our history. He fixated on the 15,000 of them who were Haitian, rather than the Reagan-protected 125,000 who were Cuban. Yet the appeals panel in Spellman said the government's description of a "massive influx" of Haitians "colors the issues." Noting that Haitians were only 2 percent of the illegals, the court added: "By almost all accounts it was mass immigration of Cubans that prompted tightening the net in which the Haitians were caught."

Giuliani was at the center of these contradictory policies, releasing Cubans with criminal records while jailing Haitians who had none. Reagan, who'd campaigned in Miami as a champion of Cuban refugees, was pressing so hard for their parole that Rudy had to spend his July 4, 1982 weekend writing a memo to him about the handling of 950 Cubans still left at Fort Chaffee.

His July 6 memo explained that the Cubans "have problems that prevent their release into the community." It listed those problems as "250 mentally ill and retarded; 400 antisocial; 100 homosexual; 100 alcoholics or drug users; 100 women, babies, elderly and handicapped." Aside from the bizarre suggestion that homosexuals could not be released into the community, much less women with babies, the memo demonstrated just how personally involved Reagan was in pushing for release.

One news account, little noticed at the time, revealed that the Coast Guard had interdicted a boatload of Haitians that had rescued two Cubans bobbing about on an inner tube raft. The Guard quickly got sanctuary for the two Cubans in Miami and sent the 161 fleeing Haitians home.

Of course the rationale was that the Cubans were escaping a dictator and the Haitians weren't. This paradox only made Rudy's job of defending these policies more impossible.

The ferocity with which he did it would come to define him. Ira Kurzban, the Haitian refugees' chief attorney, sized him up: "He wanted the government to win at any cost. He went after the Haitians as a zealous prosecutor would go after anyone committing a crime. The difference, of course, is that the Haitians hadn't committed a crime."

He was so determined to defend the policies that even after he left Washington, he tried to rationalize a decision he did not make: separate detention for male and female Haitians. He told a 1983 *Barron's* interviewer that INS kept them in separate facilities because "if you let the men into the women's camp, they go around raping them." The INS, however, said that it "had not turned up any evidence of alleged rapes."

Bruce Winick, who knew and liked Rudy as a classmate at NYU, was one of the Haitian refugees' lawyers and tried to approach him after a speech Giuliani gave at the University of Miami Law School, where Winick taught. It was shortly before the case would go to Spellman and Winick thought they should talk and see if they could find a way to settle it. Giuliani waved him aside.

The deeper the mire, the harder he tried to plant his heels. All he knew was that it was working—the combined fear of interdiction or detention was closing the coast. The number of new arrivals was plummeting. Renee Syzbala would occasionally get him to focus briefly on conditions at Krome; he'd order minor improvements and feel better. His white cocoon at Justice, where the fate of thousands of black lives could be decided without the input of black voices, reassured him.

The memory of his Kennedy past seemed more and more remote. For the first but hardly the last time in his life, he was taking on the liberal establishment, challenging liberal orthodoxy. He did not even seem conscious, to those around him, of the turning point he was living. He just knew that he would be what he had to be. Not just his party affiliation had changed. His heart had.

Seven

Mr. Untouchable

H ELEN GIULIANI COULDN'T FIND HER SON AND WAS STARTING TO GET frustrated. She had gone to his office at the Justice Department one afternoon in 1982 but was told that Mr. Giuliani had recently left to meet with Senator Alfonse D'Amato at his Capitol Hill office. The frail seventy-two-year-old made her way to Capitol Hill and navigated a maze of marble and metal detectors to find D'Amato's office in the Russell Senate office building. Parking herself in the lobby, she waited for her important, perpetually-in-motion son to amble out any minute from the inner sanctum. But he didn't. Finally, the senator himself walked out.

New York's new junior senator, D'Amato had been elected in 1980 in a bitter three-way contest against Democrat Elizabeth Holtzman and the four-term Republican incumbent Jacob Javits. A brazen but cunning political pugilist, D'Amato had beaten the ailing senator by making an ugly issue out of Javits's struggle with Lou Gehrig's disease. D'Amato was a product of the Long Island Republican machine—an organization so corrupt that it compelled county employees to pay 1 percent of their salaries as a tithe to the Republican Party. His mentor was Republican boss Joe Margiotta—later convicted by federal prosecutors. Although he would never be netted by prosecutors himself, D'Amato was already dogged by mob and ethical allegations that clung to him like an bad suit.

During his Senate campaign, his mother, "Mama D'Amato," was Alfonse's most avid spokesperson, appearing in campaign commercials and traveling the state to harvest votes for her boy. A political brochure designed like a cookbook and entitled "Mama D'Amato's Inflation-Fighting Recipes" was a big hit with traditional Republicans. Now, in the lobby of his own office, Senator D'Amato found a little old Italian lady from Brooklyn who reminded him instantly of his own mother.

After they introduced themselves, D'Amato, nicknamed "The Fonz," told Helen Giuliani she'd missed her son. He then ushered her back into his office for a friendly chat and proceeded to personally take her on a tour of the Capitol Building.

Renee Syzbala, a Giuliani aide, recalled being warned by Justice officials to avoid Al D'Amato. But after this demonstrable act of hospitality toward Mama Giuliani, "D'Amato was no longer an untouchable," said Syzbala.

From that moment, Rudy developed a bond with the crudely charismatic Republican junior senator. The two dined together on many occasions. Rudy always immediately returned the senator's phone messages.

D'Amato's prime asset, in Rudy's eyes, was his popularity and prominence not in Washington, but back home. Born in Brooklyn and raised in Nassau County, like Rudy, D'Amato was a tenacious Italian New Yorker with a cornucopia of connections in the city and state. From late 1982 on, Rudy was planning to exploit this newfound friendship to pave the way for his return to New York.

No one was happier about that than Donna. She had had her fill of Senate hearings and cherry blossoms and idle days. Most of all, she was itching to get in front of a camera again. "I needed to work," said Donna. "So Rudy said, 'How about I become U.S. Attorney in New York?'"

In February 1983, John Martin, then U.S. Attorney for the Southern District of New York, traveled to Washington to see Giuliani, who, as associate attorney general, was responsible for supervising all ninety-four U.S. Attorneys across the country. Martin told him he was going to resign and wanted to give the Justice Department a few months to find a replacement. Appointed by President Carter in May 1980, Martin still had a year left to serve in his term. But he knew the Reagan administration—in the person of Rudy Giuliani—had been pressuring Democratic holdovers to leave. Martin had not been strong-armed out of office, like others, notably Iowa's James Reynolds. His signal to leave had been subtler. The U.S. Attorney for the Southern District of New York, considered one of the nation's most prominent federal prosecutors, was traditionally asked to serve on the national advisory committee of U.S. Attorneys. The Reagan administration had pointedly not offered Martin a spot on the committee. He knew he was not wanted and decided to quietly and gracefully accept the inevitable.

After the meeting with Martin, Rudy went to see Al D'Amato. "We talked about the candidates on the list he had submitted," said Rudy. "During the conversation, the possibility of my doing the job came up. I think D'Amato brought it up. I didn't dismiss the idea."

Rudy talked it over with his mother, Donna and close friend Jeff Harris. Helen strongly disapproved. Taking the position, she told Rudy, would mean an instant demotion, like going from CEO to salesman. But Rudy saw the change as more of a switch from head coach to star player.

Donna, who desperately desired to land a TV gig in New York, told Rudy that he should definitely take the post—it was the perfect job for him. Harris agreed. It was 2-to-1 in favor. Rudy phoned D'Amato and told him he wanted the position.

Both Attorney General William French Smith and Deputy Attorney General Ed Schmults weren't exactly sorry to see Giuliani go, according to James Stewart's *The Prosecutors*. A number of Justice Department lawyers even suggested that D'Amato's private proposal to Rudy had been prompted from above. On March 16, 1983, D'Amato, backed by Democratic Senator Patrick Moynihan, endorsed Rudy as a candidate for Manhattan's federal prosecutor's post. Less than a month later, on April 12, President Reagan formally nominated Rudy, who viewed the $67,200-a-year job as the apex of his career, the ultimate opportunity to pursue his operatic crusade of good against evil. In addition to being "one of the best jobs a lawyer could have," said Rudy, "it was a chance to run my own operation and try some of the ideas I'd developed over the past six or seven years."

It could also serve as a launching pad for a New York political career. After Rudy's decision to step down as the No. 3 man in the Justice Department was announced, speculation immediately percolated about his political aspirations. Rudy's best friend Peter Powers believed at the time that Rudy saw his new job, in part, as an electoral vessel. "It was natural to think that with Rudy's interest in politics, the U.S. Attorney's office would lead to a run for public office," Powers said in an unpublished 1988 interview.

Three days after her husband was sworn in as New York City's top federal lawman, Donna got her wish: an on-camera job. Hired by New York's WPIX on June 6 as a general assignment reporter at a starting annual salary of $55,000, she owed her coveted position not to any of her former bosses—but, rather, to one of Rudy's.

"Ace Tyler represented us on a number of cases," recalled former WPIX news director John Corporon. "What he asked us to do—he said 'Donna is looking for a job. Would you interview her?'"

Tyler recalls that Rudy contacted him in the spring of 1983, after securing the nomination for U.S. Attorney, to discuss Donna's job prospects. Tyler then met Donna when the couple visited New York and was "impressed with her credentials." He contacted WPIX, his old client, on her behalf. "I was very friendly with the President of WPIX," Tyler said. "WPIX checked up on her and thought she was good."

Donna and Rudy bought a 35th-floor cooperative apartment on East 86th Street in Manhattan's exclusive Upper East Side. With a living room, a large bedroom and a regular-size kitchen, the apartment was spacious by Manhattan standards but still too small to contain all of their belongings, some of which had to be shipped to storage. The lack of space was redeemed by the spectacular view: a sweeping panorama extending from the East River to the Bronx. On the spring night when Rudy and Donna first inspected the apartment, Rudy spotted the glow of Yankee Stadium in the distance and instantly knew that this was the place for him.

The apartment also had a small extra room, eight feet by ten feet, that was intended as a study. But Donna had another use for it in mind. "We had talked about it and I definitely wanted children," she said. "Rudy wasn't driven to do it, but I was thinking ahead."

Lloyd MacMahon administered the oath of office to his protégé at 1:45 P.M. on June 3, 1983, in a third-floor courtroom in the U.S. District Court at Foley Square. Just as he had been the youngest associate attorney general, Rudy Giuliani, at thirty-nine, became the youngest man ever to lead the Southern District of New York's staff of more than a hundred crack attorneys.

Since its inception in 1789, when President George Washington established thirteen judicial districts in a new nation, what became known as the SDNY has been the pinnacle of prosecutorial prowess. Past leaders of the office filled a lofty roster: Henry Stimson, Elihu Root and the legendary Thomas Dewey. Over the years the Southern District had attracted a competitive crop of America's best and most driven young lawyers. At the time of Rudy's arrival, only one in two twenty applicants made the cut.

Headquartered in a drab, nine-story, cement-block building in lower Manhattan, with the incongruously eminent-sounding address of 1 St. Andrews Plaza, the U.S. Attorney's office looked more like a parking garage than a monolith of justice. Constructed in the late 1970s, after Rudy's stint as an assistant, it was connected by glass-enclosed walkways to the federal courthouse at Foley Square and a modern federal prison called the Metropolitan Correctional Center. City Hall, the municipal building and the police department were all less than two hundred yards away. It was within that cluster of buildings, the corpus of the federal and city governments, that Rudy Giuliani would spend the majority of his career.

Located on the eighth floor, Rudy's office was a large and oddly shaped room with five walls. A sprinkler system could be seen projecting out of a drop ceiling of acoustical tiles. The bright fluorescent lights and gray carpet conspired to create a blanched, antiseptic atmosphere. The unremarkable view revealed an exposed segment of Roosevelt Drive and a swath of buildings that had sprouted up along the highway. On the office's large mahogany desk were a collection of autographed baseballs, piles of scrawled-upon napkins and sheets of yellow legal paper and tall, neat stacks of court documents. Behind the desk was a table upon which Rudy would deposit all matters relegated to the back burner. Leaning against a wall was a folded Yankee Stadium bleacher seat, which Rudy had taken down to Washington and had just hauled back to New York.

Another piece of furniture in Rudy's office—which, like the Yankee seat, would stay with him for most his career—was Deputy U.S. Attorney Denny Young. A former assistant with Rudy during the glory days of the 1970s, Young was short, bespectacled and diffident. Functioning as the de facto chief of staff, he served as Rudy's interoffice mechanical arm, managing personalities and press releases. He was with Rudy so often that appointment logs listing meetings with the two men often neglected to mention Young. An ever loyal sidekick, he had long ago fused his public identity with Rudy's, and was widely regarded in the office as an extension of his boss.

Flamboyant and flashy, Elliot Cuker was Denny Young's extreme opposite. The luxury-car dealer would often park his Rolls-Royce on the curb outside Rudy's office to share a cigar and a story or two. Once the subject of an IRS inquiry, the ex-actor livened up the stale, fluorescently lit atmosphere.

Aside from Cuker, Rudy allowed few other distractions. Refusing to be lulled by the elation of his new, powerful position, he immediately went about the task of imprinting his insignia on one of the most venerable law enforcement institutions in America. The first and most obvious task was to distinguish himself from his predecessor, John Martin, whose management style, Rudy alleged, had been weighed down with self-congratulatory torpor.

"The office was no longer in the forefront of law enforcement, where it had been for much of its history," Rudy claimed later in an unpublished interview. "I thought too much time was spent by people patting themselves on the back. You don't just say you're terrific. You've got to prove it."

The Southern District under John Martin had been repeatedly outshone by the Eastern District's prosecution of sensational cases—notably the famous Abscam cases tried by Thomas Puccio in Brooklyn and the prosecution of Long Island political boss, and D'Amato mentor, Joseph Margiotta. Martin was a chronically cautious prosecutor who eschewed high-profile trials in favor of low-key, routine cases. Although his style was understated, even timid, he ran an efficient office.

In 1981, as associate attorney general, Rudy had ordered a staff cut in Martin's office, arguing that most important federal cases were being brought elsewhere. Now, as he took up the reins from Martin, he appealed to his contacts at Justice for a staff increase and was immediately assigned eight extra slots. Further increasing the size of his battalion by borrowing, through cross-designation, assistants from the state attorney general, Manhattan district attorney and the New York Department of Investigation, Rudy would amass, by 1986, a sizable staff of 132 assistants—the largest U.S. Attorney's office in the country, and nineteen more lawyers than Martin had had at his peak.

The new U.S. Attorney vowed to jolt the office back into action. Under his leadership, Rudy proclaimed, the Manhattan federal prosecutor would once again regain its spot as No. 1, becoming an inexorable juggernaut of justice.

"My father used to have this expression," Rudy said, "which was that he didn't want me to love him, he wanted me to respect him. After I respected him, I would learn to love him. I never quite understood how that worked at home, but it seemed to me a very good philosophy for running an organization."

Despite the fanfare, Rudy's reign as U.S. Attorney did not instantly ignite the landscape of law enforcement in New York City. The first two years, while certainly not uneventful, were primarily a period of reordering priorities and cultivating momentum.

The first order of business was the redeployment of troops. Upon discovering that the public corruption unit—which Rudy led in the mid-1970s—had been dismantled during Martin's term, he quickly reassembled it. He assigned five assistants and named Jane Parver as unit chief. Eight assistants were also pulled off various cases and moved into the narcotics unit, which soon grew to the Southern District's largest division with twenty-one attorneys. Rudy also presided over a precipitous personnel shuffle, replacing several other unit chiefs and removing assistants from stalled cases.

The tentacles of Rudy's assertiveness reached far beyond his own office. When judges were handing out sentences, federal prosecutors typically submitted memos on select cases, but treated the matter of recommending punishment with a diplomatic restraint. Rudy, however, inserted himself unabashedly into the center of the sentencing process, encouraging draconian punishments, and, in one case, recommending a life sentence for a drug dealer.

As Rudy created the Southern District's new agenda, four major areas were identified as the new prosecutorial priorities: drugs, organized crime, public corruption and white-collar crime. "It would be a mistake to decide one is more important," he told the *New York Times* in April 1983. "In the Southern District, we are gravely affected by all four."

The one that got the most initial attention, an issue designated by the Reagan administration as a top priority, was drugs. With his newly enlarged narcotics unit, Rudy pledged to relentlessly pursue drug racketeers and pushers, to support the death penalty for top-level dealers and to take on local cases from "overwhelmed" district attorneys. By using wiretaps and electronic surveillance, the new U.S. Attorney said, the location of shipments could be pinpointed and couriers could be nailed before they ever introduced dope to the street. The majority of his resources, Rudy said, would initially be brought to bear on Manhattan's Lower East Side, a widely reputed narcotics epicenter.

Newspaper reports credited the new "big gun" with having the credentials necessary to lead a citywide campaign against heroin and cocaine. While associate attorney general, the articles noted, Rudy had been behind the creation of regional drug task force units that had provided 200 new assistant U.S. Attorneys (AUSAs) and 1,200 additional FBI, Treasury and Drug Enforcement Agency agents in an expanded war on drugs.

Rudy would also make the claim that while in Washington, he had forged the merger of the Federal Bureau of Investigation and the Drug Enforcement Administration in an attempt to streamline federal anti-drug efforts. Indeed, in a thirty-three-page Justice Department booklet entitled "Challenge, Change and Achievement: The Department of Justice 1981–1985," Rudy was pictured in a photograph with Attorney General William French Smith, above a caption that read: "Then-associate attorney general Rudolph Giuliani, FBI Director William Webster and DEA Administrator Francis Mullen look on as the attorney general announces the merger of the DEA into the FBI."

The FBI-DEA "merger," however, turned out to be more fiction than fact. On February 16, 1985, the *Washington Post* published a story quoting both FBI and DEA spokespeople bluntly refuting that any kind of merger of their organizations had ever taken place. "They definitely have not merged," said DEA spokesperson Bob Feldcamp. It was only in 1984, well after Rudy left the Justice Department, that joint projects were developed to integrate the two agencies' drug-fighting efforts.

One of the earliest and most publicized of Rudy's anti-narcotics initiatives as U.S. Attorney was the "Federal Day" program, in which undercover police officers infiltrated a neighborhood, made arrests and hauled the suspects into federal, rather than state, court. The dealers unlucky enough to be netted on "Federal Day," would be subjected to far stiffer sentences than suspects brought to state court. The program debuted in September 1983, and soon spread beyond the Lower East Side to other neighborhoods in Manhattan and the Bronx, resulting in as many as 300 additional drug arrests a year. Employing what Rudy called the "Russian Roulette" model of deterrence, "Federal Day" made dealing drugs a far riskier proposition.

Several of Rudy's deputies, including associate U.S. Attorney Bart Schwartz and criminal chief Larry Pedowitz, voiced concerns that Federal Day could waste the office's time and resources on small fish in a big pond. Rudy, however, was not one to govern by consensus. "You can't run an organization on the basis of people's complaints," he explained. "You'll never accomplish anything that way."

The program also drew criticism from lawyers and federal judges who felt it administered an arbitrary brand of justice, unfairly targeting minority neighborhoods.

Rudy responded that he had gone after middle- and upper-class cocaine users by seizing the cars of people who drove into the city from Westchester County and Connecticut to buy drugs. He also ordered the drug arrests of 15 Wall Street executives, who were chained together and marched across Foley Square.

Leniency, compassion—these were not concepts Rudy applied to hard drug dealers and users. In a barrelful of vermin, they were among the dregs. Then he discovered one of those dregs was right under his nose.

Assistant U.S. Attorney Daniel Perlmutter, a bespectacled, twenty-nine-year-old Phi Beta Kappa graduate of Williams College and former editor of the New York University *Law Review,* had come to be known as "Mad Dog" for his aggressive prosecutorial style—particularly when it came to drug cases.

Tortured by a secret maelstrom of depression and alienation, Perlmutter started free-basing cocaine and shooting heroin. He hired prostitutes. He had become what he claimed to despise.

The first time he stole drugs and cash from the evidence safe at the U.S. Attorney's office was in November of 1984. For the next several months, he covertly continued to pilfer the safe. As his addiction grew, he became increasingly desperate. On one occasion, he surreptitiously signed in at 3:30 A.M., using the name of another assistant, John Savarese. He used fellow assistant David Zornow's name when dealing with call-girl services.

There is evidence in the transcript of Perlmutter's sentencing hearing that suggests Rudy had reason to know about his assistant's possible drug problem, or at least his overtly fragile emotional state, months before his arrest. Ronald Fischetti, Perlmutter's attorney, told the judge that starting in December 1984, his client, without calling in sick, frequently missed work. "No one knew where he was," said Fischetti. "He would take absences for days, weeks at a time." The *National Law Journal* reported that, within a five-month period starting in December, Perlmutter only spent a total of twenty-five days in the office.

Fischetti noted at the hearing that Giuliani became so concerned about Perlmutter that, as far back as January, he and Criminal Division chief Bart Schwartz "went out to find him." When Rudy and Schwartz found their assistant, he was holed up alone in a cold, unheated apartment. They took him to a restaurant, "in an attempt to help him," said Fischetti, who also noted that, during that period of time, Perlmutter was "hopelessly addicted to cocaine." In a subsequent interview, Fischetti said that when Rudy and Schwartz found Perlmutter in the unheated apartment, he was naked and shivering. The great crime-buster did nothing. It was months after Rudy's visit that Perlmutter committed his worst thefts from the evidence vault, even stealing the heroin he needed for a case he was trying.

Rudy later admitted in press reports that he knew Perlmutter was enduring "psychological and emotional problems," but attributed them to his separation from his wife the previous December. He never explained why Perlmutter had free rein for half a year.

When the FBI collared Perlmutter in May 1985 and the story hit the newspapers, any compassion Rudy felt for the man instantly vaporized. Perlmutter had indeed scuffed the prestigious patina of the Southern District—especially with a righteous reformer running the show. In January 1986, a few months after pleading guilty to taking $41,800 and five pounds of drugs from the U.S. Attorney's Office, he was sentenced to three years in prison. Rudy offered his opinion on the sentencing. In view of his former assistant's "personal betrayal," he believed the "appropriate sentence" should have been a hefty twelve years.

There was a time when Rudy might not have recommended such a harsh sentence, even for an anonymous junkie who had never been his assistant. Over the years his philosophy on drugs and punishment shifted significantly. The "vulnerability" study cautioned that Rudy could be accused of a "drug legalization flip-flop." The authors noted: "Giuliani never has been criticized for his flip-flop on drug legalization. However, the campaign should understand that Giuliani used to favor legalization of drugs. Today, Giuliani is firm in his opposition to legalizing drugs." The study then presented a published statement Rudy had made on drugs years earlier: "There were times in New York when I thought—back in the early 70s—that, although morally and philosophically I was very troubled by the idea of decriminalizing drugs, that it might be the practical, necessary thing to do—the

problem was getting so bad." It was in the early 1970s that his cousin Joan died after being beaten in an alleyway. Her addiction and death may have colored his
early, softer view on drugs. The authors of the "vulnerability" study advised: "If
presented directly with the quote below, Giuliani can explain how his position on
drug legalization has evolved over the years, and how he looked at the issue, like
all others, with an open mind. However, in the end, through careful analysis, he
has come to the firm conclusion that legalization would be a very harmful idea for
this country."

One of Rudy's earliest, and arguably most admirable, actions as U.S. Attorney
pitted him squarely against his boss: the Reagan administration. It was standard
practice for the civil divisions of U.S. Attorney offices to defend the federal government in a slew of varied suits, including those involving federal benefits programs. Using a 1980 law allowing for periodic reviews of Social Security
beneficiaries, the Reagan administration, in blatant disregard of court precedents,
was precipitously stripping disability benefits from ineligible and eligible recipients alike. Since March 1981, Reagan's budget battering rams had knocked hundreds of thousands of people off the rolls. U.S. Attorneys around the country were
deluged with lawsuits. It was an onerous responsibility that muddied the white
knight image of offices like the Southern District.

Howard Wilson, whom Rudy had lured away from private practice to become
his civil chief, brought the issue to his boss's attention. Though they said they
feared it might cost them their jobs, Giuliani and Wilson together decided to "aggressively refuse to defend" the weakest of the government's Social Security disability cases. They would stand up to the Reagan administration, opposing its
policy of cutting people from the disability roles.

Rudy assigned four assistants to review the Social Security cases. Any "inde-
fensible" cases were to be remanded to the U.S. Department of Health and Human
Services. In late 1987, the office was remanding roughly 50 percent of Social
Security disability cases, many for the immediate payment of benefits, and winning more than 75 percent of the remaining cases.

"One of the things of which I am most proud," Rudy said at the January 1989
press conference announcing his resignation as U.S. Attorney, "was our attempting to do justice," in the Social Security cases, "knowing that there was some risk
in doing it."

Rudy's view was vindicated when a federal magistrate issued an injunction in
May 1985 halting the Reagan administration's policy of purging the Social
Security rolls.

It was the summer of 1983, and Rudy was in the newspaper—this time having nothing to do with a criminal case. His name was side by side with Donna's, and they leapt off the gossip page in that signature boldface type reserved for celebrities. On August 21, less than three months after their arrival in New York, Donna and Rudy were already mentioned in a New York tabloid item. The item announced their plans to wed during the upcoming "Christmas holidays." Falling for Donna's reconfigured résumé, the item's authors erroneously noted that she had co-anchored in Los Angeles and dubiously gushed: "Donna's well-known in Hollywood." The reader was also let in on where and when the juicy news broke: "They spilled the beans about the wedding over dinner at Ryan McFadden's."

The announcement proved to be premature. The wedding never happened during the "Christmas holidays," despite the fact that arrangements were made. In December 1983, another gossip item mysteriously reported that "a Christmas wedding was planned but the miserable weather blocked travel plans for her family and friends who live in California." The new wedding date, the readers were informed, would be on April 15, 1984, "probably at St. Monica's Church on E. 79th St. or at Manhattan College, Rudy's alma mater." Monsignor Alan Placa, "Rudy's best friend," would be officiating.

Weather might not have been the only obstacle facing the would-be newlyweds. Rudy had already divorced Regina—but in order to marry again in the Catholic Church, his first marriage would also have to be annulled. In 1982, he had turned to Placa for help. Since he and Regina were second cousins, Placa told Rudy, they should have obtained a special dispensation to marry. If they hadn't, the marriage could be annulled, said Placa, who also had a law degree.

Placa had been Rudy's best man at his wedding to Regina in 1968. A seminarian at the time, he had dated Regina years earlier. Helen Giuliani recalled that Placa told her son and his fiancée that their consanguinity wouldn't be a problem, but Placa says he never offered such an assurance. Placa remembered that the priest who performed the marriage, Father James Moriarty, had never asked Rudy and Regina about their relationship.

But couples who filled out the prenuptial form at the time were "under oath and expected to answer all questions truthfully" according to New York Archdiocese canon law expert William Elder. If there was any question at all regarding a blood relationship, "the Church has to investigate it," said Elder. Had Rudy and Regina answered the questions and acknowledged that they were blood relatives, it would have set in motion a family tree review that would have revealed that they were second cousins and needed a dispensation.

In addition to the form, Rudy and Regina had another opportunity to inform the Church that they were cousins: a PreCana conference at which the couples discussed with a priest the meaning of marriage and the relationship of marriage to the church. Had Rudy and Regina notified the church of their blood relationship and obtained a dispensation, Placa would have had to find, if possible, some other way to manufacture an annulment.

When Father John O'Leary—who became pastor of St. Monica's Church two years after Rudy and Donna's wedding there and later arranged for Andrew's baptism—heard that Rudy had not obtained the proper dispensation for marrying a second cousin, he remarked: "Lucky guy." He explained that "it's an application of law and very often, the law favors the lawbreaker."

A Catholic lawyer familiar with annulment proceedings noted that "the Church marriage tribunal functions like a civil court, and what Giuliani did in using Placa was the equivalent of finding a well-connected lawyer with courthouse contacts to handle your case."

In an unpublished 1988 interview, Regina said she was "offended" when she found out about Rudy's plans to obtain an annulment.

"When Gina heard that Rudy wanted an annulment," said Helen Giuliani, "she was very upset. It gave Gina the feeling she was never married. She actually went to diocesan headquarters to fight it. Alan was a friend to both Rudy and Gina, but of course Gina is not Alan's friend anymore. She feels Alan manipulated the whole thing and carried it though."

Placa, who characterized Regina's reaction as "irrational," not only stewarded Rudy's annulment through the proper channels; he also claims to have arranged an annulment of Donna's marriage to Stanley Hanover. The marriage tribunal was just a few doors down the hall from Placa's office at the diocese of Rockville Center on Long Island. He collected the documents establishing that Rudy and Regina were second cousins and that no dispensation had been awarded. In 1982, despite Regina's protests, the annulment Rudy sought was granted.

Donna has never discussed the annulment that Placa disclosed in an unpublished 1988 interview. Indeed, she has refused to answer questions about their divorce as well. No record of their divorce exists in the locales where they lived after the 1972 marriage. In any event, Placa says he had the jurisdiction transferred from Donna's diocese in California to him. Both annulments were approved.

In 1989, when the annulment surfaced during the campaign, Rudy at first was indignant. "There's nothing about my life that I'm embarrassed about," he told reporters. Then his responses became equivocal. He told Maria Laurino of the *Village Voice*: "I thought of us as distant cousins. I never calculated the exact degree of consanguinity, which is how the law of the church—it's a pretty ancient law—works." He later attempted a more straightforward explanation: "She was my father's second cousin. I was her father's second cousin. That made us second cousins once removed."

The "exact degree of consanguinity" quickly became a matter of confusion. Rudy's campaign manager and buddy Peter Powers told the New York *Daily News*: "Rudy's father and Regina's father were first cousins. Rudy always assumed that he and Regina were third cousins."

In the same article, Regina said that "we knew that we were cousins. We attended PreCana and all that. It was our impression that we didn't need a dispensation." Her brother, Richard, was quoted, responding to Rudy's claim of ignorance on the second-cousin question. "That's a lie," Richard said. "He knew he was my second cousin."

In 1997, Rudy and Regina's uncle, Rudolph Giuliani, told the New York *Daily News*'s Paul Schwartzman, "I knew they were second cousins," adding that their romantic relationship had "seemed natural—they shared common interests."

Rudy and Donna lived together for almost two years prior to their wedding. They were hardly devout Catholics. Donna publicly announced years later that she was merely "raised Catholic"—the classic formulation of a lapsed Catholic. Their tax returns in the 1980s included no charitable deductions, and friends said they rarely went to church, just like much of the rest of Rudy's family. Rudy understood, however, that divorced Catholics were barred from remarrying in the church but an annulled marriage opened the church door a second time around.

If it wasn't a religious motive pushing Rudy to obtain an annulment that Regina vigorously resisted, why did Rudy go to such lengths to get it?

Rudy's college girlfriend, Kathy Livermore, remembered a conversation with Rudy about a "political annulment." She recalled it as a comment about Nelson Rockefeller annulling his first marriage, but she must have juggled Rocky's name with President Kennedy's, since there had been rumors, never proven, that JFK had an initial, annulled, marriage before the one to Jackie. "We had a big discussion about that, and how many years it would be before a president was able to be divorced and be president, and it was a very smart move on Rockefeller's part. Because it erased the marriage, it makes no record of the marriage. We had a big discussion about that."

The unmistakable inference is that Rudy got his annulment for the legions of Catholic voters in New York—with his political future clearly in mind.

On April 15, 1984, Rudy and Donna were married at St. Monica's Church on Manhattan's Upper East Side. Another gossip item soon appeared in May 1984, opening with the line: "Sometimes, life can be a bowl of cherries." Reporting that Rudy and Donna had been married the previous month, the item's authors also mentioned Donna's promotion at WPIX from reporter to anchorwoman. It came right after the honeymoon. "Does being married to a crack prosecutor help a TV woman's career?" they asked. "Nope, says a colleague at the station, explaining her promotion: 'She's got B & B—beauty and brains.'"

No matter what else he accomplished as U.S. Attorney, Rudy knew what would reestablish the Southern District as the most prestigious and feared federal prosecutor's office in the country and what would anoint him as a crusading man of the people: an all-out, take-no-prisoners campaign against the New York Mafia.

"It is about time law enforcement got as organized as organized crime," he declared to reporters in the fall of 1984.

Rudy's assault on the Mafia, he claims, began before he became U.S. Attorney. One evening he was watching *60 Minutes*. Joe Bonanno, the seventy-eight-year-old "retired" mob boss, was promoting his new autobiography, *A Man of Honor*. Bonanno boasted that the book told the true story of his career running the infamous New York crime family that bears his name.

In a sudden rush, Rudy ran to a bookstore, bought the book and trotted back to his apartment. He devoured *A Man of Honor*, noting cryptic terms that read like a code. Intrigued by Bonanno's detailed descriptions—not only of his own life, but of the lives of New York's other mob bosses—Rudy believed he'd discovered something that could translate into an indictment. In Bonanno's lavish telling of his tale, he had explicitly spelled out the history of "The Commission," the ruling body of the American Mafia—how it was created, how it operated and who belonged to it.

"Look at this," Rudy said to Donna in amazement. "This is a RICO enterprise."

RICO was an acronym for the Racketeer Influenced and Corrupt Organizations Act of 1970, which defined as a federal crime any activity that could be described as a "pattern of racketeering." Bonanno's book had triggered an epiphany: Rudy could use RICO to prosecute the heads of New York's five Mafia families as the governing body of an organization, instead of individually. The rarely used act could be wielded to hobble the mob en masse, especially since it carried heavy sentences—a maximum twenty-year prison term and a fine up to $250,000 for each count.

Sunk into his reading chair, adrenaline surging through him like a narcotic, Rudy decided that RICO would be his Excalibur.

"Joe Bonanno had really described the Commission," Rudy said. "How it started in 1931, how it functioned in the 1960s, how the members were the bosses of the five families from New York and outside families, how they coordinated disputes and put out contracts. If you allow for euphemisms, it's all there. I went back to work the next couple of days and dug out FBI reports. I determined we were going to put together the case as soon as I got back to New York."

Before the "Commission" case was ready, however, Rudy tested the power of the RICO statute in a mob case virtually ready for indictment when he arrived at the SDNY. His target was the Colombo family, which had been under investigation by the FBI since 1981. In October 1984, Rudy indicted eleven members of the family for extorting money from restaurants and construction businesses. The chief defendant was the family's ruthless leader, Carmine "the Snake" Persico. In June 1986, nine of the eleven indicted Colombo family members, including Persico, were convicted of labor racketeering.

The Colombo case tapped into an ancient rivalry between the Southern and Eastern districts. When the FBI initiated the Colombo investigation, it was agreed that the districts would work together, jointly investigating the case. When it came time for indictments, however, one office would take control. Justice officials originally decided, since most of the crimes were perpetrated in the Eastern District, that Eastern District officials should get the case. But when Rudy arrived, he used his Justice Department connections to pry jurisdiction away from the Eastern District. "I feel very strongly that case belonged in my office," Edward A. McDonald, chief of the Eastern District's organized crime strike force, told the New York Times. "Virtually every act was in the Eastern District, almost all the defendants lived in the Eastern District and we did at least half the work."

Rudy responded dismissively: "We did almost everything."

Rudy's use of the statute against an individual crime family like the Colombos was hardly innovative. John Martin had brought a RICO case against the Bonanno crime family that led to the conviction of five bosses and underbosses. In fact, two other RICO investigations were under way before Rudy arrived in the Southern District. One was the "Pizza Connection" case, which resulted in the racketeering convictions of eighteen people for running a vast international heroin operation through a network of pizza parlors. The indictments came in April 1984, and a seventeen-month trial ended in June 1986. The three-year covert investigation was the first simultaneous drug probe of American and Sicilian organized crime groups, and it long preceded Rudy's arrival at the SDNY. In another RICO case, brought against the Gambino family's powerful boss, Paul "the Pope" Castellano, Southern District organized crime chief Walter Mack won a seventy-eight-count indictment of Castellano and twenty-three Gambino family members and associates in March 1984. Six months later, Rudy rewarded Mack by demoting him and naming Barbara Jones as his replacement as the new chief of the organized crime unit. It was a move widely perceived as a preemptive attempt to prevent career mob prosecutor Mack from getting media credit for the work of the office. As Rudy would demonstrate again and again over the course of his public life, credit, in his mind, was reserved for Rudy and Rudy alone. In any event, the Castellano trial ended with several convictions.

With the early mob cases, Rudy honed a skill that would serve him well throughout his tenure as U.S. Attorney: how to run a captivating press conference. While most U.S. Attorneys traditionally handled journalists with restraint, Rudy seduced and embraced them—and they reciprocated with a hail of positive coverage. In addition to press conferences, Rudy sought exposure through lecture circuits, breakfast seminars, panel discussions, talk shows. "The only way to deliver a deterrent effectively is to publicize it," he explained to reporters. "I want to send a message."

Not everyone bought his argument. The spotlight-seeking federal prosecutor was criticized by members of the New York bar for conducting "trial by press conference." One anonymous assistant told the *National Law Journal*: "A lot of people around here feel as if they are being used to launch somebody's political career." Another assistant noted in the *American Lawyer* the high priority Rudy gave to press releases, saying he delegated Denny Young to finesse them. "Denny would review press releases as though they were indictments," the assistant said. "He'd cross out assistants' names and put Rudy's in. . . . Denny had a phenomenal devotion to press releases."

In an act that many interpreted as the peak of Rudy's scene stealing, the U.S. Attorney accompanied Senator D'Amato to Washington Heights to make an undercover drug buy in the summer of 1986. Newspapers across the country ran photos of the two dressed up unconvincingly as street thugs, Rudy in a Hells Angels jacket. The publicity stunt, designed to aid D'Amato's 1986 re-election campaign, was portrayed as evidence of the open drug market in New York—with five almost instant buys. Arrests were promised up the road. Though it was organized by local DEA chief Robert Stutman, Andy Maloney, U.S. Attorney for the Eastern District, refused to participate in the event. Sources say that only two of the celebrated buys were real drugs—meaning "the Fonz" and friend bought harmless powder in most of the stops. Robert Stutman said he couldn't remember if that was so.

Two years before the drug buy—early in Giuliani's tenure—D'Amato had asked for Rudy's help on a hush-hush matter, reflecting the senator's confidence in his cozy relationship with the prosecutor. Mario Gigante, a captain in the Genovese crime family, and brother of mob boss "Chin" Gigante, had been convicted in June 1983 of extortion and loan-sharking and was sentenced to eight years in prison. That was the same month Rudy took office. Gigante's attorney, Roy Cohn—an infamous mob lawyer and former protégé of red-baiting Senator Joseph McCarthy—had filed a motion for a reduction of the sentence. A political fixer with powerful ties to D'Amato and the Reagan White House, Cohn had helped install his partner, Tom Bolan, as a member of the senator's screening panel that cleared Rudy's appointment. In the fall of 1984, D'Amato phoned Rudy to suggest that Mario Gigante wasn't that bad a fellow and wondered if maybe the government could go easy on him.

Rudy claimed years later that, after talking to D'Amato, he immediately summoned Bruce Baird, the assistant handling the Gigante case, and instructed him to make sure he did everything possible to see Gigante's sentence was *not* reduced. Baird, however, says he does not recall Rudy mentioning D'Amato's interest in the case and that he only had a "vague recollection" that his then boss might have spoken to him about the Gigante motion. He did remember that Cohn was furious when he learned that Baird had written a letter to the judge on the case opposing any reduction in Gigante's eight-year term.

A key mob informant, Vincent "the Fish" Cafaro, later told the FBI in March 1987 that, on Chin Gigante's orders, he had delivered a $175,000 cash payment to Cohn's office. The payment was made after Judge Charles Stewart had approved, without comment, a two-year reduction in Mario Gigante's prison term.

A year after the Gigante call, in early 1985, Rudy got another call from D'Amato that was even more vexing. This time, the senator from Long Island was phoning on behalf of Paul Castellano. D'Amato asked Rudy to look "carefully" at charges pending against the mob boss. Giuliani recalled thinking it bizarre how D'Amato never mentioned that Castellano was then the most notorious criminal in the United States, accused of serious crimes, including multiple murders. Troubled by the senator's advocacy of a prominent gangster under investigation by his office, Giuliani claimed he gave his friend a mini-lecture.

"I told Al that these are the kinds of things that should go from lawyer to lawyer," Rudy said. "I said, 'We shouldn't be talking about these kinds of things.

It's not good for you and it's not good for me.' I thought I was helping him, educating him because he seemed naive. I don't know if it helped him, but it helped me because he never talked to me about a case after that."

However alarmed Rudy was by D'Amato's mob calls, he maintained close ties with the senator, and continued to make public appearances with him in addition to the drug buy. In 1985, they even traveled to Italy together, reportedly to promote the war on drugs.

Even if Rudy hadn't so eagerly courted the media, his track record at the Southern District would have made him a major media figure. Starting with the Colombo case, he presided over a stunning series of dramatic and daring prosecutions—mob and otherwise—that were the stuff of legend, even without a publicist. The media fed his burgeoning reputation—and he fed them with a regular regimen of juicy press conferences. He became a celebrity, a folk hero who, although unabashedly overzealous, even evangelical, earned apt comparisons to Eliot Ness and Tom Dewey. Giuliani was even cast by some in the media as a modern-day Savonarola, the zealous fifteenth-century Florentine priest who was burned at the stake.

The idea for the mob case that would cement Rudy's renowned crime-fighting reputation, the fabled "Commission" prosecution, had actually been bandied about for years by several New York law enforcement officials—long before Rudy read Joe Bonanno's book. In August 1983, two months after becoming U.S. Attorney, Rudy met with one of those officials, Ronald Goldstock, head of the New York State Organized Crime Task Force. Goldstock told Rudy about incriminating tapes he'd collected from a bugging device planted in the Jaguar of a reputed mob leader, who kept talking about the Mafia's "Commission." Excited by Goldstock's tapes, Rudy ordered his assistants to sift through hundreds of hours of FBI surveillance tapes and to review old Senate hearings for additional "Commission" references. In addition to Goldstock's tapes, the FBI had succeeded in March 1983 in planting a bug inside the Staten Island home of Paul Castellano, who ran the Commission. That bug, which preceded Rudy's appointment, would be crucial in the ultimate case.

A chart and thirty volumes of evidence were put together, cataloguing the crimes and delineating the leadership of each of New York's five Mafia families. First on the chart was the Colombo family headed by Carmine Persico, whose No. 2 man, or underboss, was Gennaro "Gerry Lang" Langelia; Persico, of course, was already under indictment in the Colombo case. Listed next was the Gambino family—then the largest Mafia organization in the country, with a thousand members who engaged in everything from drug running to stolen cars to pornography—headed by Castellano. The third entry on the chart was the Luchese family, headed by "Tony Ducks" Corallo. The chart would later be expanded to include the last two of the five entries: the Bonanno family, then headed by Rusty Rastelli, and the Genovese crime family, reportedly headed by "Fat Tony" Salerno.

In September 1983, a month after his meeting with Goldstock, Rudy flew down to Washington to meet with his old boss, Attorney General William French Smith, and FBI Director William Webster. He showed them the partially completed "Commission" chart and described his idea for trying the five New York leaders as an organization.

"If I go to trial today," he asserted, "I could convict two or three of the Family heads of being members of the Commission. If I can do that now, then if we investigate this thing, we should be able to convict four or five of them."

He would need their backing, he then explained, to cut into other jurisdictions. He would also need to "borrow" agents in fourteen cities to gather data on the "Commission."

French and Webster swiftly approved the case and told the ambitious prosecutor they would personally see to it that he got whatever resources he needed to get the job done.

As the investigations neared completion, Rudy flew out to Tucson, Arizona, where the man who had first opened his eyes to the possibility of this case—Joe Bonanno—lay in a hospital bed. The mobster's lawyer had claimed his client was too sick to travel to New York, although Rudy suspected the gravity of Bonanno's illness might be just as exaggerated as the man's sense of his own "honor." What Rudy wanted from the old man was a deposition regarding the existence and operation of the Commission. He was, after all, its only living founding member.

The meeting in Bonanno's room at St. Mary's Hospital was civil. Ostensibly delighted to have visitors, the amiable gangster told Rudy "off-the-record" stories about prominent figures. He seemed to enjoy telling the stories. At one point, he said to Rudy: "You're doing a good job."

Toward the end of the interview, "an anger had really started building up in me," Rudy said. The crime organization Bonanno described had tainted and troubled many Italians in America, even infecting Rudy's own family. But, as he left, the anger was replaced by intense satisfaction: Joe Bonanno had given him what he needed.

Back in New York, the "Commission" investigation had been split into two primary areas. The first was collecting interviews from cooperating witnesses, some of whom had held positions within the families. The second involved tapes of the subjects, made possible by the daring installations of bugs. On the tapes were thousands of conversations proving the involvement of each of the five bosses with irrefutable clarity. Even more incriminating was the fact that mobsters from different families in different parts of the city were heard talking about the same meetings, the same people, the same concerns. It was undeniable proof of a relationship between the families.

Also on the tapes were repeated references to payoffs made to construction companies, revealing the extent to which the five families essentially ran New York's construction industry. One boss remarked to an associate that "not a yard of concrete was poured in New York" without the mob's say-so. It became clear through the recordings that any construction company that wanted work had to pay 2 percent of the price of the contract directly to the "Commission." Some mobsters were directly involved with the companies. Salerno and Castellano, for example, became partners in S&A Concrete and subsequently saw to it that the company got a greater cut of the jobs.

In early 1985, Rudy decided he had enough evidence against the "Commission" and would try the case himself. On February 25, he signed the indictment and sent it to the grand jury for a vote. That night, fifty major mob leaders were busted and hauled before a swarm of cameras in Foley Square. When FBI agents got Castellano into an office overlooking the square, he glanced out the window.

"Isn't that Giuliani?" he asked.

The agents looked down, and there he was, standing on the courthouse steps, talking to reporters.

"Well," said the boss of bosses, "if you've got to get fucked, it might as well be by a *paisan.*"

For twenty-seven days, Rudy had worked almost without sleep. He was haggard. His nerves were jumpy. But the next day, none of that mattered. On February 26, 1985, Rudy Giuliani attained a national visibility two stints in Washington had never given him.

PBS's *MacNeil-Lehrer Newshour* was trying to book him for an evening interview in its uptown studio. Rudy had been on the show several times when he was Associate Attorney General, but he apologized, he couldn't do it—he already had two interviews scheduled that evening, one on ABC's national evening newscast, and the other on the 11:30 P.M. edition of ABC's *Nightline.* He had also agreed to appear on the same network's *Good Morning America"* the following morning at 6:15 A.M. and the *CBS Morning News* at 7 A.M.

When the press conference began at 11:40 A.M., the room was packed with more than a hundred reporters, photographers and cameramen. He was joined on the stage by Webster and several local prosecutors. Flanked by charts showing reporters how La Cosa Nostra operated, Rudy proudly announced: "This is a great day for law enforcement, but a bad day, probably the worst ever, for the Mafia." He then presented the indictment, which covered twenty-five counts and charged twelve individuals, including the five alleged bosses, with running a RICO enterprise.

The gladiatorial style that had become Rudy's trademark wasn't just reserved for mobsters and other criminals. In March 1985, a month after the "Commission" indictment was announced, he was one of several prosecutors to testify at a New York City Bar Association hearing on whether new federal anti-crime initiatives could lead to abuses by an overambitious prosecutor, especially in organized-crime cases. While others who spoke maintained a subdued tone, Rudy bluntly confronted the panel. He accused them of being "provincial" and behaving like a "trade association."

A top federal prosecutor inveighing against a panel of defense attorneys—in fact, pitching unadorned insults at them—was not only brazen but highly irregular. U.S. Attorneys and high-ranking assistants, who usually serve from three to five years, work at maintaining congenial relations with the attorneys they oppose, well aware that they will soon be looking for jobs on the opposite side of the courtroom. Not Rudy. He had other plans. There might be an overzealous downside to a politically ambitious prosecutor. But the upside—at least from a public perspective—was that he was more interested in making cases than making friends.

When the "Commission" case finally went to trial, Rudy, who had always planned to try it himself, opted instead to try a pivotal municipal corruption case that was hardly as clear-cut a winner. It was a chancy move, but Giuliani was determined to get convictions in both cases. He also relished the drama of going up against his old counterpoint from the Eastern District, Tom Puccio, who was representing a key defendant in the corruption case.

Rudy turned the "Commission" trial over to a young assistant, Michael Chertoff. Working, like Rudy, fifteen hours a day, seven days a week, Chertoff had been involved with the case since its inception. In November 1986, the defendants were found guilty on all counts. Chertoff proved that the heads of New York's Mafia families had acted as a board of directors, which had, among other things, approved mob murders and divided mob construction industry interests. On January 13, 1987, they were hit with heavy, face-blanching sentences. "Fat Tony"

Salerno, "Tony Ducks" Corallo and Carmine "the Snake" Persico were each sentenced to 100 years in prison. Five of their associates were also hit with heavy prison sentences, ranging from forty to 100 years. Castellano escaped his punishment. In December 1985, he was shot dead in front of Sparks, a Manhattan steak house. Rusty Rastelli, the Bonanno boss, had a previous engagement on the day of sentencing; he was in a Brooklyn courtroom being tried in a separate case in which he eventually got a twelve-year prison sentence.

Rudy's handling of the "Commission" case had been a professionally and emotionally taxing experience—punishing hours, ridiculous accusations of bias from prominent Italian-Americans and even threats on his life. It was the kind of heat he loved.

Many of those who worked on various elements of the case, however, felt the pugnacious prosecutor sought credit beyond what he deserved. The organized-crime indictments surfacing when Rudy arrived at the Southern District were the result of an exhaustive law enforcement effort that been on-going for at least twenty years. Robert Blakey, a Notre Dame professor who, as a consultant to the Senate Judiciary Committee in the 1960s, created RICO, put it this way in a June 1985 *New York Times Magazine* article: "It's like stuffing a pipe. You put it in at one end, and for a long time, you don't see anything. And then finally it shows. Rudolph Giuliani is the guy lucky enough to be standing at the end of the pipe."

When asked by *Newsday* in 1989 about Rudy's claim of dreaming up the "Commission" case after reading Bonanno's book, Tom Sheer, the FBI's former New York City bureau chief, replied: "That's his position." Sheer, who praised Rudy on many fronts, said the FBI had been mulling a "Commission" case since 1980, three years before Rudy's arrival. "That was always the ultimate goal," he said.

Ironically, John Martin, in addition to laying the groundwork for the Pizza Connection and Castellano cases had also sown the seeds of the Commission case for Rudy to reap.

Rudy's own organized crime unit chief, Barbara Jones, admitted in the *American Lawyer* that "all of these cases were carved out of a body of investigative work that the FBI had done and many assistants [in the Eastern and Southern districts] had done." But Rudy's prosecution of New York's Mafia leaders, Blakey, Jones and others agreed, was a bold and unprecedented feat that did extensive and lasting damage to the Cosa Nostra.

"A lot of federal agencies said it couldn't be done," said Ron Goldstock, the top state investigator. "Giuliani had the open-mindedness to see ways in which the case could be done. He raised the right issues and moved it in days."

Rudy had immersed himself in the culture of the Mafia. He saw Francis Ford Coppola's *The Godfather* enough times to memorize most of the dialogue and music. He even picked out a favorite real-life mobster—"Fat Tony" Salerno—whose clubhouse was only a few blocks from where Harold Giuliani had grown up. The U.S. Attorney, who had listened to hours of Salerno's tapes, did a convincing impersonation of the rotund, cigar-chomping gangster he had sent to prison, mimicking his scratchy, sardonic voice. "Fat Tony is the most interesting of the bosses," said Rudy, "because he has a terrific sense of humor."

In imagining which of the top mobsters would be most likely to grant clemency to a condemned man, Rudy mused: "If you had to pick one of them to appeal to, to spare you, you might have a chance with Fat Tony. I think you'd have no chance with Persico and very little with 'Tony Ducks' Corallo. With Castellano you might have a chance. With Fat Tony, I think you might be able to get a little softness, on human terms."

Rudy's favorite mobster died in prison in 1992, but he would still come back to haunt the prosecutor years later. In a 1997 federal racketeering and murder trial, assistants from the U.S. Attorney for Eastern District alleged that Vincent "the Chin" Gigante was in fact running the Genovese crime family during much of the period covered in the "Commission" case. Gigante's attorneys submitted into evidence Rudy's 1985 indictment naming "Fat Tony" Salerno as the Genovese head. Their argument was that if Salerno was convicted of being boss, how could the feds now charge Gigante with masterminding a racketeering enterprise? Genovese capo "Fish" Cafaro had testified in 1988 before a U.S. Senate Subcommittee that Salerno was once boss, but that he had been demoted in 1981 after a stroke. "Gigante allowed Fat Tony to continue to front as the boss," Cafaro told the committee. Philadelphia crime family boss Philip Leonetti testified at Gigante's trial that he was told Gigante took over as boss in early 1980. During the Gigante trial, an assistant U.S. Attorney played a tape of a conversation at Salerno's social club in 1984, in which Salerno referred to Gigante as "the boss."

Ultimately, Gigante was convicted and sent to prison for twelve years. A federal jury had implicitly found that Rudy Giuliani convicted the wrong man as boss of the most powerful crime family in New York.

Indeed, the irony is that as strong as Giuliani's record of mob prosecutions was, it cannot match that of Andy Maloney, the U.S. Attorney for the Eastern District from 1986 to 1992. In addition to taking down Gigante—whose organization was headquartered just blocks from St. Andrew's Plaza—Maloney also convicted John Gotti, the most infamous boss, whose dapper profile embodied the modern mob. Giuliani and Maloney had worked out a distribution of the various allegations against Gotti, who rose to power in 1985 by murdering Castellano in the heart of Rudy's Manhattan district. But it was Maloney who finally nailed the "Teflon Don," who had beaten three prior cases, and put him in prison for life.

Maloney also convicted Vic Orena, whom Carmine Persico installed as his Colombo successor, and Vic Amuso, who replaced "Ducks" Corallo as the Luchese chief. It was Maloney who followed the threads of the "Commission" case and sunk the mob that Rudy had helped cripple.

Eight

The War Against Greed

IN THE EARLY 1980S, WHILE ASSOCIATE ATTORNEY GENERAL, RUDY HAD characterized prosecutors who relentlessly pursued white-collar criminals as "zealots." Now, in the late 1980s, as corporate greed became the sordid leitmotif of the times, Rudy did an about-face: He declared war on Wall Street. Starting in 1986, the U.S. Attorney for the Southern District of New York became the scourge of white-collar criminals who hid behind the sterile façade of big names firms. With a Pattonesque verve, Rudy blasted open one of the biggest insider trading scandals in history.

The Securities and Exchange Commission had initiated the insider trader probe before the reign of Rudy—but as he had with the mob, he scooped up the work that preceded him and swiftly sculpted it into arrests.

Rudy's first big bust came in May 1986, with the arrest of Drexel Burnham investment banker Dennis Levine. A crass, overweight man with extravagant tastes, Levine was a well-connected rising Wall Street star who happened to have made a daring series of illegal trades. After his arrest, he agreed to pay an $11.6 million civil settlement and to cooperate with the government. Shock waves rippled through Wall Street, as many traders panicked, fearing that Levine would finger them. One of them was legendary arbitrageur Ivan Boesky. With $3 billion worth of stock-buying power, Boesky was a financial colossus who had fantasized about becoming a "latter-day Rothschild" and in 1985 told graduates of the University of California that "greed is all right." Thinly disguised as Gordon Gecko and played by Michael Douglas in Oliver Stone's film Wall Street, Boesky became a widely recognized symbol of the excesses of the 1980s. After being fingered by Levine and served with a subpoena by the Securities and Exchange Commission, Boesky decided to make a preemptive strike: he surrendered voluntarily and worked out a secret deal with Rudy, agreeing to pay a $100 million penalty. He admitted he'd traded on inside information supplied by Levine.

Rudy's office persuaded Boesky to wear a wire and cooperate with the government. Soon, with Boesky and Levine cooperating, the Wall Street swindlers fell like dominos. The next were Kidder, Peabody & Co. investment banker Martin Siegel and Boyd Jefferies, head of Jefferies & Company. The natty perpetrators of securities fraud, Rudy learned, were a lot more willing than corrupt cops to give themselves and their colleagues up—they practically got in line. In the end, a total of ten traders pled guilty, cooperated and were sent to prison. Wall Street was reeling, in a sudden siege mentality, bracing for another out-of-nowhere blow by Giuliani.

Levine and Boesky, in return for their cooperation, got relatively mild sentences. In early 1987, Levine was sentenced to two years in prison and fined $362,000. Boesky drew a three-year prison term in November 1986. Defense attorneys representing defendants prosecuted on Boesky information later discovered that Boesky had been allowed by Rudy's office to take a $50 million tax write-off on his $100 million penalty, and to put up stock rather than cash. The deal was widely faulted as a generous overreach.

On February 11, 1987, upon to returning to New York after a week's vacation in California, on-a-roll Rudy selected yet another trading target: multimillion-dollar-a-year arbitrageur Timothy Tabor. Based on a tip from Siegel, Rudy ordered Tabor arrested in the evening at his home on the Upper East Side. It was a strategic time for an arrest: too late for bail to be granted or to contact a lawyer. Tabor faced a night in jail.

Unlike the others, however, Tabor did not fold. He maintained his innocence and refused to work for the government. That left the ball in the government's court: They had to prove Tabor was guilty of conspiring to trade on illegal inside information.

The next day, U.S. marshals marched into the solemn offices of the investment firm of Goldman, Sachs and arrested Robert Freeman, a financial executive linked to Tabor by Siegel. Tabor's former boss, Richard Wigton, was nabbed at Kidder, Peabody & Co. and—in front of his colleagues—pushed against a wall, frisked, handcuffed and marched away in tears.

Such a display of sudden force is usually reserved for suspects considered dangerous or likely to flee. Tabor, Freeman and Wigton would have surrendered voluntarily, a process ordinarily arranged through attorneys. Rudy's two arrests of Gambino family crime boss Paul Castellano, for example, had both been far more genteel—the first time, the gangster was allowed to surrender at the Manhattan office of his trial attorney, and the second time, he was not handcuffed when picked up at his home and allowed to buy a Snicker's bar on the way to the arraignment.

The other oddity was that the Wall Street arrests had occurred before the case had been presented to a grand jury and before the indictments were obtained. Indictments weren't handed down for seven weeks. The raids were solely a result of Siegel's insider trading tip. While not unprecedented, such precipitous action was reserved for cases in which there was a great deal of urgency or prosecutors were exceedingly confident of their information.

Rudy, however, was defiantly defensive about the Wigton, Tabor and Freeman arrests. He told *Vanity Fair's* Gail Sheehy: "This isn't an invitation to a tea party. People are arrested in the hope they will tell you everything that happened. The important thing with Tabor, Wigton, and Freeman that gets obscured, because they're rich and powerful and have the ability to affect public relations, is that they were treated exactly the same as sixty or seventy New York City cops, and they hadn't committed violent crimes either. They were arrested for taking bribes from $50 to $5,000."

Of course, he had never arrested sixty or seventy cops—especially without an exhaustive grand jury probe. Rudy also neglected to note one difference between corrupt cops and dirty Wall Street dealers: cops carry guns. Perhaps most important, Rudy may well have acted so decisively precisely because his tipster was as well-heeled as the targets. The suave Siegel got a responsive respect from Rudy's office that someone less "rich and powerful," as Rudy put it, was unlikely to receive—especially without tapes or any other form of corroboration.

When a judge refused the prosecution's request for a trial delay, Rudy's office, faced with a dearth of evidence, withdrew the indictments against the three men. Rudy promised a new indictment in "record-breaking time." After languishing, however, for two and a half years, the new investigation finally, mercifully, fizzled out. When no new charges were brought against Wigton and Tabor, both men were, at last, cleared. In the anti-climactic end to Rudy's sensational string of insider trading cases, Robert Freeman copped a minor plea to a single count of illegal insider stock trading and received a four-month prison sentence. The story of the Wall Street Three became a lasting symbol of prosecutorial fanaticism and grist for future Rudy opponents.

"That was a gaffe," said Harold Tyler in a 1993 *Newsday* article on Rudy's handling of the Tabor, Freeman and Wigton matter. "Totally unnecessary."

Tyler is also now highly critical of another infamous case prosecuted by his protégé, a case that Tyler himself investigated as a federal judge.

Bess Myerson had a long list of notable credentials: the first Jewish Miss America; 1980 U.S. Senate candidate; New York City Cultural Affairs Commissioner; and former confidante of Mayor Ed Koch. She also had a mob-tied boyfriend who was a major city contractor caught in a successful Giuliani tax prosecution. Taken together, these attributes made for an irresistible target in Rudy's eyes.

Tyler, who submitted a report on the Myerson case to Koch, told *Newsday* in 1993 that Rudy's prosecution of Myerson was "an appalling mistake, a waste of government money . . . a tragedy. What's the point?"

It all started in the spring of 1983 when Myerson's boyfriend, Carl Capasso, was trying to wrest himself loose from a prior marriage. The judge presiding over Capasso's divorce case was Hortense Gabel. During the height of the divorce case, Gabel was trying to help her thirty-five-year-old daughter Sukhreet find a job, and sent out her résumé to dozens of people—including Cultural Affairs Commissioner Bess Myerson. After a few dinners and outings with Sukhreet, Myerson hired her as a special assistant. The story was soon in the newspapers: the Cultural Affairs Commissioner who hired the daughter of the judge who was presiding over her boyfriend's divorce case. Sukhreet, after a falling out with Myerson, left the job.

On October 7, 1987, Rudy announced at one of his trademark press conferences the indictment of Myerson, Capasso and Hortense Gabel on bribery and mail-fraud charges. In addition to the charge that Myerson had hired Judge Gabel's daughter in exchange for the judge's favorable treatment toward Capasso in the divorce case, Myerson was accused of obstruction of justice for allegedly trying to influence Sukhreet's grand jury testimony. While some questioned whether the case should have been brought at all, even Giuliani allies agreed that it was a critical mistake to include the seventy-four-year-old, nearly blind retired judge, who, at worst, was guilty of loving a clinically depressed daughter too much. That error was compounded when Giuliani put the erratic Sukhreet on the stand to testify against her mother. What particularly appalled many—on the jury and across the city—was Sukhreet's clandestine tape-recording of a conversation with her mother.

What also shocked some lawyers and judges was Rudy's attempt to get the judge assigned to the case, Kevin Duffy, to recuse himself. Noting that Judge Gabel and her lawyer Milton Gould had ties to Judge Duffy—Gould had once recommended Duffy's wife for a judgeship ten years earlier—Rudy argued Duffy was unfit to preside over the case. Duffy wrote an opinion in which he alleged that the cavalier prosecutor was trying "to throw a little mud and see if it sticks." Nonetheless, Duffy voluntary stepped down.

On December 22, 1988, more than a year after the indictment was announced, Myerson, Capasso and Judge Gabel were acquitted of all charges.

What perplexed Tyler most about Rudy's handling of the Myerson case was that his protégé, with whom he had worked closely for five years, never consulted him on the matter. "Rudy didn't want to hear from me about anything," he says now. "He could have called me. I don't think [the case] did Rudy any good. He was guilty of overkill." Tyler adds: "Rudy's a very insecure person in a way, and it takes security to seek advice."

Tyler felt Rudy could have also used some advice on the highly publicized racketeering and fraud prosecution of Philippine first lady Imelda Marcos, telling *Newsday* that his protégé "deserves" the criticism he received on the case. Marcos, who had been indicted by Rudy, went on trial after he left office and was acquitted on July 2, 1990 of charges that she had raided her country's treasury and invested the money in the United States.

Although he lost both the Myerson and Marcos cases, Rudy successfully prosecuted another prominent woman, the self-proclaimed "Hotel Queen" Leona Helmsley. Helmsley, who once reportedly said "only the little people pay taxes," was indicted by Rudy and convicted after he left office, in August 1989, of cheating the government out of more than $1.2 million in federal income taxes.

A former aide of Rudy's told *New York* magazine in September 1985: "He was striving hard in those times, with long range goals in mind. He wanted to achieve the Thomas Dewey identity, the gangbuster, the Eliot Ness crime fighter . . . on the running boards with the Tommy guns blazing—it's Rudy, Rudy, Rudy, bustin' the mob, bustin' Wall Street, bustin' the crooked politicians. So every time the FBI, whose people really did the grunt work, brought in a case with a big bow on it, he would insist on taking the lead. If anyone else held a press conference, he'd go nuts. *Nuts.* This man does not do a duet, he only does a solo."

Known as "The King of Queens," Donald Manes was the Queens borough president, Democratic county leader and, more importantly, indispensable political ally and friend to then Mayor Ed Koch. He commanded a de facto right of approval over every public project, land-use decision and development plan in his borough. Combining the perfect mix of negotiating skill, governmental knowledge and budgetary mastery, Manes had, by the mid-1980s, proven himself a highly effective politician. Taking deeper and deeper slices out of the multibillion-dollar city budget, Manes delivered the goods for Queens. He had even stanched the advancing decay of the Jamaica area by convincing the Social Security

Administration to station its regional headquarters there and arranging the opening of York College—Regina's longtime employer.

In the early morning of January 10, 1986, Manes was driving erratically on the Grand Central Parkway. Two police officers pulled him over. Peering into the car, they noticed the Queens borough president was bleeding from a two-inch gash on his left wrist. "I'm cut," Manes said.

Although Manes denied he had attempted suicide in January, he attempted it again two months later at home by driving an eight-inch kitchen knife into his heart. This time he was successful. Both attempts were a response to the pressure of a sudden Giuliani probe that had begun with undercover tapes in Chicago and would end with the prosecution of the city and state's most powerful Democratic boss, Stanley Friedman, Manes's secret partner in crime.

From the moment of Manes's first suicide attempt on, a scandal smoldering beneath the surface of the Koch administration erupted. The city's Parking Violations Bureau (PVB) had been accepting payoffs in exchange for collection contracts. A friend of Manes's, Geoffrey Lindenauer, was the deputy director of the bureau, and he'd shared a half million dollars in bribes with Manes. The Chicago tape opened the door because one Manes briber was also making payoffs there and talked about it to an FBI informant. Over the next two years, as the scope of the scandal was revealed, it became clear that dozens of city officials and pols were involved in a wide range of scandals.

Since Rudy had resuscitated the Southern District's public corruption unit in early 1984, its attorneys had been prosecuting a smattering of low- and middle-level officials. When the Parking Violations Bureau scandal broke, the public corruption unit went from being a remote outpost to central command center.

It was a time of unparalleled ethical turmoil in the city. One scandal after another was served up in the pages of city newspapers—with many of the details leaked by Rudy's office—and Rudy became the acclaimed antidote to a culture that groaned with corruption. In a tarnished, soulless city, he was Mr. Clean.

Three weeks before Manes's final suicide attempt, Rudy's office indicted Lindenauer on thirty-nine counts. The parking bureau's former deputy director quickly pled guilty to racketeering and mail fraud and agreed to testify against others involved in the bribery scheme. On March 26, two weeks after Manes's death, Rudy's office indicted millionaire businessman and former transportation administrator Michael Lazar and former Parking Violations Bureau head Lester Shafran. The indictment charged that Lazar and Shafran had conspired with Manes and Lindenauer to extort payoffs from companies doing business with the bureau.

On April 9, Rudy hooked the great marlin of the scandal: the Bronx boss Stanley Friedman, who had more influence over Koch's City Hall than anyone outside the administration. With a goatee and a penchant for gold chains, he was a powerful kingmaker, who had recently orchestrated the reelection of his puppet, Stanley Simon, as borough president. He was also a lobbyist with a bustling practice. In 1985, he pulled in $900,000 from various clients, most of whom did business with city government. He would exercise his muscle as a county leader to get people hired and then he would lobby them to get what he wanted. Rudy used the RICO statute to indict Friedman and the rest—defining a city agency, for the first time, as a racketeering enterprise and threatening its predators with the most severe punishment possible.

Friedman was charged with paying a $30,000 bribe in November to Manes and Lindenauer to obtain a parking bureau contract sought by Datacom Systems, Corp., a company he represented. He was also accused of attempting to bribe Lindenauer and Manes for help in acquiring a $22.7 million parking bureau contract for Citisource—a company in which he held $2 million in stock—for the manufacture of hand-held traffic ticket computers. The bribes came in the form of stock. The indictment also alleged that Friedman engineered a towing deal for the parking bureau that could have potentially raised $50 million in revenue for the city—one percent of which was to go straight into his pocket, and 10 percent into the pockets of Manes and Lindenauer.

Rudy wanted to try the case himself, but since it was going to trial at the same as the "Commission" case, he was forced to decide between the two. "The commission case could not be lost," one assistant told the *American Lawyer*. "It was all on tape. As Rudy put it, he had to make a choice between being a trial lawyer and being a disc jockey."

Friedman's lawyer, Tom Puccio, was a prime reason Rudy chose to try Friedman. Rudy thought the former Eastern District prosecutor and now celebrated defense attorney, who had been close to Rudy during the Leuci days, was gaining an upper hand with the judge in the case, Whitman Knapp, who had headed the Knapp Commission on police corruption. The two assistants who had been handling the Friedman case, Bill Schwartz and David Zornow, would not, Rudy feared, be a match for the formidable Puccio.

The other reason Rudy chose to prosecute Friedman was a churning contempt for public corruption. In 1987, he told *Vanity Fair*: "I don't think there's anybody much worse than a public official who sells his office, expect maybe for a murderer."

The Friedman trial was the climax of one of the worst scandals in New York City history. Rudy knew that if he lost, it would be viewed as a devastating personal defeat—diminishing his chances for high public office before they were even announced. It was Rudy's first big criminal trial since Podell's twelve years earlier and the first he had ever tried in such a fishbowl environment.

To protect against the possible prejudice that could accompany a monsoon of New York City press coverage, the trial was moved to New Haven, Connecticut. The relocation only led, however, to the siege of the New England college town by a swarm of cameras and reporters. Rudy suddenly found himself center stage in the most important trial of his life. The crush of publicity was dizzying. The stage lights were searing. The stakes were higher than they had ever been.

He went to New Haven with a seven-member team of assistants, FBI agents and a city Investigations Department attorney. They stayed in the Park Plaza hotel, a nineteen-story structure near the courthouse. One hotel suite became a document-cluttered rehearsal chamber where Giuliani, Schwartz and Zornow took their own witnesses through practice cross-examinations.

When Donna finished her nightly news show at WPIX, she would often rush to Grand Central to catch the two-hour train to New Haven and hail a cab to Rudy's hotel. As soon as she got to his suite, Rudy would devour her with kisses—sometimes in front of a reporter or staff. She would spend the night, often staying up early into the morning to listen to her husband run through the case. In the morning, she would go back to New York for work. A day or two later, she would repeat the strenuous commute.

At home was their first child, Andrew Harold Giuliani, born on January 26, 1986, within days of Manes's attempted suicide. Rudy had frantically worked on the PVB case throughout Andrew's first months of life. Grandma Helen, still living in Queens, family friends and a baby-sitter, cared for Andrew during Donna's frequent sojourns. Eight-month-old Andrew made one appearance with his mother and father in the New Haven courtroom, prompting Friedman to point his finger at the family parading before the cameras as evidence that he was the victim of a prosecution calculated to spur a political career.

During a lunch break after Rudy's morning cross-examination of Friedman, Donna became a supportive but forceful trial coach. The cross had not been stellar. Rudy was visibly nervous, stumbling through his own questions. His assistants held their tongues, but now, during lunch, Donna did not. She firmly told him he was faltering and needed to get his act together.

It was a sharp contrast with the events of the cross-examination lunch break of his last big trial—Podell—when a pre-planned plea agreement was used to turn

Rudy's performance into legend. His afternoon cross of Friedman was, however, more focused and productive, wearing the defendant down.

On November 25, 1986, after eight weeks of testimony and contentious cross-examinations and a blitzkrieg of press, Stanley Friedman and three others were found guilty of racketeering, conspiracy and mail fraud.

A stunned Friedman, flanked by his wife and children, returned to the theme of Rudy's ambitions. "I suggest when he throws his hat in the ring and when he announces his candidacy," he told reporters, "I hope you say somewhere along the line that maybe Stanley Friedman was right."

It was an unrivaled victory for Rudy. But it was not just Stanley Friedman's fate that he had altered. Rudy had presided over a radical transformation of the political landscape. The scope of his investigations of Koch administration scandals widened to include Congressman Mario Biaggi and Bronx Borough President Stanley Simon—who also both went to prison. By the end of Rudy's term as U.S. Attorney, he had ushered in the end of an era: the demise of Democratic machine politics in New York City.

It is customary after a major trial for the U.S. Attorney to take the assistants who handled it out to a fancy dinner to celebrate the win. But Rudy hosted no dinner immediately after Friedman. Finally, a few months later, he gathered up Zornow, Schwartz and the others. The location: a Chinese restaurant called Flower Drum. At the end of the evening, Rudy started figuring out how to split the tab, and the assistants, slightly surprised, reluctantly reached for their wallets.

In late 1987, after his four years at the helm of the Southern District, the persistent, gossip-fed speculation that had dogged him since the day he took office finally hardened into fact: Rudy Giuliani was mulling a run for the United States Senate.

Newspapers reported in early December 1987 that Rudy's resignation as U.S. Attorney was anticipated by the end of the year. Although he wouldn't officially announce his candidacy for several weeks, Rudy told the New York Times on December 3, "I think I'd be very good" as a senator, adding, "I don't have any question that I could do the job in an innovative and creative way."

The voice feeding Rudy political advice was the same nasal, Long Island purr that had landed him his current job—Al D'Amato's. Rudy had been prodded years earlier by a number of Republican luminaries to consider a run for governor—a suggestion that got little support from D'Amato, who had an unofficial, nonaggression pact with Mario Cuomo at the time. "Somewhere in that process," recalled Rudy, "his advice was, 'Do not run for governor, don't consider it, but I really think you should keep your mind open to the idea of running against Moynihan in 1988.'"

The two went out on a double date in the summer of 1987—Rudy with Donna, the separated Fonz with "a woman who works in Washington"—to discuss the Senate bid. D'Amato, who had promised to raise millions for Rudy's race, cranked on his churlish charm, making an all-out pitch for Rudy to run.

Donna echoed D'Amato's enthusiasm in subsequent talks with her husband, telling him that he "had a good chance of beating" Moynihan. Upstate was a locale in which Rudy would have a particularly good chance, Donna believed. "She said that I get along with those people," said Rudy. "We see eye to eye."

On January 11, 1988, the *New York Times* ran a story headlined: "Giuliani Says He Is Available for Senate Seat." Rudy was quoted cautioning that "I cannot leave unless I'm sure the right person succeeds me." He added that his successor "must be chosen within the next two weeks," or he would "remain in office as U.S. Attorney." He also noted that he had "been talking with Senator D'Amato about several possible candidates." A month later, however, Rudy would say that negotiations with D'Amato to find the "right person" had actually ended in early January.

The race to fill Rudy's considerable shoes was already becoming highly politicized, entangled with concerns about how two sensitive cases underway in his office would be handled if he left. The first was a sprawling bribery and racketeering probe that reached into the top levels of the Reagan White House.

The Wedtech Corporation was founded in 1965 as a small South Bronx-based machine shop by John Mariotta, a tool and die maker whose parents had emigrated from Puerto Rico. As the fledgling company, then known as the Welbilt Corporation, expanded, Mariotta hired a Rumanian immigrant, Fred Neuberger, as his partner. Billing their company as home-grown panacea for the plight of the poverty-racked South Bronx, Mariotta and Neuberger expanded Wedtech from a small machine shop into a prominent defense contractor by bribing a host of influential public officials and exploiting contracts designed for minority-owned businesses. Eventually acquiring almost $500 million in federal contracts, Wedtech plied a network of well-connected lobbyists and helpful pols, even winning a public commendation from Reagan himself.

The host of public officials recruited as Wedtech allies included D'Amato, Congressman Mario Biaggi, Bronx Borough President Stanley Simon and even former Reagan campaign manager Lyn Nofziger and White House counselor and Attorney General Edwin Meese III.

Rudy's probe—begun in early 1986 and based on a tip from an informant—was part of the office's wide-ranging investigation of Bronx politics and focused initially on local officials like Biaggi. With several top Wedtech executives pleading guilty and cooperating, Giuliani announced the indictments of Marriota, Simon and Biaggi and others in June, 1987. By then, the Giuliani probe had also uncovered the role of Nofziger, a lobbyist for Wedtech.

In February 1987, a federal panel of judges in Washington appointed prominent Washington trial attorney James McKay as an independent counsel assigned to investigate Nofziger—whose alleged influence-peddling on behalf of a variety of clients had attracted media attention. McKay's probe eventually widened to include Meese as well. Wedtech was also part of McKay's Meese investigation.

The link between Meese and Wedtech was a personal-injury attorney from San Francisco named E. Robert Wallach, who had known Meese since 1958, when they were classmates together at Boalt Hall Law School at the University of California at Berkeley. When Meese was appointed counselor to the President on January 21, 1981, he immediately threw a bone to Wallach, naming him to the Presidential Task Force on the Administration of Justice. Wallach invited a group of fifty local civic leaders to a dinner at Jack's Restaurant in San Francisco and announced that if anyone had any concerns or ideas they wanted brought to the White House's attention, Bob Wallach was the man to see.

As Rudy's probe into Wedtech expanded, his cooperating witnesses, and a trove of documents discovered in Washington, led him to Wallach. Wallach had lobbied Meese to help obtain a $32 million army contract for Wedtech. Between 1981 and 1986, the ingratiating injury lawyer received $1.3 million in fees from the company, while also collecting stock. He flooded Meese with memos and calls about Wedtech, and Meese did intervene on behalf of the company regarding the army contract.

Bob Wallach was no Stanley Friedman—but he was no Richard Wigton, either. When his friend attained high-level positions in the administration, Wallach paraded his influence with Meese like a kid flaunting a new toy. He was a sycophantic, self-promoting inside dealer, whose behavior invited investigation. Whether he committed crimes, however, was another matter entirely.

Rudy's willingness to pursue a man who had been widely described as the "best friend" of the attorney general—and, indeed, to pursue the attorney general himself—displayed a unusual independence and courage. It also required unusual discipline and judgment.

Rudy's office reeled Wallach in for the first time in late 1986, trying to get his cooperation. They kept the heat on through 1987, informing him in April that he was a target of the probe. That forced Meese to sign a recusal statement, removing himself from any matters involving his friend. If Wallach cooperated, however, it would be against Meese—and that would put Rudy's probe in direct conflict with McKay's, who had been charged with investigating Meese precisely to get the case out of the Justice Department's hands.

These concurrent investigations had been bumping against each other for some time. In a June 23, 1987 memo, McKay's deputy, Carol Bruce, complained of ongoing conflicts with the Southern District. "Over the last 2 weeks," Bruce wrote, "we have become deeply concerned and frustrated over our inability to move forward on information [about] which SDNY is taking the lead." As a remedy, she proposed that all matters relating to Bob Wallach—and two other Wedtech consultants connected to Meese, Franklyn Chinn and Rusty Kent London—be removed from SDNY and placed solely in the hands of the Independent Counsel's office. McKay could not, however, get the Justice Department to approve that switch.

When Rudy quietly moved to indict Wallach, Chinn and London in December 1987, he had to inform McKay, who raised strong doubts about the way Giuliani was handling the matter. A December 18, 1987 letter from McKay to Rudy began: "We have very serious concerns about both the timing and the content of this draft indictment." McKay was in the middle of plea negotiations with Chinn, who was, in addition to his Wedtech ties, Meese's personal investment advisor. "On Friday, December 11, you advised me that your office had decided that you now had sufficient evidence to indict Chinn, London and Wallach and that you wanted to return an indictment on December 23, 1987," McKay recounted, noting that the indictment date was subsequently moved up even further—to the 21st. "I expressed concern about the short turn-around time," complaining that Giuliani was "forcing" Chinn to make a quick decision on his plea offer. McKay said this also compromised the negotiations with Rusty London, who was Chinn's business associate and was contemplating a plea bargain.

McKay pointed out that his office's repeated requests for a copy of Rudy's draft indictment had gone ignored until the last minute and blasted Giuliani's attempts to lean on Wallach to cooperate. "I am particularly troubled by your gratuitous comments in your December 1, 1987 letter about the 'pressure' purportedly put on Wallach by your office," McKay's letter bluntly stated. Indicating that he was never made aware of the attempts to turn the heat up on Wallach, McKay wrote that "we never concluded that such 'pressure' was beneficial to [our] investigation."

Rudy brushed off McKay's objections and issued an eighteen-count indictment against the three defendants. What McKay didn't know was that Rudy was in a rush to indict Wallach, due more to his own personal—and political—calendar than any legal circumstances. Rudy wanted the Wallach matter settled before he took a long Christmas break. He planned on assessing his career options over the break, having promised D'Amato he would make a decision about the Senate race by early January. He had already scheduled meetings with political and public relations consultants—among them, Republican heavyweight Roger Ailes and famous TV ad whiz Tony Schwartz, who had worked on the 1964 Johnson campaign. Rudy also later claimed that he wanted the indictment done so that if he left, Meese couldn't install a replacement who would kill the Wallach case.

"When Wedtech got indicted," Rudy said in an unpublished interview, "and, right before Christmas. That was really the point at which I said, 'Now I can really devote some time to thinking about leaving and about running, and the timing of it.' Over the Christmas holidays I spent time looking at all these different polls people gave to me, talking to Denny about it, talking to [old Justice Department pal] Jay Waldman about it."

It was an extraordinary example of a character flaw that would brand Rudy's public persona: unmitigated, unconditional myopia. He forced the Christmas indictment of a pivotal figure in a national scandal to the consternation of an independent counsel so he could talk to campaign advisors without complications.

A couple of days before Christmas, around 9 P.M., Robert Wallach got a phone call at his San Francisco home. It was his lawyer, Ted Wells, in New York. Realizing it was midnight in New York, Wallach braced himself for bad news. Wells informed him that he had just spoken to Rudy's deputy, Baruch Weiss, who said that the U.S. Attorney's Office was prepared to indict Wallach by the end of the week—unless he agreed to travel to New York, sit down with Rudy and "tell him the criminal acts in which Meese engaged." If Wallach cooperated, Wells explained, the indictment would be reconsidered. A stunned Wallach instantly told Wells that "I wouldn't do it." He remembers that "Ted didn't urge me" to do it.

Rudy's ambush attempt to flip Wallach was, according to Wallach, inconsistent with a promise the office had made months before. He recalled Weiss reassuring Wells, "We will give you ample notice if we indict Bob Wallach." Frantic at the last-second notice, Wallach told his secretary and live-in girlfriend, Glenda Jones, that Rudy Giuliani was going to indict him. Then he broke down and wept.

In August 1989, Wallach and friends were convicted on racketeering charges. In June 1991, the conviction was overturned by the U.S. Court of Appeals when it was discovered that a key government witness had provided perjured testimony. The government retried Wallach, but on July 30, 1993, a hung jury refused to convict him, resulting in a mistrial. Seven years after the case against him began, Wallach was finally free.

The case against Wallach was always a close call. The ultimate outcome made it clear how misguided Giuliani was to allow his own personal agenda to dictate when he would decide it.

Meese seemed oblivious to the ethical compromise caused by his ties to Wallach. While the Wallach investigation was going on, Meese had offered his friend several Justice Department jobs, including a high-level position of counselor to the Attorney General. Indeed, it was only three weeks after Deputy Attorney General Arnold Burns had advised Meese to "distance yourself" from Wallach, that Meese presented his friend with the coveted counselor job. "Mr. Meese continued to support Mr. Wallach and to defend Mr. Wallach in the press, in testimony before the Congress, and in the public," said Burns. "This continued after Mr. Wallach was indicted by Mr. Meese's Department of Justice."

Criminal Division Chief William T. Weld was of the same view. He testified before the Senate that the relationship between Meese and Wallach "constituted the use of Mr. Meese's public office for the private gain of Mr. Wallach."

On March 29, 1988, Weld and Burns presented letters of resignation to Meese. They were shortly followed by the resignation of Burns's top aide, Randy Levine. They had all been Giuliani allies within Justice and would remain close associates of his for years. Giuliani's Wallach probe had in effect prompted a mutiny in the halls of justice.

Three and a half months later, on July 18, 1988, Independent Counsel James McKay concluded his fourteen-month probe by releasing a 829-page report stating that, although Meese had probably broken conflict-of-interest laws, there was "insufficient evidence" to prosecute the attorney general for taking bribes or illegal gratuities. Claiming he had been "vindicated" by McKay's report, Meese resigned in August.

Meese's worst public moment, however, would come less than a month later, during the racketeering trial of Biaggi, Simon and Mariotta. The trial became a volatile exchange with Meese's reputation pummeled by both the defense and the prosecution.

Biaggi's attorneys argued that Wedtech did not need to bribe their client and other Democratic politicians—the company, they maintained, only needed to put a call in to high-powered Reagan administration figures for help in obtaining government contracts.

Rebutting these contentions, assistant U.S. Attorney Ed Little said in his summation: "What's the defense here? It's very clear: The Wedtech officers would not have bought Congressman Biaggi [because] they already bought Ed Meese. Well, this is ridiculous. This isn't a who-dunnit case. . . . Wedtech bribed a whole ream of people. . . . There are two short answers to this 'Meese defense'," he continued. "The first is, Meese was a sleaze. The second is, Meese was a sleaze, too. In addition to these people."

Little got Giuliani's approval beforehand to use the word "sleaze" to describe Meese, an extraordinary event in the annals of federal law enforcement. On August 4, 1988, Biaggi and his co-defendants were convicted.

"The Wedtech investigation has been one of the most comprehensive and revealing investigations of corruption in history," Rudy told reporters. "It involved significant members of both political parties and businessmen willing to pay off those officials."

The other case that weighed on Rudy as he pondered a Senate run involved billionaire junk bond king Michael Milken and his corporate Leviathan, Drexel Burnham. Implicated by Ivan Boesky, Milken, the Drexel high-yield securities head, was targeted by Rudy's office along with Milken's brother, Lowell, and others in a massive, three-year, insider-trading probe. The eventual $650 million settlement with Drexel and the guilty plea extracted from Milken—obtained after Rudy had left office—were the crowning achievement of Rudy's war on Wall Street.

Rudy publicly acknowledged during his January deliberations about a Senate run that "four or five very, very sensitive investigations" were getting in the way of his possible candidacy. Wedtech was high on that list. The case that worried him most, though, was the one he had developed against Drexel and its infamous junk bond head.

A number of alarming coincidences had come to Rudy's attention linking Drexel to none other than Rudy's political patron, Al D'Amato. Milken had personally hosted a fundraising party for D'Amato in Beverly Hills, two months after the senator announced that his securities subcommittee would hold hearings on junk bond reforms. Rudy also learned that Drexel bankers had given D'Amato $70,000 in campaign contributions, as well as thousands more from Drexel clients, publicists and lawyers. Mike Armstrong, D'Amato's attorney and the chairman of the screening committee that would hand-pick Rudy's replacement, was on retainer to Drexel, representing Lowell Milken in Rudy's criminal probe.

After D'Amato refused to support Rudy's top aide, Howard Wilson, as his successor, Rudy's unease with the senator solidified into palpable scorn. When Rudy learned that D'Amato's screening panel was considering a slate of successors for Rudy who also represented Drexel clients or principals, the antipathy between the two men erupted, with each taking shots at the other.

Rudy even started carrying with him copies of the *National Law Journal* containing articles condemning his securities prosecutions that were authored by

Armstrong and Otto Obermaier, D'Amato's favored candidate to succeed Rudy. He was afraid Obermaier would scuttle his office's RICO and insider-trading investigations.

On February 8, 1988, Rudy announced that he wasn't running for Senate after all. "It would be wrong for me to leave this office now," he told reporters, "whatever the allure of another office or opportunity, because it would adversely affect some very sensitive matters still in progress."

D'Amato's interest in fielding a viable Moynihan challenger quickly evaporated. He barely raised a dime for Giuliani's substitute. Rudy stayed on as U.S. Attorney for nearly a year, leaving the post in January 1989.

The legendary legacy of the crime-crushing U.S. Attorney with the altar boy lisp suffered a few serious setbacks in the two years after Rudy left office at the start of 1989. In the spring and summer of 1991, for instance, a number of lauded victories, particularly in white-collar crime, were overturned in rapid-fire fashion, one after the other. From March to August, the Second U.S. Circuit Court of Appeals consecutively reversed or voided four major convictions—including Wallach's, the guilty verdict against Ivan Boesky associate John Mulheren for securities fraud, and stock manipulations convictions against GAF Corp. head James T. Sherwin. In reacting to the string of appeals decisions, the *Wall Street Journal* ran an editorial headlined "The Greed Decade Reversed." Giuliani's post-partum defeats fed the clamor of accusations that he had been a self-aggrandizing prosecutor more interested in media attention than justice.

A lengthy March 1989 piece in the *American Lawyer* on Giuliani's legacy as U.S. Attorney reported that in a survey of fifty-five lawyers and federal judges, "a majority voiced criticism of Giuliani and the office he has led." The article's author, Connie Bruck, wrote that a common theme of the various criticisms was an "unease" with Rudy, and "a sense of an ambition so raw and consuming that that which sustains it is embraced willy nilly."

In November 1989, Judge John Sprizzo dismissed charges in a major drug case brought by Rudy's office. He told Rudy's assistants: "There is in your office, a kind of overkill, a kind of overzealousness, which is not even—from my viewpoint as a person who has been a prosecutor—rationally related to any legitimate prosecutive objectives."

The vast majority of Rudy's famous prosecutions, however, remained intact, and his overall reversal rate was comparatively insignificant. That Rudy made a substantial impact as a prosecutor—however controversial or suspect his tactics—is irrefutable. His insatiable appetite for blockbuster cases—and his successful prosecution of the majority of those cases—badly wounded the Mafia and altered the face of New York politics. In discussing his legacy, Rudy told the *New York Times* on July 11, 1989: "I think we made cases more successfully during the period of time I was U.S. Attorney than ever before in the history of the office, and that's what did it. I don't think it's a myth-like thing. I think it's a matter of substance."

Posted on the city's official web page, a segment of Rudy's current biography covering his days as U.S. Attorney proclaims: "He spearheaded the effort to jail drug dealers, fight organized crime, break the web of corruption in government and prosecute white collar criminals. Few U.S. Attorneys in history can match his record of 4,152 convictions with only 25 reversals."

Assessing the performance of Giuliani's five-and-a-half year reign as U.S. Attorney, however, is not as simple as a roundup of his greatest hits or his greatest failures—or the recitation of one set of numbers. When his record is put to statistical scrutiny, the great legacy loses a considerable amount of luster.

The annual average number of total cases handled during the Rudy years, 9,933, increased 20 percent from his predecessor's annual average of 8,304. The rate of guilty dispositions under Rudy rose from 70 percent to 88 percent.

Those numbers, however, paint only a partial portrait. The rest of the canvas is wide open.

First of all, the 4,152 convictions that "few U.S. Attorneys in history can match" is a figure Rudy reflexively cites as proof of the stunning success of his record. While he'll admit he had twenty-five reversals, what Rudy won't mention is that, during his five-and-a-half-year term, he also had 540 acquittals. Nor does he mention that the percentage of criminal cases dismissed during his tenure nearly doubled, rising from 5.3 percent in 1984 to 10.1 percent in 1988. During the same period, dismissals in the Eastern District declined from 7.7 percent to 5.6 percent. Rudy also doesn't explain that few U.S. Attorneys serve for five and half years and simply don't have the time to rack up as many convictions. When the number of Rudy's convictions is annualized, it is, in fact, lower than that of the maligned John Martin. Rudy's office snared an annual average of 830 convictions, while Martin's got 940. In fact, an analysis of the overview data provided by the Department of Justice shows that Martin was a markedly more productive U.S. Attorney than Giuliani.

The average number of assistants during Rudy's term was 128, compared to 104 under Martin—giving Rudy a staff 23 percent larger than Martin's. The number of total cases—criminal and civil—handled by each assistant, however, during

Rudy's term, dropped from 79.9 to 77.6, a 3 percent reduction. More importantly, the annual average number of cases closed by each assistant fell, during the Rudy years, from 31 to 22.1, a 29 percent drop.

The performance of the Southern District during Rudy's tenure also pales when compared to the ten other largest U.S. Attorney's offices around the country in the same time frame. Although the Southern District had an annual average of 128 attorneys—the highest number of any office in the country—its annual rate of cases closed per assistant, 22.1, was the lowest among all the offices. The Texas Southern District had the highest closing rate, 56.2, more than double the Southern District's. Collectively, the ten other offices closed an average of thirty-four cases per assistant, 54 percent higher than Rudy's office.

The most striking comparison, however, emerges between Rudy's office and that of the U.S. Attorney for the Eastern District in Brooklyn. Although the Southern District, during the Rudy years, commanded a staff 80 percent larger than the Eastern District's, assistants in the Brooklyn-based district handled an annual average of 169 cases, 118 percent higher than Rudy's assistants. They closed an annual average of thirty-seven cases, a rate 67 percent higher than Southern District closings.

While the average annual number of civil cases handled under Rudy, 7,811, rose 33 percent over Martin, the number of civil cases closed by Rudy's office dropped by 1 percent (nationally, civil case closings rose by 7 percent during the same period). The average annual number of criminal cases handled during the Rudy years was 21 percent lower than in Martin's office, a drop from 2,428 to 1,921. The decline in the annual number of criminal case closings during the Rudy years was even deeper, from 1,339 to 972, a 27 percent drop.

In late 1984, Rudy released an annual forty-nine-page report spelling out the record of his office for 1983, a year he'd split down the middle with Martin. Annual reports had been issued at the Southern District for years, allowing reporters and others to measure the effectiveness of the office. A *New York* magazine story a few years earlier relied on the reports to document the SDNY's decline in the prosecution of public corruption cases. Giuliani's 1983 report came so late in 1984, it said the 1984 report would be available soon. But the second report wasn't released. In fact, Rudy never published another annual report. The effectiveness of his service was left to be judged by press conferences, newspaper articles and his own legendary aura.

Nine

Looking for Love
The Ed Koch Investigation

ON HIS WAY TO THE *NEW YORK POST* FORUM ON AIDS THAT AUGUST 6 morning in 1987, sixty-two-year-old Ed Koch was overwrought. The day before, while sitting with Deputy Mayor Stan Brezenoff, special assistant John LoCicero and press secretary George Arzt, he'd suddenly blurted out: "I am not a homosexual. I am not a homosexual."

"Do you know how much pain he must be in?" Brezenoff said when they left Koch's office. A mayor who lived with a shield around him—insulating his private life even in his best-selling memoir—was suddenly engulfed by the most personal innuendo. Arzt and his deputy Lee Jones were fielding persistent questions from reporters about a supposed former lover of the mayor's, Richard Nathan.

Newsday's Lenny Levitt was all over the story. So were the *Village Voice*'s Jack Newfield, the *Daily News*'s Marcia Kramer, the *Post*'s Joe Nicholson, the *Amsterdam News*'s Bill Tatum, the *New York Observer*'s Tom Robbins and even the *L.A. Weekly*'s Doug Sadownick. The delicacy of the story pushed reporters to collaborate more than compete—sharing information and jointly trying to figure out the best placement and presentation. Levitt, Newfield and Robbins lunched at a Village restaurant, Bradley's, on July 31 to discuss their mutual interest in the story. Newfield and Levitt tried unsuccessfully to convince a Nathan confidant, gay rights leader and Koch critic David Rothenberg, to reveal whatever Nathan told him about the relationship.

What few knew was that Nathan had also inexplicably become a subject of intense interest to federal investigators working for U.S. Attorney Rudy Giuliani. Unbeknownst to City Hall, the federal probe and the press inquiries had become surprisingly intertwined. All an exasperated Arzt and Jones knew was that suddenly a half dozen tough reporters were asking again and again about a Californian the mayor hadn't seen in almost a decade.

The crisis had been building since 1986, when Nathan had dinner at an otherwise empty Los Angeles restaurant with Larry Kramer, the legendary AIDS activist who'd helped launch ACT-Up and the Gay Men's Health Crisis. Nathan told Kramer about an alleged 1977–78 affair with the bachelor mayor that ended around the time Koch took office. Nathan had worked in Koch's 1977 campaign, co-chaired a health-care task force for the mayor in early 1978, and, when he did not get the post in the new administration he wanted, moved to California later that year.

A few months after his dinner with Kramer, Nathan came to New York and repeated the story at Kramer's Fifth Avenue apartment to Rodger McFarlane, the head of a Memorial Sloan Kettering AIDS program. Kramer and McFarlane made clear to Nathan their desire to "out" Koch. They were convinced Koch had failed to adequately fund the fight against AIDS for fear that too much concern might feed public suspicions that he was gay. Nathan said he "wanted to help" when he met Kramer in L.A.; but now he was hesitating. By mid-1987, Kramer, who literally held Koch accountable for the deaths of thousands, was telling anyone in the press who would listen about Nathan. He was also handing out Nathan's phone number and address.

"Someone is going to say something"—either directly about Nathan or the gay issue—Koch predicted the night before the *Post* forum. "I hope Larry Kramer doesn't stand up and shout from the audience." Jones recalls that they were collectively "concerned that a question might come up, either from Kramer or a reporter." The mayor's sexual orientation was, says Jones, "an active issue and a question about it would've greatly disturbed all of us."

Koch thought he'd made a mistake by refusing to meet with Kramer years earlier. He'd even asked his police detail to remove Kramer when a city commissioner introduced him at a 1982 party and Kramer launched into a tirade about the administration's indifference to the plague. Since then, Kramer had written a play, *The Normal Heart*, which chronicled, among much else, the failure of the Koch administration to confront the epidemic. It was after seeing that play in L.A. that Nathan approached Kramer at a political fundraiser and suggested the dinner. Koch merely regretted his Kramer rebuff as an ill-advised political error; the Nathan allegations, however, tormented him. Now the two issues were joined.

Koch had lived with the nightmarish specter of a gay news story most of his political life. When he ran against Mario Cuomo for mayor in 1977, Cuomo supporters sent sound trucks through Brooklyn streets, blaring: "Vote for Cuomo, not the homo." When asked directly—by *Playboy* and at a City Council hearing on a gay rights bill—he'd refused to answer. He'd once stated movingly: "If I were gay, I hope I'd be proud enough to admit it." Now, Koch was faced, for the first time, with a concrete charge. It was coming, at least indirectly, from a credible Harvard grad with a substantial health-consulting business who'd once been part of the inner circle that had attended regular Sunday suppers at Koch's Village apartment. Not even the spectacularly brusque Koch could easily dismiss it.

But it wasn't just the general press clamor that had City Hall uneasy about the *Post* forum. Rodger McFarlane had relayed the Nathan story to Nicholson, the *Post*'s medicine and science editor, and Nicholson had gone to Arzt with it. He'd told Arzt that "an ex-romantic interest" of Koch's was willing to go public about the relationship, but that Nicholson was not going forward with the story. "If the mayor is ever interested in telling his own story and is looking for a sympathetic ear," Nicholson added, "I hope he will think of me." The first openly gay reporter on a New York daily, Nicholson was queasy about the Kramer/McFarlane thesis that Koch's bumbling on the AIDS front required the exposé of this deeply personal liaison. But he did buy into the Kramer thesis enough to propose a question at a planning session for the upcoming *Post* forum.

A member of the panel that would question the mayor, Nicholson told his fellow panelists shortly before the scheduled breakfast event that he wanted to ask if Koch had been "hesitant" in dealing with AIDS "because he was a closet homosexual." Eric Breindel, the editorial page editor of the paper and another panel member, hotly resisted such an inquiry. Somehow word of the possible question made its way into City Hall, where the *Post*'s former bureau chief, Arzt, was now press secretary.

But Kramer did not appear at the forum, Nicholson did not ask his question and Koch, as always a jewel of a political performer, wowed one of the largest audiences to ever attend a *Post* extravaganza. On the way to the car, though, the mayor suddenly said to his aides: "I feel lightheaded." He spoke of a twinge.

Koch, Arzt and Bill Grinker, the Human Resources commissioner, got into the backseat of the city car, behind two cops, driver Eddie Martinez and shotgun Michael Aponte. They left the midtown Sheraton Hotel and headed toward a welfare center in the Bronx, with Grinker briefing the mayor on what to expect. Koch pitched forward in his seat, grabbing Martinez by the shoulder. "My speech is slurred," he said. "Turn around and take me to Lenox Hill." Aponte put the siren on. The car headed for Lenox Hill Hospital, a nearby private hospital with an excellent reputation. The irrepressible Koch paused and quipped—"or Bellevue," the closest municipal hospital. By the time they got to Lenox Hill, Martinez had to wrap his arm around the gangly, six-foot-one-inch mayor, who when he tried to stand up was bent at the waist and pointed headfirst toward the ground. The left side of his face sagged visibly.

It was the first time in Koch's life that he felt at risk. He would later say: "I had a stroke and I got out of the hospital in four days without any paralysis or diminution of my faculties. That was a miracle. And, in fact, that's what they told me. I came within a hair's breadth of being paralyzed." A doctor tried to put the best face on it, saying Koch had a "trivial stroke."

"Trivial to him," the mayor retorted. Koch would later make a point of telling Nicholson it was "a full-fledged stroke," as if the reporter's threatened question had prompted it. The mayor's prognosis, after a four-day hospital stay, was uncertain enough that Koch sent a letter to the City Clerk on September 25 delegating many of his powers to Brezenoff in case of a "temporary inability to discharge the duties of my office by reason of sickness or otherwise."

Three weeks before the Brezenoff letter, Richard Nathan flew to New York again, this time to prepare for a command performance at the U.S. Attorney's office at Saint Andrew's Plaza, a few steps behind City Hall. In a year and a half of federal witnesses beating a path from City Hall to Foley Square, none was summoned for a stranger reason than Nathan. A man who hadn't actually been to City Hall for nine years would now spend an hour and a half answering questions about a mayor he may have once known too well, at least as far as federal prosecutors in Manhattan were concerned.

His primary interrogator was Tony Lombardi, an IRS agent assigned to the Southern District at Rudy Giuliani's personal request. An investigator with unrivaled access to Giuliani, Lombardi had reached out to Nathan in August, calling him twice in L.A. "I was invited to New York to meet him. One way or another, he was going to talk to me," Nathan said in an interview years later. "I thought he would've subpoenaed me."

Nathan went with his attorney Jack McAvoy on September 9, 1987, for a 10 A.M. meeting that, as they recalled it, also included two other government investigators. McAvoy, a partner at White & Case, one of the most prestigious firms in the country, had flown up from Washington. "We were responding," he recalls now, "to contacts that were very much official and from within the office of the United States Attorney."

McAvoy says that the meeting took some time to put together after Lombardi's initial call to Nathan's home, which certainly occurred in August or earlier. McAvoy and Nathan had to discuss the issues that might come up, and Nathan decided to arrange business meetings in New York to coincide with his visit with the feds. Lombardi's daily appointment diaries list Nathan's name a couple of times in August, once with his phone number. It's unclear how Lombardi identified and found Nathan because he did not talk to Larry Kramer until a month after Nathan first appeared in the logs.

When they finally got together, they sat stiffly in an office on the one of the top floors at St. Andrew's, underneath two framed headshots of Ronald Reagan and Rudy Giuliani.

Lombardi's logs also indicate that he'd already been talking to reporters about Nathan, including an August 26 entry that read "Len Levitt re Richard Nathan." Marcia Kramer (no relation to Larry), who, like Newfield, also appeared often on Lombardi's logs, told Newfield on September 3: "I hear Nathan flew in to meet with Rudy's office," suggesting he arrived several days before the interview. Marcia Kramer, who ran the *News*'s bureau at City Hall and was talking repearedly to Arzt about the unfolding Nathan events, added, according to Newfield's notes: "Koch berserk—reason for stroke." Kramer's comment was clearly Arzt's chilling diagnosis, more a personal than medical assessment. But the sequence of events had convinced a few Koch insiders that the connection could be real.

In a book Koch wrote twelve years later, *I'm Not Done Yet*, he would observe in a half sentence that he believed "the corruption crisis precipitated my stroke." In fact, the two high points of the crisis—the Manes suicide and Friedman trial—occurred in 1986, many months before the stroke. The other major indictment, involving his Cultural Affairs Commissioner Bess Myerson, wouldn't happen until October. The scandal was in fact finally receding in August 1987. In the same book, however, Koch made a reference to the Kramer efforts to "out" him, oblique though it was. "Those who seek to 'out' people who may or may not be gay can be described as comparable to the Jew catchers of Nazi Germany," he wrote. His anger, so many years later, is a measure of just how deeply he still feels about the attempted use of Nathan.

"Lombardi really wanted to probe into things that I told him were of a personal nature," Nathan recalled. So did two L.A.-based reporters who came to his front door. So did Tatum, the owner and editor of the nation's largest-circulation black weekly, who pressed Nathan on the phone until he broke down in tears. Nathan was getting so freaked out he was reaching out to his longtime conduit to Koch, Dan Wolf, the mayor's closest friend and ever-present political adviser. He was telling Wolf—during his periodic New York visits as well—everything that was going on.

He was also talking to Arzt, Jones and Maureen Connelly, the mayor's former press secretary who'd known Nathan since the 1977 mayoral campaign. Connelly was brought in to try to calm the wiry and intense Nathan, who'd backed off his initial indication to Larry Kramer that he'd go public, but needed professional press advice on how to handle the heat he was getting. Jones said he and the forty-nine-year-old Nathan had a couple of jittery conversations: "You could tell he was not the kind of guy to go public."

By the time he met with Lombardi, Nathan was outraged and ready to fight. Described by a friend as someone who "never even discussed his homosexuality with his family," Nathan adopted a simple motto for prosecutors and press. He made it clear to Lombardi at the outset: "My private life is private." McAvoy recalls that Nathan "gave them a sermon"—declaring that he "would not answer questions about his personal life with the mayor"—and that they then backed off.

The rest of the questions from the press and from Lombardi, which closely dovetailed because they were feeding off each other, focused on a $12,800 consulting contract Nathan had received from the city in 1981. It was a no-bid deal, awarded by Brezenoff personally when Brezenoff was the president of the city's Health & Hospitals Corporation (HHC). But Brezenoff had also rejected Nathan's bid for a much larger contract in 1980, and Nathan's credentials as a management consultant were substantial. Nathan believed that the only reason so puny a contract was attracting such enormous interest—even after the statute of limitations would have made any conceivable prosecution involving it impossible—was because of the sex story that lurked behind it. The theory was that it could be portrayed as a public favor to hush up a disgruntled lover.

"My meeting with Lombardi had a two-part agenda: there were the HHC contracts, which was the above-ground agenda, and the private life, which was the below-ground agenda," said Nathan. "It was an open secret what he was chasing. You don't get summoned to New York to discuss your love life. They don't put that on a subpoena."

Lombardi, said Nathan, was "a hired gun looking for dirt. I guess he figured if he huffed and puffed loud enough, he could get something out of me." Instead Nathan threw the HHC deal in Lombardi's face, countering any thought that he "was bought off" by rattling off his consulting credits. Lombardi's "eyes began to glaze over," Nathan remembered. Lombardi had a slew of documents about the contract—including the two reports Nathan had written to earn his paltry fee. His eyes glaring at Lombardi like searchlights and his hands punctuating the air, Nathan recited in machinegun-like fashion the elaborate work he'd done, saying later: "Lombardi had zero interest in ambulatory care in Staten Island"—the subject of a Nathan HHC report.

When questioned by a reporter years later about this interview, Lombardi tried to describe Nathan as a "witness" in a "confidential investigation" unrelated to Koch's sex life and claimed that it was the consultant who wanted to talk about sex. "The guy gets on a soapbox about this pillow talk and all this crap," the investigator said. "We had to restrain this guy. He talked about Mr. A, B, C, D and E."

Though Nathan never revealed his Wolf, Arzt, Connelly and Jones conversations, he said in a subsequent interview that he didn't know if Koch was aware of Lombardi personally, "but he sure as hell must have been aware that people were out looking over his bedtime activities." Nathan also believed that Lombardi was partly responsible for the press barrage, saying: "I do think that there were some leaks." Lombardi listed Nathan in his diaries six times, with the last entry on September 20.

As soon as the references to Nathan ended, Larry Kramer's name appeared. On September 23, Lombardi went to Kramer's apartment at 1:30 P.M. Kramer visited the Southern District, apparently on September 30, for a second conversation. "It was a very friendly meeting," Kramer said of the Lombardi sessions. "I was amenable to giving them anything I knew. I was interested in outing Koch and he was interested in the contract I guess. Or he might have been interested in outing Koch too and used the contract." The second meeting was attended by an assistant U.S. Attorney (AUSA) Kramer couldn't identify and Kevin Ford, a city inspector general deputized to work with Giuliani's office on public corruption cases.

Kramer had heard of the alleged affair with Nathan even before the two met in L.A. and he'd told Nathan from the outset that he would go public with anything Nathan told him. He felt no guilt about a breach of either Nathan's confidence or any gay ethic. "Lombardi asked a lot of questions about who was gay in city government," Kramer recalled, adding that they even discussed prominent gay women as well as two gay male judges. "I was told by somebody that Koch would go every Monday night to a building in the West 20s; the implication being that was where his boyfriend lived. I told Lombardi that. I was given a list of names of everybody who lived there to see if I could recognize a name."

Lombardi listened, intently, always chewing gum. A six-footer with slicked-back, glistening black hair who always leaned forward in the direction of whoever he was talking to, Lombardi was a trained sponge. He had 163 carded confidential informants over a twenty-two-year IRS career, sucking information out of them with a beguiling you-take-care-of-me-and-I'll-take-care-of-you ease. He was so conscious of every form of surveillance he would take elaborate steps to avoid an overhear, picking a source up in his garish white Caddy and sitting silently until he was driving through a car wash. Then, with suds, water and brushes beating on the car, he'd speak in clipped sentences that were barely a whisper.

His slick suits, manicured fingernails and pocket-squared shirts mimicked those of the gangsters he'd put away. His stiff and wide walk advertised that he was "carrying" and, in between his interviews with Nathan, Kramer and others, he scooted off to the firing range more often than most other agents with accounting degrees.

The proudest part of a career that ranged from Richard Nixon's security detail to staffing the President's Commission on Organized Crime was the work he was now doing for Giuliani. Lombardi, at forty-four, had become an extension of Giuliani. Often leaving his wife and four kids alone in their Staten Island home, Lombardi would drive Rudy all over the city, babysit his kids and get him free tickets in skyboxes at Giants Stadium and Yankee Stadium.

As the only agent exclusively assigned to the public corruption unit at the peak of the municipal scandal, he and Rudy met often at the end of the workday, close to 8 P.M., when all but Rudy's closest aides were gone. His diaries contained Giuliani's phone numbers at his in-laws' California home during a 1987 vacation, and indicated he was invited to Rudy's birthday, "private" Christmas and anniversary dinners. Lombardi bragged that, when Giuliani ran for mayor a year and a half later, that he would get a top post in a new Rudy administration, predicting he might even become a commissioner.

Lombardi's spinning wheel of media contacts—his diaries named nineteen members of the New York press corps he spoke to—was a consequence of the widespread perception that he was Rudy's designated leaker. Reporters were so sure he was Giuliani's eyes, ears and, most of all, mouth they assured editors that when they had a tip from Tony, it was as solid as if it came from Rudy himself.

A Treasury Department report on Lombardi a few years later—when he was in some trouble himself—would quote him as saying that he "took his instructions from Giuliani." He told the Inspector General's office, according to the report, that he "basically did what Giuliani, his power base in the U.S. Attorney's office, wanted." Lombardi also subsequently testified in a federal grand jury that he "reported directly to Mr. Giuliani" and that "everyday I came to work I went to him to seek out what duties I needed to perform."

Even in a press interview about his Nathan and other politically sensitive probes, Lombardi later maintained: "I followed their direction on everything. There is not one thing I did that they didn't know about," referring to Giuliani and his top aides. "One way or another they would know about it."

Confronted in the same press interview about the Kramer questioning, he acknowledged he'd talked to the activist, but insisted that Kramer was a witness in a secret investigation, just like Nathan. He said Kramer's claim that they talked about Koch's reputed homosexuality was "absolute bullshit." Kevin Ford, however, said Kramer described "in gross detail" what he claimed to be first- and sec-ondhand accounts of "Ed Koch's sex life." Ford thought Kramer called and asked to come in, but Kramer and Lombardi's diaries indicate that it was Lombardi who first went to him.

Even before the interviews with Nathan and Kramer, Lombardi, Kevin Ford and an AUSA in Giuliani's office, David Lawrence, had begun questioning Herb Rickman, an openly gay aide in City Hall who'd been close to Koch for decades. In Rickman's case, however, the initial inquiries clearly *did* involve a legitimate law-enforcement issue. Lombardi, Ford and Lawrence were investigating criminal alle-gations against Bess Myerson, the former Miss America who had joined the administration as Consumer Affairs Commissioner. Rickman would ultimately become a key government witness at Myerson's trial.

One of the hottest cases in Rudy's office, it was the Myerson case that so ex-panded Lombardi's media rolodex. It would also prove to be Lombardi's biggest embarrassment in the Giuliani years. He was the agent who installed a bug on the phone of impressionable Sukhreet Gabel, allowing the government witness to tape her own, seventy-eight-year-old mother, Hortense, a state judge ultimately charged by Giuliani with fixing a divorce case for Myerson's boyfriend. Testimony about the taping helped turn the Myerson trial into pathetic theater and soured the jury, leading to one of Rudy's biggest prosecutorial losses.

The first of dozens of times that Rickman appeared in Lombardi's diaries was a June 15 lunch. It's unclear when Lombardi and his colleagues began discussing Koch's sex life with Rickman, but he says now that "it came up six or seven times over the course of months of witness preparation." A former Southern District AUSA, Rickman was initially considered "a potential subject" in the Myerson probe, according to Ford. But he quickly convinced the prosecutors, as he puts it, that he "was clean," and began boasting in City Hall about how well he was get-ting along with them.

Although he had been a frequent social companion of the mayor's, Rickman's enthusiastic cooperation with the Myerson investigators drove a wedge between him and the embattled Koch. It didn't help that Rickman came back to City Hall from one of his frequent visits with the prosecutors and told a top Koch aide: "Get ready for the next round. These guys are saying stories are coming on Ed and the whole homosexual issue. Reporters are coming to them." The comment fueled the Nathan fears already consuming the mayor.

"There was a great deal of candor going back and forth," Rickman says of his talks with Lombardi, Lawrence and Ford. "They never pushed me against the wall. They would mention it and drop it. I knew it wasn't proper; it wasn't germane. I said you're going outside the confines of my testimony. Lawrence's line was 'we need to prepare for any surprises' on cross-examination." Rickman said Lawrence, another close Giuliani aide, raised the issue more often than Lombardi.

"They also told me about leaks coming out on this issue from everywhere," Rickman said. "When I heard Larry Kramer's name, I bristled. They mentioned he'd been calling them. I thought this was no longer kosher. I was surprised assistant U.S. attorneys were going into that." Asked when the three began raising Koch's sexuality, Rickman said: "Almost from the start, they got involved in the whole question of cross-examination surprise."

Ford denied that they'd probed Rickman about sex-life matters, but added: "We had a series of meetings with Herb in which he would talk about the mayor's personal life and how it would be played out in the press and things that were being said, that sort of thing. Most of it had no particular relevance for what we were doing." The logs also contain several references to a Rickman assistant at City Hall, David Mack Gilbert, who was a gay activist hired by the administration to act as a liaison to gay groups. First listed on the diaries in August—the peak moment of the sex inquiry—he did not tell Rickman he was talking to Lombardi. Gilbert has since died, but Rickman says he had no involvement in any Myerson matter.

Lombardi even began calling a former commissioner of business development, Larry Kieves, who'd been dumped in 1986 in a grand display of Koch intolerance of ethical conflicts (he'd made a small investment in a company that did business with his agency). Listed four times in Lombardi's logs, starting within days of the Nathan interview, he was finally questioned at the Southern District in the late afternoon of October 22. The ostensible purpose of the interview was that Rickman had referred Sukhreet Gabel to his agency for a possible job, a matter certainly relevant to the Myerson case (a city job for Sukhreet at Myerson's agency was the bribe charged in the indictment).

"Then they said they wanted to move on to other things," said Kieves, who was also questioned by "two or three guys" but was never used as a witness at the Myerson trial. "They started asking other weird questions. It was a free-form search of who I knew and what I knew and they certainly left me with the impression that they were interested in Koch's sexual preference. Did I think Ed Koch was gay, they asked. I thought it was odd." It did not occur to the heterosexual Kieves that he might have qualified for this rather special Southern District inquiry simply because he was thirty-nine and single.

In addition to the four who confirmed the sex-life questioning, Lombardi's diaries for the same period include several other Koch associates close enough to know about his personal life. Dan Wolf was listed in mid-March 1988, as was his home address (Lombardi usually spelled out the location of meetings in his logs, whether at "SDNY" or outside). Kramer told Lombardi that it was Wolf who convinced Nathan not to go public with the affair. Henry Stern, the Parks Commissioner, was brought in for questioning the same day as Kramer that September (he "can't recall" it). Victor Botnick, the mayor's top health adviser who had trekked out to California to see Nathan at city expense, appeared on the logs on April 8, with his high-profile Washington criminal attorney, Andy Lawler. Botnick was a top HHC official overseeing the consulting work Nathan had done. In addition to this meeting, Lawler's name pops up elsewhere in 1987 and 1988.

As Lombardi put it: "We called in a number of people who would, I think, have a sensitivity about their background. And we would do the best not even to talk about it. Who the hell cares what their sexual persuasion was?" Ford added that he, Lombardi and Lawrence "spoke to a number of people who were involved with the letting of Nathan's contract." Botnick was also grilled, according to Ford, about a threat against Rickman that Botnick supposedly heard from Myerson and relayed to "both Rickman and Koch." Botnick raised the eyebrows of the sexually vigilant trio by confirming Myerson's threat, Ford said, and volunteering that "he was in Koch's bedroom when he called Rickman" to tell him about it. The innuendo of the location stuck in Ford's mind even though the thirty-three-year-old Botnick was married, with a three-year-old. Part of Koch's guarded private world since high school, Botnick was frequently described as the mayor's surrogate son.

When the Lombardi team asked Koch about the Myerson threat—and Lombardi did list three interviews with the mayor in his diary, including one in Gracie Mansion the same day as a Kramer session—the mayor insisted he'd spoken to Botnick by phone. Koch was questioned because he would also become a government witness in the Myerson trial, though a far less eager one than Rickman.

Once Nathan drew his line in the sand on sex, Lombardi never reached out for him again. The contract was such a transparent excuse they never even questioned Brezenoff, the man who had awarded it. All he remembers is putting together a package of documents on the Nathan deal to respond to "press implications of a quid pro quo."

Throughout the time that Lombardi et al. were gathering intelligence about the mayor's predilections, the logs indicate his constant exchanges with Giuliani: five entries in September; more in October. The Lombardi probe took a vacation when Giuliani briefly considered a run for the Senate against Pat Moynihan at the end of 1987 and beginning of 1988, but it resumed in March, when Giuliani had clearly refocused on a probable mayoral run.

On February 8, Giuliani announced that he wasn't running against Moynihan and the *Times* speculated that Giuliani "may be waiting to run for mayor next year" against Koch. "I guess we scratch off the Senate," Giuliani said. "Other offices in the future, it's silly for me to speculate." The *Times* reported that "early soundings by Giuliani" had revealed his name recognition and reputation "were greatest in New York City and that there were decided weaknesses among upstate conservative Republicans."

Bill Lynch, who was deputy to Manhattan Borough President David Dinkins, recalls two meetings he had at the Vista Hotel in the spring and summer of 1988 with Marty Benjamin, a close friend of Giuliani's. Benjamin was feeling out Lynch about the possibility of his taking on a managerial position in what he said was Giuliani's planned mayoral race. The city's top black political operative, Lynch was viewed as a valuable asset in winning the anti-Koch black vote in 1989. Lynch says that Benjamin and he planned a third meeting in the fall, with Peter Powers and Rudy, but by then Dinkins decided he was interested himself. Lynch wound up managing Dinkins's campaign.

Giuliani said in December that he had been talking with Staten Island Borough President Guy Molinari and others about entering the mayoral race "for four or five months." He told the callers that he had "not ruled out the option of running for mayor," but could not say more while U.S. Attorney. The Lombardi probe of Koch occurred against this background of beneath-the-surface mayoral interest, but it never led to the big-bang story that might've knocked Koch out of the race.

Newsday's Lenny Levitt anguished over doing a story, but decided not to. Bill Tatum, who wrote a weekly diatribe in the *Amsterdam News* demanding Koch's resignation, was so moved by Nathan's tears, and the quality of the reports Nathan wrote for the city, that he dropped the story. The *L.A. Weekly* published a meandering, analytical piece on October 9 headlined: "Mayor Ed Koch: Is He Gay?" It didn't name Nathan, but cited an unspecified person who supposedly had a relationship with Koch, citing Kramer and others.

The *Village Voice* followed a week later with another tepid analysis of the link between Koch's reputed sexuality and AIDS policy. It named Nathan, though, explored his HHC contracts and reached no hard conclusions about the relationship or Koch's sexuality. Throughout 1988, especially during the Myerson trial in the fall, the air was filled with talk of possible revelations about Koch's sex life. Myerson's public threats, suggesting she had information that could lead to "the downfall" of the Koch administration, were coupled with rumors about Koch's "Westhampton gay trysts," which Lombardi fed. Koch and Rickman had visited Myerson at a Westhampton summer estate.

Unbeknownst to Lombardi, he himself was, by October 27, 1987, the subject of a criminal investigation. The IRS Inspector General had opened a probe of his relationship with Arnold Herman, a New Jersey businessman who had a big tax problem. Lombardi's name surfaced in tapes made by a wired informant who was talking to Herman. A friend and confidential informant of Lombardi's for almost twenty years, Herman would eventually plead guilty to tax charges.

He testified that he had lent the agent $7,000 that was never repaid, sold the Cadillac and another car to him at a discount, paid for Lombardi's Giants season tickets for fifteen years and, on about twenty occasions, arranged and paid for rooms for Lombardi at two New Jersey hotels. IRS rules prohibit agents from having any type of financial relationship with an informant. Herman, supported by the tapes, alleged that Lombardi provided "inside information" to him on the IRS handling of his own tax problem.

On November 30, 1988, Herman had a taped conversation with his co-conspirator in the tax scam, unaware that his associate was wired and cooperating with the government. So intrigued by his friend Lombardi's work that he actually visited the then ongoing Myerson trial, Herman related his own version of the probe of Koch's sex life:

HERMAN: There's more to it than Bess Myerson.
JOE GIAMBATTISTA: Oh, really? Oh that's what you're not reading about.
HERMAN: There's more to it than Myerson, they're trying to nail Koch.
JOE: He seems so clean.
HERMAN: They don't want to understand that, so now they're saying well he's gay, he's got a lover, oh so what, who gives a shit. Does that make him better or worse or whatever?
JOE: So long as he doesn't get AIDS.
HERMAN: I say this to you very honestly, I say Lombardi what's the big deal but on the other hand, you know, he looks at it, like, this is his job.

On January 11, 1989, two weeks after Myerson, Gable and Capasso were acquitted, Rudy Giuliani announced that he was leaving the U.S. Attorney's office. As Koch had been publicly predicting since October, Giuliani would soon declare his candidacy for mayor. No gay story had appeared to drive Koch from the race, and none hung in the offing. He said he would seek a fourth term, a decision he said he had reached in the aftermath of the stroke, when he had found an inner strength.

Dick Nathan concluded that what he called "Subject X"—the not-too-veiled purpose of his SDNY interrogation—"was exposing Ed Koch in order to win for Giuliani the mayorship of the City of New York." Nathan died in July 1996 at the age of fifty-eight. The self-made millionaire left a $2.5 million estate, most of which he gave to nonprofit organizations. His will said the goals of his bequest were "to promote increased understanding of the nature of homophobia and the irrational fear, hatred and rejection of gay persons, their lives and their values." A secondary purpose was to "foster positive attitudes with regard to being gay among gay persons themselves." Like Nathan, Rickman looks back now at the sex inquiry as something done "purely for Rudy's political purposes." Even Larry Kramer, who concedes that "there wasn't anything" he wouldn't have done to get Koch, sees the probe now as "heinous, in the clear light of day."

"They were trying to get blackmail stuff on Koch," Kramer concluded. In a book that Koch co-authored with New York's Cardinal John O'Connor and published in early 1989, he referred to the *L.A. Weekly* and *Village Voice* pieces about Nathan and his sex life. He also recounted how Kramer had "decided he would bait me, cause me anguish or destroy me by denouncing me as homosexual." Koch said his staff was "more pained than I was" by the Kramer strategy, but that none of the regular press picked up on "this objectionable material." Since the incident occurred, he noted, at the time of Democratic presidential candidate Gary Hart's public sexual escapade, it was "to the credit of the New York press" that it did not publish the Kramer charges.

"I have been in 24 elections beginning with 1962," Koch wrote, clearly conscious of the campaign that was about to begin. "In every single one of those elections, my opponent would seek to defame me by spreading the rumor that I was gay." He said he decided that "people could think whatever they wanted to. My sexuality, just like my religion, is a private matter."

But in March, with Giuliani an all-but announced opponent, Koch suddenly claimed in a radio interview, for the first time ever: "It happens that I'm heterosexual." At a press conference the next day, he denied he'd made the statement on the eve of the race to defuse the issue. His aides were alarmed at this voluntary revival of the controversy, but the Nathan/Kramer hubbub had never died down in Koch's head and, as he faced his fateful final election, it haunted him.

The Lombardi sex probe contaminated an office Rudy had revered and, in many ways, uplifted. It was the ugly flip-side of the corruption prosecutions that had brought down the party pillars of the Koch regime, Manes and Friedman. It was also a harbinger of the dirty tricks operation to come. Lombardi's work was hardly done. The race for mayor had barely begun.

T e n

In John Lindsay's Footsteps

O<small>N</small> M<small>AY</small> 17, 1989, R<small>UDY</small> G<small>IULIANI</small> <small>ANNOUNCED FOR MAYOR.</small> A <small>WEEK</small> shy of his forty-fifth birthday, he was finally a candidate for something other than class president. It wasn't the office he'd always imagined, but it was the right stage—a fight to rule the world's grandest city fit him just fine.

He wrote his speech himself—in longhand on a yellow legal pad —just like he'd done his homework at Bishop Loughlin. In fact, he returned to Loughlin to give the speech. It had such a Kennedyesque cadence and message, his college girlfriend Kathy Livermore would have felt at home with it. It came out of him as naturally as a bedtime story for his three-year-old son, Andrew. Everything his church had taught him in sixteen years of Catholic education about the corporal works of mercy and a reverence for service found its way into this memoir of hope. Everything his law enforcement career had taught him about the power of evenhanded justice and government's duty to defend found its way into this statement of strength. It was a summation—not of trial evidence—but of the best in his own life.

Homelessness is not a matter merely of statistics and economics, it is a matter of conscience. Each time the administration attacks those less fortunate by exaggerated and cruel characterizations, New York loses a bit of its soul.

We must recognize that the problem of homelessness is not one problem but many. Some of the homeless are mentally ill. Others are drug addicts. But many more simply are people who can no longer afford a place to live.

New York must encourage a system of smaller and more tailored facilities to help the homeless rejoin society quickly and productively. . . .

189

Corruption in New York must be confronted and confronted directly.

As a candidate for mayor and as mayor I am seeking support on one basis and one basis alone—that you agree with me that honest, decent and effective government must be restored.

If you offer support or money expecting any special deals, forget about it, save your money.

Let me repeat it one more time—no deals for jobs, no deals for contributors.

If you are now receiving special favors to which you are not entitled, you had better be willing to give them up or you better redouble your efforts to defeat me. . . .

Most of my career has been spent in law enforcement. No one is more qualified to lead New York in the fight against crime.

As mayor I will instill a sense of fear in those who commit serious crimes...

This is the city of my roots.

It is in my heart and it is in my soul.

My grandparents and my father are buried in the soil of this city.

All of my past draws me to take on this challenge, to restore the city of my grandparents and parents, of my relatives and my friends and to offer New Yorkers hope for the future once again. . . .

Rudy opened the day at the noisy and sweltering Metropolitan Republican Club on the Upper East Side, delivering his thirty-minute speech in the large meeting room where Fiorello La Guardia announced for mayor in 1933. A three-term mayor whose name is synonymous with the city, La Guardia was one of three Republicans to win City Hall this century. He beat the Democrats as a fusion candidate—merging the Republican line with other small, independent parties and forging, said Rudy, "a movement by people of every political stripe to kick out an old, tired and corrupt administration." Giuliani said he would do the same. Taking no questions, he, Andrew and a pregnant Donna headed on a campaign bus to appearances in every other borough—Loughlin in Brooklyn, an evangelical church in the South Bronx, and predominantly Catholic sections of Queens and Staten Island.

Several of the early campaign speeches that followed—and the detailed eleven-page program on the homeless and nine-page program on AIDS—were far more liberal and daring than those of any of the four Democrats then running in a party primary. After opening with a quote from Bobby Kennedy, Giuliani's July 23 speech on race relations used the mob stereotyping of Italian Americans as a parallel for the street-criminal stereotyping of blacks, finding common ground for ethnic victims who are often antagonists. "The truth," he said, "works for blacks—as well as for Italian Americans."

Promising "a government of inclusion" and an "end to alienation," he made a commitment to "recruit and bring into government blacks, Latinos, Asians and women . . . so that everyone sees a direct connection to the governing of this city." Calling for "an end to the shame of racism," he said he would establish a Mayor's Council for Racial and Ethnic Harmony, strengthen the New York City Human Rights Commission, push for stiffer penalties for discriminatory conduct, make a "real city investment" in what he called "neighborhoods of opportunity," expand the City Youth Corps, and establish a Mayor's Championship Series for little leagues and other baseball programs.

A week later, he offered a rationale of why he was moving from the U.S. Attorney's office to City Hall in a speech at St. John the Divine titled "A City That Cares." A prosecutor, he said, "cannot ease crushing poverty, or end homelessness, or treat drug addicts, or help people with AIDS. But a mayor can. And a mayor must."

"Our city had to be sued to open emergency shelters for homeless men," he said in one of his repeated attacks on the heartlessness of the Koch administration. "And sued again to shelter homeless women. And sued once more to house homeless families. What kind of leadership leaves the governing of our city to the courts? Common decency, conscience, commitment compels us to do better." Citing the need for shelter, permanent housing, drug treatment and "an agenda driven by compassion and commitment," Giuliani said that "government's crucial role in helping people over the pains and difficulties of life" was its "most noble" purpose.

"I will face these problems as a challenge to my conscience," he said, "and the conscience of our city to help our fellow human beings." He visited shelters in the dead of night with Bob Hayes, the lawyer whose suits had forced the Koch administration to agree to a right to shelter. "I watched him walk through a sea of beds," Hayes recalled their visit to the 1,000-bed Washington Heights shelter for homeless males. "Homeless guys recognized him. He was connecting. He greeted them, talked to them, listened and this was a crowd of 90 percent African Americans. They recognized him. They seemed to like him. It was a good feeling to take him around. He was engaging."

Hayes said they spent three or four half days together, that Rudy "very much wanted me to meet his wife" and was "very excited about making change, getting her involved." The homeless plan Giuliani later announced was drawn from Hayes's blueprint. The two also toured some of the street and subway camps where the homeless gathered, and Rudy began listening as well to the television journalist who'd given homelessness its human face, WNBC's Gabe Pressman.

In an unpublished interview taped in the spring of 1989, Giuliani spoke of "the need to open hundreds of small shelters, intermediate and small term," saying you might have to "break a thousand" by the time "you're finished." With these small shelters replacing "the barracks," he said, a mayor would "have to exercise some political leadership and courage" to overcome community resistance and locate them fairly all across the city."

"It's not easy to overcome some of the stereotypes of homeless people, but I think it can be done," he said. "I think you can call on the things that are better in people. You can ask people to do things that are painful if you can show people a way to resolve this problem."

He accused Koch—in interviews before his announcement—of "beating up on homeless people." He said Koch's description of them as drug addicted and mentally ill was an example of "trying to make political points by using harsh words." Instead he tried to use his law enforcement credentials to legitimize and decriminalize the homeless, saying in one speech that it was "the advocates for doing nothing" who "dramatically exaggerate the number of homeless who are criminals or mentally disturbed."

He even tried to present his long-standing support of the death penalty through a liberal prism. In a *New York* magazine interview with Joe Klein published just before his announcement, he said, "I'm in favor of the death penalty in cases of aggravated crime—the murder of a law enforcement officer, mass murder, a particularly heinous killing. I think it should be imposed only in cases where there is a certainty of guilt well beyond a reasonable doubt." He told Howard Kurtz in the *Washington Post:* "The death penalty is an irrelevant issue," refusing to play what he called "the death penalty game" even though the vetoes of two consecutive Democratic governors had made it a proven vote-winner in city and state politics.

One of his first campaign dinners was with David Dinkins, the African-American borough president of Manhattan who was running against Koch and others in the Democratic primary. Giuliani asked for the dinner, saying he wanted an understanding with Dinkins that if they opposed each other in the fall, the campaign would not be "between an Italian-American and an African-American," but "between two New Yorkers, two concerned public servants, each offering their own vision of the city's future."

As with so much else Rudy did that spring and summer, however, the approach to Dinkins was geared to building bridges with a potential November ally in the general election race that Giuliani had always expected: a head-to-head with Koch. With Koch saying that Jews would have to be "crazy" to vote for Jesse Jackson in New York's 1988 presidential primary, he had so alienated himself from black voters that Giuliani expected to carry this core Democratic vote in November. Had Koch won the primary, Dinkins's campaign manager Bill Lynch was considering playing a role in Giuliani's November effort, independent of his 1988 conversations with Giuliani pal Marty Bergman. Efforts on Rudy's behalf were made to reach out to anti-Koch black leaders like Congressman Major Owens.

The emphasis on the homeless was a calculated attempt to position himself to the left of Koch on an issue that, for the moment, was profoundly affecting moderate and liberal Democrats.

The unwillingness to pander on the death penalty was a reminder of how Candidate Koch had milked it in the 1977 mayoral run against Mario Cuomo.

The commitment to inclusion was in contrast with a twelve-year Koch record of minority exclusion.

The "guarantee" of "drug treatment on demand" was an impassioned rebuke of Koch for the drug explosion on his watch, offered repeatedly as a gentle complement to the law enforcement focus on drugs everyone expected of him.

Certainly the ethics rap that Giuliani did everywhere—"we've had a mayor for too long who has kept his eyes closed, his ears clogged and his mouth gaping when corruption has been unearthed in his administration"—was a direct hit on Koch.

Even in his seminal announcement speech, he targeted Koch alone among the five other candidates in the race: "If you're happy with the way things are," he said, "re-elect Ed Koch."

The assumption of the Giuliani candidacy from the outset was that he had to marshal the support of disaffected liberal Democrats—turned off by the scandals and polarization of the Koch years—to defeat a renominated mayor in a tough November battle. Roger Stone, a Republican political strategist, observed later: "Giuliani was perfectly positioned to beat Mayor Koch," adding that in a race against the incumbent, "the liberal-black-Latino coalition would have opened up to Rudy the Reformer, simply because he was not Koch."

So Giuliani never mentioned his Republican roots in his announcement or any other early major speech or commercial. Instead, he fixated on gaining the endorsement of the Liberal Party, a once influential third party founded by labor leaders Alex Rose and David Dubinsky in 1944, when the Communist left took over the other progressive party with ballot status in New York, the American Labor Party. The Liberals had twice helped elect the only prior Republican mayor in the second half of the twentieth century, John Lindsay, endorsing him, together with the GOP in 1965, and alone in 1969. It had not endorsed a mayoral winner since, though it had lent its ballot line to Hugh Carey and Mario Cuomo, the two Democratic governors who'd ruled the state since 1974. It stuck with Democrats in state races to assure itself of the 50,000 votes a party must get in a gubernatorial election to maintain its automatic line on the ballot.

By 1989, the patronage-starved party, at temporary odds with Cuomo and hated by Koch, had become little more than a one-man unincorporated business, headed by lawyer/lobbyist Ray Harding. A six-figure rainmaker at a wired law firm after leaving a post on Hugh Carey's personal staff, Harding had a tempestuous relationship with Cuomo that cost him the inside track. He was, by 1989, a struggling sole practitioner in search of a new public benefactor. As skeletal as the party was—with only 23,479 members in the city, less than 1 percent of the city's registered voters—its designation could still make a Republican candidate more acceptable to the city's otherwise solidly Democratic electorate.

With Democrats outnumbering Republicans 5 to 1, and President Bush gaining only 33 percent of the city's vote in 1988, Liberal endorsement was indispensable to a Giuliani candidacy. Had Rudy faced Koch, the Liberal nomination would have been a "master stroke," said Roger Stone, because it would've given the minority/progressive coalition "a justification for backing Rudy," to say nothing of a ballot line where they could comfortably vote for him.

The party, however, had never endorsed a pro-death penalty candidate for mayor or governor. In fact, the death penalty was a major reason for its rejection of Koch in each of his four previous runs for mayor. The Liberals' other implacable principles were an opposition to tuition tax credits or any other form of publicly subsidized parochial education, and an unambiguous commitment to abortion rights. If Harding was to steer his party behind a death-penalty candidate, Giuliani would have to at least appear to support these other two core values.

That meant Rudy had to make choices that satisfied either the Liberals or his Catholic base. He attempted to position himself on both issues in ways that met Liberal needs, but Harding was so palpably eager to back him, he thought he had enough leeway he could fudge it. He became so awkward, especially on abortion, his wavering statements confounded voters. Since his conversion was forced, he did not voluntarily mention abortion in any major speech or policy statement until he addressed a women's organization in late September, dealing with it only when pressed by reporters or advocates.

The tuition tax credit issue rarely came up at all, but when it did, he initially clouded his opposition with a caveat, but eventually dumped any hedge and said straight out that any such credits "would encourage people to take their kids out of the city school system."

His "one thumb up–one thumb down" abortion ambiguity, however, became a singular disaster. Giuliani wanted to become the first candidate ever endorsed by both the Liberals and their ideological opposite, the Conservative Party, a 1966 pro-life invention of the anti-Rockefeller right that was a force in state politics, aligned with the GOP, but with little clout in the city. Giuliani first had eight courting dinners and lunches with the rotund Harding, whose party maintained a small, seedy midtown office near Manhattan's finest restaurants. Once confident he'd sealed that ballot line, Giuliani rode out to the Bay Ridge section of Brooklyn to visit Mike Long, the Conservative Party state chair who owned a liquor store right around the corner from the party's state headquarters. He wined and dined Long and the five county leaders of the party from the city.

Giuliani told the Conservatives he was "personally opposed to abortion, did not favor government funding or criminal penalties, did favor an exemption in cases of rape or incest, and was in favor of overturning Roe vs. Wade." Long then announced that Rudy's views were "acceptable" to the leaders, whose party had slightly fewer city members than the Liberals, and Harding went temporarily ballistic. For a few hours one March morning, Harding told a reporter he now had "irreconcilable differences" with Giuliani. He said Giuliani's announced opposition to funding "would mean that a poor woman would be treated differently than one who could afford an abortion."

Harding added that in his own rambling conversations with Rudy, he'd never specifically asked about funding. Instead he'd merely extracted a pledge that Giuliani wouldn't impose his personal opposition to abortion on city policy and would "administer whatever the law required." Harding logically read Giuliani's Conservative Party comments to mean that he would decline to provide the city's share of Medicaid-funded abortions or might refuse to permit municipal hospitals to perform them.

When the reporter called Giuliani for reaction, he instead called Harding, and explained that he was merely telling the Conservatives how he'd vote if he were a member of Congress or the legislature, a curious thing to do while seeking their support for mayor. He assured Harding that, as mayor, he'd use city funds to pay for abortions and let city hospitals do them. He added that while he favored overturning Roe, if it ever happened, the state's 1970 pro-abortion law would automatically become effective and he'd abide by it. Harding then called the reporter back, said it was he who'd "improperly drawn an inference" from the Conservative quotes, and announced that his problems with Giuliani had been "straightened out."

The flirtation with the outraged Conservatives was over; rubberband Rudy had discovered that even he wasn't elastic enough to stretch across the full length of the city's political spectrum.

So, on Saturday, April 8, with polls putting Giuliani from 10 to 20 points ahead of Koch, Harding hosted a morning press conference in a tiny ballroom at the Intercontinental Hotel. The unannounced candidate happily accepted the endorsement. "I would uphold a woman's right to abortion. It's a constitutional right, a legal right," he said, simultaneously dismissing the death penalty as a "phony" issue in a mayoral race. Harding included affirmative action, gay rights and gun control—as well as abortion and tuition tax credits—among the issues that brought the party and Giuliani together.

Koch charged that the Liberals "sold themselves and sold themselves cheap," insisting that they would ordinarily "throw themselves off buildings before they would surrender" on death penalty and abortion issues, and insisting that Giuliani opposed them on both. Calling it a "patronage party," Koch said, "They've been shut out, they say, from New York City jobs. They've been shut out, they say, from state jobs, and they want to come back in, so they have attached themselves to Rudolph Giuliani." The patronage hunger of the party was so transparent that even John Lindsay, who'd long ago left politics and was a practicing attorney, told a reporter in May, that the Liberals are "always worried about stuff like patronage."

Giuliani, however, apparently oblivious to the party's well-known appetite, chose the Harding press conference as the setting to promise an end to patronage in a Rudy regime. Raising the specter of the Talent Bank—a Koch patronage mill probed by prosecutor Giuliani—he vowed: "There will be no Talent Bank operating in the basement of City Hall if I'm elected mayor." Standing beside Rudy with a few other party leaders—at least two of whom, Frank Marin and Fran Reiter, wound up with top appointments in the eventual Giuliani administration—Harding could only manage a tight-lipped smile. Both of his sons would also win major Giuliani posts, and he would become a millionaire lobbyist at the Giuliani trough.

Harding was so wired into the clubhouse network Giuliani deplored that he'd borrowed $5,000 from Bernard Ehrlich, a lobbyist convicted in the Wedtech case, visited his old friend Stanley Friedman in prison in September 1988 and was still talking by phone to Friedman at the time of the endorsement. A few years earlier, Harding had rushed an early congressional endorsement of another soon-to-be

Giuliani felon, the very conservative Mario Biaggi, in order to convince a congressman with a liberal record, Jonathan Bingham, not to challenge him in their reapportioned Bronx district.

In a poisonous dispute with Mario Cuomo throughout the mid-'80s, the party leader with the license plate "Mr Lib" on his 1985 Caddy had actually only been back in control of the state party a couple of years. The dispute had gotten so bad that Harding had even helped prompt a criminal probe of the governor's son Andrew. Harding let it be known that Cuomo was now threatening not to run in 1990 on the Liberal line if the party backed Giuliani, a possible death blow to the party.

Harding defied that threat to roll the dice with Giuliani, knowing that the party's mayoral support was window dressing for a Democrat, but defining for a Republican. If Giuliani won, Harding would be a kingmaker, and jobs and contracts, he understood, are the coin of any realm. Cuomo, of course, wound up running on the line in 1990, and he and Harding eventually grew so comfortable with each other that son Andrew was honored at an annual party dinner in the 1990s.

The abortion issue, however, continued to dog Giuliani and embarrass Harding. When the U.S. Supreme Court ruled in July that states could limit abortion rights, Giuliani told reporters who pressed him at a July 4 parade that he would not lobby Albany to preserve the current state law if elected mayor. "I have a different moral view about abortion than the other candidates do and I would not be able to do that," he said, standing amidst a crowd in Bay Ridge again, the same heavily Italian neighborhood where he made the February comments that got him in such hot water.

When the New York Pro-Choice Coalition ranked Giuliani below all the Democratic candidates in August, he issued a statement "clarifying" his position again. This time he said he "will oppose reductions in state funding" for abortion, as well as "oppose making abortion illegal." He would not let his "personal views interfere with his responsibilities as mayor."

Every newspaper branded it a "flip-flop" and Koch said: "You shouldn't run from your conscience because you're afraid to lose an election." Dinkins charged: "It was interesting that he is able to alter his position on such a matter of basic principle in so short a period of time."

Giuliani himself would subsequently concede that he'd butchered the abortion issue in the campaign, but his hindsight analysis was purely cosmetic. He told the Post's Jack Newfield in 1992, while positioning himself for a second run: "I made a terrible mistake on abortion last time. I should have said I was pro-choice and stopped. But I spent so much time explaining the ideology and theology of how I reached my opinion, nobody understood what I was saying." The vulnerability study Giuliani commissioned for the 1993 campaign concluded that "most voters" in 1989 "seemed to think all the explaining by Giuliani meant he was just another pro life male politician trying to explain how he wasn't anti-woman."

The truth is that Giuliani did undergo a political transformation on the issue—utterly reversing 1987 positions like "I don't think abortion should be freely available" and "I would vote against public funding for it." He approached abortion as if it was merely one more policy arena—susceptible to polling, networking and endless readjustment. Though he constantly talked about it as a personal matter, he never searched inside for any authentic belief, or took a stand that resembled conviction.

He sat in the homes of friends and tried to figure out what the electoral market might bear. Even a favorably disposed journalist like Dan Collins wound up writing that Rudy did "more head spinning" on abortion "than Linda Blair in *The Exorcist.*" All his cheap manipulation and marketing came through to voters, and diminished him.

Rudy's other pre-primary break with the Liberal Party, as well as the liberal general electorate he hoped to appeal to in November, was on gay rights. When Koch announced a plan to grant a few days of bereavement leave to gay couples and unmarried heterosexuals who work for the city, Giuliani blasted it as "an ill-conceived political giveaway." He cited current budget problems as the reason for his attack and ridiculed "the highly questionable" expansion of benefits "that appears to include college roommates."

He also criticized a state court decision the same day that upheld the right of a nonmarital domestic partner—a gay man in the appellate case—to inherit his or her deceased partner's rent-stabilized apartment, just as a marital spouse would. Giuliani assailed the decision because it appeared "to make a gay couple a family unit." He even refused to march in the Gay Pride Parade and opposed a citywide registry for domestic partners, as well as health benefits for municipal workers who met a partnership standard.

The *Post* put this laundry list of gay rebuffs on the front page and, from then on, gay protesters from ACT-UP and GMHC—two organizations Larry Kramer had helped found—occasionally appeared at Rudy events. ACT-UP's Jay Blotcher said at one demonstration: "Giuliani's people are trying to make him a very macho candidate. They're trying to position him against Koch, implying he's the wimpy, faggot mayor." It certainly didn't help that the campaign did not have a single openly gay staff member, an unusual omission in a New York mayoral effort premised on "inclusion."

While some in the campaign thought Giuliani had simply miscalculated and adopted a legalistic stance on issues like apartment rights, others thought the intent was to contrast himself with Koch, implicitly raising the gay question. Had he faced Koch in November, the utility and significance of this strategy might have become clear. Certainly, Giuliani's posture on bereavement was strikingly out of step with his other efforts to occupy the ground to Koch's left and reinforced the heartless prosecutorial image he was trying to shed. Since Giuliani as mayor would ultimately champion extensive domestic partnership benefits, his 1989 hard line was both philosophically contradictory and politically expedient.

The gay and abortion maneuvering may also have been designed to give Giuliani enough conservative camouflage to get him through the Republican primary in September. His opponent, Ronald Lauder, the son of Estee Lauder and a perfume potentate worth $333 million, was trying to push him to the right. For example, Giuliani's abortion acrobatics momentarily mimicked Lauder's, who was pro-choice but against public funding. No poll showed Lauder making much headway—he was behind Giuliani by 40 points or more from beginning to end—but only about 100,000 of New York's 419,000 registered Republicans were expected to vote. With that small a turnout and $14 million in Lauder's campaign kitty, Giuliani had to give himself a little wiggle room to guard against the improbable.

What shaped the heart of Giuliani's early campaign, though, was a November strategy that attempted to combine the 28 percent of the electorate that year that was black with the 22 percent that was white Catholic. He wanted to take on Koch with those blocs as his core. Many of the 17 percent who were Hispanic were also Catholic, and many shared communities across the city with blacks, so he hoped to win a lion's share of their vote as well. His campaign in the primary—even his abortion and gay jockeying—was affected by his need to put that foundation in place for the general election.

But a sudden, tragic event reconfigured the Democratic race. The brutal slaying on August 23 of a sixteen- year-old black youth, Yusef Hawkins, who was attacked by a white gang in the heavily Italian Bensonhurst section of Brooklyn, doomed Koch. The murder led to black marches through Bensonhurst, headed by the activist Reverend Al Sharpton, who was taunted by a watermelon-flashing white mob. Koch called for an end to the protests, a comment that infuriated blacks and provoked Giuliani to declare that "people have a right to march." Giuliani went to the Hawkins funeral and was jeered nonetheless, but only mildly. Koch was booed so badly by the more than 1,000 people who jammed in and around the church that he had to leave through a side door.

"The last thing we need in this delicate, sensitive, difficult situation is for Ed Koch and Al Sharpton to be shooting their mouths off," Giuliani said. Lauder blasted Rudy, saying he went to the funeral "to get votes." Giuliani tried to strike a balance between his anticipated November voting blocs—repeatedly identifying himself as Italian and saying Bensonhurst should not be tarred with "a broad brush," while simultaneously supporting the protests. But even Giuliani finally realized with about a week left, as did Koch, that Dinkins was now the likely primary winner—the beneficiary of a bloodied social fabric.

The *Wall Street Journal* condemned Rudy's lefty campaign and called him a "Lindsay Republican." Al D'Amato flatly predicted that if elected mayor Giuliani would, like Lindsay, leave the party.

Throughout its first five months, Rudy's campaign was guided by the combined social gospel of the Kennedys and the National Conference of Catholic Bishops—a liberalism of the heart. It was also inspired by the political legacy of John Lindsay, who proved that a Republican could get elected mayor by drawing hundreds of thousands of black and Latino votes. It was a strategy concocted principally by Rudy himself, since the political consultants he'd inherited from George Bush's presidential campaign were too national to really understand it. Ray Harding and the Liberals had lived it, and helped him to see it. Only Koch, by losing in September as he did, could make it obsolete.

Eleven

Blood Feud
The Fight with the Fonz

No one has ever run an uglier campaign for New York mayor than Ron Lauder. He spent a family fortune on a relentless series of negative television commercials, never even throwing a major fundraiser. He only bothered to put a single positive spot on the air, and that one ever so briefly, demonstrating for all to see that his media campaign's only purpose was to damage Rudy Giuliani.

Lauder could have spent a fraction of what he did on the Giuliani campaign and secured a much larger profile for himself in New York GOP circles. In the middle of 1989, for example, upstate businessman J. Patrick Barrett was named chair of the financially distressed state GOP because he was willing to write checks that tallied in the mere tens of thousands. Lauder could've been chair for what he was spending weekly on his Giuliani smears. In his first political speech in 1988, Lauder indicated an interest in running in the 1990 governor's race. With a commitment to spend a fraction of what he lavished on his virulent anti-Giuliani ads, Lauder easily have been the GOP candidate for governor, presumably a far more attractive launch for a political career than taking on Rudy in a city GOP primary.

Nonetheless Lauder decided to make a race he was so uninterested in he rarely made a public appearance. And it wasn't an effort to lay the groundwork for a future real race. He never ran again for public office.

The ambassador to Austria under Reagan, Lauder was hard pressed to put together plausible consecutive sentences on a matter of municipal policy. He did manage, in a single sentence, however, to tell conservative NYU professor Herb London, who was considering entering the race, why he was making this expensive and impossible run: "I'd do anything for Al D'Amato," he said.

The bizarre campaign actually began in Albany on January 4 when Lauder became the first candidate for mayor of New York to ever announce 140 miles away from it. He did it there because D'Amato was visiting for a day. The announcement was held in the office of State Senator Guy Velella, the d'Amato ally who also chaired the Bronx GOP.

The gangly and shy scion had been one of the first to contribute to D'Amato's initial Senate run in 1980. Now that D'Amato was at war with Rudy—a blood feud rooted in the 1988 conflict over the Senate race and Giuliani's SDNY successors—Lauder was quite willing to buy both the commercial bazookas and popguns.

Though Lauder ads would fire most of the shots at Giuliani, D'Amato surfaced to take some himself, accusing Rudy in early 1989 of having "smeared" certain unnamed people and branding him a "publicity hound." Giuliani could not get over the irony, recalling in one interview the golden days of 1986, when he and the senator toured the drug warrens of upper Manhattan in disguise. "I do have a picture of us in our hats and uniforms," he said. "I take it out to remind myself."

If a determination to damage Giuliani was D'Amato's top priority, he was also using Lauder to help his friend and political ally Koch. The Lauder commercial assault on Giuliani during the primary was designed to leave a battered Rudy, vulnerable for take-out shots from Koch in the general election. Giuliani would make that charge publicly—saying that D'Amato "is acting on behalf of the person who supported him and who he has supported, Ed Koch"—and no serious observer doubted him. Lauder could not have made it clearer himself—his family businesses contributed $15,000 to Koch and though he was theoretically running for mayor, his attack commercials never mentioned the incumbent.

Whatever hope Lauder and D'Amato might have initially had about seriously testing Giuliani in the GOP primary ended when Guy Molinari, the congressman from Staten Island who was running for borough president, quickly moved to endorse Rudy. The suburban-like and heavily Catholic Staten Island is the heart of the city GOP, and Molinari was king there. The initial *Times* story in January about Lauder's candidacy said Molinari had "encouraged" it. Yet Molinari had been calling Rudy since at least mid-1988, by Giuliani's own account, urging him to run. D'Amato, who was so close to Molinari they'd actually shared a Washington apartment, was reported to be "furious" over the switch.

Molinari and Harding instantly became the campaign's seasoned local advisers, with Molinari named to chair it. They were the only two professional politicians to join Giuliani and his usual entourage of lawyer friends in interviewing prospective consultants for the campaign, picking three with Bush campaign credentials, including pollster Robert Teeter. Since Mike Long's wife was on Molinari's payroll, as was the Staten Island Conservative leader, the congressman also served as the temporary bridge to the Conservatives, helping to arrange

Rudy's Bay Ridge confab. In the end though, Long, a D'Amato sidekick steered the ballot line to Lauder.

Lauder's first ads—which ran in April on radio and TV at a weekly cost of $350,000—assailed Giuliani for accepting the Liberal endorsement, voting for George McGovern and supporting tax hikes. The script pointed out that the Libs oppose the death penalty and tuition tax credits, suggesting that Rudy did too.

The commercials provoked the resignation of Roger Ailes, the ex-Bush campaign consultant who had originally signed up with Lauder but became so alienated he wound up charging that the only purpose of the campaign was to "destroy" Giuliani. Ailes candidly explained why he and other top-flight consultants were attracted to a transparent loser like Lauder, calling him a "cash cow." Left to rake in the cash was Arthur Finkelstein, D'Amato's media guru.

The Lauder/D'Amato camp fired its first damaging shot the morning of Giuliani's announcement. The *Daily News* carried a story alleging that the white-shoe law firm Giuliani had joined in February, White & Case, included on its vast client list the Government of Panama, which was then controlled by Manuel Noriega, who had been indicted in the United States on drug charges. Adam Nagourney, the *News* reporter who did the story, says now that it came from "Lauder/D'Amato sources." Forty-eight hours after it appeared, Lauder followed with a shrieking TV ad that featured side-by-side photos of Noriega and Giuliani.

Giuliani wound up responding to the Noriega charge on the campaign bus that took him and reporters around the city for his announcement appearances. He insisted he'd known nothing about the Noriega representation until the *News* informed him, claimed the firm only represented the state-controlled Bank of Panama and had received no compensation in six months. He seemed to be taking what even Nagourney thought was a trivial tabloid piece so seriously that he suggested he would quit the best-paying job he'd ever had in his life. "I want absolutely nothing to do with Noriega and will take whatever additional steps are necessary to disassociate myself from him," he said, promising a review of the matter with the firm and "remedial action."

When Koch jumped into the Noriega fray, taunting Rudy for "taking drug money," Giuliani came unglued, blasting Lauder and Koch as liars. "If they really were men, they'd apologize," he whined. A one-day blip had become a campaign convulsion, lasting weeks. Acknowledging his own overreaction, Giuliani promised the fat-cat Waldorf audience at his first major fundraiser on May 23: "I will try my very best not to dignify their scurrilous lies and smears with a response, no matter how shrilly they are made." He attributed his defensiveness to his mother and father, who, he said, "raised me to believe that honesty and integrity were the truest measures of a man."

"I felt compelled to defend my honor," he said. In fact, instead of the toe-to-toe boxer Harold had trained Rudy to be, he was looking more and more like a bleeder, taking punches round after round just like Vic Dellicurti.

Barry Slotnik, the prominent criminal attorney who had taken over representation of the bank from White & Case, kept waiting for Giuliani to point out that as U.S. Attorney, he'd brought a successful action to freeze its assets. In fact, as Slotnik recalled it, W&C represented the bank when Giuliani initiated the proceeding. Slotnik never mentioned this to the reporters who cited him in stories about the campaign controversy, claiming he instead called a Giuliani aide, who said they'd forgotten about the freeze.

When other questionable W&C clients started making the news, Giuliani stormed off the set of a WNBC interview. He had always planned to take a leave of absence as the campaign heated up; so now he pushed his departure date up to June 6 and left. He was barely with the firm for four months, collecting at least $260,000 of the $700,000 a year W&C had agreed to pay him.

As ugly and absurd as the Noriega hoopla was, the Nazi attack in August was worse. Rudy was first confronted about the story as he was leaving a rather tame editorial board meeting at the New York *Post*. Jerry Nachman, the paper's editor, asked him to stop in his office for a minute and began tossing out questions about a bizarre incident that had occurred at the U.S. Attorney's office in February 1986.

Giuliani was on a tight schedule and getting late for his next event. He also had a breaking story he had to deal with that every newspaper was chasing—federal prosecutors announced that day that they were dropping charges against two of three prominent Wall Street traders, whose spectacular arrests Giuliani had ordered on 1987. "It was a mistake to move with that case at the time that I did," Giuliani was telling reporters, apologizing to the traders. He made a quick attempt to convince Nachman he'd done nothing wrong in this other, rather arcane, case. He'd heard that the *Post* was working on the story, but he didn't expect it to happen so fast. He called Nachman that night from a restaurant pay phone to discuss it further, but it was already too late.

The next morning, the *Post*'s banner screamed: "Auschwitz survivor charges . . . RUDY'S MEN ACTED LIKE NAZIS." Next to a headshot of Giuliani was the subhead: "L.I. man's SS nightmare at hands of feds." Rudy's photo caption read: "on hot seat." The story charged that a Holocaust survivor imprisoned at Auschwitz was "roused" from his Long Island home at 7 A.M. on a Sunday and taken in handcuffs to Giuliani's office, where he was seated in "an empty corridor that contained nothing but a straight-backed chair facing a blackboard." Scrawled on the blackboard were the words "ARBEIT MACHT FREI"—German for "Work shall set you free." The words were the same as those that greeted arrivals at Auschwitz, where Berger's brother and sister perished.

Nachman, who co-bylined the copyrighted story, quoted Giuliani as saying he knew about the incident and that it was "reprehensible." He said it was investigated at the time. "If we found the person who did it, and that person was with a federal agency, I'm sure we would have fired them. I think the government did precisely what it should have done: preserve the evidence and turn it over to the defense counsel." Indeed the *Post* ran a photo of the blackboard taken by the feds and turned over to Berger's attorney.

Berger, a security lock manufacturer, was eventually charged with bribing a NYC Housing Authority official to get a contract—an indictment announced by Rudy at a press conference—and acquitted at trial. The jury took barely four hours, with dinner included. The story ended with Berger's comment: "Giuliani did the same thing to me that the Nazis did and the people of New York should know this."

The AUSA who handled the Berger prosecution, as well as the internal probe of the blackboard incident, was David Zornow, a widely respected assistant who had tried the celebrated case against Stanley Friedman with Rudy. Jewish, married to the daughter of survivors and shaken by the incident, Zornow was nonetheless unable to establish how it happened. Benito Romano, a top Giuliani aide, said later that the Zornow probe did determine that the scribble was "the mindless musings of IRS agents" who had nothing to do with the Berger case. They had written it in jest and "turned the blackboard" to the wall long before the Berger arrest. Someone accidentally moved the board when Berger was brought in..

Nonetheless, regurgitating its skewed version again and again, the *Post* kept the story alive for a week, running consecutive covers on it, pushing the Anti-Defamation League (ADL) to investigate it, even getting their television reviewer to write about media coverage of it.

Though Nachman's story pointed out that the judge on the case was Lloyd MacMahon and went into details about the draft deferment and his other ties to Giuliani, it never quoted from MacMahon's opinion on the blackboard issue. "There is not a scintilla of evidence to suggest that the government intentionally directed the phrase toward Berger," concluded MacMahon.

The *Post* also ignored two letters to the judge sent by Berger's trial attorney, Ben Brafman, who called the incident "a regrettable series of horrible coincidences." Brafman, who asked that the record on this issue be sealed so that no one could "use it to malign the U.S. Attorney's office," wrote that there was "no evidence that any representative" of the office "was involved." In fact, the ADL ultimately concluded, after the election controversy was over, that "the Nazi phrase was written several weeks before Berger was arrested and was not directed at him."

Berger's lawyer at the time of his arrest was Barry Slotnik—the same lawyer who represented Noriega's bank and government. The wily Slotnik had his own agenda. A Republican who publicly entertained the idea of running for congress from Westchester in 1990, Slotnik contributed $1,000 to D'Amato on June 7, 1989, and his firm kicked in another thousand later that year, part of $4,500 in total D'Amato donations.

Slotnik claimed later that he had no idea how the *Post* got onto the Berger story three and a half years after the arrest and three weeks before the Republican primary, but he did say Berger "loved Al D'Amato." Berger, his wife and son contributed $3,700 to D'Amato campaigns prior to the story, starting when unknown Al first ran statewide in 1980 and including $200 on August 7, 1989, almost exactly when the *Post* was first approached on the story. He gave D'Amato another $900 that December.

The *Post* pieces were filled with Slotnik's quotes. To help keep the story alive, Slotnik started calling for Justice Department and congressional investigations, though he never had when the incident occurred. He now says it was "such a bullshit story" that "it blew itself out," adding that, "of course, Rudy had nothing to do" with the blackboard incident.

Giuliani attributed the story to "political bosses" he declined to name, and blasted the *Post* for stretching it "way beyond any legitimate bounds." Nachman recalls that "a couple of people told him it was out there" and that "one of them was Al D'Amato," who, Nachman said, "was jumping up and down" with outrage about the case. D'Amato told Nachman that Berger was "a constituent, a terrific guy and a devout Jew," adding that his story was "an example of what a fascist Rudy Giuliani is." Nachman said the Bergers came to meet him and brought documents: "There was a lot of sobbing and wailing." He also said that Rudy sent Arnold Burns, the former deputy attorney general and Giuliani's campaign finance chair, to try to "muscle" him into not doing the story.

D'Amato had such a special relationship with Peter Kalikow, the *Post*'s owner, that he used Kalikow's Fifth Avenue apartment as his legal address when he left his wife, even visiting the penthouse for a change of clothes now and then. Kalikow served as the chairman of D'Amato's campaign committee for years and hired D'Amato's top aide as a *Post* executive. Kalikow was also close to Lauder, yet the paper published a sizzling pre-election roast of his service as Austrian ambassador. In fact, the only major candidate spared a *Post* blast was the one it endorsed and D'Amato was covertly aiding, Ed Koch, who publicly feasted off the Berger story, chortling over Giuliani's discomfort and salivating over the thought of using it again in November.

The vulnerability study Giuliani commissioned for the 1993 campaign contended that D'Amato "created the Berger story" and urged that the senator, since he was now supporting Rudy, "be enlisted in the effort to kill it." The study, which reviewed the shortcomings of the 1989 effort, recommended that D'Amato "broker a rapprochement between Berger and Giuliani," and get "a guarantee" that the issue would not reappear. Not only did it not reappear in 1993, the Berger issue died in 1989 when Koch and Lauder lost the primaries. The same paper that had tortured Giuliani with it in August endorsed him against Dinkins in October without ever mentioning it again.

Lauder, of course, went on the air with his harshest ads right after the Nazi stories:

Why are people afraid of Rudy Giuliani? Because he's a shameless publicity seeker who used Sukhreet Gabel to tape-record her own mother. Handcuffed innocent stockbrokers in front of co-workers. And ignored the taunts of a Holocaust survivor. Because he tried to cover up his huge salary at White & Case ($700,000), the law firm that represents Panama's dictator Noriega . . . Why are people afraid of Rudy Giuliani? Because they should be.

One week after the Berger story broke the *Post* published a front-page poll headlined "Giuliani drops off charts." Buried in the fine print was a virtually unchanged forty-point lead over Lauder. But the *Post*'s numbers showed him losing by twenty-two points to Dinkins and two points to Koch, a sharp reversal of June numbers that had had him beating both soundly. Citing its own story as a possible cause, the *Post* noted a 59 percent turnaround in his favorables and unfavorables among Jewish voters.

A campaign blessed by twenty-point leads in one early poll after another was bottoming out due to months of high-octane blasts. It was broke and implementing across-the-board cuts in staff salaries. Rich Bond and Russ Schriefer, the costly consultants from the 1988 George Bush campaign, were bounced.

In the midst of all this madness, with Helen Giuliani seriously ill in a hospital for what turned out to be a five-week stay, Caroline Giuliani was born. On August 22, four days after the Berger story, Donna gave birth to a nine-pound seven-ounce girl. Under the crushing pressure of a foul campaign against him, Giuliani was running around the city wearing a patient-type wristband that allowed him to visit his mother, wife and baby daughter. He was even trying to keep the *Post* story away from his seventy-nine-year-old mother.

Still rooted in the progressive campaign he'd launched in May, he went to a day-care center in East Harlem three days after Caroline's birth and spoke of his daughter: "Four babies born in New York the same day as Caroline," he said, "are suffering the terror of drug addiction." He promised to name a Deputy Mayor for Children and vowed to make sure "pregnant women and women of child-bearing age" had "access to drug treatment."

"To Caroline, to all the children born this week and to those who will be born here in the future, I dedicate my efforts to wipe out drugs in this city," he pledged, never mentioning the tragedy of his cousin Joan, whose torment with drugs so haunted his own family.

The *Post* peppered him at the Harlem event with more questions about Berger and ignored his plan on drug addiction. He did not flinch. Maybe his overdose of family reality was just the antidote he needed to combat the unreality of the campaign media world. It certainly seemed to help him handle all the ugliness.

Donna had spent most of the first half of 1989 caring for three-year-old Andrew and maintaining her nightly anchor job at WPIX. She didn't leave the station until a week before the Caesarean delivery. She made occasional campaign appearances, and advised her husband and others in the campaign, especially about media strategies. When Rudy seriously considered boycotting the *Post* completely over the Berger story, it was Donna who convinced him not to, maintaining her equilibrium at a moment of high emotion. Level heads on the campaign staff turned to her on that and other matters.

For the second time since she met Giuliani in 1982, however, Donna was also sacrificing professionally to help his career. She'd quit her Miami job to live with him. Now his political ambitions were colliding with her news career. Questioned that March by the *Daily News* about Hanover's possible conflict, WPIX news director John Corporon said that she would remain anchor of their 7:30 P.M. show, but not handle any mayoral election news. "There's no issue here until and unless Giuliani announces," he said. Her co-anchor Brad Holbrooke said later that he did every story related to city government: "I ended up reading a lot more of the news copy than she did."

When Rudy announced in May, Hanover resisted any suggestion that she take a leave, maintaining that all she had to do was continue avoiding city coverage. Corporon, still concerned that her mere appearance was "a subliminal plug for her husband," talked to her about returning to street reporting. Rudy called Corporon, he recalls, "to reassure" him that Donna would, at most, "occasionally accompany him to events where spouses were expected." With that exception, Corporon insisted she take no active role in the campaign. Still, Lauder refused to send his schedule to the station, and David Dinkins later called its coverage biased.

"From a journalistic standpoint," Holbrooke recalled, "it was certainly a gray area and everybody had their own opinions about it. I was totally in support of Donna. It was an uncomfortable situation for her to be in. But I guess she had a little bit more of a narrow view of it, a more personal view of it. To her, it was all a matter of her own achievement and integrity as a working journalist and that wasn't the only issue. She wasn't naïve, she did know that there was this unprecedented situation where an anchorwoman in the number one market in America was married to the guy running for the number one political job."

While on paid leave with Caroline, however, she did a television commercial for Rudy that began airing in early October. "I wish all those people who think he's so tough could see him with children," Hanover said in her thirty-second spot. "That's the real Rudy." Depicted walking with Giuliani, Hanover's soothing narration concluded: "When I first met Rudy, he seemed strong and at the same time gentle, and I liked that. I thought—this was the kind of man I want to be the father of my children—and Rudy is such a great dad!" Tom Goldstein, then dean of the School of Journalism at the University of California at Berkeley, said, "It would just seem that she has put her station in a very delicate situation." Corporon took the public position that the commercial "did not embarrass the station," though Hanover hadn't sought WPIX's approval.

She may have won the battle, but she lost the war. Shortly after her six-month maternity leave ended on January 29, 1990, she returned to WPIX, but not for long. Though she came back with big plans to do a segment on "America's Children" as a weekly feature on her nightly newscast, she suddenly left the station that July. Her departure was never explained by WPIX, though Donna told an interviewer in 1993: "The whole business contracted and the show was taken off the air. I wasn't a victim of politics. The show was lost, and with it, my job."

Actually, she was the only anchor let go. Holbrooke, who also did the 10 P.M. newscast, stayed, as did the show's other anchor, Sheila Stainback. Hanover was dropped though she'd been an anchor at the station for nearly three years longer than Stainback. The two anchors of the syndicated national broadcast were also kept. "I offered her a general assignment job," says Corporon, "but she said she'd already done that. She wanted to do specialty reporting, but we didn't do that at that time."

Holbrooke adds: "They offered her a job where she would just come in and read the news and leave, like come into work for an hour and a half, and they would pay her a third of what they would have paid somebody who was a traditional full-time anchor person. She was, I think rightfully, offended. I mean Ted Knight [on *The Mary Tyler Moore Show*] would do that, but that's a parody of something that really doesn't exist much in the TV business." Corporon insists that Donna left only because it was her show that was "blown out," and that he couldn't change the 10 P.M. team: "They were established and things were going okay."

A forty-year-old woman with two young children, dropped after six years with a single New York station, was not exactly a hot property on the media market. She would never get another evening anchor job, and she didn't get another television job of any type until May 1992, when she began doing freelance street reporting for the local Fox station.

Whatever impact the 1989 controversies had on Donna's news career, she was able, once she recovered from Caroline's birth, to play a stronger role in the campaign than she had prior to her leave. Peter Powers had by then also taken over as campaign manager, and Liberal boss Ray Harding, a savvy hand at city politics, had moved into the headquarters. Roger Ailes, the Bush consultant who had quit Lauder, was on the team as well, and the four became the nucleus of the day-to-day decision making.

Ailes was giving Rudy sound-bite lessons designed to cure his rambling ways. His early performance reviewers had labeled him "wooden," "robotic," "solemn," "medieval." The *Times* reported that he "came across as an arms length candidate, shaking hands stiffly and rarely shedding his suit jacket." He was so formal at first that when he stopped at a stickball game in East Harlem, he kept his suit jacket on until aides convinced him to take it off and wound up pictured in the tabloids swinging at a pitch with a tie on. He would speak at Town Hall gatherings designed so he would interact with folks from the neighborhoods and deliver such compound answers he would only have time for a handful of questions. *New York* magazine's Joe Klein fixated on his "severe" appearance at a March GOP dinner, noting that "his very presence seemed a reproach." The *Voice*'s Dan Collins watched him at street fairs and on walking tours and wrote that he "looked ominous at times."

"If he held up a baby," concluded Collins, "it might cry."

But most pundits conceded, as the weeks wore into September, that he was getting more relaxed, smiling, engaging. "I didn't really start running last time until August," he said four years later.

His sole debate with Lauder in early September was vintage Giuliani. Taunting Lauder by calling him "Ronnie," Rudy slammed Lauder's indifference to the homeless: "Suffering to him is the butler taking the night off." When Lauder called for stringent measures against street vagrants, he said that was "cruel." He extended his hand to Lauder offering to support the winner of the Republican primary and asking if Lauder, who was on the Conservative line, would do the same. "If Ronald Lauder was a real Republican, he'd support the winner of the Republican primary," Rudy declared when Lauder balked. Each of these on-target shots at the time would come back to haunt a future Giuliani.

Rudy smashed Lauder by 50,000 votes in a September 12 primary when three out of four Republicans stayed home. But, thanks to Lauder's millions, the damage had been done.

Every postmortem on the November loss to Dinkins, including Rudy's, would lay the blame on D'Amato. The *Times* analysis cited the Lauder hammering and quoted Giuliani as saying: "There's no question that it hurt. And to the extent that Al D'Amato was a larger part of it, then he has to take responsibility for that." D'Amato did do a speaker-phone endorsement of Rudy from Washington, praising him to a roomful of reporters but never climbing into a photo frame with him. In the aftermath of the loss, Giuliani would not answer questions about the possibility that he might challenge D'Amato in the 1992 senate campaign. "Would I rule out such a thing?" he said in early 1990. "I just don't know what the future is going to hold."

The *Times* said D'Amato waged this extraordinary war because he was "angered" about Giuliani's "presumptuousness" in insisting on selecting his Southern District successor in 1988. The explanation satisfied few. Could so minor, and even understandable, a Giuliani slight have prompted so nuclear a D'Amato response? Neither D'Amato nor Giuliani would talk publicly about the real reason—the politically sensitive investigations, especially the Milken probe, that had sparked and followed the succession fight. These prosecutions were still going on in 1989, and were driving D'Amato and some of his closest political friends nuts.

In early 1989, D'Amato lost the battle in Washington to install Rudy's immediate replacement. Rudy's old friend from Justice, Attorney General Dick Thornburgh, appointed ex-Giuliani aide Benito Romano interim U.S. Attorney over the vigorous opposition of D'Amato. It was a vital assist to Rudy's campaign. Had a D'Amato appointee been installed instead, the new U.S. Attorney could have found a hundred ways to embarrass Giuliani in the middle of the mayoral run. From the beginning, Romano's appointment was only for a year, when D'Amato's designee, Otto Obermaier, was set to take over.

One of Romano's first acts—on March 29—was to indict D'Amato allies Michael and Lowell Milken. Giuliani had forced the Milken investment bank, Drexel, to its knees shortly before his departure. But plea discussions dragged on with the brothers for months—with Lowell still represented by Mike Armstrong, D'Amato's personal attorney.

The juxtaposition in the timing of the Lauder candidacy and the Milken case was convincing evidence of their interconnection. Lauder hurriedly announced in early January, just days before Romano's selection was revealed. Soon after the Milken indictments, on April 19, the Conservative Party gave Lauder its line, solidifying his candidacy, and on April 26, Lauder's first commercials blasting Giuliani aired. On May 26, D'Amato launched a verbal broadside at Rudy, blasting him for going "to any length to aggrandize himself, regardless of the guilt or innocence of a person." The senator had never before criticized the handling of any case in Giuliani's office, and did not specify what cases he was talking about now. "I'm for people's rights," he said. "And I don't think you take people and smear them the way Rudy Giuliani has without conscience."

On August 7, Romano announced that an expanded indictment was coming Milken's way by October 1, shortly before Romano's scheduled departure. Romano later said: "I wanted to resolve the case before D'Amato's replacement got there. Whether they were waiting for Obermaier, you'd have to ask them." Milken was later quoted as viewing Romano's threatened superseding indictment as "the Giuliani method, still going strong." Romano says plea negotiations had begun at an AUSA level before he left in October.

Within a couple days of the news of a revised Milken indictment, D'Amato went to the *Post*'s Nachman with the Simon Berger story. It appeared two weeks later. On August 23, D'Amato told the *Times* that appointing Giuliani was "the biggest mistake I ever made."

"I certainly don't hold Rudy in any esteem," D'Amato continued. "And because of his shortcomings I don't want to see him in a higher political position." The titular head of a state party was setting a public ceiling on how high a rising star could climb. The new indictment threat proved to be enough, and Milken ultimately pled guilty, cutting a 1990 deal with Obermaier's office.

"We're in the realm of speculation," Romano said years later. "But the coincidence of events"—linking the Milken prosecution and D'Amato's anti-Rudy hostilities—"is striking." Insisting that nothing D'Amato did affected his own determination to resolve the Milken case, Romano said: "It may have prevented Rudy from getting elected mayor the first time."

As nicely as the Milken and D'Amato pieces fit, however, Milken wasn't the only reason for the enmity that would dominate New York GOP politics for years. The Wallach trial started in April, featured a withering cross-examination of Meese and ended with a conviction on August 8. It offended an inner circle of

Reagan and other national Republicans. D'Amato's statewide allies were still incensed about the 1988 indictment of State Senator Richard Schermerhorn and the reported attempt to wire him up against the state's second most powerful Republican, Senate Majority Leader Warren Anderson. The only reason these two cases did not become larger factors in the state party's response to Giuliani was that Anderson and Reagan left office, by January 1989.

Perhaps more important than any of these cases was the fact that, beginning in 1988 and running right through the 1989 campaign, key Giuliani aides were coming after D'Amato personally. Rudy had put the pieces in place for these probes before leaving the Southern District. His old friends, watching the campaign slugfest from Foley Square, were ratcheting up an attack on the senator that would cut him like a knife. It was hardly, however, the first, or, for that matter, the last time, that the Giuliani crew would target D'Amato with lethal intent.

Three days after Rudy Giuliani and Al D'Amato launched their initial succession attacks on each other in 1988 news stories, Tony Lombardi, Giuliani's favorite G-Man, made an eerie entry in his diary: "Rudy mtg re D'Amato." It was January 16, 1988, and it was the first time Lombardi had ever listed a meeting regarding any D'Amato matter, much less one with the boss.

On January 13, the dispute over Rudy's SDNY successor had erupted on the front page of the metro section of the *Times*. D'Amato, who had been trying for months to convince Rudy to step down and run for Senate, described the conditions Giuliani was setting as "provocative and not too smart." The *Times* said D'Amato was telling friends that Giuliani had put him "in an untenable position."

On February 8, Giuliani announced that he would not run for the Moynihan seat, indicating that he hadn't spoken to D'Amato since early January, when their negotiations ended. Lombardi's appointment logs suggest that Giuliani's closest aides began targeting D'Amato criminally as soon as Rudy broke with him politically. These dry details implicitly confirm the political origins of the investigator's Koch probe as well, since they reveal how readily Lombardi embraced an investigation of a Giuliani opponent.

The logs carry six references to Jack Libert, all in 1989. Libert was the treasurer of D'Amato's campaign finance committee, the ex-counsel to the Long Island board of supervisors D'Amato dominated and a law partner of D'Amato's brother Armand. The Southern District would develop a tax case against Libert, after investigating him for years on fraud and other charges. In his 1995 book, *Power,*

Pasta and Politics, D'Amato says Libert was "very close to me" and says Libert "suffered greatly" because he knew D'Amato. He cites the prosecution of Libert as one of "the meanest examples of dirty politics run amok," contending "the criminal justice system was used and abused for transparently political purposes."

In an embittered four-page account of the case, D'Amato never mentions Giuliani. Yet, from the outset, the point of the Libert probe was to flip him to get D'Amato, a purpose apparent to everyone, including the targeted senator.

Lombardi's references to Libert come between July 12, 1989 and August 11, 1989. One reference refers to the investigation as Libert/D'Amato. Another on August 10 refers to an 8 P.M. meeting with Romano. The logs indicate he was supposed to make a "Libert report" to Romano. In addition to the Libert references, Lombardi's diaries contain another "D'Am" reference on August 17, indicating he should make a call to a source about the senator. Just as the SNDY's Milken decisions dovetailed with D'Amato's 1989 actions against Giuliani, Lombardi's entries on Libert also coincide. Lombardi's last D'Amato listing comes the day Rudy was confronted by Jerry Nachman about the Simon Berger story.

Lombardi was certainly aware the Berger story was brewing. On August 15, he listed the Federal Records Center in Bayonne, New Jersey in his diary and Simon Berger's name twice. The only other entry that day are the names of Benito Romano and Louis Freeh, Romano's deputy, who is now the head of the FBI. A large arrow is drawn from the top of the day, where the records are listed, to the bottom of the day, where the meeting with Romano and Freeh is listed. Romano recalls getting pre-publication information about the *Post*'s story on the Berger blackboard allegations and discussing it with Freeh. He doesn't recall meeting with Lombardi about it, though he says Lombardi "knew the IRS agents who were working in the room" where the Nazi slogan was written.

Not surprisingly, as soon as the Berger story broke, Rudy's campaign was handing reporters the affidavits and other documents from the file that proved how intensely the office had probed the incident. Liberal Party head Ray Harding even did it at a press conference. Reporters, lawyers and the general population can wait weeks to review an archived court file, but the U.S. Attorney's office can get it virtually overnight. Romano says he doesn't know how the federal file wound up in the hands of the campaign.

Lombardi's entry about the Berger file is one of many that indicates his continuing political involvement with Giuliani after Rudy left the U.S. Attorney's office. He listed three Rudy campaign dinners or announcements in March and May. He also listed Rudy's primary and general-election night parties at the Roosevelt

Hotel and was seen at both. He wrote "security" as a function for himself at the November party.

The same day as Rudy's first fundraiser at the Waldorf on May 23, Lombardi wrote: "RWG meeting—W&C," indicating he was going to Giuliani's office at White & Case. He also recorded two other meetings at the law firm, including one on September 14, two days after Rudy and Dinkins won the primary. The only two numbers listed in the back of Lombardi's 1989 diary were Giuliani's and Young's at W&C.

A 1990 U.S. Treasury Department "report of investigation" indicated that the department's regional inspector general found that Lombardi "did engage in prohibited political fundraising activities on behalf of former NYC mayoral candidate Rudolph Giuliani." The report noted that this allegation, as well as three others against Lombardi, were "corroborated" through "a covert investigation." As Romano later put it: "Tony was permitted a good deal of roaming room."

The timing of Giuliani's meeting with Lombardi on D'Amato in 1988, coupled with the subsequent events, underlined just how connected Giuliani's prosecutorial and political objectives were.

D'Amato had called Rudy on behalf of Mario Gigante and Paul Castellano in 1984 and 1985 and yet Giuliani continued to maintain his close ties with the senator, telling virtually no one about the shameful interventions of a U.S. senator. Rudy even did the 1986 pre-election drugs-in-drag raid for the senator after the calls.

It wasn't until D'Amato defied Giuliani on succession and publicly criticized him that the senator became a Lombardi target. It wasn't until late 1988 that Giuliani first revealed the Gigante and Castellano calls, and then only to two trusted biographers, Dan Collins and Michael Goodwin, whose book was scheduled to appear in late 1989 (it did not). Yet the senator's ethics had been the subject of sizzling headlines for years prior to 1988, as had his character testimony in Brooklyn federal court for a mob-tied disco operator. Probable cause for Giuliani, at least in some cases, was Personal Cause.

The D'Amato inquiries inspired by Giuliani went beyond Lombardi, and lasted long after the 1989 election. As pivotal a factor as these probes may have been in framing the enmities during the first mayoral run, they continued to haunt the relationship for years to come.

Lombardi worked with an AUSA named Jim McGuire on the Libert investigation. The logs contained twenty references to McGuire, starting in early February

1988. Several entries in the summer of 1989 cite the Libert case. (When they started working together, Lombardi would freely gossip with McGuire about "Koch's gay liaisons.")

McGuire was such a tiger that D'Amato made rabid attacks on him in his 1995 book, contending that "many who worked with McGuire" said he had "a real fixation on me." Citing Libert's attorney, Robert Fink, D'Amato writes that McGuire made "a corrupt offer" to drop all charges against Libert if he would "give us D'Amato." When Fink returned to McGuire and told him Libert was "not aware of any wrongdoing by either Al or Armand," McGuire insisted that Libert come in anyway. "After we hear what he has to say, we'll talk about a deal for him," Fink quoted McGuire as saying.

Fink added in a later interview that McGuire said that "the only way" for Libert "to avoid indictment" was to provide information on the D'Amatos.

Rhodes Scholar, point guard on the Yale basketball team and Harvard Law grad, the thirty-three-year-old McGuire joined the SDNY in 1987. When Giuliani interviewed him for the job, they swapped Brooklyn neighborhood stories and compared notes about McGuire's high school days at Brooklyn Prep and Giuliani's at Loughlin, two of the borough's premier Catholic high schools.

McGuire volunteered to handle the Hells Angels drug cases, winning a half dozen convictions, three at trial. The black leather motorcycle vest Giuliani wore on his 1986 drug buy with D'Amato was seized in the case McGuire tried. When Hells Angel "Wild Bill" Medeiros saw pictures of Giuliani with a vest with his colors on it, he told McGuire he wanted to sue Rudy. Medeiros was a cooperating witness who admitted on the stand that he'd committed countless rapes, and his vest had been seized in a raid at the Angels' Lower East Side headquarters.

The sandy-haired and single McGuire went on a post–Hells Angels vacation in January 1988. When he got back, Rudy moved him up from general crimes to public corruption. Almost from the beginning, he was given pieces of whatever was in the office on Rudy's drug-buying partner, the senator whose succession dispute with Rudy had apparently turned him into a target just as McGuire was reassigned to the corruption unit.

D'Amato was already deeply involved in the far-flung Wedtech case. He had intervened countless times in Washington on behalf of the defense contractor, usually at the behest of Congressman Mario Biaggi. After Biaggi's conviction, Ed Little, one of the AUSAs handling the case, asked McGuire to look at D'Amato's role in the scam. D'Amato had received $30,000 in illegal contributions from the company. Giuliani's office had also learned that D'Amato had met with the Biaggi defense team—a serious breach for a sitting U.S. senator about to testify for the government. Little said Rudy wanted McGuire to include it in his grab bag of d'Amato inquiries.

In May 1988, D'Amato had testified in the Biaggi trial. The *New York Times* reported that though D'Amato was a government witness, "he often seemed more helpful to Mr. Biaggi," claiming that the assistance he and Biaggi had given Wedtech was "aboveboard." Asked if he would have helped the company if he had been aware that the congressman's son Richard was set to soon receive stock in it, D'Amato did say: "I think it would have given me some pause to reflect. I don't know." That was his only damaging statement. His performance managed to anger both sides. Even before this appearance, D'Amato had been a government witness in another successful case against Biaggi tried by Brooklyn federal prosecutors in 1987.

Biaggi says now that "Giuliani's guys"—McGuire wasn't one—tried to flip him against D'Amato. Biaggi can't remember when the meetings occurred though he believes they happened before his and his son's July 1988 SDNY conviction. He says two meetings occurred—both were in the office of his lawyer—and that prosecutors "offered to take care of me and my son."

"Their original information that I was not on friendly terms with D'Amato was correct," Biaggi says. "They thought they could get me to zap him. They brought me just so far. I thought my son would benefit. For some, it could have been tempting. There was an interest the first time so they came back for a second meeting. They had my diaries. They said I met with D'Amato fifty-three times. They were looking for me to say that I saw Al take money from contributors. I couldn't do what they wanted me to do. I'm not made that way."

The attempted flip of Biaggi was a measure of just how serious the office was about D'Amato. McGuire recalls that Rudy made it clear—in three or four different conversations—that he thought D'Amato was dirty. Giuliani talked about D'Amato's "reputation in office," about his ties to wise guys.

Then, just as Rudy was leaving the U.S. Attorney's office in late January or early February 1989, McGuire was called to meetings with Giuliani and Romano. He was asked to handle a number of D'Amato probes in the office. He was told to talk to Lombardi and Little, both of whom had files. He subsequently collected FBI memos, surveillance reports, "a boatload of newsclips" and Lombardi's tips.

McGuire felt honored.

He got a witness from the Long Island board of supervisors who was damaging to Libert and, at the very start of 1989, the case went to the top of his deck. He followed the trail right into Armand D'Amato's law firm. By September, a top aide to Romano was telling two reporters that Libert might flip, a measure of how well the McGuire/Lombardi probe was going. McGuire even went to Romano to get authority to subpoena the law firm's records. But it was getting so close to Romano's scheduled departure and Obermaier's ascendancy in October that Romano demurred.

In addition to Libert, agents working with McGuire were also involved with an attempt to wire up a lawyer named Jack Solerwitz, who'd been convicted in a state scam case. Solerwitz volunteered to approach two individuals tied to the senator, one of whom was another member of Armand's firm.

McGuire had free rein on these cases until Romano left in October, shortly before the November election. But soon after Otto Obermaier took over, McGuire found himself in trouble, reduced suddenly to an unprotected pawn in Giuliani's chess match with D'Amato. McGuire recalls receiving a new D'Amato allegation around Thanksgiving, though it hardly turned out to be something to be thankful for. He would later tell investigators an IRS agent brought the allegation to him, though subsequent news accounts indicated the agent denied he had. The allegation was that several executives from a major investment banking house had offered to bundle a quarter of a million dollars in contributions to D'Amato if D'Amato would install Obermaier as U.S. Attorney. McGuire went to his immediate superiors about the allegation and the next thing he knew he was in the eye of a storm.

The allegation was referred to the Public Integrity Division in Washington, but it could not be confirmed. McGuire was grilled at SDNY about the inflammatory charge, yanked from the corruption unit and informed that his cases were being taken away from him. The Libert case was sent to the main tax division at Justice. The division eventually indicted Libert and in 1992 a jury took all of three hours to acquit him. Washington officials killed the Solerwitz sting shortly after McGuire was put on ice.

The investigations of Armand D'Amato's firm that began with McGuire and others in Rudy's office were a prelude to Armand's eventual indictment and conviction in the Eastern District. Al D'Amato called his brother's case, involving his law firm's billings, the worst "nightmare" of his life. It ended with an appeals court unanimously overturning the conviction. D'Amato told associates for years that he blamed Giuliani for Armand's prosecution. Since it was an Eastern District case brought long after Giuliani's departure from the U.S. Attorney's office, the only possible connection was the door-opening McGuire probe of the firm.

The persecution of McGuire that followed Romano's departure continued for much of the years in between Rudy mayoral runs, and was a measure of the tensions between the senator and the mayoral-candidate-in-waiting. In February 1991, McGuire was suspended with pay from the U.S. Attorney's office. The only explanation given was that the Justice Department in Washington was trying to determine if he'd fabricated the allegation involving Obermaier. On leave until this probe ended, McGuire began sinking into a tailspin.

As McGuire's limbo entered its second year in February 1992, he took another hit, this time on the front page of the *Daily News*. A drug case he'd worked on years earlier—with the same IRS agent who he said brought him the Obermaier tip—was blowing up in federal court. The three defendants had filed papers contending that they were only prosecuted because they were gay. One claimed that McGuire told him: "If you were not who you are, you would not be indicted." Subsequent stories quoted Obermaier as saying that this, too, was under investigation by Justice.

Newsday's account said that Justice officials appeared in court and asked that the charges be dropped because McGuire and the agents had used "falsified evidence" against the gay men. They would not disclose what it was.

By May, McGuire finally worked out a deal with the department. He resigned and the SDNY put a negative letter in his file. The letter reportedly indicated he was resigning to preempt a dismissal. He was not charged with fabricating either the evidence in the drug case or the allegation in the Obermaier case. The IRS agent, however, was indicted on charges of manufacturing a memo of an interview in the drug case that October and acquitted at trial.

D'Amato wrote that McGuire "was censured for trying to launch an undercover investigation of his own boss" and "fired" for a "personal vendetta against gays and minorities." McGuire insists he was neither censured nor fired, and Justice won't comment. The anti-gay allegation against him was never explored in the public record beyond the self-serving affidavit of a felony defendant (no anti-minority charge was ever made).

McGuire was no babe in the woods. His supporters at the office said he was a tough prosecutor—even a cowboy—who tested the limits. That was probably why Rudy handpicked him to carry on the D'Amato job during the 1989 mayoral showdown. That was probably why the Court of Appeals reversed and upbraided him for telling a jury: "While some people go out and investigate drug dealers and try to see them brought to justice, there are others who defend them, try to get them off, perhaps even for high fees."

Yet at McGuire's lowest moment—in the middle of the 1992 Justice Department review of his conduct—Rudy certainly didn't walk away from his loyal soldier in the holy war with the Fonz. Giuliani submitted what McGuire describes as "a fabulous letter" of support for him to the Justice Department. And either Rudy or Denny Young, he says, put in a good word for him when he eventually became a partner at his current law firm, none other than the prestigious White & Case.

Twelve

Political Possession of Stolen Property

A L D'AMATO AND RUDY GIULIANI SHARED A SINGLE POLITICAL assumption in 1989: both believed that Rudy would wind up in a tough general election race with Ed Koch. The purpose of the Lauder smears, from D'Amato and Koch's perspective, was to soften Giuliani up for a November kill. Similarly, it was Koch's wounded and weary government that convinced Rudy he could win in the first place. History told all three that David Dinkins could not become the first black mayoral nominee of a major party in city history, overcoming the advantages of a three-term incumbent. History was off by about nine percentage points.

It wasn't just that the post-primary Giuliani had an unanticipated November opponent. His campaign lost its aura of grand mission, its Catholic clarity. What had seemed so pure a May crusade against the tarnished Koch was suddenly a murky November conundrum. Instead of facing his first election astride a white horse, Rudy's only hope now was to be carried into office by a wave of white fear.

The man he faced in the general election was so disarming he reminded Giuliani's core voters of the butler Rudy had cleverly mentioned during the Lauder debate. This surprise Democratic nominee spoke as if manners were more important than manipulation. He warmed to people of all backgrounds. He embodied racial peace at a moment in the life of the city when Yusef Hawkins proved color could still kill. He was a black man who did not shrink from his blackness yet had earned a death threat in Madison Square Garden from Louis Farrakhan. He was a mediator, yet marine enough, after a tour of non-combat duty, to go to battle three heartbreaking times before winning the borough presidency, which he then gave up to take a chance against Koch. If "tough" was the first adjective that came to mind when New Yorkers spoke of Giuliani, "nice guy" was the common first impression of David Dinkins.

Worse yet, Rudy was now the trooper blocking the schoolhouse door. He was history's obstacle. Instead of leading the reform movement he'd imagined at his announcement, he was impeding one so much larger than his, a struggle that had started on slave ships centuries before and had finally arrived at this summit of power, the mayoralty of America's empire city. What was most remarkable about Rudy—poised at this racial crossroads—was that he did not even seem to notice. What was chilling about him was how readily he attempted to adjust to this unexpected moral and political challenge, how eagerly he became whatever he needed to be to win.

He no longer spoke of small homeless shelters in every community, or identified with crack babies. He made no more cathedral addresses about the unity of African Americans and Italian Americans. The death penalty he had blasted as a "phony issue" in March suddenly became a crusade he promised to lead as mayor, vowing to "lobby and fight very, very hard for it" in Albany. The administration he had condemned as corrupt was magically extended to include Dinkins even though the borough president had been one of its staunchest Democratic critics. The peace dinner he and Dinkins had had at the start—its promises broken—prompted only "agita" now for Dinkins, and amnesia for Giuliani.

A campaign mounted in May to bond a partitioned city would, by November, divide it into polarized blocs. The Rudy who launched his first run for office, listening to the finest heartbeats of his life, would disappear in its final weeks. He would prove that all he wanted was to win, that all he feared was losing. No one would have expected him to simply lie down and lose, but few who knew him thought he would do whatever it took to win. He had waited until he was forty-five years old to run, leaving little time for comebacks if he was to achieve the fate he felt should be his. Not even history could get in the way of that destiny.

Down by twenty-four points to Dinkins by late September, with Koch and all the rest of the Democratic establishment supporting Dinkins at a mass unity rally at City Hall, Rudy went on the attack. His first post-primary commercial revived the question of Dinkins's failure to file tax returns from 1969 to 1972. It aired on Donna's station, WPIX, during the newscast.

"Some people will try to tell you this is a negative commercial," an announcer said as scrolling text repeated the message. "But it isn't because it's fair and the facts are true." Dinkins disclosed the facts himself in 1973, when he had to step aside because of his tax delinquencies after Mayor Abe Beame had picked him as a deputy mayor. He'd paid $28,645 in penalties and fines for four years of avoidance. It had already cost him one seat in the sun and had been used against him every time he ran for office.

Dinkins claimed that at their dinner in February, Giuliani told him "the income tax matter was very, very old and was not an issue." Giuliani changed his mind, Dinkins concluded, "because of the polls." While Giuliani personally responded to Dinkins's charge that the ad was a sign of desperation, he left it to his press spokesman to discuss the dinner promise: "He does not remember the tax issue coming up."

Simultaneously with the commercial, which bought far more free press coverage than the campaign bought airtime, Giuliani also placed an ad in the largest Yiddish newspaper, the *Algemeiner Journal*. It cost only $800 but reaped a whirlwind. The ad counterposed a picture of George Bush and Rudy with one of Jesse Jackson and Dinkins. It read: "Let the people of New York choose their own destiny." The ad was a holiday greeting for Rosh Hashanah, the Jewish New Year.

Giuliani denied that the ad had anything to do "with the color of your skin, your religion or your ethnicity." Yet almost anyone who'd ever pulled a lever in a New York voting booth knew it was a naked appeal to Jews, connecting Dinkins with the turbulent tide of black anti-Semitism. The dishonesty of it was transparent since Dinkins, who led a boycott protest of Farrakhan, had a track record on Jewish issues no one could question. Richard Cohen in the *Washington Post* called it "anxiety by association."

Rudy said it was tit for tat—likening it to Dinkins's branding of him as a Reagan Republican. He could not see the difference between his role as Reagan's associate attorney general and Dinkins's endorsement of the first black presidential candidate. He could not distinguish between the high-water marks of his career—which were a consequence of two appointments by Ronald Reagan—and Dinkins's identification with a symbolic candidacy.

The ad was reprinted on the news pages of every tabloid, and while it was called "troubling" by the American Jewish Committee, it began to take a toll on Dinkins, eroding his Jewish support. Dinkins had kept Jackson at bay until the 1989 murder of Yusef Hawkins, when the celebrity preacher finally came to town and turned the protests into a rallying cry for Dinkins. He and Dinkins didn't make a joint appearance until September 2. But Dinkins allowed Jackson to dominate his victory party the night of the primary, talking to the cameras for fifteen minutes and opening the door to this Giuliani hit.

The irony was that if Koch had won the Democratic primary, Giuliani no doubt would've welcomed Jackson's support. After all, his emissary, Marty Bergman, had sought out Bill Lynch as a possible campaign operative for Rudy, and Lynch was one of the directors of Jackson's 1988 New York presidential campaign. Bergman in fact met Lynch at a fundraiser Bergman threw in his home for Jackson.

At the same moment as the explosive Jackson ad, a furor arose over the racial monologues of Jackie Mason, the borscht belt comedian and Orthodox rabbi who had been accompanying Giuliani on campaign appearances. First, Mason told the *Village Voice* that Jewish support for Dinkins was based on guilt and that Jews were "sick with complexes." Once that story broke, *Newsweek* revealed that Mason had earlier referred to Dinkins as a "fancy shvartze with a mustache," a Yiddish expression that had become the colloquial equivalent of "nigger."

Mason made the remark at a luncheon with Giuliani and four *Newsweek* reporters weeks earlier, but *Newsweek* did not report it until after the *Voice* piece. Giuliani maintained he had not heard the remark, but according to *Newsweek*, "Giuliani joined in the nervous laughter, making no attempt to rebuke Mason." Giuliani aides cited the same punctured eardrum that got Giuliani out of the Air Force ROTC in 1963 as the reason he'd missed the slur at an intimate lunch.

The prominence of Mason in the campaign was a reminder of how Kochphobic it was from the outset. Giuliani had met Mason in January 1989 when Mason debuted an anti-Koch shtick at the Village Gate, where Giuliani, Dinkins and other soon-to-be mayoral candidates were celebrating the publication of *City for Sale*, a chronicle of the Koch scandals, with Rudy as hero.

Mason invited himself to the Gate, coming with constant sidekick Raoul Felder, whose representation of Andy Capasso's wife had helped bring to light the tawdry details of the Bess Myerson case. Mason's ridicule of Koch's "didn't-see-nothing-don't-know-nothing" defense had Giuliani giddy all night, and a marriage from heaven, at least for a race against Ed Koch, was made. Mason even did an anti-Koch commercial for the Giuliani campaign. But a comedic bonanza against Koch turned out to be a bust against Dinkins.

What no one in the press noticed was that Rudy acknowledged that his press aide had raised the issue of the shvartze comment with Giuliani immediately after the August 31 luncheon. All Giuliani did—with Koch still in the race—was ask Mason's manager to make sure he never used the phrase again (and this was the day after Giuliani's visit to the Hawkins funeral). But when the much milder Mason comments broke a month later in the *Voice*—and Koch was no longer in the race—Giuliani asked the comedian to leave the campaign. It was obviously a combination of the difference between getting caught (*Newsweek* didn't publish the shvartze comment until October) and Mason's diminishing utility. Mason's slur itself was not a cause for decisive Giuliani action.

The attraction to Mason was not just that he was Giuliani's "ambassador" to the Jewish community, as the *New York Times* put it, but that he helped show that Rudy "has a sense of humor." This rationale was openly stated by Giuliani's press secretary. The assumption was that Rudy was such a lead weight the only way to lighten him up was to let people see him laugh at someone else's jokes. He did that whenever deadpan Jackie opened his mouth. This wit deficit was only a problem when Rudy was counterposed to the jocular Koch, since Dinkins was as heavy-footed as Giuliani.

With the Mason incident and the Jackson ad as a backdrop, the underlying dynamic of the campaign had clearly become race. That theme would be repeated again and again in October, with Rudy's campaign targeting four Dinkins aides, all black, in news revelation after news revelation.

Newsday revealed that Dinkins manager Bill Lynch had approved $10,000 in campaign payments to a nominal organization, the Committee to Honor Black Heroes, controlled by notorious race-baiter Sonny Carson. Carson had been convicted in Brooklyn in 1975 of the kidnapping of a black man. Depicted as an anti-Semite in follow-up stories the Giuliani camp encouraged, Carson obliged by holding a press conference in the black Brooklyn neighborhood of Bedford-Stuyvesant, surrounded by bodyguards in nationalist colors, and declaring how offended he was. "I'm anti-white," he boomed. "Don't limit my anti-ing to just being one little group of people. I think you'd insult me if you tried to do that."

The reporter who broke the story, Lenny Levitt, says he noticed the strangely named committee, without an address, on the Dinkins campaign filing and tracked it to Carson. Levitt said he made the discovery without a Giuliani tip, but that after the story, the Giuliani camp called to congratulate him. Levitt can't remember if it was Ray Harding or Peter Powers who spoke to him, but whichever one it was said the story was "perfect" and that it allowed the campaign "to put out other stuff we have" but previously couldn't, presumably because of the racial climate. Giuliani immediately threw an ad up on the tube focusing on Carson's kidnapping conviction and Rudy said: "This ex-convict was set out on the streets to get votes."

Another Giuliani target, Jitu Weusi, was a public school teacher during the racially explosive citywide strike in 1968 who at that time read a stridently anti-Semitic poem on the radio that had been written by a student of his. He had since founded a successful, Afrocentric private school and, unlike Carson, been a positive nationalist force within black Brooklyn, respected by leading black elected officials. When Giuliani found him on the Dinkins payroll, the leaked stories pigeonholed him as an anti-Semite based on a single, distant, event. "I have spent the last 20 years apologizing as well as suffering," he told the *Post*. "When do I get a reprieve?"

Harding was quoted in the lead of the story, which was headlined: "Liberal Chief: Dinkins Aide Is a Jew-Baiter," leaving no doubt about where the well-shopped allegation was coming from. Weusi, whose name alone beat drums in white ears, said the poem did not represent his views then or now, and that he found it "deeply offensive." The combination of the Carson and Weusi stories—which the Giuliani campaign kept alive for weeks—helped provoke cries of "Jackie Mason was right" from Jewish crowds greeting Giuliani.

Word of the Carson and Weusi roles with Dinkins traveled a strange route to Giuliani headquarters. Giuliani knew about Carson in fact before Levitt wrote a word. The campaign's original source, ironically, was the Brooklyn-based Reverend Al Sharpton. Dinkins was keeping Sharpton—another alarm bell for Jewish voters who happened to be under indictment on state tax charges at the time—as far away as possible. Without an indirect assist from street-savvy Sharpton, the Giuliani campaign wouldn't have had the slightest idea who Weusi and Carson were. Sharpton heard that Carson was putting together a breakfast for Dinkins at Junior's in downtown Brooklyn and running a registration and pull operation for the candidate in Brooklyn projects. Sharpton told Brooklyn GOP leader Arthur Bramwell about the Carson/Weusi roles, and Bramwell relayed it to the campaign, citing his source and precisely why Sharpton was talking.

"Yes, he fed me the information," said Bramwell, a Bedford-Stuyvesant GOP district leader active in the Giuliani campaign. "I was the only guy he'd talk to." Bramwell had known Sharpton's mother for years, as well as the bishop Sharpton credits with bringing him into the ministry, and had helped deliver a Sharpton endorsement of Al D'Amato in the 1986 Senate race. Bramwell even told the Giuliani people how deep the enmity was between Sharpton and Dinkins, recounting a story of how Dinkins, as a private attorney, had overcharged Sharpton years earlier for incorporating an organization then run by the young minister. Bramwell was the vice chair of that organization. Chris Lyon, the research director for Giuliani's campaign, recalls that they first heard about Carson and Weusi via this bizarre pipeline and that, on a weekend, he hurriedly did Nexus and other searches on these targets.

Sharpton says he doesn't remember the incident, though he acknowledges talking to Bramwell during the campaign. "I knew Sonny and them were working voter registration," he recalls. "If I told them anything, I told them these guys were involved in the campaign."

Jim Bell, the vice president of a United Auto Workers local who took a leave from his union job to coordinate security and travel for the Dinkins campaign, was nailed in an October television story by WNBC-TV's John Miller. Bell's yellow sheet featured a 1971 misdemeanor conviction for hitting a police officer and was being circulated to reporters by none other than Tony Lombardi. He offered the story to one reporter who turned it down. When Miller went with it, he cited unnamed "law enforcement sources."

Miller's name appears in Lombardi's logs several times, including once a few days after the Bell story. Miller would not confirm that Lombardi gave him the rap sheet, but several sources knowledgeable about how he got the story confirmed that it came "from the Giuliani camp." Bell's swipe at the cop was so minor he was fined $100, and he claimed that the cop had called him a "nigger."

Phil Thompson, who earned a meager total of $515 as a consultant to Dinkins and was a fellow at the Robert Wagner Sr. Institute of Urban Public Policy at New York University at the time, was blasted in a *Post* story for having a "fiery red past." At one time a member of the central committee of the Communist Workers Party, the Harvard-educated Thompson was red meat for the Rudy machine. Lynch had brought Thompson to Dinkins after meeting him in the Walter Mondale campaign of 1984, and Thompson is now a full professor in Columbia University's political science department. Hardly Maoist credentials. But the *Post* story—and one in a weekly that quoted from decade-old speeches of his—convinced him that "someone had been going through my FBI file." The scandal also cost him a job at the Ford Foundation.

Strangely enough, Harding, who was fast becoming the campaign's garbage dispenser, made his own living on legal cases referred to him by the Yugoslav mission. Confronted by a reporter, he could not see the contradiction between smearing a young black once tied to a fringe left party and his own fees from a communist government.

"Many of the stories that surfaced this week," the *New York Times* concluded in the midst of the Carson, Thompson and Weusi stories, "had circulated widely as rumors, but it was not until the Giuliani campaign made them into campaign issues, that they were picked up by the press."

This collection of negative New York stereotypes about blacks—criminals, anti-Semites, communists—led Giuliani to conclude: "So some real questions now have to be raised about Dinkins's judgment, the kind of people he surrounds himself with. And then, importantly, if he were mayor, what kind of people would he have surrounding him in City Hall." He said Bill Lynch should be fired for hiring this questionable crew.

In fact, Lynch too was apparently targeted. On September 28, 1989, two weeks after the primary, Lynch got the first of three letters from the IRS about his 1985 tax return. The return had been filed on time and no question about it had been raised in the intervening three years. When Lynch got the notice, which was resolved in 1990 without any additional tax or penalties, he thought it was routine. In fact, the IRS says auditing a return that old is not ordinary.

Around the same time as the audit letter, a top deputy in the SDNY personally close to both IRS agent Tony Lombardi and Giuliani, told two reporters that Lynch had a tax "problem," though he refused to be specific. The deputy appeared "tickled" about the "problem," said one reporter. Lombardi, who has not conceded any role he might have played in the audit, later said in an interview: "I don't recall if another agent could have said that they had him under investigation. I don't rule that possibility out."

In addition to the audit, Lombardi, who had met Lynch and Bell at a June garden party, mentioned matter-of-factly to a reporter that he tailed Lynch during the final weeks of the 1989 campaign. Pressed about the surveillance in an interview in 1993, Lombardi said: "I can't ever remember that happening." Lombardi went on to talk about Lynch as if he had, at some point, been a subject of sordid interest: "I don't recall anybody ever coming to me to say that Bill Lynch has done anything wrong. I heard a story about his son. I heard some matters that I would think he would be pained about as a father. I only knew of what little rumors one might want to have floated about the guy." Lombardi, the rap sheet expert, was apparently referring to a dismissed disorderly conduct charge and a farebeating arrest.

Lynch said that he and Bell, who has since died, believed that they were followed on several occasions during the campaign as they left the West 43rd Street headquarters: "We'd leave anywhere from midnight to 2 A.M. and pick the car up in a parking lot on West 44th Street. We had the same routine: drive up 8th Avenue, then over to Broadway and 72nd Street," where they would buy hot dogs and newspapers. "We'd go north on Central Park West or Amsterdam Avenue. At some point, we both were sure that we were being tailed by the same car each night. I didn't really think about it that much until it happens for like the fourth or fifth time. So we pulled over one night at 105th Street and jumped out of the car and ran back towards the guy behind us. That's when he backed up and cut out." Lynch said the tails ended that night.

Lombardi freely admitted he investigated a reputed girlfriend of the very married Dinkins. "There was one case which was given to me to handle in a very, very delicate way. And that was Dinkins having a love liaison with a woman who was on his staff and that he was doing whatever was necessary in order to get this woman promoted," he said in a taped interview. "Everybody knew about it. The thing was if there was some criminality to it."

While Lombardi declined to name the woman and claimed he conducted the inquiry when Dinkins was mayor, his 1989 diaries contain a detailed entry about 605 Water Street in Manhattan, the home of a Dinkins aide named Cindy Ng. The entry occurred on October 30, nine days before the election. Peter Powers told the *Times* the same day that "New Yorkers deserve to know the facts concerning Cynthia Ng's apartment."

Ng had already taken an ugly news hit in the *Post* back in August, when a reporter and photographer surprised her at a meeting of a Chinese-American political club where Dinkins was speaking.

The thirty-seven-year-old aide, when stopped by the *Post*, fled to a phone booth and hid in the dark for twenty minutes. Dinkins's angry "explosion" at the reporter was reported in the *Post* as "unusual." The story detailed how Ng's salary had doubled—reaching $49,000—since she had joined Dinkins's staff in 1984. It also charged that she submitted false income affidavits to qualify for her city-subsidized apartment near Dinkins's office. Someone in Dinkins's personnel office had verified Ng's understated income, according to the story. The Ng story had faded off the news pages until Powers tried to revive it in October.

The fixation on Ng had more to do with what was suspected to have gone on in the apartment than the subsidy for it. *Newsday* revealed in 1987 that the $95,000-a-year executive director of the New York City Housing Authority, who lived alone, was illegally occupying a subsidized apartment reserved for a low-income family of five. No other newspaper even reported it, including the *Post*, and the city investigation commissioner declined to investigate. As soon as the Ng story was published, however, a Department of Investigation (DOI) probe was publicly announced.

The *Post*'s Jerry Nachman defended the selective focus on Ng, contending that "it didn't matter" if her low-balled income claims were "commonplace," they should still be examined. The *Daily News*'s Barbara Ross, who was assigned to the Giuliani campaign, had passed on the story before the *Post* went with it, but only after Ross asked Dinkins to his face if he was having an affair with Ng. When Dinkins was elected, his DOI commissioner referred the case to the Manhattan district attorney to investigate "to avoid any appearance of conflict of interest." The DA soon announced that no charges would be filed. After a stint in Dinkins's City Hall, Ng moved to California, where she works in a management position at Stanford University today.

The Giuliani campaign was prepared, however, to go much further than Ng on the Dinkins sex trail. They had a time bomb they wanted to detonate as close to the November 7 election as possible. Shortly after the September primary, they obtained a devastating fifty-four-page file of letters, with seventeen photographs, taken from Dinkins's public office.

The letters were from eight different women, and the photos were of him with his arms wrapped around them or sometimes posing cheek-to-cheek, often in tennis whites. Dinkins had apparently traveled from one public position to the next with the letters, since the earliest were addressed to him at the New York City Board of Elections, which he used to chair, and the latest were sent to him at the City Clerk's office, which he headed until 1986.

One woman signed her name but referred to herself as "cupcake"; another addressed him as "my chocolate button." "Cupcake" wrote on January 7, 1983: "I thought of you at the dawn of 1983—wanting so to feel close and share memories of our special moments together. Always my mind returns to Philadelphia and how you swept me off my feet (smile)." Shelley wrote: "Thanks for the loving so sweet and so free—searching, exploring, being with me." One from PeggyAnne in Puerto Rico written at 7:10 A.M. said: "You have changed me with your touch." Collected over an eleven-year period, the letters, which clearly referred in some cases to physical relationships, came from Puerto Rico, Spain, Florida, and California. The candidate who failed to file his taxes apparently never misplaced a love letter.

The route the letters took to campaign headquarters would've set off stolen-property alarms were Rudy still at the U.S. Attorney's office. Research director Chris Lyon says he was given the letters "in an open shoebox one Saturday at the midtown campaign office by Raquel Vidal," Dinkins's secretary until July 1986. After Dinkins was elected borough president in 1985, Vidal expected a significant position in the new office. According to Vidal, Dinkins said at one major fundraising dinner: "You want to see my committee. Here's my one-person committee," pointing at Vidal. Angered by promotions Cindy Ng had achieved, Vidal was so offended by her own contrasting treatment, she quit and took at least one file and a rolodex with her.

Vidal's sister Sara was a regular volunteer in the Giuliani campaign, even though she was on the payroll of City Council President Andrew Stein, a Democrat. Dinkins had run against Stein for Manhattan borough president in both 1977 and 1981 in bitter campaigns. A covert ally of Giuliani's in 1989, Stein had "no problem" with Sara's frequent involvement in the Giuliani campaign, Vidal now says. Occasionally joined by Raquel, Sara Vidal accompanied Giuliani to Hispanic events throughout the campaign, also working on outreach efforts to Hispanic voters. Sara raised $3,575 from twenty-nine individuals for the Giuliani campaign, all on October 2, 1989. The sisters also donated $635 to Rudy's mayoral campaigns over the years.

Raquel Vidal's decision to turn over the letters was not simply a product of three-year-old anger. Half Dominican and half Puerto Rican, the sisters lived with their mother Ercira in a one-family home in Queens. Their mother, who'd met Rudy once, died on June 17, in the middle of the campaign. They were deeply moved when Giuliani showed up first at the funeral home. He got there at 1:45 P.M. for the 2:30 funeral, the sisters recall, prayed, and left a mass card, amazing even the funeral director. "You never forget that," Sara says now. Though Raquel had worked for Dinkins for years and Dinkins knew her mother, he did not call or come. "Joyce Dinkins sent flowers," Sara recalled, referring to Dinkins's wife. Raquel did not turn over the love letters to the campaign until well after her mother's death, and soon after Dinkins' primary win.

In an extended interview in 1999, Raquel Vidal would neither directly confirm nor deny delivering the letters. "You can write what you want to write and I will have no comment," she said, after listening to a detailed description of her visit to the Giuliani headquarters. "Talk to Dinkins and Lynch. They would understand why I did what I did. I don't have anything to add to what they have to say." Lynch said Vidal was "livid" and "flipped out" when Dinkins's office refused to rehire her. She tried to return months after she'd quit, says Lynch, and got "angrier and angrier" when she could not get another job "for a long time," adding that he certainly believed she took the letters when she left.

Raquel acknowledged she was quite familiar with the letters, saying they went to "the character of the person involved" and argued that they were a legitimate public issue, even though none of the women who wrote them had any connection with Dinkins's official position

Sara Vidal wound up a deputy commissioner of human rights under Giuliani, earning a city salary twice her Stein paycheck as soon as Rudy took office in 1994. Since then, she's received several salary increases and now makes $80,000 a year as the director of the city's office on Census 2000.

Raquel Vidal got a secretarial job in 1987 with the Federal Home Loan Bank of New York, a congressionally chartered quasi-public bank. She rose from the secretarial ranks, starting as a temp, to an executive position as public information officer after Giuliani became mayor. Guy Molinari, the Staten Island borough president close to Giuliani, chaired the bank board when she was elevated to her executive post. The bank will not disclose her salary increases or discuss her references, political or otherwise. By all accounts, even those of the Dinkins camp, the Vidals are competent and hardworking staffers.

The day the letters arrived, campaign headquarters was abuzz about them. "Everyone" at a senior staff meeting—Harding, Peter Powers, and others—"had one in their hand," according to Lyon, who was present at the meeting. "They were filled with glee," says Lyon. "It was the giddiness of teenage boys looking at Playboy. I felt, and so did most people in the room, that if the letters were printed, Giuliani wins." Rudy was at the meeting himself, but cautionary. Since the letters indicated Dinkins was taking trips, sometimes with women and sometimes to visit them, Giuliani focused on it as a financial scandal, contending Dinkins could not afford these trips. The question he posed, says Lyon, was how to link the trips and the women to city funds. No immediate decision was made about how to deal with the letters but they were taken from Lyon and "kicked upstairs."

The first attempt to get the content of the letters out was an anonymous mailing to selected members of the New York press. On October 4, the three-page memo appeared in the name of a concocted organization called the Independent Democrats of Chinatown and the Lower East Side. The memo defended Giuliani, dismissing attacks on him written by columnist Jimmy Breslin, and charged that Dinkins was "enjoying immunity from the press in the name of racial harmony." It called Dinkins "a gigolo in a permanent state of mid-life crisis."

"Although he has been married to whom he refers as 'his bride of 36 years,' evidence is available which shows that he has been involved in extramarital affairs as far back as 1970. With so many problems in the Black family structure, does NYC need Dinkins as a role model? Yes, there is a need for role models within the Black community, but no one who has no respect for wife and home. He speaks of high roads, yet leads a low life."

The press memo named Ng, who contributed no letters to the old file, and eight women, most of whom were identifiable from the letters. The memo contained information about several of the women—including identifying one as "blond and blue-eyed" for obvious racial purposes—that could not be obtained from the letters alone. The places of work of some were listed. That's where the Vidal rolodex may have come into play. The memo also challenged reporters to ask Dinkins about these women and promised that "if and when he denies these facts, we will present you with the evidence."

Chris Lyon remembers getting a copy of the flyer, though he says his research unit had nothing to do with producing it. When it got no press response, a debate erupted at the highest levels of the campaign about what to do with the letters. Lyon and several other campaign sources recall that the biggest fear was that if a story about the letters was printed, their release might be traced back to the Giuliani campaign and wind up hurting Giuliani as much as it did Dinkins. Too many people within the campaign knew about them, and any planted story would be traced back to Giuliani. It was decided at that point not to give them to reporters.

But in the final days of the campaign, public polls started showing the once wide gap between Dinkins and Giuliani narrowing to a very winnable margin. The pressure to use the letters grew. No subsequent high-level meeting was held re-examining the earlier decision. Instead, on Thursday, October 26, the *Post's* Fred Dicker, a skillful, hard-boiled reporter with a decidedly Republican/conservative tilt, got a phone call and a tantalizing offer. Three hours later, he had the letters, given to him, according to three sources, who asked not to be identified, through Ray Harding. Lyon remembers that the custodian of the letters, after he turned them over at the staff meeting, was Carl Grillo, Harding's aide.

So Dicker started working the phones, trying to locate the women who'd written the letters. The next day he called Bill Lynch and set up a meeting for 2 P.M., when he gave Lynch copies of the letters and asked for comment. Dicker soon got a call from Andrew Cuomo, the governor's son.

The *Post's* regular Albany bureau chief, Dicker knew the Cuomos well. Unofficially aiding Lynch in the Dinkins campaign, Andrew Cuomo said he was calling to give Dicker "friendly advice to be careful with the matter." According to a memo to file Dicker wrote at the time, Cuomo warned: "people will be going after you." Efforts were being made, Dicker learned, to go around him to his superiors. That night Cuomo called back to "make sure nothing got into print," Dicker said.

That night, a Friday, Cuomo and Lynch took copies of the letters to Dinkins, who was staying at a suite at the Sheraton Centre. It was twelve days from election day, and Dinkins, who met the two in a bathrobe, shifted quickly from denial to desperation. The attention-grabber was Cuomo's question about whether the phrase "my chocolate button" meant anything to him.

The Dinkins camp reached out to Peter Kalikow, the *Post's* owner, talking first to Kalikow's top adviser, public relations consultant Marty McLaughlin. Nachman and McLaughlin talked. They agreed that there were lots of editorial and political problems with the story. No city employees were involved; none of the women were talking. It was obvious that publication of the letters, with the first black mayor on the verge of election, would be racial dynamite, to say nothing of the possible electoral backlash if a paper endorsing Giuliani printed them.

Dinkins, who rushed out to a black-tie dinner after the session with Lynch and Cuomo, reached Kalikow at his home. Kalikow was uncomfortable with the story. He liked Dinkins personally. He bought Nachman's and McLaughlin's arguments. When Dinkins got off the phone, he seemed reassured that the *Post* would not print the letters. The next morning, Cuomo was the first to inform Dicker that his story would not be published. He presented it as a done deal.

That same Saturday morning Cuomo called a *Village Voice* reporter at home, having heard that he might have the letters and write a story. It took half an hour for the reporter to convince Cuomo that he'd turned down the letters when they were offered by a Giuliani source. It had been rumored for days that the *Voice* was doing the story, although in fact no one at the paper was even considering it. The scuttlebutt, encouraged by the Giuliani campaign, was designed to induce a daily to scoop the weekly *Voice*. Instead, the paper was getting calls from other news organizations promising to credit the *Voice* if they could get an advance copy of the fantasy story.

Dicker called Nachman at his Connecticut home after his Cuomo conversation and Nachman said he had "a million questions" about the story, putting him off to Monday. Another editor told him on Monday that the *Post* didn't want the story. Nachman said years later that a Dinkins call to Kalikow killing the story was "plausible," but the editor was so dismissive of the letters himself that he contended they were "in crayon without any pictures," which is not true.

Dicker said he had "an icy feeling" when he learned the story was spiked, calling the decision making one of "the shabbiest and most poorly handled things" in his long *Post* career. By Monday afternoon, however, word about the letters had spread to every newsroom in the city. Josh Barbanel of the *Times* called Dicker and said he'd heard the *Post* had killed the story; Dicker declined to comment. Arthur Browne, a top editor at the *Daily News*, called a Giuliani political consultant asking about the prospect of a *Post* story.

Giuliani's efforts to expose Dinkins's romances were apparently unaffected by any concerns about his own. Ironically, Kathleen Smith, the ex-secretary he'd dated in his Justice Department days, was working as the director of volunteers at Rudy's campaign headquarters. Smith's sister Therese McManus was another top campaign aide, in charge of scheduling. Smith had left a Washington job to come up to work in New York for Rudy. Single and attractive, she'd been the subject of internal campaign gossip, with many aware of her once intimate ties to the candidate.

In late October, with the press awash in talk about the love letters, Dinkins had a warning letter hand-delivered to Giuliani headquarters. "If you persist in your present course," Dinkins wrote without any specifics, "you will learn something I learned in the Marine Corps. Marines aren't very good at picking fights, but they certainly know how to end them." Shortly thereafter, the Dinkins camp reached out to Regina Peruggi, hoping to turn her story into a weapon against Rudy. Jim Hall pressured her to help, according to Hall's closest friends. Gussie Kappner, her mentor and confidant, was seen by others at CUNY headquarters pressuring her to meet with Dinkins's people. Friends say she even playfully wore a Dinkins button. Her black and white worlds were colliding.

Regina talked for the first time to a reporter—Maria Laurino of the *Village Voice*—the same week the letters were delivered to Fred Dicker. She had been fighting reporters off up to then. Laurino was focused on the annulment and Giuliani's contrived loophole that won it—namely that he had originally thought they were "distant cousins."

While Regina's minimal quotes did not directly counter that, Peruggi's friends and a relative did. Peruggi's maid of honor, Pat Rufino, who lived in Florida, called Rudy's contention "baloney," saying they knew exactly how close the ties were. "Regina was extremely upset. To turn and tell someone not only is this marriage over, but it didn't exist, is a real slap in the face."

Another friend, Jackie Moore, cited the same anger: "It kind of negates fourteen years of your life." Moore and Rufino confirmed that Regina, who decided that a divorce was necessary, had sent a letter of protest about the annulment to the archdiocese. Her brother Richard said of the Rudy rationale: "That's a lie. He knew he was my second cousin." That, of course, meant that Rudy knew at the time of the wedding that they were closely enough related to require a dispensation.

Laurino's point was that Giuliani had engaged in an "obvious public prevarication" to gain the annulment, undermining the image of probity he was trying to sell to the electorate. As damning as the Laurino facts were, the dailies shrunk from the story. Regina's friends said she had wanted out "because of problems in the marriage," but the story shed no light on what those problems were and Regina's friends would not spell them out in detail. The cloud long cast over his first marriage—with its separations and on again/off again ambiguity—now hung over the campaign.

The Regina story—and the threat of more of it—was driving the Giuliani campaign berserk. Rudy told the *Daily News* that the Dinkins campaign had prepared a TV commercial focusing on his first marriage but hadn't aired it because of adverse reaction from a test audience. The *Amsterdam News*, a strong Dinkins supporter, ran two stories in its pre-election issue on the Peruggi annulment, one on the front page. Peter Powers, armed with the love letters and facing the Regina rumors, offered a telling analogy to a consultant with friends in both camps: "Tell the Dinkins people it's like the Cuban Missile Crisis."

Dave Seifman, the *Post*'s level-headed City Hall bureau chief, wrote a column headlined "Low Blows" that vaguely listed the invisible punches and counterpunches in what a source in his story called "the most vicious campaign" he'd ever seen. Seifman blamed both camps, concluding: "The Giuliani camp is clearly the more active."

Giuliani aides pushed on to try to get references to the love letters published in any fashion that might open the door, even if it was a trick story about how the *Post* had killed its own scoop. Right up to the Sunday before the Tuesday election, everyone at the highest levels of both campaigns was on edge. One top Giuliani campaign operative said: "There was a lot of joking and intense speculation about whether the letters would appear. Rudy was involved in it himself. We were counting on the letters. We didn't think we'd win without them."

Most of the focus in the last week was on the *News*, where Adam Nagourney came in for unusual Saturday duty four days before the election. Though Nagourney, Arthur Browne and others at the *News* said they never saw the letters, they did not want to get scooped if the *Post* made a last-minute decision to publish them. A story could be done about the buzz surrounding the letters without citing them directly, and Nagourney and his editors were also considering that option. Nagourney says, "We were getting faked out by the Giuliani people; they were trying to convince us that the *Post* was doing it." Another *News* reporter involved in the coverage said, "The Giuliani people were trying to steamroll us into doing the story."

Andrew Cuomo calmly reasoned with Nagourney in mid-afternoon. He appealed to Nagourney on the basis of the confidentiality of a public official's private life. Jack Newfield, a *News* columnist at the time, saw paragraphs on Nagourney's screen he thought were the beginning of a piece and argued against a story, pointing out to Browne and others that the private lives of many white politicians had never been so publicly exposed. The editors were on the phones with lawyers, who had raised questions about the legality of receiving, much less printing, the letters. One attorney, as Newfield recalled it, contended that the letters might be the copyright property of the women who wrote them, making their use more difficult.

That same weekend, Chris Lyon approached Powers for a final conversation about the letters. Lyon told Powers that he thought someone he knew at the *Washington Times* would print a story if the New York papers wouldn't and that local tabloids would have to follow the Washington story. "Peter told me we couldn't do it because our fingerprints at this point were all over the letters," Lyons recalls. "The New York follow-up story, Peter said, would be about how the Giuliani campaign planted the letters in Washington." Lyon says he knew then that "the campaign was over."

Finally, the Sunday sex bombshell so coveted by the Giuliani camp fizzled out, just as the Regina ruckus died down. Raquel Vidal complained years later that the story was "squashed," saying all the letters did was bring city and postal investigators to her door in the 1990s, another event she blamed on Dinkins, who was mayor at the time. Rudy had pressed every chocolate button he could, but he would have to face Dinkins on November 7 without a word of it in type.

A year or so after the loss, Rudy and Donna went to Philadelphia to the annual regional awards dinner of the Radio Television News Directors' Association. WPIX director John Corporon had invited them, and the three were having drinks in a cocktail lounge at the hotel when Corporon raised the love letters. Ever since Corporon heard about them during the 1989 campaign, he'd wondered why no story ever appeared. He'd once bumped into Jerry Nachman and grilled him about it, recalling that Nachman said he didn't know if it would've been "appropriate" to publish them.

"We were chatting about politics," Corporon recalled his conversation with Rudy and Donna, "and I said, by the way, I meant to ask you . . . about those love letters. It was just curiosity and gossip as far I was concerned. But Rudy wasn't playing that game." Corporon said he couldn't remember precisely what Rudy said, but he indicated he "didn't want to talk about it." It was "absolutely clear that he heard about the letters," said Corporon, and it was just as clear he "didn't particularly want to discuss it."

Though Rudy spent the four years in between mayoral elections running against Dinkins, and Dinkins spent them fending off Giuliani, the dueling dynamite of the letters and Regina had been defused. Neither would appear on Rudy's radar screen again, even when Harold Ickes, the counsel to the Dinkins campaign, became *Post* owner Peter Kalikow's lobbyist soon after Dinkins took office. Ickes successfully steered a major development project for real estate baron Kalikow through the city approval process. And Rudy Giuliani, the daily commentator on everything else that happened in the Dinkins administration, did not say a word about the Kalikow decision that might've decided an election and cemented a mutually beneficial political friendship. The episode was potentially so embarrassing to everyone involved Rudy could never mention it.

I t wasn't as if sex and race were the only weapons available to Giuliani in his run against Dinkins. *Newsday* and the *Village Voice* broke stories about Dinkins's only significant personal asset, the stock he owned in a cable company. As Manhattan borough president and a member of the city's Board of Estimate, Dinkins had voted twice on franchise issues affecting the company, despite an ethics opinion advising him not to. He supposedly transferred the stock to his son, but proof of the transaction was as dubious as the lowball value he placed on it in his financial disclosure statements. The media storm over the cable revelations was so hot Rudy's electoral stock soared.

With help again from Raquel Vidal, who was identified as a former Dinkins secretary and quoted in one *Daily News* story on the stock, the Giuliani campaign extended the original conflict-of-interest stories into another tax evasion controversy. One paper after another did stories raising questions about Dinkins's failure to pay gift taxes, and Giuliani rightly connected that to the otherwise ancient history of evasion. *New York* magazine revealed the day before the election that the quotable secretary who'd helped prepare the disclosure forms was the sister of Giuliani's "Latino coordinator Sara Vidal," suggesting the source on the tax story was biased.

While Rudy's campaign aides quietly fueled the sex firestorm, the candidate himself brilliantly worked the cable scandal. Dinkins faced a supposed tell-all, standing-room-only press conference on the stock in the unaired heat of his strobe-lit headquarters, but his answers were more sound bite than substance. He handed out a "Dear Dad" letter from his son that theoretically memorialized the stock sale for $58,000, but could explain why years of financial disclosure filings had never divulged it. More than Carson or any of the other racial flare-ups of the campaign, the cable scandal damaged Dinkins and narrowed the polls. Democrats who wanted to vote against him for wrong reasons were hand-delivered a right reason.

As effectively as Rudy rode this issue, he didn't believe it could win the election. So in the final week, he tried a new race formulation. At Columbia University, he started saying race wasn't a reason to vote for anyone. He said "the potential for their frustration"—by which he meant the possible anger of Dinkins's black supporters if he lost—"is not a rationale for the election of David Dinkins, any more than the potential for the dissatisfaction among my supporters is a legitimate reason for electing me." He downplayed the importance of racial harmony, saying it wasn't pivotal. "It's wrong for David Dinkins to expect the voters to choose him because he's black," he said, "just as it would be wrong for me to expect the voters to choose me because I am white."

It was his second speech on race since the campaign began, and one was the inverse of the other. By saying now it wasn't the issue, he was making it the issue. The first time, in the liberal phase of his early campaign, he was talking to blacks; the second time he was talking about them.

Similarly, when pressed about his Haitian actions in the early 1980s, Candidate Giuliani said, "I defended that policy and still do," adding it "saved a lot of lives." Yet he issued a four-page statement entitled "Issues That Concern Irish New

Yorkers," saying he was "a strong proponent of amnesty for undocumented immigrants." He even promised to press for "extending the cutoff date for amnesty applications from 1982 to 1989," meaning he wanted to grant immigration status to the Irish for precisely the years he'd worked to deny it to the Haitians.

Incredibly, he said "it does not make sense to deport people who are hardworking, law-abiding individuals," though he had admitted, in his testimony years earlier in the Haitian case, that the Haitians he was excluding were both. For the Irish, he favored "full legal status to people who are here already and who are contributing to society," as well as "complete and unimpeded access to municipal services" for all residents—"citizen or alien." No Krome for Celts!

His turnaround on Koch was just as drastic. Three days after the primary, Rudy's campaign sent a letter to Koch contributors saying that their support of the mayor demonstrated their "commitment to the future of our city" and their "concern about the quality of leadership that will guide New York." With every poll showing that Koch Democrats were reluctant to vote for Dinkins, Giuliani went out of his way to praise Koch, even saluting him on a corruption issue a week before the election.

In less than a year as a politician, Rudy had mastered the art of reinvention. He could recondition himself overnight. The Rudy who might have been mayor had Ed Koch won the primary would not be seen again—a Rudy the *Wall Street Journal* said was "the last thing either the city or the national GOP needs—another Lindsay liberal to give Republicanism a bad name." The dynamic of the campaign had turned Rudy into a political carousel, spinning round and round with a hundred, ever changing, faces.

Shortly before the election, Fiorello La Guardia's granddaughter Katherine stood up at an Italian-American political breakfast and announced her family's choice for mayor—David Dinkins. She said Giuliani had made "improper comparisons" between himself and her grandfather. John Lindsay in the end said Dinkins, not Giuliani, represented the coalition that had elected him.

The night he lost, Rudy's party was at the Roosevelt Hotel. Tony Lombardi was there, doomed not to be the commissioner he'd long been talking about. The gang from Foley Square and Justice was there—Ken Caruso, Denny Young, Randy Levine, Arnold Burns, all of whom had played key roles in the campaign. So was Mike Mukasey, who was telling stories about D'Amato though the senator had supported his appointment to the federal bench in the fall of 1987, when Rudy and Al were still talking about a Moynihan race.

The ballroom was filled with the frustrated supporters he'd closed the campaign invoking—white, male and mad. It was also filled with ugly untruths about how blacks had stolen the election at polls in Harlem and Bed-Stuy, where the dead had supposedly voted by the thousands.

Rudy gathered himself in a suite upstairs. His three-point, 44,000-vote loss was a miracle finish—the closest mayoral election since 1905—and he knew the numbers meant he had a future. He had feared a ten-point loss, since public polls in the final days had indicated a Dinkins surge. While other races, like one against Mario Cuomo in 1990 or D'Amato in 1992, were being discussed, it was already almost an assumption among the inner circle in the suite that he'd be back in a mayoral contest again. Destiny had only been delayed, briefly and narrowly.

Downstairs, when he tried to concede, he came face to face with the anger his hard dash to election day had unleashed. The clamor of booing and hissing that greeted Dinkins's name was a legacy of his own campaign. But he was already preparing for the next one. That was yesterday's baggage. He wanted everyone on the same page. He began bellowing at his supporters until his voice broke. His face contorted. His eyes popped. The press would say for years that he had told his own people to "shut up." Again and again. But all he said was, "No, no, no . . . Stop that! Quiet! Quiet!" It wasn't that he was out of control. He was outraged that they were out of his control.

He had already moved on and, as the years that lay ahead would prove, he was impatient with anyone on his side who could not keep pace with his shifting political moods.

Thirteen

A Season of Compromise
Preparing for 1993

DEFEAT WAS A STRANGER IN RUDY GIULIANI'S LIFE. FROM Manhattan College, NYU and MacMahon to Foley Square, Patterson and Justice, he had rarely suffered a setback. He'd been embarrassed a bit by Haiti, McDonnell Douglas, Myerson, Wigton and Tabor. But each had barely provoked momentary reflection. The 1989 election, however, yanked him to a halt, altered his career calendar and tested his gut.

Losing a terribly public slugfest—even by a margin he'd managed to miraculously narrow—also left him, for the first time since he became associate attorney general in 1981, just an ordinary man, albeit one still brimming with extraordinary ambition. He was again, as he had been almost a decade earlier, merely one of 62,000 lawyers in a city of clamoring courthouses. His return, in his discount suits, to an obscure private practice made him more certain than ever that it was not enough for him.

He went back to White & Case after the election, but lasted less than six months, rarely appearing at his office but still drawing hundreds of thousands in income. In January 1990, he bought a third apartment at 444 East 86th, moving Helen downstairs to the 18th floor. Settling in for the most domestic period of his and Donna's life, they knocked down the wall between their two units on the 35th floor and turned the renovated apartment into a reasonably spacious home for four. Rudy owned Helen's apartment alone, beginning a separation in his and Donna's finances that would widen over the years. He listed the apartment on his 1993 financial disclosure form, filed with the city, as valued at between $100,000 and $250,000, putting his Citicorp mortgage in the same range.

By May 1990, he left W&C for Anderson Kill Olick & Oshinsky, a twenty-two-year-old upstart of a litigation-heavy firm that specialized in defending asbestos companies. Once again, as he had with W&C, he convinced Anderson Kill to take on his sidekick Denny Young as a full partner. John Gross, the former AUSA whose apartment Rudy had retreated to when he and Regina first separated in 1974, was Giuliani's champion at the firm, convincing his partners that Rudy was the right fit.

The firm's records indicate that Rudy brought only a couple of clients with him and that, over the course of the next three years, added few to its list. His biggest new client was AT&T, which hired him to defend the company against a racketeering lawsuit brought by a Venezuelan communications company.

Drawing on his extensive RICO experience in the SDNY, he bottled the case up on technical motions, preventing a trial on the issue of whether AT&T had driven the Venezuelan firm "from the marketplace, misappropriating its technology and proprietary business information." His opponent, Myles Tralins, a Miami attorney, said Giuliani's "briefs and arguments were superbly prepared" and that "avoiding a trial was a significant service to his client." An entry in Anderson's client list also indicates that AT&T retained Giuliani in March 1992 with regards to "legislation," though the entry doesn't indicate whether the bill it was interested in was under consideration at a federal, state or city level.

Another Giuliani client was Towers Financial, a collection company controlled by Steve Hoffenberg, who'd been accused by the Securities and Exchange Commission of selling $34 million in unregistered securities in the 1980s and had reached a civil settlement with the SEC. With ten separate entries for Towers matters in the firm's client list, Hoffenberg was a major, Giuliani-generated, addition. He also became an extraordinary headache.

An Anderson lawyer was sanctioned by a federal judge for filing a frivolous lawsuit on behalf of Towers against Wang Laboratories and Giuliani had to personally sign the settlement agreement. Worse yet, when Hoffenberg faced indictment on a $460 million fraud charge in 1994, he offered to cooperate against an Anderson attorney, who he charged had told him to lie under oath to federal prosecutors. The false charge took a year and a half to disprove.

Hoffenberg was hardly Mr. Clean when Giuliani brought him to the firm. Convicted as far back as 1971 of larceny, he also used a lawyer to register Towers for public trading who was convicted of tax fraud. Yet Rudy had not only opened the door for him at Anderson, he'd collected thousands in contributions from Hoffenberg entities.

The SEC filed new scam charges against him in Giuliani's final weeks at the firm. Ultimately, a federal judge sentenced Hoffenberg to twenty years in prison, saying he'd destroyed "the savings and investments of thousands of people" and blasting Towers as a pyramid scheme.

While Hoffenberg was a corporate client who proved to be a criminal, Rudy did apparently do criminal law work for other clients. The firm's list says he represented one client involved in an "FBI investigation" and another in a "grand jury investigation." But surprisingly, with all the hoopla about his purported trial skills, he never tried a civil or criminal case at Anderson or W&C. His only known trials as a private attorney occurred way back at Patterson, and involved two libel matters.

In Giuliani's first full year at Anderson—1991—he made $578,000 in salary and bonuses. That dropped to $294,000 in 1992, when his honeymoon at the firm began to wear so thin some partners started openly griping about him. Ann Kramer wrote a January 6, 1993 memo to another partner including Giuliani and Young on a list of "attorneys who should be asked to leave."

A January 20 memo from Bob Horkovich, reviewing "the 1992 hours that each attorney devoted to billable, pro bono" and other matters, ranked Giuliani and Young lowest. It noted that Rudy was 1,740 hours under budget and Young 1,456. An accompanying chart revealed that Giuliani had only billed for three hours in the entire month of December, and a scant 177 hours that year, without a second of recorded pro bono time. At $375 an hour, he was budgeted to generate over a half million dollars, but instead came in dead last in the firm's workload scorecard.

Three days after the Horkovich memo, John Doyle, one of Giuliani's former Southern District friends at the firm, reported at a meeting of its board of directors that Giuliani and Young had reached an "agreement" with Anderson Kill "regarding a departure date and leave of absence." March 31 was selected as the date both would leave. While the firm's managing partners later claimed that they were fully satisfied with Giuliani's performance, Eugene Anderson, the lead partner, wrote a memo in the middle of the January 1993 skirmish acknowledging that "the present distribution" of firm profits "overcompensates for 'political clout'."

By the time Rudy left Anderson, he'd been a private attorney at three firms, including Patterson, for a combined eight years, all quite undistinguished. It was not a question of ability; it was a question of focus. He'd proven, as both a young AUSA and as U.S. Attorney, what a sharp legal mind he had. The work just didn't turn him on. He said when he came to Anderson that he wanted to resume the First Amendment practice he'd specialized in at Patterson and that he wanted to do securities regulation compliance for foreign and U.S. companies. He left without doing either.

Instead, Giuliani used the office as a campaign headquarters. He involved other partners in the campaign, naming Gross his treasurer. When he put together a skeletal staff, they worked out of a conference room at Anderson Kill through most of 1992. From the moment he arrived at the firm, he was a mayor-in-exile, and he spent more time plotting a democratic coup than collecting lucrative clients.

He flirted with a 1992 race against D'Amato, teasing reporters and his nemesis now and then with public winks, but his eye was fixed on the vulnerable opponent who'd barely beaten him. He became a magnet for anyone disaffected by anything David Dinkins did, a political paramedic parked at City Hall to respond to a four-year state of emergency, diagnosing the wounded and comforting the aggrieved. On the electoral rebound himself, he positioned himself to rebound every missed Dinkins shot. To win the inevitable second race, he would spare no effort or personal value.

The mistakes of 1989 convinced Rudy that he would have to step outside his reflecting pool of confidants for policy and political advice. He recognized his own need for municipal remedial education, so he designed an informal course on city governance. He reached out to Ray Horton, the finance guru at the business-funded Citizens Budget Commission, Henry Stern, the ex-Parks Commissioner who ran the city's leading good-government organization, and Robert Wagner Jr., the Koch deputy mayor raised in Gracie Mansion during his father's three terms. He met with Rodger McFarlane, the gay activist and ally of Larry Kramer's, homeless honcho Andrew Cuomo and teachers' union president Sandra Feldman, whose election-day field operation had been so key to Dinkins's 1989 win.

Later on, he even secretly met with William Bratton, the future police commissioner who was then head of the Boston police, and George Kelling, the criminologist whose advocacy of quality-of-life arrests had largely been adopted by Bratton. A tape of the March 25, 1993 interview with Bratton reveals the absence of any clear Giuliani crime plan, with Rudy asking if it was "conceivable to assign police officers to the task of restoring order on the streets," removing "the panhandlers and squeegee operators." Giuliani also seemed concerned about what he called "minority sensitivity and police brutality," asking if complaints had gone up when Bratton launched a quality-of-life arrest offensive while he was the head of New York's transit police in the early 1990s.

The guise for these sessions was an open ear. But Rudy was also hoping that policy bridges might either neutralize potent enemies from 1989 like Cuomo and Feldman or recruit new allies. Wagner did a pivotal commercial in the end, lending Rudy the legitimacy of the state's most famous Democratic name other than Roosevelt (his grandfather was U.S. senator and his father was mayor). Stern posed as a civic critic, assailing the ethics of the Dinkins administration, then quickly assumed his old Parks post when Rudy took office. Horton, the most quoted overseer of city management for twenty years, praised Giuliani's campaign white paper on fiscal policy, undercutting Dinkins's attempt to belittle it.

Rudy also attached himself to the Manhattan Institute, a think tank backed by rich, right-wing foundations that was trying to achieve a new urban politics by bankrolling thinkers and commentators who would popularize pieces of its ideology. Rather than talk to poor people, Rudy decided to listen to the Institute talk about them. He came away from periodic tough-love luncheons at the Institute's midtown dining room with a welfare and homeless philosophy more focused on dependency than decency, better suited for saving money than saving lives. These trendy poverty lessons at least guaranteed Rudy wouldn't reappear in 1993 as a Lindsay liberal, a hopeless niche anyway in a contest against a black mayor.

Though a tax-exempt nonprofit insulated from partisan politics, the Institute was named on the seating list for Giuliani's first big fundraiser—held in May 1992—as responsible for sending ten people, mostly staff. In addition, some of the heavy-pocketed Institute donors wound up buying tickets to the fundraiser, as well as to those that followed. The $1,000-a-head grilled-chicken dinner at the Sheraton, featuring Giuliani client Willie Mays and jazz xylophonist Lionel Hampton as the only black men in the ballroom not carrying a tray, was an opportunity for Giuliani to display for a thousand supporters his newfound municipal competence. "New York City needs more than a symbolic mayor," he declared. "New York needs a substantive mayor, a mayor dedicated to a fundamental restructuring of our city."

William Weld, his Justice friend who was the new governor of Massachusetts, appeared as both a speaker at the dinner and the embodiment of the candidate Rudy wanted to be, a social moderate as pro-business as pro-choice, as fiscally firm on finances as he was physically fierce on crime. The Weld model was also mildly pro-gay, friendlier than the no-bereavement-leave Rudy of 1989, but restrained enough to draw the line, as Rudy did, on issues like a new Board of Ed curriculum that exposed grade school kids to lifestyle facts about gays.

A couple of months before the dinner, Giuliani boycotted the St. Patrick's Day Parade, joining Dinkins and expressing outrage at the refusal of organizers to allow gays to march as a banner-wielding contingent. Declaring that he didn't "buy the notion that the parade is a religious event," Giuliani stayed away because the Hibernians, the church-tied group that sponsors it, "didn't resolve the inclusion issue." Not only did Giuliani announce his agreement with "the point that gays and lesbians are making–that the parade is not private and is essentially a political parade"—but he did precisely what Weld was doing in Massachusetts. Weld explained his own boycott by calling Boston's gay ban "discriminatory" and "wrong."

Giuliani's ambivalence on gay issues was so strong, however, that he marched in 1993—just seven and a half months before the election—and criticized Dinkins, who was still boycotting. When Dinkins tried to award the permit to a new group that would've allowed a gay contingent to march, Giuliani said: "The legal rights are clear. I'll give the mayor some free advice: Permits should be given to the Hibernians because failing to do so violates their First Amendment rights." The Civil Liberties Union agreed, and so did an Irish federal judge, leaving the parade in the same hands that continued to bar the gay group.

Neither Rudy nor the media noted that the Hibernian parade chair went to the organization's 1992 national convention and tried to bar from future parades the unit of his own organization that had allowed gays to march with them in 1991, calling them "the fag division." Weld also marched in 1993, but only because a court in Boston had ruled against the gay ban.

Rudy's 1993 turnaround may in part have been prompted by Cardinal John O'Connor's public comments when Dinkins and he boycotted. The cardinal praised one city leader who showed, Council Speaker Peter Vallone, and said "we will not forget" that he came, emphasizing that he would "personally remember." An editorial in the archdiocesan newspaper, printed with the obvious imprimatur of the cardinal, added that politicians who shunned the parade had "gone public with their priorities," thus indicating that "the Irish and the Catholics are pretty far down the list."

When Rudy also marched in a later St. Patrick's parade on Staten Island, he got a hero's welcome to chants of "Save Us Rudy," "Dinkins Sucks" and "No Queers Here." When asked about the bombast from his supporters, Giuliani said, "The anger level, or the irrationality level, is not disproportionate on one side or another of this thing. It's on both sides." His cosmic reference went well beyond gays or blacks. It was an apparent commentary on the conflicting mindsets that were increasingly cutting the city in half.

Giuliani's ambivalent groping on gay issues was mirrored on a host of fronts. Like his oscillations on gay matters, his unpredictable repositioning on a variety of other issues began in the early Dinkins days and continued right up to the election.

He refused, for example, until mid-September 1993 to say anything substantive about homelessness, initially accepting and then declining a spring invitation to speak at a housing conference with Dinkins. After making the homeless a "matter of conscience" in 1989, he dramatically shifted gears in late 1993, announcing a plan whose centerpiece was a tough new ninety-day limit on the shelter stays of what he called the chronically homeless. He also said the city had to abandon its long-standing commitment to a right to shelter, saying he would seek "legal relief" from court orders won by Bob Hayes, the advocate who had walked him through shelters four years earlier.

The plan was so transparently in violation of the consent decree Hayes won that Giuliani never attempted to implement it when he became mayor. Its purpose, however, was to show a willingness to flex municipal muscle at what the *Post* now called the "intimidating" homeless, just as his 1989 embrace of the homeless was designed to implant a charitable heart in a prosecutorial profile. With "liberals" like Pete Hamill reflecting the changed public attitudes about the homeless in a *New York* magazine cover story that advocated quarantining them in unutilized military camps, Giuliani's plan also called for stepped-up police enforcement of quality-of-life ordinances to get them off the streets. It referred to some homeless as "menacing individuals."

Hidden beneath these headline-grabbing, tough-love initiatives were remnants of the compassion that characterized his 1989 approach. He still promised that "a cornerstone of the Giuliani policy" would be "substantially increasing drug treatment availability" for the 50 percent of homeless singles he estimated were chemically addicted. In separate comments unconnected to the homeless plan, he continued to favor treatment on demand. He made similar, ambiguous commitments to the mentally ill homeless, supporting their "right to receive treatment in the community." Gone was the concept of small shelters in every neighborhood in the city. Gone was the forceful commitment to permanent housing.

There was still, however, enough political uncertainty about how this "round-'em-up-move-'em-out" Rudy floated politically that when advocates assailed the approach, Giuliani softened. The *Post* accused him of "retreating within days" because he started talking about "exceptions" to the ninety-day rule, and how people might "have their stays 'extended.'"

Giuliani also adopted the harsh and hurtful rhetoric of Dinkins's severest critics in a bitter dispute between blacks and Jews, only to try to moderate his language in the final weeks of the campaign. He capitalized immediately on a 1991 riot in the Crown Heights section of Brooklyn, when a black mob killed an Orthodox Jewish scholar, Yankel Rosenbaum, and assaulted at least forty others over a three-day period. The riot was triggered by the death of a seven-year-old black boy, who was killed by a car traveling in a motorcade that carried the world leader of the Lubavitcher sect, a large Orthodox community centered in the heart of the otherwise black neighborhood.

Rudy joined the outcry against Dinkins, blasting police paralysis during the outbreak. When the only youth indicted for Rosenbaum's murder was acquitted by a largely black jury in October 1992, an angry crowd of Lubavitchers, led by Rosenbaum's brother Norman, marched across the Brooklyn Bridge to protest at City Hall, though Dinkins had nothing to do with the criminal case. Those most outraged began calling the riot a "pogrom," Yiddish for Nazi-like, state-sponsored-or-sanctioned violence against Jews and—Giuliani soon embraced the term.

Ultimately, by the summer of 1993, he said he would no longer use this incendiary expression, even as he continued to bore in on Dinkins's provable Crown Heights passivity. Rudy's reversal was prompted by a state finding that neither Dinkins nor the police commissioner had issued any sort of a stand-down order that led to the police inaction. But Rudy still wouldn't concede that "pogrom" was excessive, saying only that he wouldn't initiate the use of it again. If asked, he would continue to discuss its relevance to Crown Heights.

Backing away from this hyperbole was part of an on-again, off-again Giuliani effort to make Crown Heights another competence issue, turning the hamstrung cops into a management rather than a racial failure. Giuliani vacillated between attempts to defuse the suggestion that Dinkins was more concerned about police violence against black rioters than he was about terrorism against Jews in their homes, and attempts to exploit that charge.

Even as Rudy soft-pedaled the use of "pogrom," he remained closely aligned with the Lubavitcher plaintiffs and attorney who sued the city in 1992 and charged that Dinkins consciously permitted blacks "to vent their rage at the expense of the lives and property of Jews." He invoked this "pogrom" lawsuit in a television ad, feeling no apparent need to distance himself from the smirking lawyer who derisively asked Dinkins during a Gracie Mansion deposition if he knew "what a yeshiva was."

Rudy's penchant for having it both ways was particularly acute whenever the issue was black and white. He swung back and forth between explicit and coded appeals to race, on one hand, and conscious retreats from it, on the other. In the space of two weeks shortly before the election, he at first derided Dinkins for granting a permit to Louis Farrakhan for a Yankee Stadium rally, but subsequently said: "I would protect Farrakhan to the same extent as I'd protect someone that I agreed with."

Giuliani's initial declaration that he "would not allow Farrakhan to use city property"—comparing the planned rally to allowing "neo-Nazis or skinheads to rent Yankee Stadium"—boomeranged in the press and polls. So with just four days to go before the election, he said: "Farrakhan has a right, unfortunately, from the point of view of the sensibilities of people, but fortunately for the First Amendment, to express that viewpoint."

Other shifts were stretched out over the years of pre-election positioning. As far back as the end of 1991, Giuliani did an extended interview on WNBC-TV and accused Dinkins of "playing racial politics" to get himself "out of political difficulty," saying the mayor "was as responsible for creating ethnic or racial divisions" as the people attacking him. Dinkins was hiding "behind black victimization too often," Giuliani charged, claiming that the mayor was "whining" that he was being "held to a different standard" because he was black. Rudy said such victimization was "very destructive—he did it when he was running; and he does it now."

By planting so early a seed that Dinkins was seeking special treatment—a kind of affirmative action program for thin-skinned black mayors—Giuliani was laying the groundwork for future, unbridled attacks. Yet by July 1993, he was claiming that it was he who was being judged by an unfair double standard. "From a cold political calculation," he told the *Times*, "you take the issue of race out of this and I win by 15 to 20 points." Make this "a normal American election," he insisted elsewhere, "and I win." He could not make up his mind if he wanted to paint himself as a race victim, or his opponent as a race whiner. All he knew was that it helped him to talk about race.

So he figured out a way to talk about race while pretending he wasn't. "I've got to get this city to stop thinking in categories, to stop thinking in terms of black and white and Hispanic, gay and heterosexual. I've got to get New York to stop thinking about all this symbolism." When confronted with the fact that only two of his thirty-seven campaign aides in 1993 were black, Giuliani's campaign spokesman said "we don't believe" in keeping numbers like that and accused the *Daily News* reporter who raised the issue, Paul Schwartzman, of being a "racial arsonist." The Giuliani brass railed about Schwartzman to his bosses.

Rudy accused Dinkins of relying on "symbolic hiring and not on selecting people of quality" in putting together his administration. He promised to find "people of quality," adding that a government that is "a cross-section of the city" was a "secondary" consideration. The candidate extended the same color-blind reasoning to a Dinkins set-aside program for minority businesses, calling anything that was race-based "terribly divisive."

Yet, when Giuliani appeared at a July 1992 Institute for Puerto Rican Policy forum, he was quite willing to "think in categories," as well as to champion "symbolic hiring," suggesting that the color-blind rhetoric only applied when he was talking to white media about Dinkins's supposed favoritism in hiring blacks.

"I know that there are more than enough qualified people in the Latino community to take over any of the positions in the government in New York City," he said, suggesting, as he did more explicitly on other occasions, that Dinkins had not appointed enough Latinos. "And it is the art and science of governing effectively to find these people, empower them, put them in positions where they can truly represent the community.

"I believe very, very much in role models. I believe that the young people have to see people in significant positions in government in the City of New York that they can look up to and they can identify with, whether they're Puerto Rican or otherwise Latino, or Jewish or Italian or African American. The single most important change the city has to make is people have to get appointed to public office for the right reasons." Giuliani not only stressed this "view on appointments," as he put it, to high-level positions—vowing "to share power in an appropriate way"—but he berated Dinkins for "not recruiting cops at all in the Latino community."

This was another specially tailored Rudy Affirmative Action Program— designed solely for the community that could give him a decisive swing vote, and it went unreported in the white press.

By the close of the campaign, any celebration of a consciously inclusive government was forgotten and the chameleon candidate was instead insisting that all his appointments would be based solely on merit, "irrespective of race, religion, ethnic background and sexual orientation," just like his virtually all-white and all-heterosexual campaign staff. With less than a week until election day, Rudy took to accusing Dinkins of hiring by race.

While 180-degree turns—on Saint Patty's, homelessness, Farrakhan, racial double standards and inclusiveness—were easy pirouettes for the dexterous Rudy, he seemed to only be able to flip in one direction, ever rightward. By the time he got to election day, in fact, it was a wonder that the entire right side of his body wasn't gripped by carpal tunnel syndrome, that cruel consequence of repetitive motion.

Giuliani flipflops were also occurring on the crassest of political levels, where Al D'Amato still hovered. Rudy lived in fear of another D'Amato-inspired Republican primary. Arnold Burns, the 1989 finance chairman for Rudy, talked openly about how disastrous a repeat Lauder-like scenario would be, calling it a "plague." D'Amato, of course, did all he could to suggest that another challenge was in the offing.

A millionaire Republican businessman who'd long given to D'Amato, David Cornstein, was floated as a possibility. He even paid for focus group research on the race in the summer of 1992. Cornstein was also reported to have retained Arthur Finkelstein, the D'Amato and Lauder campaign consultant, and was talking to GOP leaders.

So was Andrew Stein, the City Council president whose rich father, Jerry Finkelstein, was so close to D'Amato that the senator made him the first non-lawyer to sit on his judicial screening panel. D'Amato allies talked of allowing Stein to run in the Republican primary even though, as a Democrat, he would require a waiver from three of the city's five GOP county leaders to do so. With the Bronx's Guy Velella and Brooklyn's Bob DiCarlo in his pocket, D'Amato was within striking distance of the majority he needed for the waiver.

When Stein threw his biggest campaign bash in January 1992—hosting a Waldorf grand ballroom extravaganza with Frank Sinatra and Liza Minnelli—a D'Amato army attended. Velella and DiCarlo were listed on the seating arrangement at the same table as D'Amato clones like Charles Gargano, the senator's top fundraiser. Also listed were Conservative Party county leaders Serph Maltese and Jim Molinaro, who were D'Amato allies targeted for the same Stein waiver, making him a possible Conservative candidate.

This group—as well as Stein's welcome at a Conservative Party cocktail party honoring Lauder—was an announcement of D'Amato's threat to back Stein. Freely talking about the possibility of running in a GOP primary, Stein also declared early, like Lauder, that he would opt out of the expenditure and contribution restrictions of the city's Campaign Finance Board system. That meant he was ineligible for public matching funds, but could raise virtually limitless sums from his family, and tons of tawdry tycoons tied to Finkelstein and D'Amato.

Rudy did not fear losing a GOP primary to Stein, but he couldn't afford another spate of ugly primary ads. He feared another well-financed spring and summer battering that might squeeze him ideologically and damage him personally, weakening him for November.

What was most disconcerting to Giuliani early on was the courting of Guy Molinari, the head of the 1989 campaign who controlled the only Republican borough, Staten Island, like a fiefdom. His daughter Susan was the Island's representative in the House, inheriting Guy's old seat, and both the GOP and Conservative leaders from the county were close allies. Finkelstein was wooing the Molinaris with donations. Guy Molinari could be heard offering tributes to Stein, one in a late 1991 *Times* story that sounded like a virtual endorsement.

Molinari was even more important in 1993 than in 1989 because a referendum on the possible secession of Staten Island from the city was scheduled to appear on the same ballot as the mayoral election. That meant turnout in the city's whitest borough—where secession had become a hot cause in the Dinkins years—would be up dramatically.

Giuliani would milk the secession issue in 1993, using a previously undisclosed letter Dinkins wrote to Mario Cuomo opposing the secession referendum. Dinkins merely quoted from an Abraham Lincoln speech about the need to oppose a minority breaking up the government "whenever they choose." Yet Rudy used the invocation of Lincoln as evidence that Dinkins was trying "to put his opposition to secession in racial terms," making "things worse." When Dinkins insisted he had "never, ever come remotely close" to injecting race into the battle, Giuliani contended that "comparing the Civil War South to Staten Island clearly raises it," justifying his own fanning of the flames.

With just a little rhetorical kerosene and Molinari's organizational support, Giuliani expected to get the margin he needed on Staten Island alone. Molinari's message, when D'Amato boycotted the first big Giuliani fundraiser in May 1992, was clear: "I would hope that he and D'Amato can have some sort of détente," he told the *Times*. "It's very important to both of them. I've been trying to negotiate something myself, since I'm probably one of the few people who's very friendly with both of them. But not too much luck so far."

Giuliani reminded reporters at the same fundraiser that D'Amato "supported me about six weeks before the 1989 election and he did it on the telephone." This comment was designed to respond to pressures on him, from Molinari and others, to endorse D'Amato, who was facing a tough re-election challenge that November. Refusing to say he would back D'Amato, Giuliani bristled over the heat he was getting from GOP county leaders: "I've never been persuaded by threats, including when the Mafia threatened to kill me," he declared.

One of those leaders, thirty-six-year-old DiCarlo, had taken over the Brooklyn party in the fall of 1991. Financed by $30,000 in Lauder donations, he defeated a slate of Giuliani allies in a county committee battle (DiCarlo had run Lauder's campaign in Brooklyn in 1989). DiCarlo's ties to the D'Amato crew were so strong that when he joined a small venture capital firm in September 1992, he listed Lauder, Cornstein and Gargano as investors he was bringing into the business on a schedule attached to his employment agreement.

A recent bankrupt with a spotty employment history, DiCarlo executed this business agreement two days after he successfully beat back an attempt by Giuliani backers on Brooklyn's GOP executive committee to engineer an early mayoral endorsement. DiCarlo made it clear at the executive session that he would only entertain an endorsement after Giuliani announced he would back D'Amato. The Brooklyn leader's successful rebuff of the 1992 endorsement suddenly became a key factor pushing Rudy toward a painful peace with the senator.

Giuliani had lost the frontline prosecutorial weapons he'd tried to use against D'Amato—Lombardi and McGuire were gone. Otto Obermaier, not Benito Romano, was riding herd at Foley Square. As late as 1992, a Giuliani loyalist in the Southern District, David Lawrence, was trying to flip a felon who'd pled guilty, Arnold Biegen, to use him against D'Amato. Biegen allegedly had information implicating D'Amato in an attempt to get a top Housing and Urban Development (HUD) Department official to lie before a federal grand jury.

Prior to Lawrence's efforts, Randy Mastro, one of Rudy's closest Southern District friends, left private practice in early 1990 to become an aide to Arlin Adams, the independent counsel named to investigate HUD. D'Amato had been cited in many of the scandal stories involving the agency and Mastro freely told friends, including Pulitzer Prize–winning columnist Sydney Schanberg from *Newsday*, that "the main reason" he was joining Adams was to probe D'Amato. Larry Urgenson, a top Justice official in Washington who oversaw a myriad of D'Amato investigations during that period, recalled that Mastro "came on very, very strong," pushing a D'Amato agenda.

A Philadelphia lawyer, Adams turned out to be a do-next-to-nothing independent counsel, making no major HUD cases—with the exception of the former Interior Department secretary James Watt, who was allowed to plead guilty to reduced charges in the mid-90s, ultimately serving only probation. Mastro was quickly frustrated and left the office in six months.

While the case that started with Lombardi and McGuire—the tax indictment of D'Amato treasurer Jack Libert—resulted in a quick acquittal on June 25, 1992, brother Armand D'Amato was indicted by Brooklyn federal prosecutors that March. Armand D'Amato's pending indictment, as well as a mixed bag of findings on an array of ethics charges against the senator by the Senate Ethics Committee, made Giuliani's endorsement even more important to the tarnished and embattled senator.

Telling friends just a few days earlier that he would never endorse D'Amato, Giuliani did it on October 13, less than three weeks before the election. He made the announcement at his own headquarters, without any D'Amato photo-op, just as the senator had in 1989. Two weeks after the endorsement, Lawrence filed a memo in the Biegen case specifically citing the HUD allegation against D'Amato and noting that Biegen's information on the subject was not "even sufficient to warrant this office entering into a cooperation agreement with him." Coming shortly before the election, Lawrence's memo rebutted news accounts damaging to D'Amato.

Rudy used the most transparent rationale for his decision to back the senator—

namely that D'Amato's Democratic opponent Bob Abrams had called D'Amato a "fascist" at a Binghamton rally. Abrams's one-word temper tantrum had occurred the night before the Columbus Day parade, so D'Amato, at times faking televised tears, had walked around during the festivities handing out copies of the upstate news story. Seizing on this comment as an anti-Italian slur, D'Amato said he saw it "as a clear reference to Benito Mussolini," and threw a television commercial up on the air about it.

Giuliani said he was so "disturbed" he called D'Amato as soon as he heard about the remark and promised to endorse him the next day. "The use of the term fascist was ethnically divisive and beyond the acceptable bounds of even the toughest kind of negative campaigning," he said soberly. The day after D'Amato won re-election, the *Times* ran a front-page gloat—quoting D'Amato's top campaign advisers boasting about how they'd "turned" this foolish reference "into an anti-Italian attack" and kept it alive "for a week and a half." The *Times* said the consultant was "chuckling with professional pride" over the "sheer gall" of it. No one in the press noted that the D'Amato camp's post-election bravado had exposed Rudy's rationale as a joke.

Those who knew Giuliani and had shared confidences with him at Foley Square or suffered with him through the Lauder and Simon Berger assaults of 1989 understood how strongly he felt about D'Amato and how profound a surrender the endorsement was. He was backing someone he had tried to indict, and he was doing it with a six-year term in the U.S. Senate at stake. He was endorsing someone who had maligned him, who had cost him the mayoralty, who had caused him and his family wrenching pain.

It was not just a low point in his still-new political life. It was also a deeply personal defeat that harked back to his days in Brooklyn, when his dad was proud and tough and teaching him to box. Rudy was backing down in the middle rounds of a fight, staying in his own corner with the bell clanging for all his world to hear. When D'Amato narrowly won re-election, Giuliani was at the Hilton victory party, his teeth flashing, greeting a ballroom crowd of fat-cat donors and political heavyweights. He saw Mike Long, the Conservative Party honcho who'd spurned him in 1989 and was acting as the emcee, and he and Long agreed to get together.

"I don't know if he wants to talk about the mayoral election or what," Long said. "My thoughts? I'm open. . . . Hey four years is a long time. I'm not looking to hurt anybody." Long said there was no question "the Republican Party would like to see us endorse Rudy." But when Rudy later insisted on running on the Liberal line, Long tried to be helpful by putting up a nominal candidate who barely registered on the general election scorecard.

Bob DiCarlo pushed a Brooklyn GOP endorsement of Rudy through immediately, claiming at his executive committee meeting that he had "made peace between D'Amato and Giuliani." DiCarlo's investment "partner" Cornstein disappeared. One Giuliani loyalist from Brooklyn who fought DiCarlo, Gerry O'Brien, was pained when Rudy came to a 1993 campaign event and "swerved in a wide berth" around four leaders who'd always been with him "as if we didn't exist," walking across the street "to join DiCarlo." Determined to play by D'Amato's rules, Giuliani wound up running with DiCarlo, who used his control of the Brooklyn party to designate himself as the Republican candidate for a State Senate seat when the incumbent resigned in July 1993.

The Bronx's Velella became an instant vice chair of a Giuliani fundraiser on December 2 at the Sheraton, where all five GOP county leaders were, for the first time, seated on the dais. Velella would ultimately head Victory 93, an offshoot of the State Republican Committee, which would raise and spend $1.4 million to aid the Giuliani campaign. Another D'Amato devotee, State Chair Bill Powers, was seated at the main table with Rudy at the December fundraiser, the first time he'd appeared at a Giuliani event.

No one in the media remembered that Velella owned the two-story building in the Bronx that housed his and his father's law firm on the first floor and Stanley Friedman's Democratic headquarters on the second, a concrete symbol of the collusion between parties that permeated the borough's politics.

Few recalled that Giuliani had denounced Velella in 1989 for appointing his seventy-five-year-old father, Vincent, to the Board of Elections. Demanding "an explanation" for what Giuliani charged was "a close friendship" between Vincent Velella and the Genovese crime family boss Rudy prosecuted, "Fat Tony" Salerno, Giuliani recounted the senior Velella's decades-long ties to mob figures. The *Voice* had repeatedly referred to the two-member Velella law firm as "in-house counsel to the Genovese family," and reported that the junior Velella had just used a major mob figure to renovate his house. Rudy's knowledge of the Velella history was partly personal. Vincent Velella had been the East Harlem GOP counterpart in the 1940s and 1950s to Democratic district leader Lou Carbonetti, who'd taken Harold Giuliani under his wing and supplied Rudy with his first set of law books.

D'Amato's new alliance with Rudy killed the Stein GOP boomlet overnight. It even helped convince Stein to pull out of the race altogether in May 1993. Lots of factors led to Stein's withdrawal, but he would not have quit so quickly had D'Amato stayed in his corner, cutting deals and raising big bucks.

D'Amato money also started flowing into unfamiliar Giuliani coffers. David Cornstein, for example, who didn't give a nickel to Giuliani in 1989, donated the

legal maximum of $6,500 in 1993. The Mack family, whose real estate and enter-
tainment company had been a gargantuan source of contributions for D'Amato,
went from a paltry $1,000 donation to Giuliani in 1989 to $36,500 in 1993. Asked
if the family would've given to Giuliani if he hadn't endorsed D'Amato, Fred Mack
said: "I've got to really play dumb on that one." D'Amato would later claim that
he personally "raised" more than $50,000 for Giuliani, but D'Amato-connected
donors clearly gave more than that.

Strangely enough, Rudy's D'Amato endorsement also helped him with a powerful Democrat, Ed Koch, who was so close to the senator that he joined D'Amato,
D'Amato's mother, Gargano and Finkelstein at a private dinner the night of the
1992 election. As late as June 27, 1991, Koch, who had already become a Dinkins
critic, told the *Los Angeles Times*: "I don't think Giuliani has the kind of personality that you want in a mayor. You don't want somebody who's a killer, even a legal killer." Giuliani pursued Koch's endorsement at a half dozen lunches and
dinners before the popular ex-mayor, a columnist at the *Daily News* deeply af-
fronted by Dinkins's handling of Crown Heights, finally endorsed him. Had
Giuliani not backed the senator, Koch would've probably sat it out or aligned himself with D'Amato's candidate.

Just as the war with D'Amato had undermined Rudy in 1989, peace appeared to
pave the way for a win the second time around. At the first meeting of his seven-
member core campaign staff on November 9, 1992—held in his law office—Rudy
announced that his "endorsement of D'Amato bought him out of a Republican
primary and possible attacks from the right." According to a nine-page memo
summarizing notes taken at the meeting, Rudy said the endorsement "would position him much better in 1993 than in 1989."

T he collapse to D'Amato wasn't Rudy's only moral accommodation of the
new mayoral season. Four months before he endorsed the senator, he joined
Molinari in a bizarre crusade the borough president was leading against the
Southern District. As quixotic and unpredictable a public official as there is in the
city, Molinari, allied with police union chief Phil Caruso, was championing the
cause of an INS agent, Joe Occhipinti, who had been convicted by the SDNY on
seventeen counts of civil rights violations, principally against Dominicans.

After thirty-six witnesses testified against Occhipinti—from harassed mer-
chants to seven law enforcement officials (including an assistant district attorney
named John F. Kennedy Jr.)—he was sentenced to thirty-seven months in prison

for false reports, illegal searches and improper imprisonment. Occhipinti, who ran an anti-drug operation in the Washington Heights section of Manhattan when these abuses occurred in 1989 and 1990, began his prison term when he lost his appeal unanimously at the Circuit Court in May 1992.

Rudy's old friend David Lawrence, the head of the SDNY public corruption unit, had branded Occhipinti a "rogue agent" and authorized his prosecution. Several SDNY agents who had worked for Rudy helped make the case, hardly something one federal agent wants to do to another. Giuliani's old friend Dick Thornburgh was the attorney general who had signed off on the indictment. Yet the Police Benevolent Association's Caruso charged in a letter to Justice that Occhipinti was "definitely the pawn of a conspiratorial plot perpetrated by known drug dealers who wanted him out of the way," a view echoed by Molinari.

The onetime head of a New Jersey PBA local for federal agents, Occhipinti tossed wild charges at Rudy's old office, saying at one point that the prosecutors attended "sex and drug parties" with Dominican drug lords. According to a letter written by the head of the Jersey PBA, Occhipinti had developed evidence "implicating a former AUSA from SDNY of suspected drug trafficking activity."

For reasons that baffled Molinari supporters, including the editorial board of the *Staten Island Advance* (which said Occhipinti "acted as if above the law"), the borough president became so obsessed with the agent's case he quit as the head of Bush's statewide re-election committee in June 1992. Molinari said he did it because Justice Department officials had "refused to listen" to evidence clearing Occhipinti.

In fact, John Dunne, a top Justice official and former GOP state senator from New York, said he'd had "repeated conversations with Molinari" but that Molinari presented "nothing new." Justice's Office of Professional Responsibility, still run by the man who had brokered Giuliani's blind date with Donna, reviewed the case and found nothing wrong with the department's handling of it.

Incredibly, that's when Giuliani, who had spent a lifetime dismissing this kind of hysterical critique of federal prosecutions, entered the controversy. In early July, Giuliani met with Steve Frankel, the attorney who had handled Occhipinti's unsuccessful appeal. A former AUSA who'd worked with Rudy and remained a social friend, Frankel was no longer representing Occhipinti, but was asked by Molinari to meet with Rudy at Giuliani's office and explain the facts of the case to him. Molinari attended the meeting too and, as Frankel recalled it, pressed Giuliani to put together a case for a pardon. "Rudy wasn't actually doing this for Joe," Frankel says. "He was probably doing it for Molinari. I think he liked Guy Molinari." Frankel turned over briefs and other legal documents to Giuliani and never heard another word about it.

Giuliani said publicly after the meeting that he was trying to help Occhipinti get a hearing on new evidence that he was framed, though he indicated he was not Occhipinti's attorney. The supposed evidence had been gathered by an unusual group of investigators Molinari had put on his borough president's payroll. Giuliani said he'd "studied" this evidence and was determined to get a "fair" assessment of it. Suddenly on July 20, within days of Giuliani's meeting, Attorney General William Barr asked the FBI to review Molinari's evidence.

An FBI report in December found that Molinari's materials included "fabricated affidavits." Three of Molinari's new witnesses failed polygraphs. Audio cassettes of recanting witnesses provided by Molinari probers were said to sound like scripted statements. An FBI memo of September 17 reported "there appeared to be the possibility" of a new "obstruction of justice case against Occhipinti." Molinari was so overwrought during the FBI probe, he was calling reporters and telling them that an FBI helicopter was circling Borough Hall.

Deputy Attorney General George Terwilliger wrote Molinari that the FBI investigation "provided no credible information upon which the Department of Justice could base a position challenging the integrity or propriety of Mr. Occhipinti's conviction." Molinari dismissed Terwilliger's findings as "garbage" and called Giuliani's successor Otto Obermaier a "disgrace." Undeterred by the Terwilliger letter and the FBI report, Molinari began personally lobbying the outgoing president for an Occhipinti pardon. He even went to the White House on January 6, 1993, pressing Bush on the issue.

On January 16—just four days before Bush left office—he commuted the rest of Occhipinti's sentence. The agent was immediately released from prison and flown to New York, where Molinari and Caruso greeted him at the airport. He'd served only eight months of a sentence that was the lowest he could receive under federal guidelines.

Four days after the commutation, according to an FBI memorandum, Justice asked the Eastern District to investigate the new obstruction case against Occhipinti and others, involving the phony Molinari evidence that Giuliani had urged the department to review. The Justice letter was based on an October 26 report by DOJ assistants fully available at the time of Bush's bizarre commutation. The Eastern District closed the case in December 1993, with the FBI noting that prosecution was declined because "the case would be difficult at best" and because "it was best not to give subjects in this case a platform on which to gain publicity."

Giuliani bragged later that he "played a role in delivering" the commutation, adding that he had "stated my position in writing to the Justice Department." He did all this, he said, "seeking justice" in the case, not as the agent's lawyer.

Occhipinti says he knew Giuliani from their days in the Southern District and went to Rudy when he was indicted. Giuliani referred him to a criminal attorney he could not afford. Later, when he was in jail, "Rudy and Guy Molinari put forward the paperwork to file for my executive clemency," which he said consisted of "an application and whole variety of legal papers." He said Denny Young, who was then Rudy's law partner, pitched in as well.

After the commutation, "I met several times" with Giuliani, Occhipinti says. He told Giuliani that his Washington Heights sources had convinced him that illegal Dominican votes had stolen the 1989 election from him, a view that Giuliani began publicly expressing. "Rudy asked me if I would help him by lobbying on his behalf, going around doing speaking engagements, explaining how powerful the Dominican druglords were in New York." Occhipinti made many appearances for Rudy "all around the city," he said, from January through September 1993, precisely when the Eastern District probe was underway.

Occhipinti's ex-attorney Frankel said he was "pretty shocked" by the commutation. Frankel acknowledges that when he prepared the appeal, he found "the evidence pretty overwhelming." The appeal focused on a nervous breakdown Occhipinti's prior attorney supposedly had during the trial. "They couldn't say he was wrongly accused or wrongly convicted," Frankel said. "Rudy's a careful guy. I don't know how much he'd put in writing on this case. I would have thought it was about phone calls and meetings and rooms where no records are kept."

Frances Saurino, whose husband Ben was both one of the SNDY agents who investigated the case and one of Rudy's longtime admirers in the office, wrote an op-ed piece in the *Staten Island Advance* shortly after Occhipinti's release. "Molinari and Giuliani, men who claim to be consummate respecters of the ideals of equal justice and the rule of law, have resorted shamelessly to blatant political influence," she wrote. They have used "their substantial connections in Washington to gain special favor for Occhipinti," insulting "all law enforcement officers who work with honor, dedication and professionalism within the guidelines of their mandate to enforce the law." Shame on them, she concluded.

Her sentiments were widely shared in Rudy's old office. But Giuliani knew his Occhipinti actions had solidified his relationship with Molinari and Caruso, and in his new life, that was all that mattered.

On September 16, 1992, ten thousand cops rallied, and then rioted, at City Hall. It was not only a dark day for the Big Blue. It was a political disaster for Rudy Giuliani, who joined Molinari and Caruso in speeches off a flatbed truck that fueled an anger so racial the city shook.

Cops carried signs that said "Dump the Washroom Attendant," "Mayor, have you hugged your dealer today" and "Dinkins, We Know Your True-Color—Yellow Bellied." Drawings on their homemade posters depicted the mayor in a '60s Afro with giant lips, or engaged in kinky sex acts. They broke through police barricades and stormed the steps of City Hall, cheering "Take the Hall!" and banging on windows. They blocked traffic for an hour on the nearby Brooklyn Bridge. They climbed on top of the cars of city officials parked in the lot in front of it, jumping up and down until they dented them. And they chanted "Rudy," "Rudy" in thunderous rhythm, as he worked his way through the nearly all-white mob, beaming, backslapping, posing for photos, pumping his fist.

WCBS-TV cameraman John Haygood was called a nigger. Una Clarke, a city councilwoman from Brooklyn, was stopped by an off-duty cop with a beer in his hand who said to his sidekick: "This nigger says she's a member of the City Council." Another black councilwoman, Mary Pinkett, was stuck on the bridge, her car rocked and shaken by cops. Fifty-three officers would wind up charged with misconduct—eleven would go to an administrative trial and ten would be convicted. Even Caruso would go to Police Commissioner Ray Kelly the next day and apologize, conceding he had lost control of his own union's rally.

When Rudy spoke, surrounded on Murray Street by cops pouring in and out of bars with open beer cans, the next mayor launched into a litany of Dinkins's offenses against the police. Dressed in a starched white shirt and tie with his sleeves rolled up, Giuliani bellowed into a mike, standing next to a chain-locked dummy in a police uniform. He put his glasses on, but rarely looked at the handwritten scrawl gripped in his clenched right hand. He screamed "bullshit" twice in a condemnation of Dinkins actions—saying later that he was only repeating Dinkins's use of the word a few weeks earlier when he responded to a confrontational cop at a precinct meeting. The expletive, captured by television cameras, provoked a tumultuous response from the crowd, as did his laundry list of grievances.

The union wanted a rich new collective bargaining agreement, said Dinkins. They were also mad that Dinkins opposed issuing 9mm guns to them, favored legislation creating a Civilian Complaint Review Board (CCRB) and used city funds to pay for a funeral for a Dominican with a drug record who was killed by a cop a month earlier. Giuliani railed against Dinkins on each issue—calling the CCRB, for example, "a board made up of civilians who know nothing about policing and who share the same biases against police as the mayor." He vowed that when he was mayor, cops would be given "the benefit of the doubt" in controversial incidents.

The protesters were also upset about a mayoral commission Dinkins had named to investigate police corruption. It was the first such commission since the early 1970s—when the Knapp Commission helped give young Rudy his start. Filling the air with more invective, Giuliani shouted that the commission was created "to protect David Dinkins's political ass."

When the two-and-a-half-hour demonstration was over, and Rudy returned to his office at Anderson Kill, he was ecstatic. He said he'd hit "a grand slam." After a lifetime of imaginary at-bats in a Yankee uniform, he couldn't tell the difference between clearing the bases and ending an inning. He would soon discover he'd hit into his first triple play.

A *Daily News* editorial called his conduct "shameful," blasting his "pandering rhetoric" for not including "a word of condemnation." Unlike Rudy, the police commissioner "knows rabble when he sees it," said the *News*, saluting Kelly's "investigation into the lawlessness." The *Times* said Giuliani now claims "implausibly" that he was unaware "officers were out of control." It blasted Rudy's "barnyard" performance and asked: "Where was his concern for the city? His decision to address the police was reckless, as were some of his harsher comments." David Garth, the political consultant who would a few months later take control of the Giuliani campaign, said Giuliani looked more like "Hot Hand Rudy" on TV than "Cool Hand Luke."

Even while Caruso apologized, Rudy went on the attack. Two days after the madness, he said, "One of the reasons those police officers might have lost control is that we have a mayor who invites riots." He again assailed Dinkins as a "hack." The closest he came to remorse was a reference to his own family history: "I had four uncles who were cops. So maybe I was more emotional than I usually am."

Twelve days later the drumbeat of criticism was still music to his ears. He said Kelly's report citing cop misconduct was an attempt to make them "scapegoats for political gain." The real issue, as he saw it, was whether "the relatively minor occurrence of racial epithets, if they occurred at all, has been made the focus of this rally for political purposes." The *Times* concluded that Giuliani's continued attempts to "gloss over the rioters' conduct" was a political calculation. He is "betting—irresponsibly—that divisiveness will win votes."

It did solidify his blue-collar base. The PBA, which had backed Koch in the 1989 primary and stayed out of the general election, became his ready ally. It did not formally endorse him, so it could spend thousands on his behalf outside the constraints of the Campaign Finance Board. The union, whose executive board was still all white, bought a stream of ads filled with vile anti-Dinkins assaults (one Crown Heights ad carried the headline "Never Again," as if Dinkins were Hitler).

During the primary, it spent a reported $100,000 promoting Roy Innis, the counterfeit civil rights leader and Giuliani friend who sat at the head table at Rudy's December 1992 fundraiser and soon thereafter ran against Dinkins in the Democratic primary. Afterwards, Dinkins filed a CFB complaint against the union's continued duplicitous ad campaign, but could not prove what logic dictated: Even though the ads never mentioned Rudy, the union expenditures were clearly designed to benefit him.

The union also steered at least $24,650 to the campaign, some of it through its political action committees and some through vendors who worked for it, ranging from their lawyers to firms that service their annuity plan. The ads and donations aside, an army of cops volunteered eventually for election day duties, manning the polls for Rudy all across the city.

The Giuliani camp feared that this rally rant would haunt Rudy. The vulnerability study commissioned by the 1993 campaign featured up front a section entitled "The Human Scream Machine: The Cop Riot." The confidential study said the "shrieking performance may be Giuliani's greatest political liability this year." In smaller subheads, the report described his behavior as "disturbing " and "no portrait of probity." The two quick lessons to be drawn from it, the study concluded: "No shrieking. No swearing." The study went on:

When dealing with direct questions about the rally, Giuliani should acknowledge and criticize the underlying racial nature of the protest. The biggest problem most voters may have with Giuliani's participation in the rally is his unwillingness to criticize those taking overtly racial pot-shots at the Mayor. Giuliani has yet to admonish those who attacked the Mayor with racist code words on signs and banners. Why not?
When answering Dinkins' attacks on this issue, Giuliani should never engage in the kind of personal sniping at the Mayor that characterized his responses last fall. Mean-spirited counter-charges will do nothing to disprove Dinkins's assertion that Giuliani is an out-of-control hot-head incapable of governing the city; they only reinforce what Dinkins is trying to prove.

Instead, Giuliani declared four days before the election: "I don't regret speaking down there. I regret the fact that false statements have been made about this. The fact is, there was no riot. There was misconduct. So that's a false statement." The closest he ever came to admitting error was to say he "used unfortunate words," though he still maintained that the depiction of him was "mythology."

Not one news station ran the footage of his personal explosion during the campaign. Not one newspaper ran a photo of his contorted face. Magically, Giuliani succeeded in defining unedited pictures of his own biggest public performance as partisan and negative. He tossed out crazy arguments to try to confuse the situation factually. He claimed he was trying to cool things when he left the steps of City Hall and moved to the nearby flatbed truck, taking thousands of cops with him. How screaming vulgarities at a street running in beer could be construed as a calming influence was never addressed.

A leading *Times* columnist, Sam Roberts, quoted him a week before the election as saying he "didn't know what had happened earlier at the rally." But what everyone reported was that the insanity went on before, during and after his sustained visit. Rudy was right that the cops had overrun police barricades before he got there, but the barricades and the cops who overran them were still in the same positions when he arrived. If everything was quiet when he arrived, why was he saying he cooled things by moving a few hundred feet away?

What was most ironic about this defense—though no one in the media noted it—was that the same candidate who berated the mayor for not knowing how terrible the violence was in Crown Heights was using his own ignorance as a defense for participating in a rally that turned riotous.

The Dinkins campaign mysteriously waited until the last four days to go on the air with their own cop rally commercial and a Giuliani ad immediately denounced it as "downright lies" and "vicious" even though the Dinkins ad's only memorable image was a straight shot of Rudy cursing.

The riot performance occurred shortly after Rudy joined the Occhipinti crusade and shortly before he joined D'Amato's. It was a season of pre-electoral bottoming-out, a succession of personal collapses. For another candidate in another time, that single seismic moment at the rally would have finished a career. A black politician at a police brutality rally where he and the crowd went bonkers would've disqualified himself, at least in the view of editorial boards, from public office.

Rudy learned he could not only stonewall his way past the critics; he could get an uptick in his base for toughing it out, for snarling at anyone looking for a regret. It was a lesson he would take with him the next time he went to City Hall.

Fourteen

Seizing City Hall

N O ONE IN THE GIULIANI CAMP WOULD ADMIT IT, AND THE candidate might not have even acknowledged it to himself. But Rudy would not have run in 1993 if David Dinkins were white. Certainly Giuliani challenged Dinkins because he thought Dinkins was beatable, not because Dinkins was black. But Dinkins was only beatable, contrary to every historical precedent, because he was black.

No mayor in the twentieth century who served a full term and ran for a second has lost a general election. Mayors have only lost re-election attempts three times—always, like Ed Koch, in Democratic primaries. Indeed, incumbency is so hard to overcome that John Lindsay won a second term in 1969 after losing the Republican primary. He ran in November on the Liberal line alone.

The concentrated budget powers and daily media exposure of the mayor are so extraordinary that four years is enough time for anyone to do enough favors to put together a re-election majority.

No Republican since the party began in the middle of the nineteenth century had ever defeated an incumbent Democratic mayor. The technical exception was Fiorello La Guardia in 1933, who beat John O'Brien, a Democrat who succeeded scandal-ridden Jimmy Walker after Walker was driven from office. O'Brien, the corporation counsel under Walker, was hand-picked at a Tammany Hall county committee meeting in Madison Square Garden and served as mayor for a few months before losing to La Guardia. Even then, La Guardia only beat this nominal incumbent because the Democratic vote was split between O'Brien and another candidate backed by President Franklin Roosevelt.

Republicans usually ran so badly in the city that Al D'Amato, a two-term senator, got 38 percent of the city's vote in 1992. George Bush, a one-term president, got a mere 23 percent the same year. Both were better-than-average totals, achieved just months before Giuliani launched his mayoral bid. GOP candidates for president, senator, governor or mayor who weren't incumbents frequently garnered less than a fifth of the city's vote. The party was so moribund it gave its line to Ed Koch in 1981 and got less than 10 percent of the vote against him in 1985. Lindsay's 1965 win was the only Republican victory since La Guardia, making the mayoralty almost as much a Democratic franchise as McDonald's was a hamburger franchise.

Republicans did much better in state races, winning more Senate races, for example, than Democrats over the past fifty years. If Rudy was looking for a winnable launching pad, state attorney general, comptroller and governor, as well as the Moynihan Senate seat, were all up in 1994, and elected incumbents would certainly not be running for two of the four spots.

Registration changes suggested it might even be harder for Giuliani to win in 1993 than four years earlier. When Giuliani met with his campaign staff in November 1992, according to the memo summarizing the meeting, his first question was how registration had changed. "It was observed that between 1989 and early 1992, registration had held up in African American and Latino assembly districts, but had fallen in all white ADs," the memo read. "It was surmised that the surge in registrations for the 1992 presidential elections was probably located in areas most likely to have supported Clinton-Gore, namely African American, Latino and white liberal areas."

Yet, even with the outmigration of older whites reflected in the assembly district numbers noted at the Giuliani meeting, the racial dynamic of the city electorate was still the opening that beckoned Rudy to run again. Since there is no racial question on registration cards, it is impossible to factually break down city registration by race. But the assembly district analysis done by Giuliani, coupled with exit polls and other data, left no doubt that, while the majority of New Yorkers were minority in 1993, the majority of registered voters was still decidedly white. Even the Dinkins camp estimated registrants at 53 percent white; while other analysts pinned it at 55 percent or more. The registrants who actually turned out in 1993 would wind up 60 percent white.

To beat Dinkins, Rudy would have to run twelve points ahead of D'Amato's 1992 total. How could a mere lawyer who'd never been elected to any public office, and whose last public service ended almost five years before the 1993 election, expect to do that? What besides race could explain why, according to exit polls, 64 percent of the city's white Democrats and 77 percent of all white voters would vote for him? What else could explain why 59 percent of white Democrats voted for Giuliani in 1989—before Crown Heights or any of the other Dinkins failings occurred?

Rudy knew the racial numbers as well as he knew his conviction rate as U.S. Attorney. In 1989, Giuliani expected to face Koch and got Dinkins. In 1993, he passed on other opportunities, preferring to run for an office history said he could not win. He did it because the vote he got four years earlier convinced him that all he had to do was increase white turnout, or do marginally better among Latinos, and he would win. He did it because he understood that race was creating an opportunity to make history. The underlying dynamic was so apparent that a July cover story in the Sunday *Times Magazine* dubbed it "New York's Race Race" and predicted: "Even if Giuliani wins, he may be the last white man for years to lead his city."

Once Rudy decided to challenge Dinkins though, he had to turn upside down the racial calculus that was the secret rationale for victory. He had to make white voters feel that their predisposition to vote for him was not a consequence of race, nor should it be a source of guilt. So his campaign and the pundits who backed him kept talking about the 95 percent of blacks expected to vote for Dinkins, equating the Caucasian swing to Rudy with this countervailing tribal instinct. A *Times* column so bought into this argument that it suggested whites were less tribal than blacks, pointing out that Dinkins would get "more than 90 percent of the black vote—a proportion that Mr. Giuliani does not come close to matching among whites or even among Italian Americans."

What this facile reasoning ignored was that white Democrats, including the two on the ballot with Dinkins in 1989, also typically got 90 percent or better of the city's black vote. A black candidate like Dinkins might push the share up a measly four or five points. It was white Democrats who were altering their voting patterns and leaving their party in droves to vote for Rudy—even the much more Republican Rudy who ran in 1993. Many of these voters were driven by race.

That's why Giuliani kept talking about it—from Farrakhan to affirmative action. That's why Rudy ranted at the cop rally. That's why the commercial theme of the campaign became "One City/One Standard"—which, coupled with the Giuliani refrain on the campaign trail that "no one group can have all their agenda"—was designed to convince anyone who wasn't black that Dinkins favored his own.

The strategy, as that November 1992 memo made plain, pivoted around an effort to maximize white turnout, to get the unmotivateds who vote in presidential elections but sit out others to the polls. The Giuliani code about how he'd be an "evenhanded" mayor was designed to convince the guy on the couch in Staten Island or Queens who usually just stews and spews to realize Rudy was for him, and to get up and do something about it.

Two Dinkins supporters gave Giuliani just the opening he needed in the final weeks of the campaign to drive the race point home. A Brooklyn minister, William

Jones, got himself quoted in the dailies saying that Giuliani supporters included certain "fascist elements" that were branding Dinkins a murderer over the Rosenbaum slaying. Eric Adams, the leader of an organization representing black cops, charged that Giuliani's running mate, City Comptroller candidate and former congressman Herman Badillo, could not understand Latinos because he was married to a non-Latino. Dinkins disavowed both statements—and neither Jones nor Adams were in any way formally connected to his campaign—yet Giuliani threw press conferences to denounce them and put his wife on the air for a thirty-second spot to defend him.

Dressed in a red plaid jacket and discreet gold earrings, Donna nodded and looked directly into the camera, just as she did at WPIX:

"As a journalist, I thought I'd seen everything. I was wrong. I'm Donna, Rudy Giuliani's wife. My husband was called a fascist by a group of ministers endorsing David Dinkins. And while people who support the Mayor are called proud, people who support my husband are called racist. This election shouldn't be about race, it should be about competence. Of course I want people to vote for Rudy Giuliani. But I want people to vote for Rudy because he's the best man for the job, not for any other reason."

If the script had been a Hanover news story, the fact-checking department at her former station would've killed it. A single minister, making a group endorsement, talked about "elements" around Rudy. As the *Times* review of the commercial by reporter Todd Purdum put it, "Jones did not call Giuliani a fascist." Neither had anyone in the Dinkins campaign called Giuliani supporters "racist." Instead, Dinkins had often said, as Purdum recounted, that it was an "expression of pride" for either a black to vote for a black or an Italian for an Italian, saying it was only when someone voted against a candidate because of his origins that racism was involved.

Badillo did another commercial on Adams's comments aired at the same time. Badillo explicitly argued that Giuliani was the true victim—of guilty liberal voters reluctant to oppose a black candidate.

Purdum's review of Donna's ad concluded that it "risks seeming disingenuous: While ostensibly saying that race should not be an issue, it actually goes to great lengths to highlight and trade on racially inflammatory remarks." Donna's "sorrowful tone as she stands by her man," wrote Purdum, "puts a soft edge on a tough message. It trades on Ms. Giuliani's reputation as a former news anchorwoman to make its case in a Checkers meets Diane Sawyer vein." Rudy and company obviously thought the ad worked so well they did a second with Donna a week later—this one responding to old hat and unfair charges against Giuliani on abortion.

In unusually strong commentary from the *Times,* an editorial blasted the initial Donna and Badillo ads as an attempt to "make a campaign that stands to benefit from racial fear appear to be the victim of those fears." Calling them "the politics of disinformation played at a very dangerous level," the *Times* concluded: "Not since the heyday of Lee Atwater have we seen such devious artistry when it comes to stirring feelings of racial paranoia among whites."

Jones and Adams were easier targets than another Dinkins supporter who had actually raised the subject of race with Dinkins at his side, Bill Clinton. At a late September fundraiser, the president said that Dinkins deserved re-election on his record, but was facing a tough campaign because "too many of us are still too unwilling to vote for people who are different than we are."

"This is not as simple as overt racism," Clinton told a thousand cheering supporters of Dinkins. "That is not anything I would charge to anybody who doesn't vote for David Dinkins or Bill Clinton or anybody else. It's not that simple. It's this deep-seated reluctance we have, against all our better judgment, to reach out across these lines."

The words were not in Clinton's prepared text though he went on for some time about how troubling this phenomenon was. He said that on the flight from Washington with the mayor on Air Force One, he'd begun to wonder why Dinkins—who he saw as having reduced crime, hired cops and stabilized the city's budget—should face a competitive race in a city that was five-to-one Democratic. "It is the inability to take that sort of leap of faith, to believe that people who look different than we are really are more like us than some people who look just like us but don't share our values and our interests."

Giuliani never directly took these comments on, a tribute to Clinton's stunning popularity in the city. His muted response was that he was "going to put the best possible interpretation on it, which is that the President was showing his support for David Dinkins," adding that "a president never really intends to create division." Instead he seized on the Jones and Adams canards. He followed that with a press conference blast about a year-old *Amsterdam News* editorial that he said "compared me, Guy Molinari and Phil Caruso—all of whom have Italian American last names—to fascists" (he did not mention that the *Amsterdam* endorsed "fascist" D'Amato at around the same time).

Contrary to Clinton's idealized view, there were plenty of good reasons for Dinkins to face a hearty challenge, and Rudy Giuliani was hardly wrong to give him one.

Giuliani was genuinely outraged over Crown Heights and the polarizing incident that preceded it—when Dinkins allowed black protesters to picket a Korean grocery store in Brooklyn for weeks in violation of a court order. He believed he could weld together a disintegrating social compact and that Dinkins could not. He thought Dinkins ran an ineffectual government that only got itself organized when Dinkins deputies were trying to steer a contract to a friend. He still talked, years later, about how the 1989 election had been stolen from him by vote fraud in black and Dominican districts, a conviction that fueled his desire to win a payback election.

As compelling as Rudy and many other citizens of the city found the critique of Dinkins to be, Clinton was right that no Republican would have had a chance to beat a white mayor with his record, all the pluses and minuses considered. The city had to nearly file Chapter 11 for Ed Koch to beat incumbent Abe Beame in a Democratic primary in 1977. Robert Wagner only beat Mayor Vincent Impelliteri in 1953—again in a Democratic primary—because screaming scandals convinced New Yorkers that the mob had taken over his government. And in the only other example of a defeated incumbent, Ed Koch simply overstayed his welcome, going for a fourth term beleaguered by scandal and sapped of sound bites, losing to Dinkins—in a Democratic primary one more time.

The 1993 ballot might as well have been black. Race was the rationale for the campaign, the door-opener. And Rudy ran through it so fast all the city saw was a white blur.

Once Rudy recognized that his old gang of friends wasn't going to get him the mayoralty, it was only a matter of time before he wound up hiring Dave Garth as his campaign consultant. Garth is City Hall. He had elected Lindsay and Koch, winning five of the previous seven mayoral races. One of his losses was in 1989, when he nearly raised Koch from the dead and savaged Rudy Giuliani along the way. While Rudy took what D'Amato said about him personally, his experience as a lawyer taught him never to begrudge a mercenary advocate.

When Garth and Giuliani met on a television panel show in 1991, they found themselves agreeing about the need for police reform and decided to get together for dinner. Giuliani talked to Roger Ailes about a repeat performance, but Ailes, who announced at a Giuliani fundraiser in December 1992 that if Rudy didn't win the city was "going to turn into Detroit," suggested Garth instead.

At sixty-three, the bald, potbellied Garth reminded Rudy of his father: "He makes me argue my case," said the candidate, who actually wound up spending most of his time listening to Garth argue his. The decisive Garth expects candidates to do what he demands. He dictates message and mediums, deciding where what he wants said will be said. Garth thought, according to his aide Richard Bryers, the 1989 campaign had "spun away from Giuliani's strengths to Dinkins's strengths," aided by the Yusef Hawkins case. He wanted Rudy "projecting competence," carrying himself as if he were ready to make the city manageable again. Bryers said Garth had no interest in "great gossip like the love letters" of 1989, thought they "would not be decisive," and instead "believed Giuliani would win by being tightly focused" on a few solid issues.

While Giuliani had a forbidding image from his prosecutor days, he was actually accessible, expansive, even open. Garth would make him the tough candidate and mayor he has become—tight-lipped, dismissive and commanding. Bryers, who was the campaign's press secretary, explained in a later interview: "Intelligence is a weakness for a candidate; it's a liability. You have to be very repetitive. Intelligent people want to discuss issues, but that's not going to help you. You need someone who's disciplined."

Until he met Garth, Rudy thought he had to at least try to answer reporters' questions. Garth sent him off periodically with a script and Rudy's job was to see to it that he said nothing to compete with the designated theme. While Garth certainly did not invent this "candidate protection program" mode of campaigning, he was skilled at enforcing it, and Rudy was one of its pioneers.

Answer no questions about the law practice, Garth ruled.

That's all Rudy's done the last four years? Too bad. It's nobody's business who his clients were.

And the stories, by and large, went away.

The strategy—implemented by Bryers, who Garth brought in from Pennsylvania and Washington partly because he neither had nor coveted any relationships with New York reporters—was to mau-mau anyone with a question Garth didn't like. Berate them. Accuse them of being biased. Go over their heads to editors or owners. Stonewall or spit at them. Make access a favor and keep score.

Bryers assailed a *Times* reporter, David Margolick, who was doing a profile of Rudy's legal career. WNBC-TV's Pablo Guzman was married to Giuliani's SDNY press secretary, but when he tried to do a piece on Rudy's outlandish claims that he was once the CEO of a Kentucky mining company, the Giuliani crew descended on his bosses screaming. *Newsday*'s City Hall bureau chief Michael Powell had to take a screed so loud almost everyone in Room 9—the pressroom at City Hall— heard each barb.

An auto dealer who backed Rudy and advertised on the twenty-four-hour news channel NY 1, pulled his ads for a while over the station's supposed anti-Giuliani bias. Giuliani refused to participate in debates that included the Conservative Party candidate and Dinkins refused to participate if he was excluded. So WCBS-TV put Rudy on alone for an hour shortly before the election, a boon especially unusual for a candidate never elected to any office. Both camps agreed to a *Newsday* idea to submit ten questions apiece, with each side answering the other's most pointed queries. When Garth got Dinkins's questions, the campaign reneged and refused to answer any of them. *Newsday* printed Dinkins's answers to tough questions, and Rudy got a walk.

The vulnerability study commissioned for the '93 campaign described Giuliani's "habit" of answering reporters' questions "abrasively" or, on some occasions, "attacking the interviewer." The study, which was finished by April, said these responses "contribute to the impression some have of Giuliani as cold, hard, mean and humorless." The recommendation was that Giuliani "make a conscious effort to curtail this behavior to foster a more positive, friendly image." While Rudy did keep this side of himself in check through much of the year, his press handlers adopted it, but their coarseness was invisible to the public.

The press style of the campaign, it turned out, was merely an audition. That's how the Giuliani team would eventually run City Hall, too, oblivious to the contrasting public information obligations of a campaign marketing a candidate and a government serving a city. Cristyne Lategano, Bryers's inexperienced assistant, was hired in part to make sure a female press aide was highly visible with him on the campaign trail (the all-boys team of 1989 had not done well among women at the polls). When she became Rudy's press secretary after the election, Garth's approach was virtually all she knew. As comfortable as Rudy already was with it, this press style moved with them to City Hall from day one, where nothing like it had ever before been attempted. It effectively became both his and Lategano's public personalities.

This scheme would not have worked—in 1993 or thereafter—if the two prime tabloid owners hadn't been so aboard with Rudy they accepted it. The tabloids have the power to punish such arrogance in bold type. TV stations follow their news lead. But Giuliani had uncritical support from the *Post*, reacquired by Rupert Murdoch in early 1993, through the campaign and the first term. *Daily News* owner Mort Zuckerman was also a Giuliani man. Zuckerman, who doubles as a real estate developer, had made a $33.8 million deposit during the Koch administration on the publicly owned and exquisitely-located Coliseum site, and the Dinkins administration, together with state officials, were not disposed to letting him keep it. He had failed to develop anything, and his deadline had long expired. When Dinkins would not let him off the hook on the deposit, the *News* backed

Giuliani. Early in his first year, Giuliani bailed him out on half the deposit, helping him keep more than $17 million.

In addition to media management, Garth also put together the fusion ticket that proved crucial to the campaign. Giuliani had no running mates in 1989 because he did not control the Republican line. To put together a ticket featuring Democrats Badillo and Susan Alter, the candidate for Public Advocate, Rudy had to be able to deliver the GOP line, which meant he had to be able to steer at least three county leaders behind candidates of his choosing early in the election year. Once he made peace with D'Amato, Rudy could do that.

Badillo, who'd known Garth for almost thirty years, was drawn to the ticket in part because of his presence. The onetime borough president of the Bronx and the city's best-known Latino politician, Badillo had been talking for months about running for mayor himself. He'd done it four times before, but no one was taking him seriously this time. He toyed for four months in early 1993 with a candidacy, pulling out in late May. Badillo's law partner Rick Fischbein, according to Badillo, negotiated the fusion deal with Garth, Giuliani and Peter Powers, meeting over a couple of weeks, often at Fischbein's Park Avenue apartment. He wanted assurances that the Giuliani campaign would help foot the costs of Badillo's run.

Dinkins could not offer Badillo a spot on his ticket since the incumbent comptroller was a Democrat, Elizabeth Holtzman, who was supporting Dinkins. The Badillo bargaining dragged on because Badillo was trying to get the Republican and Liberal lines immediately, but to delay his endorsement of Giuliani until after the Democratic primary for comptroller in September.

When he finally agreed to endorse Giuliani in May, he doomed any chance he had to win the Democratic primary, meaning he was running solely to help Rudy. Everyone understood, including the Dinkins camp, that an active Badillo, traveling the city with Giuliani in the campaign van for months as he did, would move at least several points of the Latino vote to Rudy.

Susan Alter was also a Garth concept. She would add a woman's touch to the army of suits that seemed to always surround Giuliani. A city councilwoman from Brooklyn, she had reform credentials and a perky intelligence. She was also an Orthodox Jew with a rabbi emeritus for a husband. After Crown Heights, Giuliani already had the Orthodox vote. Alter might boost turnout, especially of Orthodox and other women.

It did not seem to bother Giuliani much that Alter was a carpetbagger. Her husband's synagogue was in fashionable Lawrence, Long Island, and it provided her husband with a rather lavish home. His voter and car registration listed Lawrence. He'd recently applied for a public job in Brooklyn and listed Lawrence as his home.

The address she used in Brooklyn was in the heart of a black neighborhood and her political opponents said she was rarely there.

After Rudy called her in mid-May to invite her to join his ticket, she considered it for an hour or two, calling friends for advice. She was in Lawrence when she made the calls, though it was a weekday and she claimed, whenever her Brooklyn residency was questioned, that Lawrence was only an occasional weekend getaway. That's where she decided to run for the office that is the charter-mandated successor to mayor.

Three days after Alter's gala press conference with Rudy, *Newsday* reporters found her at home in Lawrence on a Tuesday. She had spent the night there. As columnist Gail Collins put it: "Yesterday Alter was spinning a story that had the rabbi driving regularly from Long Island to Rockland County to Flatbush, just to sleep in the politically appropriate bedroom. If any of this is the least bit true, the husband deserves to be named American Automobile Association Man of the Year."

Alter wasn't the only carpetbagger encouraged by Rudy to join the 1993 campaign. Congress of Racial Equality (CORE) head Roy Innis, who lived in Westchester and maintained a legal city address, challenged Dinkins in the Democratic primary. So close to Rudy he was listed at the head table of Giuliani's December 1992 fundraiser, Innis announced his candidacy just a few months later. Innis lent a black face to the Giuliani critique of the incumbent, assailing Dinkins as soft on crime in preparation for the November run. Not only did Innis frequent Giuliani fundraisers, Rudy went to CORE's annual gala before and during his mayoralty, oblivious to the findings of two Anti-Defamation League directors that Innis had an alleged anti-Semitic past.

What was most surprising about Badillo's alliance with Giuliani was that Mario Cuomo did nothing to try to prevent it. Badillo was so close to the Cuomo administration that the governor had appointed him chair of a pivotal state housing board and recruited him to run for state comptroller on the 1986 ticket. Fischbein's wife was also a Cuomo appointee on the board of another state housing agency and, in December 1991, when Cuomo almost ran for president, Fischbein was one of the key people setting up finance committees for him around the country.

"I have no advice for Herman and can't give him any instructions," Cuomo said, a peculiar position for the titular head of the state party known to intervene in anything that affected his own interests. "My prediction is he won't do it, but I could be wrong—and if he does, it will hurt Dinkins." The Cuomo administration awarded the Fischbein firm its first state bond business in 1993—a coveted plum it was so ill equipped to perform that its handling of a $24 million hospital bond was blasted in two internal memos written by state officials.

Schools Chancellor Rudy Crew was the mayor's closest black friend. He now feels betrayed—personally and professionally. (© Robert B. Levine)

Ray Harding, the Liberal Party boss and wired lobbyist, exchanges victory kisses with Rudy at a 1997 party, with master of ceremonies Charlie Hughes looking on. A top municipal labor leader, Hughes later pled guilty to stealing $2 million from his members—thousands of kitchen workers and hourly school aides. (© Frances M. Roberts)

When Giuliani met "Baby Doc" Duvalier, the boy king of Haiti, he reached the expedient conclusion that there was no political repression in a land where thousands were executed. (© AP/Wide World)

Posing before their 1986 "drug buy" in Washington Heights were Giuliani and Al D'Amato, who was running for re-election. The press never found out, but three of their five buys were bad. When their friendship fractured two years later, they fought like Hell's Angels rivals. (© AP/Wide World)

Denny Young and Giuliani announce their departure from the U.S. Attorney's office in the Southern District of New York in January 1989. They joined white shoe firm White & Case before Rudy's first run for mayor. (© AP/Wide World)

Thirty-eight-year-old Rudy, the youngest associate attorney general in history, in a Miami appearance in 1982, the same year he met Donna Hanover there. He's always done an involuntary eye roll in public performances, particularly when making a strained explanation. (© AP/Wide World)

Classic car auto dealer Elliot Cuker was a client at
Patterson, Belknap in the late '70s who took on
Deepak Chopra proportions in Rudy's New Age life.
(© Bill Turnbull/*Daily News*)

U.S. District Court Judge Lloyd MacMahon was, after Harold
Giuliani, the single most important mentor in Rudy's life. All
the judge and the father shared was an appetite for anger.
(© AP/Wide World)

Cristyne Lategano, the twenty-eight-year-old press secretary who became the second most powerful person in Rudy's government, was his indispensable companion until she became very dispensable. (© Richard B. Levine)

Judith Nathan was the other "path" Donna said Rudy chose in the fall of 1999, with the Senate race of the epoch staring him in the face.

(© Helayne Seidman)

Giuliani the Prosecutor nailed a corrupt city administration. As mayor, he looked the other way while friends compromised his government. (© Catherine Smith)

Nine hundred people a day line up for food at the Holy Apostle soup kitchen in Chelsea, with hunger skyrocketing in the Giuliani era. (© Catherine Smith)

"Nice trenchcoat" was Rudy's only comment when NYPD commissioner Bill Bratton was pictured on the cover of *Time* magazine. It was code for "Get out." Bratton was bounced a couple of months later.

(© AP/Wide World)

Former U.S. District Court Judge and Deputy Attorney General Harold "Ace" Tyler, a wise early mentor, brought Giuliani to Washington as his aide in the '70s, then into his law firm. Rudy shut him out when he indicted former Miss America Bess Myerson in the '80s. (© Harvey Wang)

Cuomo certainly had the leverage to kill the Giuliani/Badillo fusion with a single grumble. But he also had ties to Giuliani he hadn't had in 1989, and he faced a tough re-election in 1994, unlike the far less competitive 1990 race. Ray Harding, who delivered his Liberal line immediately to Alter and Badillo, and Garth, who was already positioned to become Cuomo's top consultant in 1994, were clear conduits between the Democratic governor and the Republican challenger. One indication of how tight this circle of connections would become was that right after Giuliani's election, Harding joined Badillo's law firm.

Badillo was actually the weakest indicator of the covert alliance between Cuomo and Rudy. Two early Cuomo decisions also helped Giuliani. In 1990, Cuomo approved the bill that would put the Staten Island secession referendum on the ballot in 1993, when every politician in the state understood it would increase turnout in the most anti-Dinkins borough. The Democrats in the State Assembly passed the bill to help two Democratic Assembly members from the island, but they expected the governor to veto it. The bill created a commission to complete a time-consuming study of the implications of secession and to issue findings by the time of the '93 election.

Cuomo, who was up for re-election in 1990, signed the bill with great fanfare at a Staten Island ceremony. He and the legislature made sure that the referendum wouldn't appear on the ballot when either of them was running again—in 1992 or 1994. Two weeks after the bill signing, Giuliani, who had been speaking at GOP functions around the state, ended speculation that he might challenge Cuomo. "I've got a law practice and other things I've got to do both personally and professionally," he said.

Early in 1993, Dinkins wrote Cuomo, trying belatedly to get the governor to delay the referendum. Cuomo claimed he couldn't. To this day, Cuomo maintains he approved the referendum "on the merits," pointing out that it "was not a bill I proposed or moved" and blaming it on the Assembly. "It had nothing to do with Rudy Giuliani," says Cuomo. Dinkins attributed his loss to secession and added: "I figured the governor would never sign it."

Though Staten Islanders overwhelmingly approved secession, the issue disappeared when Giuliani took office, confirming the racial impetus that in part drove it. A legal opinion issued by Assembly attorneys indicated that the City Council had to approve what's called a home rule message for secession to actually proceed—exactly what Dinkins had contended for years to no avail. By the time the assembly killed it, however, the issue had given Giuliani 26,000 more votes in Staten Island than he got in 1989.

The other Cuomo actions that contributed to Dinkins's defeat revolved around

Crown Heights. In October 1992—a day after a jury acquitted the only man charged in Yankel Rosenbaum's murder—Cuomo asked a top aide, Richard Girgenti, to "conduct a comprehensive review of how the criminal justice system functioned in this case." Girgenti drafted an executive order limiting the inquiry to "the investigation and prosecution" of the murder and sent it to Cuomo on November 16.

But Girgenti's mandate was then changed to include "the August 1991 disturbance in Crown Heights," as well as the response of the NYPD and the Dinkins administration to the deadly riot. In between the original and final versions of the order, Al D'Amato was re-elected, campaigning at Norman Rosenbaum's side and collecting an astonishing 40 percent of the Jewish vote. With the governor up for re-election in 1994, that vote set off alarms in Albany. Cuomo now has no recollection of participating in any decision to broaden the mandate, contending that it always made sense to examine the handling of the riot. Yet Cuomo's initial public statements attributed Girgenti's assignment solely to the acquittal, and the fact that federal prosecutors had not yet announced their own investigation of the murder. He said nothing about investigating the city's response to the riot.

When the Girgenti report was issued in mid-July, it found that Dinkins "did not act in a timely and decisive manner in requiring the Police Department to quickly restore peace and order to the community." Cuomo actually pushed television news producers to put the release of the report on live, the only time he did so in a dozen years as governor.

While the findings were meticulous, they were also selective. A Dinkins deputy mayor who was also close to the governor, Milt Mollen, was spared even a line of criticism. Others who weren't close to the governor were denounced as "simply not credible" when queried about their similar failure to respond to warnings from Jewish leaders about the lack of police action.

Though Girgenti would concede later that many of the same Jewish leaders whose warnings Dinkins and his top staff downplayed also spoke to Cuomo, Girgenti never questioned Cuomo about whether he relayed those concerns to the mayor. Since the leaders were calling Cuomo to ask him to send the National Guard to the neighborhood, they were obviously making precisely the same points to him about the lack of NYPD response as they had to the mayor.

Worse, Girgenti investigated but never reported on a conversation between Cuomo and Dinkins that had become the battle cry of Crown Heights, cited endlessly by critics like Ed Koch. Cuomo told the *Jewish Press* in a taped interview: "The mayor on the second day of the trouble in Crown Heights said that the night before had been a sort of day of grace to the mob, and that wouldn't happen a second day because it was abused and because there were crimes perpetrated that were not prevented."

Though the governor's sound-bite prowess made this quote the central theme of Dinkins detractors, Girgenti never mentioned it in his 360-page report. When one reporter pressed Girgenti about it a week after the release of the report, he said he'd personally visited the offices of the *Jewish Press* and determined that "the *Jewish Press* quoted the governor correctly." He conceded, however, that he also determined—by asking the mayor and "looking at the governor's notes"—that no such conversation with Dinkins ever occurred. Girgenti said the governor "took a lot of different conversations and news reports" and "reduced" them to this one-day ventilation theme. Even the phrase "day of grace" had more of a Catholic Cuomo than a Protestant Dinkins ring to it.

The Crown Heights plaintiffs and lawyer relied on this quote so strongly that the federal judge who denied a motion to dismiss the suit cited it a dozen times, saying it was the most compelling evidence supporting the claim.

Cuomo finally testified in this suit in 1995—nineteen days after he was out of office and a year after Dinkins's departure. For the first time, he acknowledged that he had not even spoken to Dinkins until the fourth day of the riot, when police finally had taken control of the situation. "Mayor Dinkins never said that to me at any time," the ex-governor declared, when asked about the day of grace. "No agent of Mayor Dinkins, no deputy of Mayor Dinkins, no agent of the police contacted me and said that the mayor had participated in or ordered a day of grace."

Had Mario Cuomo said the same words in 1993, he might have changed the result of a close election. Instead he let Dinkins twist in the wind. Dinkins says now that Cuomo's "attitude about Girgenti's report was that it could have been much worse, like he had saved me from a worse report." He is baffled about why Cuomo didn't deny the grace quote in 1993.

The Giuliani camp was awash in leaks about Girgenti's findings long before the release, and when it came out, Rudy seized on it as the strongest indictment of his opponent. The false quote and the skewed report—which, of course, ignored the question of why Cuomo waited until the fourth day to call the mayor—damaged Dinkins in 1993, while winning Orthodox allies for Cuomo in 1994.

While Cuomo's image as a national Democrat has been secure since his 1984 blockbuster convention speech, he played a bipartisan brand of politics within New York that revolved around his own balance-of-power interests. Mild-mannered Senator Pat Moynihan told the *Times* that Cuomo and D'Amato had a "mutual non-aggression pact" for years. In the 1992 Senate race, for example, Cuomo, like

Giuliani, joined in the D'Amato "fascist" hoax, lending Democratic credibility to the notion that Democratic nominee Bob Abrams's use of the term was an anti-Italian slur. He was far closer to Senate GOP leader Ralph Marino than the Democratic minority—so much so that Marino tried to block George Pataki's 1994 nomination to run against him.

Cuomo endorsed Dinkins for re-election, but his own social service commissioner refused to criticize Giuliani's transparently illegal, ninety-day-shelter-limit, homeless proposal, even suggesting it might be the kind of change that was necessary. Giuliani presented the fifteen-page strategy paper in mid-September, contending that it "fully incorporates and builds on the recommendations" of a city commission appointed by Dinkins and chaired by Andrew Cuomo. In fact, its most punitive elements were never contemplated by the Cuomo Commission report, yet neither Andrew Cuomo, nor anyone in his father's administration, pointed that out.

Andrew Cuomo had been a key to Dinkins's '89 win, suffocating the love-letter story. But he'd since given Giuliani off-year lessons on homeless policy and, in one taped session, the two swapped jokes and insights like old friends. He stayed far away from the '93 race, having just been appointed the Clinton administration's new Housing and Urban Development (HUD) undersecretary. Similarly, the governor, who'd vigorously attacked Giuliani in 1989 and threatened Ray Harding over the Liberal endorsement, limited himself in 1993 to occasional, long-distance comments supportive of Dinkins. The only time Cuomo criticized Giuliani was a muted and barely reported comment connecting Rudy disparagingly to "the new federalism of Bush and Reagan."

The day after he won, Giuliani said he didn't anticipate any problems in dealing with Cuomo, noting they had "mutual friends"—an apparent reference to Garth and Harding—and that Cuomo had given him advice during the race on how to make the transition from lawyer to candidate.

Bill Lynch, David Dinkins and others in the Dinkins inner circle were convinced that the governor had two-timed them, nominally supporting Dinkins while simultaneously making sure that a potential new Republican mayor wouldn't hurt him in his Democratic base—particularly among Jews—in 1994. Brooklyn D.A. Joe Hynes, a onetime appointee and ally of Cuomo's, titillated the audience at a 1993 roast with this tale: "Some years ago, the governor was brought in for a physical and an interview by the draft board. His interviewer asked him if he could kill someone if necessary. Mario thought for a moment, and then he said: 'I don't know about strangers—but friends—DEFINITELY.'"

Garth, who was publicly named Cuomo's media strategist less than four months after Rudy's election, was not only a key link for Giuliani with the governor, he was critical to bringing Koch aboard. In April, Koch told a television interviewer that he was "going to string out" his apparently inevitable endorsement of Giuliani. "It's helpful," he said.

"To you or him?" he was asked.

"To me," he said.

Richard Bryers says now that they "were never unsure of Koch." His endorsement didn't occur until mid-September, when Koch swallowed any distress he might have had about the sex inquiry Giuliani's office had conducted of him years earlier. Friends of Koch say that Giuliani assured the former mayor—shortly before the endorsement—that he didn't know about the Tony Lombardi probe. These friends say that Koch accepted that explanation initially, but began to doubt it, particularly after watching Giuliani's hands-on management style—what Koch would characterize as a one-man government.

When the *Village Voice* published a story in July 1995 revealing that federal prosecutors in New Jersey who were "considering" indicting Lombardi had described him in open court as a "spy" working inside the government , Koch was so upset he called a friend at 7 A.M. and told him to go buy the paper. The story also reported that Giuliani had just vouched for Lombardi in a sworn stipulation taken by prosecutors at City Hall. Rudy conceded in that stipulation that Lombardi had "attended meetings and planning sessions" with him. Koch was already distancing himself from Giuliani on a variety of policy matters. He now had a personal bone of contention: Giuliani may well have lied to him to secure his 1993 endorsement.

Though no longer at the IRS and no longer directly involved with Giuliani, Lombardi still had an effect on the 1993 election. Before he left the government, Lombardi launched the probe that would haunt and tarnish Dinkins. As soon as the 1989 campaign was over, in late November and early December of 1989, he played a key role in jumpstarting an investigation of Dinkins's cable stock transfer and steering it out of the Southern District and into the Eastern District. Uncertain of his status in the office just taken over by Otto Obermaier, Lombardi pushed Eastern District U.S. Attorney Andy Maloney to take over the case. Maloney did and his eventual report raised questions about the authenticity of the letter transferring the stock from Dinkins to his son. Lombardi also launched a preliminary tax inquiry of the cable company's principal, Percy Sutton, a powerful Dinkins ally.

In addition to the post-election Lombardi role in the cable probe, David Lawrence and Kevin Ford, the AUSA and the city investigator who had worked with Lombardi on the Myerson and Nathan cases, also conducted damaging probes of the Dinkins administration over the next four years.

Ford spearheaded a special investigation of asbestos inspections at the Board of Education that forced a nearly month-long citywide delay in the opening of schools in September 1993. While there was no doubt the inspections were faulty, Ford, who oversaw asbestos and other environmental investigations for the School Construction Authority (SCA) at the time, was informed of the false reports long before he and others sounded the alarm that August. The *Daily News* reported that Ford's unit knew for two years that the asbestos reports were "unreliable." The SCA was so sure the reports were faulty, it began conducting its own tests. Yet it told no one in law enforcement until the eve of the pre-election school opening.

The asbestos crisis, angering the parents of a million school children, was seized upon by the Giuliani campaign as another example of Dinkins mismanagement. Confronted with the first citywide shutdown ever (except for strikes), Dinkins appeared daily to be trying once again to grab hold of another self-made emergency.

Shortly after Giuliani became mayor, he named Ford deputy commissioner of the Department of Investigation, an agency run by Giuliani's most trusted law enforcement confidants. Ford quit DOI in 1998 to rejoin Lawrence, who was working in the counsel's office at the prestigious Goldman, Sachs investment firm.

Lawrence stayed in the Southern District until mid–1993 and remained so friendly with Rudy he attended a Rudy fundraiser in 1992 while heading the office's public corruption unit. He and his wife are listed on the seating arrangement for that fundraiser, though no contributions were recorded on the campaign filings. At the same time as he was appearing at the fundraiser, Lawrence was conducting numerous probes of Dinkins associates, including sending two major Dinkins fundraisers, Arnold Biegen and Joe Barnes, to jail. Lawrence pushed Biegen for information on both Dinkins and D'Amato.

Lawrence tried to flip Barnes and Biegen before and after guilty pleas, but eventually recommended the thirty-five-month prison sentence imposed on Biegen, who had been the treasurer of Dinkins's committee. In an October 1992 presentencing letter to the judge, Lawrence wrote that Biegen "provided no meaningful assistance to any federal investigation," dismissing Biegen's own claims to have done so as "simply without basis."

Lawrence also probed the Dinkins administration's award of a multimillion-dollar sludge contract to a firm represented by Ron Brown, then Democratic National Committee chair, and Harold Ickes, who was counsel to the Dinkins campaign. In addition, Lawrence subpoenaed city records regarding a Corrections

Department contract won by a client of Sid Davidoff, the leading lobbyist of the Dinkins era who was a constant target of Giuliani public attacks. The prosecutor even investigated Laura Blackburne, the chair of the Housing Authority under Dinkins who was forced to resign principally over revelations that she had spent $3,000 on a pink leather sofa for her office.

None of the Lawrence cases ever gave Giuliani any campaign ammunition, though Rudy certainly included Biegen, Blackburne, the stock transfer and other publicized probes in the litany of ethics questions he cited surrounding the Dinkins administration. But with competence the up-front issue of the campaign, and race the subliminal one, Rudy spent little time with the corruption themes he had ridden so hard in 1989.

Garth and the memories of 1989 combined to give Rudy a new campaign personality. He began smiling like a trained seal, baring teeth with every handshake, discovering what would prove over the years to be an inexhaustible supply of surface friendliness. He put on sports glasses with wine-colored rims, and that plus a slimmer build and a tighter haircut enhanced his image of energy and competence, especially when compared with the sixty-six-year-old Dinkins. The snappy "Rudy!" posters were said by *Newsday's* Mitch Gelman to "scream, rock-star-like."

When Garth yelled at Rudy for dressing "like an undertaker," he found bright colors in ties, and accepted "coaching" on when and where to roll up his sleeves. Giuliani started the campaign by getting away from dark themes like crime, but in the homestretch, his speeches were laced with references to "slaughter" and the dramatic image of criminals "roaming unhindered" on the streets.

At $25,000 a month plus a percentage of the media buy, Garth was meeting with Giuliani every night, usually around midnight, reviewing the day and planning the next. Powers and Harding started most mornings with him. When Giuliani got testy toward the end of a race that was closer than he anticipated, Garth cooled him out by making a tough commercial that went after Dinkins's weaknesses but keeping it in the can. Just the knowledge that he had such a weapon in his arsenal calmed Rudy and helped keep him at least mildly positive in the final days.

Garth also decided to involve Donna in the initial screening of all the commercials—joining just Rudy and Powers, according to Bryers. In sharp contrast to 1989, Donna was all over the 1993 effort, campaigning with and without him, meeting volunteers and attending executive staff meetings at the headquarters. With only part-time, freelance, work at Fox's Channel 5, she was unencumbered by restrictions like those imposed on her by WPIX.

Her total TV earnings in 1993 were $32,773 and they spent $23,848 on child-care, suggesting how often Donna was out of the house for campaign, rather than professional, reasons. Both Garth and her husband respected her media judgment, as well as her sense of what would work with women voters. "She's my closest ad-viser," Rudy would say shortly after taking office. "She has a lot of understanding of how the city works. She's good at assessing who's strong, who's weak."

Brad Holbrooke, her WPIX colleague, neighbor and friend, contrasted her 1989 and 1993 campaign roles: "A lot of people, some of the campaign advisers, laid Giuliani's defeat at the feet of her unwillingness to campaign for him. That's not my evaluation, but other people have said that he's not a warm and fuzzy guy, and she could warm and fuzzy him up and she didn't because she wanted to maintain that integrity as a journalist apart from the political fray. And I think in the next campaign she did campaign for him fairly vigorously and a lot of people felt that was a major improvement."

Toward the end of the campaign, Donna was hired by TV Food Network to be co-anchor of *Food News & Views*—her first real broadcast job in almost three years. Reese Schonfeld, the network president who'd known Donna and Rudy for years, says he hired her because "she's terrific" and because he "thought it was un-fortunate that she was caught in a journalistic bind when your husband is a politi-cian and you can't be on the air." Schonfeld said he talked with John Corporon, Donna's old WPIX boss, "about how she got screwed over by her association with the mayor, or the mayoral candidate" in 1990. "He loved Donna. I loved Donna."

Donna taped a two-hour sneak preview "taste test" with Robin Leach prior to the election, showcasing her skills at debriefing the personalities of the food and nutrition businesses. She did not, however, assume her on-air responsibilities un-til 1994. But the job that evolved sounded much like the one she'd rejected when she left WPIX. Joe Langhan, a network executive, described her daily routine: "She'd come in around 4 P.M. with her escorts"—she had a city-paid staff of four and Langhan said she'd "have at least two, sometimes three, with her." She'd im-mediately "read the script, talk to the producer and look at the tapes." Then she'd go on the air at 5:30, mostly just reading the news. What started as an hour-long show was eventually reduced to half an hour, which she'd split with her co-anchor. Though a free-lance, Donna still makes an annual six-figure salary at the network, which blossomed into a cable colossus.

Holbrooke, who wound up working with her there as well, said her decision to work at the network was a "testament to her ambition or to her love of television," since Donna "has never cooked a meal in her life." Holbrooke said "her kitchen was full of law books and newspaper clippings—and I actually saw it—and the stove was never turned on."

The great fear of 1989—the mysterious Regina Peruggi story—never even threatened to return in 1993. In anticipation that it might, the campaign's vulnerability study, which was authored by Lyons at Garth's suggestion, devoted a lengthy analysis to the possibility that "the Dinkins campaign might leak negative personal information" about the Peruggi marriage. It said that the marriage and annulment raised "questions about a 'weirdness factor'" afflicting Giuliani's "personal life." The study reviewed what it described as Giuliani's "wide array of conflicting answers" about the marriage, which it said "brings the soundness of his judgment into question—and the veracity of his answers."

A five-page recapitulation of Rudy's answers to prior questions identified "numerous inconsistencies and questionable circumstances about how long the two were married, whether Giuliani knew he was marrying his second cousin, whether he dated other women while still married, and ultimately how consistent he has been about his personal life." The study referred to Rudy's "raucous social life" during the Peruggi marriage, adding that the media saw the marriage itself "as an extremely bizarre event." It recommended that Giuliani "deflect as a shameless act of negative campaigning any attempt to question the legitimacy of Giuliani's first marriage or his fidelity." By assuming this "personal defense strategy," the study concluded, "the campaign will find it exceedingly difficult to attack Dinkins with personal charges," signaling the death of the love-letters assault.

Giuliani was so unnerved by this and other passages in the study that he had a campaign aide sit down at the computers of the two authors and erase it from their hard drives. The aide also confiscated discs. Copies were only given to Powers, Garth and Giuliani, and it was never discussed again.

Some of its analysis of Giuliani weaknesses proved prophetic. In a section entitled "arrogance," the study reported that critics charged he "doesn't listen to people, doesn't take advice, attacks critics and is insensitive to those who do not share his position on an issue." It concluded that "this charge is not without some justification." The review of "ruthlessness"—after noting that he was viewed as "the Machiavelli of the legal community"—found that there was "lots of evidence demonstrating" that as a federal prosecutor he "certainly pushed the envelope of the permissible."

"Rudy Giuliani has plenty of 'inoculating' to do on several fronts," the authors wrote in the introduction, specifying his "reputation for overzealousness," the reversals of his federal convictions, flip-flops and the cop rally. "This study is tough and hard-hitting. It is not intended to shock or offend, but to prepare the candidate and his staff for the kinds of no-holds-barred assault they should expect" from the Dinkins camp.

The third paragraph of the five-inch-thick bound volume, though, sounded its death knell. Rudy Giuliani was hardly prepared to look into a mirror that bared everything from his hairline to his eyeroll. "The readers of this vulnerability study are urged," the preface read, "not to dismiss or take lightly any of the negatives discussed in this document. Taken together, the negative issues presented in this study offer a compelling argument against electing Giuliani mayor."

Though Mayor Rudy would bar Public Advocate Mark Green from making an apolitical appearance in a city senior center in 1995, Candidate Rudy spent his final day of the 1993 campaign shuttling between seven such centers. He swung through all five boroughs, finishing that night, of course, in Staten Island with the Molinaris.

His election-day operation—featuring thousands of off-duty cops, firemen and correction officers, assigned to "monitor" black districts—was denounced by Dinkins at a noon press conference as "an outrageous campaign of voter intimidation and dirty tricks." A poster that warned Dinkins supporters they might be arrested if they voted was put up—particularly in Latino areas—by four men riding in a car registered to a city cop. The poster—headlined "Re-Elect Mayor David Dinkins"—said that federal agents and immigration authorities were at the polls ready "to arrest and deport undocumented illegal voters." The Dinkins campaign, of course, said it had nothing to do with the poster, a position echoed by both the PBA and Rudy.

In the campaign's closing days, Rudy put Helen D'Avanzo Giuliani into a commercial, just as Al D'Amato had done with his mother. She said her son was a "nice guy." When the firemen's union endorsed him, he mentioned Eddie D'Avanzo in his speech, recalling how his fireman uncle was "seriously injured in the line of duty" and calling him a "hero." His extended family—particularly George Giordano, the son-in-law of William D'Avanzo and Olga Giuliani, and Cathy Giuliani, the daughter-in-law of Uncle Rudy Giuliani—was very active in the campaign, with Giordano accompanying him on many street appearances.

Lou Carbonetti, the son of Harold Giuliani's best friend who'd gone to Yankee games with Rudy as a kid, and Lou's son Tony were on the campaign staff, with Lou assigned to help his fellow graduate of East Harlem politics, Herman Badillo. In fact, the fusion ticket debuted at a 116th Street rally at Badillo's suggestion, and

Rudy, Badillo and Carbonetti returned to Harold's old East Harlem haunts to launch the campaign that would fulfill his dream.

Lou had also worked in the 1989 campaign, having visited Rudy at the U.S. Attorney's office when he first heard Giuliani might run and offered his services (he ran his own East Harlem Democratic club). Carbonetti recalls that he brought a "beautifully framed photo" of Harold and his father when he saw Rudy—for the first time in many years—and that Giuliani kept the photo and returned the frame, saying he couldn't accept gifts.

With Donna, the kids, Giordano, Cathy Giuliani and Carbonetti around, the campaign, whose first TV ad featured a relaxed Rudy doing his Brooklyn shtick from native Brooklyn, had a comfortable, family, feeling to it. The ethos, though, went beyond family. The Dinkins campaign charged that Rudy's "make-things-the-way-they-were" appeal was a conscious effort to "manipulate nostalgia," aimed at the elderly in particular, with a not too subtle racial edge. The Sunday *Times Magazine* described him on its cover, however, as "A Wonder Bread Son of the '50s," buying into this purebred image as authentic: "It's as if his cultural and psychic sensibilities froze about 1961, the year he left the tutelage of the Christian Brothers at Bishop Loughlin."

"I used to hide my personal side," Giuliani said. "People thought I was a machine. People want to get to know you, to get to feel you. I was holding part of myself back." Nonetheless, he still refused reporters' requests during one campaign swing to alter his route a few blocks and pose for photographs in front of 419 Hawthorne Street, concerned no doubt about the reception he might get on the virtually all-black block.

Joined on election morning by Donna, Andrew and three-year-old Caroline, Rudy voted shortly before 9 A.M. A family campaign culminated in a family scene. No one noticed that neither Rudy nor Donna had much of a voting history—with both of them registering on January 1, 1984, and then missing the 1984 and 1988 presidential elections, as well as the 1986 gubernatorial and Senate races and the 1985 mayoral race. Ronald Reagan, George Bush, Al D'Amato and Mario Cuomo weren't enough of a lure to get them to the polls. Incredibly, neither voted in the 1989 mayoral primary, when Rudy's name first appeared on the ballot, running against Ron Lauder.

Rudy beat Dinkins by almost the same margin as he'd lost four years earlier, completing a 50,000-vote circle. He managed to get to the top—one of the most visible and powerful public positions in the nation, in control of its fifth largest public budget—without ever serving in another elective position. No mayor had done that since John O'Brien, the interim successor to Jimmy Walker who was mayor in 1933 for a few months. Koch had served in Congress and the city council for years; Dinkins had been borough president and an assemblyman. Giuliani had discovered a new path to power, circumventing the clubhouse career ladder.

In addition to the 26,000-vote boost he got out of Staten Island, he carried Queens by 17,000 more votes than he did in 1989. He also lost Brooklyn by 29,000 fewer votes and Manhattan by 22,000 fewer. Exit polls said 85 percent of his vote was white, 9 percent Hispanic, 3 percent black and 3 percent other. Catholic turnout was up to 72 percent, accounting for 59 percent of all Giuliani voters. Dinkins voters were only 27 percent white. The city had split itself in two.

Rudy sat on a bed in his Hilton suite on the 44th floor, getting results from aides and hugs from Donna. Cops and firemen filled the ballroom below, while the balcony was crammed with bearded Orthodox Jews. It was as white and male a crowd of 1,500 as had assembled to celebrate a New York electoral win in decades. When Rudy finally spoke, he thanked the NYPD and the fire department for helping him win. Bob Wagner Jr., whose father was the mayor who'd welcomed hundreds of thousands of southern blacks to the city in the 1950s and early 1960s, was so shaken by the homogeneity of the crowd and what it said about his divided city, that he went home early and mourned. The man whose sweater-clad, cozy TV commercial had reassured Democrats and helped elect Giuliani wasn't having second thoughts about Rudy personally. It was just the aura of Rudy's narrow base, he said later, that made him "uncomfortable."

Giuliani pledged that his administration would be "universal in its concerns, sensitive to our diversity and evenhanded in every way possible." In a clear attempt to reassure blacks who voted against him in large numbers, he promised: "Nobody, no ethnic, religious or racial group, will escape my care, my concern and my attention." The *Times* editorial said Giuliani might "never fully erase the memory of his inflammatory speech" at the cop rally. But, it argued, "he could begin to make amends by sending police a wholly different message: that he expects them to match the same standards of probity and fairness that he demands from the rest of the government."

Rudy was so excited all he got was an hour's sleep. Bryers went to get him at 4:30 in the morning; he was scheduled for four morning television appearances. Donna sat in on every one. At Koch's urging, he went to City Hall to embrace Dinkins and signal a smooth transition and a unified city. He decided to visit all five boroughs, a day-after pledge he'd made in 1989. "It was his idea," Bryers recalled. "He wanted to convey that he was an agent of change." Cristyne Lategano took the victory lap across the city with him, refueled by a bare two to three hours' sleep.

They made it a point to go to Harlem first, where his five-vehicle caravan went to a church whose pastor, the Reverend John Brandon, had done a TV commercial for him. Brandon, who would be forced to resign shortly after Giuliani made him youth commissioner because of tax problems, greeted him, as did housing advocate Evelyn King, another endorser who would have to quit a Giuliani transition post within months because she lobbied the commissioner she'd just helped appoint. The only leader at the carefully orchestrated event who had not endorsed Rudy was the Reverend Calvin Butts, Harlem's most prominent minister. Butts would, by the end of Rudy's first term, become the first black leader to call him a "racist." Promising the small group an inclusive administration, Giuliani said: "I need to spend time with you."

The highlight of the daylong swing was ebullient celebrations in Borough Park, where his Orthodox Jewish supporters "met him with all the passion and excitement of a rock star," Bay Ridge and Staten Island, cornerstones of his Catholic base.

At forty-nine the youngest mayor since Lindsay, Rudy was a deep well of drive and intellect. His win had renewed his confidence, revived his ambition. He knew he could ride a crest—crime had already been dropping for thirty-five consecutive months under Dinkins, as quiet as he and the media had kept it, and the job hemorrhage that had so wounded the city was turning around, belatedly mimicking national economic trends. He had faith in his ability to manage—his Justice Department career convinced him of that—and he believed a well-run New York could be a showcase for the Big Job. He had already broken every precedent by becoming mayor; he was destined, he thought, to be the first to get beyond it, to win a higher office when his two terms were done.

A week after the election, he, Donna, the kids, Lategano, a babysitter, the security detail and a group of transition aides went to Palmas Del Mar, a 2,750-acre resort in Puerto Rico for a four-day vacation, accompanied by a half dozen reporters. Every day, he tried a different sport—tennis, basketball, a driving range. He walked the white-sand beach in a loping, oversized, striped sportshirt and baseball cap, with the press at his side. He didn't take either off when he waded into the water. The hairdo that often seemed pasted to his head never got wet. His pale skin hid from the rays and did not change color. He looked chunky and ponderous.

He did daily press briefings, detailing the transition that was going on back in the city. At one, he returned to the ethics theme he'd emphasized in 1989 and downplayed in '93, promising an independent Department of Investigation, a vow that even his most ardent admirers would later see as a joke. He talked repeatedly about the search for a new police commissioner, which had already become the most important decision facing him.

Donna was with him at the photo-ops, briefly joining the basketball game. She never took a public swim either, appearing silently at his side in knee-length shorts and flowery blouses. They got a two-bedroom villa with a kitchen (she brought a housekeeper with them) and stayed out of sight most of the week, except for the scheduled press availabilities. Despite the presence of four transition aides and constant calls to New York, Rudy said he was trying to have "as close to 100 percent vacation as possible."

The resort was so spread out the Giulianis traveled around it in gas-powered golf carts, security detail behind. The first day, while Rudy answered press questions in the hotel lobby, everyone suddenly noticed the cart weaving recklessly off into the sun, ramming into a curb, with only seven-year-old Andrew at the wheel. When Rudy hit the golf range, a reporter celebrated each of the long balls he drove into the trees by naming them after each one of his courtroom grand slams ("Friedman!" "Boesky!" "Biaggi!" Milken!!!") and Rudy howled.

No one knew it, but this would be the last Giuliani family vacation. Donna would go to Disneyworld in 1996 with the kids, but without the man who had proposed to her there. In 1998, she'd take the kids to Ireland without him, the sort of vacation no New York politician would miss except for deeply personal reasons. She would take them to Paris too—in April 1999, just days before her and Rudy's fifteenth anniversary. But he would stay in the city. The official explanation, when the *Post* asked in 1999, was that he was too busy to travel. In fact, right after his re-election in 1997, he'd launch a national speaking tour that would take him to twenty states in a matter of months. If a family that plays together stays together, Rudy wasn't playing.

The power and the limelight would, as soon as he moved into City Hall, become his life. He would adapt immediately to his new, almost kingly, status, with a realm envied by politicians everywhere and virtually unchecked by any countervailing force, legislative or otherwise. He would relish his role as commander-in-chief, with an army of 40,000, the nation's second largest militia, and it would so consume his attention he would approve detective promotions. Every important word of his would be televised, every mood analyzed. He could not enter a room again in his vast city without every eye following him. Their whispers were about him. Their hands reached for his. That would become all the intimacy he needed, and for a while he found it affirming, elevating.

He no longer feared being ordinary or wanted what was commonplace. From November 2, 1993, on, history was his only companion, greatness his only goal.

Fifteen

Metamorphosis of
a Mayoralty

RUDY'S FIRST YEAR AS MAYOR SHOWCASED THE AMBIGUITIES OF HIS five-year pusuit of the office. Just as his two campaigns had oscillated wildly from political pole to pole, 1994 would be a year of uncertain searching, guided by neither party nor ideology.

He knew he wanted to make a focused fight against crime the bedrock of his administration. That pushed him to go ahead with the hiring of a new class of 2,400 recruits and to name a wildcard police commissioner, Boston's Bill Bratton, whose ego was as unmistakably large as the mayor's. Rudy's adamant insulation of the NYPD from budget cuts in the face of a $2.3 billion gap—resisting the sage urgings of the *Times* and two comptrollers that he achieve modest savings by substituting cheaper civilians for deskbound cops—made his priorities and resolve unmistakable. So did his willingness to buck his own party and campaign in Minnesota at Bill Clinton's side for the passage of the federal crime bill.

He knew he wanted to launch a tax cut program, undaunted by the size of the gap, and he did it by picking his prime target wisely: an onerous hotel tax that he saw as discouraging tourism yet delivering little real revenue in a $32 billion budget. Cutting a symbolic tax even slightly (from 6 percent to 5) while simultaneously slashing the city workforce by nearly 7,000 jobs—primarily by offering a lucrative severance package to induce employees to leave—sent a signal to business that the new mayor meant business. He would later claim that his tax cut and fiscal plan spurred the city's economic revival, but in fact, private-sector employment grew in Dinkins's final two years and was up 21,000 in early 1994, even before Giuliani proposed his budget.

By exempting police and fire from the severance package and initial cuts, he concentrated the real damage on the Human Resources Administration (HRA), the Health & Hospitals Corporation (HHC) and the Board of

Education, bureaucratic behemoths whose overwhelmingly black and Latino users had little to do with his election.

The fiscal iron wall he built around the fire department suggested a partially political motive, since there was no policy rationale for it and the fire union had been even more helpful to his campaign than Phil Caruso's PBA. He denounced Fred Siegel, one of his former Manhattan Institute gurus, for suggesting that millions could be saved if firemen were rescheduled so that fewer worked day shifts, when fires occurred infrequently. In any event, the mayor made his hard choices with relish, almost savoring the howls they provoked.

He knew also that he wanted to establish a new public culture, embodying a toughness that would not blink in moments of crisis. His first opportunity came just ten days into his term, when police and the Nation of Islam wound up in a late-night standoff at a Harlem mosque.

Cops had been summoned to the scene by a bogus 911 armed robbery call, made by drug dealers angry at Louis Farrakhan's followers for driving them off the block. The first officers on the scene tried to push back the Black Muslim guards and instead were thrown out, losing a gun and a radio in the scuffle. Bratton and Giuliani instantly defended the cops in phone call interviews with reporters, though neither was on the scene. While Bratton's two top black aides tried to negotiate with mosque leaders, Giuliani kept calling the new commissioner and demanding action.

"You have stolen police property. Why aren't you going in?" Giuliani asked, according to Bratton years later.

"I want arrests!" demanded the mayor, who was trying, says Bratton, to show "how he was going to be different from Dinkins." Bratton warned of "the potential to have this escalate," and insisted on allowing "the negotiation process to work." It did. Cops were allowed in to search the premises and recover the gun and radio. Months later, the Muslims who fought the cops were arrested.

When the Reverend Al Sharpton, the portly prince of provocation who had tormented both of Giuliani's predecessors, tried to join a subsequent meeting at the NYPD involving the Muslims and Bratton, he was stopped at the door. The mayor said he wouldn't meet with Sharpton either, even warning black elected officials who criticized police handling of the melee: "They're going to have to learn how to discipline themselves in the way in which they speak." If New Yorkers "can't stand up for those police officers despite the color of our skin"—he declared, noting that the nose of one female cop was broken at the mosque—"this city's in more trouble than I think people believed it was."

The combination of the Sharpton rebuff and the vocal defense of the cops sounded the bugle on a new day in New York.

A day after the mosque incident, Rudy had his first controversial police shooting to deal with—an unarmed seventeen-year-old killed by three police bullets in a Brooklyn basement. The son of a prominent Muslim cleric, the boy also had a drug conviction. The new mayor was in a rush to declare: "The officer reacted both properly and bravely."

The controversy dissipated quickly, and no one noticed when the city subsequently settled a lawsuit filed by the family, paying $318,000. An Amnesty International report on the case in 1996—also ignored by the media—contended that no cops were indicted because the Nyclad bullets were untraceable and it couldn't be determined which cop's shots killed him. The family attorney says an autopsy established that he was kneeling and raising his arms, "elbows bent and palms forward," when killed.

While the settlement prevented any definitive review of the facts of the case, what was important from Rudy's standpoint was that he had seized the first two incidents of his mayoralty to draw a line in the sand. The benefit of the doubt in favor of the police that he had promised at the infamous 1992 cop rally was now unambiguous policy.

Beyond these core, preconceived, principles of governance, first-year Rudy was an open book. The issue that had underscored both of his campaigns and shaped every modern mayoralty—race—would, predictably, arrive on his desk in so many different forms, he had endless opportunities to define and redefine himself.

He recognized that defeating the first black mayor had created a chasm; he could consciously try to close it or accept it as his inevitable fate. John Lindsay had proven that being a Republican was no bar to also being a bridge to blacks. With no black among the likely challengers he would face in four years, the power of the mayoralty gave him the chance to change minority minds. All he had to do was decide he wanted to, then listen to those who could tell him how.

He recognized just as surely that there was no way to achieve his fundamental immediate goal—cutting the citywide crime rate— without lowering it significantly in minority communities. That's where most of the crime was. He could either enlist those communities as partners in this crusade or make them its target. He had to understand that any cop-is-always-right license to frisk, bust or shoot would turn neighborhoods into suspects, crunching crime at the price of pride.

The government he put together demonstrated his indecision about which path to take in his overall relations with minority communities. He named no black deputy mayor. Since Abe Beame attempted in 1974 to appoint young David Dinkins—an appointment nixed when Dinkins admitted in the screening process that he hadn't filed his taxes—the city had always had a black deputy mayor. As poisoned as Ed Koch's relations were with the black community, he named a succession of black deputies. Not only did Rudy decide not to, he simultaneously hired a thirty-member executive staff at City Hall that included only two blacks, one a holdover from Dinkins who supervised AIDS programs.

He ridiculed the liaison offices Dinkins had set up to service each ethnic community and said he disbanded them, while in truth installing his campaign aide Bruce Teitelbaum as a liaison to one, the Orthodox Jewish community. The African American/Caribbean, Latino and Asian Affairs offices were abolished.

On the other hand, he installed blacks at the helm of the Human Resources Agency, the Health & Hospitals Corporation, the Department of Health, the Department of Business Services, the Tax Commission, the Youth Bureau and the Housing Preservation and Development Agency, as many key agencies as were run by blacks under Dinkins.

He also appointed Latinos to head the Housing Authority, the Personnel Department, the Brooklyn Navy Yard Corporation, the Department of Juvenile Justice and the Department of Mental Health and Retardation, while naming one, Ninfa Segarra, both a deputy mayor and one of his two representatives on the Board of Education. Especially compared with what it would eventually become, the administration began as a picture postcard of inclusiveness.

On the heels of this mixed appointment record, as well as the mosque and Brooklyn shooting incidents, Rudy moved in late January 1994 to shut down a minority set-aside program created under Dinkins and designed to deliver 20 percent of city contracts to black, Latino, Asian and women vendors. While one element of the program was under legal challenge, Giuliani gutted it without a hint of any reformed replacement. The *Times* bellowed that his "wrongheaded and hardheaded" decision to eliminate "one of the most socially beneficial and cost-effective programs of its kind" might have been designed to "play to the exaggerated sense of white embattlement that helped him as a candidate."

"The theory of it is to remedy past discrimination," Giuliani said. "Now you can agree or disagree with whether that is necessary." Obviously believing it wasn't, the mayor and his chief of staff, Randy Mastro, promised that, without a program of preference, the city would nonetheless award more minority contracts than with it. They would never again—over the course of more than six years—provide any comprehensive data on the percentage of contracts minority firms won. Rudy simultaneously decided that the screening panel he had named to recommend new family, criminal and civil court judges was no longer required to consider diversity as a factor in making their selections.

John Dyson, the new deputy mayor for economic development, put the negatives swirling around the administration in context with two disturbing comments. In February, it was revealed that he'd written a memo to First Deputy Mayor Peter Powers after a newspaper article questioned whether they could run a diverse city. "Do not worry," he wrote. "Two white guys have been running this city of immigrants for over 200 years." The seven-page memo, which started with this sarcastic reference to the *Daily News* story about Giuliani and Powers, upset an aide so much he stole it from a City Hall desk and delivered it to the paper.

Sent the day after he was hired in December, Dyson's memo did not evoke any outrage from City Hall before or after it was leaked. "I think if you read it in context and you don't want to get offended, you won't get offended. If you want to get offended, you will," Giuliani deadpanned before storming out of a press conference when questions about it persisted. In fact, the full context of the letter was a laundry list of racially controversial proposals from the elimination of parole to the appointment of "a revolutionary with a smile on his face" to upend "the goofy welfare structure."

Just four months later, the irrepressible Dyson turned entertainer in a taped newspaper interview, rebuking the Democratic comptroller, Alan Hevesi, for pushing for the retention of a black-owned financial management firm. He told a reporter that Hevesi "ought to know a bid from a watermelon." Mild-mannered City Council Speaker Peter Vallone said it was "clearly a racist statement" and demanded a retraction or removal.

The One City/One Standard mayor did more press conference jujitsu. He defended Dyson when few doubted that similar acid spilled on an ethnic group that had voted for him would have cost the miscreant his job, or, at minimum, elicited a rebuke. "He was referring to a watermelon, which in and of itself doesn't suggest a racial slur," said the mayor. "You can interpret it either way you want." Dyson was, according to Giuliani, "a very straightforward, very direct, very honest person." He was also extremely close to Liberal Party boss Ray Harding, having largely financed Harding's recapture of the party in 1986.

"I apologize to those who took offense at it" was the best Dyson could do. A multimillionaire who'd served as Power Authority chair under Mario Cuomo, Dyson added: "I would use a different word. A bid and a baby carriage. A bid and a fruit—pick one, a peach or a raspberry." The only explanation he offered for using watermelon was that it was "an expression we happen to use in upstate New York." Though he maintained a city apartment, Dyson actually lived in Millbrook, a stylish town a couple hours to the north where his family owned a winery. He helicoptered home most Fridays, the city's first carpetbagging deputy mayor. Incredibly, he did not even bother to change his voting registration to the city while deputy mayor.

The *Times* said Giuliani was "torn between an awareness of the importance of good race relations" and a "mysterious urge" to stand by Dyson. In fact, he had managed, halfway through his first year, to convey a tolerance for intolerance he would never overcome. Yet no one around him seemed to recognize the lasting impression these biting words were leaving.

Dyson also dropped a bomb at a City Council hearing in the spring of 1994, casually mentioning that the city was going to use "home relief recipients at Sanitation, Parks and Transportation to clean your districts better." Dyson's timing could not have been worse since the mayor was then negotiating the severance deal with the unions, who agreed, for the first time, to allow the city to redeploy workers from agency to agency, filling holes left by departing employees. The threatened use of welfare workers infuriated Stanley Hill, the state's most powerful black labor leader and head of the largest municipal union, who declared: "We've gone past slavery days. We don't operate that way in New York City, we're a union town. Maybe he would like to clean the streets for nothing."

Giuliani tried to retreat from Dyson on this one: "There is no plan. There is no proposal. It's an idea. We will discuss it." That's also what he'd said when Dyson's workfare vision first appeared in the infamous December memo.

Workfare would become a linchpin of Giuliani social policy up the road, but at this moment, the mayor was so nervous about labor's opposition—the sanitation union head called Dyson's proposal "a crazy idea"—that he backed off. "This is precisely the area that creates questions about these programs," Giuliani said.

Instead of workfare and other radical alterations of city policy, the 1994 Rudy was passive on public assistance policy, silently acquiescing to new record highs in the city's caseload. Between July 1994 and January 1995, the average number of recipients each month was 1,151,083, an increase of 47,933 over the same period in Dinkins's final year.

It was also almost 100,000 more recipients than the number cited in Giuliani's campaign position paper on economic recovery, issued to great fanfare in late 1993. That paper blamed soaring welfare rates on "a collapsing job market," adding that "many who struggled to maintain their independence and sense of pride had to turn to welfare" during the recession of the early '90s. It was a supportive depiction of recipients rarely heard in the Giuliani years to come.

But as late as February 1995, the administration was still projecting small increases in the rolls for the coming months, leveling out only when "an increase in available jobs" reached the bottom rung of the labor ladder. Giuliani's first executive budget, released in May 1994 for the fiscal year that began July 1, actually contained an increase of $33 million in city funds for public assistance—a 2.6 percent hike. As antagonistic as the administration's relations with the welfare poor would soon be—with chilling attempts to squeeze the rolls—it was hardly that through 1994.

The administration's lobbying agenda in Washington that year also had a liberal coloration on health care. In the 1994 *Federal Program*, its annual needs report to Congress, the city weighed in on the comprehensive health care debate, calling for "universal coverage" for the city's "1.3 million uninsured." Complete with a cover letter from the mayor, the seventy-three-page program staunchly defended the city's Medicaid and Medicare expenditures, rallying to the cause of everything from teaching hospitals to nursing homes. It warned that Medicaid and Medicare cuts "would ravage the city's hospitals." The city's 1994 budget added $190 million for the city's share of Medicaid.

The homeless program announced in May abandoned the harsh rhetorical edge of the campaign document. Its ninety-day limit was now an attempt to compel assessment and appropriate placement of the addicted, mentally ill, alcoholic or other chronic homeless singles, rather than a threat to throw them on the street. It restored $52 million cut from the city's proposed capital plan for the development of permanent supportive housing for singles and offered to convert one of the worst large shelters into housing. There was no talk of clearing the streets of the "menacing" homeless.

To be sure, advocates were still upset about the language of "mutual responsibility"—the attempt to require the sheltered to accept individually drawn "living plans" and to participate in programs addressing their particular needs. But the worst that would happen to a homeless single who rejected the city's prescription for him was that he might, theoretically, be charged rent for what Rudy called "semiprivate accommodations"—a hollow bluff never really implemented. The campaign promise to undo hard-won court decrees protecting the homeless was temporarily over, the right to shelter was implicitly acknowledged and Rudy was trying to implement a policy he described as "both compassionate and effective."

These approaches were hardly surprising in light of the social and political views of much of the government he'd assembled. Joan Malin, for example, a soft-spoken forty-three-year-old former Fulbright Scholar who'd worked in various city social service agencies for nearly twenty years, was the new head of the Department of Homeless Services. She had been deputy commissioner under Dinkins, coordinating the city's efforts to get out of the business of directly running shelters and contracting specialized shelter services out to a variety of nonprofits. It was an initiative Rudy admired.

When Giuliani took office, she was running the agency while he searched for a replacement. A major snowstorm hit and Rudy, in his emergency mode that would suit him so well throughout his mayoralty, was rushing through round-the-clock meetings assessing the city's response. Malin impressed him at a City Hall session with a detailed accounting of how shelters were handling the frigid crowd.

Then she met alone with him at Gracie Mansion for an unusual job interview. He did not ask her about her background, only about her policy views on moving homeless singles out of general shelter beds and into treatment programs quickly, as well as structuring a more reciprocal relationship with the client population. Without the get-them-off-the-streets question ever coming up, she got the job.

Malin and the mayor got along so well they wrote the May homeless report together, each with a pen in hand going over a DHS draft at City Hall, he in an armchair, she on a couch. Giuliani was involved line by line in the plan. It was clear to Malin that he had decided that homelessness would be one of a handful of issues he believed he could have a measurable impact on in his first term.

The press coverage and advocates' reaction to the report infuriated him—with everyone turning the carefully moderated language about accountability into a threatening bark. But he continued to convey a sense of personal ownership about the plan, and Malin immediately went to work on the least controversial aspects of it, turning over a dozen shelters for singles to nonprofits, creating a menu of options for placement.

Malin wasn't the only Dinkins holdover Rudy retained—so were his health and mental health commissioners. Top former Koch aides included Paul Crotty, who'd actually run Koch's campaign in 1989, and was named to the pivotal position of corporation counsel, running the city's vast legal department. Crotty, a Democrat, had clerked with Rudy for Lloyd MacMahon and attended his wedding to Regina Peruggi, giving him Giuliani credentials as well. Another former Koch commissioner Henry Stern, a Liberal who was back running Parks, earned his stripes with Giuliani by turning the prominent civic organization he ran into an arm of the '93 campaign.

Giuliani's circle of top aides included two deputy mayors who were Democrats, Dyson and Segarra, one who was a Liberal, Fran Reiter, and only one Republican, Powers. His chief of staff, Mastro, was also a Democrat, as was his City Planning Commission chair, Joe Rose. So was his patronage dispenser, appointments secretary Tony Carbonetti, the twenty-five-year-old son of Lou Carbonetti Jr., who became director of the Community Assistance Unit. Richard Schwartz, who had been the key campaign issue staffer since 1992 and became Rudy's special policy adviser, was also a Koch Democrat.

High-ranking Republican aides were counsel Denny Young and labor commissioner Randy Levine, a Justice Department friend with ties to the state party. Budget director Abe Lachman commuted from his Albany home, where he'd long been a top finance aide to the Senate GOP majority. Bill Diamond, the general services commissioner, and Joe Lhota at finance, were Republicans at key agencies, where contractual and tax assessment decisions worth millions were made. Fred Cerullo, a Republican city councilman from beloved Staten Island, got the highly visible consumer affairs post. John Gross, his pal from the U.S. Attorney's office and Anderson Kill, was the treasurer of his campaign committee and a political adviser.

Much of this key staff met—early in the administration—for a weekend retreat at Gracie Mansion to hear Philadelphia mayor Ed Rendell, a new Democrat who'd been reforming a stricken city, explain how it's done. The Big Three outside the government—Donna, Harding and Garth—spoke frequently with one voice, and only Donna was a Republican, having dumped her Democratic registration shortly before marrying Rudy. Garth has been a registered independent since 1966, when Lindsay first took office.

It certainly appeared to be a mixed enough team to include diverse opinions, even if it did not include people of diverse origins. Yet an anonymous and annoyed commissioner told *Newsday:* "Don't worry, the city is being run by Rudy, Peter [Powers], Randy [Mastro] and Denny [Young]. They're getting to every issue one by one." Everyone of the four horsemen but Powers had been a prosecutor, and all were white males who'd lived within blocks of each other on the East Side of Manhattan, suggesting a monolithic core concealed beneath a variegated veneer. Whether it was one, four or a larger decision-making combine who were getting to the issues, they did seem to be getting to them one-by-one. But with everything about city policy so new to this inexperienced core team, even Rudy, at the outset, was willing to listen.

The biggest decision of all, however, was a political, not a policy, one. Yet Rudy's gubernatorial endorsement in 1994 would wind up shaping the mayor's policy agenda for the rest of his first term.

M ario Cuomo has a way with words, no doubt. But when he was governor, his favorite mode of political communication was the unspoken "understanding." The master orator was also a master at weaving wordless webs of intrigue, conniving alliances out of a mesh of humor, convenience and mutual comfort. He may never have had an explicit deal with Rudy Giuliani. But they had an "understanding" that began in 1993, when a Democratic governor helped defeat a Democratic mayor, and culminated in 1994, when a Republican mayor jolted the state with a Democratic gubernatorial endorsement.

An actual endorsement was more than "old baggy eyes" expected. He liked his quids to come in the same form as his quos. He never endorsed Rudy Giuliani in 1993. In fact he endorsed David Dinkins, making each punch he threw Dinkins's way all the more telling. He was after a nominally neutral Rudy, whose running commentary on the 1994 race was an only slightly subliminal ad for him. A rousing endorsement might be better, but that was too much to ask. This "understanding" was channeled through the mediums of Garth and Harding, who had themselves struggled through a decade and a half of intense and shifting relationships with Albany's man of many moods.

The seduction of Rudy Giuliani started with Staten Island secession, Crown Heights, homelessness tutoring by Andrew Cuomo and the Badillo candidacy. When Rudy became mayor and proposed a 1 percent dip in the city's hotel tax, Cuomo pushed a phasing out of the state's 5 percent version of the same tax. The combined reduction preceded a tourism boom, and though Cuomo was first out of the starting gate on it, he let Giuliani pose as the man whose policies were spurring the surge.

After the Democratic majority in the Assembly vowed to block Rudy's proposal to fingerprint welfare recipients, Cuomo approved it administratively. Both Cuomos—Mario and son Andrew, the HUD undersecretary—helped out on the homeless, with state officials acquiescing to the new Giuliani homeless plan though the *Times* had predicted combat, while Andrew brought an unexpected $73 million in extra housing aid for the homeless to a City Hall meeting with Rudy. The governor also amended his executive budget to offer the city $130 million in Medicaid assistance in response to a public Giuliani complaint—something the *Times* noted Cuomo "never did" for Dinkins.

Governor Cuomo even went to City Hall to announce the Times Square deal with the Disney Corporation, letting Giuliani take center stage for a turnaround deal that had actually been arranged by Cuomo's and David Dinkins's staffs. At a personal level, the governor routinely took Giuliani's calls whenever they came, whereas he usually had an aide contact a Dinkins or Koch deputy to see what the call was about before getting on the phone with Giuliani's predecessors.

But most importantly, the governor encouraged a state authority, the Municipal Assistance Corporation, to provide the instant $200 million to finance the severance program that salvaged the first Giuliani budget. Asked in Albany in March if he might back Cuomo, Giuliani said: "Nothing is out of the question. Everything is open for discussion." The MAC funding—indispensable to the closing of a record-setting deficit that Rudy had inherited—was approved by the corporation's reluctant nine-member board, most of which was appointed by Cuomo, shortly before the May GOP state convention.

Rudy was Cuomo's covert ally at that convention, quietly working to get 25 percent of the delegates to vote for Herb London, the 1990 Conservative Party candidate for governor who was positioning himself to challenge George Pataki in an upcoming Republican primary. Pataki, then a little-known state senator hand-picked by Al D'Amato to run against Cuomo, was engaged in an all-out war to block the 25 percent and avoid a primary with London. Yet the officially neutral Giuliani got much of the Queens delegation to vote for London during the nail-biting, three-hour roll-call vote.

Peter Powers called delegates the weekend before the convention, looking for London votes though the anti-abortion and pro-gun professor was to the right of pro-choice Pataki. London had little chance of defeating Cuomo, who'd routed him in 1990, and the attempts to get him on the ballot by Giuliani and Senate Republican leader Ralph Marino were widely seen as indirectly benefiting Cuomo. London narrowly missed the qualifying threshold, thwarted by Pataki's top backer and Rudy's longtime nemesis, D'Amato.

On July 1, 1994, Matilda Cuomo was Donna Hanover's guest on her Food Network show. When Matilda finished describing her recipe for lamb shanks and Mario's penchant for apple pie and cinnamon toast, she and Donna had a good talk about child care, adoption policies and the good old governor. Reese Schonfeld, Donna's boss at the network, later singled out that "exclusive" as the highlight of Hanover's six-year stint on the show.

The seduction of Donna had actually started in early 1994 when Matilda visited Gracie Mansion for two hours, chatting, as Hanover put it, "about how we, as First Ladies, can work together." Donna eagerly enlisted in the Garth/Harding team, pushing for a Cuomo endorsement early on and telling Republican friends of the mayor that Pataki had "flipflopped on abortion." Rudy would later note in a pre-election speech that Donna told him she intended to vote for Cuomo long before he made up his own mind.

"A large part of it," Giuliani said, "had to do with the Governor's very strong record, 100 percent record, supporting women's rights, the rights of children and the things that are necessary for women and children in our city and state." Donna became an enthusiastic Cuomo campaigner, returning with Matilda to up-state Utica, where Donna had launched her broadcasting career, and, the next day, touring the mostly Italian Belmont section of the Bronx together. While no one, including Donna, knew it at the time, the Cuomo endorsement turned out to be her last hurrah. A key adviser in 1989 and 1993, she would never again play so influential a role in a crucial career decision.

In early September, at a press conference endorsing London for comptroller and another Republican for attorney general, Giuliani was asked if he would also soon be endorsing Pataki. "Most likely that is what I will do," he said, predicting he'd probably do it by the end of the month. A couple of weeks later, Cuomo went public with his pressure: "The mayor's in a bind," he said in a press conference at City Hall Park. "He has his own personal political problem, and he has the welfare of the city. If he wants to help this city, then it would be very good for him to help me." Cuomo noted that "the mayor himself has said over and over" that the governor has been a friend to the city, adding that Pataki wasn't.

Cuomo says now—and Giuliani's public comments since confirm it—that he never asked for an endorsement, just a wily wink. "I said to the Liberal Party," he recalls, referring to Harding, "that the best position for Giuliani is to say 'I know the governor has been good to us. I know Pataki says he'll be good to us. I believe I should not choose between them. I will give the public the five major issues important to the city. I will ask the public to consider the position of both on the following.' I told the Liberal Party I would be satisfied with that, I wouldn't expect anything more." What makes the "pass" Cuomo insists he gave Giuliani plausible is that it was his own favorite trick—he did it with D'Amato, GOP comptroller Ned Regan and the Republican Senate leadership that played ball with him.

On the Republican side of this tug-of-war, Randy Levine and John Gross, two of Rudy's closest friends, were pulling hard for Pataki. Gross appeared three times on Giuliani's October private schedules, far more than usual. Randy Levine's fax machine at the Office of Collective Bargaining was flooded for weeks with communiqués to and from state GOP boss Bill Powers.

But Rudy's Republican advisers were up against a stiff financial wind. In October, barely three months into the new fiscal year, the budget Rudy had pasted together in May was coming apart. An $800 million deficit loomed—a result of falling tax receipts, skyrocketing police and fire overtime and overly optimistic economic forecasts. Rudy had to go back to MAC for a second round of funding to finance another severance package, again designed to induce thousands of city workers to quit. Just as in May, the only alternative to a state-financed severance deal was mass layoffs, a disaster that had not occurred since the near bankruptcy of the city in 1975. The Cuomo board agreed to a $230 million financing.

Ironically, Levine was negotiating a corresponding redeployment deal with the unions—which also included health care givebacks—when he learned of Rudy's endorsement decision. The night before, he and budget director Abe Lachman had cornered the mayor at Gracie Mansion after a Sunday budget session. Levine left thinking they'd talked him out of backing Cuomo, at least for the moment. But unbeknownst to Levine, Rudy had talked with Garth five times that day, as he wove through a schedule that took him to Mass in Queens with a GOP congressional candidate, and included a stop at the honors convocation for Marymount Manhattan College, whose president was Regina Peruggi. On the eve of his most liberal political decision, he coincidentally touched base with his own liberal roots.

Levine got the word that Monday while at District Council 37, the largest municipal union. He was teary-eyed, upset that his friend had made a decision that might forever tarnish his Republican credentials. The union leaders erupted in cheers. Giuliani had already scheduled a 5:20 P.M. press conference for later that day, ostensibly to announce the budget deal, but instead, before a live television audience, he crossed the Rubicon.

With a deer-in-the-headlights glaze, a somber Giuliani read from a prepared text, his bowed head presenting a thinning comb-over to the phalanx of cameras. Gone was his usual defiant certitude; he was drenched in sweat on a cool late October evening. He could not flash his practiced toothy grin, the tension locked his lips in a straight yet quivering line. He said Pataki was the personification of the status quo, running a campaign "out of a political consultant's playbook." He praised Cuomo as "his own man," assailing Pataki as "guided, scripted and directed by others."

He revealed he'd decided to vote for Cuomo two weeks earlier because the governor was better for the city. "But I weighed the option of remaining neutral and not expressing an opinion on the race," he said, echoing the advice Cuomo would later say he gave Harding. Specifying that he'd "talked to my wife," he said he'd "finally decided over the weekend."

Bill Clinton was pictured on CNN raising his arms in celebration. He called Giuliani from Air Force One and thanked him. Harding reached Cuomo on his car phone shortly before the announcement to tell him it was coming. Cuomo listened on the radio, parked outside a Fifth Avenue synagogue, and reveled. It was a "surprise" gift, he insists, more than he sought. A Giuliani aide recalls seeing the governor walk into City Hall one night in the middle of this period—so late it was dark and quiet—and watching Rudy and Cuomo "hug like schoolboys."

Giuliani began campaigning for Cuomo with and without him. They did an appearance on the Brooklyn waterfront together, boosting development projects there. They went to the Liberal Party's annual dinner, a $500-a-seat celebration of all that Harding had wrought. The boss sat beaming between the two on the Sheraton dais, and Giuliani saluted Cuomo as "a man of conscience." They went to

Long Island together, where polls indicated Giuliani was popular. But Giuliani's decision to do a Saturday swing through five upstate cities predictably boomeranged. Republicans had already been saying that the endorsement "plays into our hands upstate," where anti–New York City feelings abound.

So Rudy met protesters at every airport, often chanting "let's make a deal"—a suggestion that would soon become the theme of a massive Pataki television blitz. The ad charged that Cuomo "cut a deal with the mayor of New York to send our tax dollars down to New York City to bail them out of their budget problems in exchange for political support." Cuomo says now: "I spoke to Garth on the phone. I said this is not a good thing for him to do. I said Rudy would be seen as the mayor of New York. They would think I was going to give all the money to him." Denying the apocryphal story that he charged up to Garth's office and screamed about it, Cuomo said: "It was better for both of us that we weren't in the same room together. I don't know what his motive was."

Rudy was riding so high after the endorsement—which was depicted as having momentarily pushed Cuomo ahead of Pataki for the first time—that his upstate tour was clearly designed to position him as kingmaker. He also began trying to build an anti-Pataki Republican alliance, effectively recruiting the predisposed London and going out to Nassau County to try to woo Tom Gulotta, the county executive.

This strategy, too, boomeranged when Bernadette Castro of convertible-couch fame, the GOP candidate for U.S. Senate, said Giuliani had invited her for a Sunday schmooze on a Gracie Mansion couch, where he asked her to abandon Pataki and endorse Cuomo. "I have to take George out," Castro said Rudy told her. Giuliani said he wanted Pataki defeated, according to Castro, "because he feels that if George is elected, he [the mayor] will be destroyed," ostensibly by a Pataki/D'Amato cabal. The maneuvering with Castro and the alliance with London—who issued a stinging statement demanding that Pataki "lead or get out of the way"—cheapened the Giuliani endorsement.

Originally presented as a matter of principle, it quickly took on the appearance of a power grab. Giuliani started predicting a "realignment" within the GOP after the election that would obviously revolve around him: "I don't by any means intend to play the only role. I don't think any one person should control a political party. I think that's part of the mistake that was made here," he said, taunting D'Amato.

The *Times* concluded that a Cuomo win would make Giuliani "one of the most popular Republican officials in the state with no clear party rival for the gubernatorial nomination." It did not add the possibility of a third phase to the

Giuliani/Cuomo "understanding"—in 1998, the presumably departing, four-term, governor would at least wink, and possibly nod, in a familiar direction.

Finally, on the Saturday before the election, Giuliani volunteered for surrogate duty to lead the last-minute negative assault on the suddenly rebounding Pataki, hosting an extraordinary press conference at City Hall. His fate was, by then, so joined with Cuomo's that he behaved as if he was fighting for his own political survival.

He appeared with the city's most liberal elected Democrat, Mark Green, the former Naderite who had been Dinkins's consumer affairs commissioner. Crushed by D'Amato in the 1986 election, Green's formal complaint about a legion of alleged D'Amato transgressions had prompted a damaging formal Senate investigation of the senator. Now the city's Public Advocate (and, according to the City Charter, next in line of mayoral succession), Green brought evidence of a HUD deal between Pataki and D'Amato to the press conference, waving several documents obtained from the records of the Westchester town of Peeksville, where Pataki had been mayor.

Rudy let himself go. All the pent-up memories of his 1988 and 1989 wars with D'Amato—as well as the resentment he still felt about his forced endorsement of D'Amato in 1992—rose to the prickly surface. The glib Green would prove a verbal popgunner when compared to the artillery Giuliani was ready to fire. Pataki's election, he said, would turn the state into "a government of D'Amato, for D'Amato and by D'Amato." If the D'Amato/Pataki "crew ever get control," he charged, "ethics will be trashed." No one at the press conference pointed out that in September 1993, when Rudy was running for mayor with D'Amato's support and the senator threw a Sheraton fundraiser in anticipation of a possible race against Cuomo himself, Rudy sat on the dais in support.

Asked about Rudy's harsh attack on D'Amato, Cuomo retreated: "He has information I don't have. He's very close to these people. He was out in a flak jacket with D'Amato."

Ironically, Giuliani had "information" about Cuomo, too, dating back to his U.S. Attorney days. A confidential FBI memo dated April 24, 1986 reported an "unsubstantiated" tip a FBI special agent had "received" from Giuliani himself. The U.S. Attorney had personally informed the agent that "a company called Comstock Electric made a $25,000 campaign contribution to Mario Cuomo and, several days later, was awarded a large contract" at the Jacob K. Javits Convention Center. -

The agent, who was then investigating bribery allegations at the convention center, wrote that Giuliani indicated: "Comstock allegedly got the contract through a minority front company called Luis Electric. After an unidentified general foreman learned of the alleged payoff, he was killed." Giuliani gave the agent the name of an individual "who may know about this incident or may have been involved."

In fact, a Comstock general foreman working at the Javits Center was found in a company van shot in the head in 1985. Comstock and Luis had $52 million in Javits contracts, and Luis's owner was killed execution-style after the Giuliani memo. No criminal case was ever made based on Rudy's "information."

Bob Grant, the right-wing radio talk-show host who became a friend of Giuliani's while Rudy was U.S. Attorney and who said he "would have swum the Hudson to learn something negative about Cuomo," contends that Rudy helped him get dirt on the governor. "Once I heard from an inmate at the federal pen at Fishkill who claimed to have some juicy information about Cuomo, and I asked Rudy if he could get me in to see the guy. He made the phone calls and got me inside, though it turned out to be a wild goose chase."

There were even tales about how Rudy's office had tried to flip a Cuomo bodyguard when he was busted in the Southern District on gun-running charges. The guard was questioned about any "information" he might have on the governor, according to the Cuomo camp.

Obviously these tidbits couldn't compete with what Rudy knew about D'Amato, but they indicated that Rudy had his own suspicions about Saint Mario. He swallowed them. He also chucked the memories of George Pataki paying homage in 1992 at a Giuliani fundraiser, brought there by Robert Costello, another old friend of Rudy's from the Southern District days. Giuliani even disregarded any sense of obligation to state GOP boss Powers, who raised over $1 million for the Victory 93 effort that helped elect Rudy.

The denunciations and threats from his own party ranged from D'Amato, who said Rudy "didn't give a damn about the city or state," to Molinari, who "guaranteed" a GOP primary challenge against Giuliani in 1997. "The only thing that makes sense is that he becomes a Democrat," said Molinari. What particularly galled Republicans was Rudy's attack on Pataki for having a "very, very strong right-wing voting record" and being "pushed by the Conservative Party"—though Giuliani himself was backing London, who fit that description far better.

Pataki won by four points, buoyed by the largest turnout of upstate outrage in a state election ever. In a post-election appearance on Don Imus, D'Amato charged that Giuliani had "betrayed a trust" and lied about his reasons for endorsing Cuomo, saying he "got caught with his pants down," a phrase with a personal family history for Rudy that D'Amato could not have known. Pataki wrote an autobiography in 1998, saying that Giuliani's endorsement was "a knife in the back" that left him "stunned," "speechless," and feeling "as if the wind had been knocked out of me, after a sucker punch."

Rudy did not just endorse, "it was an all-out trashing of our effort," Pataki concluded, carefully choosing Rudy's words. The new governor described the endorsement as "too great an opportunity for the mayor to pass up," adding that Rudy would be "to New York State what Michael Jordan had become to the Chicago Bulls" if Cuomo had won. Pataki did not mention what those who knew him and Rudy well agreed was a related, primary, motive—Giuliani feared that a Republican governor would dwarf him.

When the Pataki autobiography was published in the middle of his re-election campaign, all the key passages about Rudy that had appeared in the galleys were deleted. Another détente had been arranged with D'Amato, who quietly backed Rudy's re-election in 1997. The next year, Giuliani endorsed both the governor and D'Amato, even doing a television commercial for Pataki. But the enmity remained both mutual and transparent, with dozens of internecine wars over development and other policy issues, ranging from a Manhattan stadium for the Yankees to the naming of the West Side Highway after Joe DiMaggio.

I n the days after Cuomo's loss, Rudy was at another high-stakes political cross-roads. Cuomo had won 72 percent of the city's vote, so if all Rudy had in mind was being mayor of New York, his endorsement of the loser was still a winning choice for him. But Giuliani saw himself as larger than that. Pataki's win was part of a national GOP sweep, from statehouses across the country to both houses of Congress for the first time in half a century. An ascendant Reagan right had pushed a young Rudy to reregister in 1980. Koch's loss in the 1989 mayoral election had shoved him rightward again, as had two runs against Dinkins. Now Newt Gingrich and George Pataki were doing it once more, propelling him in the direction of another personal sea change. He floundered for weeks, uncertain about his own philosophical definition.

The Sunday after the election, he went to a Baptist church in Bedford-Stuyvesant where black parishioners greeted him with unusual warmth. He talked for twenty minutes, expressing no "regret" about his Cuomo endorsement. "Let's try to forge new alliances," he said. "He wants to be heard in the black community and to be understood," said the minister's brother. Rudy seemed, for just a moment, as comfortable in Bed-Stuy as he usually was in Staten Island. He laughed and hugged and kidded.

Two days earlier, he sat in the Museum Room at Gracie Mansion with Richard Cohen, the *Washington Post*'s syndicated columnist. They talked for two hours—the mayor sitting with the phone in his left hand awaiting a return call from Pataki. He told Cohen about his upcoming visit to the church. They talked about race and Republicans so much Cohen used him in a column the next week as a model of conciliation. Giuliani's approval rating among blacks, he told Cohen, was "somewhere in the 30 percent to 40 percent range, maybe even higher."

"He has been able to mold a multiracial coalition," wrote Cohen, "that should, in the name of a better America, be the goal of the Republican party. Whatever his reasons for endorsing a Democrat, Giuliani has something important to tell his party. Too bad it doesn't call."

Giuliani faced a re-election campaign that would start in two short years. The crime rate had just begun its descent and he did not know if it would continue and re-elect him on its own. He had choices to make. If he enthused too vocally about the Gingrich and Pataki gestalt, he'd wind up too far to the right to win in New York City. If he did not perceptibly attach himself to some of it, however, he would appear awkwardly out of step with the party and the times. He might even get the Republican primary Molinari threatened. He could tumble off this highwire act in either direction, depending on how firmly he planted one foot after another.

His now unambiguous abortion position was an accepted minority view within the GOP. Before the 1997 election, he would also stake out stronger liberal positions on two issues with powerful electoral constituencies in New York City—gay and immigrant rights. If he was to do all that without alienating the party, he had to come aboard on its core economic issues, each of which had a racial underside.

A New York mayor who cut welfare and expanded workfare could bond with the new Washington and Albany gang. A New York mayor who echoed the national and state party's insistence that less was more—a stop-sign open palm instead of a gimme one—might be quite useful. A tough-love and law-and-order mayor who tamed yet angered the tribe in the race capital of America would be just the symbol the party wanted to whet the appetite of the emerging majority of white voters that had just gone GOP in the midterm congressional election.

He could not be the coalition mayor Cohen thought he discovered and fit the niche in the new Gingrich galaxy that beckoned. The national future he still envisioned for himself required a makeover. The Contract for America timetable and the resolve of the new governor to act quickly gave him little time to adjust—he would have to react to their initiatives by early 1995. A Lindsay reprise, such as the one Cohen celebrated, would only mean he'd have to leave his party up the road, just as Lindsay had. The center had shifted, especially the one within his own party, and he would either shift with it or risk irrelevance.

On January 18, he went to Yale for the Chubb Fellow address and laid out his version of a new politics. He said cities "deserve some of the blame" for the way they're perceived around the country. "We go to Washington almost as urban panhandlers, asking for more money and more money and more money." Cities have to "stand on their own more," he said, "which we are willing to do." In a March 31 speech at the National Press Club in Washington, he said: "The political revolution in Washington has caused concern over the prospect of reduced federal aid for cities. In fact, this correction in course can work in favor of the new urban agenda. America's cities can deal with the prospect of less aid, provided they are given the latitude to devise local solutions to local problems."

Giuliani said he "applauded" the block grants that would set annual lump-sum limits on federal social service contributions to each state and eliminate individually triggered entitlement spending on welfare and Medicaid. At the National Press Club, he urged passage of a bill that "strips welfare of its entitlement status, embraces reciprocity and workfare, and gives states and cities more flexibility to decide how to impose time limits on welfare benefits."

Even a Democratic congressman who would ultimately endorse him in 1997, Floyd Flake, said in the budget battles of 1995 that Rudy's determination "not to offend Gingrich makes for an offense to the people he is representing in this city." Ron Anderson, the top appropriations committee staffer to Syracuse's Republican congressman Jim Walsh, said Giuliani "supported certain parts" of Gingrich budget bills, adding that he "certainly wouldn't say the mayor opposes the cuts; he's more silent on it."

The mayor's financial plan, issued in mid-February, boasted that it differed from prior plans, including Giuliani's 1994 edition, because "the City is not seeking additional State or Federal aid to help solve its problems." It is "instead," said the plan, identifying savings "by reducing entitlement spending." Giuliani's lobbying office in Washington only objected, albeit mildly, to cuts in one of the five, severely slashed, education programs. It had opposed similar reductions virtually across the board in 1994. The same switch occurred on cuts in emergency food assistance. While Giuliani made an exception and actually sought an "increase in funding" for AIDS, he made no objection to dramatic GOP-backed slashes in foster care, food stamps, college assistance and transit.

He explained his support for capital gains and other Gingrich tax cuts that benefited the rich by actually arguing that the city had "a disproportionate number of people in the upper income categories." Reductions in their federal tax burden would, he argued, "leave more money in our local economy," suggesting that he believed that lower taxes for Donald Trump could compensate for less aid to Bed-Stuy.

Giuliani cited his mayoral mentor Rendell from Philadelphia in the Yale speech, as well as Chicago's Richard Daley Jr., both of whom had championed reform policies similar to his. But Rendell was simultaneously denouncing the Gingrich revolution as a "horror show" and "a freight train bearing down on us." Daley said the block-grant approach, eliminating "the crucial safety net aspects of these entitlement programs," had "the potential to divide our city."

Rudy was in fact separating himself so dramatically from the rest of urban America that Norman Rice, the Seattle mayor who headed the U.S. Conference of Mayors, said he couldn't get Giuliani or a surrogate to return a phone call. When the conference did a survey of 145 mayors across the country about the Gingrich plan, 96 percent said they believed it would have "negative effects on their cities and residents." Giuliani did not respond. "I've tried to call him, I've tried to engage him, but I haven't been successful. I can't understand why any city would be silent."

Finally, in late October 1995, after ten months of pliant acquiescence, the mayor said the Medicaid and Medicare cuts would be a "catastrophe" for the city. His complaint followed Pataki's by days. But he went beyond Pataki. He spent a half hour with Bill Clinton at the Waldorf-Astoria and stunned reporters, and even his own budget staff, when he announced that he'd urged the president to veto the Republican budget. His studied objection was to the suddenness of the cuts—saying they should be "phased in" under a fairer formula. Giuliani nonetheless declined a November invitation to join 20,000 protesters at a rally organized by the Greater New York Hospital Association to cheer the veto and oppose the cuts. Hillary Clinton came to New York to join it.

The suddenness of his swing—as late as October 15 the *Times* was calling him "unusually muted" on the budget issues—suggested that he was moved mostly by the hostility to the cuts reflected in New York polls and the powerful pull of the health care lobby. Rudy had tried to ride it out, but caught in a dilemma that pitted his national repositioning against his reelection imperatives, he had to oppose at least one crucial area of cuts.

His reaction to Pataki's first budget was an even more jolting reversal than his national passivity. Pataki vindicated everything Rudy had said when he endorsed Cuomo, proposing a budget that cut $800 million in welfare and Medicaid payments to the city. Brushing aside appeals from the Democratic majority in the

Assembly to join them in resisting the cuts, Giuliani proposed a financial plan that sought $400 million more.

For the first time, a New York City mayor decided that a reduction in state entitlement aid was a fiscal positive. It meant, from Rudy's perspective, that the city could slice its own entitlement expenses since it was required to match state funding. Rudy was literally discovering that less was more—less aid from the state for the city's poor allowed the city to slash its own expenditures by similar amounts. So a state budget that set time limits on benefits for adults without dependents on home relief, or squeezed the amount of support payments, was suddenly seen by City Hall as a budget-balancing boon.

The governor and mayor started talking about New York as if it were still the welfare magnet it had been decades earlier. But the maximum monthly grant made it the seventh most generous state, and if you took inflation into account, it went to the middle of the pack. The Citizens Budget Commission—the business group Rudy had depended on in 1993—calculated that total welfare spending had declined 17 percent in the prior two decades. Families on welfare were living way below the poverty level.

When Rudy endorsed Cuomo, he said he was doing it because Cuomo, unlike Pataki, understood "our quest for equity from Albany to recover some of the deficit in the balance of payments," pointing out that the city pays much more in state taxes than it gets back in state benefits. By aggressively pushing for cuts in the chief source of state and federal funding flowing to the city—namely, social service subsidies—Giuliani was deepening both of the deficits he had, until recently, railed against.

In the same Cuomo endorsement and on the stump, Giuliani had attacked the centerpiece of the Pataki campaign—a gouging promised tax cut. Suddenly, he was backing it.

His budget was a color-coded stacked deck. Police, fire and sanitation took 1 percent cuts while Medicaid, public assistance, foster care, day care and child protective services plummeted 28 percent. City University, the blackest and brownest major public university system in America, faced a Giuliani-proposed reduction of 17 percent. The Health & Hospitals Corporation, whose users and employees were overwhelmingly minority, was slated to take a $100 million hit. Youth Services was almost cut by half, while the Department of Aging took no cut at all. The mayor tried to end the forty-seven-year history of city-subsidized transit passes for 500,000 school kids, while preserving the reduced-fare subsidy for senior citizens. For the second straight year, the Board of Education cuts were the most devastating, even targeting the sports programs Candidate Giuliani used to talk about expanding.

Though tuition at community colleges was twice the national average, Giuliani backed a hike, saying it would be a good thing if it encouraged more students to work, thereby "preparing them for the rest of their lives." His own, mostly jobless, days at Manhattan College were apparently a faint memory, and he did not seem to know that a third of CUNY students already worked full-time and another third part-time. While college students would pay more, co-op and condo owners would pay less in property taxes, as would developers and corporate tenants who moved into a new tax-free zone downtown—all part of a second round of Giuliani tax cuts.

In the midst of the debate over this budget, Rudy was reported to have told executives at WNYC, the city-owned radio station, that it would be "a good thing" for the city if the poor left. "That's not an unspoken part of our strategy," he was quoted as saying, "that is our strategy." The mayor challenged the quote, insisting that the departure of the poor might be the "natural consequence" of welfare, Medicaid and other social service cuts, but not "the intention of our policy." He readily acknowledged that he'd said such "mobility would be a good thing."

A top budget official said that if the cuts, combined with the high cost of living, "leads people" to conclude that "they'd be better off getting welfare in other places where the cost of living is lower, fine." The *Post* cited one of Rudy's "chief policy architects" as saying that "the poor will eventually figure out that it's a lot easier to be homeless where it's warm" and boasting that making the city inhospitable to the poor was the best way "to clean it up."

The anomaly of a mayor talking openly about scattering to the wind the very people he was elected to serve set off no spark in a desensitized time. While a single commissioner in the bankrupt days of the Beame administration ignited a firestorm with similar "planned shrinkage" rhetoric—and lost his job—triage was now a one-day story. The first Republican/Liberal mayor since Lindsay was deconstructing the support systems his predecessor had erected and no one with power was howling. The lady in the harbor with the torch was shifting with the current, lighting the way out of town now, and no one was insisting that the city's "huddled masses" weren't cargo.

Rudy was becoming an explicit war-on-the-poor mayor, unrecognizable to those who recalled the softer moments of his five-year campaign, or of his first year in office. As tough as he liked to pose, he was bending to powerful exigencies. Had Cuomo won, he would have been a starkly different mayor. Had the Democrats won fourteen more House seats, the city might well have seen another

Rudy. If Cuomo were governor, he and Giuliani would probably have been ag-gressive bipartisan allies in a public war against the Gingrich budget. That would have driven Rudy even further away from his party. He was just that malleable.

Irving Howe, the historian, wrote once that Ed Koch came to the realization during the Reagan years that "to remain a liberal would mean to pit himself, maybe hopelessly, against the powers of Washington," and so the onetime Mississippi civil rights marcher accommodated himself to the times. He eventu-ally came "to enjoy the violation he was staging of his earlier self." Koch was to Reaganism, concluded Howe, what La Guardia "had been to Roosevelt's New Deal—the municipal broker for the dominant social force in the country." While Howe was writing about Koch before he completed his final-term reprieve—transforming blighted neighborhoods with the largest city housing program in history—he did somehow anticipate the New Giuliani.

To secure his own reelection, he waited until the last minute in 1996 to half-heartedly endorse Bob Dole, who would set a modern record with a dismal 17 per-cent of the New York City vote. Rudy succeeded in doing it—and placating his Republican enemies D'Amato and Pataki—while appearing so tepid he angered few Democratic voters. The truth is that as much as he liked to describe himself as above partisan politics, Mario Cuomo was the only major Democrat in a contested race he ever endorsed, compared with dozens of GOP candidates in senatorial, con-gressional, councilmanic and other elections. More important than endorsements, though, were policies, and he resolved to make himself the embodiment, as Howe would put it, of Republican urban policy.

From 1995 on, his mayoralty pivoted around a carefully crafted national por-trait: Rudy was the take-charge, no-nuance, antithesis of New York's lofty liberals. His favorite numerical sound bite after the murder rate—recited, particularly af-ter his 1997 reelection, in studios and hotel ballrooms across America—was the ever increasing tally of the departed dependent, the hundreds of thousands sepa-rated from the welfare rolls. Neither the media nor the mayor had any idea where these half million were now, or how they were living.

The mayor claimed, without citing a shred of evidence, that welfare's discards were somehow miraculously independent. In truth, they were New York's "disap-peared"—a lost city no television camera could find. They stood in the longest lines at soup kitchens since the 1920s, swept the streets in the orange-vested workfare uniforms of the nation's last conscripted army, crowded shelters and out-of-the-way sidewalks in growing numbers, left town or hid in its invisible crevices.

If Giuliani was Howe's new urban broker, his role was that of welfare pioneer, a born-again, big-city, preacher of the gospel of work. Roosevelt wanted to put a

chicken in every pot; Giuliani was determined to put a broom in every city-subsi-
dized hand. Taking a page from Gingrich, he was out to slay a dinosaur system of
dependence with a regimen of forced labor, creating overnight the largest sweep-
for-benefits workforce in modern American history. He also immediately moved
to shut down poor people's access to subsistence with a new battalion of city
sleuths, sworn to the sacred duty of penetrating the pretense of poverty and dis-
qualifying anyone who would fake it for benefits. Gingrich could only talk about
welfare reform; Clinton could only bow to the power of its constituency. Rudy
could do it.

He could do it in the largest laboratory in the country, with 1,150,000 recipients
awaiting re-education, a head count of opportunity that could make him the hero
of every smug, long-distance critic of welfare sloth.

Sixteen

Brutal Blindside
No Benefits, No Doubts

T HE CHANGE IN RUDY GIULIANI CAUGHT HOMELESS COMMISSIONER Joan Malin by surprise. As central as homeless issues had been in 1994, when she and the mayor worked so closely together on a groundbreaking plan, they were off the table by 1995. A political mood swing had occurred. Rudy's social engineering focus had shifted. As the year wore on, he was less and less interested in the complexities of the policies she was charged with implementing. By his count, he had room on his plate for only one social initiative that would leave a mark he could cite in a thirty-second commercial. He now knew it would be welfare.

When the squeeze on public assistance recipients began—and adults without dependents were the first forced off the rolls—Malin went to City Hall with the predictable bad news: Homeless numbers were going up. Though the word came down from the mayor not to talk about the hike in homelessness and the connection to welfare policy, Malin was pushed by Steve DiBrienza, the chair of the City Council's general welfare committee, and conceded it at a public hearing. No one wrote the story anyway.

Between 1994 and 1996—when Malin finally stepped down in August—her agency's spending plummeted 22 percent, while its average daily census of families and singles grew from 23,337 to 24,609. As the Independent Budget Office put it years later: "DHS [Department of Homeless Services] spending reached its nadir in 1996 at the same time as shelter census peaked."

Massive cuts in the capital budget hit DHS, killing millions for homeless housing. Average annual funding for housing construction dropped 34 percent over the Giuliani years, and he spent only one in twenty capital dollars on housing, compared to one in ten during the Dinkins years. While almost two thousand new apartments for the homeless would be completed in Giuliani and Malin's initial fiscal year, the total slid to a paltry 264 units in the final budget of his first term. In Dinkins's last full fiscal year (1993), 3,225 units were produced.

In addition to the shelter and housing construction cuts, Rudy did nothing to expand the drug treatment programs central to his homeless plan, abandoning any pretense of achieving the treatment-on-demand promise of his two campaigns. Instead he relied on the state to finance the only significant battery of programs and, without any Giuliani protest about Pataki cuts, the number of residential beds dropped over Rudy's first four years. Only 27 percent of the needed slots for outpatient services were funded as of March 1999, a far cry from treatment on demand. Admissions to outpatient programs were virtually unchanged from 1993 (10,117) to 1997 (10,624), while inpatient admissions fell 50 percent. So much for the memory of Rudy's cousin, Joan D'Avanzo, whose death at an early age was an argument for treatment.

The only policy attention Giuliani paid to treatment modalities was a visceral condemnation of methadone, a chemical substitute for heroin embraced by the National Institute of Health and used by 36,000 addicts in New York City. At a 1998 press conference, he suddenly vowed to end all methadone programs in the city, though 92 percent of the funding for them was state and federal. Eliminating the availability of this three-decades-old stabilizing agent would, of course, have been the opposite of the option plan for the addicted homeless he had once proposed.

Assailing Clinton's drug czar, General Barry McCaffrey, as "a disaster," he suggested that those who supported methadone were part of "the politically correct crowd that favor a lot of different kinds of drug experimentation." His antimethadone rant led to such an outcry from everyone who knew anything about drug treatment that he had to back off, a rare retreat.

The mayor who also vowed as a candidate that it wouldn't require a court order to force him to care for the homeless got hit with one after another. His administration was fined $5 million for forcing hundreds of homeless families awaiting placement to sleep nightly in the offices of the Emergency Assistance Unit. In an end run around court orders on the EAU, the city put families—for the first time in years—in the old barracks-style shelters Rudy once deplored.

In another lawsuit, Bob Hayes returned to the judge who had issued the right to shelter decision and won a January 1996 order forcing the city to open a new twenty-four-hour shelter with 200 beds. His affidavit contended that approximately 170 men were being bused late each night to a Queens temporary facility for a few hours sleep, awakened at 6 A.M., and bused back to 42nd Street, where they were put back on the street to start the cycle again.

The mayor who had once envisioned hundreds of small shelters all over the city instead sharply increased the number of homeless singles bused out of town to upstate Camp La Guardia, a dilapidated former prison frequently filled near its 1,000-bed capacity. With shelters in the city housing up to 850 beds, he got Pataki to dump a state requirement limiting them to 200 beds. He twice vetoed a City Council bill sponsored by DiBrienza to impose 200-person limits on new shelters, and when the council moved to override his veto, he served eviction papers on the operators of a program for the mentally ill who were using a city-owned facility in DiBrienza's district. He claimed, in a transparent threat, that he needed the facility for shelter space if the councilman persisted on the bed-limit bill.

Malin also faced two new homeless strategies that came out of City Hall in early 1996: massive police sweeps and strict shelter eligibility standards. Lou Anemone, the NYPD's chief of the department, announced at a high-level, late-spring meeting that the police "were going to empty the streets." Prior to that, under both Dinkins and Giuliani, the police had worked with DHS outreach teams to break up large encampments of the homeless, but now the watchword was expansive sweeps of most of Manhattan. Rudy sat in on the meeting, saying little while Tony Coles, a former partner at Anderson Kill who was now deputy counsel at City Hall, described the offensive. A few weeks after this secret meeting and the launch of the initiative, Malin announced her resignation.

Police Commissioner Howard Safir, who'd succeeded Bratton that April, put out a ten-page "reference guide" to "quality of life enforcement options" in July. It spelled out a dozen infractions useful against the homeless. The DHS monthly outreach report for July revealed that "the NYPD has begun a quality of life initiative in Manhattan from Battery Park to 110th Street, river to river." An NYPD memo described the purpose of this "major initiative" to be to "displace those who engage in quality-of-life offenses" and "permanently correct those conditions which give rise" to those offenses. Police would be enforcing violations from carrying an open container of alcohol to "blocking sidewalks" to panhandling.

"In anticipation of the initiative, DHS Outreach staff started to inform clients on the eastside of midtown," said the report. "Many clients without ID have been taken to the police station. In some cases, the Sanitation Department or Parks Department has taken their remaining postal carts and possessions after they have been arrested." From then on, for months, the outreach reports referred to continuous coordination with NYPD sweep activity until location after location was described as cleared of all homeless.

At the same time, the administration revealed an eligibility review procedure for shelter applicants designed to reduce the mounting population. Rudy announced that the city was no longer giving families who arrived at the EAU "the benefit of the doubt" (only cops got that). "When you go and investigate, you find that a large percentage of people that were coming to that unit were not homeless," he said. "They were just seeking other accommodations."

Starting just as Malin departed in August, investigative teams grilled applicants—as well as visited relatives and prior addresses—to determine if they had any other shelter options, "even for a short period." In the first six months, 2,400 families were rejected. Eighty percent of the rejected families who filed for a fair hearing to appeal DHS's initial determination either won the appeal, if represented by Legal Aid, or forced DHS to change its mind. Only 365 families had been rejected for services by DHS in Rudy's first fiscal year. In his fifth fiscal year, 14,041 family applications for emergency shelter were denied, sometimes the same families again and again. The shelter census, of course, temporarily dropped.

The use of what advocates called "the criminal investigation model" on homeless pretenders was actually a strategy borrowed from Rudy's already up-and-running welfare plan, the policy priority that displaced homelessness on his personal hit parade. While thousands of service jobs were cut at HRA, the city moved to hire 1,500 poverty inspectors, who began using finger-imaging, financial checks, home visits and hard-boiled interrogation to discourage or reject applicants.

Rejection rates immediately doubled, soaring from 27 percent in Rudy's first, rather benign, year to 57 percent in 1998. With the mayor suddenly promising to end welfare by 2000, the pressure on welfare centers got so intense, a Bronx intake facility set a record between December 1998 and April 1999, turning away 90 percent of the 3,000 people who came seeking benefits. Just 7 percent got assistance, compared with 61 percent the prior year.

While in 1994 only 14 percent of the caseload filed for fair hearings—which mostly involve appeals of denials of assistance—45 percent were appealing by 1999. Clients won nearly 90 percent of the cases throughout the Giuliani years.

Ray Horton, the Citizens Budget Commission president who'd met with Candidate Rudy to advise him on policy three times between elections, issued a report in 1997 that found that "the vast majority" of people removed from the rolls were actually "entitled to benefits and had not committed fraud." Some were removed simply because they weren't home when an "eligibility specialist" paid an unannounced visit, or because of "administrative errors." Without challenging a fact, City Hall dismissed the report as "political," though Horton had actually served on Giuliani's budget transition team.

Besides eligibility screening, the other Giuliani mechanism for slashing the rolls was that old John Dyson favorite, workfare. Given mandatory jobs in city agencies like Sanitation, Transportation, Parks and HRA, recipients were "sanctioned" for minor infractions, losing all or part of their grants. A home relief recipient could see his case closed for missing as little as a single hour of work.

In 1997, for example, 69 percent of the adults without dependents in the work program were "sanctioned off the rolls," according to the *Times*. The 1997 sanction rate for all public assistance clients was an astonishing 59 percent, leading observers in and out of government to conclude that a primary purpose of the program was to squeeze people off the rolls, even while City Hall babbled on about the value of work. Compelling the truly able to perform useful public service was one thing, but using picayune work requirements to deny those new to work any benefits at all was another.

While an average of 32,000 did work in the program at any given time over the next four years, few were able to move on to real jobs. Giuliani blocked any tracking of the departed, citing, strangely enough, their privacy rights, though the city was in a unique position to do simple social security number matches and determine a rate of employment. City Hall consciously chose not to do such matches, because the mayor and his top aides convinced themselves that such checks would miss thousands of ex-recipients who found off-the-books jobs that wouldn't show up in social security records. The administration hid behind an almost mystical confidence in the absorbing power of the underground cash economy, assuming, though never publicly stating, that it supplied the subsistence income the city was now denying to hundreds of thousands.

The best HRA could come up with was a study by phone of 126 recipients who left the rolls. The study claimed that 54 percent found jobs. But this slim sample included only those individuals with the same phone number as when they were on welfare—a weakness the survey acknowledged may have biased the results by only eliciting responses from the stable sample. No one took the in-house spot survey seriously, and a critical review by the state comptroller undercut its validity.

More realistically, the *Times* reported that at one "Job Center"—the euphemism Rudy invented for former welfare centers—3.5 percent of 1,000 clients were placed in jobs. Five percent of the first 5,000 recipients at Job Centers found employment. Since the city manual for Job Center workers described employment as a "secondary goal," these numbers were hardly surprising. The "primary" goal of the centers was diverting people from applying for public assistance, and they were so discouraging, applications dropped dramatically.

When Jason DeParle of the Sunday *Times Magazine* asked Giuliani which figures were more important—job placements or diversions—the mayor picked "decreasing the numbers of people dependent on the government." DeParle concluded that the left "made the mistake of assuming that a check" was all the poor needed. "Now the right is on the verge of the same error, confusing the loss of an entitlement with a social elixir." Swept up in his "exuberance" over the "reforms" in one of his talks with DeParle, Rudy gave this advice to the poor: "If you can't get a job, start a small business. Start a little candy store. Start a little newspaper stand. Start a lemonade stand."

With Giuliani proclaiming in speeches all over the country that his welfare schemes were "by far the best thing we're doing for the city," the drive to deny benefits reached irrational and illegal dimensions. City University students on welfare were given twenty-hour workfare assignments that made college impossible—and 62 percent of the 27,000 students trying to lift themselves up by their bootstraps either left college or got off public assistance.

A Republican senator from Staten Island, John Marchi, was so upset about the impact of the Giuliani philosophy that "welfare is not a scholarship program," he steered a bill through the legislature requiring HRA to try to give students on-campus workfare assignments. But the administration largely ignored it, losing lawsuits, including one that involved nineteen-year-old high school students who were given workfare assignments that prevented them from finishing school.

The U.S. Department of Agriculture, a federal judge and George Pataki's Department of Social Services all found that Rudy's Job Centers were improperly denying people food stamps. The state social service commissioner wrote a letter describing city practices as a "mess" in "flagrant disregard" of food stamp rules. Giuliani got so personally involved, he spent a Sunday morning at City Hall pouring over federal regulations, reversed his HRA commissioner's public promise to change practices, and began charging that food stamps had sometimes been used "to buy drugs."

A half million people, many of them children, lost the stamps that filled their stomachs, and Rudy dismissed the arguments of the program's defenders as "emotional." Ironically, food stamps don't cost the city a cent and were originally a Republican idea, promoted by that left-wing ideologue Giuliani supported for president in 1996, Bob Dole. Nonetheless, Rudy was standing at the New York border, blocking hundreds of millions of federal dollars from entering the city and, not incidentally, making it more difficult for citizens of his own city to eat.

The courts also ruled that the city was improperly denying Medicaid benefits to deserving families, presumably on the theory that the poor should be able to purchase their own health care. In fact, in 1999, a federal court found a pattern—affecting all public assistance—of misleading applicants, pressuring them into withdrawing applications, refusing to accept applications, wrongful denials and failing to give recipients their appeal rights. The state's highest appeals court also concluded that the city was systematically frustrating the rights of people with HIV/AIDS to get assistance.

Giuliani even lobbied in Albany for a bill that would impose what's called "full-family sanctions" on any recipient who failed to meet a workfare or other welfare requirement. Had it passed, entire households, including children, could be denied benefits. The worst the Giuliani administration could legally do, absent that change, was impound the adult share of a family's payments.

The brutality of all this was papered over in quotable bromides. Rudy talked again and again about Harold Giuliani and their mutual respect for work, invoking his father's recognition of value in the most menial labor. He said he was trying to erase a "perverted social philosophy" that robbed the poor of their ambition. How dead-end servile labor, or the use of work rules to end benefits, restored ambition was left to the imagination.

In fact, the "ennobling experience" he offered 5,000 Work Employment Program workers—until the city lost a court case— included sending them into vacant lots to remove feces, animal carcasses and every other form of diseased waste without uniforms, gloves, face masks or boots, plus denying them access to toilets and drinking water. Horror stories also hit the papers of WEP workers forced to work despite serious medical conditions who dropped dead—one on the Coney Island boardwalk, another on his way from cleaning a park on a blistering summer day.

A madness had settled in. With each successful month of declining rolls, Giuliani drew nearer to his moment in history, when he could say, as he did at the dawn of a millennium, that he had ended welfare. It was, of course, as false a claim as it was fearful a goal. There were still, despite all the torment, 622,128 people on public assistance on January 1, most of them children. Rudy asserted that all able-bodied adult recipients were in workfare or some other "work-engagement" activity, a boast no one believed. Even HRA conceded that 60,000 able adults weren't actually working or in training, counseling or treatment programs. They were counted as "engaged" when they got a referral letter.

If Rudy was just going to manufacture success at the end, why the painful push to get there?

The number. Every time he made a national appearance, HRA would give him a new number. The off-the-dole odometer was constantly flipping upward. He didn't have to share this one with Police Commissioner Bill Bratton, the *Time* magazine coverboy, or anyone else at the NYPD. It was his and only his. People gasped when they heard that 550,000 were gone, dumped, deleted. They looked at him with awe. And he got that half smile on his lips, a curl of self-congratulation. The scope of it was a measure of his greatness, and the scandal of it was mired in obscure detail. He thought he could ride it to Washington.

Lillian Barrios-Paoli lived through this nightmare at Rudy's side. She was the Joan Malin of HRA.

Mexican-born, she came to New York to get a Ph.D. in urban anthropology, becoming a citizen in 1978. She shuttled between city and nonprofit worlds, usually in social service arenas, serving as Koch's commissioner of the Department of Employment. When Giuliani took office, she became personnel commissioner, then head of Housing Preservation and Development. Most of what she knew about housing came from the fact that she'd personally directed the construction of three homes of her own—from scratch. She had also been a member of the board of Marymount Manhattan College through 1994, recruited by her old friend, Regina Peruggi, and she saw the mayor there at major college events.

Her management skills, Latino origins and team-player qualities won City Hall's trust and, in January 1997, she took over HRA. Rudy declared her "one of the most exceptional administrators in city government." By the time of her appointment, the eligibility review and workfare programs were in full swing. Her role—in an election year—was to put a gentler, kinder face on policies that were giving Rudy some heat.

Much of her history, however, had been in job training. She thought recipients would benefit from a mix of work and education. She said so at a City Council hearing in April. It was heresy.

Tony Coles, who oversaw HRA from City Hall as if it was his own agency, laid the company line on her again and again. "He insisted that they only learn to work by working," she recalls. "He was adamantly opposed to placing them anywhere but WEP. All they need is an alarm clock was his position." A high-pitched, wide-eyed tax lawyer, forty-one-year-old Coles described himself as "the smartest person in City Hall," a billing that could have cost him his job if the mayor ever heard it. Coles, a registered independent, replaced Richard Schwartz as special adviser to the mayor at the same time Paoli took over HRA.

When Paoli told Coles in one of their daily conversations that some recipients needed language training, he responded: "What in? Swahili?" Paoli realized he "didn't know the caseload at all," that he had no idea that thousands of clients couldn't get jobs because they had limited English skills. Russians, Latinos, Asians—it was a city of a hundred tongues and Coles was deaf to it.

They had many other issues. "We had ten million arguments about tracking," she says. "I told him we could not have a reasonable program unless we knew outcomes. He said it was intrusive." Coles also told her that if clients refused to go to WEP, their children should be removed, a precursor of the Giuliani plan for homeless families that would not appear for two years.

Poverty was, to Coles, "something you willed yourself out of," Paoli says. "People chose to be poor. They had to get up and say they didn't want to be poor anymore. They had to find a way." While only Coles made these arguments to her, her best sense was that he reflected Rudy's view. There were "deserving poor" in the Coles/Giuliani view—the elderly, the handicapped, children. But jobless adults without physical disabilities were their own worst enemy, and their own responsibility. Despite unemployment rates during the Giuliani years that far exceeded the national average, hovering around 10 percent in 1997, Coles maintained that anyone could get a job who really wanted one.

By December—with Rudy re-elected and in search of his next conquest—he refocused on welfare. That's when he decided to make the end-it-by-2000 pledge. That's when he started talking to Jason Turner, the workfare wizard of Wisconsin. Paoli got a call shortly before Christmas from City Hall. She had previously been told she would not be one of the new term administrative changes, that she was safe. But at a weekend meeting, there was a shift in attitude.

"You would be better off leaving HRA," Paoli says she was told. "The administration thinks you should leave because it would want you to do draconian things that you wouldn't have the stomach to do." It was handled so quickly and clumsily that they gave her a post as president of one of the public hospitals and announced it without telling the current president. He heard it on his car radio on his way to the hospital Christmas party.

As traumatic as the offensive begun in 1995 was, the war on the welfare poor had a new general with a reclusive and rigid personal air. A onetime Reagan and Bush administration junior official, Turner had already converted the Giuliani creed into a three-word slogan—"everyone can work." He was so midwestern he told PBS halfway through his first year in New York that "work sets you free" without realizing it was the slogan on the gates of Auschwitz, the quote on the blackboard in the U.S. Attorney's office used against Giuliani in the 1989 campaign.

A year after Paoli's departure, Rudy told the *Times* that she and her African-American predecessor at HRA, Marva Hammonds, "did not have the same strong philosophical commitment I have."

"My philosophy has been," he said, "first make the changes and have them moving in a very, very strong way—then announce them. At that point, there isn't terribly much that people that oppose it can do."

In the closed circle of an administration that had no real experience with poverty and listened to virtually no minority voices, the blessing of ignorance is certitude, and the surest consequence of certitude is decisive action. Who gets hurt in the outer reaches of a centralized media city is an abstraction, a rumor, a bias, an antiquated ideology. His welfare charts on the other hand—with multicolored lines diving by hundreds of thousands—were the hard stuff of practical life, the only snapshot the broader world would see. A mayor could freeze the frame, define the visible city, invent his own legend.

Giuliani's put-down of Hammonds and Paoli was his way of making it clear that he, with the help of Richard Schwartz and Tony Coles, ran welfare policy for years from City Hall. But it was also a public belittling of two of his most significant minority appointments. Turner, who was praised by Giuliani in the same article and clearly did share the "same philosophical commitment," ended a string of three consecutive minority HRA commissioners, going back to Koch's day.

The implicit message of Paoli's good-bye call was that City Hall wasn't sure it could count on any minority to do what had to be done at HRA. In fact, the ten or so top staffers Turner brought to City Council hearings seldom included any blacks—an astonishing new face on an agency that had blacks in leadership positions four decades ago.

The ethnic transformation at HRA was part of a pattern. All but one of the seven black commissioners named at the start of the administration were replaced by white or Hispanic ones within three years. Two of the four Latino agency heads selected in 1994 were replaced by whites (and one agency was eliminated).

When Ninfa Segarra, a figurehead as deputy mayor for six years, was finally given a sinecure at CUNY, Coles took her job. Rudy Washington, a black contractor whose small company had leased space from the city's Brooklyn Navy Yard Corporation and left owing thousands in back rent payments, was elevated in 1996 from Business Services Commissioner to deputy mayor. Active in Giuliani's campaign against Dinkins, Washington was a marginal adviser at City Hall, but his imposing new title was apparently seen as sufficient inclusiveness to camouflage the void of blacks at the top of agencies.

The only agencies run by a succession of Latino commissioners were the Housing Authority and Juvenile Justice, and the only one headed by an unbroken series of black appointments was Business Services. The only one of these agencies with a substantial budget is the Housing Authority, though it is almost entirely federally and state funded. A black commissioner followed Paoli at HPD when she moved to HRA, so it has been run by either a black or Latino in the Giuliani years, as has Health & Hospitals, whose initial black president was replaced by a Latino.

The rest of the city's dozens of agencies—including police, fire, sanitation, planning, finance, budget, parks, environmental protection, correction, law and general services—have been run by white commissioners throughout the administration. The transportation commissioner is now a former top police commander who is black.

The workforce underneath these commissioners also changed color. The percent of workers who are black in mayoral agencies—excluding HHC, where thousands more blacks lost jobs—declined from 37.2 percent at the very end of the Dinkins administration to 34.7 percent in 1999. This 2.4-point drop was a dramatic reversal of a steady growth in the share of city jobs that went to blacks, particularly since the fiscal crisis of the mid–1970s. Under Rudy, the percent dipped five of six years, ending a decades-old tradition of more and more blacks using city jobs as an entryway to the middle class.

The change in the mayor's personal office was dramatic. The number of blacks whose City Hall positions were classified as administrators and managers dropped from thirty in 1993 to thirteen in 1999, falling from 17 percent to 10 percent. The total for all blacks on the mayor's staff dropped from 211 to 110, and the proportion of City Hall jobs held by blacks plummeted 28.5 percent.

With the explosion of hiring in the NYPD, the number of white administrators and managers increased by thirty-one in the six Giuliani years, while blacks went up by six, their percent of the brass actually dropping a fraction of a percent. Even after the NYPD's merger with the transit and housing police, the percent of its total workforce that is African American, including civilians, crawled up a mere 1.8 percent by 1999. Since transit and housing had a far higher percent of black employees than the NYPD, this minuscule increase is the best indicator of just how white the new NYPD hires were.

Wilbur Chapman—the highest-ranking black in the NYPD under Giuliani, who is now transportation commissioner—told the twenty-four-hour cable news channel, NY1, in 1999 that the department missed a golden opportunity to change its racial profile early in the Giuliani era in 1995. Chapman had run the most successful minority recruitment drive in the history of the city in 1993, while Dinkins was mayor. Of the 37,926 applicants who passed the 1993 police exam, a quarter were black and a quarter Hispanic. Yet the department decided to junk that civil service list and ordered another exam, hiring thousands of new cops from a new, whiter, pool.

The fire department—whose administrative ranks grew under Giuliani by 111 percent—had exactly one black manager more in 1999 than in 1993. There were fifty-three more white administrators and managers named in the same period, dropping the black share of top jobs almost in half, from 15.3 percent to 8 percent. Similarly, there were 100 more white uniformed fire supervisors and forty-nine more white firefighters, while the number of black supervisors fell by nine and the number of black firefighters by forty-two. Remarkably, over Giuliani's first six years, both the paltry 2.5 percent of fire supervisors and 4.4 percent of firefighters who were black declined by 0.4 percent. As impossible as it might have seemed, the 94.4 percent white supervisory ranks and 90.9 percent white firefighter ranks of 1993 actually got marginally whiter by 1999.

Almost 6,000 fewer blacks were employed at HRA's Department of Social Services. Part of this job loss was due to the 1996 creation of the Administration for Children's Services, a new agency overseeing child protection, foster care and related services that employed 4,901 blacks in 1997, almost all of them transferred from HRA. But the percent of blacks left in the shrunken HRA still dipped two percent.

At the Department for the Aging—a political jewel servicing high-voting seniors at 335 centers—the number of white administrators grew by 160 percent, while the paltry number of blacks (only five) remain unchanged. The black share of high-level jobs at Juvenile Justice plunged by 30 percent, at the Taxi & Limousine Commission by 71.4 percent and at the Department of Mental Health by 24.7 percent. The percentage of blacks in the total workforce of some agencies also plunged—at Consumer Affairs by 11 percent and at Transportation by 26 percent (this was partly due to the transfer of the Parking Violations Bureau).

The Department of Citywide Administrative Services (DCAS), which is charged with monitoring the city's equal employment program, saw a 62.5 percent drop in the percent of administrators and managers who were black and a 49.3 percent decline in all agency staff. There were 568 fewer blacks in the agency than when Giuliani took office (this is adjusted to account for the merger in 1996 of the personnel and general services agencies into DCAS).

Latinos fared better than blacks in most of these agencies, and their portion of the total workforce grew by 1.8 percent, almost as much as the black share dropped. The only agencies that saw a substantial boost in the share of managerial jobs going to blacks were Business Services and Housing Preservation and Development, the two agencies led by blacks through almost all of the Giuliani years. Agencies headed by Latinos also saw a hike in managerial hires that were Latino.

The appointment, managerial and workforce numbers were, as Rudy saw it, a result of color-blind hiring on a merit-only basis. Not once in six years did he express a whiff of public concern about an inclusive government. Instead he defied a charter mandate that he consult with the Equal Employment Practices Commission, a quasi-independent body whose members he and the City Council appoint to monitor minority hiring. He was supposed to confer with the EEPC about the development of an Affirmative Employment Plan, which the charter requires the city to maintain at all times. Giuliani quickly discarded the Dinkins plan and took nearly his entire first term to replace it with an operative one of his own.

Then he refused to call it an affirmative plan, contrary to the precise wording of the charter, and instead labeled it an Equal Opportunity Employment Plan. A collection of level-playing-field platitudes, the Giuliani plan did not even require advertising job vacancies in minority newspapers. The EEPC, chaired by Charlie Hughes, an African-American labor leader who endorsed Giuliani in 1997, mildly criticized the plan, urging a change of name and other revisions. It also said the delays had "negatively impacted on the administration of equal employment opportunity programs in city government." Rudy brushed these objections aside.

He had swung back and forth on the question of affirmative action as a candidate for mayor, but he now pretended, as he accommodated himself to many mainstream Republican ideas, that an aversion to racially conscious hiring was a matter of ideology to him. He did continue, especially through the 1997 election, to take minimal steps to maintain ties to the Latino community, partly through high-level appointments. But blacks were outsiders almost by definition, regarded as an overreaching special interest. It was as if Rudy believed that any concession to black concerns—from affirmative action to homelessness to welfare—would be viewed as a sign of weakness by his core constituencies and, conversely, any resistance would be seen as strength.

All his life he'd occupied a milky universe—raised in blanched Nassau suburbs, educated at insular Loughlin and Manhattan, shuttling twice between the colorless cubicles of the Justice Department in Washington and the U.S. Attorney's office in Manhattan, practicing law at three premier law firms where not just the shoes were white.

As a kid, he'd rooted for the all-white Yankees while Jackie Robinson crossed the color line just a couple of miles from his home. His father and uncle sold the family bar when the neighborhood changed, and Harold spun his favorite oven story about blacks in his garden conversations with Lina Merli. His first wife left a long-troubled marriage to spend the next twelve years with a black man, who expressed a racial fear of Giuliani. He never lived, like so many white New Yorkers, on a block alive with human diversity—preferring Woodside in Queens, West End Avenue and the homogeneous East 80s.

He quarantined Haitians. He exploited race to win the mayoralty. Even when he ran for re-election in 1997—opposed by a liberal Jewish woman, Ruth Messinger—he tried to make her Dinkins's candidate, repeatedly trying to tarnish her by tying her to the former mayor. And again, in the putative 2000 Senate race, he tried to use race against Hillary Clinton—at first, suggesting she was a dupe of the Dinkins crowd, then depicting her as a stand-in for Al Sharpton. Perhaps the ugliest stunt in any of his campaigns was his appearance in 1997 on the steps of City Hall with state prison guards from Attica—the site of the bloodiest massacre of mostly black prisoners in American history. Already up by 18 points in the polls over Messinger, he used a party thrown in her house decades earlier on behalf of a released Attica inmate to try to paint her into a radical and racial corner.

He refused for the first five years of his mayoralty to meet with Carl McCall, the state comptroller and the highest-ranking black official in the state. He stonewalled Manhattan borough president Virginia Fields as well, the highest-ranking black in city government, and refused to talk to the Council of Black Elected Officials, a statewide coalition of legislators that represents 2.5 million people. Charlie Hughes, the EEPC chair who did a television commercial for Rudy in 1997 and was his most important black backer, now says that he never had a single private moment with the mayor, dealing almost exclusively through emissaries.

Rudy's virtual elimination of the city's once half-billion-dollar subsidy of the public hospital system has curtailed services and slashed jobs in an agency that primarily serves blacks and Latinos. He browbeat the City University into adopting a plan to end remediation programs, which John Morning, a black Pataki appointee on CUNY's board, said would "significantly impact on minority access" to college. Since the Giuliani plan continued remediation for students born in non-English-speaking countries, blacks would be affected the worst, argued Morning. (Morning has also been appointed to another public board by Giuliani.)

Giuliani said nothing during an on-air appearance with old friend Bob Grant when the talk-show host with a talent for race-baiting referred to Harlem congressman Charlie Rangel as a "pygmy." Asked by the *Washington Post* to defend his record on minorities, he said: "They're alive, how about we start with that?"

(He later explained this comment as a reference to plunging homicide rates.) With a $10 million kitty for his 1997 re-election campaign, he did not spend a cent on black media, though he certainly targeted other ethnic communities.

Joseph Dolman, a *Newsday* columnist, asked La Guardia's biographer Thomas Kessner, to compare the two mayors. Kessner told him La Guardia wasn't like Giuliani. "He did not have a permanent disagreement with a whole part of the city," Kessner said, referring to the divide that separated City Hall from New York's millions of African Americans.

City Councilman Lloyd Henry, a soft-spoken black minister who remained neutral in the 1997 election, recalls that during one long conversation with Giuliani on a boat ride after an Ellis Island event and briefer exchanges at public events, Rudy appeared "uncomfortable" and "bashful."

"I don't know if that's how he relates to people of his own pigmentation," said the two-term, Caribbean-American councilman. "I'm certainly not saying he's prejudiced. But he's not compassionate enough about our problems. I think he's fearful of being too identified with the black community. I don't know where that fear comes from."

Even black Democrats who endorsed his re-election have been sharply critical of him since—State Senator Ada Smith, for example, says his "relationship with the black community is nonexistent." Arthur Bramwell, the only black Republican to lead a county organization in the state, hosted fundraisers for Candidate Rudy in his Brooklyn home in 1989. He now says: "I don't think he has any empathy for blacks. He was brought up as a prosecutor. On that side of the fence, you have everything going your way. This tends to give you an arrogance toward people in general and toward certain people in particular. He thinks most criminals are blacks. He doesn't know when to show respect." Bramwell said neither Giuliani nor his aides "ever discussed any policy issues," adding that "they just set a firm policy and expect everyone to follow."

Ed Koch weathered a dozen years of tortured relations with blacks. David Dinkins was tormented by the Crown Heights riot, gutting his credibility with Orthodox Jews in particular. John Lindsay was seen as the ally of anti-Semitic blacks during a racially charged teachers strike in the late 1960s. Race politics is an inescapable part of the landscape of New York.

But Giuliani's predecessors tried, often without success and sometimes half-heartedly, to build bridges to communities they'd alienated. Rudy has just seethed. He has welcomed opportunities to flex muscle, but never to reveal heart. He's mistaken wounded anger for enmity, and let it become enmity. Maybe his own political antennae told him reaching out would only hurt him. Whatever the motive, the result is a fault line of mistrust. It's erupted whenever the cops who've made Rudy a national hero got too aggressive.

A madou Diallo was a West African immigrant shot at forty-one times in the vestibule of his Bronx home by four cops, hit nineteen times. Reaching into his pocket for his wallet was his fatal mistake.

Abner Louima was a Haitian sodomized with a stick in a precinct bathroom. His intestines and bladder were punctured and he was dumped in a holding cell while hemorrhaging blood. Cops mistook him for someone who had tried to punch one of them outside a nightclub.

Anthony Baez was a Puerto Rican choked to death by a cop so brutal his commander had earlier tried to get him off the street. Baez's mistake was an errant football. These three cases would dominate the news though there were many other shocking cases of police abuse in the Giuliani era, as there had been in New York long before he was elected. The difference was how the mayor handled them.

Even Rudy's harshest critics praised his initial response to the Louima case. As soon as he learned of it, he went to the hospital and promised the battered thirty-three-year-old security guard to "make examples" of the officers who committed these "reprehensible crimes." One cop was immediately arrested by Internal Affairs. The mayor said charges against the cops "should result in the severest of penalties, including substantial terms of imprisonment." Every supervisor at the precinct, including the commander, was dumped.

But the brutal attack occurred in August 1997, on the eve of Rudy's re-election. He'd seen how the August 1989 racial murder of Yusef Hawkins, which did not involve police, had cost Ed Koch the mayoralty. So Rudy declared that the Louima crisis was "a real opportunity, one that only gets presented to you for a period of time, to permanently change the way in which the police department relates to the communities in New York City." He named a twenty-eight-member task force to examine systemic problems he'd never before acknowledged. He even appointed "enemies" like New York Civil Liberties head Norman Siegel, a classmate of his at NYU law school who had been blasting his police policies. Their report wasn't due until after the election.

Five months into his new term, Rudy turned what Siegel called his "best 48 hours as mayor" into a hoax. He held a press conference to ridicule the one-inch-thick report of his own task force. Its recommendations "made very little sense," he said. The only one he'd bother to adopt was the suggestion that the title of the NYPD's office of community affairs be switched to community relations. "That's a good change," he wisecracked. The "real opportunity" he cited in '97 had become a joke in '98.

Giuliani's response to the Baez case was just as political.

The twenty-nine-year-old was kicking a football around with his brothers in front of the family home on a dead-end street on December 22, 1994. The ball accidentally hit two parked patrol cars. Nine brutality charges had been leveled against one of the cops on the scene, Frank Livoti. While only one of the complaints had resulted in a finding against him, Livoti had been placed in the department's special monitoring program for a while. His commander had asked that he be assigned to a desk job or transferred out of the precinct, the only time he'd ever made such a request.

But Rudy's favorite cop, Chief of Department Lou Anemone, the NYPD's highest-ranking uniformed officer, put in writing that Livoti's transfer was not "practical" because of his "PBA status." Livoti was a PBA delegate close to Phil Caruso, the union boss who had helped elect Giuliani.

Several of the complaints against Livoti involved chokeholds, a banned arresting technique. That's what he put on Baez. He knelt on Baez's back while handcuffing him as Baez lay face-down on the ground. He ignored warnings from Baez's father that the kid was a chronic asthmatic, keeping him in a prone position for ten minutes, then dragging him into a cop car without attempting to resuscitate him. Baez died an hour later in a hospital.

The mayor declined to comment. Six weeks after Baez's death, Anemone publicly described Livoti as having "a distinguished career of service to the community, doing the kind of work that the citizenry of the city and certainly this country are looking for." Livoti, who was also facing an assault indictment in another chokehold case, opted for a non-jury trial. Caruso made several appearances at the trial, hugging and kissing his protégé. Judge Gerald Sheindlin, now the star of the TV show *The People's Court*, acquitted Livoti in October 1996. Rudy then uttered his first words on the case, calling Sheindlin's ruling "a careful, well-thought-out, legally reasoned opinion."

But SDNY U.S. Attorney Mary Jo White opened her own civil rights investigation of the Baez incident. Bronx borough president Fernando Ferrer, the highest ranking Latino in city politics and a Democratic candidate for mayor, began making a major issue out of Livoti's protected status on the NYPD. So on February 21, 1997, Howard Safir dismissed the cop from the force. During a debate with his

Democrat opponent in October, Giuliani declared that the Livoti verdict was "a failure of the criminal justice system."

Livoti was eventually convicted twice—in state court on the other chokehold case in 1997 and in federal court on Baez in 1998. After Livoti was found guilty of choking a teenager, Steven Resto, for running a red light in a go-cart before the Baez incident, Baez's mother told reporters: "It would have made a big difference if someone had listened to Resto in the beginning. My son would be alive right now."

The federal judge who sentenced Livoti to seven and a half years said much the same thing. She condemned the NYPD for "letting him remain on the streets knowing a tragedy would occur." The judge said the department "should have known he was dangerous" and that "senior police officials rejected repeated demands to transfer him."

The city simultaneously settled a civil suit filed by the Baez family for $3 million, the largest settlement in a cop case ever. Almost two years after the state trial—when the state judge called the testimony of the cops with Livoti that night "a nest of perjury"—Safir announced that he'd relieved three of them of their guns and placed them on modified assignment. All had supported Livoti's bogus story, and Safir had taken no action against them, even though they had testified that a mystery black man had appeared at the scene, choked Baez and then disappeared. It wasn't until a federal prosecutor called them "absolute liars" in his summation at the second trial that Safir took action.

By the time Diallo was killed in February 1999, Rudy was an all-but-declared candidate for the U.S. Senate. With Louima, he made election-year adjustments in his benefit-of-the-doubt mantra to placate white liberals; with Baez, to placate Hispanics. His response to Diallo was dictated by what would sell to his new statewide constituency—white and conservative, much of it upstate and suburban Republican. With a strong majority of the city's white cops living in the suburbs, the Senate race, had Rudy stayed in it, would have been the first time they could have voted for him.

Unarmed and never arrested—just like Baez and Louima—Diallo could not be muddied up, as Giuliani and Safir routinely did with others shot by cops. That did not stop the NYPD from trying—they ransacked his Bronx apartment looking for any discrediting information. The city exploded in weeks of demonstrations, featuring the arrests outside police headquarters of Dinkins, Rangel and even black leaders who'd endorsed Giuliani, like Floyd Flake, the ex-congressman and minister. The mayor said the shooting was a mere "tragedy," the demonstrations were "silly" and the demonstrators were "the worst elements of society."

After he met with a delegation of African diplomats and leaders, one member of the group told the press that Rudy had expressed sorrow over this "regrettable mistake." His press secretary rushed to correct this interpretation, telling reporters that Rudy had never called it a mistake, only a tragedy. None of the officers was suspended, as two Louima cops had been. Though none answered the NYPD's or DA's questions about the circumstances of the shooting, Rudy left the unmistakable impression that he believed they'd behaved properly. He also did chart presentations at City Hall and national television interviews claiming that the city's police were "the most restrained" in America.

Within fourteen hours of the shooting, the mayor left town for Pennsylvania to regale a banquet room of Republicans with the story of how he'd tamed New York. Safir flew to Hollywood for the Oscars. Had he not been caught on camera glad-handing stars, the commissioner would have got away with missing a City Council hearing on the Diallo shooting that Monday, having phoned in a "schedule conflict" excuse. Giuliani defended Safir's safari, saying: "Frankly, there is no crisis or emergency going on and things have been proceeding quite normally."

When Safir returned, he decided it was perfect timing to announce, at a press conference with the mayor, that the department was switching to hollow-point bullets. These deadlier, new bullets corkscrew into a target and stay there, forcing him or her to the ground quickly. The full-metal-jacket bullets used up to then passed through a body without causing suspects to drop.

Police sources told the Post that Safir agreed to change bullets in the aftermath of the Diallo incident. They said the theory was that the cops continued firing at Diallo—two emptied their 16-shot Glocks—because he remained standing, effectively pinned upward by the fusillade. That turned out to be precisely the defense the cops used at their trial a year later—a strange coincidence since the department said the cops had refused to answer questions. The bullet switch prompted another outcry, and Rudy insisted it had been in the works for months.

Under sustained protest and editorial and City Council pressure, the mayor announced a $15 million recruitment drive ostensibly to attract more minority cops. The eventual television advertising buy, however, was more a salute to the NYPD than a genuine recruitment effort—especially since next to no time was bought on black media. The number of blacks in the next police class grew, but only modestly. It fell a far cry short of the success of Dinkins's recruitment effort, which had produced the minority-heavy list the Giuliani team spiked.

He and Safir also made cosmetic changes in the unit that the four cops who killed Diallo belonged to—the Street Crime Unit (SCU). This elite undercover operation was the model of aggression in the Giuliani age—making the lion's share of gun arrests and boasting that they "owned the night" in the mostly minority neighborhoods where they roamed. Only 3 percent of its members were black, though Safir did add minority cops to it after Diallo.

Safir had tripled the size of the unit to 400 cops as soon as he took office, a move that so rankled SCU commander Richard Savage he quit, concerned about too little training and too little supervision. In 1997 and 1998, the SCU "tossed"— meaning frisked—45,000 people, yet made only 9,500 arrests. Its arrest figures actually dropped while its frisk reports soared. A Brooklyn grand jury declined to indict two SCU cops in 1997 after they fired twenty-four times at an unarmed black man sitting in his car, killing him. But the grand jury did issue a muted, thoughtful, thirty-five-page critique of SCU operations. To any caring police and city administration, the report would have sounded an alarm.

Issued by a Democratic district attorney, Joe Hynes, who had all but endorsed Giuliani, the report said there were "no formal criteria or testing" for joining the unit but that the prime characteristic of recruits was "arrest activity, a willingness to be proactive." It faulted the absence of specialized training. It said the cops on the street "had too much discretion," a finding that anticipated Diallo, since the cops involved, when they finally testified at trial, could only justify approaching Diallo because he was "peering" side to side as he stood on his stoop.

Disturbed that one of the cops in the Brooklyn incident had emptied his Glock, the grand jury found that "the goals of the NYPD with respect to controlling the number of shots fired had not been achieved." Giuliani denounced Hynes for "engaging" in "a political exercise." The grand jury's nine recommendations were junked.

When an appellate court moved the Diallo case to Albany, Rudy praised the decision, agreeing that the cops could not get a fair trial in the city he governed and seizing another opportunity to blast the protesters for poisoning the air. When the upstate jury, which included four blacks, acquitted the officers on all counts, he announced his own vindication. Yet polls said most white New Yorkers rejected the notion that all the cops, including the two who emptied their Glocks, did nothing wrong.

Rudy went out of his way to undercut any possible federal charges, saying there was no basis to second-guess the jury, though that was exactly what he'd urged when the only defendant charged with the murder of Yankel Rosenbaum was acquitted. He also unleashed his patented attack on those he said were consumed with anti-cop bias, equating it, for the umpteenth time, with racism. The difference between hating a people for who they are, and denouncing individual cops for what they do, was apparently too subtle a thought for the ever-enlarging forehead at City Hall.

In addition to the big three cases, Rudy twice assailed the parents of sixteen-year-old unarmed black boys shot by the cops, even while their sons lay in hospital beds in critical condition. Michael Jones was fired at seventeen times and hit six times while riding his bike in his Brooklyn neighborhood with a large toy gun. Giuliani said: "Adult supervision would have prevented the gun. It would have also prevented him from being out at 2:30 in the morning for whatever purpose, and I don't think the purpose for which he was out was a salutary one." There was no evidence that Jones, who survived, was involved in any criminal activity.

Three months after Diallo, the mayor said much the same about the parents of sixteen-year-old Dante Johnson, who was shot while running away from an SCU cop at 12:30 in the morning. Giuliani and Safir mused about why Johnson's family allowed him to roam the street after midnight and Giuliani concluded: "There appear to be facts that would explain and justify what happened here, including the actions of these men—what are they—16-year-olds at 12:30 in the morning?" The cop grabbed Johnson through the window of his patrol car and shot him once in the abdomen. The chase began, the cops claimed, because either Johnson or a friend appeared to them to possibly be carrying a gun. Neither was.

As ugly as Rudy's responses to individual cases were, his policies were worse. A city commission recommended the creation of a permanent independent monitor to oversee police misconduct and the City Council passed a bill to do it twice. Rudy's vetoes were overridden by the council, but he bottled the issue up in endless court cases. The former prosecutor who made his "Prince of the City" reputation by supposedly targeting bad cops declared: "A much better way to improve the police department is to get it to investigate itself."

He also tried to gut the only oversight vehicle already in law: the Civilian Complaint Review Board, which is charged with probing allegations against cops filed by citizens. Created by Dinkins, the CCRB spurred the police riot Rudy joined in 1992. Blacks and Latinos file three quarters of its complaints. Nonetheless, the proportion of CCRB staff that is black declined by 49.9 percent between 1995 and 1999.

Though complaints jumped 56 percent in Rudy's first four years, he proposed cuts at the board in each of his first four budgets, totaling $2.4 million at a $5 million agency. The council restored most of the board's funding. The mayor also derided it for years, though he appointed successive former SDNY friends of his to chair it.

After the Louima incident, Giuliani finally boosted its budget and toned down his blasts. Complaints leveled off in recent years as well, though they are still far higher than under Dinkins, when there was both more crime and more felony arrests. In 1998, an NBC *Dateline* piece exposed how precincts repeatedly refused to take CCRB complaints, or to give complainants forms to fill out. The data showed much of the initial decline in complaints was at precincts, while those filed at the CCRB continued to go up. Lawsuits filed against the department also climbed 52 percent from 1993 to 1999.

Most disturbing about Giuliani's CCRB record was how Safir handled the paltry 5 percent of complaints that are substantiated by the agency. According to a New York Civil Liberties Union report, Safir "nullified" two thirds of the 635 CCRB cases he reviewed between January 1996 and July 1998, refusing to take any action against the cops. But when a probe of the NYPD announced by U.S. Attorney Zachary Carter zeroed in on the handling of these cases in 1998, Safir imposed discipline in 58 percent of the ones he reviewed between July and December of 1998.

Rudy, predictably, branded the federal probe political. He resisted efforts by Public Advocate Mark Green to review Safir's handling of substantiated complaints, losing a two-year court battle. He or Safir dismissed criticisms from Amnesty International, an unofficial House Judiciary subcommittee and Attorney General Eliot Spitzer.

The 178-page Spitzer report analyzed 175,000 stop-and-frisk reports and found that, after adjusting for different crime rates among racial groups, Latinos were stopped 39 percent more often than whites and blacks 23 percent more often. In addition, 15 percent of black and Latino "tosses" did not meet the legal definition of "reasonable suspicion"; another 25 percent of the reports did not contain enough information to determine the constitutionality of the searches.

Not even the experience of his only black City Hall adviser, Deputy Mayor Rudy Washington, affected the stonewall. Washington told Giuliani in the midst of the Diallo protests that he, too, had been pulled over by a cop in 1998, while riding with his wife in his chauffeur-driven city limo. When Washington asked why they'd been stopped, the cop said: "Shut up. I don't need a reason to stop you." When Washington persisted, the officer responded: "I ask the questions. Not you." A high-ranking police official happened by, recognized Washington and asked what was going on. The cop explained that Washington's car "looked very suspicious." Washington told Giuliani the confrontation was so traumatic, his wife began to cry.

Washington told the story—and others as well—in a roomful of Giuliani aides and someone leaked it to the *Times*. A retired black police lieutenant who was a close friend of Washington's, Woodrow Gist, told reporters that Washington told him the story when it happened and that the deputy mayor had deliberately not taken down the officer's name and badge number. "He just didn't want to get into it with the Police Department, knowing how the mayor feels about the department," Gist explained. "He is a member of the administration. So he could not raise it in the context of race."

Washington still didn't "want to get into it" when the story broke. He refused to discuss the incident with the press. The most Giuliani would say was that it was a "confidential" but "useful" bit of advice, and that he hoped police would treat blacks "respectfully." He added that he also wanted others who "try to create an exaggerated, false impression of the police" to deal with cops "in a more respectful way."

Giuliani's only defense in the face of the evidence of police abuse was the numbers he trotted out repeatedly, documenting a decline in fatal police shootings. He preferred to talk about 1999, when only eleven people were killed in cop shootings, the lowest since 1985. He ignored the 36 percent increase in cop killings in his first three years, a reversal of the 44 percent drop in Dinkins's final three years. The rise from twenty-two killings in 1993 to twenty-nine in 1994, twenty-six in 1995 and thirty in 1996 was particularly inexplicable since every other form of gun violence was plummeting.

For two decades prior to Rudy's taking office, the number of people killed by the NYPD "mirrored fairly closely the number of civilians killing each other," according to John Jay College criminologist Andrew Karmon. That correlation came completely apart in the first three Giuliani years. It was also out of synch in 1997 and 1998, when the rate of police shootings finally dropped—to twenty and nineteen, only 13 percent less than in Dinkins's last year. Meanwhile, the murder rate had dropped 67.4 percent during the same five-year period. And since Rudy was only talking about police fatal shootings—excluding deaths like chokehold victim Baez—the more relevant comparison would have been civilian handgun homicide, which fell 81 percent. Even the 50 percent drop in fatal police shootings between 1993 and 1999 (from twenty-two to eleven) doesn't keep pace with either decline.

Similarly, there was a 52 percent drop in shots fired by perpetrators at cops between 1993 and 1997, but only a 12 percent decline in shots fired by cops. Shots fired by cops exceeded the number in Dinkins's final year right up to 1997, even though the "perps" were carrying and using guns less and less often every year. It was as if the only guy firing away at the O.K. Corral was Wyatt Earp.

I n March 2000, Patrick Dorismond, a twenty-six-year-old Haitian who, like Louima, worked as a security guard, was killed by an undercover narcotics detective. Giuliani's inflammatory exploitation of the case would disconcert his strongest allies, even those on the editorial page of the *New York Post*.

Dorismond was standing outside a midtown bar with a friend looking for a cab to go home to Brooklyn, where he lived with his girlfriend and their one-year-old daughter. According to the police, a single cop approached Dorismond and asked: "Hey, do you have some Krill?" Angered by the suggestion that he was a crack dealer, Dorismond replied: "What are you doing asking me for that shit?" He and the undercover then got into an exchange of as many as eight punches, with differing accounts about who threw the first one. Two backup cops standing just a few yards away rushed up to the altercation, and one of them shot Dorismond in the chest. Police concede that when the altercation began, the undercover had not identified himself as a cop, though they claim one of the three officers yelled "police" just before the fatal shot was fired.

After initially assuming a wait-and-see public posture, Rudy launched into daily assaults on the character of the dead man. He told Safir to release a sealed juvenile record indicating that when Dorismond was thirteen, he was arrested for robbery. While touring upstate Saint Patty's Day parades as part of his Senate campaign, he recited other arrests on Dorismond's rap sheet, including attempted robbery, assault and gun possession. Next the mayor unearthed a domestic violence complaint filed by his girlfriend, who told cops he had punched her.

The facts slowly emerged: The juvenile case never got so much as a docket number, meaning it was dropped before it ever went before a judge. No gun was found in the alleged possession case, which involved a traffic dispute. He was never charged with attempted robbery, just simple assault when he punched a youth for cheating him out of some marijuana. Dorismond pled guilty in these cases to disorderly conduct—a violation, not a crime. The cop who took the domestic violence report noted on the form: "No injuries. No complaint of pain." The girlfriend withdrew it.

Though Dorismond had never been convicted of any crime, much less an assault, Rudy was still maintaining: "That he spent a good deal of his adult life punching people is a fact." This record established, in the mayor's view, Dorismond's "propensity" for violence. "He engaged in an assault and that's what caused his death," said Giuliani.

The outrage reached a fever pitch. With no convictions, all of Dorismond's adult record was also sealed. Giuliani explained that it was not illegal for him to break the seal on any of it because Dorismond was dead. "Privacy interests and rights expire with you," he declared. For the first time, the *Post* published two editorials criticizing Safir and the mayor. Legal ethics experts, a state assembly committee and editorial boards roundly denounced the release.

David Diaz, a veteran WCBS-TV reporter whose respected professionalism led to his selection as the head of the Inner Circle (an association of city journalists), put the question that was on everyone's mind to Giuliani at one of the Dorismond press conferences. "Mister Mayor, how would you respond to the people who feel that not only is the Police Department out of control, you're out of control, that you are the lawless one in the city?" Diaz asked. "You set the tone. You disregard court opinions when you don't like them. What is your answer to those who say that Giuliani is out of control? Giuliani is the chief lawless one?"

"Oh come on," Giuliani said. "Let's move on to a serious question."

Diaz insisted: "Mr. Mayor, what is your answer to that question?"

"My answer is let's move to a serious subject."

The only defense the mayor offered was that he released the records on "sound legal advice," declaring that he would defend his decision anywhere. But his corporation counsel, Michael Hess, one of the good old boys from the Southern District, testified before a State Assembly committee that the mayor neither sought nor received an opinion. Safir suggested at the same hearing that an assistant corporation counsel had given them an informal opinion in a similar 1996 case—but he offered no opinion letter or other evidence to support it.

In fact, the NYPD had also unveiled the sealed records of Michael Jones and Dante Johnson, the sixteen-year-olds shot by cops and denounced by the mayor for being out too late at night. In the Johnson case, Safir was personally quoted as saying the kid was on probation at the time of the shooting, though that would have been part of the sealed record if it were so. Johnson's lawyer contends he was never on probation.

Giuliani was just as defensive about adopting any reforms that might be seen as a concession that anything had gone wrong. City Council Speaker Peter Vallone tried to use the Dorismond incident to get Giuliani to back the creation of an independent monitoring board—the bill Rudy had vetoed twice and stymied in the courts—but the mayor refused. In his rejection letter to Vallone, Rudy misspelled Dorismond's name as Dorismand.

Rudy and Safir also resisted any material changes in narcotics undercover operations, which had led to the deaths of four unarmed black men in four weeks (counting two carrying toy guns killed right after Dorismond). The department was putting 500 additional officers on the streets every day—paid for with $24 million in overtime—to raise drug arrest totals. But 75 percent of the new busts were for misdemeanors and violations. Felony drug arrests were actually down 9 percent, while petty possession cases, mostly of marijuana, were up 68 percent. Former Police Chief Bill Bratton wondered out loud why such a massive manhunt for potheads was necessary if New York was as safe as Rudy perpetually announced. The reasoning obviously had as much to do with keeping the lid on crime stats until the expected Senate election was over as any real law enforcement objective.

It certainly escaped few in the city's vast Haitian community that Dorismond was the second Haitian involved in a celebrated Giuliani brutality case. Giuliani's name was already a curse on Haitian radio, but the trashing of Dorismond raised the anger to a new level. Unbeknownst to the mayor, Dorismond was the son of the lead singer in one of Haiti's best-known bands during the 1950s and 1960s, a twenty-piece ensemble that played to huge crowds all over the island. Dorismond's brother Charles had become a hit reggae artist called Bigga Haitian. The Dorismond name was so well known, Rudy again became a major news story in the land he'd visited almost twenty years earlier.

Jocelyn McCalla, executive director of National Coalition for Haitian Rights, inadvertently raised the specter of Rudy's nearly two-decade-old orchestration of the detention and blockade of Haitians. "In a way, what Giuliani has been doing is far worse than anything he has done, on this issue where he insists on demonizing Patrick. This is the kind of thing that happens in Haiti, and it's absolutely outrageous."

"We are the sons and daughters of seekers of freedom," said Vladimir Rodney, a lawyer and vice chairman of the Haitian-American Alliance, referring to the Duvalier days a younger Giuliani had so warmly embraced. "The mayor has done unspeakable harm to the bond of trust between the police and our communities." In the protests that followed, signs and chants in Haitian Creole blasted the mayor, some comparing him to a "loup garou," a Haitian demon who preys on the blood of babies.

One of a group of Flatbush ministers who met with Safir during the controversy was Monsignor Gregory Sansaricq, the pastor of a Catholic church near Dorismond's home. He is related to Bernard Sansaricq, the Florida-based leader of a failed Haitian insurrection who Giuliani agreed to prosecute during his 1982 visit with Baby Doc. The first child Monsignor Sansaricq ever baptized was one of the children later killed when Papa Doc ordered the slaughter of fifteen members of the Sansaricq family in 1964.

The monsignor remembers calling Giuliani at the Justice Department in the early 1980s near Christmas. "I pleaded with him for a half hour to release some of the detainees for Christmas," says Father Sansaricq. "It was a polite conversation, but he said they didn't respect set procedures, they didn't use legal channels to emigrate. I used the image of two houses next to each other. I told him if one was on fire and people ran from that one to the other, no one could accuse them of breaking in. He didn't move one inch."

The Flatbush ministers asked Safir for "a public apology to the Dorismond family and the community at large," Sansaricq says, and Safir said he "could make no apology because the case was under review." He also declined to make any public gesture concerning the release of the record. "The mayor came into the meeting when we were already about to leave," says the monsignor. "We politely continued to leave."

The mourners at Dorismond's three-mile-long funeral procession—10,000 strong—sang the Haitian national anthem, and then turned tender, singing "J'ai Besoin de Toi," or "I Need You." Clashes with police, many in riot gear, led to twenty-seven arrests and twenty-three cop injuries. Giuliani visited the injured cops at nearby hospitals, but stayed away from the funeral. His press secretary explained: "In situations where the person involved may have been involved in a crime, the mayor does not attend the funeral." Several months later, he tried to arrange a private meeting with the family, but they insisted on having their lawyer present, and he demurred.

It was not just the echoes of Rudy's tortured history with Haitians that the Dorismond case sounded. Patrick Dorismond grew up two blocks from 419 Hawthorne Street, where Rudy lived his first six years. Dorismond graduated from Bishop Loughlin High School. "How much connection can you have?" asked the Haitian priest who performed Dorismond's funeral. "Just different colors, that's all."

Of course, the father who raised Rudy on Hawthorne Street had a bit of a punching history himself, to say nothing of the documented pathology of aggression found in court records. His angry outbursts were such a family legend Rudy himself has acknowledged them. It was Harold Giuliani who wrapped boxing gloves around Rudy's hands before his mother taught him how to read a word on a dead man's rap sheet. And—unlike Dorismond—Harold, Leo D'Avanzo and Lewis D'Avanzo had real criminal records, including a juvenile record in Harold's case, available to credibly defame them if they ever mistook an undercover cop for a thug.

Also swirling around Rudy—in the throes of the Dorismond controversy—was his own, deeply personal, history with cops. "There's never been a mayor who understands the psyche of the police department the way I do," he said in 1997. It was a reference to the five uncles who were cops, including Vincent D'Avanzo, busted himself, a front for a mobbed-up bar. It was also a reference to his lifetime in law enforcement, especially the days when Bob Leuci and Bill Phillips taught him how thin the blue line was between cop and criminal.

"People do act in conformity very often with their prior behavior," he said of Dorismond at a Blue Room press conference, invoking and distorting his record. He could just as easily have turned those words in on himself.

Battered from every direction, even the right, for his Dorismond actions, Rudy decided to play psychiatrist. "There's a process called projection in psychology. It means accusing someone of what you're doing," he said. His Democratic rival in the Senate race, Hillary Rodham Clinton, was engaging in "projection," he charged, when she said he was polarizing the city. He also psychoanalyzed why the press refused "to face the facts" about Dorismond, noting that "people rarely accept things that are going on in their unconscious."

On a strict diet for campaign purposes, his sallow face tightened in a grimace, as his own unconscious roared in his ears.

Seventeen

These Statistics
Are a Crime

I F YOU BELIEVE CRIME HAS BEEN REDUCED," CANDIDATE RUDY declared three weeks before the 1993 election, "you are living in never-never land." Without offering evidence or explanation, Giuliani ridiculed FBI stats that revealed a 16 percent drop over David Dinkins's final three years: "He declares victory on crime, and people laugh at him."

The *Times* did a single front-page story on the decline. It ran just as the dip started, in April 1991, and never mentioned Dinkins's name. The headline announced: "Even Criminals Credit Police." When the FBI released its national numbers in October 1993, the *Times* ran a scant 400-word story on page 42 and led with state figures. In the second paragraph, the story noted that the "largest drop occurred in New York City."

The only other *Times* reference to the numbers in 1993 was in an April campaign story, devoted to Dinkins's frustration at getting opinion makers to acknowledge that crime had plummeted in all seven FBI categories "for the first time in 36 years." The reporter, James McKinley, closed his analytical piece with a definitive declaration: "Mr. Dinkins will never be able to prove his policies have curbed crime." Between Dinkins's first year (1990) and his last (1993), murder fell 13.7 percent, robbery 14.6 percent, burglary 17.6 percent and auto theft 23.8 percent—yet no one noticed.

As muted as the *Times* was, the tabloids were even quieter, especially the *Post*, whose "David: Do Something" banner headline during an upsurge of murders in 1990 forced Dinkins to win state legislative approval for a tax surcharge that would finance the hiring of more than 6,000 new cops.

The reluctance to credit Dinkins for the crime reduction was hardly unusual. Neither the media nor the public had ever regarded crime stats as the measure of a mayor. When the murder rate first broke a thousand in 1969,

John Lindsay was re-elected, with the endorsement of the *Times* and most of the city establishment. The Democrat who opposed him tried to make an issue out of the 1968 jump in the murder rate—still a record 32 percent—and was widely dismissed as a demagogue.

Rupert Murdoch's *Post* literally drafted Ed Koch for governor in 1982 despite three consecutive years of escalating murder culminating in a 1981 historic high of 1,832, which came after drastic police cutbacks. The *Times* backed Koch in 1981, 1982 and 1989 amid horrific homicide surges. It did the same in 1985, following a two-year drop of significant proportions, and never cited the improving numbers in their endorsement. Until Rudy Giuliani, mayors were neither blamed nor praised for cyclical shifts in death data.

When the city's overall crime index increased at a rate 60 percent higher than the nation's in 1980, Phil McGuire, who was the NYPD's chief crime analyst then and now, said: "No one really knows why crime in the aggregate goes up or down." The *Times* matter-of-factly reported that the city "generally reflects and MAGNIFIES the national crime trends." It barely noted at the bottom of the story that the department had lost 9,000 cops since the fiscal crisis of 1975 and was at a longtime low of 22,000.

Lee Jones, who was Dinkins's press secretary, said: "We only had one press conference announcing crime statistics that involved the mayor. We thought if a politician stood next to a set of numbers, the credibility of the politician attached to those numbers. Then the people who liked David believed the numbers, and the people who didn't like him didn't believe them. We didn't want the figures in any way tainted by a politician."

Dinkins's biggest political mistake may well have been delaying the hiring of 2,100 new cops at the start of 1993, citing budget considerations. Combined with the 3,000 he'd already hired, the swearing-in of that new class could have given him just the spotlight he needed to claim credit for the sustained reversal of crime trends that had gone steadily upward for seven years prior to 1991. Instead, Giuliani got credit for that deferred class and the one paid for by his own first budget, totaling 4,200 new cops in his first year. Over his years as mayor, the NYPD grew from 29,000 to over 40,000, partially because of the surcharge Dinkins engineered and partially because of new hires Giuliani financed himself in 1998. Merging the Housing and Transit police with the NYPD was also a giant factor.

Giuliani had a meager crime program as a candidate. He blasted the reduction in drug arrests and promised more. He said he'd put more cops on foot patrol and make more gun arrests. He talked about drug- and gun-free zones near schools.

He vowed to let cops carry 9-mm guns. He supported the death penalty and opposed parole.

Beyond hiring Bill Bratton as police commissioner, Giuliani also had a meager program as mayor. Bratton wrote in his 1998 book *Turnaround* that two of Giuliani's transition aides "presented us with a 16-item list of campaign promises" before the new government took office. Bratton politely said he'd "handle some of the requests," though he also told them he had his own "series of initiatives" planned. In an interview now, Bratton sneers at the list and calls it "a joke."

When Bratton sent his first written strategy over to City Hall—a war on guns—"they nitpicked it endlessly." Getting City Hall approval "for each successive strategy," Bratton concluded, "was a tortuous process and to the best of my recollection never added anything substantive to the documents." John Miller, the WNBC-TV reporter who became Bratton's press aide, says the mayor and his aides "had no idea of a plan." Bratton says: "Giuliani provided authorization. He had no input whatsoever. The ideas came from within the Police Department. I'd be hardpressed to cite a single strategy other than domestic violence that originated with his office." Bratton and Miller agree that all Giuliani did at the outset was repeatedly ask Bratton—who had achieved substantial crime reductions as the head of the Transit Police in the early 1990s—"can you do in the street what you did in the subways?"

In his book, Bratton adds that at some of the later joint meetings, "the mayor's staff actually spoke of themselves as the principal authors" of some of the strategies. "We had sweat blood developing these strategies; now they were drinking it," contends Bratton, whose top advisers, John Timoney and Jack Maple, were heard to wisecrack, "When Rudy was a kid, did he ever once get to school with his lunch money?" Instead of generating ideas, City Hall was branded "the black hole of law enforcement" by Bratton because it dawdled with so many suggested initiatives that the NYPD began launching them before the mayor announced them.

Rudy did have a very clear idea, however, about how to control whatever media credit might come with a crime reduction. When Miller released the stats for the first five months, showing an estimated 11 percent drop, Denny Young ordered him to "stop doing that." City Hall would "decide when the numbers would be released," Miller was told. "Hold them back for a big announcement."

Giuliani wasn't quoted until the final paragraph of the *Times*'s page one story on the first stats. "I have never been one who strongly relies on statistics as a way of measuring what you're doing," dead-panned the man who had ended the publication of annual reports in the Southern District. "Obviously, you prefer the trend in the direction of declining crime, but I don't want the department to be overly focused on statistics."

This ruckus over press was foreshadowed by a showdown at the end of Bratton's first week on the job. He recounts how Deputy Mayor Peter Powers and Young, who was named Giuliani's counsel, raked him over the coals at a Sunday night meeting in January because of a front-page profile of him that appeared in the *Daily News*.

"I've known Rudy since we were kids, okay?" Powers said. "I'm his best friend, and I couldn't get away with this. If you can't work that way, he'll get someone else." Young added: "WE will control how these stories go out. The mayor has an agenda and it's very important that everybody stay on message and that the message come from the mayor."

City Hall's fixation on crime credit would ultimately force Bratton's resignation in 1996, but only after combat so intense that Rudy once summoned Miller to Gracie Mansion to dress him down for announcing a major bust without putting the mayor before the klieg lights. Actually, Miller had beeped Press Secretary Cristyne Lategano, who was with him at a Yankee game, and she hadn't responded. But he dared not defend himself by attempting to put the blame on Lategano. Rudy concluded: "I have the distinct impression that someone over there is putting someone else's agenda ahead of mine."

From the first numbers on, it was clear that the downturn begun under Dinkins was only going to get deeper, just like it was in cities across the country. That's why Giuliani was so desperate to seem personally in charge of it. Bratton had instituted sweeping management reforms that neither he nor Giuliani anticipated when they took office. The principal innovation called Compstat—or computer statistics meetings—evolved by the spring of 1994 from a new focus on weekly crime figures. Eventually, Compstat sessions occurred in the command center at NYPD headquarters, usually attended by 200 top precinct and executive staff from Bratton to detective squad commanders, all in full dress with polished brass.

Grilled by Maple, Timoney and other chiefs, precinct captains for the first time had to come up with concrete strategies to combat specific crimes spotted on pin maps within their jurisdiction. By 1995, huge, eight-foot-by-eight-foot computer monitors mounted on the walls could, as Bratton put it, "call up each map, each crime" and make "crime clusters visual." Commanders were held accountable for the numbers and every precinct had its day in the sun at least once a month. "Compstat was police Darwinism; the fittest survived and thrived," said Bratton.

This mechanism made the numbers the heart of the department, dictating deployment and tactics. Though Rudy observed only three Compstat sessions himself (according to Bratton), it also quickly became the heart of his government, talked about everywhere but duplicated nowhere. His Cabinet sessions at City Hall were hardly a facsimile, with him dominating a scattered, cheerleading talk-around. "Compstat was going on well before Rudy was even involved," Bratton says now, adding that the sessions Rudy attended were "a learning experience for him." Giuliani knew nothing about the organizational technique until he saw it in practice, insists the commissioner who pioneered it.

The second major strategy was what Giuliani took to calling "zero tolerance" for quality-of-life violations. Bratton had pioneered the concept without ever using the terminology, which he says "implies zealotry and a lack of cop discretion." Working with criminologist George Kelling while running the Transit Police from 1990 to 1992, Bratton began busting fare-beaters, graffiti artists and panhandlers. Prosecuting minor offenses had, in his view, transformed the culture of subway life, convincing criminals to take their act elsewhere.

That's what he painstakingly explained to Giuliani in their off-the-record sessions at the start of the 1993 campaign. "He didn't understand quality of life," Bratton recalls, "but he was a sponge." By then the police chief in Boston, Bratton sneaked into town at Giuliani's request and met with him at Anderson Kill for two hours. Rudy pressed him to discuss his Transit Authority strategies. "He caught the wave," says Bratton. "He understood the frustration about fear of crime. He understood that Republicans needed to do something about it."

Rudy also met with Kelling, and his campaign borrowed Bratton's monologue and Kelling's "Broken Windows" theory, which holds that just as unrepaired windows signal the abandonment of a building, untended disorderly behavior, no matter how minor, can lead to more serious disorder and crime. That was the basis of Giuliani's 1993 rhetorical assault on squeegees—the swarming crew of windshield-wiping vagabonds who were posting themselves at major intersections around the city in search of pocket change. Bratton came up with a battery of enforcement priorities—focusing on public drunkenness, harassment, menacing, urination and disorderly conduct and pushing street cops to trivialize nothing.

Third was a punishing plan to bolster drug and gun arrests, neither of which was an FBI index crime. The thought was that taking users, dealers and weapons off the street would reduce the pool of scavenging and frequently armed criminals, thereby driving downward the seven index crimes of murder, rape, aggravated assault, robbery, burglary, larceny and auto theft. The trick was that if drug and gun numbers went up, it wouldn't push the index up. The drug arrest part of this strategy was a Giuliani refrain from the 1989 campaign—indeed he'd tried to do it as U.S. Attorney—while the gun emphasis was principally another Bratton innovation.

These strategies became the foundation of Bratton and Giuliani's simultaneous claim that they had, as a *New York* magazine cover story put it in 1995, "ended crime as we know it." Despite the statistical success, celebrated on page one of the *Times* three times in 1995 alone, Giuliani dumped Bratton when polls showed that 60 percent of New Yorkers credited him, while only 18 percent cited the mayor, for the two-year, 26.3 percent drop in felonies. The fatal triumph was when *Time* magazine put Bratton in a trenchcoat on its cover in January 1996. Leaking damaging stories to tabloids and blocking key promotions and approval of his book contract, the mayor pushed Bratton toward the door.

Calling it a "death by a thousand cuts," Bratton at first resisted quitting, confident that firing him "would have been seen as remarkably petty." But having watched Giuliani browbeat Schools Chancellor Ramon Cortines into leaving, he concluded that it was not the mayor's practice to let opponents depart with honor. Stories were dropped banging Bratton for taking trips paid for by millionaire friends. A book contract he signed was handled by City Hall as if it belonged on the crime blotter and referred to counsel for scandal review. "I observed the slow strangulation of my ability to run the organization. He created a situation in which I had no choice but to resign," concluded Bratton, ironically the man most responsible for handing Giuliani the record that has made him a national hero.

Though the mayor went through the motions of considering Bratton's designated successor, John Timoney, as a replacement, he'd offered the job to Howard Safir well before Bratton had even resigned. Safir was the fire commissioner, a friend of Giuliani's since their joint days in the Justice Department in the 1980s when Safir ran the witness protection program for the U.S. Marshals. Though he'd never been a cop, the somber, jut-jawed, fifty-four-year-old was prepared to look like one, standing erect beside the mayor at what must have been an all-time municipal record for joint mayor/commissioner press conferences. According to Bratton, Giuliani even took charge of the seating chart at Safir's April 1996 inauguration.

Routinely depicted as a cardboard cutout of a commissioner, he wound up in a media frenzy about one of his own trips. In March 1999, he was dubbed "Oscar Howard" after he took a private jet junket to Hollywood for the Academy Awards even though he was scheduled to testify before a City Council committee about the police slaying of Amadou Diallo. The city's Conflict of Interest board, chaired by ex-U.S. Attorney Benito Romano, has been looking into charges about that trip—a gift from a Manhattan millionaire that included four nights at a Beverly

Hills hotel—for more than a year. The board is also examining Safir's use of two detectives to investigate the other driver in a car accident involving his wife, and the use of eight to chauffeur guests at his daughter's wedding.

Giuliani, however, has been far less troubled by Safir's trips and other indiscretions than the ones he tried to pin on Bratton. After all, a 1999 poll reversed the numbers that cost Bratton his job: 63 percent saw Safir as a "figurehead," with only 21 percent identifying him as his "own man." The overwhelming majority said Giuliani ran the NYPD.

Safir cannot lay claim to a major innovative strategy of his own, though he did continue Compstat and other Bratton tactics. Asked by the *Times* in 1999 to list what programs he'd "be remembered for," the commissioner mentioned his "call for taking DNA samples from everyone arrested" and "the installation of security cameras" in a few city housing projects.

The only other achievement was Safir's claim that he'd "expanded anti-drug initiatives," which, by definition, is not an innovation he launched. He did implement a modified version of Bratton's Operation Juggernaut, a late 1994 idea of Maple's that was to put 5,000 cops into a Normandy-like citywide anti-drug unit targeting street dealers everywhere, starting in Queens and redeploying again and again until the city was swamped with narcos. When the *Daily News* published an exclusive on its front page headlined "Bratton's Juggernaut," Giuliani reversed field on a concept he'd initially embraced.

Instead of going after dealers, the mayor was suddenly far more intent on pursuing leakers. "I want the people responsible found," he told Miller, a prime suspect himself. "And I want them dealt with." The plan stalled for more than a year when it finally began in Bratton's final days, redesigned as the Brooklyn North Drug Initiative. Even Bratton says Safir effectively orchestrated it after his departure, producing instant plunges in shooting and other statistics—"an effect, but for politics, that we would have had eighteen months earlier." But Bratton blasts Safir for "not replicating" the program across the city, and felony drug arrests, after three years of increases, dropped in 1997 by 10 percent even with all the additional manpower (they have rebounded a bit since).

The FBI index continued to decline in 1996, the last full year of statistics before Rudy's re-election campaign, implicitly indicating that it was Rudy, not Bratton, who was driving the numbers. That is precisely what Safir's empty suit was meant to suggest. By the 1997 campaign, Giuliani's TV ads were proclaiming, over black-and-white footage of a burnt-out neighborhood followed by color shots of happy children in a Brooklyn playground: "In less than four years, murders in Bushwick have fallen 55 percent. Overall, crime in Bushwick is down 50 percent. Some still want to turn the clock back. With Rudy Giuliani, Bushwick and neighborhoods across the boroughs will keep moving forward. And we're a whole lot safer for it."

Manhattan borough president Ruth Messinger, the Democrat who ran against him, wrote a 1996 letter to the city's two most powerful Democrats, Council Speaker Peter Vallone and Comptroller Alan Hevesi, asking them to examine the crime data. She did it after a Bronx captain close to the departed Timoney was deposed by Safir for doctoring numbers, but neither Vallone nor Hevesi did a thing. The chairman of the council's public safety committee, Sheldon Leffler, said he tried to hold a hearing on the stats, but quit when the NYPD wouldn't cooperate. Hevesi released an audit exposing NYPD mismanagement in 1998, but its focus was on the uneconomical use of cops to perform civilian functions. In it, he detailed nearly three years of stonewalling NYPD resistance to the study.

State Comptroller Carl McCall, another Democrat, launched an audit of the crime statistics, as well as performance probes of four other agencies. Giuliani had McCall's auditors thrown out of city agencies. He defied subpoenas. McCall sued and won at a lower court level, but Giuliani, even after losing a unanimous appellate decision as well, insisted on taking the case all the way up to the state's highest court, where he again lost unanimously in April 1999. Rudy promptly announced that he expected the court to rule as it did. Despite the losses, Giuliani succeeded in preventing a police probe for two and a half years. Then McCall dallied for ten months, waiting until February 2000 to finally launch it.

Ironically, Giuliani's position in the litigation against McCall was that the state comptroller was usurping Hevesi's charter-mandated function, even while the NYPD was vigorously blocking Hevesi, too. The end result was just what Rudy wanted: accountability to no one. The crime stats have never been examined by anyone outside 1 Police Plaza and City Hall.

Rudy questioned these numbers himself in 1993, and that was before four commanders in the Giuliani era had to be disciplined or fired for doctoring them. When the first full-year figures for 1994 were released, the mayor observed: "Nobody can be sure exactly what is going on," adding that he and Bratton could only lay claim to "about half" the drop in rates. No such caution has guided his comments for years. Instead the stats are worn like a badge—in Giuliani appearances all over America. The front-page *Times* story Dinkins never got has been printed twelve times in Giuliani tenure.

The manipulation of this data, as well as the attempt to steer observers away from any analysis that might cast doubt on Giuliani's role in the decline, has become a municipal science:

Total Index

The FBI just receives the data on the seven index crimes from local law enforcement agencies. It does not generate or confirm it. Yet most people think the numbers carry an FBI imprimatur.

In fact, the crime composite is a statistical nightmare. Murder your mom with a sledgehammer and it counts as one crime on the index. Take a twenty out of her purse and it counts the same. In fact, just try to take a twenty out of her purse, get spooked and run away without the twenty. A botched attempt at a crime counts the same.

That means a deep drop in any city's numbers could be deceiving. Thirteen percent of the total decline in the New York City crime rate between 1993 and 1997 was due to larcenies under $50; seventeen percent, larcenies under $200. Less than half of one percent was attributable to murder. Larceny in New York City fell 16.5 times the rate of decline in all cities over 100,000 in population, while its murder rate sunk at 2.3 times the average. Criminologists estimate that "no contact" occurs between thief and victim in 95 percent of all larcenies, so it is the least threatening crime.

Yet who can doubt that the overall decline in the first Giuliani term was outstanding? There was a 40.5 percent reduction in the index, better than in any of the other twenty-four cities with a population of 500,000 or more. Instead of just saying that, Giuliani started claiming—in a June 2, 1997 *Good Morning America* appearance, for example—that New York City was "the safest major city in the U.S.," adding "and those are the FBI statistics." That's the definition of gilding a lily.

If you were a piece of property, New York City was the second safest of the top twenty-five cities in 1997. If you were a person, it was thirteenth. It dropped to fourteenth in 1998, the latest available national breakdown of rates per 100,000 population. Since property crimes—burglary, larceny and auto theft—overwhelmingly outnumber violent crimes, New York City's overall rate did rank second lowest, right behind San Jose, California (population 861,000). But New York City was still eighth in murder, seventeenth in robbery and thirteenth in assault in 1998. Among violent crimes, the city's only number two ranking was in rape, the smallest category by far. It's only number one ranking was larceny. But visions of secure $20 bills inside mom's purse were not exactly what the term "safest city" conjured up.

Ahead of all but forty-one cities out of the 201 with populations over 100,000 — at the 80th percentile—wasn't a solid enough statistic for Rudy either. Even second of twenty-five wasn't. So his operations staff came up with a chart of their own, using FBI figures, ranking New York City first of the nine cities with populations over a million. As handy a sound bite as the chart for 1997 was, two of the cities—Philadelphia and Chicago—couldn't be counted because of incomplete data. Five had lower rates of violent crime, a comparison Giuliani's chart never mentioned.

The FBI, by the way, doesn't do any of these rankings themselves. They warn against them in the report that contains the numbers, saying "direct comparisons should be guarded against" because "dissimilarities" between cities "may bias the results."

Murder

Giuliani launched his 1997 re-election campaign by making a January 1 five-borough tour celebrating what he said was the first time in thirty years that the murder rate had fallen below a thousand. The *Post* ran a murder odometer throughout December 1996, culminating with the NYPD claim that only 983 homicides occurred. No one reported it when the Department of Health released its annual Vital Statistics report after the election, indicating that Medical Examiner Charles Hirsch, a mayoral appointee, actually found that there were 1,018 murders in 1996 (even the police later raised their total to 987). Since the difference of thirty-five between the initial NYPD total and the medical examiner's was only six greater than the year before, it was perfectly predictable when Giuliani was touting the number that the magical 1,000 barrier would remain intact in 1996.

The homicide rate is widely regarded as the least subjective of the otherwise soft crime numbers. Yet, one of the ways the city rate was artificially lowered in the past was to classify hundreds of probable homicides as "injury undetermined whether accidentally or purposefully inflicted." This means that the medical examiner could not determine if the death was an accident, a suicide or a homicide—the three categories of what are called deaths by external circumstances.

When Hirsch took over in Ed Koch's last year (1989), he was outraged at the extraordinary number of undetermined external deaths. Created as a new category in the 1960s, annual undetermineds grew to over 1,000 in the early 1970s and averaged over 700 in the 1980s, a far higher rate than elsewhere in the country. Hirsch immediately hired physician assistants as medico/legal investigators to make hard determinations. The number of mystery deaths plummeted as if on command, from 727 in 1988 to 186 in 1989. It went from two a day to one every two days.

Ellen Borakove, a spokeswoman for Hirsch, says: "Up to 1989, we didn't have anybody doing scene investigations. We had to depend on the police and there was an insufficient investigation of cases. Dr. Hirsch reached an agreement with City Hall when he was hired that he would be able to hire these investigators. We started out with eight. Now we have twenty-four. That's exactly why the number of undetermineds came down." After Hirsch closed the loophole, the murder rate seemed to soar in 1990, presenting David Dinkins with consecutive years of 2,000 plus murders.

The electorate was so alarmed by what appeared to be a city draped in blood, it handed the reins over to Rudy. But in fact, the real murder rate had exceeded 2,000 through most of the 1980s when everyone thought it was averaging around 1,750. The homicide share of an annual total of 700 undetermineds certainly topped the 250 more homicides required to reach 2,000.

As surely as undetermineds skewed Koch's and Dinkins's murder rates in opposite ways, they have had only a marginal effect on Giuliani's. The number is slightly lower under Giuliani than under Dinkins, but external deaths across the board are down. The percentage of external deaths that are undetermined has risen in the Giuliani era. It averaged 3.4 percent under Dinkins, and 4.9 percent in the first four Giuliani years. If the percent of undetermineds had remained flat under the two mayors, there would have been a total of 183 fewer undetermineds between 1993 and 1997. If most of those were murders, it would temper New York City's rate of decline, bringing it closer to the rate for a number of major cities.

The other category of external deaths that has, on at least one occasion, been a repository for a misclassified homicide is "other accidents." In 1996, Doris Roditi, a seventy-five-year-old resident of the Upper East Side, was beaten to death near her ATM, but for three weeks the case was listed by the NYPD as an accidental fall. The police changed their finding when the holdup team that killed her was caught mugging another elderly woman near the same ATM. Roditi's ATM card was found on one of the perpetrators.

Dr. Andrew Levine, who did the initial evaluation of Roditi in the Lenox Hill Hospital emergency room, said: "It's kind of a stretch to think it was an accident, but the police didn't do a full medical exam. It definitely looked like she was beaten up." Roditi's attorney Richard Bernstein said "her purse was missing and she had no identification on her." Yet the police who traced her through her apartment key did not figure out that she'd been robbed. Nor did they determine that thousands were taken from her ATM. Bernstein's secretary asked police why they assumed it was an accident, especially in view of Roditi's many broken bones, and "they said it was because her bones were frail."

While two categories of accident (auto and home) dropped slowly in the Giuliani years, "other accidents" like Roditi's, which occur on sidewalks and in other public places, grew in 1994 and 1995 by sixty-eight, or 19 percent. This growth followed years of a precipitous slide, with the 1993 number a third of what it was when Dinkins took office. The total did dip in Giuliani's third year, but rose in 1997 and fell again in 1998. "Other accidents" is the only form of external death to wind up higher in 1997 than 1993. Its share of all external deaths grew by 4 percent. Since the medical examiner barred a review of death certificates in this category, it is impossible to determine whether there are other cases like Roditi's (the ME had listed Roditi's case as "pending" until the ATM card was discovered). So even in the murder count, there is a subtle interplay of factors confounding the results.

The real issue, though, with the murder rate is what caused the 66 percent drop between 1993 and 1998? Drug dependence deaths decreased by 24 percent in the same five years, drug overdose poisonings by 71 percent. AIDS deaths dropped by 68 percent, AIDS cases by 65 percent. The infant mortality rate fell by 38 percent, and teenage births by 15 percent. Did Rudy do all of this? Did Jack Maple or Bill Bratton? The crack and AIDS chaos of the 1980s was replaced in the 1990s by a new culture that took firm hold in poor and minority communities. The worst part of the Giuliani expropriation of all credit for the crime turnaround is that communities get none.

When murder soars, the police aren't blamed. Ray Kelly, on his final day as Dinkins's police commissioner in 1993, attributed the crime wave in a rambling CNN interview "to family values . . . young people out there on the street with no supervision . . . the out of wedlock birthrate." No one in the city administration or the media reverses that diagnosis when crime plummets, even when every other social indicator points to a transformation of the culture of poverty.

What's the evidence that Rudy's crime strategies were the primary agent of change? The NYPD breaks murders down into two categories—those visible to police—that is, streets, stoops, parks—and those not visible to police, inside houses, office buildings, and so on. If a greater police presence caused the murder decline, incidents visible to cops would have dropped at a far faster rate than those not visible. Instead this figure has fluctuated from Giuliani year to year without any clear pattern.

Year	Decline in Visible Murders	Decline in Not-Visible Murders
1994	29%	4%
1995	22%	28%
1996	8%	28%
1997	29%	8%
1998	15%	22%

Not-visible murders fell faster than visible ones three out of five years and at a slightly faster overall pace.

The only police strategy cited as a plausible explanation for how it pushed murder down is the guns offensive boldly announced in early 1994 as Crime Strategy #1. The Giuliani theory is that aggressive policing caused criminals to stop carrying guns and, as Rudy put it in a 1999 congressional appearance, "led to a reduction in handgun-related homicides." Yet felony arrests for possession of dangerous weapons averaged 7,388 for the final three Dinkins years, peaking in 1991 at 7,820. Under Giuliani, the same arrests averaged 4,885 from 1994 through 1998.

The Giuliani team has explained its own declining weapon arrests by contending that criminals got the message after an initial wave of busts, leading to a reduction in subsequent arrests. But arrests dropped from the moment Giuliani took office, falling by 6 percent in 1994, the first Giuliani year. In the second year, they fell 25 percent. By 1999, felony weapon arrests were a third of what they were in Dinkins's last year. In fact gun seizures, according to NYPD records, dove 9 percent in 1994.

If weapons arrests and seizures changed criminal behavior, these numbers document that the busts happened on another mayor's watch, namely the mayor whose anti-crime record Candidate Rudy called a joke. That's the same mayor who got the surcharge financing that put 6,000 extra cops on Rudy's payroll. In fact, as little as it is known, murders fell by 299 (or 265, according to the medical examiner) in the same final years of Dinkins that weapon arrests peaked and new cops were hired. Sure, the tally tumbled at a far faster pace in the first two Giuliani years, but if either mayor deserves credit, which should get more? David Dinkins, during whose term a seven-year trend of upward murder figures was finally reversed? Or Rudy, who presided over the deepening of an already downward trend?

The truth is the murder plunge is not provably connected to either mayor's gun strategies. Neither is there any evidence that quality-of-life arrests had an appreciable impact on murder. Even Jack Maple, in his book *The Crime Fighter,* has debunked the Giuliani-promulgated notion that bolstered quality-of-life busts for urination or panhandling convinced serious criminals to go straight "because they picked up on the prevailing civility vibe." As Maple put it: "Rapists and killers don't head for another town when they see that graffiti is disappearing from the subways."

While increased drug arrests under Bratton (far less under Safir) may have had a minimal impact on murder numbers, the causal connection between a drug bust and reducing homicides is far more tenuous than the link between arrests for a loaded gun and killings. Either correlation is guesswork, but if the choice is between the effect of gun or drug arrests, the weapons numbers of the Dinkins era were undoubtedly more telling than the drug numbers of Giuliani time.

This is especially true since arrests of dealers increased between 1993 and 1997 by 15.8 percent, while arrests for use or possession rose an astonishing 138 percent. Similarly felony drug arrests rose 6.8 percent and misdemeanor busts 140.7 percent. With 88 percent of the upsurge due to possession and use arrests, the NYPD offensive was hardly focusing on the drug universe most likely to commit murder.

The final Giuliani argument is that better-deployed cops, with assignments determined by Compstat pin maps, have lowered murder and other crime rates. Bratton concedes that Compstat "didn't really get going" until the late summer of 1994. Like any other management innovation, it must have taken additional months for it to begin to impact on crimefighting in seventy-six precincts. Yet the biggest drop in murder—400 by the medical examiner's numbers—occurred in 1994. How could Compstat have caused it?

Contrary to Giuliani mythology about his supposedly fine-tuned military machine, the department's performance slipped since 1993 when judged by prime efficiency standards used prior to Rudy—the percent of cops on patrol and response time to emergencies. Even with thousands of additional cops, the average number of cops on daily patrol at the end of Giuliani's first term was no more than when Dinkins left office, making Giuliani's percent decidedly less.

Response time rose by two minutes during the first term—a 24 percent hike that has gotten even worse since. The number of emergencies simultaneously fell by 34 percent.

Only 27 percent of felony arrests in 1998 led to indictments, the lowest in decades. In Dinkins's last year, the rate was 38 percent. Criminologist Michael Jacobson, who was a commissioner under both mayors, sees the drop as "evidence of a diminution in the seriousness of the felony arrests."

By 1999, only 58 percent of the force was assigned to precincts, with a 14 percent increase in uniformed executive management positions since April 1997 and a 15 percent jump in cops doing administrative work at headquarters. Overtime is setting breathtaking records.

This mess is why Rudy resorts to the FBI stats as the sole measure of the department's effectiveness. But that's hardly the story in other cities where murder is way down.

The *Time* magazine story that cost Bill Bratton his job ranked Seattle ahead of New York City in the rate of homicide decline, so *Newsday*'s Lenny Levitt called Seattle's police department to ask them how they did it. While Giuliani and Bratton went to blows over credit, Seattle said: "In all honesty, we don't know why. It's too soon to tell whether it's a trend or a fluke." When murders hit a ten-year low in Orange County, the sheriff's office said: "As much as I'd like to give law enforcement the credit, I know there's a million other contributing factors." In San Diego, where dramatic crime drops have occurred despite the lowest ratio of cops per capita (a third of New York's), the police chief says: "The problem with claiming better policing is responsible is that someday crime is going to go up again, and I wouldn't want to be on the other side of that question."

The other factors that Rudy mugged a city, and now much of a state and nation, into ignoring range from the collapse of crack to the toughening of federal gun laws. Criminologists point to the fivefold increase of the state prison population since the introduction of the harsh Rockefeller drug laws—a boom that long predates Rudy. The record-shattering economic growth and job market had its effect. The downward drift of alcohol consumption rates—a bitter companion to violence—are featured in Justice Department studies.

Outside of New York, law enforcement officials praise trauma units for lowering murder rates, citing the 1990s explosion of lifesaving emergency techniques that have led to survival rates for shooting victims as high as 90 percent. Auto and home accidental deaths in New York City dropped a combined 28 percent from 1993 through 1998, a success story Rudy has yet to appropriate. With the particular success of trauma care in New York City, the murder plunge may be more an episode from *ER* than *NYPD Blue*.

Instead of making his personal focus on crime and organizational improvements like Compstat one limited cause among many for the drop in murders, Giuliani has given himself superhero status, as if he and his army caused killers to stop in their tracks. Instead of approaching the stats as flawed and cyclical measurements that undoubtedly overstate the downturn, he prattles on about them on every national television appearance, in his campaign ads and whenever he has a major budget, management or State of the City speech to give.

The problems with the data beyond murder, however, are far worse.

Larceny

Auto and Auto-Part Theft

These two crimes account for 42 percent of the total decline in the first four years. New York City's 60,197 drop in auto thefts between '93 and '97 exceeded the decline in the rest of the twenty-five largest cities combined by almost 12,000 stolen cars. The rate of auto theft per 100,000 population plummeted in New York three times faster than in these other cities.

The theft of parts and accessories—which is a category of larceny—dove 85.5 percent, from 48,722 in 1993 to 7,078 in 1997. Fifty-four percent of the overall decline in larceny—which is broken down into nine categories ranging from purse snatching to shoplifting—was due to this unprecedented, 41,644 drop, in cases involving the theft of vehicular parts. In Safir's first year, 1996, this category decreased by 16,163 or over 70 percent.

While Safir has claimed that auto-theft decline "has all been a part of aggressive law enforcement efforts," the only strategic change was a heightened NYPD pursuit of chopshops. It has never offered any numbers, however, documenting an increase in chopshop arrests. In any event, a 1989 Justice Department survey estimated that chopshops only accounted for 10 to 16 percent of car thefts, and since then, the department, and other law enforcement officials, have indicated that these operations are becoming increasingly obsolete.

The only auto theft initiative was announced in 1995, and stolen vehicles had already dropped by 17,044 or 15 percent in 1994, the second deepest reduction of any Giuliani year. In fact, motor vehicle theft was diving by 34,664 in Dinkins's final three years, far faster than any other crime.

The decreases had virtually nothing to do with policing since the NYPD reports that, from the beginning of Giuliani's first term, the only index crime that witnessed a minuscule upward trend in the ratio of arrests to complaints is auto theft. While the ratio doubled for murder, and nearly did the same for other index crimes, it was flat for auto theft. For every 100 auto thefts in 1993, seven arrests were made. For every 100 in 1997, nine arrests were made, by far the lowest ratio and lowest rate of increase for any index crime. (This does not necessarily mean the arrests were for crimes committed in the same year.)

The arrest ratio for auto theft (0.09) remained precisely the same for the last four available Giuliani years (1995–98). The actual number of arrests fell every Giuliani year, declining by 46.7 percent between '93 and '98. Arrests for felony possession of stolen property—a charge frequently filed against chopshops—also fell every year, dipping 34.5 percent.

Larceny arrests—for auto parts and every other category—increased a paltry 2 percent over the same five years. Despite a drop in larceny offenses that outpaced every other large and medium-sized city in the country, the city's ratio of arrests to complaints remained the lowest of any index crime other than auto theft (15 arrests per 100 occurrences). If cops weren't causing the downturn in auto or auto part theft, what did account for it?

One explanation is a dramatic improvement and proliferation of effective auto security systems, the sales of which particularly boomed in areas like New York City with high long-term rates of auto theft. New York is also one of the few states that has mandated insurance discounts for the installation of these devices, and industry analysts confirm that sales of these systems have risen disproportionately in areas of the country like New York City where auto theft has been historically high. Studies indicate that when auto-makers add engine-immobilizing systems to cars, theft falls as much as two-thirds from one model year to the next.

Another reason is the passage of federal auto theft bills in 1992, 1994 and 1996. Among many changes, the legislation put in place the National Motor Vehicle Title Information System and the National Stolen Auto Part Information System. These bills made dealing in stolen parts a federal crime, and reinforced requirements that went into effect into 1987 requiring the Vehicle Idenitification Number (VIN) marking of fourteen major parts. A 1998 Justice Department evaluation of the effect of these legal changes indicates that cars with marked parts had "lower theft rates as strong as 20 percent." By 1996, the department concluded, auto theft investigators thought marking was having a significant impact on part and auto theft, "with the greatest effect on chopshop operators." New York City was historically the chopshop capital of American car theft.

Technology, too, has been pushing the theft of parts down. By the mid-1990s, cars were increasingly equipped with radios that were inoperable if stolen. Other frequently stolen parts, like an accessible computer chip once often stolen from General Motors cars, disappeared in new models. Many of the new security systems that made auto theft more difficult also made part theft tougher. While higher drug arrests, for example, might have removed potential amateur car thieves from the street, no other Giuliani-era action is cited by insurers as in any way contributing to the auto and part drop, which drove the overall reduction in index crimes.

Theft from an Auto

A second category of larceny involving stolen packages, suitcases or clothes from a vehicle has followed an entirely different pattern than the theft of parts or cars. Its small 12 percent drop in the same four-year period when part theft fell 85 percent reinforces the inference that security systems and part marking, not police tactics, are the primary agents of change.

The theft of loose items in a car dropped from 55,865 to 49,302 between 1993 and 1997, a decline of only 6,563 compared to the virtual elimination of vehicular part theft. Thieves are only slightly less likely to steal a camera from a car than they were before Giuliani, believing apparently that they can get away quickly with a salable item. Radios that won't work if stolen, parts with VIN numbers, screaming alarms and the rest of the security revolution have combined to make package theft the most attractive remaining option for street thieves.

The relative stability of this figure compared with the theft of parts is also attributable to insurance and police reporting practices. Insurers are far less likely to require a police report to cover the cost of a stolen part. But they always require a police report for a stolen package. The insurer has no evidence other than a client's written claim to the police that a camera was stolen. When an airbag is stolen, however, the repair shop bills for installing a new one. The bill is all the paper needed for payment.

The NYPD has increasingly required people reporting a stolen part to go to the precinct and fill out a report. It does not usually send cops to the car or home, nor will it take the report over the phone. Since insurers do not routinely require a report, victims don't bother to go to precincts. On the other hand, since insurers require reports for stolen packages that are covered, victims make sure one is filed even if they have to visit a precinct. Police will often come to a vehicle if a valuable package is taken and write a report. Insurance requirements appear to have more to do with the level of these two index crimes than any Giuliani-era strategy.

Shoplifting and Coin Machines

The only specific form of larceny to increase between 1993 and 1997 was shoplifting, which went up by 5,185 incidents or 33 percent. It is also the category least susceptible to police adjustment since it is determined by complaints filed by businesses. Just as with auto package theft, insurers require stores to file police reports to make shoplifting claims, so the complaint figures come closer to reality. How does Giuliani explain why shoplifting would explode when other forms of theft whose measurement is more malleable to police are plummeting?

On the other hand, the larceny and full FBI index category of greatest decline, decreasing even faster than auto parts, was theft from coin machines. Never a large number, coin machine thefts practically disappeared during Rudy's first term, nosediving 90 percent from 5,983 to 574. Not even Safir has claimed he's put a cop by every Snickers bar dispenser.

Fred Miller, a security consultant with the National Automatic Merchandising Association, says the 574 is "ridiculously low," adding that Giuliani's drop is "due to underreporting or extremely conservative statistics." Miller also believes that vending machine theft is down because of a number of security advances—pick-resistant locks inside and outside the machine, camera systems and pagers that activate if a machine is opened. Frank McLoughlin, a Bell Atlantic executive, cited four innovations that have made city payphones more secure—including new electronic systems that warn the central office when a coin box is getting full and when a phone has been broken into, as well as carbon-treated, specially reinforced steel bars.

Public Buildings

In the same league as coin machine theft is larceny from public buildings—particularly, in New York, office buildings. This is to be distinguished from *burglary* in public buildings, which involves illegal entry. Larceny occurs during business hours and the perpetrator is an employee, a messenger or a visitor who entered legally. Building larcenies fell 11,750 or 23 percent between '93 and '97. The slide was so large it accounted for 15 percent of the entire larceny drop. Like Snickers bars, not even Safir claims the NYPD has been guarding every loose laptop on the 25th floor.

Mike Julian, an ex-NYPD commander under Dinkins and Giuliani now in building security, says the reduction in these thefts is largely due to new procedures in most office buildings, requiring outsiders to get sign-in lobby clearance before boarding elevators, as well as surveillance techniques throughout buildings. He also said he knew of attempts to increase restaurant and midtown building collars, but the overall ratio of larceny arrests to complaints has remained so low throughout the Giuliani years, crimebusting couldn't have much to do with the drop.

If these four categories are added together—auto, parts and accessories, coin machine and building theft—they account for nearly half (48.8 percent) of the total decline in index crime during the first Giuliani term. In the rest of New York State, the decrease in these four categories accounts for only 34 percent of the drop. Technology, insurance requirements or reporting changes are responsible for most of this reduction.

Burglary

Attempted Force

The one number in the index that screams "manipulation" is the stunning decline of this form of burglary—one of the three categories of burglary that appear in the FBI breakdown. The other two categories are forcible entry and no-force burglaries. The first category dropped during Rudy's initial term and the second rose—both within the range of possibility. But attempted-force burglaries virtually disappeared. The NYPD's top statistical analyst, Anthony Voelker, told the

Times in 1982 that the city's statistics were honest, but spelled out how easy it would be to change them: "You just don't count attempted burglaries or attempted robberies and your burglary and robbery numbers will look much lower."

Essentially a victimless crime since no entry is made and no property stolen, burglary attempts fell from 17,223 in 1993 to 1,813 in 1997, an 89 percent plummet exceeded by only one other category of crime—coin machine theft.

What is even more astounding is that the figure rose under Bratton and then, in Safir's first year (1996), sank from 30,602 to 4,131. This 86.5 percent dive in a single year is unparalleled in any other New York City crime category. Policing can't begin to explain so dramatic a descent since there was only a 5 percent increase in burglary arrests over these four years, and the ratio of arrests to complaints went from eight per 100 incidents to sixteen. The number of additional arrests is so small—414—it can't possibly have deterred that many putative burglars.

The 15,414-incident drop in this category over four years is so out of line that it more than triples the combined 4,525 decline in the other twenty-two major cities combined. Attempted-force burglaries tumbled in New York City by a rate of 209.7 per 100,000 population, while they dipped in the other cities by 22.9. New York City went from the city with the highest rate to one of the four lowest. The fall-off in the percentage of attempts was seven times more in New York City than in any of the top cities.

In the rest of New York State, attempted burglaries held virtually steady at 7 percent of all burglaries for four years. In New York City, where the percentage of attempted burglaries had fluctuated little for several prior years, it suddenly went from 17 percent in 1993 to 41 percent in 1995 to 3 percent in 1997.

The police tactics that changed this number involved reporting procedures—it is a paperwork, not a crimefighting, triumph. Victims of attempted break-ins were increasingly told they had to come to the precinct to report it, where lines or obnoxious clerks awaited them. With nothing stolen, no police report was necessary for insurance reasons, so few made the trip.

The data also indicates that many burglaries were downgraded to felony possession of burglary tools, a charge that does not count in the index. At a time when burglaries were falling 46 percent, burglary-tool arrests exploded 1,050 percent, from 735 in '93 to 8,449 in '97. This leap includes a one-year bounce—Safir's 1996—of 3,130 cases. Before this unprecedented burst, burglary-tool arrests averaged 743 during Dinkins's last three years. The total for this usually rare crime in the rest of the state fell from 350 in '93 to 286 in '97.

The near-disappearance of attempted-force burglary in New York City was responsible for 34 percent of the burglary and 5.5 percent of the total index decline.

The 26,471 plunge in 1996 accounted for 45 percent of the entire drop in the index that year. Without it, Safir and Giuliani would have been stuck with running in Rudy's re-election on a meager 7.3 percent decrease, instead of the announced 13.3 percent drop. Since Bratton's overall rate of decline the year before was 16.6 percent, a decline less than half that size would have invited damaging press and public questions about the effect of Bratton's forced exit.

Public Buildings

Burglaries of all types that occurred in nonresidential buildings during the business day dropped from 9,607 to 800. This 92 percent reduction was almost double the rate of decline for residential burglary during the day and nearly triple the rate of decline for nighttime burglary in residential or nonresidential buildings. Daytime nonresidential burglary elsewhere in the state slipped a mere 7 percent in the same period.

This wholesale burglary drop in public buildings is similar to the larceny downturn in the same locations. (Larceny involves legal entry, burglary illegal entry.) The combination suggests that some of the nonresidential burglary reduction was prompted by the factors cited by former commander Julian for the drop in building larceny—namely, sign-ins and surveillance cameras. Sophisticated security systems in homes and offices have boomed in New York City in the last few years as well, making all forms of burglary more difficult.

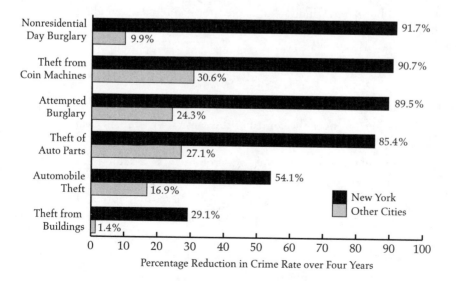

Percentage Reduction in Crime Rate over Four Years

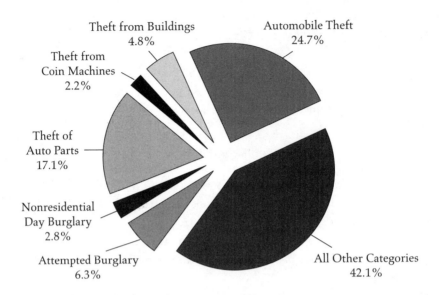

Theft from Buildings
4.8%

Automobile Theft
24.7%

Theft from
Coin Machines
2.2%

Theft of
Auto Parts
17.1%

Nonresidential
Day Burglary
2.8%

Attempted Burglary
6.3%

All Other Categories
42.1%

In any event, no one at City Hall or the NYPD has claimed to have introduced a policing strategy responsible for the public building decrease, which lowered the total index by 3.6 percent. When that part of the index decline is added to the percent prompted by the slashing of attempted-force burglaries and the four questionable categories of larceny, 57.9 percent of Giuliani's much-ballyhooed plunge is either up in the air or primarily attributable to causes that have little to do with effective police work. (This figure is adjusted to account for the overlay between the two subcategories of burglary included—attempted-force and public-building burglaries.)

Assault

Downgrading

Why would arrests for the index crime of aggravated assault, a Class B felony, increase by 16 percent over the course of the same four Giuliani years that arrests for third-degree assault, a non-index Class A misdemeanor, shot up by 82.7 percent? Why would arrests for simple or second-degree assault—a Class D felony that does not appear on the FBI index either—grow by 60 percent? Since the gravity of injury is the primary difference between these three forms of assault, were arrested assailants just getting gentler—committing assaults that "inflicted" less "bodily harm"? The sharp upturn of these lesser categories of assault—which depend on a cop's reading of the circumstances and the statutes—indicates an attempt to classify assaults downward.

Strong-Arm Assaults

The precipitous drop in this type of aggravated assault—which involves the use of fists and feet—also suggests a conscious pattern of downgrading. Between '93 and '97, these physical-force assaults fell by 5,009, according to the FBI index break-down. This 61 percent decline was exceeded only by the slide in handgun attacks among the five kinds of aggravated assault.

Strong-arm attacks bottomed out in Safir's infamous 1996, when they hit a low of 1,877 cases, a better than four-fold drop in Giuliani's first three years. These weaponless attacks were 13 percent of all assaults when Giuliani took office and still 10 percent in 1995. But in 1996, they plummeted to 4 percent. The absence of a weapon in these assaults gives police the maximum discretion in reporting them. Many may well have wound up classified as simple or third-degree assaults.

Similarly, cops also have more discretion when an assault occurs on a street, as opposed to a residence or public building, where complaints are frequently more formal and taken in front of witnesses. Assaults on streets and other undefined lo-cations accounted for 89 percent of the drop, while assaults in residences barely decreased at all (from 19,838 to 18,739 in four years). In fact, assaults in residences rose from 32 percent of all index assaults in '93 to 42 percent by '96.

The proportion of the decline in index assaults attributable to the two categories most susceptible to ambiguous classification—strong-arm and street—dovetails with the inexplicably disproportionate rise in non-index felony assault arrests. The only explanation for these simultaneous trends is an effort to artificially shift assaults out of index classifications and into categories no one in the media ever notices.

Robbery

Convenience Stores vs. Streets

The largest increase in index crime by far over these four years was in store holdups, which went up an astronomical 518 percent, from 174 to 1,076. The Giuliani administration has never discussed this figure, which is based on calls, alarms and complaints from the looted businesses. Like the rising number of shoplifting cases, store holdups minimize departmental reporting discretion.

Maximum discretion on robbery incidents, like assaults, occurs on streets/high-ways and in alleys, where robberies have declined by 23,227 or 46 percent. These street muggings account for 56 percent of the total drop in robbery. Robberies at banks and residences decreased at a slower pace, though gas station holdups fell by 59 percent in 1997.

Also like assault, the police have more reporting discretion when a robbery is committed without a weapon. Strong-arm robberies, too, have fallen disproportionately, accounting for 51 percent of the drop in the five categories of robbery. Moving from 37 percent of all robberies to 24 percent, the drop in the city's number of robberies that are committed by physical force alone is three times greater than the average of the twenty-two top cities. Only one other city, Memphis, had a 13 percent slide.

A large part of the robbery downturn consists of street muggings without a weapon—the most easily fudged stickup. Since attempted robbery and attempted assault are not broken down in publicly disclosed data, unlike burglary, it is impossible to tell how much of the strong-arm and street reductions in either category are merely attempts, where nothing was actually taken.

O ther than rape, the decline of every index crime is suspect. Sometimes the issue is a calculated misappropriation of credit, as in motor-vehicle or coin-machine theft. Sometimes, it's a resistant reporting protocol, as with attempted force burglary or auto part theft. In other categories, particularly murder, the incongruous magic-bullet theory is transparently designed to credit a lone achiever.

Assault has become an all-in-the-eye-of-the-beholder happenstance, public buildings a videotaped sanctuary of private security. Unarmed robbers are suddenly almost extinct, and burglars who almost never commit a burglary prowl the streets in historic numbers equipped with the tools of an abandoned trade.

This combination has turned Rudy's self-proclaimed triumph into a dark doubt. Clearly, no one in polished brass has stepped forward to confess to participating in a conspiracy of feigned crimelessness. But the numbers do indeed speak for themselves. They are being misused.

The hocus-pocus started with squeegees. Candidate Rudy promised to wash them out of our hair. While they seemed everywhere, an NYPD report found that there were only seventy-five of them in 1993, planted like Calvin Klein billboards in unavoidable locations. So Ray Kelly, the police commissioner who worked for Dinkins, heard Giuliani's campaign cry and drove the squeegees off the streets before Rudy raised his own Windex-free right hand on inaugural day.

The whole world, years later, thinks Rudy did it—the predictable result of endless repetition. But Bill Bratton himself conceded in his 1998 book that by the time he arrived at police headquarters, the squeegees were gone, noting that "ironically Giuliani and I got the credit for the initiative." Only politics, Bratton concluded, "prevented David Dinkins and Ray Kelly from receiving their due."

Mike Julian, the top commander under Dinkins who devised the squeegee strategies and stayed under Bratton, says he heard Giuliani salute himself for stopping squeegees at a 1995 event and approached Cristyne Lategano. "I told her you ought to drop that. I said Dinkins did it and that the records are there. I said they didn't need to do this, they had their own record. She seemed to agree."

Two days before Christmas in 1997, recently re-elected Rudy, gloating at a press conference, was asked about squeegees: "That one started with me," he declared. "I remember when I called Bill Bratton and told him to do it. I don't even think he was aware of the squeegee operators when I told him about it." Squeegees were the debut of the real Crime Strategy #1: Make Rudy Marshal Dillon.

Graffiti was another Giuliani fantasy. In a 1999 keynote address at the Heritage Foundation in Washington, Giuliani said that he'd recently been watching a tape of the John Huston movie *Prizzi's Honor*, and noticed, "at one point in the film, a subway traveling on an elevated part of the tracks" that was covered with graffiti. "When I saw it, I was sitting at home. I said to myself, 'Subway trains don't look like that anymore.' And then I said, 'Oh yeah, you did that.'" A year earlier, on the *Today Show*, he proudly proclaimed: "We've reduced graffiti by 90–95 percent."

Actually, a state agency, the Metropolitan Transit Authority, runs the subway system. Its web site lists May 12, 1989 as the date of one of three "key events" in subway history—the day the last graffiti-covered train was taken out of service. Rudy was just about to announce his first failed run for the mayoralty and the MTA had just put 1,775 new cars and 2,810 refurbished cars into service. What kept the graffiti off the cars was the much-publicized campaign of the then new Transit Authority police chief, Bill Bratton, whose pioneering quality-of-life campaign in the subways between 1990 and 1992 was what attracted Rudy to him in the first place.

Between the Bratton graffiti busts and a new MTA effort to wash trains with new, powerful, cleaning solutions within hours of any new graffiti—all instituted while Rudy was at Anderson Kill taking lessons on how to be a mayor—the system was widely celebrated as graffiti-free when the Democratic convention came to New York in 1992. "Did I get off the plane in Toronto or what?" asked Bill Geist on CBS.

In fact, by the time Rudy was striking his Mr. Clean pose at the Heritage Foundation, the MTA was sadly declaring that nearly all of the system's 5,800 cars were afflicted with scratchitti—the etching of nicknames into subway windows and walls, using everything from razor blades to keys. On many cars, every window is defiled. It got so bad that the agency stopped measuring scratched graffiti on passenger environment surveys. Why keep writing 100 percent each quarter?

The mayor might not have noticed scratchitti since the only time he actually sees a subway, by his own admission, is on a VCR.

The single most damaging shot at the Giuliani crime façade was fired in March 2000 by Fox Butterfield, the *Times*'s trenchant crime reporter who did a story that showed that other big cities, unlike New York, had managed to record "as big or even larger drops in violence while employing strategies that have ended up improving race relations." Citing San Diego and Boston as "national models of policing," Butterfield found "a sense of sadness" about the "great opportunity squandered" in Giuliani land.

Rana Sampson, a former NYPD sergeant who is director of public safety for the University of San Diego, told Butterfield: "New York has paid a huge price." Jeremy Travis, a former NYPD deputy commissioner who runs the National Institute of Justice, said the challenge was to bring crime down while enhancing public confidence in police. "That is what dropped out of the picture in New York," he said.

Butterfield—in this and other pieces over the years—has been an exception in the coverage of the New York crime phenomenon. Despite the frequent transparency of Giuliani's media manipulation of this data, his self-serving bluster on crime has worked. Even his critics have ceded him credit for the cut without demanding a logical explanation of just how his strategies produced these results. Ruth Messinger, his 1997 opponent, paid homage on crime, mostly to try to establish her own reasonableness. She knew that to do otherwise—in the face of a media mountain of tributes—would be to quarrel with common wisdom. When Hillary Clinton squared off against him in early 2000, she seemed to take the same tack.

Rudy's zero tolerance on crime for auditors, citizen groups or reporters with questioning minds has helped him keep his secret. He has spent millions on commercials—in the 1997 election and more recently during his brief Senate campaign—convincing everyone in the city or state with a television set that he killed crime. His partisan and ideological fans have celebrated him for it. None of that will make it so.

Eighteen

Soap Opera Schools

S CHOOLS CHANCELLOR RUDY CREW WAS, FOR A MOMENT, THE PERFECT
match for his namesake and champion.

An imposing bear of a black man, he was lucid and lettered, smoothly comfortable in a white world, privately engaging and publicly discreet, resolute yet accommodating. Born in upstate Poughkeepsie, he lost his mother at two and was raised by an exacting father who played jazz clarinet, worked three jobs, put him in Catholic school and opened his ears to the sounds of Ellington and Coltrane.

By the time Crew married his Italian-American high school sweetheart in his early twenties, he had already adopted her family as his own second family. Even after their twenty-year marriage ended, he thought of their four children as half-Italian and himself as part-paisan. Two of his three closest aides as chancellor were Italian-American women—deputy chancellor Judith Rizzo and press secretary Chiara Coletti.

Though Crew was hardly the mayor's first choice in October 1995, Giuliani had helped make him the $245,000-a-year chancellor, moving him from the 65,000-kid Tacoma, Washington system to the pinnacle of his profession, running schools with 1.1 million young lives on the line. With a Ph.D. from the University of Massachusetts and a charisma that turned on urban kids, Crew had the street swagger to go with his shades and black leather jacket and the sophistication to awe a tuxedo-clad business dinner at the Waldorf.

In addition to Tacoma, the forty-five-year-old, velvet-toned Crew had been superintendent in Sacramento and deputy superintendent in Boston. He brought a couple of top aides from Boston to New York, making the schools a second Bostonian outpost, akin to Bratton's NYPD, in the Giuliani realm.

The seven-member Board of Education actually hired Crew and only two were Giuliani appointees (the rest were named by borough presidents). But Giuliani controlled the board's budgetary purse strings. He'd driven Crew's predecessor, Ramon Cortines, out of town. And when the board temporarily picked a replacement for Cortines the mayor didn't like, Giuliani used his mayoral clout to get the appointment rescinded overnight. Crew knew he could only succeed if Rudy Giuliani let him. He also knew Rudy would only let him if he liked him.

Cortines was an object lesson in what happens to a chancellor Giuliani doesn't like.

Cortines was named to the job in a four-to-three vote in the summer of 1993, while Giuliani and Dinkins were in the middle of their second campaign. The so-called Gang of Four that voted for him was, strangely enough, aligned with Candidate Rudy. Dinkins's two appointees voted against Cortines. Two of Cortines's backers—Staten Island's Mike Petrides, an appointee of Guy Molinari, and Ninfa Segarra—were active in Giuliani's campaign.

The Gang got its name when it forced Chancellor Joseph Fernandez out of his job, joining Cardinal John O'Connor and Giuliani in blasting Fernandez for introducing a curriculum designed to teach tolerance for gays to kids as young as first and second graders. Since the board president in 1989, Robert Wagner Jr., gave Candidate Giuliani veto power over Fernandez's appointment, he was the first chancellor hired with Rudy's approval to be forced from office by Rudy or his allies.

Cortines's selection by the same foursome—led by Petrides, who was playing a managing role in the Giuliani campaign—deflected any criticism that the dismissal of Fernandez was anti-gay. Cortines came to New York from San Francisco, where he'd been outed as gay by a local magazine. When Cortines got to New York, ACT-Up demanded that he announce his sexual orientation. Single and sixty-two years old, Cortines refused and the issue disappeared.

But after Rudy was elected and intermediary Petrides resigned due to illness, Cortines could never get comfortable with the Giuliani team at City Hall. He had an intensely private correctness about him, a stiffness that did not mix well with the locker-room style of Giuliani's old-boys network. Giuliani's early budget woes led him to target the Board a month after his 1994 inauguration, demanding cuts Cortines was institutionally obligated to resist. Rudy took the resistance as personal. A Mexican-American born in Texas who'd run three substantial school systems in California, Cortines was offended when the mayor kept insisting he cut 2,500 jobs. Cortines insisted Giuliani did not have the authority to specify what cuts would have the least damaging effect on the system. That was his right.

So he was summoned alone in April to Gracie Mansion for a late-night emergency meeting, kept waiting for an hour and then threatened. Surrounded by several aides, Giuliani demanded Cortines fire his top press and finance staffers. The mayor said he was going to name Herman Badillo, his former running mate, as a fiscal monitor over the schools. Cortines waited a day or so and quit. Only the intervention of Mario Cuomo, who was still in the process of building his relationship with Giuliani, resolved the dispute. Cortines agreed to stay, Badillo took his post and an armistice was reached. Within days of Cuomo's defeat, however, war broke out again.

That December, Rudy began what the *Times* called "a vitriolic public campaign" to force Cortines to quit. Some of it was budgetary, with the mayor announcing a second year of slashing cuts. Some was of it was serious policy differences, with Rudy pressing to get the NYPD to control school security. But the undercurrent was decidedly personal.

Cortines "spent yesterday whining," Giuliani told reporters in June, "which he does all the time and you fall for it." He branded Cortines "the little victim." His admonition that Cortines should not "be so precious"—a reference to what Giuliani called Cortines's hypersensitivity to criticism—was a strange choice of language. It had a gay-baiting tone to it that may not have been intended, but was widely suspected.

The mayor made several significant gay appointments at the start of his administration, like Taxi & Limousine chairman Chris Lynn. His policies over the years became increasingly pro-gay, such as his 1997 extension of medical benefits to the gay partners of city workers. But there had not been any high-level gay involvement in his campaign or at City Hall. Pulitzer Prize–winning columnist Sydney Schanberg reported top aides to Giuliani were telling reporters that Cortines was peculiar. "He is not married, they say. He has no children, his lifestyle is reclusive." The columnist quoted one aide as saying: "This guy is weird. Would you want him alone with your family?"

When Cortines quit a second time—on June 11, 1995—he told the *Times* that he believed Giuliani "simply disliked" him. "I won't discuss that"—he said, refusing to elaborate about the perceived animus—"I will never discuss that." Shortly before he left town in October, Cortines allowed a *New York* magazine reporter to join him and Ed Koch, a Cortines friend and ally, at a midtown restaurant for lunch. Asked if the epithets Rudy tossed at him injected sexual orientation into the debate, Cortines said: "I don't know if that's it. You know, I've dealt with innuendo all my life." Koch, who'd had his own experience with Giuliani innuendo and was just beginning to slam him, said that "forcing Ray's resignation" was "the worst thing Rudy did as mayor."

What happened in the aftermath of Cortines's resignation was also an object lesson for Crew.

The board began interviewing candidates and settled on a first choice, Bernard Gifford, a black former vice chancellor with impressive corporate consulting credentials. Giuliani insisted Gifford support his call for line-item mayoral budget control and an NYPD takeover of school security. Gifford withdrew.

Then in September, the mayor made his own public pick—Leon Goldstein, the president of a CUNY community college awash with Democratic patronage hires, including the wives of two assembly speakers and the spouses of five other powerful Brooklyn pols. A sixty-three-year-old shmoozer and showman, Goldstein's academic background was in hotel management. The only CUNY president without a Ph.D., he had been rejected five prior times in chancellor searches at the board and CUNY. Goldstein's candidacy was quickly attacked in a swath of scandal stories, yet Rudy stood by him. The leak of a confidential report to the board—replete with charges against Goldstein—finally forced him to withdraw.

Rightly or wrongly, Rudy blamed the leak on an aide to board president Carol Gresser. She had been an ally of his going back to the 1993 dismissal of Fernandez, but their disagreement on Gifford and Goldstein changed all that. When Gresser next championed a Long Island Hispanic, Daniel Domenech, getting four votes for him at a Friday meeting in early October, the mayor leaned on one member of Gresser's majority, Jerry Cammarata. The Staten Island appointee of Guy Molinari, Cammarata collapsed after a Gracie Mansion visit and switched his vote twenty-four hours later, sinking Domenech. "The press will be on me for a couple of days," Cammarata explained to Domenech, "but the mayor will be after me forever."

Cammarata was a character right out of the Molinari circus, changing his party registration four times in eight years. He ran for a district school board on Staten Island in 1993 on a church-backed slate, proclaiming that he would ensure that parochial schools, where his three kids went, were safe from gun-toting public school kids. Then he was ejected on election day from a public school polling site after police discovered he was carrying a licensed .38 caliber pistol.

He also lay claim to three Guinness Book world records. He sang for forty-eight straight hours at Nathan's Famous hot dog stand in Coney Island, seventy-five hours while sitting in a bathtub perched atop a flatbed truck riding all over the city and ninety-six hours in a subway songfest celebrating Richard Nixon's resignation. It was unclear if Guinness was keeping track of breakneck conversions by public officials who couldn't take the heat.

Chancellor for a day, Domenech was actually the third Latino forced from the post by the Giuliani team in two years. Unlike Fernandez and Cortines, however, Domenech had not come to power with Giuliani's support. In promoting Goldstein and blocking Domenech, Giuliani forged an alliance with Brooklyn board member Bill Thompson, the only black on the board and a supporter of a candidate waiting in the wings, Rudy Crew.

Gresser had leaned toward Crew before the Goldstein and Domenech battles, but Crew demurred, only willing to take the job with Giuliani's endorsement. "If you didn't have both people on board," he said later, "it was going to be near impossible to do the job, let alone get it." So Crew flew to the city without anyone in the press knowing, quietly meeting with Giuliani at the mansion. He wanted Giuliani to hear three things: "I'm a Democrat. I'm a black man. And I'm not afraid of you. That's what I am about."

Crew wanted to establish from the outset that he "would not work in an atmosphere of fear" and the Cortines experience taught him that he had to make that explicit. He and the mayor also talked policy, even getting to the issue that would be their eventual undoing: vouchers. "I spoke plainly about my history of opposition to them at our very first meeting," he recalls. "And he said he wasn't interested in them either." Giuliani and Crew also agreed that the system needed to be shaken up, reformed, challenged.

With two years to go before re-election, the mayor had what he thought he needed: a black chancellor with a commanding presence and résumé who could serve as a prophylactic in 1997, protecting him against criticism on school performance. A professional and personal relationship began at that first meeting and lasted three years, until the mayor's changing political ambitions killed it. Though Giuliani would lay claim in the good years to having installed Crew, the truth is he turned to him only after a series of false starts.

Giuliani was as uncertain about what to do with the school system as he was about who should head it. He knew he wanted cops in the schools—tackling crime was always his first instinct. He knew he could rail about administrative bloat day in and day out, demanding dramatic reductions to the salute of every editorial page. That was it; that was his education program.

He could count on the fact that no one would notice—while he ranted for six years about board bureaucracy—that the number of police department managers grew by 79 percent, and fire department managers by 120 percent between 1993 and 1999. Neither would anyone note a 46 percent jump in administrators and managers in all the mayoral agencies directly under Giuliani's control, with an astounding 943 percent jump at the city's law department.

As limited as his school repertoire was, he never talked to Crew or Cortines about teaching and learning—only governance and budget. "He thought schools were a series of episodes, Round I, Round II," Crew says now. "He had no pedagogical commitment, no educational philosophy, no grounding in a belief system." Without any

real ideas about how to make schools work, Giuliani was unsure if he'd ever be able
to conjure statistics out of the system salable in a thirty-second campaign commercial. He wound up wandering from one side of school issues to the other:

Candidate Rudy championed the breakup of the central board, the establishment of borough boards and "forceful" actions to "assure that responsibility for
educational policy is established at the community school board level." As mayor,
he dropped the idea of borough boards and backed a new state law that vastly diminished the powers of community boards, centralizing power.

Candidate Rudy assailed Dinkins for responding to the "chaos" of the system
by simply demanding "that he should have control" of the board. "The truth is
that there is much that a mayor can do with the current arrangement that has not
been done," Giuliani contended in a nineteen-page issue paper. Though he accused
Dinkins of seeking "dictatorial power" over the board, Mayor Rudy adopted the
same position on mayoral control, portraying himself in recent years as an out-
sider and critic, unaccountable for its failings.

Candidate Rudy favored "increasing the opportunity for choice" within the
public school system; Mayor Rudy became a champion of private and parochial
school vouchers.

Candidate Rudy bemoaned chancellor turnover, saying the city's only response
to school failings "has been to change centralized leadership." Each new chancellor, he said, "has been brought to the job with great fanfare and a hope that their
particular style or initiative will be able to turn the system around." But these
leaders "of the slow, overburdened system have not been able to improve the system's performance in any measurable way." He even objected when Dinkins in-
terceded in the chancellor selection process in 1993, contending a mayor should
only comment when the board came up with a candidate.

With that much equivocation, and the baggage of Giuliani's two years of school
wars, the mayor needed Crew almost as much as Crew needed him. Crew understood that and, from the beginning, he demonstrated a political agility in leverag-
ing their mutual needs that none of Giuliani's other top appointees, including
media master Bratton, could equal.

Crew immediately replaced the finance deputy Giuliani had pushed Cortines to
fire with the analyst in the mayor's office who monitored the board's budget. Crew
set up weekly meetings at City Hall with the mayor. He produced a mind-numbing,
forty-one-volume set of books detailing how the board spent every cent, winning
the mayor's praise for laying bare the labyrinth. He navigated the turbulent NYPD-
takeover waters masterfully, attributing his hesitancy to the board, most of whose

members were opposed. But he kept an open mind and quietly negotiated a deal the mayor could buy, taking three years to do it.

He also joined Giuliani in a 1996 coup to topple Gresser as board chair. Giuliani complained about her to Crew, calling her "a housewife who lacked the intellectual weight to warrant conversations." The mayor put the four board votes together over the July 4 weekend, while Gresser was in Maine, preparing for her newborn granddaughter's arrival from the hospital. Crew dropped one negative quote on her in a June interview and stayed out of the way when the ax fell, letting Giuliani take center stage alone.

Most importantly, Crew reinforced the critical political alliances Giuliani had with the United Federation of Teachers and District Council 37, establishing excellent ties of his own with the two unions that represented most board employees.

Giuliani was particularly conscious of the power of the 90,000-member UFT; its phone bank and field operation had played a key role in his 1989 defeat. Their neutrality in the 1993 election—combined with their million-dollar "apolitical" ad campaign assailing Dinkins—helped Giuliani win. Giuliani attempted to ingratiate himself with UFT president Sandra Feldman early on, going to a rare private dinner at her home on December 2, 1994, along with Peter Powers and his wife Kathleen, who worked at the board.

When Ray Cortines suggested reducing such UFT perks as sabbaticals and preparation periods to close the board's 1995 budget gap, Feldman went ballistic and Labor Commissioner Randy Levine called Cortines aides to oppose the workrule savings.

Giuliani simultaneously supported state legislation authorizing early retirement bonuses for teachers in 1995 and 1996 even though his campaign issue paper criticized Dinkins's 1991 bonuses for inducing the most experienced teachers to leave prematurely. The UFT loved the incentives, and 18,000 teachers walked out of classrooms. Ultimately the union sat out the 1997 election, a boon to a mayor whose school cuts set records. Neutrality was the best Feldman could do with a membership that predominantly opposed the mayor. But when Feldman was the honoree of an American Jewish Congress luncheon in the middle of the campaign, Giuliani's Democratic foe, Ruth Messinger, was barred from attending. An AJC member armed with an invitation, the embarrassed Messinger was cornered by reporters in the lobby while Feldman and Crew chowed down inside.

DC 37's Local 372, which represents 19,000 kitchen workers, school aides and other paraprofessional staff, was also a significant player in city politics. Their president, Charlie Hughes, was so anxious to establish an early rapport with the administration he contributed the maximum permissible under city law to the Giuliani '97 committee by 1995 ($7,500), and raised thousands more.

He then started contributing to the Liberal Party, donating $17,500 in 1996 and 1997. In the same time period, Hughes bought seven tickets for the Giuliani committee's $2,500-a-plate Lincoln Center fund-raiser for an identical total of $17,500. Seven tickets were attributed to him on the committee's seating list for the event, but no contributions from him or anyone else from the union were filed for that time period. He now acknowledges that he "made out the checks to the Liberal Party" to go to the Giuliani committee dinner. "I'm sure that's the way it was," he said in a recent interview. Since these donations would far exceed city limits, the solicitation of such end-run contributions by the Giuliani campaign would be a clear violation of law.

In addition to financial support, Hughes became such a linchpin of the re-election effort that he anchored a Democrats-for-Rudy television commercial and City Hall rally. Not only did he deliver the endorsement of his local, he played a pivotal role in getting DC 37, the largest municipal union with 120,000 members, to back Rudy. All Rudy Crew remembers is that the mayor made it clear that he "liked Hughes very much," that he thought Hughes was "a good labor leader."

Hughes backed Rudy primarily because of a sweetheart deal the mayor had arranged that simultaneously pleased Feldman. In contract negotiations with the UFT, Giuliani agreed to relieve teachers of cafeteria and hallway monitoring duties, giving them an extra, free, forty-five-minute, period a day. Teachers were theoretically supposed to use this period for professional or curriculum development or tutoring (they already had up to two preparation periods a day). This bonanza for teachers was widely denounced by business groups and editorial pages as a productivity loss.

The mayor initially proposed replacing teachers with workfare workers, but he shifted, with Crew's encouragement, to the increased use of Hughes's 6,600 school aides as monitors. The decision meant additional hours for the aides, who made less than $10 an hour and earned an average of $10,000 a year. Giuliani then upped the ante by agreeing to create a new supervisory title for school aides that paid as much as $3 an hour more.

The union newspaper reported that "the path" to "the first promotional title ever created" for school aides "was cleared" in late 1996 "in informal discussions Hughes held with Giuliani and Crew." Hughes negotiated specific terms with Crew's counsel in early 1997 and a thousand aides were expected to be upgraded. Hughes's extra-legal donations to the Liberal Party dovetailed with the timing of the new title decisions. Hughes says now that the decision to "not use welfare mothers" and promote school aides was "why I endorsed him." Board officials es-timate that covering the lost teacher-monitoring period costs the school system $90 million a year.

This double whammy for the unions almost came unglued when the UFT rank and file voted down the contract in December 1995, shortly after Crew's arrival. The rejection was inspired by Giuliani's announcement of a $35,000 raise for him-self and substantial raises for his top staff at the same time that he was publicly celebrating Feldman's agreement to a two-year wage freeze for teachers. (They got 11 percent raises in the final three years of the pact.)

Harry Spence, Crew's deputy who was participating in the second round of ne-gotiations necessitated by the rejection of the initial deal, says that he and Feldman agreed to drop the new free-period provision. The union hoped to use the savings that would accrue from restoring the teacher's cafeteria and hallway assignments to sweeten nonsalary benefits. But, Spence says, Giuliani "adamantly refused," insist-ing on giving teachers a free period their union was no longer demanding.

Spence believes Hughes was the reason. The free period remained in the other-wise slightly revised contract and the UFT membership ratified the deal in a sec-ond vote in 1996.

Citing the UFT's extra forty-five minutes and similar losses in the new fire union contract—including the requirement of a fifth man on every truck and an extra week of vacation—CBC's Ray Horton said Rudy was "bugling a full retreat" on the labor front. Instead of paying higher wages for more work, Horton pointed out, these contracts "would pay more for less," giving "new meaning to the con-cept of productivity bargaining." The unions were backing Giuliani because they'd learned "to dance with the highest bidder," Horton charged. While Giuliani's array of five-year labor contracts counterbalanced double zeroes in the first two years with substantial raises thereafter, Horton charged that the mayor protected en-tirely the fine-print "bureaucratic entitlements," like sabbaticals and wash-up time for cops, that affect the way services are delivered.

Unbeknownst to Horton or the press, Hughes also won a secret 3 percent raise in a side agreement. "When everyone else got zero in the first year," says Hughes, "we got a 3 percent shot out of a severance-related benefit fund."

Crew had again learned from the Cortines example. In his departing interview with Koch, Cortines blasted Giuliani for caving to the unions. "He obviously doesn't want to stand up" to them, said the outgoing chancellor, who was forced out just as contract negotiations with the UFT began. "Instead of educating kids," Cortines charged, using the same terminology that would later become a Giuliani mantra, "we've become an employment agency." Still at his ex-linebacker weight,

Crew was hardly one, like Cortines, to tilt at windmills. Mayors had long dominated board contract talks, and Crew knew the unions were more important to
the mayor than his own continued tenure.

But facilitating the mayor's labor relationships wasn't the only useful role Crew
played. When reading scores rose 3.6 percent in June 1997, a pleased Giuliani used
it as the focus of his first campaign commercial. The ad was a preemptive strike, designed to undercut Messinger's core issue. Proclaiming reading scores "up in every
district" and calling it "the highest one-year increase in the past decade," the commercial showed Giuliani reading to a culturally diverse group of schoolchildren. It
also cited a new $125 million Project Read program Giuliani had just funded in his
new budget and claimed the administration "was rebuilding and renovating our
schools."

The truth was that reading scores were down since Rudy became mayor. The
1996 scores were 5.9 percent lower than in 1995. Even Crew's mini-spurt was partially attributable to a decision to exclude a large number of non-English-speaking
kids from the reading exam. Project Read was part of the first new infusion of city
funding since Rudy became mayor. But he'd cut the projected school budget by
$1.3 billion in his first three years and was the only mayor to ever go to Albany
and ask for less state operating aid. He'd also just put $275 million in new capital
construction money into the budget, hardly compensating for reductions totaling
$4.8 billion in the capital plans of the first three years.

Newsday's commentary on the ad stated matter-of-factly: "Giuliani restricted
the flow of money to the schools more severely than any mayor since the city's
fiscal crisis of the mid-1970s, forcing many schools to reduce services." Crew, understandably, said nothing. A month later, Giuliani put this radio ad on the air.
"When a mother comes up to me and says, 'Thank you, Rudy, for fighting back to
save our schools,' I tell her you should thank another Rudy—Schools Chancellor
Rudy Crew." With Messinger saying she could work with Crew but remaining
noncommittal about retaining him, the chancellor had become a campaign issue,
one Giuliani thought helped him.

When Messinger finally did her own first media buy in late August, it was, predictably, an ad aimed at Giuliani's education record. It depicted Messinger as a former teacher and public school parent and it hammered at the cuts, overcrowding
and lower test scores. The footage was of kids taking class in a school bathroom.
One kid appeared to be sitting on a urinal. Just like Giuliani's commercial, the ad
was staged and shot in a private school, since it is illegal to film one in a public
school. As soon as it hit the screen, the chancellor hit the ceiling.

The letter he wrote Messinger and released to the *Times* accused her of "deni-
grating the public school system for political gain." He called the urinal scene

fraudulent. "I am shocked that you would recruit children to take part in such sordid duplicity," he wrote. "You seem determined to mislead the public and demoralize our children with lies about their public schools."

Crew was both angry—offended, recalls an aide, at the picture of "a little black boy sitting on the loo"—and delighted. He knew he could turn what Messinger hoped would be her best press day into her worst. Cristyne Lategano, the mayor's press secretary, called when the letter went public, "mad with glee," according to Crew's press secretary Chiara Coletti. With 91,000 more kids than classroom space, the system did, according to Crew's office, put some kids in converted bathrooms, closets, hallways and locker rooms. "The question," as the *Times* put it, "was whether students were learning in operational bathrooms," or ones with the urinals removed.

As fine a distinction as this was, the *Times* published an editorial blasting Messinger for "manufacturing an illustration of school overcrowding that is worse than anything in the city's system." Crew's tough letter was the obvious hook for the editorial angst, but a news story a few pages away was headlined "Schools Often Turn Bathrooms into Classrooms." A television reporter went to a school in the Bronx and, though barred from entering, interviewed a teacher who said she had to teach over the sound of flushing toilets in a bathroom classroom. The Messinger campaign released photos from the UFT newspaper of a classroom with a table placed against a bank of urinals, students around the table, and the urinal tops being used as a bookshelf. It accused Crew of "appalling political partisanship."

When Crew orchestrated a relatively smooth school opening in September (overcrowding had caused a mess in 1996), the mayor declared: "There hasn't been a chancellor making this kind of progress in at least the last decade."

The Giuliani campaign aired a rebuttal commercial praising Crew and highlighting Project Read again, as well as $25 million in new school arts funding Giuliani had put in the '97 budget. From Crew's point of view, these expensive new initiatives, as well as the first overall increase in the board's budget in years, more than justified his indirect aid to the Giuliani campaign. "They could call me an Uncle Tom," he said later. "I'd take all of that for the arts money and the reading money. If I was going to get blasted for looking appropriately deferential to the mayor of the city, that's not a problem for me."

In the final weeks of the campaign, Crew's press office barred the media from Joseph Pulitzer Junior High School, where Messinger was invited to speak to a seventh grade class. Ironically, Candidate Rudy had appeared at the same school in 1993. Messinger's campaign claimed that Giuliani had been allowed to bring cameras and reporters to fifteen public school appearances in the prior twelve months; Crew's office quibbled about the numbers. At the first mayoral debate in mid-

October, each candidate had only a couple of questions they could direct at the other. In a final bow to the wedge issue Crew had become, Giuliani used one of his to ask if Messinger would keep him as chancellor. Messinger squirmed and said she'd have to talk to Crew first.

Polls showed that voters thought the schools were sliding, yet Crew got a five-to-one favorable response. Giuliani wanted some of that to rub off on him. Crew's aggressive advocacy had already turned Giuliani's prime weakness into a mixed bag at worst.

What no one who knew Rudy Giuliani could have anticipated was how well he and Crew would get along personally.

They became such fast friends Giuliani would call Crew at 2 A.M. just to chat. They did scotch and cigars together dozens of times, at the mansion and at an East 58th Street cigar bar owned by Elliot Cuker, one of Giuliani's closest friends. They stunned their respective staffs on April 1, 1997, when they played an April Fool's joke and switched roles, Crew showing up at City Hall and Giuliani at the Board of Ed. They went to Yankee games, often with Andrew. They could make each other roar with laughter—and not just with Messinger swipes—amid serious talk about futures, families and fears.

Giuliani liked to talk about his great man theories of history, moving from La Guardia to Roosevelt. Crew said Giuliani read often about great men, and spoke comfortably about his sense of historic destiny. "Courageous and bold" was Giuliani's definition of greatness. "His sense of leadership was to take a position and hold it," recalls Crew. "The tighter and longer and more tenaciously you held a position, the greater a leader you were."

Crew and he also compared notes "easily and regularly" on "exacting" fathers, both of whom were dead. Giuliani told Crew that he had worked in his dad's bar "for a bit of time, maybe a summer, and watched his father and uncle rough a drunk up and throw him out." The way Giuliani told the story left Crew feeling it was "a sad commentary" on Giuliani's yen for "bravado."

"Stern" was the fatherly adjective each favored. Crew also told Giuliani about his longtime Italian father-in-law, also dead: "He was a guy from Brooklyn, in construction, a World War II vet, who moved to Poughkeepsie but was a real New Yorker. I told Rudy about how he handled the hard parts of an interracial marriage—the intimacy, the growth. He understood the strength and the character I was talking about."

Their love of the Yankees was a bond too. Crew's father had been a fevered Dodger fan, drawn by Jackie Robinson, but when the club left for L.A., the love died. A baseball and football player as a teenager, Crew saved boxtops to try to qualify as a Yankee bat boy. He loved Elston Howard, the first black Yankee. When his long reach helped him beat eleven-year-old Andrew to a foul ball at a playoff game, a cop on the security detail said he had to give it to the kid. "No way I'm giving this up," he laughed, and the mayor, sitting one seat away, laughed approvingly with him.

"In the core of his being," Crew says, "there's a person who's very easy to get to know. There's a youngness, a boyishness to him. It got to be a guys-night-out thing, with gestures of youth. I decided to deal with it as authentically and honestly as I could. I would give whatever I got. Not just in terms of friendship. If it was a fight he wanted, which he sometimes did, I gave it back. If it was a hard reform agenda, I'd give it back."

Since Crew had met Andrew, he wanted to make sure Giuliani met his brood. "My kids were frightened for me," he remembers. Giuliani's press clips scared them. "They thought there was a storm hanging over me all the time." So Crew took his kids to City Hall for pictures with Giuliani, and they got a little more comfortable.

"I didn't want to cower. It's not in my makeup. So over wine, I would tell him so-and-so is afraid of you and he would ask why. We had lots of conversations about the fears he creates. In a moment of vulnerability, he said he really didn't want to be feared. He had a rationale about why fear was not a good organizational trait.

"But I came away with the sense that this is a man who really respects power. He understands it. He loves to use it and deal with those who have it. He loves individual bravado. He wants to see if anybody else has it in him. It is his emotional drug of choice. He pushes. He tries to break others. It is as natural as drinking water to him."

They were dog lovers as well—Giuliani had Goalie as his constant mansion companion and Crew had Chance. Both were retrievers, one golden and the other Labrador. Music was another common thread: Crew was as obsessed with jazz as the mayor was with opera. Crew played his favorites so loudly at the board that aides had to ask him to lower it, while Giuliani has been known to spontaneously plunge into an aria. Neither could ever get the other to appreciate their special sounds.

Giuliani called Crew "a regular guy" in press interviews, a clear contrast with how he felt about Cortines, and wrapped his arm around him warmly when they met at public events. The mayor also made a big display of giving Crew a box of

Dominican cigars with a red bow on top for his birthday in 1996, and took a trip with him to the black rodeo.

When an article appeared in *Vanity Fair* in early 1997 charging that Giuliani was having an affair with his press aide, Cristyne Lategano, Crew was sympathetic, deploring the media's preoccupations. He called Giuliani and Lategano, who had sometimes joined the boys-night-out cavorting, and said "hang on to your hats, don't let life turn you sour."

Crew had remarried in 1992, and he and his wife Kathy, a forty-five-year-old mother of three grown children, were living in the Brooklyn brownstone near the board that chancellors get gratis. He took Kathy to Gracie Mansion for dinner shortly after his arrival in 1995 and met Donna, who hosted the dinner for ten or so. When problems later developed in Crew's marriage, he and the mayor quietly mused over their troubled marriages to California blondes.

"We did talk about these issues," he recalls. "Public life is so different in New York. You pay an enormous price. I did discuss my own domestic situation." Giuliani was guarded, but the scene at the mansion spoke volumes. Crew was there at least twenty times, he estimates, often until the early hours of the morning. He never saw Donna other than at the first formal dinner, when she and her husband barely spoke. The Giuliani marriage was, he quickly recognized, "difficult space" and he "respected" that by staying away from it.

The mayor and he usually sat on the patio or in a small green room off the patio, where they could open a window and smoke cigars. They were not allowed to smoke in the more spacious sitting room, what Crew observed as the "only oblique reference" to the fact that Giuliani was living with someone else and had to accommodate to her rules. With Giuliani outside the mansion another thirty times or so, he observed "no cell phone or other contacts with Donna."

The underpinning of the Giuliani/Crew relationship, though, was always mutual need, crystallizing in the 1997 election. Crew was no rubber stamp for Giuliani—he had, for example, stopped the NYPD from collecting junior high school and high school yearbooks and using prom photos as if they were mugshots, banning a practice Giuliani publicly championed.

The mayor tolerated Crew's independence because it worked for him—it was one of the reasons the Messinger attack was treated with credibility. He also couldn't afford a confrontation with Crew on the heels of the Cortines, Gresser and other board messes. But as much as their agendas and personalities meshed for the first two years, Crew told his top staff he anticipated "big problems" after the election.

Crew saw Giuliani as the definition of single-minded. Until he was re-elected, winning big was his solitary synapse, literally the only thing on his mind. Every muscle movement was an electoral exercise. When Giuliani was certain what his goal was, he could subordinate everything in life to achieving it. But when he didn't know what his next move was, he flailed at the air, loose, disembodied, dangerous. For a year after his win, until Pat Moynihan announced he wasn't running for his Senate seat again, term-limited Rudy had no plan for himself. Likewise, he had no plan for the city.

He got into pointless wars—with jaywalkers, street vendors, community gardeners and taxi drivers. He threw up barricades on sidewalks and bridges, as well as around City Hall Park—trying to change the way pedestrians crossed streets, cabbies protested and citizens visited the seat of their government. The bridge blockade stopped a convoy of striking cabbies from entering the city at all, having been branded a "terrorist threat" by sidekick Safir. The cabbies were trying to protest the same sort of onerous rule-changes that had 350 licensed sidewalk vendors suddenly barred from blocks and blocks of midtown and the financial district.

When he wasn't bulldozing community gardens, he was losing case after case in federal court over his refusal to grant permits to gather or march to demonstrators he didn't like. The crudest was his refusal to allow World AIDS Day mourners to read the names of the newly dead in City Hall Park. The 150 demonstrators who showed were led through metal detectors into a parking lot surrounded by a newly installed chain-link fence. Sharpshooters were positioned on the roof of City Hall to monitor them.

He visited twenty states between December 1997 and December 1998 and became Mayor MIA, sporting transparently premature presidential or vice presidential ambitions. Chicken dinners in Arizona assumed the role in his life that broken water mains once had. He set up three fundraising committees—one useful if he ran for governor, one for senator and one a federal PAC that was seed money for this mystery national run. All his crazed quality-of-life initiatives—especially against jaywalkers and cabbies—got him taming-the-beast time on network news. That seemed to be the point.

A new Yankee Stadium on the West Side of Manhattan became the fixation of the first year of Rudy's second term and millions were spent studying it. To stop a referendum on the stadium he knew he'd lose, he named a commission to revise the City Charter, which legally displaced any other referendum. Then he named a second commission in 1999, though charter revisions usually occur every decade or so. Neither commission came up with a single meaningful change, and in 1999, the Giuliani proposals lost three to one.

It was a mix of government by groping and government by tantrum. Crew sensed that it was only a matter of time before this runaway train ran into the schoolhouse. "I knew Rudy needed to set his sights on something else and I knew he'd try to do so almost immediately after the election," Crew remembers, unsure at first what the electoral goal would be. "He was either going to completely embrace this work and this 80 percent minority system or he was going to distance himself from it. And he was going to make that determination on the basis of whether it was performing well enough to earn him acclaim and whether or not we still had a good relationship and I was ready to do his water carrying."

With Giuliani unfocused and traveling so much, he had less time for Crew in 1998, though they certainly did continue to get together, closing the year with a particularly warm Christmas dinner and exchange of gifts. The mayor was particularly pleased because Crew had just turned over school security to the NYPD in December, allowing Giuliani to finally fulfill a five-year-old campaign promise. The reading scores also went up two points in June, a two-year hike of 5.9 percent, the largest sustained hike since 1980 and 1981. The moment was, however, the calm before the storm.

Giuliani certainly found out during a 1996 contretemps over Catholic school scholarships that vouchers were a matter of principle to Crew. The chancellor was sandbagged on the scholarship issue, questioned about it during a live television interview in September, shortly after a disastrously overcrowded school opening. The reporter, Marcia Kramer, cited a so-far unreported offer from the Cardinal to enroll a thousand low-achieving public school kids in the parochial schools. Giuliani had spoken with Cardinal O'Connor about the idea the same morning as the Crew interview, and given Kramer quotes supporting the concept as "generous" without saying a word to Crew.

The chancellor kept his cool on the air, calling it an "interesting offer," but cautioning: "I think we've got to be a little bit careful about the glitz of all of this." He said he had a meeting scheduled with the Cardinal, which in fact had been set without any knowledge of the scholarship offer. He said they'd talk about it. Then he went right to the phone. Days of jockeying with the mayor followed, including a thirty-five-minute face-to-face at City Hall.

The mayor implored him to help. "I need you to go along with this one. You have no idea what the church does for the city. You have no idea what they do for me," he said. The mayor had already gone public with quotes lambasting any educator who might oppose public funding of the tuition payments for these thousand kids as "afraid of success" and a captive of special interests. "He could put on this prosecutorial look that said I will snuff you out," Crew says. "I never got that look. The closest I came was over the Catholic schools.

"He said it was a little experiment and I shouldn't overreact. I called the archdiocese's school director, Catherine Hickey, and asked what kind of a program had been negotiated. She said, 'What negotiations? There is no program. It just appeared in the news.' I confronted Rudy and said there is no there there. It's political hooey. He said we have to work it out. He spoke about the political importance of the church. I sensed he almost had a deal, a quid pro quo. He would provide resources and they would lean in his direction. I told him I was going public with the fact that there's no plan."

When Giuliani found out how implacably opposed Crew was, he shifted and acknowledged that public funding would be unconstitutional. "You cannot use public funds to subsidize religious education," he said. He still called on Crew to help place students in the privately funded program. Crew thought of his father, who taught him to never be afraid of people who yell and scream. "Just yell and scream back," he said. "I knew there was nothing behind the curtain but a Victrola."

Crew declared he would not help identify the 5 percent lowest-performing students, recruit children or administer the program. "Our function, our role, our devotion, is to public school children, and it will never waver," he told reporters, adding that his advice to parents considering Catholic schools was "you should stick with us." Giuliani backed off, but it was hardly the mayor's only attempt to do a deal with the Cardinal.

"I got a call once from Rudy about textbooks," recalls Crew. "He said the Cardinal had called him. He wanted me to go beyond the state textbook allocation to help the Catholic schools. I tried to figure out how close to the line he was asking me to walk. As long as our kids weren't hurt, I would try to help. But where it didn't make sense, where it would gut the public school system, where it was malevolent redistribution, he knew where I stood." In 1997, Crew did agree to allocate an extra $14.7 million to private and parochial schools for textbooks, after adding over $2 million in 1996.

As helpful as he was on textbooks, Crew's implacable opposition to the scholarship plan should have been enough to convince the mayor that he would also stoutly resist any voucher scheme. In fact, before Giuliani's two-day dalliance with the facsimile of publicly funded scholarships in 1996, Candidate Rudy and

Mayor Rudy had also repeatedly opposed vouchers. In 1993 he told Sandra Feldman that "as a lawyer, he believed vouchers were unconstitutional." In a May 1995 appearance at a UFT conference, he said vouchers "would bleed the public schools of needed funds" and be "a terrible mistake." In a Wharton Club speech in August 1995 he declared: "Vouchers would weaken, if not create the collapse of the New York City public school system."

Despite all that, with a Senate race looking more and more plausible, Giuliani decided to include vouchers in his January 1999 State of the City speech. He told Crew it was going to be vouchers with a wink. "Don't worry about it," Giuliani said. "It's just a political thing, a campaign thing. I'm not going to do anything. Don't take it seriously." Crew agreed to maintain his public posture of opposition, but to "keep a low profile."

Ironically, in Giuliani's hour-long speech, he inadvertently referred to the very reason why he should not have taken the risk of starting down the voucher path. "The present board, the chancellor, City Hall, and the whole operation works together better than it has in over a decade," he said. "The reason that happened is because very good, strong personal relationships have developed, and an understanding that if we don't figure out a way to get along, then we hurt the kids."

He promised to "continue" those strong relationships, saying that the changes Crew had achieved were "absolutely remarkable." Then he dropped his Parental Choice Program bombshell, an experiment allowing parents in one, low-performing, district to buy access to a private or parochial education with a publicly funded voucher. "I hope people who for all different reasons oppose this—some on a matter of principle, some for other reasons—I wish they would just suspend judgment on it for a few years."

Giuliani praised the Schools Choice Scholarship Program, which he had launched in 1996 independently of the board after Crew opposed the Cardinal's proposal. The mayor believed that the 46,000 kids who'd filed applications for tuition assistance under the privately financed program justified a public voucher experiment. Consultants retained by the program had identified reading and math upticks in two of the three grades where scholarship children were placed. But their study also found that the biggest gains were in attendance at religious services. While Giuliani saluted the program as a successful precursor of vouchers, boosting attendance at Mass was hardly what Crew saw as a constitutional way of spending tax dollars.

Crew, Coletti and Rizzo were at City Hall for the speech. As Crew and the mayor had pre-arranged, the chancellor made muted, critical comments to the press. The three went to Sammy's Noodle Shop in Greenwich Village for a late lunch afterwards. They agreed that Giuliani had been supportive of Crew in the speech, incorporating many of his suggestions. They thought his voucher proposal was so vague and tentative it was more an idea than a plan, just as he had promised. They thought a confrontation could still be avoided.

The next night, Giuliani and Crew did one of their still regular "social" dinners. Giuliani spent much of the mid-January evening talking about bilingual education, half suggesting that he had a strategy to junk it. He had alluded in the State of the City speech to "a group of other changes that will emerge as we move along throughout the year." A silent Crew listened as Giuliani auditioned another one.

The two did another night out the next weekend, this time at Cuker's bar. An uneasy wisp hung in the air, but it was still all smiles. It would be the last boys-night-out for the two Rudys. Crew and his oldest son Rudy Jr. did return to the cigar bar the following Sunday for a Super Bowl evening, but Giuliani was surrounded by top aides, from Cristyne Lategano to Tony Coles, and they had no opportunity for real conversation.

In early February, when Amadou Diallo was killed, the mayor was suddenly ensnarled in the worst sustained media crisis of his administration, with daily pickets and mass arrests arousing intense national interest. His handling of the police shooting was infuriating to most black New Yorkers and Rudy Crew was no exception. He offered to talk. He told Giuliani advisers that the mayor was "looking callous and uncaring." Giuliani was refusing to meet with the most prominent city and state blacks and Crew, who viewed himself as Giuliani's closest black confidant, wanted the mayor to reach out. But Giuliani did not respond to Crew's entreaties. No cigar, no night at Cuker's, not even a return phone call. Crew was mystified.

Then the mayor sent a budget modification to the council with $4.5 million in it for voucher funding in the fiscal year that was already half over. His February financial plan, which contained the outlines for the new budget year that began July 1, called for $12 million to launch the voucher plan. For the first time, Giuliani's budget office did not tell Crew's budget office about a line item until it was in print, according to Harry Spence. What really drove the chancellor batty, though, was when the *Times*'s Dan Barry reported on March 3 that mayoral aide Tony Coles was "intensely" lobbying nonmayoral members of the board to get them to back the plan, another unprecedented secret maneuver.

Crew was in California when Coletti reached him with the news. He had been hearing rumblings about a lobbying effort, even learning that Coles had told one borough president that Crew wasn't really opposed to the voucher experiment. But Coles had now publicly acknowledged the effort. He saw this end-run around him to gain board approval for a plan Giuliani told him was merely a campaign stunt as a duplicitous violation of their understanding. He called the mayor's office immediately, but Giuliani was in the air, on his way back from an out-of-state fundraising swing.

Coletti was getting press calls from everywhere. One call was particularly imperative—from Karen Hunter, an editorial writer from the *Daily News*. Though the paper was a constant thorn in the chancellor's side, he had an excellent relationship with Hunter, who was working on an editorial against vouchers. He decided to talk to her.

He told her the mayor had given him no warning about his voucher lobbying. "What will you do if he pushes it down your throat?" Hunter asked. "Nobody pushes anything down my throat," said Crew. "I wouldn't stay here if that happens," he heard himself say without ever planning to say it. "Always in your life you come to the proverbial hill to die on. This is mine." He called vouchers "doing something for some at the expense of many."

When Giuliani landed, the chancellor reached him in the GMC Suburban that took him all over the city. Why? Crew demanded.

"I thought for the purposes of debate, we'd have an experiment," the mayor replied. "Don't turn a deaf ear."

"That's fine for an intellectual exercise, but this is real," said Crew. "You never told me you were going to do this. We've had this conversation about this type of program before. I want you to know that I've already talked to the *Daily News* about this and I told them I would quit over this."

"You didn't do that, did you? You don't mean it, do you?"

"I do," said Crew. "I'm not playing any artful games." Crew felt he had always been straight with Giuliani, "not bullshitty or guileful."

Giuliani called the *News*. The anti-voucher editorial was temporarily killed. The quotes from Crew were turned over to the news desk and became a story instead of an editorial. The *Times* learned about the threat to quit too, and threw it on the front page. An escalating cycle of news stories began. Crew, who was suffering with an ear infection after a conference, stayed in California an extra day, ill and flustered.

The *Times* reported that Giuliani met the next day at an undisclosed midtown Manhattan location with the new board member from Queens who had replaced Carol Gresser, and with Queens borough president Claire Schulman, a Democrat who had endorsed the mayor for re-election in 1997. Assured of the votes of Jerry Cammarata and his own two appointees, Giuliani was looking for a fourth vote for vouchers.

"The damage was already done," Crew now realizes. "That was the turning point. I had dared to say no on his national issue. The questions about my charac-

ter started right away. At first, it was just, 'Was I a prima donna?' His choice was
to embrace us or distance himself. From that moment on, I knew what he would
do." When Crew told him of his fixed determination to fight the proposal, Giuliani
moved into submarine mode. "To him, I was Arafat. I was Bratton. I was Al
Sharpton," Crew says in retrospect.

Giuliani certainly wasn't going to let it look that way. He was already taking a
beating in the press for forcing Crew toward the door. Crew extended an olive
branch, telling reporters he would not quit if Giuliani ran the voucher program
out of City Hall and his board was not "contaminated" by it. He still promised to
"rail against it." At a meeting in the mayor's office, Crew reminded Giuliani of his
prior statements on vouchers. "I just changed my mind," the mayor explained.
"The change in the schools isn't happening fast enough." Crew thought the comment was "a sucker punch." Giuliani was the kind of guy, Crew was suddenly suspecting, "who could go to a Yankee game with you one night and cause you to lose
your job the next." These abrupt swings were a personal perversion of his, Crew
thought. "Some people see it as venal, scorpion-like. I just think of it as perverse."

The board met privately with Crew and pushed a voucher vote off the table. The
City Council and State Assembly Democrats vowed to kill it. Crew began to think
he could lie back and let Giuliani's ploy die its own natural death.

Then, in late April, Giuliani formally proposed his executive budget. He wanted
council approval to spend $7,000 a year per capita to send 3,000 kids from one
school district to private or religious schools. Since Crew was opposed, he offered
to run the program out of City Hall, draining as much as $24 million out of the
board's budget in addition to the program's $12 million operating cost. The *Times*
called it "another badge" for Giuliani to wear "on the national stage."

Though it was only two days after the massacre at Columbine High School in
Colorado, Giuliani also said at the budget briefing that "the whole school system
should be blown up" because it was "dysfunctional." He announced the withhold-
ing of $6 billion in city funding for the board's construction budget, charging that
"there was money going to boroughs that didn't need that much money" because
Crew and the board majority "had to get the vote of that borough" to pass the
plan. In fact, Giuliani was demanding a shift in capital funds to Queens, the borough whose vote he needed—to pass vouchers, dump Crew or make any other
changes he might want.

When the blow-up speech provoked a press outcry, he turned the heat up another notch. He said he could not "be held accountable" for the state of the city
schools because "you don't give me enough control of it." He called for the aboli-
tion of the board, demanding that he be allowed to run the schools. The mayor

who'd campaigned for re-election seventeen months earlier citing school improvements he claimed to have caused, was obviously preparing for a Senate race of obfuscation.

Crew released a blistering letter, faxed to hundreds of opinion makers, accusing Giuliani of "reckless" and "destructive" remarks about the school system. He called the voucher plan "an attempt to dismantle" public schools. "When the mayor declares that the whole system should be blown up, he tells 1.1 million children and thousands of parents, teachers and administrators that they are wasting their time in schools that he has suddenly dismissed as no good and beyond redemption."

Giuliani then refused to answer questions about whether he wanted Crew to remain, saying only that the chancellor should "present an agenda of reform and not just defend the status quo." When Crew had assailed Ruth Messinger in 1997, Giuliani had happily declared: "You create an unfair depiction of the system he's running, he's going to fight you." Having done it himself and provoked a similar Crew retort, he decided to ignore a week of Crew phone messages. A *Daily News* poll showed most New Yorkers solidly behind Crew in the head-to-head with the mayor, with 54 percent saying Giuliani was proposing vouchers to help his Senate campaign, while only 30 percent thought he was "serious" about improving schools.

"When Rudy sees a need to take someone out," Crew says now, "he has a machine, a roomful of henchmen, nicking away at you, leaking crazy stories, usually to the *Post*. He is not bound by the truth. I have studied animal life and their predator/prey relations are more graceful than this. You either capitulate to it or you die politically." The death by a thousand cuts that Bratton had described was under way again.

In May, Giuliani put the votes together on the board to defeat the Crew capital plan the mayor had called "realistic" in January. The TV station New York One reported that mayoral insiders were calling Crew a "complete moron" on the budget.

The *Post* ran a story written by a City Hall reporter that derided Crew for taking thirteen work-related trips in twelve weeks—mostly to education conferences around the country. Starting back in March, the story said, an administration official had begun talking about Crew's "love of California," as if he was always there.

The mayor hosted his first big Senate fund-raiser and the guest speaker was Jeb Bush, the Florida governor who'd just steered a voucher plan through the state legislature. Tony Coles traveled to Chicago, where the Board of Education had been abolished, even though Giuliani had pointedly contended in his State of the City speech that New York's system was performing better than Chicago's.

When the reading scores dropped five points in June, and math scores ten, Crew was left twisting in the wind. Giuliani said he was "very alarmed and concerned." Positioning himself anew as more critic than culprit, he called for radical reform with himself in charge. He stopped short of directly blaming the chancellor he'd saluted for more than three years. Crew has "done a very good job within a system that is totally nonfunctional," he said.

A month later, a new state test found only a third of the city's kids meeting language arts standards, a devastating blow that sent Giuliani running as far away from the system as he could get. The combination of scores made it a political imperative for Giuliani to pin responsibility for this failure elsewhere.

The board appointed a subcommittee headed by Jerry Cammarata, the Staten Island member close to Giuliani, to evaluate Crew's performance. The chancellor's five-year contract was up for review in December and Cammarata was open about his intention of doing a tough, comprehensive assessment.

In mid-June, Hillary Clinton, who was then contemplating a Senate run, visited a couple of Manhattan schools, one with Crew. Giuliani blasted both of them. "Did I think that the appearance of the chancellor and the First Lady was basically a politically motivated event? The answer is yes." It was actually the second time Crew had appeared in a school with Clinton. On April 30—just days after Crew released his stinging letter—Clinton was a volunteer principal for a day. Crew and Clinton wound up in a *Times* photo at the end-of-the-day session for all volunteer principals. Giuliani was invited but didn't show.

"When Hillary was invited to visit a school by the principal," Crew recalls, "Cammarata prepared a memo demanding to know who gave the principal the authority to invite her and whether the superintendent knew. I called the mayor directly. I told him this is the First Lady of the United States of America and that I could not bar her. This was not Ruth Messinger. He told me she was using her White House status to leverage her campaign. I told him I am not saying no."

Crew says he also got livid calls from Tony Coles about a third Clinton appearance at a school and that Ninfa Segarra, one of Giuliani's board appointees, told him over dinner just how upset the mayor was over his principal-for-a-day picture with Giuliani's putative opponent.

The worst of it hit on August 3. Giuliani sent Crew a "Dear Chancellor" letter: "I am concerned that you have canceled our last six regularly scheduled meetings on education. Whatever may be your reasons for canceling these meetings, I hope you will be able to put them aside so that we can continue to work together to reform our school system." It was leaked to the *Post* and *News,* together with a blind quote from a mayoral aide: "It seems he's got one foot out the door."

Coletti responded by pointing out that Crew's top deputies Spence and Rizzo were on vacation in July, saying "the chancellor really feels he needs one of them with him." With memories of Cortines dancing in his head, Crew wasn't about to meet with Giuliani alone anymore. The other reason he wasn't meeting—which Coletti did not mention—was the death of his first wife, Angela.

"I had four kids all over the country," Crew remembers. "I had to go out to California, where she died of breast cancer, and go through one funeral. Then bring her body back to Poughkeepsie and do another. The day of the *Post* story I was delivering a eulogy for her upstate. The people at the Italian Center in Poughkeepsie didn't want anyone to see the story. The whole thing told me a lot about this man. This is a maniac. On the day I was burying my wife, I have these people concocting this world of treachery."

Someone at the funeral incensed about the mayor's potshot called the *Post*. The *Post* called Crew's office. Coletti pleaded with the reporter not to write anything about Angela's death since Crew regarded it as a private family matter. Notice of the death had appeared in the Poughkeepsie paper, though, so the *Post* saw it as a legitimate story. It went with a single line buried in an account of the continued strain between Giuliani and Crew that made no explicit reference to the hurtful timing of the mayor's letter.

City Hall claimed in quiet conversations that it knew nothing about Angela's death when the letter was released. With two Giuliani-appointed board members on the same floor as Crew, his aides doubted it. From Crew's standpoint, it didn't matter. He thought the letter and release were horrid acts no matter what Giuliani knew—"a phone call would've sufficed." When Giuliani's secretary called and asked if they could send flowers, Crew told them "not to send a thing."

What was also simmering just beneath the surface was the suspicion in Crew quarters that Giuliani's "henchmen" were leaking stories about his current wife, Kathy. "I was getting calls right and left about Crew's marriage being in trouble," Coletti recalls. "Reporters said it was coming out of City Hall. The contention was that it was affecting his stability." Crew's missing wedding band was noticed by a gossip columnist who never went to the board. The *Daily News* got Kathy on the unlisted number at the brownstone, then they reached Rudy Jr. at his corporate job. Everyone was upset.

"There were inquiries about Kathy and myself that occurred close to some of this stuff," says Crew. "It was off limits, personal stuff, rumor and innuendo. The staff kept most of it away from me."

A week after Giuliani's letter, he and Crew got together at City Hall. Surrounded by aides, they talked for forty-five minutes about summer school and the planned September opening. The mayor was less antagonistic than he had been at the last meeting in June. "As opposed to a more friendly relationship," Crew told reporters afterward, "this is much more businesslike, operational, and that's fine."

A second meeting occurred on August 24. Crew suspected something was up when he got a call that morning at home from Giuliani's gadfly friend, Elliot Cuker. "Has the mayor called you?" asked Cuker. "He wants to get it to be right. The mayor thinks the world of you." Crew remembers telling Cuker that he was not afraid of the mayor and that he would not "cower"—terms that had become second nature to him during this war. When the meeting at City Hall ended a few hours later, Giuliani asked his and Crew's staff to leave his office. Crew had unsuccessfully sought a private moment with the mayor when their relationship fell apart over the blow-up speech, but Giuliani had rebuffed him. Now the two old friends were alone again, for the first time in many months.

"I'm sorry to hear about your wife," Giuliani said. He walked over to Crew, who was standing, wary, drained. He wrapped his arms around the chancellor and hugged him. "I miss you," he said. "I want things to be the way they were." Crew felt his own body stiffen involuntarily. "I miss you too," he replied, uncertain about what to say or do. "This is very sudden." He wanted to get ahold of himself, to think this through.

The anger about everything—from vouchers to the funeral—stewed inside of him. So did the suspicion that Giuliani had used the confidences they'd shared about his marriage to stir the pot. "I would not be surprised if they tried to plant the stories," he says. "It had something to do with why I stiffened. These were examples of how low they would go to get the goods on you. There was nothing they wouldn't do."

"We need to bury the hatchet," said the mayor. "Call and we'll set up a dinner." Crew says he had his secretary call four times and mark each attempt in her book. He never got a date. "Rudy was playing a game," he now thinks. "He is the quintessential artful dodger, saying one thing and doing another. None of it was true."

Three days after the meeting, Crew disclosed to the *Times* that he was considering an offer from the University of Washington to head a new research institute. He talked about "the very slippery slope" of the political landscape in New York. He said the last two meetings with Giuliani had been "refreshingly harmonious," and that he certainly wanted to stay through the end of the next school year.

But Crew had come to believe that the only way he could make himself acceptable to Giuliani again was in a Stepin Fetchit prone position. "I don't like to fight," he said afterward. "I like to fix things. There was no guile in my relationship with him. I didn't go after press. He knew I wasn't there to make a name. But he never understood who I was.

"If Rosa Parks could do what she did, if my people were hosed and spit on so I could walk in the front door of City Hall, did he really think I would get there and surrender? Didn't he know from whence my heart was speaking? He thought I was engaging in some political gibberish, that I would change under fire. He never knew me. He doesn't understand issues of race and class." All of the combat and intrigue had left Crew so uncertain he wavered, Hamlet-like, about staying or going, sending out such mixed signals even his supporters were dismayed.

On December 23, 1999, exactly a year after the two Rudys had exchanged Christmas presents over dinner, Rudy Giuliani put four votes together to fire Rudy Crew. Two investigative reports that the *Times* called "damaging but flimsy" had been issued shortly before the vote—one about inflated attendance was released by the governor; the other about cheating on standardized tests had been rushed out by an investigations commissioner appointed by Giuliani. A frazzled Crew had embarrassed himself by saying a Republican city councilman who called for his resignation was "too short," at five foot six inches, to criticize him. The chancellor contended he was saying the newly elected councilman was "too short" on experience.

The vote took ten minutes. Crew stayed with his children at the brownstone, a spokeswoman saying he preferred to be "lynched in absentia." Giuliani claimed the board members made up their own minds, but that he talked with them and wholeheartedly agreed. "There was no willingness to try to take on the kind of reform that was necessary," he said. "I don't see how they would come to any other decision." Dan Barry, the *Times* reporter who'd chronicled the demise of the friendship, concluded that the mayor "became fed up with the long-playing Crew psychodrama and let it be known that the chancellor's ouster would make a fine Christmas present."

Steve Sanders, the chair of the Assembly's education committee, called the mayor at the last moment to try to convince him to pull back, but the mayor didn't return the call. Sanders did reach Randy Levine, who had become a deputy mayor, and Levine reportedly tried to persuade Giuliani to stop it. "People were trying to calm him down," a source told Barry, "but he was gone on this one."

Crew said: "I could tell that the same storm that brought me here was brewing to take me away." In his later retrospective, all he could see was the mayor's flash-point temper. "There is a very, very powerful pathology operating inside this man," Crew says now. "I don't believe he's driven by race. I believe there is an anger he feels about ▮▮▮▮▮ce of his life that just takes over."

"Change is good," ▮▮▮▮ ▮ayor.

"I think they sh▮▮ ▮▮et someone new—quick—so all the boys and girls don't stop learning▮ ▮▮fford Hall, eight, a Brooklyn third grader quoted in the *Times*. "Some ▮▮▮▮ght not know a lot of math or how to spell if they don't get somebody▮

In fact, City Hall had no game plan. Crew left overnight and the board had to rush to find an interim successor, who would be offered a six-month contract while the board searched for a permanent successor. Giuliani tried unsuccessfully to block the appointment of Harold Levy, but he got the job anyway. The Queens member who'd voted with Giuliani to oust Crew resisted him to go with Levy, a businessman who sat on the State Board of Regents and enjoyed powerful support from state assembly Democratic Speaker Sheldon Silver. Giuliani then refused for months to talk to the new chancellor and turned his State of the City speech into a demand that the board sell its headquarters building—a new version of the old blow-up rhetoric.

A nationwide chancellor search early this year netted a paltry number of applicants. The newspaper spin was that others hesitated to apply because Levy might want the long-term appointment and have an inside track. The other possibility was that the Legend of Rudy was scaring prominent applicants away.

The system was meanwhile spinning out of control. As a bone to Giuliani in the throes of the spring combat, Crew had agreed to accelerate his schedule for getting rid of social promotion, the time-honored practice of passing below-standard kids. For the first time since taking office, Giuliani started pushing extremely hard on promotional practices when the voucher issue stalemated in May. It was clear the City Council would kill vouchers, leaving Giuliani still in need of an education initiative he could point to in the Senate campaign.

Flunking thousands of minority kids had just the right pizzazz. If done right—using more than test scores to select the kids and offering the chosen ones lots of well-planned remediation—Crew believed enforcing new standards could be as educational as it was punitive. But the Giuliani push forced him to rapidly put a program in place for the summer of 1999. Using only the scores, 35,000 kids at three grade levels were required to take classes in schools without air conditioning during one of the hottest summers in city history. Only 14,000 passed the exam when the summer was done, dooming the rest to repeat their grade, at least theoretically.

But then, in September, the board's testing company admitted they'd made a mistake in grading the tests. They'd sent 8,668 kids who'd actually passed to the summer session. "This is a good thing that happened. If I were a parent," said Giuliani, apparently forgetting he was one, "I'd say thank you. . . they got more education."

Crew's successor Levy spent most of his first weeks in office preparing for the chaotic summer of 2000, when as many as 250,000 kids may have to take class, with social promotion eliminated systemwide. He wound up locked in a constant war of words with Giuliani about how to recruit the teaching staff for this massive undertaking. Giuliani insisted that his latest education innovation—merit pay—be introduced as part of the summer program. He wanted bonuses to go to the teachers whose kids increased their scores.

This position, of course, pitted him against his onetime friends at the UFT. They'd already broken with him over vouchers and were openly aligned with Hillary Clinton. That made them fodder for his mill. He derided incentive deals Levy structured to try to induce teachers to work. He went out of his way to assail the union as a bar to reform. No one could tell how it would all turn out, but the system was in unmistakable disarray: no real relationship between the mayor and the chancellor, maybe no headquarters, an end to social promotion and recurring cycles of tumult.

Six and a half years into Giuliani's reign, reading scores were up by a single point or down by three points, depending on how you tabulate the mistake-ridden 1999 scores. Math scores were down three points. School overcrowding worsened by 6 percent in elementary schools. Attendance was down in junior highs. Without the luck of a national wave to ride, as on the crime front, the magical mayor had no numbers to bandy about as evidence of his educational genius. All he had was Alibi High.

He'd huffed and he'd puffed, even threatening to blow the house down. But, with the capital budget cuts, there weren't even any bricks left for a sturdier one. His classroom fairy tale certainly had no storybook ending.

Nineteen

Sex and the City

DONNA HANOVER WAS THE FIRST WOMAN TO ACTUALLY RUN FOR FIRST lady. The mayoral spouses of the last half-century—Susan Wagner, Mary Lindsay, Mary Beame and Joyce Dinkins—were housewives without careers or public profiles of their own. Donna, on the other hand, had been a broadcast journalist for nearly two decades by the time she arrived at Gracie Mansion. As consumed with winning the mayoralty as Rudy was, she'd merged her career ambitions with his, confident that they'd hit grand heights together.

So she became a strategic and humanizing presence in the 1989 and 1993 campaigns, appearing in four television commercials and narrating some of them. She was one of the inner circle of five that reviewed all of the commercials, and, by her own account, she helped "write speeches and raise money." Key campaign aides in 1989 and 1993 described her as the quickest route to Rudy's saner side, a media-wise and forceful counselor.

Visible almost daily at the campaign headquarters, particularly in 1993, she saved him from his own clumsy indecision on abortion, convincing enough women in a stridently pro-choice town that she would not let him waver in office as he had on his way to it. "I think I was helpful in attracting women to the campaign," she said, understating her role the day after the win. Moderately modern in outlook, effusive yet smart in person, and accomplished by all but the loftiest professional standards, she was just what this hardened son of the fifties needed to make himself marketable.

"I can't think of an important decision I've made that I haven't talked about with Donna," Giuliani told *New York* magazine three months after moving into Gracie Mansion in 1994. "She has a remarkable understanding of history and politics." In a *People* magazine interview published in June, he called her "my closest adviser."

Rudy was not just talking about campaign decisions. He might well have never become U.S. Attorney had it not been for her, urging him to leave

Washington out of what she saw then as mutual career interests in New York. She trained him in camera management while he was U.S. Attorney, teaching him the art of the sound bite, and what to do with his hands, his eyes and his smile.

Her extraordinary pilgrimages to New Haven for the Friedman trial in 1986, shoeless and red-eyed, were a measure of her understanding that this world-is-watching case was indispensable to their next joint step. She talked on those train trips with a reporter about her own ambitions for Rudy, and the breathlessness of it told him she saw no limits to where they could go. The mansion that beckoned wasn't just Gracie. She asked the reporter what he thought Rudy should run for and he said her husband should remain U.S. Attorney, contending Giuliani could do more good there than anywhere, as a forcefield of deterrence that would make every corrupt pol, Wall Street trader or mobster think twice. Her eyes went blank, the conversation ebbed, the bubble she strains to carry inside her burst.

Donna and Rudy understood that if she was to successfully rub off on him, lightening his public gravity, they would have to put their private life on display. They did it self-consciously. He was certainly the first U.S. Attorney in New York photographed on his bed with his wife, both of them playfully hugging in Yankee caps for a magazine photographer. They told reporters they danced to Frank Sinatra records alone on New Year's Eve. Donna detailed nuances of their earliest exchanges in Miami. Rudy recounted how he conceived the commission case in a private moment with her in their Washington townhouse. They dropped gossip items each time they set a wedding date in 1983 and 1984. Two days before Andrew's fourth birthday in 1990, Donna told the *Daily News* he would be getting glow-in-the-dark sheets. Their staged kisses—for still photographers and *Inside Edition*—were full mouth.

In a 1993 campaign interview with *Newsday*, Donna announced: "My husband is the most virile man." She added that he was "so strong and wonderful," as well as "the most good-looking man in the city as far as I'm concerned." In case the reader still hadn't gotten the point, she concluded: "I love him just the way he is." The gush machine went on to ask the reporter: "I'd love to have you put something in about how wonderful my mother-in-law is as a babysitter. I do have a wonderful mother-in-law."

In the 1989 campaign, she told reporters that they went out of their way to keep the family together on holidays, recounting how Rudy came to WPIX with Andrew if she had to work. "We go to the same events," she said, "incorporating our family life with our professional lives."

When Giuliani considered running for the U.S. Senate in December 1987, Donna openly discussed the impact of a Senate seat on their family. She told the

Times it might require too prolonged a separation, given her job in New York. "That's definitely one of the major things on both of our minds," she said. "How much it would mean him being away from us. We waited a long time to have this little boy." (Andrew was born two years after their 1984 marriage.) She said she would ultimately support a race "if he says, 'You and Andrew are #1 in my life.'"

Rudy and Donna's public intimacy did not end when they won. The inaugural was a giant family affair, with her parents, Bob and Gwen Kofnovec, flying in from California to take second row center seats next to Uncle Rudy Giuliani and wife Viola, right behind Governor and Matilda Cuomo. Grandpa Bob advertised his Texas roots by donning a white cowboy hat on the walk up Broadway, lugging four-year-old Caroline in his arms.

Seven-year-old Andrew stole the show by joining Rudy at the podium throughout the inaugural address, waving, yawning, echoing his father's words, even punching his fist in the air for emphasis. Donna, from her seat, tried at one point to stop Andrew from moving around the lectern, demanding that he "stay there." But he ignored her, carrying on so outrageously he made himself an instant David Letterman celebrity. When Rudy appeared on the show afterwards, Letterman deadpanned: "We wanted to have his son Andrew, but tonight Andrew is with Koppel on *Nightline*."

Donna stood with her husband and two children when he took the oath of office, just as she had during the two private ceremonies that preceded it. In an unusually emotional display, Rudy saluted her in his inaugural address, calling Donna "my wife, my partner, my inspiration and my lover." Donna, he said, "is one of three people I believe most responsible for my standing here." He named Peter Powers and Dave Garth as the other two.

Rudy and Donna touched affectionately all day, he grabbing her shoulder at times and she reaching backwards to clasp his hand. Just like on their wedding day, they cut a giant cake together with a single knife, this one embroidered with the city seal and consumed by a few of the five thousand who gathered at a Pepsi party afterwards.

"I made two resolutions," he said on New Year's Day at City Hall. "One was to be the very best mayor I could be. And the other was to be the very best father and husband I could be." The inaugural stretched out over two ceremonial days, with Rudy and Donna inseparable, traveling to every borough, visiting precincts and firehouses with boxes of chocolate chip cookies. Giuliani's signed, three-paragraph message on the first page of the inaugural program began: "Donna and I are humbled by the faith you have placed in us." The rest of the message was a series of plural pledges.

Monsignor Alan Placa, who married them and baptized their children, said they were resolved to create a "Fortress Giuliani" within the two-story, creamy yellow Gracie Mansion that replicated as nearly as possible their modest, joined apartments on East 86th Street. To furnish this real home within so public a space, Donna said they brought with them only their own old furniture, which she described as "what Rudy had when we were married, and what I had, modified by Toys 'R Us."

She told an interviewer that April: "When Rudy was elected, I said I want to raise a family, but I want to have an impact." She announced that "one of the reasons" she became a journalist was because she "always wanted to know what was going on on the inside." Now, she smiled, she was "as on the inside as you can be." So she made sure she was included in high-level discussions at City Hall and the mansion, declaring she would be the mayor's "adviser and confidant." Likening First Lady to being the wife of a CEO, she described herself as "the person who says 'I love you very dearly but you're not right about that.'"

She allowed a *Daily News* reporter to accompany her for a month in the spring of 1994—on everything from a stint at her Food Network job to a Harlem Week visit—and she was still telling chirpy Andrew jokes four months after the inaugural. Described by the *News* as "a 90s incarnation of a 50s wife and mom," she raved about the compatibility of her french fries and focaccia cable life and her role as First Lady. "It's a perfect working mother's job. I can do a first-lady breakfast and a first-lady lunch and then either go and put my kids to bed or do another first-lady event."

In addition to a vast mansion staff, she hired four personal assistants at a public cost of $127,000 a year, headed by a press secretary and another assistant who told a reporter she advised Hanover "on confidential issues." After a couple years of raises for all four, they were up to $167,000. This staff—far more than any prior First Lady's—was put on a city payroll that was shrinking in the first two Giuliani years faster than at any time since the near bankruptcy of the mid-'70s.

Fiscal woes were also not allowed to intrude on happy time at the repainted riverfront mansion, where most of the colors in the living quarters were instantly changed to lighter shades on sunny Donna's orders. Donna started fundraising for major renovations at the mansion from the moment she moved in, raising $421,630 in 1994 from private donors, and spending almost all of it to strip the chimneys down to the original brick, replace railings and carpets and acquire antiques. It was twice what David and Joyce Dinkins had spent in four years, and the most raised for the mansion since a major 1984 renovation. At the same time, the NYPD installed a high-tech $150,000 security system, even though the mansion was surrounded by fences and had twenty-four-hour police details.

Donna's "Cool Schools" project—with her presenting a $2,500 check, a wall clock and t-shirts each month to two good public schools—was announced at the same time that her husband was unveiling the worst school budget cuts in decades. While Rudy became the first mayor in history to ask Albany for less school aid, and his deputy mayor Fran Reiter endorsed federal education slashes championed by congressional Republicans, Hanover bustled around the city to create what she called a "positive perception" about working schools.

She also tried to meld her professional and mayoral lives. Asked by a reporter which name she used, Donna responded: "I can never remember how I left the dry-cleaning. Since I got married, I've used all combinations of the names. Donna Hanover is my professional name. The mortgage is Donna Hanover Giuliani; the taxes, Donna Hanover Giuliani. . . . I would prefer Donna Hanover Giuliani, although in a professional capacity, I would continue to use Donna Hanover. I'm comfortable with any combination."

The mayor was drawn into her business life in minor and major ways. When she did a cameo appearance in the movie *The Paper*, Rudy rushed back from his first Washington visit as mayor to attend the March 15 premiere with Donna (he left midway through because a cop was shot). He was also attentive to her TV Food Network (TVFN) friends. In fact, the fledgling network's association with the new First Family played a behind-the-cameras role in its gaining a channel in New York City—another example, just like WPIX, of how Donna's ties to Rudy influenced her career.

On February 28, two months after the inaugural, Giuliani took the unusual step of attending what his private schedule called "the management luncheon" of the network, though mayors rarely appear at corporate events for start-up companies. TVFN debuted in some markets on November 23, 1993, but it was unable to find even temporary space on the congested New York City cable dial until February 1, 1994. All it could get then, however, was a channel that NBC's America's Talking was slated to take over that July. Shortly after TVFN lost its NBC channel, Reese Schonfeld, its founder and CEO, brought his family to the mansion for a private Thursday dinner with the Giuliani family. It was Schonfeld who had hired Donna. In addition to the dinner, Schonfeld, who says he's been close to the Giulianis for years, recalls a Sunday lunch at the mansion. He insists it was all family chitchat at the gatherings.

Schonfeld acknowledges, however, that he was then frantically searching for a spot on the dial. He says a Manhattan channel is worth "five channels in any other market because that's where the advertisers are." While Schonfeld says his fledgling network was entitled from the beginning to a New York channel as a result of complicated national cable transmission agreements, he was unsure how he would get one when he hired Donna in the summer of 1993. While he denies it was a factor in her hiring, TVFN may well have seen Donna's identification with the network as a potential asset in gaining NYC access should her husband win the mayoralty.

Time Warner controlled the Manhattan dial—but its city-awarded franchise was regulated by a Giuliani agency and up for renewal in Giuliani's first term. Donna's presence at TVFN certainly couldn't have hurt with T/W, whose president, Dick Parsons, was a close friend of Giuliani's going back to their joint days at Patterson, Belknap, as well as a top campaign and transition aide to the new mayor. T/W facilitated the network's temporary use of the NBC station, as did Roger Ailes, the former Giuliani campaign manager who was then running America's Talking.

When the NBC option ran out, though, T/W could not deliver a permanent channel. Dick Aurelio, the T/W executive who ran the city franchise, says now that media companies "were standing in line to get on our system." Aurelio and Fred Dressler, another T/W executive who negotiated with Schonfeld, say that TVFN had no transmission rights to a channel that put them ahead of others on the waiting line.

Schonfeld's first meeting with Aurelio was a 1994 breakfast at Michael's Restaurant on the East Side, arranged by none other than the mayor's media consultant, David Garth. Garth called Aurelio to set up the breakfast and, as Aurelio remembers it, he told Garth on the phone that he didn't think there was anything he could do to help Schonfeld get a channel. It was Garth, says Aurelio, who broached the notion of TVFN "getting one of the city public-access channels" at the breakfast. "The impression I had was that Garth was wearing a Giuliani hat," said Aurelio, a onetime deputy mayor in the Lindsay administration. Aurelio had last seen his old friend Garth at a 1993 dinner, when Garth blasted him about T/W's campaign coverage of his client, Candidate Rudy.

"Garth never said explicitly that he was doing this for Giuliani," Aurelio says. "But I definitely had the impression that he was. It was implicit that the mayor was involved. I just assumed I was getting more pressure from the Giuliani people." Aurelio says he told Schonfeld and Garth it would be "political dynamite" because of Donna's ties to the network. He also warned that use of a public access channel for commercial purposes posed a possible legal problem. In fact, when Giuliani tried a few years later to deliver a city channel to Fox, another Donna employer, a federal judge barred it.

Schonfeld acknowledges Garth's role in pushing Aurelio and seeking a city channel, saying Garth and he live in the same West Side building and that Garth did it as a personal favor. Told that Aurelio saw it as pressure from Giuliani, Schonfeld said: "He couldn't have read it more incorrectly." With Aurelio unable to deliver a city channel, Schonfeld says Garth talked directly to Rudy. "The mayor said there was no way he could help us, particularly because Donna worked at the network," Schonfeld recalls.

Schonfeld says T/W had meanwhile put him together with a channel controlled by a New Jersey public television station, NJN. The best T/W could do, though, was get the Food Network on from midnight to 3 P.M., when NJN aired no programming. Donna's show, as Schonfeld recalls it, was a prime-time newscast outside New York City, but on at the crack of dawn in the city. So Schonfeld launched a protracted political campaign in New Jersey "to find the right person" to sell him NJN's New York rights.

Since it was a state-owned channel and Christie Whitman was governor, Schonfeld wound up meeting with Candy Straight, a top Whitman fund-raiser and lobbyist. Straight, who sat on an NJN board, had also been involved in both Giuliani campaigns, donating $6,500 to the 1993 effort. Straight was such a close friend of Donna's that Donna had attended her private birthday party. "I can't tell you if I did or didn't talk to Donna about Straight," says Schonfeld. "I can't remember if Schonfeld mentioned Donna," adds Straight, who concedes she "certainly knew Donna was on the network." Straight steered him to other insiders close to the governor, Schonfeld says, and he eventually got the support of the Whitman-appointed chair of the state Public Broadcasting Authority, Joseph Montuoro, another GOP fund-raiser.

Schonfeld acknowledges he bought the valuable channel's air time for eight years without any competitive bidding for a piddling $4.3 million. He maintains that no one else could have purchased the channel since T/W had assigned it to the network; NJN echoed Schonfeld in their own statement. But Aurelio says "anybody could have made that deal" and that he had "no idea" why the state didn't auction it. Aurelio recalls receiving a letter from Whitman's office authorizing the sale to TVFN. "There might have been some particular influence," says Aurelio. As soon as Schonfeld closed the Jersey deal, he left as managing partner, having created what is now a cable colossus.

The Food Network job—Donna's first in three years—started the turnaround in her financial condition. Her 1994 income of $114,659—most of it from the network—more than tripled her 1993 freelance earnings of $32,773. With most living expenses covered by the city, she was, for the first time in her life, free to salt away a substantial percent of what would prove to be a mounting yearly income. Donna's total Food Network earnings alone through 1999 were $720,321.

Not only was 1994 a good year for Donna financially, it was a good year for her and her husband personally, at least most of it was. Rudy and she hosted dozens of the private dinner parties she loved, turning the official dining room, with its table for twenty-two, ornate off-center fireplace and finely detailed wallpaper of French monuments, into a buzzing hive of high-energy networking. Donna estimated that they were doing "one or two dinner parties a week," as well as "the usual four or five receptions."

Most of the receptions occurred in the mansion ballroom, which seats 120 under high ceilings, with tall, gaping windows, Greek columns, candle chandeliers and a rare, ornamented mahogany commode. When it was warmer, the receptions spilled out, past the aqua-green shutters, onto the northeast porch and the back lawn, from which the Giulianis and their guests could catch a panoramic view of the Triborough Bridge, connecting Manhattan in a string of lights with Queens and the Bronx. The lawn, bordered by a high wooden fence and thick shrubs, is part of the eleven-acre Carl Schurz Park, all compacted landfill overhanging the FDR Drive. Rudy and Donna could stand in their backyard and hear and feel the humming city they were such a part of beneath their feet.

In addition to a rather mundane and messy office for four in the basement, Donna had her own sitting room on the main floor, off the southwest corner of the ballroom. It was named the Susan Wagner room in honor of Robert Wagner's wife, and it was modeled after a tearoom in a little girl's dollhouse. Opposite the portrait of Susan Wagner, one of a doting Donna was hung. Donna gave interviews here, lots of them in 1994. She entertained friends in one-on-ones and small groups. Rudy had his den nearby, with a large leather couch and a pillow embroidered with the phrase: "It ain't easy being king."

Rudy's private schedule the first year revealed a remarkable number—at least for him—of family dinners and other family time, particularly on Sunday. On February 15, Donna's birthday, the schedule commanded that Rudy "depart City Hall for Gracie Mansion at 6:15 SHARP!"—the only such invocation that year. The rest of the night is marked "personal time." He helped fix a dinner for two that night and they danced to Johnny Mathis, with the kids secreted upstairs.

On Rudy's birthday in May, the words "DAY OFF" dominate the calendar, the only time they appear in 1994. On their anniversary in April, the calendar indicates a 7 P.M. City Hall departure for the mansion and "personal time," an atypical early end to his day. Each was an earmark of Giuliani's attempt to get some balance between family and a job so vital it consumed him.

In their private time at the fourteen-room mansion, they managed to make the main floor—which is open to tourists one day a week—a homey and natural setting. Donna told stories of family runs through it, sometimes after Goalie, the lab they bought when they moved in. But the private second floor, up a curving staircase or an elevator in Rudy's den, was a sanctuary, and joyously their own in the early months. It was the first time in twenty years—since John and Mary Lindsay—that a family with children occupied the mansion, and the creaky wood floors seemed to celebrate.

Donna was on such a roll she was celebrating as well—most effusively in an interview with *Town & Country*, done in the early fall for their Christmas edition. She spread eight years of family Christmas cards out on a table, every year since Andrew's birth—revealing "changing hairlines and hairstyles."

She talked about how their festivities always start with the night before the Thanksgiving Parade, "when we take the children to West 77th Street to watch the balloons being blown up." She said they'd take the Rockefeller Center window walk, have Helen over for Christmas Eve memories about "life in her old Brooklyn neighborhood," watch *It's a Wonderful Life* for the hundredth time and trim the tree with, among other things, a Virgin Island seashell she and Rudy had saved from a trip years before.

"There is a sense of continuity, of history having happened, of it happening right now," she said. "We wouldn't want to be anywhere else."

Donna Hanover, then forty-four, married ten years, a Donna Reed throwback from a Jimmy Stewart dream, finally back before the cameras she'd sought since high school in Sunnyvale, had no idea that her world was unraveling as she spoke. The winter chill that soon entered their lives seemed, at first, like a passing phase. Donna and the friends close to her and her husband thought it would bow to the warming bonds of young children and a dozen years of intimate entanglement. But when mutual withdrawal hardened into habit, she knew that the comfort she felt all around her that day in *Town & Country* would never return.

The twenty-eight-year-old woman who was named City Hall's youngest press secretary in history understood that getting a top job was often a result of a strong underling relationship with a superior, in Rudy's world and in many others. Cristyne Lategano, a sneaker saleswoman at Super Runners on the Upper East Side just a couple of years earlier, made herself an appendage of Rudy's through a long campaign of forced smiles and callused handshakes. She matched his energy and his desire, looking for votes on park benches and sidewalks from one end of the city to the other, and one side of the clock to the other. She proved to him that she cared, and he rewarded her with a powerful position whose traditional standards she could not meet.

Those who worked with her in the 1993 campaign and in the years that followed at City Hall said Lategano never wrote a press release. She and the mayor, always at each other's side, edited drafts of some releases together, but no one knew if she could actually compose the stock-in-trade of her profession. She was so ill at ease with reporters that she announced her discomfort at a press conference in 1995, declaring "I usually don't talk to you guys and I try not to, as you know."

A Rutgers graduate with less than two years of experience in press relations before joining the Giuliani campaign in the spring of 1993, Lategano had worked on the congressional staff of a Republican congresswoman from Maryland, and the New Jersey campaign staff of George Bush's 1992 re-election committee. One pro-choice press release bearing her name was repudiated by the national Bush campaign, which was publicly baffled by the issuance of a statement that it said "appears to be contrary to the president's position."

Garth and Giuliani decided they needed a female press aide to accompany the candidate on his constant swings through the city. Rudy was too often surrounded by white males, they reasoned. Lategano's résumé came in over the transom and she impressed Garth aide Richard Bryers, the press secretary, who passed her name on to Peter Powers, the campaign manager. It was a demanding, yet low-paying, position made for a young single with discipline and discretion.

A marathoner and vegetarian, Lategano mixed an airy confidence with a sweet shyness. When she pulled her long, reddish brown hair back, her lean and open face might've reminded Rudy of a young Regina. Her clunky, muscular legs dominated her waistless body, and she could be heard pounding her way in high heels or flats from far off—assertive, emphatic.

Her other asset was that she, like Bryers, knew no one in the New York press corps. Since the campaign press strategy was a straight-arm to the mouth of any overly inquisitive reporter, her out-of-town ignorance made her a perfect buffer, unconflicted by any media relationships.

The *Daily News* reported that during her first interview with Giuliani, she impressed him with her firm grip on Yankee baseball trivia. "She is a real Yankee fan," the mayor said later, "and I can usually tell the difference." That wasn't their only common bond. She was born in Brooklyn and moved to Long Island as a kid, graduating from Lynbrook High School, where Harold Giuliani had once tended the grounds. Indeed her best-known public propensity—a stonewalling antipathy to reporters—was merely a reflection of Rudy, one of countless ways she molded herself in his image.

The night of the 1993 win, she was with Rudy and Donna at hotel victory parties until the early hours of the morning, and when Rudy finally followed Donna to bed for a couple hours' sleep before the morning rush of interviews, he was heard calling her "Crissie." Few challenges can compete with campaigns as a bonding experience—the intensity of it merged these two, already sympatico, personalities, long before anything deeper may have started.

In her first months as press secretary, she took a beating. She had no experience managing anyone, yet she suddenly had to oversee a City Hall press and research staff, as well as public information offices in dozens of agencies. Reporters were in a constant state of fevered dismay; with deadlines breathing down their necks they couldn't get answers to basic questions.

She embarrassed herself in May by calling reporters to tell them the new administration had evidence of gross mismanagement by Dinkins's just-departed Youth Services commissioner, Richard Murphy. The false alarm, ultimately refuted by Giuliani's own Department of Investigations, was transparently designed to deflect attention from charges against the agency's new commissioner that were just coming to light. Murphy had to wait a year for his exoneration, while Giuliani's appointee had to resign immediately.

She was caught bragging about how she got a *Times* editorial killed. Even her apartment became a minor scandal, when *Newsday* revealed that she was one of several top campaign and administration aides who'd gotten discounted apartments from top Giuliani fund-raiser William Koeppel, a real estate developer.

John Miller, Bratton's press aide, became a close friend of hers in 1994 and recalls her frequent teary days. Once that fall, Miller, Lategano and Jack Maple went to lunch at a coffee shop neat the Hall and "she broke down, complaining that everyone had lined up against her." She said her opponents within the Giuliani inner circle—which included Garth and Powers—thought "she couldn't do anything right."

Garth said flat out in subsequent interviews: "I did not think she was qualified to be the press secretary, and my opinion hasn't changed." He kept interviewing candidates to replace her or serve over her head in a new position of communications director, and Giuliani kept rejecting the recommendations. Garth grew so frustrated, he broke with Giuliani by that fall, declaring later: "I don't want to work anywhere I'm not comfortable."

With an office to run, Lategano refused to give up her old campaign role as Giuliani companion, traveling with him almost everywhere in the specially equipped white Chevy Suburban wagon. That kind of schedule, often including parts of a weekend, crushed her social life. She'd dated another campaign aide, Ron

Giller, during the 1993 race and into the first year. She was enchanted by City Planning Commission chair Joe Rose, the son of a millionaire developer with golden-boy charm. She also went out early in the first year with Michael Lewittes, a *Daily News* gossip columnist.

Everyone thought she was dating Miller, too, but the TV hunk, who usually juggles a very full dance card, insists the relationship hovered between a friendship and a romance, without ever becoming a romance. Ironically, Cristyne "started going to Elaine's with me," recalls Miller, "and then without me." Denny Young once told Miller to "stay out of Elaine's because this is a blue-collar administration" and the mayor doesn't want his top people depicted in the press as part of "some café society." Giuliani, of course, later made Bratton's visits to the Upper East Side watering hole a count in the indictment against him.

Miller trained for the November 6, 1994 New York City marathon with Cristyne. It was his first race, and she was already a seasoned runner. "She worked me like a dog," said Miller, acknowledging that they spent so much time together, doing Central Park "in the middle of the night," that it was widely assumed they were dating. The day of the race, with both Miller and Rose running, the mayor fired the starting cannon from a naval station in Staten Island and was then helicoptered to Brooklyn and driven to the finish line. Around 12:45 P.M., he and the race organizer, Allan Steinfeld, started holding opposite ends of the tape—first for the men's winner and then for the women's. There was a twenty-minute-or-so respite between the end of the race and the awards presentation, which also featured the mayor. Usually, says Steinfeld, the mayor leaves after the awards are done.

But Giuliani waited for Lategano. She did the race in four hours and twenty-six minutes, meaning she came in at 3:16, almost two hours after the female winner. Giuliani was supposed to be appearing with Donna at a hotel press conference and rally for Mario Cuomo. Billed as a "unity" event precisely because of Giuliani's cross-party endorsement, the event was the culmination of the campaign, with the election just a day away. It was on his schedule for 3:15 P.M., but he was still waiting for Cristyne at the finish line then. He left for the rally after greeting her, and before Miller dragged himself over the line. (Rose never finished.)

Miller, once the acknowledged top TV crime reporter in New York and a friend of Giuliani's from his U.S. Attorney days, had already been through a spat with Rudy involving Lategano. When the mayor read a news story indicating that a parade to celebrate the 150th anniversary of the NYPD was to be held on Bratton's birthday—a pure scheduling accident, according to Bratton—he canceled it. Then Lategano dropped a couple of hostile quotes on Bratton in a news story. Miller objected to the comments in a conversation with Lategano, saying Giuliani "didn't have to squeeze" Bratton like that. A protective Giuliani called Miller, screamed at him for reprimanding Lategano and hung up on him.

A couple of weeks after the marathon, Miller found himself in another bitter exchange with the mayor, this time over a Sunday *Daily News* headline: "Bratton's Juggernaut." The December 11 story announced a major new drug initiative and Giuliani was incensed about "the leak," demanding that he wanted "the people responsible found and dealt with." No one doubted that if the headline read "Rudy's Juggernaut," it would have been toasted. The mayor killed the plan and zeroed in on Miller as a prime suspect.

Then, on December 23, the blond, curly-headed, six-foot-tall Miller was standing in the marble-pillared rotunda at City Hall when Lategano spied him on her way out of the press office. She ran to him, leaped in the air and wrapped her legs and arms around his $2,000 suit. He spun her around. To Miller, it was a zestful, Christmas-break farewell. The mayor, however, was just a few steps behind Lategano. He stood and watched. Joe Rose was also, coincidentally, in the hallway, having strolled over, like Miller, from his nearby office. "The mayor scowled and walked past them without a word," said Kevin Davitt, an aide to Rose and witness to the spectacle.

Cristyne gave Miller a Hermès tie for Christmas. "She said she'd given it to Rudy first," Miller recounted, "but he said he couldn't accept a gift from an underling." She asked Miller to "try not to let him see you wearing the tie."

Miller says that after the Christmas/New Year's break, he got a phone call from Denny Young, the consigliere, as mob reporter Miller calls him. "Don't call Cristyne again," were his instructions. A few days passed and Miller was preparing to handle press inquiries on a major new NYPD initiative. He left Lategano a message and got another call from Young. "I thought I told you not to call Cristyne," Miller recalls Young saying. "Well, this was a purely press business matter. I didn't realize I wasn't to call her on a press advisory." In that case, said Young, it's okay to call her. But five minutes later, he got another call from Young: "No," said the lawyer attached to the mayor's hip, "I was wrong about that. Don't call her about anything."

The stunned Miller kept his distance, smelling a final confrontation in the air. He couldn't sort out all the motives—was this jealousy or pique over the Bratton publicity machine? In February, the Hall suddenly insisted that Miller's entire public information staff be replaced. It was such a challenge to Bratton's authority that he and the rest of his top staff huddled and talked about quitting en masse. Miller slipped out of the meeting and fell on his own sword, announcing his res-

ignation to a group of reporters and a live NY1 audience. "Now loyalty is important," he said.

> Loyalty runs up. I'm loyal to the mayor, I'm loyal to the police commissioner
> . . . but there were loyal Nazis too. Loyalty runs down too and I'm loyal to
> my people. . . . Now they want to find places for everybody to go. So what do
> they say, the captain is supposed to go down with the ship, right?
>
> Somebody in this administration said, trying to summarize the company
> line, "We want to have more control over the information." The information
> that we put out here is not information that we are supposed to "control." It's
> not the mayor's information, it's the public's information. That's why they
> call this Public Information.

Miller convulsed in televised tears.

Giuliani returned fire: "It seems to me that John had difficulty accomplishing
what is a very difficult management task. Some people are very good at one thing,
they're not very good at another." He dismissed the media furor, saying that it was
certainly "not a tumultuous day in New York City when the deputy commissioner
for public relations of the NYPD resigns."

"Big deal," he wisecracked. Giuliani sacked the press heads of four other city
agencies and fired three dozen press aides the same day, consolidating a scaled-
down press operation under the tight control of Lategano. The dismissals and dramatic Miller resignation were an object lesson. Anyone "off-message," as City
Hall put it, would soon be off-premises, and the message was only four letters
long: RUDY. Though the Bratton team would hang on for another year, their fate
was decided in the Miller fracas, and no one was ever able to separate the personal
and policy causes that drove Rudy to make that war.

While simultaneously using a mutual friend to discreetly assure Miller that she
was not behind the attacks on him, Lategano went after the Bratton press machine. "Public relations was put before any kind of substance," she said. "When
you put glamour over fighting crime, it leads to serious problems. This is a reality
check. We're here to fight crime, not to be Hollywood stars. This is real-life cops,
not *NYPD Blue*." Her willingness to implicitly attack Miller drew her even closer
to the mayor, who told reporters: "I think she put it quite accurately."

In March, Lenny Alcivar, the deputy press secretary, began organizing a thirti-
eth birthday party for Lategano. He called former beau Michael Lewittes, who
helped with names of friends unknown to the City Hall crowd. The party was set

for Sunday evening, March 19, the day before her birthday. The mayor, who'd encouraged Alcivar to put it together, asked him the Friday before how it was going. He wanted Alcivar to read him the guest list. He told Alcivar he wanted Lewittes and Joe Rose "disinvited."

Alcivar protested that Lewittes had helped him organize the party, but the mayor was insistent. He even checked again with Alcivar to see if he'd followed the instructions. Rose, who was known to beep Lategano in the early-morning hours, and Lewittes were told not to come. No one, of course, considered inviting Lategano's near-dear friend John Miller.

The mayor's private calendar that Sunday included a 6 P.M., pre-party, "communications meeting" at City Hall, attended by Lategano and a dozen other top aides, most of whom were shoehorned into the party at Jim McMullen's restaurant. The schedule has him leaving City Hall at 8 P.M. and going to a "private meeting" thereafter. It's an unusual entry since it says nothing about the location and purpose of the meeting and lists no departing time. In fact, contrary to the overwhelming majority of calendar listings in this time period and the security protocol, there is no indication that the mayor ever departed for or arrived at the mansion.

Giuliani was with Lategano the next Sunday as well—the day he and Donna had agreed would be a family day. *Newsday* spotted him and Cris "pawing through the racks at the Ann Taylor and Laura Ashley stores on East 57th Street." A saleswoman at one store was quoted in the gossip item: "She picked out a couple of skirts and asked him what he thought. And the mayor would say 'Oh, that looks fine.'" The subsequent explanation offered by City Hall was that the mayor was due at an Orthodox Jewish function that evening and Cristyne's short skirt would've been inappropriate.

What no one knew was that immediately prior to leaving City Hall for the midtown event—which was just fifteen blocks from Lategano's 73rd Street apartment—the mayor had held another Sunday afternoon "communications meeting" at City Hall. The room was filled with alternatives to Lategano who could have accompanied him to the National Council of Young Israel dinner, including Bruce Teitelbaum, Giuliani's liaison to the Jewish community.

On March 31, Giuliani announced a $25,000 raise for Lategano, from $77,000 to $103,000, and a promotion to a new title at City Hall, director of communications. Powers and Garth had suggested the title as a way of installing someone with management ability over Lategano. Instead, she got the title herself, and won subsequent raises all the way up to $141,000 in 1999. When she got the promotion, the *Times* quoted from a three-day-old directive sent by the budget office to all agency heads. It said that "increased responsibilities, reorganization or reassignment does not necessarily justify a level change, promotion or salary adjustment." Cristyne actually explained that the funding for her raise came out of the savings from the dismissal of Miller and many others in press offices.

In May, Cristyne moved downstairs to an office right next to Rudy's. Her new office was a converted conference room that was being used by another top aide, who moved elsewhere. She quickly filled her large office with framed magazine covers of Rudy and a photo of her with Barbara Bush. Rudy had an office on the main floor that was used primarily for ceremonial purposes. He spent most of his time down a hidden circular stairwell that led only to the joined, two-office complex he and Cris now shared. To get there, even top staff had to be cleared through Giuliani's secretary on the main floor. There was a shower and a bathroom, a kitchenette, two desks and two sofas, a conference table, VCR and two television sets in the suite, a cozy setting for the constant companions.

Between the time they spent in the basement offices and on the road in "the ice cream truck," as the Suburban was called, Lategano and Giuliani were rarely apart. Gossip items had them at late-night dinners. When he put on weight, she put on weight. When he got into cigars, she was seen taking a puff from one of his. They'd ride in the van eating from the same slice of pizza and drinking from the same diet drink. They wore similar double-breasted pinstripe suits. She'd fix his tie before a TV or major public appearance and he'd ask: "How do I look?" He'd make a scrunched-up face and she'd mirror it, saying: "Oh, you look like a bunny rabbit." They'd both wind up with bunny-rabbit faces that broke into smiles.

The 1994 New York marathon was her last. She trained for the 1995 marathon but didn't run. By 1996, she was still a jogger, but no longer had the energy or the inclination for the rigorous preparation that was once the inner discipline of her life. She also stopped dating anyone regularly, making herself available to him any hour of any day he wanted. She embraced opera and red meat. Friends who visited her bare-walled apartment—just a short walk from the mansion—said it "didn't look lived in." When around him, she even took to wearing a custom-made police badge bearing four stars as a sign of her precocious power.

Her body language at evening events was wifelike. She'd get "all glammed up," as an aide described it, and "carry a little purse and cell phone, with no schedules, speeches, memos or briefcase" (another staffer, Manny Papir, usually carried the work). During the day, she had a tote bag full of paper. But at night, she was frequently empty-handed, as if out on a date. He'd pick her up at the crack of dawn and drop her off in the dead of night. When they walked together, they'd lean close to each other, whispering and often touching. Neither she nor the mayor took vacations, except for an occasional Lategano visit with her parents in South Carolina. They were so often together late at night that they were noticed by the press arriving in the same car at a 1 A.M. building collapse, the twenty-four-hour mayor and his twenty-four-hour accessory.

The whispers were getting so loud Donna could hear them. She had joined Powers and Garth at some point in urging that an experienced press manager be installed above Lategano. Instead, Cristyne was elevated to communications director. If Donna had once been his "closest adviser," Lategano was now. Rudy was even increasingly on the road on Sundays—his promised family day—and Cristyne was almost always with him.

While his 1994 private schedule demanded he head home at 6:15 SHARP! on Donna's February birthday, he went to a Waldorf-Astoria dinner for the Manhattan Republican Committee on her 1995 birthday. The schedule had him arriving at 7:15 P.M. and staying at the dinner until 8 P.M., when he was supposed to depart for the mansion. That would have him home about two hours later than 1994, but one GOP partygoer remembers him staying at the dinner even later.

The day before Donna's birthday, Valentine's Day, lists Cristyne covering eight events with Giuliani, an hour of "personal time" at City Hall and an evening at a Citizens Union dinner. Just as the schedule specified no departing or arriving time for Gracie Mansion on Lategano's birthday, it had none on Valentine's Day either. Both were highly unusual omissions. In 1994, on the other hand, he was listed as leaving City Hall at 7 P.M. on Valentine's Day for "personal time" at the mansion.

Their eleventh anniversary fell on an April Saturday in 1995, yet Giuliani had a nearly full day of outside events, mostly with Cristyne, ending in the Bronx at a banquet sponsored by an Hispanic minister who'd backed him in 1993, the Reverend Ruben Diaz. He did bring Caroline on a Central Park Easter egg hunt that morning—it was the day before Easter—returning her to the mansion before heading out again.

The events surrounding the anniversary suggest it was a particularly critical moment. The day before, his schedule listed a two-hour, mid-afternoon, meeting with Elliot Cuker, who functioned as a go-between with Donna. The two Saturdays after the anniversary, he trekked out to Long Island to meet with his old friend Monsignor Placa. Cristyne was listed as with him for mayoral appearances before and after his first trip to Placa, and before his second, but she is not listed as accompanying him there. It was the only time in a year and a half of schedules that such sustained meetings with Cuker and Placa were listed.

In June, the tensions exploded when Giuliani disappeared for most of Father's Day. He did one press event that morning and when reporters asked what else he had planned for the day, he said he was going back to the mansion to play ball with Andrew. One reporter went back to City Hall, however, and saw Rudy and Cristyne arrive and head to the downstairs suite. Three hours later, they were still there. Bruce Teitelbaum, another mayoral aide, was upstairs in an office and the reporter later asked if he knew what Lategano and the mayor were doing. Teitelbaum put his hand up as if to bar the question, smiled, and said: "I don't know." The reporter finally left.

An enraged Donna finally drove there, demanding to see her husband. According to a news account published two years later, she was kept in a side office by Rudy aides. When he finally came upstairs to leave, the husband and wife who had so publicly announced their affection and interdependence sixteen months earlier on the same City Hall steps came apart as a couple.

Life in the mansion turned frigid. Donna issued edicts that Giuliani dared not defy. Cristyne was never to appear at an event that the mayor and Donna attended together. Kim Serafin and others from the press office substituted for her; they told staffers they were instructed to replace Lategano at Hanover events. Informed at the last minute that Hanover was attending an August speech Giuliani was delivering at the Wharton Club, Lategano left the van in a rush. Eventually this rule of avoidance became a virtual nullity since there were so few joint appearances.

In late September, *New York* magazine's Craig Horowitz wrote a cover story headlined: "Thirty-year-old Cristyne Lategano Has Suddenly Become the Second Most Powerful Person in NYC. And the Most Controversial. What Does Rudy See in Her?" The article asserted that she'd surpassed Peter Powers as the "ultimate insider" in the administration, and raised the question of "an extra-professional relationship."

What Horowitz could not know at the time was that Powers was so frustrated by Lategano's incendiary influence on his lifelong friend that he, too, like Garth, Miller and Bratton, would wind up leaving the administration in part because of her. Ironically, Lategano managed in short order to drive a wedge between Giuliani and all three of the people he'd cited at the inaugural as "most responsible" for making him mayor.

Horowitz spent more space rebutting any hint of an affair than he did supporting it, but the piece, undoubtedly read by everyone Donna knew, cast a cloud that hung over the mansion for years. City Hall charged that any suggestion of a relationship was sexist because Lategano was merely doing her job. But, in fact, no press secretary had ever "followed the body" like Cristyne. Usually, a changing guard of lower-level press aides accompanied a mayor, while the chief sat in the Hall, much like an editor in a newsroom.

When Lategano was hospitalized with chest pains in November, Giuliani raced to the hospital and remained at her side for hours. The next morning, he was hospitalized himself. He needed stitches to close an inch-long cut in his forehead. His aides said he cut his head on a shower door because he was exhausted from a lack of sleep.

In addition to the ban on Cristyne at joint Donna/Rudy events, Hanover also insisted that Cristyne no longer interact with her children. When Rudy and Cristyne went to a Yankee game from City Hall or another location, Andrew frequently went too, driven by his own police detail. Andrew, Rudy and others, usually Elliot Cuker and Manny Papir, would sit in the box seats near the Yankee dugout, but Cristyne religiously located herself elsewhere in the stadium, out of Andrew's sight. (The only exception members of the entourage could remember was the final game of the 1996 World Series; Cristyne was allowed in the box.)

When the games were over, Rudy would tell someone to get Cris on the phone and they'd talk. Sometimes Giuliani would go home with Andrew. On other occasions, especially if it was an afternoon game, Lategano and Giuliani would leave together, letting the detail bring Andrew back to the mansion.

Likewise, the days of rolling in the grass behind the mansion with Giuliani's kids were over for Cristyne. In fact, by 1996, the once regular receptions at the mansion, with Donna introducing Rudy to the assembled, had tapered off so dramatically everyone on staff noticed. Donna rarely attended Rudy's receptions at all. Sometimes Rudy would speak and leave, and then Donna would appear, speak and leave.

For a while, Cristyne stayed clear of the mansion as much as possible, especially if Donna was there. Marty Rosenblatt, a former aide to Mario Cuomo, was recruited to run Giuliani's research operation in mid-1996 and was supposed to meet Lategano early one morning. Lategano told him she "couldn't go to the mansion," so she asked him to meet her at a diner a couple blocks away from it. They had breakfast and then the mayor arrived in the van at the diner to pick her up.

Cristyne came to some of the mansion receptions, but remained in the den, usually with other mayoral aides. She might come out near the end, saying hello to those she knew. The staff saw it as a conscious effort on her part not to appear to be the hostess, a First Lady in Waiting. The private dinners at the table of twenty-two also dwindled dramatically.

The Donna who was indifferent about which last name she used was gone too. She changed it on their tax returns. She changed it as a director of the Gracie Mansion Conservancy, the private entity that maintained the mansion. Her staff called reporters to insist on the use of Hanover. She corrected anyone who addressed her as Mrs. Giuliani, snapping at a nurse who made that mistake on a visit to a hospital emergency room with Andrew. Her California- and Texas-based family stopped contributing to Giuliani's campaign committee. The Kofnovecs had made fifteen contributions since 1989, totaling $685, but they never made another donation after June 1994.

Donna took the kids on vacation over the next few years to Paris, Ireland, Disneyland, Yellowstone, her family home in California and Memphis while Rudy stayed in New York. He pretended his city business prevented a vacation, but when he fashioned himself a national figure after the 1997 reelection, he flew to twenty states in a year, without ever bringing his family. Donna went to Memphis in 1996 to shoot her first major movie. She played Ruth Stapleton, the evangelist and sister of President Carter, in the movie *The People vs. Larry Flynt*. The kids hung out on the set, toured Graceland and visited the motel where Martin Luther King was shot.

When the movie was screened in December, and *George* magazine threw a dinner honoring Hanover for her widely praised portrayal of Stapleton, Giuliani was nowhere to be seen. "He wanted the focus of the evening to be on her professional life" was City Hall's explanation. He apparently didn't feel the same way in 1994 when he went to the screening for *The Paper*, though she only made a cameo appearance in the picture. Donna spoke briefly at the *George* dinner, thanking her agent and press secretary for "helping me get through these last two difficult years."

In the same time frame in 1996, Donna and the kids rode on a float in the Yankee World Series parade, but decidedly not the float Rudy was on. She skipped the annual Christmas party for city workers though her name appeared on the invitation. When she also missed the annual Christmas party at the mansion for the media, Cristyne took her place at the mike. Finally, at the end of a year that clearly was a turning point, Donna gave a carefully calculated December interview to Elizabeth Bumiller of the *Times* that was widely seen as a formal announcement of the separation anyone could see.

"We had Thanksgiving together," she said, as if it were an indication that they still were still a couple. "But as professionals, we are pursuing separate careers." Hanover's spokeswoman told Bumiller that she was "moving away from attending political events."

For the first time, she boycotted the 1997 Inner Circle dinner. She'd played a role in all three of the annual skits that the city's journalistic community sponsored, but in '97, she started a four-year run of loud absences. She was so removed from the government by then that when a friend on the city payroll called to talk about difficulties at her agency, Hanover said there was nothing she could do. She "withdrew from anyone who had anything to do with the administration," said the friend, whom Donna had helped get her city job. She also announced that she would not participate in the mayor's campaign, including his television ads.

In mid-May, she attended the screening of *Night Falls on Manhattan*, a film directed by Sidney Lumet, whose *Prince of the City* had helped put Rudy on the map nearly two decades earlier. Hanover played a newscaster in the movie, and Cuker had a small part as well. She went with Cuker, who was her acting coach and Rudy's speech coach. Giuliani had issued a proclamation declaring it Sidney Lumet Day. He was scheduled to hand the scroll over to Lumet at the post-screening party that night. A couple of hours before the event, Giuliani confirmed his attendance and said he was staying for dinner. But moments before he was scheduled to arrive, his office called and said he couldn't come. Hanover went home after the screening, missing the party, too. In their apparent anxiety to avoid each other, they'd both skipped the gala.

The biggest bombshell was a *Vanity Fair* piece in August. Two deputy mayors called the magazine repeatedly to try to bottle it up—one was "crazed, rude and bullying," according to editor Graydon Carter. But the nine-page story ran anyway. It charged that the mayor and Lategano had begun an affair in October 1994 during one of three trips out of town and that an extra pair of footsteps—identified by Giuliani as Lategano's—had been overheard by the security detail in his mansion bedroom one afternoon. It also quoted an aide who claimed the two "touched in a way you wouldn't normally touch a co-worker." The story was assailed by City Hall and much of the press for relying on anonymous sources. The administration quickly pointed out that two of the three trips weren't overnight, as the article contended.

The mayor ranted at press conference after press conference. He said it was "trash," "garbage" and filled with "vicious" falsehoods strung together with "malicious" intent. There was, in Lategano's view, "no need to comment on malicious works of fiction." While Giuliani said the article was "untrue," neither he nor Lategano ever specifically denied that they were having an affair. Since some of the supporting facts cited by the magazine were demonstrably wrong, Giuliani's insistence that the story was "false" was in fact merely a finely parsed commentary on the details rather than a flat rejection of the substance of the story.

Nonetheless, reporters took the bait and reported that the two had denied the affair.

In a peculiar form of indirect confirmation of the charges, police brass immediately summoned members of the mayor's security detail to a meeting and instructed them to respect the mayor's confidentiality or face severe penalties.

What gave the story legs that have lasted for years, however, was Donna's reaction. She refused repeatedly to deny the allegations in the story, which revolved around the dissolution of her own marriage. She issued a statement on her personal Gracie Mansion stationery, citing her charitable work and concluding: "Above all, my family is deeply important to me and will remain so in the years ahead." The night the story broke, Rudy hosted an outdoor barbecue for City Hall interns at the mansion. Donna stayed inside; Cristyne outside. At a moment when a simple joint appearance of any type would have calmed the rumors, Donna went her own way, stalked for days by reporters.

"My private life is my private life," said the mayor who'd investigated Ed Koch's and David Dinkins's. He denounced NY1 reporter Dominick Carter for "embarrassing" himself and "showing that you have no decency" because he persisted in asking about the allegations. In the weeks before the *Vanity Fair* story, he'd anticipated it in comments to the *Times*'s Maureen Dowd. "Exploiting my private life is something I've never done," he said, turning ten years of publicized bliss upside down.

One citizen caller got through on Giuliani's weekly WABC radio show and raised a subject that had only been mentioned in a single graph in a *Post* column by Jack Newfield—the 1989 attempted leak of the Dinkins love letters. "How can you be mad when people are looking at your affair," asked "Jesse" from the West Side, "in view of your own attempted sex smear." Faced publicly for the first and only time with this bit of forgotten history, Giuliani dodged the subject: "Jesse, I've said everything I'm going to say about these allegations. They're scurrilous, and it sounds like you are, too."

As the days wore on, Linda Yglesias of the *Dallas Morning News* finally got an interview with Donna. Given a clear opportunity to denounce the story for its reliance on anonymous sources, Donna declined. "I haven't really considered how I would look at the story as a journalist," Hanover said. "I'm looking at the story as a mother, for the most part." She said she'd made sure the children were "in a situation where they hadn't seen a newspaper, TV"—clearly far out of the city. Hanover wouldn't say whether she loved her husband. "I'm not going to comment on the mayor." She vowed: "My children and I will continue to live at Gracie Mansion with Rudy as a family, after the election, if he wins."

The furor died down and Donna's disappearance from the re-election effort was again barely noted in the media. Giuliani circled the city in the final days of the '97 campaign in an open-ended bus, accompanied by an entourage including Lategano and Annemarie McAvoy, the Republican candidate for comptroller who'd never run for anything, would lose by more than fifty points and wasn't even known on her Queens block. Rudy would raise the hand of his nominal running mate in triumph, and reporters moving through the crowds saw people pointing and saying to one another: "There's Donna." Light-haired and vivacious, McAvoy was the perfect stand-in.

Election night, Donna and the kids, ever present four years earlier, were nowhere to be found. They had kissed for the cameras at the 1993 victory party. When she voted in 1997, she refused to tell reporters whom she voted for. Shortly before the second inaugural, City Hall revealed that the couple was taking an overnight trip to an undisclosed location. The only public concession that came out of this mystery mission was the announcement that Donna would in fact appear at the inaugural.

Though people were covered in blankets on an icy January day, Donna sat center stage in a skimpy green leather outfit with sheer stockings. She pressed her aides on the platform to check her lipstick and her hair. An intense treadmill workout schedule in the small gym she'd equipped at the mansion had left her looking lean and attractive. The massive media attention for this ever auditioning actress and television personality may have been more of a lure to come than whatever Rudy said to her. There were no more full-mouth kisses, however. All she offered Rudy was a cheek. In sharp contrast with his 1993 deeply personal salute, he thanked Donna, "who does so much to help our city, particularly our schools and our children." The Kofnovecs were nowhere to be found.

For a 1997 profile in *Vogue*, she did six sit-down interviews with writer Jonathan Van Meter. She only mentioned Giuliani three times, referring to him twice as the mayor and once by name. "Do you care to address the constant rumors about your marriage being in trouble?" he asked. "No," she said. Pressed over coffee about what it was like to be First Lady—the complications, the conflicts of interest, the strangeness of the role, she said: "I don't really think of myself as the first lady of New York."

Twenty

More Sex and the City

ONNA'S INAUGURAL APPEARANCE WAS HER LAST AT CITY HALL. There were only a couple of reported sightings of her with her husband over the next two and a half years. She laid such claim to the rest of her family, however, that the mayor's press office was instructed to refer all questions about Goalie to Donna's press secretary on the theory that he was Andrew's dog. One former staffer recalled that when the press office accidentally answered a question once about the Labrador, Donna called to complain. "I signed the adoption papers," she reportedly pointed out. Similarly, no pictures taken of the children by city photographers could be released without her approval. Her attitude was so proprietary, staffers observed, it was as if she had won sole custody of the children in an unacknowledged yet binding agreement.

Though Caroline spent part of "Take Your Daughter to Work" Day with the mayor in April 1994 and 1995, she has not appeared at City Hall for that event in years. When the beloved Yankees were knocked out of the playoffs in 1997 in a decisive game in Cleveland, Rudy watched it at a midtown bar with Lategano and other hangers-on, rather than at home with Andrew. While Rudy staged touch football games on Superbowl Sunday in the early days at the mansion, he had to move the gang, minus Andrew, to Cuker's cigar bar in the later years. Howard Safir had to sub for the mayor at a more unusual "family" event, delivering a speech at a January 1999 authors' affair at the Four Seasons attended by both Donna and Regina Peruggi, who was by then the president of Marymount Manhattan College.

In 1998, when Giuliani did his national Republican tour of twenty states, an aide said flatly that Hanover talked to one member of his City Hall staff "more than she did to Rudy." Friends like Herman and Gail Badillo, who were close to Rudy and Donna, sidestepped Gracie Mansion events rather than choose between private affairs hosted by one or the other.

In February 1999, Donna granted another interview to the *Times*'s Bumiller and, when asked if she was committed to her marriage, replied: "I'm committed to my family." Bumiller wrote that during the hour-long interview, she was "warm when the subject was her career and children" but "icy when the questions turned to her husband." She did not make it clear, Bumiller observed, that "her future necessarily included Mr. Giuliani," noting only that she planned on staying in New York when he left office.

"Oh, I never moved out of Gracie Mansion" was her way of dismissing years of speculation about her living arrangements. In fact, for years she had not slept in the specially equipped master bedroom where Rudy had to stay for security reasons. Sources familiar with her mansion life say she frequently used the apartment in the attic that Ed Koch built for his chef. She was also spending large blocks of time out of the mansion altogether, principally in California.

Finally, in May 1999, the ice mansion began to heat up, with the first public indications that Donna and Rudy might have discovered some new common ground. Cristyne Lategano was a big part of the reason. Shortly after Giuliani announced the formation of the finance committee for his Senate run in April, City Hall was filled with rumors about Lategano's possible departure. The *Daily News* reported that she was seeking a job with George W. Bush's exploratory committee. Lategano was said to have talked with Roger Ailes, who already employed Donna at Fox Television. Howard Rubenstein, the city's most powerful publicist, called and offered her a job.

Wise heads were nodding that Rudy had finally come to his senses and would not go into the most important campaign of his life—a run against Hillary Clinton—with Cristyne at his side, a public reminder of his gravest personal weakness.

The *Daily News* did a gossip item in October 1998 that had Rudy "cursing" Lategano out at an East Side morning breakfast spot so loudly three witnesses reported it. The two were seen less and less often at the restaurants around Lategano's 250 East 73rd Street apartment. The owner of Simon's, a nearby noodle house, said that the couple used to stay late there, talking "for three hours, past closing time," but that the last time she saw them was on March 7, 1999. A picture of Rudy inscribed "food is delicious" appeared on the restaurant's window, signed the date of their last visit.

They'd also dined at Café Greco "half a dozen times," Baraonda, Café Tosca and EJ's Luncheonette, all close to Lategano's apartment. The manager at the luncheonette said they'd come there "at least once a month," freely describing "the chemistry" between them. "They sat with their faces very close," he said. But the frequency of their appearances at each of these places plummeted that spring. No one at any of the neighborhood restaurants had ever seen her there with any other man and, in fact, since the demise of Miller et al. in 1995, those who knew her at City Hall said she didn't date anyone for years.

On May 23, shortly before Rudy's fifty-fifth birthday, Adam Safir, the son of the police commissioner, got married at Gracie Mansion. Under a tent on the back lawn, Rudy and Donna went from table to table together, "very much the host and hostess," according to one guest. The band went through a series of medleys, starting with the '50s and working up to the '90s and they danced again and again.

"They went from the jitterbug and the twist all the way up to hip-hop," the *Post* reported, quoting an unnamed partygoer. "They were jumping up and down like monkeys." Rudy, whose dancing feet have won praise from partners since college, was in a dapper dinner jacket. Donna was "very glamorous in a strappy black dress slit up the side," according to another friend, who said: "She was happy. He was happy. Everyone was happy."

Monday, the blind quoters planted items in both tabloids—an extraordinarily rare occasion when competing gossip pages were led by the same story. They even used the same "cheek-to-cheek" image. The *Post* suggested the politics of its sourcing by concluding that the "rekindling of the marital fires" might be connected to Lategano's rumored departure for Bushland, and then denouncing as "unsubstantiated" and "scurrilous scuttlebutt" any suggestion that "Lategano was having an affair with the mayor." Saying there was "even less reason" now to believe the "rehashed rumor," the *Post* predicted that Rudy and Donna were "just a step away from full-blown canoodling."

Donna back-pedaled when she saw the stories, as if everything was moving a bit too fast for her—with the public reconciliation getting far ahead of a private one that, in her view, had just started. Her press office called the papers and warned about over-interpreting a spin on the dance floor. But privately, she was calling old friends and expressing "hope" that "things might work out" for the first time in years. In the weeks that followed the wedding, Rudy and Donna did family dinners and barbecues, sharing what Hanover's spokeswoman called "lots of private moments."

Donna did not attend Rudy's birthday fund-raiser that immediately followed the wedding, but she did put together a family gathering at the mansion. And when Lategano came to the mayor's bash at the Sheraton—his annual major fundraiser—she came late and alone, joining a table of friends off to the side. She did not even attend the private cocktail party before the dinner, held in an upstairs penthouse for the heavy hitters. She used to dominate these events—handling introductions, fending off prying reporters, orchestrating the seating and the program—just as Donna had hosted Rudy's major fundraising dinners in the early '90s.

But this time, Cristyne and the mayor did not speak to each other all evening, and she left as alone as she arrived. Three days later, she took a break from City Hall for a South Carolina visit with her parents. At thirty-four years of age, with her friends married and pregnant, Lategano was getting restless. She was also getting dumped. Her father told the *Daily News* in an early June phone interview from South Carolina that she was learning how to play golf. She came back to the Hall ever so briefly in mid-June and announced she was going on an indefinite leave of absence, returning to South Carolina for a long stretch on the links.

Ironically, Rudy also began explaining his noticeably reduced Friday and weekend schedules by telling reporters, through his press office, that he had a "new love": golf. He was said to be teaching young Andrew the game as well.

"Donna put her foot down," one Rudy insider told the *News*, saying she wouldn't stand by Candidate Giuliani even "tacitly" if Lategano remained "a daily presence of innuendo." Lategano said she'd be back in September, citing an illness in her family as the reason for the protracted departure, but the mayor was doling out quotes that sounded like a delicate farewell.

He offered "a spirited defense" of Lategano's press strategies in one interview, calling the reporter back a second time to add a single specific: that she had come up with the idea of renaming the Interborough Parkway after Hall of Fame Dodger Jackie Robinson. Ironically, the dedication ceremony for the newly named highway, with the mayor and Lategano joined by Robinson's granddaughter in a major news event, occurred on April 15, 1997, Rudy and Donna's thirteenth anniversary.

As soon as Lategano was out the door, albeit she thought temporarily, she got the Bratton treatment. The Sunday *Times Magazine* collected blind anti-Lategano quotes at City Hall as if the glossy was printed on flypaper. Jim Traub wrote that the jettisoned Madame DeFarge, as Bratton called her, was "considered transparently opportunistic rather than bright." Traub quoted two "senior" aides to Giuliani who said things like: "She would froth him up." Reading the August 1 story with her new golf clubs and newer boyfriend, Lategano surely recognized the sanctioned assassinations she'd once performed on others.

Though she never responded in print, she ranted about Traub's piece to a Yale student editor, David Altschuler, during a campus visit a couple of months later, calling the anonymous sources "cowards" who should have "the decency" to tell her "to my face" what they had told the *Times*. The queen of malicious whispers was suddenly squealing about them. After Traub's story, everyone understood that Lategano would never be back. City Hall watchers certainly expected that her departure would foreshadow Donna's return, but it never happened.

As mysteriously as the two had warmed up in May, they'd cooled down by early fall. In fact, there were no post-wedding sightings of the two—cheek-to-cheek or jaw-to-jaw. In October 1999, A&E announced that Hanover would host a new weekend series, *House Beautiful*, produced by Hearst Entertainment. Billed as "an insider's tour of the world's most fascinating homes," it promised shows on "romantic living," which would offer "tips on creating a romantic home through sensual style, inviting bedrooms and bathrooms to indulge in." Hanover was adding this new A&E show to a repertoire that already included the Food Network, Fox feature reporting, tiny movie and TV roles and a potpourri of special corporate appearances she makes through agencies.

The A&E tapings, however, were frequently shot at a studio in Pasadena, California. It was just one of several reasons that she was spending more and more time in California, even taking courses there with her old friend from the Pittsburgh *Evening Magazine*, Art Greenwald. "She's here in L.A. quite a bit for acting," says Greenwald. "She's been coming to my writers/actors workshop. It's a closed group of professional writers and actors, with the writers presenting their work, the actors performing it, and the group critiquing it."

Donna spent Oscars week in L.A. this year, for example, staying at her parents' house in Santa Clarita. For the first time, Rudy's and Donna's tax returns for 1999 contained four different California forms, including filings for investment earnings for Andrew and Caroline. In a complicated maneuver, they claimed a real estate write-off on a California form. Some of the filings were merely an indication of California nonresident earnings, but the "passive activity loss" filings on property suggested a new property tie to Donna's home state.

Long before the spring thaw of 1999, Donna had settled into a comfortable life of her own, centered around a career that was nonetheless indisputably connected to her husband's prominence. When their brief fling was over, she simply returned to her separate yet rewarding world. In 1998, Hanover's earnings had hit a high of $354,447, a 1,006 percent increase over what she made the year before Rudy became mayor. Over the course of the first six years of the mayoralty, she earned over $1,370,000, more than twice Rudy's income.

Her biggest paycheck was always the Food Network's, rising to $157,264 in 1998. Next was Fox's New York Channel 5, where she was hired in February 1995 as a street reporter for *Good Day New York*, the popular morning news show. Her 1998 income there was $123,250. The Fox job had all the earmarks of a political hire. When she got it, she hadn't worked as an anchor for almost five years and hadn't held a street reporting job for thirteen years. Yet, at forty-five, here she was, back in a daily news format. It wasn't a question of competence—she quickly demonstrated a mildly appealing on-air feature and interview style. It was a question of opportunity, and few in the business doubted that her husband's very large profile had helped create the opportunity.

Fox's owner Rupert Murdoch was a major Giuliani booster who would benefit twice from lucrative tax abatements granted by the Giuliani administration. In late 1996, Giuliani went so far out of line to try to force Time Warner to give Fox's twenty-four-hour cable news show a channel in New York he was rebuked by a federal judge. It was a repeat of the Food Network scenario, only this time Rudy did, ever so briefly, put Donna's employer on a city-owned public access channel. After the city lost the court case, T/W's Dick Parsons gave Fox its channel anyway, fearful that Giuliani would delay the renewal of its New York franchise.

Hanover's Fox income quadrupled after the fight with T/W. She earned $31,000 there in 1995 and $123,000 in her peak year, 1998. Her 1996 income—the year Giuliani went to bat for Fox—soared to $94,000. Even her Larry Flynt movie debut had a mayoral connection—director Milos Forman said he met her at a Gracie Mansion dinner and decided to offer her the part.

In addition to the interplay between Donna's broadcast career and the mayoralty, her growing real estate income was also linked to it. The two apartments she and Rudy jointly own on the 35th floor of 444 East 86th have been sublet since the beginning of 1994. They reported earning $58,050 in rental income from the apartments in 1999, a 95 percent increase over their 1994 rental earnings. With depreciation, mortgage, maintenance and other costs, Rudy and Donna have been able to report a tax loss on the apartments almost every year. They have also made more than $157,000 in total mortgage payments over the six years, substantially reducing their principal while the value of their asset grew.

The reason they were able to sublet this long, however, was because the co-op board voted to exempt them from the four-year limit on subletting. Other co-operators in the building faced an automatic initial limit of two years, which the board could, at maximum, extend for a third or fourth year. The Giulianis, on the other hand, were allowed to exceed that limit by as much as four years—an enormous financial benefit granted, understandably, because of Rudy's public service. The property expenses reported in their tax returns made no reference to the sublet fees that other cooperators must pay the co-op, ranging up to 20 percent in the fourth year, suggesting that the building's board also waived those fees.

The third Giuliani apartment in the building—Helen's on the eighteenth floor—is a mystery. Rudy listed it in his financial disclosure forms from 1993 through 1996 as a property he owned alone, while simultaneously listing the other two apartments on the same page of the form as owned by Hanover and himself. In 1997, however, he suddenly listed it as jointly owned with Hanover. He reported no earnings on his tax returns or in his disclosure forms for granting an interest in the apartment to Hanover, who had an implicit spousal claim to it anyway.

So it would appear that he transferred title to the apartment to the two of them sometime in 1997. The forms continued to list it as a joint asset in 1998 and 1999. The apartment was valued on the disclosure forms at $100,000 to $250,000, but cooperators in the building say that apartments in the same line are currently going for as much as $290,000.

The transfer of the apartment was not the only personal financial change that occurred in 1997. A Merrill Lynch margin account—reported as both a $20,000 to $60,000 asset and a debt jointly held with Donna—was listed in Giuliani's disclosure forms continuously prior to 1997. It disappeared from Rudy's forms in 1997. Giuliani's disclosure forms only cover his own and joint assets or obligations.

The Merrill account did continue to appear, however, on the joint tax returns filed by Donna and Rudy, albeit listed as assigned to an unspecified "nominee" (perhaps the children). The switch in this account, plus the apparent restructuring of their interests in Helen's apartment, suggests that Donna and Rudy redefined their financial relationship at some point during 1997. With the appearance of the *Vanity Fair* article, 1997 was also a decisive moment in their personal relationship.

In any event, the woman who came to Gracie Mansion as an unemployed former broadcaster with freelance earnings of $32,000 a year is undoubtedly now a millionaire, with a substantial investment portfolio. Her publicly subsidized personal staff of four—abetted by chefs, maids and a vast mansion staff—serve her every need, and her personal police detail scoots her around the city in tinted-glass limos. Her friends at the Food Network say she is often accompanied by several staffers and cops when she reports for her brief reading gig at TVFN. Her children receive similar police and mansion attention.

While many tabloid readers have wondered out loud for years why she has stayed in a transparently dead marriage, the answer may well have been in the fine print. The financial largesse of her mayoral years, as well as the incomparable lifestyle of the mansion for her and her children, have at least helped make the personal pain bearable.

Donna, however, wasn't the only woman in Rudy's life to prosper. Not only did the on-leave Cristyne Lategano get four months at full pay from the city—using accrued time until October 1999—City Hall gave her an $8,780 raise in July though she was already on leave. Then the mayor's allies on the board of the city's Convention & Visitors Bureau, which obtains nearly half its financing from the city, created a grand opening for her. A year and a half earlier, the board had installed former deputy mayor Fran Reiter as president. Reiter had just successfully managed Rudy's re-election campaign and her appointment was criticized as politicizing the historically independent tourism bureau.

From the moment Reiter arrived at the bureau, she made her intentions to run for mayor clear to everyone around her. In April 1999, she announced that she was forming an exploratory committee to consider a possible 2001 run and changed her registration from Liberal to Democrat, so she could run in the Democratic primary. The board took no action, however, until July, when Lategano was on leave and looking for a place to land. Then they told Reiter she had to make up her mind: stay at the bureau or run for mayor. A severance package that included full pay for the remainder of her contract and totaled approximately $300,000 helped persuade her to go quietly.

Then, with deputy mayor Randy Levine on the search panel, the board settled on Lategano for president. *Crain's*, the city's weekly business magazine, reported that Lategano was "the nation's only CVB head without a day of professional experience in the tourism industry." Usually a strong Giuliani supporter, a *Crain's* editorial said the appointment "embarrasses the city" and urged her to "withdraw her candidacy." It noted that no one dared "speak up against Ms. Lategano" because they would be "labeled enemies by the mayor," adding that "would-be critics" in the industry "fear that city agencies will find ways to make their businesses suffer." The mayor publicly praised the board.

Dan Barry, the *Times*'s bureau chief, wrote that Lategano's only experience in the tourism business was "tirelessly promoting the premise that Mr. Giuliani single-handedly returned luster to a tarnished metropolis." Incredibly enough, Cristyne said she knew business travelers' needs because she'd once lived out of a suitcase as a GOP advance person.

The bureau divulged Lategano's $150,000 starting salary, but refused to reveal the term of her contract or whether salary hikes were built into it. One board member says she has a three-year contract, which could entitle her to a Reiter-like buyout. Lategano ducked New York press questions out of habit, but told Altschuler, the Yale student editor, that she "cut the salary" herself because she "didn't want to be making more than the mayor." The mayor then made $160,000, but his salary has since been hiked to $195,000.

The junking of a national search and selection of Lategano was an outrage so transparent that only a cowed city elite would've stood for it. Jennifer Raab and William Diamond, two far more seasoned Giuliani commissioners, were among the bypassed applicants. But other than in *Crain's*, it was barely a one-day story.

When Lategano started at the tourism bureau in the fall of 1999, Giuliani tried to justify the appointment by crediting her with inventing the media strategies that had made him "the best-known mayor in the world." The mayor who wouldn't share any crime-reduction praise with Bratton said it was Cristyne's idea to end-run the print media and communicate directly to voters via Air Rudy. Just in time for the planned Senate race against Hillary Clinton, he'd found a hiding place for his gravest personal scandal. Freed from the Stockholm syndrome of life in the van, Lategano flourished, marrying a golf writer in a South Carolina ceremony in February 2000. Rudy did not attend the wedding.

"I think his time is best spent in New York, or wherever he needs to be," said Lategano. The day before the wedding, the *News* published photos showing the mayor with and without his wedding band, noting that he hadn't worn it since the start of the new millennium. In the past, the mayor had so determinedly worn the ring that when he jammed his ring finger, he switched it to his right hand. Giuliani refused to comment, but the ring did not reappear.

Though Donna still wore her ring, she was just as busily sending out signals of separation.

Just before Christmas in 1999, she made a rare public appearance at a Madison Avenue shopping fair where 160 stores agreed to donate 20 percent of the day's sales to the Children's Aid Society, a charity she supported every year. She bought a socklike change purse at Mac Kenzie-Childs and nude-colored lip liner at Versace. But the *News* reported that she opted not to stop at the men's floor. "I'll skip that and head back downstairs," she quipped. When a Chicago tourist approached and said: "Mrs. Giuliani, I love your husband," she replied: "Hanover, Hanover." Though the irony went unreported by the media, the mayor held a press conference at the same shopping fair a few hours later.

When Donna got her first major soap opera role in January 2000 and reporters called, she talked about how she, Andrew and Caroline watched tapes of her various performances, never mentioning her husband. On Valentine's Day, she appeared at a charity fundraising gala with New York's other First Lady, Libby Pataki, but she and Libby left before the speeches. Libby met her husband at Jean

Georges, where they shared a Valentine's dinner; Donna exited "because she planned to be home with her children for a family dinner," her spokeswoman said. There was no mention of Rudy, even though this was the night before Donna's fiftieth birthday.

A month later, Donna did a surprise interview with Heidi Evans that the *Daily News* plastered all over its Sunday edition. It was another carefully coded bit of self-promotion and half-hearted disclosure. In between all the career chatter, she made it clear that if Rudy won the Senate seat, neither she nor the children were moving to Washington with him. She tried to soft-pedal that unilateral declaration by pointing out that many New Yorkers who "work in Washington leave their families in New York." But the message was clear: Donna planned on moving back to East 86th Street.

Asked if she had any regrets about life at the mansion, she paused, giggled and said: "Why don't we move on to something else." She did the same when Evans raised the Senate race and Hillary. Evans noted that a precondition to the interview was that "the R word (Rudy), the M word (marriage), and the H word (Hillary)" were not to be mentioned. Apparently, neither was the T word (truth). Evans had nonetheless cajoled the post-Senate-race separation comment out her, accompanied by cold stares from Donna, who was clearly annoyed that she'd gone beyond the ground rules.

The day the story appeared, Rudy was in Buffalo, doing his third straight day of Saint Patty's Day parades. He met with Buffalo's Catholic bishop privately. He shook hands on the parade route for hours, baring his inexhaustible smile all the time. Not even the public announcement of his separation from his children could crack the facade.

Judith Nathan is a registered nurse who doesn't see patients. All she needs is a phone and a computer and she can work at home alone, with her rhinestone-collared cocker spaniel, Matilda. Her work for Bristol-Myers Squibb is more a billing and sales operation than an ER. While she lived at 136 East 55th Street between 1995 and 1999, her leased four-door Chevy Lumina was usually filled with boxes of pharmaceutical samples, and she'd do business meetings with purchasers around a coffee table in the lobby of her fourteenth-story residential tower. She was one of 7,000 "drug reps" that Bristol leased cars for across the country from Wheels Inc., a national chain.

Divorced and well-heeled, Nathan lived with her daughter Whitney and her boyfriend Manos Zacharioudakis, a psychologist at Brooklyn's Woodhull Hospital. Located off Third Avenue, their building was home to a notable collection of residents. Lew Rudin, a developer who chaired the influential Association for a Better New York, owned the building and occupied the penthouse. Bill Fugazy, the legendary limo king and lobbyist, lived there too, as did Madeline Cuomo, the eldest daughter of New York's ex-governor.

The building was right around the corner from P.J. Clarke's, the onetime trendy bar and restaurant, and Nathan liked to get a drink there. She also enjoyed Coopers Classic Cars and Cigar Bar, the usually desolate East 58th Street bar owned by Elliot Cuker, just six blocks from her home. She was just a short walk away from Equinox, her snooty fitness center where she worked out regularly.

Zacharioudakis says their relationship "ran out of steam" in February and March of 1999. With nowhere to move, the forty-four-year-old Nathan stayed with Zacharioudakis until June, though they rarely spoke and retreated to separate ends of the two-bedroom unit. "She started living kind of the single life again that spring," recalls her ex-boyfriend, who was nine years her junior. "We were essentially living separate lives. We would not really interact more than a half hour a day, usually around six P.M., and then she'd go out."

A doorman noticed a black Suburban with dark windows would drop her off at the corner of Lexington and 55th, but never directly in front of the building. "It looked like a government vehicle," he said. Once after the doorman saw her get out of Suburban, he asked Nathan if that was an important client. "She seemed embarrassed and said: 'Something like that.'" The doorman recalls that as she withdrew from Zacharioudakis's life that June, she began staying "at a family member's place" in Manhattan, returning periodically to "pick up more and more of her stuff."

She also started that spring spending long weekends at her condo facing the bay in Noyack, a tiny hamlet in South Hampton. She drove out without Zacharioudakis, who had regularly accompanied her there during the years of their romance. After Whitney finished school on June 13, Nathan stayed much more often in the Hamptons duplex at 400 Noyack Road that she had bought in 1997 for $155,000.

With front and back decks and bedrooms and baths on both floors, the apartment was filled with wicker chairs, paintings and small carpets tossed on tile floors. Zacharioudakis said Nathan was part Greek, part Anglo on her mother's side and, despite a maiden name of Stish, Italian on her father's side. Though usually slathered in strong sunblock, Nathan loved the nearby beach and pool, as well as days of summer tennis, bridge and backgammon. Her on-the-phone job allowed her to work from the condo some weeks and see the new man in her life most weekends.

Every one of his visits was a bit of a scene.

There was certainly nothing secluded about the condo, one of six apartments located in a gray-wood-siding townhouse on a main road dotted with marinas and single-family housing developments. There were four townhouses in the development, built in 1988 and called The Narrows. The thirty apartments circled a common parking lot. That meant that every time Nathan's new "very good friend" pulled into the lot, accompanied by an SUV or Town Car entourage of six or seven cops and backup cops, there were enough neighbors watching to fill future tabloid and divorce transcript pages with damning eyewitness accounts.

Many of the units, of course, were the summer getaways of city residents who rarely got to see up close so many of their tax dollars at work. The *Post* would later put the public price tag in overtime and hotel accommodations at $3,000 a day. It should hardly have surprised that some would gossip about it back home. Yet Rudy Giuliani seemed to believe that the two-hour ride allowed him to take overnight risks he certainly did not take on East 73rd Street, where Cristyne Lategano lived. He started coming in May, the very month of his cheek-to-cheek "reconciliation" with Donna, and he did not stop his regular visits until September. There were even occasional sightings as late as October. Golf with Andrew was the alibi used at City Hall to explain to reporters why he had no weekend schedule; no one but Donna knows what the alibi at home was.

The mayor who'd recruited and dispatched an army of welfare investigators into the homes of thousands, searching for undeclared companions, did not care how public his extra-familial sojourns were becoming. They made some minimal efforts to hide—he and Nathan would eat on the empty, enclosed patio of a Southampton restaurant, holding hands; she would go to the local deli for takeout lunch with him waiting in the car; the shades on her condo would be drawn day and night. But word about his Southampton life drifted back to the city by late summer. Even reporters began hearing about it.

He was already in the throes of the biggest news story and political challenge of his life, yet he would still do what he wanted. He had a chance to put his family back together and counterpose Hillary Clinton with a wife and children at his side, yet he would still do what he wanted. He faced the extraordinary demands of running the city and what promised to be a $40 million campaign, yet he was instead doing what he wanted, all the while complaining to confidants about how much time she required. What he wanted was Nathan, a woman with a nursing nature and an East Side veneer of sophistication.

Born Judith Stish and raised Catholic in the coal-mining town of Hazelton, Pennsylvania, Nathan got her nursing license in 1974, shortly after high school. Her family name is really Sticia and her great aunt, Mildred Stish Anella, says they come from Monte Calvo near Milan. In his own way, Rudy was coming home: Judi Nathan's roots were more northern Italian than his own Tuscany background.

In 1979, she married Bruce Nathan, a sales rep for an architectural group in Charlotte, North Carolina, where Judi was working for U.S. Surgical. After six years in Atlanta, they moved to Manhattan in 1987 with their two-year-old, adopted, daughter. "When I met Judi," Bruce Nathan says, "she stopped working." She didn't have a job, he says, until they moved to Los Angeles in 1991, when she worked "for a few weeks at an art gallery" and for a couple of months selling surgical supplies again, as she had in North Carolina more than a decade earlier. Asked what she did during the day, her ex-husband said: "I don't know. As time went on, she became involved in Junior Leaguey things."

Divorce papers indicate that in March 1992, Judi suddenly left L.A. with her daughter, returning briefly first to her parents' home in Hazelton, then to a friend's apartment in New York later that year. She later moved into the Monterey, a new, massive, 502-unit, rental building at 175 East 96th Street and finally got a New York nursing license.

Bruce Nathan called her a "social climber" in the divorce papers, saying her "main goal in life was being involved with whatever was 'the in thing' at the moment." She "thought nothing," he charged, "of playing bridge two to three nights a week, clubbing at bars one night a week with single friends, going to movies, shows, etc.," all to the alleged detriment of their daughter. An executive with a flooring company now, he also accused her of "anti-Semitic abuse," calling him "a rich little Kike, Jewish boy" and "Jew Boy." In his affidavit, he called her "a manipulator, pathological liar and exaggerator."

When she countered this mishmash of allegations with charges of physical abuse he later denied, a judge ordered a detailed shared-custody program, though still granting Judi primary custody. She had filed an affidavit from a teacher at Whitney's school that directly countered her husband's claim that he regularly took Whitney to school; the teacher said Judi was "always" the one who did it. He wasn't apparently as far off on her social habits, however—Zacharioudakis, doormen and neighbors on the East Side confirmed her more recent out-on-the-town habits.

Neither glamorous nor dowdy, Nathan had a wide-eyed, easily dazzled look, always bejeweled with pendants and pearls around her neck and bracelets on both arms. "She was married to a rich man and living the high life for many years," Zacharioudakis observed. "She had a lot of expensive jewelry from those years." Bruce Nathan, however, insists he is not the "millionaire" Zacharioudakis says he is, though he says "she lived a nice life" when they were married. Though he did not dispute her contention in the divorce papers that they had several luxury cars and a $75,000 yacht in Southampton, he says he pays only $1,600 a month in alimony now.

She kept toned with gym workouts and a calorie-counter in her head, and was often seen going in and out of East 55th Street in jogging outfits. When she wore glasses, she seemed professorial. Her mix of moderately priced fashion and wildly expensive accessories—like a $4,900 Hermès handbag—suggested shifting shopping moods and resources. "She can buy the $2,000 purse," says Zacharioudakis, "or the $20 purse if it's stylish and tasteful. She would shop as much in Bloomingdale's as she would in Daffy's"—a discount department store, which, like Bloomies, was close to the East 55th Street apartment.

Her allure for Rudy was all in her gaze. When she went to a press conference at City Hall in late December, she never took her eyes off him, magnetized by a performance that day that swung from joking self-assurance to a mastery of a complex variety of issues. Politics was suddenly fascinating to her.

A registered Republican in New York since 1988, she didn't vote in any of Rudy's three mayoral races, missing presidential elections as well. Her cousin, Tom Stish, also raised in Hazelton, was the area's Democratic state legislator until he switched to Republican in 1994, giving the GOP a one-vote majority in the state House of Representatives (he was later defeated for re-election). She rarely watched TV news and preferred the business section of the *Times* to the metro section. Her idea of a good book was a murder mystery set in the Hamptons. Zacharioudakis said she and he "wouldn't get into extensive discussions about politics" and after five years of dating or living with her, he couldn't say if she was conservative or liberal. "I think she's a Republican," he said.

When she was sued in 1994 for hitting a pedestrian on a Brooklyn street while driving her rental car, she insisted in a deposition that no accident had occurred. She claimed the injured man, a thirty-one-year-old black messenger named Gary Wilson, actually "jumped" up on her hood, throwing himself against her windshield while she was making a slow, left-hand turn. She also said he was playing a Walkman so loudly she could hear the music and that, while he sat on the ground after the accident, she yanked it off his ears "because he smelled like alcohol."

Taken semi-conscious to a hospital with a fractured head and other injuries, Wilson said he had his Walkman headset under his jacket because it was raining when he was hit while crossing the intersection with the "Walk" sign. Four years after Nathan's deposition, in January 2000, Wilson won a $100,000 settlement, according to his attorney.

Zacharioudakis says the first he heard about her meeting the mayor was around February—he will not say where they met, but others have indicated it was at Cuker's bar. She next came home from a March or April fundraising event she went to with her daughter—probably at Spence, the elite private school Whitney attends—and said she'd seen Giuliani again. This time, she produced a photo. "It was her, Whitney and the mayor in the middle, a blue and white awning in the back. They were both smiling," said Zacharioudakis. By then, he and she were "essentially over."

It was during this early spring period that the Suburban started dropping Nathan off. Rudy was spotted in 1999 having a three P.M. lunch with a group of men and women at Shun Lee Palace, an upscale Chinese restaurant across the street from her building that Nathan frequented. He went to The Old Stand, a bar at the corner, for a soda, alone in August, sipped it for a few minutes as if waiting for someone and then left. The owner of Yorke Fashion Comfort Center, next door to 136 East 55th, said he saw Rudy crossing the street one day and walking into the Moscow Restaurant and Cabaret, which is directly opposite Zacharioudakis's building. A sales rep at nearby Bloomingdale's recalls Rudy coming in in the spring of 2000 "to buy a fragrance." It was quite a public crossroads for rendezvous—in fact, Ray Harding's law firm was at precisely the same Third Avenue intersection.

"We still lived together after it ended, but it was formally over in June," Zacharioudakis. "They probably began spending much more time together in the summer." She didn't move the bulk of "her stuff out until September 1," when she got a new apartment on East 94th Street. Her daughter started ninth grade on September 8. She had to be back in the city most of the time by then, though the two still took their separate cars to Noyack for occasional weekends into October.

That's when Rudy had to figure out how to integrate her in his Manhattan life. She was certainly not one to be stuffed in a closet. At first, people at City Hall were told that the increasingly visible Nathan was visiting Denny Young.

Louisa Young, the mother of Denny's two children and wife for two decades, had filed for divorce on August 16. She finally recognized that alter-ego Denny, who had been at Rudy's side for almost seventeen years as executive assistant, law partner and counsel, was "married" to him. Though the divorce would not be granted until the spring of 2000, Denny was available that summer to chaperone Rudy's new friend.

She began appearing at City Hall in August, attended the dedication of City Hall Park in early October and a Yankee victory party at the mansion in November. She and Young went to the December press conference together.

In addition to Young, she was described as a friend of Kate Anson, a fortyish, longtime City Hall aide who would later catch the bouquet at Lategano's wedding. At some points, Nathan was even passed off as a member of the mayor's security detail (impersonating a police officer is a crime). Judi and Rudy became such regulars at Cuker's, they found their own special space—a curtained-off, six-by-eight-foot, reservable room complete with TV and dark, u-shaped, leather couch fitted against the wall—for sipping diet sodas. Cuker called it the Romeo y Julieta Room. If they came in a larger group, they sat out at one of the glass tables in the bar amid old movie portraits of Sophia Loren, Humphrey Bogart and Cary Grant, unwinding in a cloud of smoke.

Her appearances at the emergency command center the night of the Millennium, one Town Hall meeting after another, the State of the City speech, the Saint Patrick's Day parade and on upstate campaign swings began to set every insider tongue in the city flapping by March. When she showed up seated next to him at the Inner Circle on March 10, almost as many eyes followed her every move as followed Hillary's. The annual political lampoon hosted by the city's press corps was the first time the two met as Senate rivals, but Clinton and Rudy weren't the only headliners.

Donna had quietly accepted the failure of the short-lived May reconciliation, saying later that whatever hope she had had for it ended in the fall. The years, however, had so disconnected her from Rudy's real life that she did not know about Nathan until the early months of 2000. She may have known the symptoms but not the name. Within days of the Inner Circle spectacle though—which had mouths flapping everywhere—she gave her separation interview to the *News*'s Heidi Evans. While much of the interview reinforced the chill in the marriage that the city anticipated, Donna couldn't resist one contrary tidbit, perhaps meant as a taunt tossed at her new rival. Asked if Rudy had given her a fiftieth-birthday present in February, she looked at her aide with a "Should I?" smile, and said he had.

"I guess I can say. A necklace and earrings," she said. "Carolee [an upscale costume jeweler] is the designer. Sort of a silver-tone chain with pearls and earrings to match."

On April 20, Donna announced that she'd agreed to join Kirstie Alley and Hazelle Goodman in a two-week run of the off-Broadway hit *The Vagina Monologues*, a spicy show written by a close friend and supporter of Hillary Clinton's. The announcement was widely perceived as a slap in the mayor's face, with *Post* columnists printing salacious slices from the play. Friends of the mayor would later tell reporters that for months early in 2000, Rudy was asking Donna to talk about a legal separation and she was refusing. One said he started asking as far back as the spring of 1999. If the protracted Cold War over Lategano had been tortuous, the new one seemed about to get hot.

A week before Donna announced her off-Broadway debut, Rudy learned he had a high prostate-specific antigen count. Nineteen years earlier, he had watched his father die of prostate cancer. He did not tell Donna, or almost anyone else, about the test results, which were part of a routine physical. The doctors put him on antibiotics before giving him a second PSA test. "It all sort of started there," he later said. "Just the contemplation of it"—for the two weeks that followed—"makes you think about what's important in life." The second test was just as alarming so Giuliani checked in at Mount Sinai Hospital for a biopsy on April 26 at 7 A.M.

David Seifman, the *Post*'s bureau chief at City Hall, was standing at the hospital door at dawn. He is said to be able to hear a deputy mayor inhale from his desk on the opposite side of City Hall's Rotunda. Seifman's source got the time right but didn't know why the mayor was going to the hospital. The veteran newsman waited until the mayor emerged three hours later and did a quick story that reported the visit without mentioning the cause. Giuliani decided, however, that Seifman's presence meant he had to go public the next day. He had kept his secret so close to the vest even his top aides didn't know what was going on. Now, to prepare for his press conference, he widened his circle of advisers. As soon as he did that, the *Times* and NY1 had the scoop.

Rudy's prostate cancer diagnosis was on the air before he could do his morning press briefing. It was an extraordinary performance, with adversarial Rudy open, warm, responsive and authentic. He said he'd told his wife the night before and the children early that morning. He choked up only when he recalled his father's death. He said he needed time to assess his treatment options—which were basically radiation or surgery. He had no idea how it would affect the Senate run. In the Blue Room, for once, the profound had replaced the petty.

There's little doubt that Judi Nathan knew long before Donna. In fact, she went to the hospital with Rudy for the prostate tests. Zacharioudakis says that Nathan "has very extensive training in terms of treatment and medication," particularly with regard to cancer care. "She will nurse him in more ways than one."

The day after Rudy's stunning announcement, he went to upstate Saratoga Springs for a campaign appearance. Nathan was with him. He introduced her to several people at the county's Republican Women's Club, and everyone "just assumed she was a member of his City Hall staff or someone from the campaign." He taped a commercial at the event, where he got a standing ovation and cries of "Rudy, Rudy" from the thousand people in attendance.

"We should be for real," he told the crowd in the sound bite featured in the major media buy. "We should be honest with each other." The Saratoga event ended around 8:30 P.M., and even though Giuliani was due in Buffalo the next morning for breakfast with GOP leaders, he and Nathan went back to New York.

That night, a Friday, they were seen eating mussels in marinara sauce at 11:30 P.M. in a rear alcove of an East Side restaurant located in between Gracie Mansion and Nathan's new 94th Street apartment. The inevitable SUV and two cars were parked outside. That Sunday, they returned for another dinner.

Ironically, the restaurant, Cronies, is directly across the street from Elaine's, the too-chic joint Giuliani had railed against when he forced Bill Bratton out of his administration. "He went to Elaine's too much," Giuliani told *Esquire* in 1997. "I thought the emphasis on the heavy nightlife, the drinking, did not give the kind of image to the police department that it needed. You lead by example or you don't really lead." In fact, Bratton was a bigger Diet Coke man than Rudy.

Roger Friedman, a Fox online gossip writer, was eating at Elaine's that Friday and a friend told him the mayor's detail was parked in front of Cronies and that he was inside—very definitely not alone. Jammed with its usual media crowd, Elaine's dispatched one curious customer after another across the street. As brazen as the Inner Circle joint appearance had been, at least Rudy and Judi hadn't gone alone. Dining opposite Elaine's—which apparently they'd done often—was a demand for coverage.

Friedman told Mitchell Fink, a *Daily News* gossip and a friend, about the sighting on Saturday. On Monday, he told another friend and gossip Richard Johnson, the crown prince of Page Six in the *Post*. Friedman says that at around 4 P.M., Johnson told him that his editors wouldn't publish the item. Fink sent a reporter to Cronies on Monday, got confirmation and a no-comment from City Hall, and wrote an item for Tuesday, May 2, that neither named nor described her. Friedman wrote a story, too, and his Fox editor said, according to Friedman, that they were "definitely going ahead with it." Fink agreed to cite the Friedman story, which was precisely why Friedman was so willing to share his scoop.

But around 8 P.M., Friedman's vibrating cell phone started hopping around in his pocket. "It was my copy editor asking if I knew that they had decided not to do it. There was some discussion up the line and they weren't going to do it. I just laughed."

The *Post* had been sitting on photos of Rudy, Judi and Whitney walking out of another East Side restaurant, Hanratty's, on April 22. They had an "apolitical" tipster who told them the two regularly ate there, just a few blocks from Nathan's apartment. A freelance photographer was sent there on April 15—Rudy and Donna's anniversary—but never saw them. When he was sent again the next Saturday, he got brunch shots and rushed them to the paper. The editor took his negatives, but printed nothing. For eight days, no one at the paper even asked the City Hall staff to ID the woman in the pictures, though the editors only had a first name.

When the *Post* got Friedman's tip, they knew that Giuliani had gone to Cronies with Nathan fully aware that the *Post* had already photographed them at Hanratty's the week before. Rudy was doing everything but hire publicist Howard Rubenstein to get his relationship into the headlines, and no one would publish it. Friedman had egged the *Post* on by telling them the *News* was. He'd let the *News* know the *Post* had a picture shot elsewhere, pushing them. And still, all that ran was the tiny, blind Fink item.

It was enough, unleashing the *Post* and Fox. Johnson got a name and the old East 55th address, then sent a reporter with the photo to confirm it. The story the *Post* ran on Wednesday carried two large pictures underneath a "mystery brunch pal" headline. Friedman finally got his story online. When the *Post* pictures appeared, Giuliani declared: "She's a good friend, a very good friend." A Rudy "confidant" was freely telling reporters: "They're an item. They seem to be very affectionate. They're very open about it." There was no mistaking Rudy's eagerness to affirm the relationship. It was only six days after the prostate announcement, and Rudy had already topped himself.

The press conference was quickly eclipsed, however, by the death later that Wednesday of Cardinal O'Connor. The next day's tabloids still did page after page of stories about Nathan, inside an outside wrap of cardinal plaudits and obits. Donna was silent, with a spokeswoman repeating the five-year-old mantra about how she was with the kids. A media firestorm started and Donna, rattled and embittered, picked an awkward moment to respond. Her aides started calling a favored reporter or two on Friday and whispering that Donna would have something to say on Saturday at 12:30 P.M. outside St. Patrick's Cathedral on her way to the wake. By Saturday, it was a media mob and Donna's wake sideshow would earn the published ire of Church officials.

She carefully chose the tense of her verbs, saying she would "be supportive of Rudy in his fight against this illness, as this marriage and this man have been very precious to me." She also issued an ominous warning: "The well-being and safety of Andrew and Caroline will be my primary concern in any decisions that have to be made, as has always been the case." Though her aide told reporters she would answer questions, she took none. Standing in a black dress, with black high heels, she was so shaken, dead silence followed her canned statement. Reporters dared not intrude with shouted questions.

That morning's *Post* reported that Nathan, too, had taken a trip to St. Pat's. She was marching a few feet behind the mayor up Fifth Avenue at the St. Patty's Day parade just a month and a half earlier. But the Donna declaration was not just a response to Nathan.

She had pulled out of *The Vagina Monologues* five days after he announced his cancer, citing "personal family circumstances" and promising to do the show in the future. A *Post* columnist branded the statement she issued "the coldest get-well card ever mass-faxed around town," noting that she never mentioned cancer or Rudy. The column was an indication that her "aloof" posture was clouding her "wronged" public image. She was also incensed that Rudy had announced he would be going alone to the cardinal's funeral on Monday, locking her out of an event commemorating the life of the priest who had often counseled them, particularly her, in an effort to keep the marriage together.

Rudy sat with George and Libby Pataki, Bill and Hillary Clinton, Al and Tipper Gore, George W. and Laura Bush, a lonely figure at the front of the cathedral and the crossroads of his life. His mortality, marriage and manhood flashed before him in the solitude of a funeral Mass.

The next day was a horror. *Post* reporters toured the homes of Stish family members in Pennsylvania, asking great-aunts about Nathan's affair with the mayor. They rebuked her. Rudy looked so weak at a public appearance he had to promise the audience he wouldn't collapse. He claimed he was taking an antibiotic to counteract an infection caused by the biopsy. His security detail was so upset that unbeknownst to the press, they summoned an ambulance he rejected. The press stakeout of Nathan lost her. She wasn't at East 94th Street or Southampton for twenty-four hours. The mayor was missing part of the time too. It was a day of decision.

A pallid Giuliani, accompanied by Young, Cuker and other top advisers, turned Wednesday morning's routine press briefing at a Bryant Park event into the news shriek of the week. His eyes fixed on his feet, his shoulders slumped forward, his voice a whisper, he announced: "For quite some time it's probably been apparent that Donna and I lead, in many ways, independent and separate lives. It's been a very painful road and I'm hopeful that we'll be able to formalize that in an agreement that protects our children and protects Donna." He said he wanted "a separation agreement; it's not a divorce."

His immediate motivation for announcing the separation, he claimed, was "the tremendous invasion of privacy that's taken place in everyone's life, my family's, Judith Nathan's family." Since there hadn't really been any new reporting on his own family, he was clearly referring to the press swarm in Hazelton and at 94th Street. Asked about the effect on the Senate race, he detoured into an extraordinary salute to Nathan, calling her "a very, very fine person" who's been a "very good friend" before his illness and since, saying "I rely on her and she helps me a great deal."

"I'm going to need her more now than maybe I did before," he declared. Asked if she'd been more supportive than Hanover, he wouldn't answer. He called Donna a "wonderful woman and mother" and left it there.

He had not told Donna he planned this announcement and she was not watching the televised stunner. A friend called her to tell her it was on. Her press aide's talks with a reporter early that day indicated that nothing special was expected. When Rudy was finished, Donna's office promised a quick press conference, and then pushed it back again and again. Finally, just before the afternoon deadline, she walked out to the mikes in front of Gracie Mansion. Her tightly written statement delivered directly to the cameras, just as she had taught Rudy years earlier, was as strong a summation as Rudy had ever delivered at any of his thirty-three criminal trials:

Today's turn of events brings me great sadness. I had hoped we could keep this marriage together.

For several years it was difficult to participate in Rudy's public life because of his relationship with one staff member. Beginning last May, I made a major effort to bring us back together. Rudy and I re-established some of our personal intimacy through the fall. At that point he chose another path.

She said she and Rudy would now discuss a legal separation, but that for the next few months at least, she and the kids would remain at the mansion for security reasons.

Her spokeswoman said the staff member was Cristyne Lategano and the relationship was intimate. So the cameras had one more head to hunt. Cristyne tried a cute, smiling, dismissive retort, saying she "had no desire to speculate" about why Donna Hanover issued her statement, called it "a difficult time" for them, and put in a plug for Giuliani as one of "the greatest mayors in our city's history."

Reporters started shouting questions about the affair and she tried to leave the room, but they blocked her way. She said something about standing by her prior statements and they demanded she repeat them. New York's official welcome wagon bulled her way out the door. The next day Rudy took an identical position, as if it was one last release he and Crissy wrote while sharing a slice of pizza.

"I said everything I was going to say about that a long time ago," he ruled, lying that he had "definitively" answered those questions when all he'd done in 1997 was rant and duck, assailing *Vanity Fair* without ever explicitly denying the affair. He was back to his old habits of berating and demeaning reporters who were asking questions now not about his private life, but about what went on between the two most powerful people in the government.

The city was in an emotional tizzy. But Rudy wasn't through.

Donna retreated to Los Angeles with the kids for the Mother's Day weekend. She, her parents and the kids did a family shot for the staked-out reporters—her dad again in the cowboy hat he wore at the inaugural. Caroline looked more like her grandmother than Rudy. The kids were Kofnovecs. Her parents gasped in shock to reporters. Donna doled out quotes to reporters, taped two A&E segments and kept the kids out of school for half the week.

Her first night in L.A., a Friday, Rudy's office did a media alert, making sure the press would be out to cover the First Official Mayoral Date. The *Daily News* said it with the headline: "Walkin' My Baby Back Home." He met Nathan at an East Side eatery, dined with her and three City Hall aides, including Anson, the winner of the Lategano bouquet sweepstakes. Then he took a ten-block stroll to her building with her, the entourage and the security detail. Engulfed by cameras and reporters, Nathan beamed and so did Rudy. "It's a great night," the mayor declared. Customers in outdoor cafés cheered as they passed. She gave him a goodnight kiss at the door, indistinguishable from the ones she planted on his aides. He walked to the mansion, with the shame of his separation press conference already history.

Donna was picking up Andrew at the airport just as Rudy and Judi sat next to each other at Tony's Di Napoli. The stroll was a stab at her heart. She and Rudy used to love long walks, often on East Side streets. "Pray for me," he said to the last reporter with him on the walk to the mansion. He was referring to his health. The city was wondering about his soul.

There was certainly something familiar about the saga of Judi Nathan. For most of the '70s, Rudy's opening line with women was that he was separated, and no one could tell when he was and when he wasn't. As a young assistant in the Southern District, he dated openly and even started the unannounced nocturnal visits at a paralegal's apartment. "Can I come up?" was his clandestine slogan.

Later, his friends at Patterson, Belknap thought he was leading the bachelor life in 1977—three years before it actually began.

Regina Peruggi remained with him until February 1980, but their co-op apartment on West End Avenue was just a precursor to Gracie Mansion, a life of icy, unfinished sentences and human walls. When Rudy became mayor and Regina was president of Marymount Manhattan, a small East Side Catholic college, he cochaired and appeared at its biggest fundraising event every year, stirring contributions from donors who funded his own campaigns. Whether it was his intent or not, his help might well have sealed lips that once threatened his career with secrets.

Rudy began introducing Donna as his fiancée in May or June 1982, while he was still very much married to Regina. Rudy declared his love long distance, proposed in six weeks and was obsessed with Donna. Everything happened so fast she gave up her Miami job and condo a bare three and a half months after they met. Virtually the day she arrived in Washington, Rudy and Regina filed a separation agreement in New York. Five months later they were divorced. Of course then, Donna was all googooeyed.

Reminiscent of those days, the tabloids reported that Nathan was wearing a heart-shaped diamond on the ring finger of her left hand worth up to $20,000. The *Post* noticed it first, saying that a "source close to Nathan" pointed it out and noted that she's "done nothing to dispel the notion that it's an engagement ring." The *News* reported that Nathan "has not been shy about flashing it around when she walks her dog." The forays with Matilda had actually taken on the air of a paparazzi performance and choosing to wear the ring on these excursions was an invitation to questions that both Nathan and Giuliani then declined to answer. If the ring was Rudy's, he was, as usual, just a step ahead of himself, pushing every envelope, as if separations were merely a question of interpretation.

When Rudy ran for mayor in 1993, he had his aides researching the John Lindsay campaign to see what political lessons might be transferable. He told them that years earlier, while he lived on West End Avenue, he'd noticed Lindsay's city limo parked repeatedly in front of his building. He asked and was told that Lindsay had a mistress there. He was hardly shy about spooning up such salicious and unsupported gossip, recounting the story with a smile, as if such adventures were part of the allure of the mayoralty. If true, it would turn out to be the only part of the Lindsay legacy his Republican successor imitated.

Rudy Crew, the schools chancellor who became his cigar-chomping buddy, recalls one conversation in early 1999 at Cuker's bar when Giuliani cited Al D'Amato approvingly. The senator had once told Giuliani that he ought to do a statewide race because, as Giuliani told Crew, there'd be a babe in every town who would want a piece of him. "I remember it was cold, a wild locker-room conversation," says Crew. "It was words to the effect of 'There's plenty to pick from, a lot of action out there.'" Crew was actually dropped from the Cuker scene just as Nathan became Giuliani's regular companion there—such was the fate of education policy in Rudy's realm.

A public marriage on the rocks was a door-opener to Giuliani. He behaved as if he believed that there was no point in being estranged if you couldn't also be available. The man who was busily destroying social entitlements was developing a very personal one of his own. And he was advertising it. There are even those close to Rudy who said Nathan learned he was a virtually nightly visitor to Cuker's and went there looking for him. Asked recently if Rudy was at Cuker's often with his new girlfriend, a 5'9" honey-blond bartender in the spaghetti-string tank top and tight-fitting black skirt said, "She's not his NEW girlfriend."

At the center of Rudy's social swirl was Cuker, who is said by Rudy confidants to have made the introduction to Nathan, a charge he vaguely denies. Cuker, fifty-six, has been a constant with Rudy since the IRS probe of the late '70s. Beyond the four classic cars Cuker supplied him over the years, he was one of seven or eight close friends who'd showed up in 1989 at the first meeting of the Giuliani campaign committee. He'd given or raised $16,500 for Rudy's campaigns since.

Cuker had opened the cigar bar, right around the corner from the Plaza Hotel on East 58th Street, in late 1997, having gotten permission from the State Liquor Authority to park one of his cars in the center of the bar, beneath suspended hubcaps and available for sale. To make sure he got the unusual permit—a mix of matches, booze and gas is hardly ordinary—he had hired a Republican attorney who used to chair the city's Alcohol Control Board. With low ceilings, cement pillars, red-orange lighting, triangular red stools and black-and-white photos of movie stars, the bar had an old Hollywood garage look. Rudy made it his second home, or possibly his first, holding forth there night after night. With no food other than pâté and caviar, all it offered was stogies and companionship.

The bar made Cuker an almost daily presence in Rudy's life, allowing him to gradually fill the void left by Peter Powers, the lifelong best friend who had retreated to private life in 1996. That's when Cuker became, as other Rudy friends see it, a Svengali-like influence on the mayor, turning a '50s remnant into a New Age pioneer. Cristyne hung out at the bar with Rudy early on, alone and in larger groups. Her birthday party occurred there. Fran Reiter threw a Convention & Visitors Bureau party there. The gang gathered there, just to be near their hero. Cuker presided over a bar that became Rudy's playground, but attracted little other business. By the fall of 1999, he was trying to sell it.

Cuker also started appearing more and more often at City Hall. Appointed the chair of Giuliani's Film and Theatre Advisory Committee, the frustrated off-Broadway actor won bit parts in three or four films after Rudy took office. He wrote and directed all of Giuliani's garishly successful skits and dance routines for the annual Inner Circle revue, a spoof thrown by the city press corps. He even acted as master of ceremonies at Rudy's fundraising galas.

Cuker is so exotic (which is what his telephone book ad calls his cars) that he has spelled his own name five different ways over the years, using Cooper, Cukor and Cuker as last names and Elliot and Eliot as first names. He spouts psychobabble acquired in over twenty-five years of therapy. He wears bow ties deliberately untied most of the time because he "likes the look." He has a country house in Putnam County a stone's throw from George Pataki's and acted as a go-between with the governor for Rudy. He was Rudy's speech coach and Donna's acting coach, serving as one of their mediators as well until news of his Nathan connection reached Donna.

Divorced once, he lived with twenty-something Bernadette Hession, an Irish immigrant who did the paperwork in his garage, until he fell in love with her even younger sister, Noeline. He married the twenty-five-year-old at Gracie Mansion in 1997 and she now works in the car company, which Dun & Bradstreet estimates as a $6 million-a-year business. In July 1999, Cuker sold the garage and associated Village property for $6.3 million to a developer who is building an eleven-story tower on the land; he is reportedly opening a new garage nearby.

A social friend of Cuker's, who met Rudy through him, remembers sitting opposite him in the garage office and gazing at a twenty-foot-by-twenty-foot mural of the dealer hanging behind his head. A photo of Cuker's wife staring at him hangs in his bar—the only color shot on the wall. His business card also carries a picture of him with a cigar in his mouth. Self-absorption as a religion was what he sold to Rudy, who had only thought of it previously as a way of life.

"Look into your inner self, trust your heart, climb away from the real world and into a spiritual world" was how one Rudy friend characterized the Cuker message. He rationalized pleasure and indulgence as forms of expression, said another. "Breathe-deeply" relaxing lessons with Rudy were so common Cuker began to sound like a City Hall swimming coach. He told the *Times* that when he "put Rudy in the parts" he played in the Inner Circle skits, "he gets a fuller sense of his complete being than when he's in his business suits." And Rudy said: "Elliot gives me ways of trying to discover the character. It's very much trying to discover your own feelings about things. I used to think about acting that it was making something up, as opposed to trying to find how you honestly and legitimately react to something."

Peter Powers, Randy Levine and many others in Rudy's buttoned-up crew began to see Cuker as a dark cloud hanging over Rudy's life, but no one could break his hold.

"We lost him," was what these friends whispered.

He had become a citizen of Cuker's world, rubbery and elusive, superior and posturing. That world, Nathan and cancer would combine to unravel him.

Twenty One

Soiling Mr. Clean

T HE ARROGANCE THAT IS LIKE BODY ODOR TO RUDY, REPELLENT TO others but undetectable to him, is rooted, strangely enough, in his concept of clean hands. He is never wrong, his swagger says, because he has spent his life uncovering and combatting wrong, a knight besieged but undaunted by the compromised, confused and corrupt. It is not just his eyes that do not blink; it is his rectitude.

He used to talk about tracking a crooked cop who started each day at Mass and took a bribe by afternoon. He told the story with a sneer that suggested that no form of human duplicity could surprise him, and that the hypocrisy of it bothered him more than the payoffs. As a young assistant in the Southern District, he swept the floors for dead case files no one else would try and found a way to get indignant about bootlegging in Harlem. It wasn't just criminality that upset Prosecutor Rudy whenever he found it in public life or on Wall Street; it was every form of insider trading, every tilt of the balance of justice.

At the peak of the Koch scandal hysteria in December 1986—with Donald Manes dead and Stanley Friedman convicted—Giuliani talked about "a certain kind of frustration" he felt in the pursuit of municipal wrongdoing. "Much of what you're looking at really isn't criminal," he said, "but raises questions about how politics is practiced." He called this pattern of conduct—specifically citing lobbyists who profited from public power—as the "noncriminal, unethical behavior" of New York's political players. And later, when he was mayor-in-exile during the Dinkins reign, he regularly derided the influence of power-broker lobbyists like Sid Davidoff, promising to shut down the inside track.

Giuliani also waged war against "the corrosive effects of money on politics," appearing after his loss in 1989 before the Campaign Finance Board and recalling his own role in creating the city's new system of restrictions on contributions and expenditures:

As someone whose work as U.S. Attorney laid at least some of the foundation to this law by the exposure of municipal corruption, I am a very, very strong advocate of it. I believe that it is demonstrable that public officials in New York City very, very often over the last 10 to 15 years were incapable of making decisions in the public interest because of the huge amounts of money donated by some.

And therefore, the title of the book that was written several years ago, *City for Sale,* was certainly the reputation that New York City was obtaining, a city that could be purchased. If you look at some of the history pre this new law, it really isn't just an appearance problem. That's one part of it, that people are donating $40,000 and $50,000, and that looks bad. So, also, you can see a pattern of vote changing, benefits giving, zoning variances, there's a whole history out there of an absolute impact on the way in which public decisions are made.

We have to explain to people that, in fact, their generally held notion that you can buy and sell politicians actually does happen, has happened, and will continue to happen if we don't have laws intervene to try and create limits.

These comments were not just an outgrowth of his 1980s probes of the Koch administration. His 1974 prosecution of Congressman Bert Podell was a pioneering effort to define both a political contribution and a legal fee as bribes.

He was just as hostile to patronage, promising in his first mayoral campaign "to make certain the corrupting influence of patronage is removed from government once and for all." Where government jobs "are turned over in blocks to political leaders who have been in power for a long time," he said, obviously referring to Stanley Friedman and Donald Manes, "that almost always leads to corruption." He vowed: "There will be no patronage in my administration. Not under this mayor's nose."

He loved to showcase his fine-tuned antenna for probity in personal settings. For example, when Lou Carbonetti Jr., the East Harlem clubhouse clone of Harold Giuliani's close friend, visited him at the U.S. Attorney's office in the late '80s and offered him a framed picture of Harold Giuliani, Rudy took the picture and returned the frame, too pure to accept a gift from the likes of Carbonetti. But when he became mayor, he named Carbonetti a commissioner until news leaks about his questionable past forced his resignation, whereupon Carbonetti miraculously rebounded with a better-paying job at a city-assisted development entity. Rudy also installed Carbonetti's twenty-five-year-old, college dropout, son as his patronage chief at City Hall, eventually elevating him to chief of staff, and Carbonetti's ex-wife in a six-figure post at the Housing Authority.

Similarly, when Cristyne Lategano gave him an expensive tie for Christmas, he said he couldn't take a present from an employee. He then started a relationship with her so close it shook his administration and his marriage. In four years, her public salary nearly doubled. Then he rewarded her with a sinecure that was a scandal.

He's raised almost $50 million in three mayoral races and the Senate race, all the while claiming to have never solicited a giver one on one, which would certainly make him an anomaly in American politics. Yet his campaigns have been financed by the grifters and wire pullers who flock to him at his birthday fundraisers, negotiate with his government by wink and nod and believe that the maximum legal contribution is the minimum threshold for access. So long as whatever quid pro quos that are involved weren't part of a conversation that included him, Rudy could pretend they never happened.

The lines he's drawn in the sand, as he moved from prosecutor to politician, have shifted with each gust of wind—if one's covered, he's just scratched out another. Engulfed in City Hall by the very "noncriminal" conduct he once abhorred—his friends leeching off his government as lobbyists and "consultants"— he looked at no one else's hands but his own, still pale white underneath all that dark hair. "As you get used to this job," he said in 1999, "you realize that some of the things that would get you upset when you started don't really matter. The only thing that still upsets me is when people question your integrity or your honesty."

R ay Harding was broke on January 1, 1994. He owed the IRS a quarter of a million dollars. He hadn't been a partner in a law firm for almost a decade. He claimed to be a copyright specialist, but his only known litigation history was knocking Liberal Party opponents off the ballot on obscure technicalities. One of his sons, twenty-nine-year-old college dropout Russell, had a summer job with EMI Records before joining the Giuliani campaign staff in 1993, where he was in charge of sending surrogate speakers to lesser events. The other, thirty-six-year-old Robert, told the *Times* his last job was as the Cuomo-appointed counsel to the state's Facilities Development Corporation.

A couple of months into Rudy's first year, Fischbein & Badillo made Ray a partner. The firm's lobbying clients with the city soared from three to seventy-two, twenty more than the second-place finisher. His hourly rate climbed to $375. When a flashflood of news stories hit the Harding firm in 1997, it adjusted its disclosure filings with the city, hiding clients with city business under a self-serving redefinition of lobbying. Harding said he wouldn't lobby personally—whatever that meant—but he'd actually said that in '94 when it all started. No one believed F&B had really lost nearly half its lobbying clients when it filed for only forty-one in 1998.

Both Harding sons were given jaunty new titles as soon as the administration took office, with Robert eventually rising to deputy mayor, and Russell, to the head of the city's Housing Development Corporation. Their combined salaries exceeded their father's old IRS debt, hitting nearly $300,000. Both got chauffeurs. As *Times* columnist Elizabeth Kolbert pointed out, Russell had "no background in financing housing" when he took over HDC, and Robert "had no background writing budgets" when Giuliani put him in charge of the fifth largest in the country. "Tammany had higher standards than this," said Richard Wade, the urban historian who was once a Harding ally in the early days of the Liberal Party. "How could you have a nationwide search and come up with the kids of Ray Harding?"

By 1997, Libs were named to twenty-three key city posts, controlling agencies from Parks to Economic Development to the Board of Standards & Appeals, which handles zoning variances. Twenty-four city officials listed as having been lobbied by Harding's firm attended the Liberal Party's gala annual fund-raiser that year at the Grand Hyatt, as did twenty-one members of the firm. Fran Reiter, the party's ex-chair who was deputy mayor for most of the first term, was listed on F&B's disclosure forms eleven times, and her office nineteen times—some measure of how frequently the firm lobbied her.

In a dismaying paradox, F&B wound up representing all three of the clients Giuliani had cross-examined Stanley Friedman about years earlier. As party boss and predator lobbyist, Harding also embodied precisely what Friedman, who has always maintained his innocence, conceded was his worst ethical failing. His lawyers said in a pre-sentencing memo that Friedman had "exploited" a system that permitted him to reap profits "from law clients who employed him to call upon public officials whom he helped place in positions of public authority through his political influence."

Harding's lobbying success was a model followed by others in the Giuliani orbit, including the wife of his Senate campaign manager, Bruce Teitelbaum. When Rudy endorsed Mario Cuomo in 1994, Teitelbaum, then the deputy chief of staff, left City Hall to help in the Cuomo campaign. Liaison to the Jewish community for Giuliani, Teitelbaum was dating Suri Kasirer, who held the same job for Cuomo. After Cuomo's loss, Kasirer joined a lobbying firm with Democratic roots but Giuliani connections.

Then she quietly formed her own firm, assembling at least two dozen clients, many of whom were chasing city funding, contracts or permits. She did not file as a lobbyist until the *Daily News* reported in 1998 that she had secretly arranged high-level meetings for two powerful corporate clients. By then she was Teitelbaum's wife and he was chief of staff, one of the most powerful enforcers inside the government. In her first filing, she listed eleven clients paying her $350,000. It soon grew to fourteen clients. By the time she filed, Teitelbaum was moving across the street from City Hall to take over Rudy's political operations and changing his registration to Republican. Ironically, Rudy had railed about the impropriety of Dinkins lobbying king Sid Davidoff reportedly dating a City Hall aide who handled a contract with a Davidoff client.

Randy Mastro returned in July 1998 to the same law firm he'd left when he joined the administration in 1994, Gibson Dunn. He was then a junior partner in the Los Angeles–based firm that once represented Ronald Reagan and included William French Smith and others from the old Giuliani crowd at Justice. Mastro came back as co-managing partner of a larger, 100-attorney, New York office. He boasted to a friend that potential clients who wanted to do business with the city were banging down his door, but he had to wait the one-year legal requirement before he could represent them.

His firm had no lobbying clients through the first five years of the administration. It filed for nine in 1999, with Mastro listed as a principal lobbyist for each. Much of the lobbying was described as starting as soon as the first year elapsed. Candidate Giuliani used to vow to stretch the conflict of interest bar to five years, but as mayor, he dropped the idea. The *Times* reported that by the summer of 1999, Mastro had "collected 50 clients and found time to vacation in Rio de Janeiro."

One focus of Mastro's work as deputy mayor had been spearheading the effort to drive the mob out of the private carting business, which handles all commercial trash in the city. He also created the Trade Waste Commission to regulate the industry. The commission immediately licensed subsidiaries of national companies like Waste Management (WM) to operate in the city, but delayed the licensing of an estimated 200 small companies, many with no provable organized crime connection. It also had to approve the merger of Waste Management with another major operator, which made the company the dominant force in the New York trash business.

When Mastro wound up representing Waste Management, an attorney for the small operators called it "unseemly" and said that Mastro had "overwhelmingly favored WM" in designing the system. With WM also winning an $86 million contract to truck waste exports out of the city—the down payment on what will become a billion-dollar garbage export policy also fashioned by the Giuliani administration—reporters started writing about the apparent conflict.

Mastro responded by saying his firm had represented WM before he rejoined it. But that explanation—in view of his previous association with Gibson Dunn—raised more appearance questions than it answered. He did not list WM as one of his city lobbying clients, representing it instead in connection with a state agency. WM's lobbyist with the city was Dennis Vacco, the former state attorney general close to Giuliani who approved the settlement of a huge antitrust suit with WM on his final day in office in 1998.

Peter Powers, the mayor's lifelong friend and former first deputy mayor, also took on Waste Management as a client, though Powers insists he does no direct city lobbying. A tax lawyer before going to City Hall in 1994, Powers did not return to a law firm when he left the administration in 1996. After a three-year stint with an investment company, he set up a one-man consulting business and moved into space he rented from public relations czar Howard Rubenstein, the most influential constant in New York politics over the last three decades. The only other first deputy mayor of the '90s, Norman Steisel, the scandal magnet of the Dinkins administration, had also moved into Rubenstein's office after leaving City Hall.

Closely allied with Dinkins and weighed down with the baggage of ex-clients like Stanley Friedman, Donald Manes and Leona Helmsley, Rubenstein was at first warned by Deputy Mayor John Dyson that he was not welcome at Rudy's City Hall. Then his blue-chip clients started calling the Hall on his behalf. He represented Bill Koeppel, Giuliani's biggest donor and fund-raiser who offered apartments to a dozen Giuliani staffers, including Lategano. He represented George Steinbrenner, whose Yankees would spend two terms negotiating a stadium deal with Giuliani. And in fact, by the time the first term was over, he also represented John Dyson's upstate winery and got the center row seat at the second inaugural, right behind Giuliani and Powers. He even took on Elliott Cuker as a client, handling the opening of the infamous cigar bar, and offered Cristyne Lategano a job when she needed a route out of City Hall.

Though Rubenstein had appeared before a special state ethics commission in the throes of the municipal scandal of the '80s and vowed to never again combine his dual role of lobbyist and fund-raiser, he was back doing both in the Golden Giuliani era. Rubenstein's lobbying clients grew from six in 1995, when the early hostility of the Giuliani administration was hurting him, to twenty-six in 1999, though he still dismisses lobbying as a minor part of his firm's $30 million-a-year business. He threw a $1,500-a-ticket party in his Fifth Avenue apartment for

Giuliani in 1998, raising $140,000. He said he and Powers were also "collaborating"—with each recommending the other to clients.

Richard Schwartz vowed publicly when he left the city government to form Opportunity America, a job placement company targeting welfare recipients, that he wouldn't profit from the welfare-to-work program he helped create for Giuliani. This year, however, Comptroller Alan Hevesi blocked a $104 million HRA welfare-to-work contract for a Virginia firm, Maximus, that retained Schwartz's company as a major subcontractor. Schwartz was scheduled to get 30 percent of Maximus's city fee.

Hevesi charged that city officials had granted the Maximus partners "huge preferred treatment," with "conferences, meetings and exchanges" occurring between HRA and the contractor four months before the initial open session with other providers. HRA commissioner Jason Turner had used Maximus while running a similar program in Wisconsin. A month before HRA solicited bids for the project, Turner's father-in-law was hired in Wisconsin by Maximus's New York project director at the suggestion of Turner's wife. Maximus also hired a longtime Turner friend as a consultant and Turner let him function out of an office near his on HRA's executive floor. Recommended to Maximus by Turner's deputy, the consultant was actually allowed to sit in on agency meetings with potential Maximus rivals, who did not know he worked for Maximus.

Randy Levine, who went from labor commissioner to a top job with major league baseball and back to City Hall as deputy mayor for economic development, left the administration in 2000 to become president of the Yankees. Drawing $900,000 in deferred payments and a $1,000-a-month consulting fee from baseball between June 1997 and May 1998 while deputy mayor, Levine signed a written agreement with the city ethics board to have nothing to do with the city's dealings with the Yankees and Mets. But he acknowledged telling Steinbrenner at a breakfast that Staten Island Borough President Guy Molinari wanted to discuss a minor league stadium deal with him—one that will ultimately cost the city about $80 million.

Levine also initiated discussions and signed the closing documents for city assistance for a forty-four-story office tower that Mets owner Fred Wilpon was building for Bear Stearns investment company in midtown. Though Wilpon, like Steinbrenner, was on the baseball executive council that gave Levine his job and his severance package, Levine saw no conflict in arranging $75 million in tax incentives and $1.5 billion in low-interest, tax-exempt bonds for Wilpon's project. Levine, who had a white phone on his City Hall desk directly connected to baseball's switchboard, had represented Steinbrenner before Giuliani's election and was personally close to Bud Selig, the commissioner of baseball. His post–City

Hall Yankee job surely had more to do with those connections than any he had to Rudy.

John Gross, who moved over to Levine's old law firm and was the treasurer of all three of Rudy's mayoral election committees, earned Rudy the sole official sanction of his public life, an extraordinary $242,930 fine from the Campaign Finance Board in 1997. The only larger fine in agency history was levied against David Dinkins at Giuliani's urging. Despite months of warning letters from the CFB, Gross continued to stockpile hundreds of thousands of dollars in contributions in excess of the $7,700 limit by a person or entity. He ran up a tally of over 150 violations of the statute Rudy had proudly laid claim to prompting. Many of these excessive contributions came from firms who had just done, or were seeking to do, a deal with the Giuliani administration.

Giuliani squawked when the fine came down, and Gross vowed to appeal. Ken Caruso, another old Justice Department ally who was now representing clients like developer and *Daily News* owner Mort Zuckerman, was brought in to argue the committee's case. Instead of appealing, however, Rudy began undercutting the board, which was chaired by his own appointee, the Reverend Joseph O'Hare, the president of Fordham. The administration refused to honor matching-fund checks the CFB wrote to City Council candidates, frustrated the implementation of legally adopted reforms, and even tried to move the offices to Brooklyn. Shortly after taking office in 1994, Giuliani had declared that for the board to work it had to "be and appear to be independent of political vindictiveness."

When Giuliani set up two federal and one state fundraising committees in 1998, he put Gross in charge of all of them, a display of the contempt he felt for the CFB findings against him. He also named Gross to run his Senate finance operation. The state committee Giuliani formed in 1998—and the soft money Senate committee he put together in 2000—were raising donations that dwarf CFB limits. Since Giuliani is no longer running for city office, he has no legal obligation to abide by those limits. But the logic of his own comments about the system in the '80s and early '90s—that it was created to discourage the excessive donations that compromise city officials—still applies.

As the first sitting mayor to run for higher office since the CFB was created, Rudy's solicitation of contributions of as much as $50,000 from those doing business with the city guts the very reform he championed. "It's like a return to the Wild West days of the 1970s and the 1980s," said Gene Russianoff of the New York Public Interest Research Group, after a *Daily News* analysis revealed that as early as February 1999, Giuliani's new committees had already collected $1.2 million from city vendors. The reformer Rudy saw the receipt of such big-buck donations as a sign of personal weakness. "It has to do with their wanting to spend huge amounts of money because they really believe they are not adequate candidates," he said. "They feel they need a tremendous amount of money to package themselves on television."

Gross, Caruso, Levine and Mastro were, of course, Giuliani friends from his SDNY or Justice days, and one of the early common bonds between them was an intolerance for the kind of insider collusion, embodied by either top-dollar donations or cozy lobbying, that the Rudy team now accepted as endemic.

The mayor hardly seemed alarmed by any part of this pattern of conduct. When Harding and Kasirer's lobbying reach was exposed in news accounts, Giuliani insisted only that the two not individually appear on behalf of clients with members of his administration, saying others from their firms could. He did nothing for years at a time prior to the news stories to spotlight or curtail the invisible hand of connected friends reaching into his administration. A few months after the worst of the Harding stories appeared in 1997, Giuliani moved him into the campaign headquarters, right next to his protégée Reiter, whom his firm had lobbied so often.

Unlike the fine lines he once drew about taking a picture frame from a family friend, Rudy was now willing to sketch facile lines to blur transparent conflicts of interest. He called the charges of the incestuous intertwine ensnarling the HRA welfare-to-work contract "all created stuff." When a State Supreme Court judge ruled that Maximus's $104 million deal had been "corruptly" awarded, Rudy said: "Democratic judge. Democratic decision. Jerky decision." His appeal to overturn it, however, rested on whether Comptroller Hevesi had exceeded his authority, not whether the contract was clean.

Rudy was just as willing to engage in the sort of patronage practices he once called "a plague"—going far beyond the Carbonetti and Harding families, as well as the two dozen Libs in high places. Halfway through the first year, Randy Mastro dismissed patronage charges published by every city newspaper with the claim that they'd only hired 500 from the 7,000 résumés sent their way. "Of course we are hiring supporters," he said. "Who else would we appoint?"

Guy Velella, the Bronx Republican county leader who Giuliani denounced as mob-tied in 1989, recommended several top appointees as a member of Rudy's transition team. Leonard Piccoli, one of Velella's recommendations, was named the head of a city hospital even though a damning audit had forced his resignation from a similar position in the Koch era. Giuliani plunged ahead with the appointment even after news stories revealed Piccoli had written a character reference on behalf of a Luchese crime family capo convicted in an attempted murder case.

Only when it was revealed that wiretaps had picked Piccoli up having social conversations with one of the city's most brutal gangsters did Giuliani relent on the appointment. Though he lost on Piccoli, Velella did anoint the new commissioner of the Department of Information Technology and Telecommunications Technology.

The other Guy—Staten Island's Molinari—was given control of the sanitation department. Claire Schulman, the Democratic borough president of Queens who endorsed Giuliani, hand-picked the commissioner of the Department of Environmental Protection. Tom Von Essen, the head of the fireman's union that was key to Giuliani's election, was installed as fire commissioner. Bernie Kerik, Rudy's driver and bodyguard in the 1993 campaign, was made corrections commissioner. Neal Cohen, a Mastro in-law, became health commissioner. New Consumer Affairs Commissioner Jules Polonetsky, who ran for public advocate on Rudy's ticket in 1997, displaced old Consumer Affairs Commissioner Jose Maldonado, who had turned down a Giuliani offer to run for the same post.

Diane McGrath McKechnie, a onetime Republican candidate for mayor, took over the Taxi & Limousine Commission. One Republican city councilman after another ran the Finance Department, and a third headed the powerful Economic Development Corporation. Homeless Services was turned over to a Democrat who'd changed his registration to Liberal. David Cornstein, who toyed with becoming Al D'Amato's water-torture candidate against Rudy in '93, was installed atop the Off-Track Betting Corporation. Though technically a gubernatorial appointment, Herman Badillo, with Rudy's help, became chairman of the City University Board of Trustees. Ken Caruso was named a director of the Metropolitan Transit Authority.

The worst patronage decisions included the hiring of the sister of a top Pataki aide at the same time that the city was negotiating a multibillion-dollar watershed agreement with the aide, the blocked attempt to install the unqualified Leon Goldstein as schools chancellor and the dumping of two Criminal Court judges in favor of politically wired replacements. The judicial appointments prompted the final public break between Giuliani and Ed Koch, who joined the state's chief judge, Judith Kaye, in condemning them.

When a mayor with Rudy's track record as a prosecutor adapted so readily to the patronage, lobbying and fundraising mores of the city's compromised political culture, it lowered the ethical standards more than the acquiescence of another pol might have. It infected the air at City Hall. No one in the Giuliani administration was indicted, but then, neither had anyone in Dinkins' been. Giuliani the Candidate had claimed there was an "ethos of corruption" at the core of the

Dinkins reign. But more of those close to the Giuliani administration committed crimes than those in Dinkins's day—and sometimes the crimes were directly connected to their business with the city.

Rudy's favorite union leader, Charlie Hughes, the man who introduced Rudy at his re-election victory party, pled guilty to stealing $2 million from his union, even billing tens of thousands of dollars of Victoria's Secrets lingerie to the union. He was one of nineteen District Council 37 officials who pled guilty, many of whom admitted they rigged the vote to get the five-year labor contract negotiated with Levine and Giuliani approved by the membership. The fix was so apparent that opposing union leaders publicly begged Giuliani's Department of Investigation to look at it, but it wouldn't. When Hughes was indicted, Giuliani said: "I find it hard to believe he might do anything allegedly dishonest."

Rudy's favorite fund-raiser, Bill Fugazy, the former limo king who was the master of ceremonies at Giuliani's first major campaign event in 1989, pled guilty to perjury in a bankruptcy proceeding in 1997. Though news accounts in 1996 had already reported that the FBI had raided Fugazy's office, Giuliani appointed the lobbyist who'd raised $40,000 for him to a prestigious immigration panel. He let Fugazy remain on the panel after a federal prosecutor in New Jersey filed an affidavit in a case against a lobbying client of Fugazy's charging that Fugazy had paid $72,613 in "kickbacks" there.

Even after Fugazy pled guilty in the 1997 perjury case, Rudy kept him on the panel and wrote a letter of support to the sentencing judge. Not even the testimony of one of the government's most important witnesses against the mob stating that Fugazy was a Genovese crime family associate could deter Giuliani.

Gregory Rigas, a construction contractor who raised $31,800 for Rudy and attended a private dinner at Gracie Mansion with him in 1995, pled guilty a year later to SDNY charges of bribery, conspiracy and mail fraud. He admitted that he inflated costs on contracts the city awarded him even after the School Construction Authority had barred him from bidding on its work, and after the feds informed city investigators about the execution of a search warrant at his corporate offices.

In fact, two months before Rigas's dinner at the mansion a city investigator wrote a widely circulated internal memo flatly stating that Rigas "will be charged with serious crimes related to government contracting." A week after the dinner, Rigas raised $10,000 from subcontractors for the Giuliani campaign, having already contributed more than the maximum himself. Though Rigas pled guilty to forcing subcontractors to make illegal contributions to Giuliani and other politicians, Rudy's committee returned Rigas's donations after his guilty plea but kept the subcontractor contributions.

The committee also kept $25,000 raised by apartment king William Koeppel in 1996 after he pled guilty to a scheme to force his tenants to make campaign contributions—again to Giuliani—in exchange for apartment leases. Having raised over $200,000 for the 1989 and 1993 campaigns, Koeppel was also named, like Cornstein, to the board of the Off-Track Betting Corporation.

George Sarant, a major Giuliani donor and director of a Queens social service agency awarded $43 million in HRA contracts, pled guilty to Southern District illegal contribution charges in 1997. Very close to Giuliani's cousin Cathy, who shuttled from one major patronage job in the administration to another, Sarant's agency won the contracts even though it was not ranked first in an agency review and was more expensive than other bidders. U.S. Attorney Mary Jo White said "there was insufficient evidence to support federal criminal charges relating to HRA's awarding of the contract," but that "irregularities in the administration of the city's contracting process were uncovered." Though she referred the irregularities to the city Department of Investigation, DOI never issued any findings.

While Giuliani's cop-union ally Phil Caruso was never convicted, the triumvirate that surrounded him—two lawyers and one insurance broker—were nailed in a 1998 SDNY racketeering case. Caruso was so tied to this trio that the law firm hired him—though he wasn't a lawyer—as a $200,000-a-year consultant after he left the union in 1995. They also hired his daughter and three children of Caruso allies at the PBA. The union, the lawyers, an insurance firm owned by their wives, and several other companies that serviced the PBA combined to give $25,000 to Giuliani in 1993, all orchestrated through Caruso. The insurance company was still giving $1,000 as late as 1996, right before the indictment.

It was just not possible that the moral radar and compass Rudy Giuliani carried with him after fourteen years in law enforcement couldn't detect or deter the swirl of alliances that was so visibly compromising his government. He had to have chosen to discard his special, professionally honed, ethical intuition, as if it was now a handicap in his new trade. He'd let himself become an overeager casualty of the culture, worn down by too many sweaty handshakes in hotel ballrooms with men on the make. When he began to think of Ray Harding as a true and valued friend, for example, it was all too clear to those who had known him as a prosecutor that he had lost his way in a mire, effectively abandoning his former self.

He had decided, as a matter of practical necessity, to trade in the integrity laser beam of Saint Andrew's Place for the timeless sneer of the pack that perpetually circled City Hall, which still sits directly in front of the Tweed Courthouse, that enduring Corinthian symbol of past city corruption.

The SDNY was only a few hundred yards away from City Hall, but the walk across Centre Street had transformed him.

He made City Hall more impregnable to the public than the Southern District had been, with everything from sharpshooters on the roof to protest bans on the steps, almost as if he was ashamed to let anyone see what was happening inside. He replaced indictment press conferences with deal press conferences, hoarding information with the same energy he had once dispensed it, and leaving reporters to deconstruct his almost daily pattern of deception the same way defense attorneys used to search for weaknesses in his briefs. He lost more pivotal lawsuits as mayor—nineteen of the twenty-three decided, First Amendment, cases alone—than he had lost key criminal cases as U.S. Attorney. Having learned in the Southern District that even a quasi-independent investigations commissioner could be a dagger in a mayor's back, he appointed ex-prosecutor friends Howard Wilson and Ed Kuriansky, who ran DOI as if they were still his protective assistants.

John Feerick, the dean of the Fordham Law School who chaired a state integrity commission that worked with Rudy's office in the 1980s, and the leaders of several other good-government groups wrote him within days of his 1993 election, asking that Giuliani "consider appointing a task force to review the adequacy of the city's campaign finance, conflict of interest and ethics." Paul Crotty, the corporation counsel, met with the groups, conveying what New York Public Interest Research Group's Gene Russianoff described as the new administration's attitude that a stringent ethics code "gets in the way of running an efficient government." No further meetings were scheduled, and not a single serious reform was ever put in place during six and a half Giuliani years.

All Rudy knew was that he wasn't on the take himself. He was earning far less than he had at White & Case or Anderson Kill, a sacrifice he made to serve. He did not cut deals himself either; he merely allowed them to happen. He wore his reputation like an old suit, and few in the media or the public noticed it no longer fit.

When Rudy began positioning himself for a Senate run against Hillary Clinton in early 1999, he also moved to complete his own ideological and geopolitical reconfiguration. He knew from the start that he would have to run against his own city—at least on some issues—to get the upstate votes a Republican needed to win. A Democrat like Koch, who ran for governor in 1982, could not turn on the city without diminishing his vote in the party's base. But Pataki had proven just a few years earlier that a Republican whose upstate commercials were driven by downstate animus could be carried to the Capitol by envy and hate. Rudy could not go that far. After all, his prime political credential was the record he laid claim to in the city. But he could send measured signals of his eagerness to bend to interests often at odds with the very city he was still sworn to represent.

So he switched overnight on protection of the city's upstate watershed, yielding to demands from upstate developers, town officials and legislators who wanted to build to the reservoirs' edge. Robert Kennedy Jr., the state's most vigorous defender of the New York City water supply system, rallied environmental groups against the Giuliani move and he wavered.

Next, he did an about-face at a Binghamton barbecue by backing milk price supports. Cheered by upstate dairy interests, he reversed his position on an Albany bill he had previously said could add twenty-one cents to the cost of a gallon of milk. He conceded consulting with an upstate GOP congressman before adopting a position utterly antithetical to the needs of his constituents. He knew he would pay no political price since Hillary Clinton had the same position—but she was not mayor of the city whose residents would pay the bill.

Similarly, he settled a six-year-old lawsuit with an upstate county executive opposed to the way the city ran its vast homeless shelter, Camp La Guardia, located near Orange County malls. City lawyers and commissioners trekked to a peace parley at the county GOP headquarters.

Even his handling of the Diallo and Dorismond police cases appeared more customized for upstate and suburban voters than it was designed to balance equities in a torn and troubled city. The contrast with his response to Louima—when he was a city candidate—was stark. His support of the gargantuan capital-gains and other tax cuts backed by House and Senate Republicans—which would gouge the federal budget to the detriment of the city—was likewise in sharp contrast with his belated endorsement in 1995 of a Clinton budget veto.

But the Senate race was not just a matter of adjusting to the exigencies of the upstate/downstate rivalries, or even identifying with congressional GOP agenda. It required a remaking of Rudy's core municipal appeal.

Just as he had switched his registration to Republican to join the Reagan revolution in 1980, he was now altering his self-description to Republican so he could fundraise and run in a state Republicans were increasingly able to carry. He had begun the process before Senator Moynihan announced his retirement in November 1998, as part of his national forays earlier that year. But to become his party's uncontested Senate candidate, he would have to complete that circle.

He had gone to great lengths immediately prior to the 1997 campaign to strike a nonpartisan pose, declaring as early as June 1996 that he "rarely thinks about partisan politics" and observing that voters "have soured" on it. "I think they're tired of the Republican notion that only Republicans have the answers to problems," he explained.

Shortly before his last-minute endorsement of Bob Dole in the 1996 presidential election, he told the *Post*'s Jack Newfield that "most of Clinton's policies are very similar to most of mine." The *Daily News* quoted him as saying that March: "Whether you talk about President Clinton, Senator Dole. . . . The country would be in very good hands in the hands of any of that group."

Revealing at one point that he was "open" to the idea of endorsing Clinton, he explained: "When I ran for mayor both times, '89 and '93, I promised people that I would be, if not bipartisan, at least open to the possibility of supporting Democrats." Ray Harding corrected him: "It's not bipartisan. It's nonpartisan." Rudy even expressed his pleasure when he wasn't invited to the Republican National Convention in San Diego. "If I take three or four days off from city business, I want to do it for a substantive purpose. It didn't seem to me any substantive purpose could be served by going to the Republican convention."

Nonpartisanship became the theme of the 1997 re-election effort, when he garnered the endorsement of dozens of prominent Democrats and the Central Labor Council. He even found a Democratic assemblyman, Jules Polonetsky, to run with him. It was a return to the 1994 Giuliani, when he endorsed Cuomo, and a reversal of his 1995 spin in the direction of decidedly Republican social policy. The whirling dervish's most recent, post-1997, shift, though, was more emphatically partisan than any prior incarnation. He now knew, of course, that he would never again have to run in so Democratic a town.

No longer concerned about spending what added up to weeks on the road and appearing before mostly tiny Republican audiences all over the state and country, Giuliani declared that the changes he'd supposedly wrought in New York were "quintessential Republican programs." Proclaiming that "we darn well better have a Republican president" and assailing Clinton as "the first president in a long time that hands America over weaker than he found it."

As much as he tried to distance himself from the Reagan administration in his initial runs for mayor, he traveled to the Ronald Reagan Presidential Library in California in late 1999 to be feted as the annual winner of its acolyte prize. After spending a day at the library, he said, he was reminded of "just how much this country is in need" of Reagan-like leadership. He called his appearance there "a labor of love." Since he'd previously claimed "I was never a partisan Republican; I was not involved in the Reagan election campaign," his new posture was enough to make New Yorkers wonder if their mayor, too, had Alzheimer's.

The Giuliani Senate committee was simultaneously sending anti-Hillary fundraising letters, signed by Rudy, to conservatives around the country with the same Reaganesque message. "The left-wing elite opposes me," he wrote, "because I have shown that a Republican can win elections by wide margins even in a

Democratic stronghold like NYC with a bold unapologetic Ronald-Reagan-style conservative agenda." In truth, he'd only won once by a wide margin, he'd run as a Liberal and he'd never mentioned a Reagan agenda in any of three races. "I guess what I'm most angry about is how the Clintons have attacked and belittled Ronald Reagan and his legacy," the letter concluded.

Spending $5 million on direct mail appeals and using right-wing mail gurus like Richard Viguerie, the new Rudy also became a religious zealot. He denounced the Hillary "left-wing elite"—using derivatives of that put-down eighteen breathless times in an eight-page letter—for opposing everything from school prayer to the posting of the Ten Commandments in public schools. He went on for two pages about his attempt to block the showing of an exhibition at the city-funded Brooklyn Museum of Art because it contained an arguably profane painting of the Virgin Mary that incorporated elephant dung, denouncing Hillary's "free speech" objections to his defunding of the exhibit as "hypocrisy." He accused Clinton of "hostility toward America's religious traditions," depicting her as a soldier in "a relentless 30-year war" against that "religious heritage."

New Yorkers discovered for the first time that Rudy favored school prayer and the posting of the Ten Commandments only when a letter sent to a Virginia Christian Coalition mailing list wound up in the hands of a city reporter. They also found out that a mayor who ran as a cultural Catholic but never talked about re-ligion was suddenly telling social conservatives across the country: "I think America needs more faith and more respect for religious traditions. . . not less." The letter made no reference to his abortion, gay rights and gun control views— all of which were anathema to the Viguerie pen pals. Neither did it mention that he did not just defund the exhibit, he defunded the museum, potentially putting it out of business, until he was blocked by a federal judge.

When the letter hit the press in February 2000, Rudy reacted to questions about his churchgoing practices as if he'd been asked about his marriage or his wander-ing ways, blowing them off as invasions of his privacy. Almost a year earlier, he was asked if he "attended Mass regularly" by two conservative journalists, Karl Zinsmeister and Bill Kauffman, of *The American Enterprise* magazine. Sitting in Syracuse City Hall, accompanied only by Lategano, Giuliani was visibly taken aback by the question.

"You know, I really don't think you should ask me questions about my religious practices," he said. "No, I don't attend Mass regularly, but I go to Mass occasion-ally." His tax returns suggest it's very occasional since he and Donna give a col-lective $200 a year to Saint Monica's, the church near City Hall he was married in and has identified as his family's parish. They give less, roughly $100 a year, to Alan Placa's church in Long Island. Occasionally they deduct for $100 contributions to another church or two and every year they give $1,000 to St. David's, Andrew and Caroline's school. Their returns for several years in the 1980s claimed no deductible church contributions.

Jack Tice, a retired detective and an usher at St. Monica's, said in October 1999, just as Giuliani was sending the Christian Coalition letter, that the last time he saw Giuliani and Andrew at mass was June or July, when they came without Donna and Caroline. The time before that was Easter. The pastor, Monsignor Thomas Modugno, was vague, saying the last time he saw the mayor or any members of his family was "not long ago."

When Rudy ran for mayor in 1993, he told the Educational Priorities Panel in a taped discussion: "I am a Catholic, but I would not consider myself a strict Catholic." But when he ran again in 1997, he assailed his Jewish opponent, Ruth Messinger, for skipping the Mass that preceded the Columbus Day Parade. "This is a community she doesn't care much about," Giuliani said, refusing to specify what "community" he meant. "She wasn't at the Mass today. She drops out of the parade at 70th Street"—nine blocks short of the thirty-five-block parade. Likewise, his Senate campaign was unmistakably predicated on chasing the Catholic vote—from his exploitation of the Brooklyn Museum case to wrapping himself around a dying Cardinal O'Connor to marching every St Patty's route in the state several times.

T he Catholic posturing was, of course, just one more piece of theater. Like his ideological and partisan pretenses, it was all part of the sham drama of a life he'd crafted for democratic consumption. But, after decades of reinvention, his meticulous artifice disintegrated all at once—in two shocking weeks of spring 2000 bombshells, starting with his cancer disclosure of April 27, continuing to his "very good friend" admission of May 3, and ending with his May 10 separation stunner. A Senate campaign he'd launched with a defense of the Virgin Mary was suddenly under siege by revelations that would have embarrassed Mary Magdalene.

In the immediate aftermath of these revelations, the media watch on Rudy's Senate fate was cosmic. His every cancellation and nuance was deciphered, his network of friends probed and decoded. He had press conferences to announce that he had no announcement to make. *Newsweek* had a Senate withdrawal scoop he debunked. Doctors were interviewed to see if reporters could forecast his political choice by determining what his inevitable treatment conclusion would be. The motives of those who whispered one course of action on the Senate race in his ear were critiqued by everyone who offered opposing advice, and some of the mutual inner-circle suspicions sneaked into news coverage.

Giuliani's closest friends tried to disarm the most lethal missile fired at him in these explosive weeks—Donna's charge that his "relationship" with Cristyne Lategano had locked her out of his public life. The advisers told reporters that Hanover's press aide had described the relationship as "intimate" not "sexual," an almost Clintonesque parsing of Hanover's unmistakable accusation. Having refused to answer direct questions at her press conference, Lategano subsequently took the offensive in a *Times* phone interview from Yankee Stadium, where she was attending a game with her husband. She insisted that "the only relationship" she "ever had with the mayor was a professional one." She said: "There is nothing to prove other than a close personal friendship." As much as that sounds like a denial, Lategano still did not flatly say that there was no sexual affair.

Lategano's no-tapes, no-pictures, no-stained dress assertion hardly rebutted Donna. Was it the Giuliani/Lategano position that a wife who loved the limelight and exulted in her First Ladydom hid in the mansion for almost five years on a hunch? Were they arguing that when Hanover said she couldn't participate in Rudy's public life because of Cristyne, she was merely contending that there was only room for one in the backseat of the Suburban and that Lategano was too close a buddy to the mayor? Were they suggesting that Hanover was speculating, or lying, when she finally said the words she'd swallowed half a decade, pushed by her husband's surprise separation announcement?

Try as the friends might, nothing could soften the sting of Donna's comments, which left little doubt with all but the Kool-Aid brigade that the mayor had admitted as much in a tense face-to-face with his wife years earlier. The desperate search for a defense on the Lategano issue revealed just how deadly a charge the Rudy team thought it was, as well as how pivotal it might become in framing whatever the future might hold for Giuliani. The strategy was to try to keep the media focus on cancer, rather than character, as the shaping factor in his decision-making process.

The state GOP convention was May 30 and party leaders from Washington to Albany were hungry for a resolution, with Congressman Rick Lazio waiting in the wings and the clock ticking loudly. Rudy said he changed his mind again and again, day after day, and those who talked to him agreed. On Monday, May 15, after a weekend of powwows at City Hall, a decision seemed imminent. He called his commissioners to a remote spot in Staten Island for a cabinet meeting, but when they got there he had nothing to say, and the meeting ended in twenty minutes. They left perplexed. The same day Governor Pataki announced he would "probably" seek a third term, boxing Giuliani in, leaving him nowhere to go after his mayoral reign ended.

By that Thursday, the common insider wisdom of a week earlier that he would pull out had become the common insider wisdom that he wouldn't. He had a rally planned before his appearance on MSNBC with Andrea Mitchell, shot at the 92nd Street Y. But a torrential electrical storm shook the city, and no announcement came. He started the hour-long interview with Mitchell, saying he was still undecided about running. He acknowledged that he'd "made a mistake" on the Patrick Dorismond police brutality case, an admission so rare it stole the *Post* front page. But he pointedly did not say it was wrong to release the dead man's criminal arrest record.

"My thoughts were to try to get out all the facts that would show that the situation might arguably be more justified than the way it was presented," he said. "I should have also conveyed the human feeling that I had of compassion and loss for a mother. I think if I could do it over again, I would have tried to have balanced it more. You don't get to do things over."

A questioner from the audience pushed him on how he could be a moral leader in light of the revelations about his personal life. "I would just ask people to take a look at me and see I'm a human being," he replied. "I've never pretended to be a religious leader." The contradiction between his Ten Commandments letter and this response forced Mitchell to cite it, but Giuliani contended he had not posed as one in the letter either, a rejoinder so disingenuous Mitchell visibly dismissed it.

When Rudy insisted that "even public officials are entitled to have some zone of privacy," Mitchell asked if he hadn't violated that zone when he surprised his wife with his separation announcement. "I thought it was necessary to do that. I explained why at the time, and I'm just not going to dwell on it," he insisted. He said he hoped "that's the end of it," suggesting that his public problems with Donna might already be over, as if he believed he could close the book in one week on a marriage he'd spent a decade insinuating into the public consciousness.

It was in that moment that the stormy uncertainties hanging over his Senate run appeared strong enough to kill it. Mitchell had spared him any reference to Lategano, much less the comparatively benign Nathan, yet the mere mention of Donna had brought him back to earth. No one would let him pretend that all of this had not happened. In a momentous Senate race, he would face inevitable questions he could not answer and, unlike Hillary, the questions would not involve the conduct of his spouse.

Giuliani would later say that he got home that night so fired up by the national spotlight of it all and so turned on by the jujitsu that he thought he'd stay in. He would say he wrestled with it most of the night. He would claim that the only factor he weighed in making his decision was what was best for his health. He had said all along that he needed to make the medical decision first and the Senate decision second, analyzing what the treatment he selected would let him do. But now he concluded that the political decision was getting in the way of a medical judgment.

Men his age with this disease ordinarily have surgery—a virtually certain cure—but surgery carried higher risks of incontinence and impotence. His advisers preferred to tell reporters he worried about having to piss every ten minutes on campaign swings, but impotence threatened his lifeblood and he resisted surgery primarily because of it. With the weight of medical opinion leaning toward surgery, he preferred radiation treatment, which was a far from certain cure but involved lower risks of life-altering side effects. Of course radiation also was the choice most compatible with staying in the Senate race, though City Comptroller Alan Hevesi had weathered the same surgery four years earlier, at precisely Rudy's age, and been back at work in four weeks.

There was every reason to believe that Rudy could run for Senate with either treatment option, fully restored by September at the latest. State GOP leaders were so confident he could win that they were willing to give him the nomination even if he only ran a media campaign, making appearances around the state rarely or not at all. The party brass that had boosted him most enthusiastically said privately that if he used cancer to pull out, he was hiding behind it.

That night, as he mused in the mansion, Donna was home, just back with the kids from California. She had spent part of the day talking to her newly retained divorce lawyer, a woman with twenty-five years' experience whose partner represented Christie Brinkley and Mia Farrow. The *News* had busily reported a story about Donna's lawyer that Thursday that would become Friday's front page. Hardly a good omen for the maritally impaired Rudy, the story said Hanover would probably be able to stay in the mansion until he left office and that Nathan could be barred from the mansion as "poisonous to the home environment." The *News* also reported that Donna would likely be entitled to a goodly share of Rudy's future earnings based on her role in creating his celebrity. Obviously, those future earnings would be greatest if he was forced from public life.

Depositions up the road about Lategano were a possibility. His entire secret life, involving more than Lategano and Nathan, could be laid bare long before the depositions. Reporters were already calling women he'd known well and asking how well. There might be leaks or more press conferences like the one on May 10 that ended with Donna's statement that she would "have no further remarks TODAY."

Just as uncertain was how Nathan would handle it all. She wanted to be part of his public life—a choice that forced much of these contretemps to the surface. She had even appeared to relish some of the early publicity. But when the press went to Hazelton, Pennsylvania —knocking on every door she'd opened as a kid—she'd used her discomfort to push him to act. The separation announcement clarified matters. But a Senate withdrawal would lower the spotlight even further. Were he to run, she would be hounded. Were he not to run, she might even be able to share his coming medical trauma with him.

So the day after the Mitchell interview, at the largest press conference of his life, Rudy finally withdrew from the Senate race, calling it "a health decision." He decided, he said, "to put my health first" and "devote the focus and attention that I should to being able to figure out the best treatment—and not running for office."

Walking into the conference in an upstairs chamber of City Hall, he was immediately preceded by Cuker, in a dark blue, open shirt, his emotions masked by his ever present poker face. Nathan was watching a pained and stumbling Rudy on television and the *Post* would report that she cried so much she traumatized an eye and had to be taken to Manhattan Eye, Ear and Throat Hospital, where the mayor rushed afterwards. This time, he called Donna before the conference, and told her of his decision. He would have been kinder if he'd urged her not to watch it.

He mentioned "love" twelve times in a thirty-minute epiphany. He never used it in connection with his family, which he did not mention until three-quarters of the way through the conference. Instead he kept saying how "fortunate" he was to "have very good friends"—that other new favorite word of his—and "people that I love and that love me." He said he used to think that "the core of me was in politics" but he now knew "it isn't." He talked about learning he wasn't "Superman," "confronting" his "mortality" and realizing he was "just a human being." When asked if cancer had drawn him "closer to God," he made a joke of it, saying he hoped God was closer to him. In fact, the two most common instinctual responses to such crises—turning to family and church—had no apparent allure for him.

He nonetheless portrayed himself as a changed man who'd rediscovered what was "important in life," and admitted for the second time in two days that he might have made mistakes. The allusion was to minorities again. He said he was going to "try very hard" to find ways to "overcome maybe some of the barriers that maybe I placed there." He reminded everyone of his 1997 victory party and 1998 inaugural pledges to reach out to the left-out and he renewed that forgotten pledge, saying he wanted to make sure "every New Yorker feels I'm dedicated to them."

But when pressed by a reporter about how he intended to do that, he suddenly blurred his message, insisting that he was "just not capable of doing it as a racial, ethnic, religious thing" and contending that "there are people in all different groups" who feel excluded. His contradictory impulses about the unmistakably racial consequences of his reign meant he was still in denial—unwilling to genuinely accept the existence of a problem he nonetheless wanted to appear to be solving. Ironically, the budget he proposed at the same time that he learned of his cancer killed a $750,000 program for prostate cancer screening for the poor despite the largest surplus in city history and the fact that black men were much more likely to get the disease than whites.

Neither of the two prominent New Yorkers who'd just weathered the same health crisis—Hevesi and Giuliani hero Joe Torre—ever put in so maudlin and self-indulgent a performance about it. What was particularly bizarre was that Rudy's press conference just a few weeks earlier when he actually revealed his cancer was such a sharp contrast. He did that one without a note of self-pity. It was at a conference announcing a political decision—and simultaneously saying how little politics mattered—that he wallowed, rambled, exposed himself. He was the post-surgical Lyndon Johnson lifting his hospital shirt for the cameras. He was Warren Beatty's Bulworth without either Halle Berry or a social reality check. He was a Cuker character, breathing entirely too deeply.

Was he in mourning over the ending of a Senate run he was so ambiguous about that he never announced for it and rarely campaigned?

Was he setting the stage for a grandiose comeback?

Was he trying to shift the media spotlight off the personal debacle he caused and onto the one he was a victim of?

Was he in meltdown or just in love? Had he spent too much time on Cuker's amateur couch?

All of the above.

A day later, he taped an exclusive *Meet the Press* interview with Tim Russert. Again there was no mention of Lategano or Nathan. He hit his new "love" note twelve times once more. Cancer was his claimed exclusive rationale for withdrawal, reflection the exclusive mood on display. He was asked if he still believed what his father had taught him—that respect was more important than love. And, for the first time in his public life, he broke with Harold Giuliani.

"My dad taught me a lot of really good things, and he was a wonderful man, but no—as I've told, you know, my son, daughter—no father is perfect. You know fathers—fathers make mistakes and fathers are human beings, and I tend to think now that love is more important than I thought it was."

It was just one paragraph, however, in a rewrite of the autobiography he'd spent a lifetime concocting.

The shift on Harold still left a mountain of myths. In fact it's possible to write a biography of Rudy Giuliani from news clips that's entirely fictional. By gaining control of the information around him, and cowing those who knew him, he has over the years manufactured a life story. His auto-novel would sometimes be the opposite of what was real, sometimes merely a grossly exaggerated version of it. But each step of the way, through a life of prominence and impact, he had twisted the truth, melding it with his imagination and feeding his illusions.

The father he celebrated so often was a pathological predator. His extended family harbored a junkie, a crooked cop and a murky mob wing. He dissolved his first marriage with a lie so he could appear Catholic when he remarried. The very personal jewelry his first wife found in her bedroom wasn't hers.

His Perry Mason trial debut was staged shtick. His *Prince of the City* hero never gave him a crooked cop. Unassisted by the canned assets of a government case, the self-celebrated trial attorney tried a bare trickle of cases, all civil, in eight years on the other side of a courtroom. Instead he turned a multimillion-dollar favor from a judicial mentor into a claim that he was a successful corporate CEO.

The only black leader he bonded with in early life was the hemisphere's bloodiest tyrant. His sworn testimony in a Florida courtroom was delusion in service of the tyrant. As the most powerful figure in federal law enforcement, he stole medals from honest prosecutors in Washington who had served justice.

The Commission memoir that made his mob reputation was plagiarized. He mistook Jimmy Caan for Marlon Brando and convicted the wrong Godfather. He hid the numbers that exposed his Southern District record as if they were embarrassing relatives. The very impersonal, steel-silver, jewelry that honest stockbrokers found on their wrists *was* his.

The IRS agent at his side was a sex spook. Possession of the stolen letters he marketed to make himself mayor was a criminal misdemeanor. He planted probes in his old office to cripple a political foe he then endorsed. He mistook a mayor for a washroom attendant and led a rally that was a riot. His path to power was the bias of birthright.

His single-standard city was a single-race city. The targeted homeless replaced the punching bag of his childhood. The publicly dependent could be forced to stand on their own feet, he said of half a million people, only if their stomachs were as empty as their pockets. His crime stats were more P. T. Barnum than Marshall Dillon, especially after he traded in a cover-boy commissioner for a clownish cipher. His school strategy was more about establishing rhetorical distance than encouraging reading improvement. The only black leader he bonded with later in life would become the city's most bloodied chancellor. His ethical antennae couldn't make it past the metal detectors he installed at City Hall Plaza.

The first mistress displaced the First Lady. A second displaced the First Family. New Age insights displaced '50s values. His children were ghosts in a haunted public house, invisible to the city's families and reminders of a life that was. The wife he once made speeches about delivered one of her own and in three sentences crushed his character. For years, their joint demand for privacy was all they shared—a cry made hollow by the punishing excursions he'd taken into the lives of others. A man whose closest aides probed one Nathan's love life could not protect the privacy of another. And now, with him and his wife turning their marriage into public spectacle, all they shared was bitterness.

His family a fraud, his achievements a boast, his integrity a whim, his judgment a memory, his health a fear, his beliefs a mirage, Rudy Giuliani hunkered forward, the simulated smile as broad as the shoulders were bowed, still chasing a dream worthy of his destiny. Beating Hillary, he believed, could have made him an instant Washington power and led to her husband's job, the grail that had guided him from the outset. He would have to find a new path, or seek a new grail. Donna was gone, Garth was gone, Cristyne was gone, even Powers was barely a presence. The pros like Mastro and Levine were off making money, with Harding also in search of his next mayoral meal ticket. Helen was too ill and too old to notice.

Denny Young was still there, so constant and ego-less a companion that his marriage was dead. But Denny was a silhouette. Elliot Cuker was there, too, though the business wizard couldn't put enough smoke in the cigar bar to keep it open. Judith Nathan was certainly there as well, and to be with her where no camera could catch them on the eve of his fifty-sixth birthday, he'd watch a Yankee-Red Sox game in a box at a sports bar rather than that old love shack of his, Yankee Stadium. In the throes of his now-discarded Senate campaign, Cuker and Nathan had become two of his key political advisers, despite the fact that Cuker wasn't registered to vote and Nathan never voted. They could still be part of his clapping kitchen cabinet when he moved, post-cancer, to carve out his future. Teitelbaum, Tony Carbonetti and the other neophytes he had invented from whole cloth were also still with him—but they were mere pieces he moved around the board.

He would submit to no discipline or definition. He would invent his own magical message and take his own personal poll. It was his stage anyway, and he did not mind being on it alone. That way he knew he was still in control. And control was what mattered now, in a world where, more than ever, all he could really trust was himself.

Notes

Chapter 2

"He had no use for priests" (19): Quotes from Helen Giuliani, Rudy himself and several other individuals identified in the preface were culled from unpublished interviews conducted in 1988 and 1989.

William was Rudy's godfather (21): In addition to William, Vincent and Roberto, Edward D'Avanzo was a transit cop until 1942, when he switched to the fire department. Harold's brother, Rudolph Giuliani, entered the police force as a patrolman on February 20, 1956.

whose family borrowed money from Leo (26): This source, referred to subsequently as "Lewis's friend," provided critical details of the criminal histories of Leo and Lewis D'Avanzo and Harold Giuliani, including the fact that Harold had done time at Sing Sing. Court documents and other records confirmed more than a half dozen pieces of critical information he supplied. None of his information proved to be incorrect. A close friend of Lewis's, this source is also a felon whose convictions date back to the 1960s.

The Viscontis' candle business originally began as a small, family-run operation, headquartered in the garage of Fanny's mother-in-law's house on Devoie Street in Williamsburg.

Chapter 3

A man whose sporadic (64): Harold's new employer, however, like his old one in Flatbush, Brooklyn, had its legal problems. Less than six months after Harold listed the company as his employer on his Queens voter registration card, Teamster leader Francis C. DeBrouse was convicted of using his position with the union to persuade two companies to accept extermination contracts from Gotham Maintenance. The city's Department of Investigation later found the Department of Real Estate had engaged in questionable bidding procedures by giving Gotham its noncompetitive contracts.

Chapter 4

Bob Leuci said he would think about it (78): Robert Daley, *Prince of the City* (Boston: Houghton Mifflin, 1978), pp. 10–15.

ACKNOWLEDGMENTS

I'd like to thank the following people who made this book possible.

First are the people who financed it. John Donatich and Jack McKeown at Basic demonstrated their faith in this project from the beginning. They put the money on the table. David Schneiderman and Don Forst from the *Village Voice* granted me a leave and a greatly reduced workload, subsidizing this book and making me remember once again just how special a place the *Voice* is.

Bill Moyers and the Schumann Foundation, Neil Fabricant, and the Community Service Society helped me raise the additional funding that paid the salaries of Adam Fifield and Jennifer Warren, my two assistants on the book. Kim Nauer at the Center for an Urban Future acted as the fiscal conduit for these research grants and was an enormous help. Susan Lehman at *Talk* magazine bought serial rights. Fran Goldin, my agent, took me on two great rounds of sales pitches until we made a deal.

Second are the people who worked on it. I sang the praises of Adam Fifield in the Preface. Jennifer Warren is another ex-intern who became an indispensable research asset to this book. She worked with me for almost ten months, a reporting rock who did document and database searches, interviews and analysis, often deep into the night. She has a genius for organization and an enthusiasm for reporting that make her own first book inevitable. Ephraim Smith was the statistician whose volunteer work on the crime, Southern District and minority employment data was vital to this book. Other researchers who made major contributions were David Altschuler and Nicole Gesauldo, two interns who worked tirelessly on time-off from their studies at Yale and Columbia.

Ruth Ford, a reporter for the *Brooklyn Paper*, did some fine spot research for me on church-related issues. Chisun Lee, now a *Voice* staff writer, mastered all the Times Square material while working as my intern last summer. Ex-intern Rashmi Vasisht hunted court records. Lauren Dunn, a SUNY-Binghampton student editor, did good work up there on Rudy's family roots. Brian Mealor, Matt Leising and Lina Katz also helped.

Eddie Borges, another ex-intern, was my constant computer consultant, raising me from the dinosaur dead and introducing me, during the course of this book, to communication possibilities I instinctively resist as a threat. Eddie, who works for the *Hollywood Reporter*, also did some reporting on Donna Hanover for the book. Joseph Jesselli was the computer expert at the *Voice* who also helped.

Liz Nagle, Richard Miller, Norman MacAfee, and John Donatich, who edited the book, were the folks from Basic who did the impossible—turning out a massive book on overdrive. Kevin Goering was the outside counsel who did a thorough job of vetting it.

Third are the people who went beyond interviews and actually helped provide access to records or sources, in no particular order: Vincent McGhee, Anna D'Avanzo, Jack O'Leary, Elizabeth Lockwood, Jeff Harris, Charles Miller, Fred Dicker, Danny DeFrancesco, Herman Badillo, Bill Stern, Gerson Borrero, David Neustadt, Rachel Gordon, Harry Spence, Chiarra Coletti, Tom Robbins, Jack Newfield, Jonathan Rosner, Dave Seifman, Bob Hardt, Michael Finnegan, Jon Bowles, Patricia McCarthy, Michael Tomasky, Timothy Williams, Ken Cobb, Bill Bastone, Ray Horton, Tom Touposis, Paul Schwartzman, Charlie Bagli, Bruce Lambert, Irwin Stotsky, Ira Kurzban, Jean-Jean Pierre, Patrick Markee, Liz Kruger, Brendan Sexton, Mary Brosnahan, Marcus Baram, Bill Lynch, Marvin Smilon, Joe Conason, Ken Frydman, David Garth, John Corporon, Reese Schonfeld, Harold Tyler, Bill Bratton, Mike Julien, Jay Tannenbaum, Evan Halper, Dr. Tom Toia, Jack Bonomi, Lenny Levitt, Joe Calderone, Tom Apple, Dave Lewis, Ian Michaels, Frank Barry, Dan Walfish and Frank Castro.

Fourth are the people who did excavating spadework in book or article form that we relied on: Todd Purdum, Jennet Conant, Paul Schwartzman, Connie Bruck, Michael Powell, Jesse Drucker, Joe Calderone, Michael Winerip, Barry Bearak, Dave Lewis, Jim Traub, Rob Polner, Dan Janison, Jonathan Van Meter, Linda Yglesias, John Leonard, Dave Saltonstall, Mitchell Fink, Richard Johnson, George Rush, Joanna Molloy, Craig Horowitz, Heidi Evans, Gail Sheehy, Josh Gitlin, Elizabeth Bumiller, Jason Deparle, David Seifman, David Firestone, Martha Sherrill, Charlie Bagli, and Dan Barry. They consulted books by Robert Daley, Gene Mustain, Jerry Capeci, James Stewart, Jim Traub, Robert Orsi, Marilyn Thompson, Tom Puccio, Dan Collins, Bill Bratton, Jack Maple, Evan Mandery, John Mollenkopf, Edward I. Koch, George Pataki, Kevin

McAuliffe, Jack Newfield, Jessie Kornbluth, William French Smith and Elizabeth Abbott.

Fifth are the people who nurtured me and the gang. Frances McGettigan Barrett is the best partner a frequently unshaven, unshowered, stressed-out, embattled, aging writer could have. She's been with me for thirty-one years, and I never appreciated her more. My son Mac took off for Colgate in the middle of this project, and his excellent freshman year made this grueling workload worth it. Kathy Powers was kind enough to lend me Adam Fifield for months at a time, and her sacrifice was a generous contribution to the book.

My brother Larry Barrett and his wife, Eileen, put up Adam on his visits to Washington. My mother Helen, my brothers Chris and Tim, my sisters Loretta and Tia, as well as the rest of the family, were wonderfully forgiving when this book prevented me from going home to Virginia for Christmas and my father, Lawrence G. Barrett, died three weeks later. Now all I have to do is figure out a way to forgive myself.

This book tested me physically (I should also thank my doctors, particularly Dr. Edward Fitzpatrick) as well as creatively. My eyes, my leg and other body parts gave way under the strain of endless consecutive days of work. The deadline was immutable, and there's nothing like an immutable deadline to motivate and discipline. The Lord, maybe as a favor to Dad, helped me to the finish line. Thank Him, too.

INDEX

Note: The initials RG refer to Rudy Giuliani.

Abbott, Elizabeth, 125
Abortion, 306
  and RG's stand in 1992, 198
  and RG's stand on in 1989 election,
    194, 195, 197–198
Abrams, Bob, 254, 278
ACT-UP, 176, 198–199, 368
Adams, Arlin, 253
Adams, Eric, 268, 269
Adelphi Institute, 98–99
Advisory Committee on Trade
    Negotiations, 127
Aguiluz, Carl, 80, 81, 82
AIDS, 190, 307, 319, 352
Ailes, Roger, 169, 203, 210, 400, 420
Air Force Reserve Officers Training
    Corps (AFROTC), 50
Alcivar, Lenny, 408–409
Algemeiner Journal (Yiddish newspaper),
    223
Alley, Kirstie, 434
All Star Café, 5, 9
Alpha Sigma Beta fraternity, 50–51
Alter, Susan, 273–274
Altschuler, David, 422
American Jewish Committee, 223
American Jewish Congress, 373
American Labor Party, 194
American Lawyer, 69, 148, 154
  and RG's U.S. Attorney legacy, 172
America's Talking, 399, 400
Aminex Resources Corp., 99–101
Amnesty International, 291, 334
Amsterdam News, 175, 179
  "fascist" comments, 269

and Peruggi annulment and 1989
    campaign, 235–236
Amuso, Vic, 156
Anderson, Eugene, 243
Anderson, Hibey, Nauheim & Blair, 127
Anderson, Stanton, 126
Anderson, Warren, 213
Anderson Koll Olick & Oshinsky,
    241–243
Anemone, Lou, 315, 329
Anson, Kate, 434
Anti-Defamation League (ADL) and Nazi
    (Berger) incident, 204–205
Apfelberg, Benjamin, 16–17
Aponte, Michael, 177
Aristide, Jean-Bertrand, 122
Armour & Co., 104
Armstrong, Mike, 171, 172, 212
Arzt, George, 175, 177, 179
AT&T, 242
Atwater, Lee, 269
Auletta, Nicholas, 152
Aurelio, Dick, 400–401
Aurelio, Thomas, 27

Badillo, Gail, 419
Badillo, Herman, 268, 273, 284–285, 369,
    419, 447, 454
  campaign ad of 1993 election, 268–269
Baez, Anthony, 329–330, 335
Baird, Bruce, 149–150
Barbanel, Josh, 234
Barnes, Joe, 280
Barr, William, 258
Barrett, J. Patrick, 201

Barrett, Matthew, 48
Barrios-Paoli, Lillian, 320–321, 322, 323
Barron's National Business & Financial Weekly, 97, 132
Barry, Dan, 385, 426
Baseball
  and Rawlings baseball factory, 124
  and RG's childhood, 22–23
  See also Dodgers, Brooklyn; Yankees, New York
Bayard, Henri, 118–119, 125–126
Beame, Abe, 222, 270, 291–292
Bell, Jim, 226, 227, 228
Bellmore, North, 32
Benjamin, Marty, 186
Bennett, Ernest, 125
Bennett, Franz, 125–126
Bennett, Michele, 126
Bensonhurst protests of 1989, 199–200
Ben Veniste, Richard, 79
Berger (Nazi) incident, 204–208
Berger, Simon, 204–207, 214
Bergman, Marty, 193, 223
Bernstein, Richard, 351
Berrouet, Edouard, 115, 123, 126
Biaggi, Mario, 165, 166, 170–171, 197, 216–217
Biambi, Roger, 114
BID. *See* Times Square Business Improvement District (BID)
Biegen, Arnold, 253, 280
Bingham, Jonathan, 197
Bishop Loughlin Memorial High School, 33–37, 56–57, 189
Blacks
  appointed in 1994 by RG, 291–292
  being stopped by NYPD, 334–335
  Brooklyn, 29
  Civilian Complaint Review Board (CCRB), 333
  and Diallo case, 330–331, 332
  and Ed Koch, 291–292, 327
  election in 1997, 330
  employment for city positions, 322–325
  Garden City, 29
  and Harold Giuliani, 64
  homeless, 191
  and Jackie Mason's comments, 224–225
  and police misconduct, 328–339
  and RG's personal relationship with Rudy Crew, 378–380, 382, 467
  and RG's relationship to, 325–327
  vote in 1989 campaign, 199
  See also Race
Blakey, Robert, 154
Blotcher, Jay, 198–199
Boesky, Ivan, 157–158, 171
Bogan, Carl "Kojak," 60–61, 76–77, 84, 124
Bohan, Owen, 15–16, 17
Bolan, Tom, 149
Bonanno, Joe, 146, 151
Bond, Rich, 207
Bonomi, Jack, 90
Bonventri, Peter, 34
Borakove, Ellen, 350–351
Bork, Robert, 92
Botnick, Victor, 185
Boxing, 20, 27, 339
Bradley's Restaurant, 175
Bramwell, Arthur, 226, 327
Brandon, John, 287
Brasco, Frank, 87
Bratton, William (police commissioner), 244, 343–347
  appointment of, 289
  crime rate statistics, 353
  firing of his press staff, 407–408
  marijuana manhunt by Safir, 338
  Nation of Islam fracas, 290
  Operation Juggernaut, 347
  and RG insisting on credit for crime reduction, 344
  squeegees, 364, 365
  Time magazine article, 346, 354
  Transit Authority, 345, 365
  Turnaround, 343
Breindel, Eric, 177
Breslin, Jimmy, 232
Brezenoff, Stan, 175, 178, 185
Bristol-Myers Squibb, 428
Brombwich, Michael, 106
Brooklyn, East Flatbush, 24
Brooklyn Academy of Music, 35
Brooklyn North Drug Initiative, 347
Brown, Ron, 280
Browne, Arthur, 234, 236

Bruce, Carol, 168
Bruck, Connie, 172
Bryers, Richard, 271, 279, 281, 404
Bucknam, Bob, 239
Bumiller, Elizabeth, 414, 420
Burkert, George, 75–76
Burns, Arnold, 170, 206, 239, 250
Bush, Barbara, 410
Bush, George, 110, 210, 258, 265
Bush, George W. and Laura, 3, 420, 438
Bush, Jeb, 388
Butterfield, Fox, 366
Butts, Calvin, 287

Cafaro, Vincent "the Fish," 150, 155
Cahill, Tom, 68
Caiola, Benjamin, 79, 82
Camiel, Pete, 93
Cammarata, Jerry, 370, 386, 389
Camp La Guardia, 315, 458
Capasso, Carl, 160
Capozzoli, Louis, 15
Carbonetti, Louis, 27–28, 29, 53, 90, 255
Carbonetti, Lou Jr., 27, 28, 284–285, 296,
    446
Carbonetti, Tony, 284, 296, 446, 468
Carey, Hugh, 194
Caribbean Basin Initiative, 117–118
Carr, Joel, 100–101
Carson, Sonny, 225, 226
Cart, Matthew, 76
Carter, Dominick, 416
Carter, Graydon, 415
Carter, Jimmy, 95, 103
Carter, Robert, 88, 89, 90, 131
Carter, Zachary, 334
Caruso, David, 1
Caruso, Ken, 107, 108, 239, 452, 453, 454
Caruso, Phil, 256, 258, 260, 269, 290, 329,
    456
Castellano, Paul "the Pope," 148, 149, 150,
    154, 156, 158
Castro, Bernadette, 302
Castro, Fidel, 116
CBS Morning News and "Commission"
    indictment interview, 152
Centrella, Joe, 36
Cerullo, Fred, 297

Chapman, Wilbur, 323–324
Chertoff, Michael, 153
Chiappa, Richard, 59
Children's Aid Society, 427
Chinn, Franklyn, 168
Choate, David, 110
Christ Stopped at Eboli (Levi), 19
Church World Services, 128
Citizens Budget Commission, 244
City for Sale, 224, 446
City University of New York (CUNY), 310,
    318
Civil Aeronautics Board, 86
Clarke, Una, 260
Claude, Silvio, 128
Clinton, Bill, 269, 289, 301, 308, 389, 438
Clinton, Hillary Rodham, 308, 340, 366,
    394, 434, 438
    See also Giuliani, Rudolph William
    Louis (Rudy), and Senate race with
    Hillary Clinton
Cody, Dave, 82
Cohen, Neal, 454
Cohen, Richard, 223, 306
Cohn, Roy, 149, 150
Coles, Tony, 315, 385, 388, 389
    overseeing of HRA, 320–321, 322
Coletti, Chiara, 367, 377, 384, 386, 390
Collins, Dan, 65, 198, 210, 215
Collins, Gail, 274
Colombo investigation, 147, 150
"Commission" Mafia case, 146, 150–156
Committee to Honor Black Heroes, 225
Common Cause, 109
Community Assistance Unit, 297
Compstat statistics meetings, 344–345, 347,
    354
Condé Nast building, 4, 8
Congress of Racial Equality (CORE), 274
Connelly, Maureen, 179
Conservative Party, 195–197, 212, 251, 254,
    272, 304
Construction company payoffs, 152–153
Conti, Luigi, 120, 127, 128
Contract for America, 306
"Cool Schools" project, 399
Coopers Classic Cars and Cigar Bar, 378,
    429, 433, 434, 442–443, 450

Coppola, Francis Ford, 155
Corallo, "Tony Ducks," 6, 151, 153–154,
    155, 156
Cornstein, David, 250, 255, 454
Corporon, John, 135, 208, 209, 210, 237,
    282
Cortines, Ramon, 346, 367–369, 373,
    375–376
Costello, Frank, 27–28, 68, 73, 304
Council of Black Elected Officials, 326
Crains and Lategano appointment as CVB
    head, 426
Crew, Kathy, 380, 390
Crew, Rudy (schools chancellor), 367–368,
    371–394, 441–442
    personal relationship with RG, 378–380,
        382, 467
Crew, Rudy, Jr., 385, 390
Crew, Rudy, school vouchers, 371, 382–388
Crime
    absence of plan relative to in 1993, 244
    "Broken Windows" theory, 345
    Compstat meetings, 344–345, 347
    factors which lower, 355
    graffiti, 365
    plummeting of in New York City, 2
    punishing plan and drug and guns
        arrests, 345
    and RG as mayor, 289, 341–365
    and RG's taking credit for what was
        done previously, 364
    squeegees, 363–364
    Times Square, 10
    "zero tolerance" for quality of life
        violations, 345
    See also Crime rate statistics; New York
        Police Department
Crime Fighter, The (Maple), 353
Crime rate statistics
    assault, 362–363, 364
    attempted force burglary, 359–361
    auto and auto-part theft, 355–357
    burglary from public buildings,
        361–362
    call for audit of New York, 348
    evidence that RG strategies created
        decrease, 352–354
    murder, 341–342, 350–355
    robbery, 363–364

shoplifting and coin machines theft,
    358–359
theft from an auto, 357–358
theft from public buildings, 359
total index, 349–350
Cronies Restaurant, 436
Crotty, Paul, 71, 296, 457
Crown Heights riot, 247–248, 269
    defeat of Dinkins in 1993, 275–277
Cubans, protection of, 131
Cuker, Elliot, 99, 391, 415, 438
    and Coopers Classic Cars and Cigar Bar,
        378, 429, 433, 434, 442–443, 450
    as RG's friend, 137, 411–412, 413,
        442–444, 468
Cuomo, Andrew, 197, 233, 234, 236, 244,
    278, 298
Cuomo, Madeline, 429
Cuomo, Mario (NY Governor, 1983–1994),
    166
    campaign against Koch, 176
    and Comstock Electric contract, 303–304
    and Crown Heights, 275–277
    election of 1993, 274–279
    gubernatorial election of 1994, 297–303,
        309
    and Liberal Party, 194, 197
    non-aggression pact with D'Amato, 276
    renewal of Times Square, 6, 7
Cuomo, Matilda, 299
Curran, Paul, 77, 88, 91

Daily News
    and Crew's quitting over voucher issue,
        386
    and Crew vs RG, 388
    and Dinkins love letters, 236
    and Donna Hanover, 396, 398, 428, 434,
        464
    falling out with Lategano, 420
    and Leuci, 78
    and Noriega and RG's law firm, 203–204
    number of RG black campaign aides in
        1993, 249
    Operation Juggernaut, 347, 407
    and Patterson Belknap, 97
    and Podell, 88
    profile of Bratton, 344
    racism and Dyson, 293

and RG participation in NYPD riot and rally of 1992, 261

and RG's marriage to his cousin, 145

support of RG from 1993 on, 272

Daley, Richard, 1

Daley, Richard Jr., 308

Daley, Robert, 78

Dallas Morning News

and Donna Hanover interview, 416

and Stanley Hanover, 111

Daly, Peter, 82

D'Amato, Alfonse (US Senator, 1981–1999), 133–134, 202, 211, 239, 251, 299, 300, 311

available women, 442

backing of RG in 1997, 305

encouragement of RG to run for Senate in 1988, 165–166, 169

fight against RG in 1989 mayoral election, 197, 200, 201–219

investigation of by Lawrence regarding HUD indiscretions, 252–253

links to Milken, 171–172

and Mama D'Amato, 133

and Mario Biaggi, 217

and McGuire, 215–219

mob calls to RG, 149–150, 215

and Nazi (Berger) story, 206–207

percentage of NYC vote in 1992, 265–266

Power, Pasta, and Politics (D'Amato), 213–214

and RG's endorsement of Cuomo in 1994, 302, 303

and RG support in 1992 Senate race, 252–256

threat of backing others in 1993 mayoral election, 250–251

undercover drug buy, 148

and Wedtech case, 216

D'Amato, Armand, 216, 217, 218, 253

Damn Reading! (A Case Against Literacy) (Hall), 101

Danforth, John C., 108

Dano, Jimmy, 24

D'Avanzo, Adelina Stanchi (maternal grandmother), 18–19, 28, 43, 45, 61, 63

raising of RG, 20–21, 23

D'Avanzo, Anna (maternal aunt), 18, 19, 20, 22, 23, 31, 45–46, 47, 53

D'Avanzo, Edward (maternal uncle), 31, 45–46, 47, 48, 62, 284, 469(n2)

D'Avanzo, Evangeline (cousin), 21, 44

D'Avanzo, Helen (cousin), 55

D'Avanzo, Helen. *See* Giuliani, Helen D'Avanzo (mother)

D'Avanzo, Joan Ellen (cousin), 21, 44, 62, 142, 314

D'Avanzo, Lee Ann (cousin), 55

D'Avanzo, Leo "Tullio" (maternal uncle), 23–25, 26, 27, 37, 46–47, 55–56, 58, 106–107

D'Avanzo, Lewis, 26–27, 31, 35, 37–38, 46, 56, 59, 106–107

and criminal career of, 56–59

D'Avanzo, Lois (cousin), 46, 56, 57

D'Avanzo, Luigi (Louis) (maternal grandfather), 18–19, 23

D'Avanzo, Olga Giuliani (paternal aunt), 19–20, 21, 44, 284

D'Avanzo, Robert Jr. (cousin), 61

D'Avanzo, Roberto (maternal uncle), 21

D'Avanzo, Veronica "Betty," 24, 31, 55, 58

D'Avanzo, Vincent (maternal uncle), 21, 24, 46, 340

D'Avanzo, William (maternal uncle), 19–20, 21, 44, 284

D'Avanzo Contracting, 55

Davidoff, Sid, 280–281, 445, 449

Davis, Bob, 126

Davitt, Kevin, 407

Death penalty, 192

DeBrouse, Francis C., 469–470(n2)

DeConcini, Dennis, 104–105

De La Salle Christian Brothers, 33

Dellicurti, Vic, 27, 90

DeMeo, Roy, 58, 59

Democratic Party

and mayoral politics in New York City, 265–266

and RG's affiliation, 103

and RG's circle of top aides, 296–297

and RG's early allegiance to, 52

strength in New York City in 1989, 194

DeParle, Jason, 317–318

Dewey, Tom, 150

DHS. *See* New York City Department of Homeless Services

Diallo, Amadou, 328, 330–331, 332, 346, 385, 458

Diamond, Bill, 297

Diaz, David, 337

Diaz, Ruben, 411

DiBrienza, Steve, 313

DiCarlo, Bob, 251, 252, 255

Dicker, Fred, 233–234

DiMaggio, Joe, 305

Dinkins, David (NYC mayor, 1990–1994), 221, 286, 291–292
  and Bill Lynch, 186
  and Campaign Finance Board fine, 452
  decrease of crime during his administration, 341
  and Disney's rebuilding of 42nd Street theater, 6
  general mayoral election of 1989, 192–193, 221–240
  homeless programs of, 313–314
  investigations of his administration after its conclusion, 279–280
  and Jewish issues, 223, 327
  love letters and affairs of, 228–235, 236, 416
  mayoral election of 1993, 265–286
  renewal of Times Square, 7
  and RG's criticism of educational policy of, 372
  and RG's criticisms of his police policies, 61
  supposed affair with Cindy Ng, 229

Disney Corporation and Times Square, 6–7, 8, 9

District Council 37, 373–374, 455

Doctors Without Borders, 2

Dodgers, Brooklyn, 22–23, 379

Doherty, John, 11

Dole, Bob, 311, 459

Dolman, Joseph, 327

Domenech, Daniel, 370–371

Dorismond, Charles, 337–338

Dorismond, Patrick, 335–340, 463

Douglas, Michael, 157

Dowd, Maureen, 416

Dow Jones case, 97

Doyle, John, 243

Draft, military, and RG's deferment, 71

Dressler, Fred, 400

Drexel Burnham Lambert, 1, 157, 171–172

Drug Enforcement Administration (DEA), 80, 125, 126

Drugs
  enforcement as NYSD Attorney, 139–142
  initiative as mayor, 345, 347
  and narcotic undercover operations, 337–338
  RG's philosophy on, 141–142
  trafficking in Haiti, 125–126
  treatment programs, 314

Dubinsky, David, 193

Duffy, Kevin, 160

Dunne, John, 257

Durst, Douglas, 8–9

Duvalier, Jean-Claude "Baby Doc," 115, 129, 338
  drug smuggling, 125–126
  and Haitian refugees, 117, 119, 123
  lawyers for, 126–127
  promise not to prosecute returning refugees, 119–120

Duvalier, Michelle, 125–126

Dyson, John, 8–9, 296
  as deputy mayor for economic development, 293, 450
  racist remarks in 1994, 292–294
  workfare, 316–317

Eagleburger, Lawrence, 117

Eagle Party, 50

Ebbets Field, 22–23, 24

Edmonds, Charles, 76

Ehrlich, Bernard, 196

Eisenhower, Dwight D., 67, 92

Eisner, Michael, 6–7

Elaine's restaurant, 406, 436

Elder, William, 144

Emergency Assistance Unit (EAU), 314

Eppolito, James (Jimmy the Clam), 24

Equal Opportunity Employment Plan, 325

Esposito, Ralph and Joseph, 58

Estime, Jean-Bertrand, 118, 123–124

Evans, Heidi, 428, 434

Farrakhan, Louis, 221, 223, 248, 267, 290
Federal Bureau of Investigation
    crime statistics, 341, 347, 349, 350
    drug enforcement, 139
    and Podell investigation, 85
    and RG as associate deputy attorney
        general, 92
Federal Crime Bill, 289
"Federal Day" anti-narcotics program,
    139–140
Federal Times and Nard case, 105
Feerick, John, 457
Feinberg, Ken, 60–61, 83
Feldcamp, Bob, 139
Felder, Raoul, 224
Feldman, Sandra, 244, 373, 374, 384
Fernandez, Joseph, 368
Ferrer, Fernando, 329
Fields, Virginia, 326
Fink, Mitchell, 436
Fink, Robert, 216
Finkelstein, Arthur, 203
Finkelstein, Jerry, 251
Fischbein & Badillo, 447–448
Fischbein, Rick, 273, 274, 447
Fischetti, Ronald, 140–141
Fisher, Jeffrey, 129
Fitzsimmons, Robert J., 16
Flake, Floyd, 307
Florida Atlantic Airlines, 86
Food stamps, 318
Ford, Gerald, 91, 95
Ford, Kevin, 181, 183, 184, 279, 280
Ford Center for the Performing Arts, 9
Forman, Milos, 424
Fox Television, 282, 401, 420, 423–424
Frankel, Steve, 257, 259
Freeh, Louis, 214
Freeman, Robert, 158, 159
French Connection case, 75, 76
Friedman, Nancy, 84
Friedman, Roger, 436–437
Friedman, Stanley, 1, 162–165, 196, 255,
    448, 450
Fugazy, Bill, 429, 455

Gabel, Hortense, 160, 183
Gabel, Sukhreet, 160, 183, 184

Galante, Carmine, 69–70
Gambino family, 150–151
Ganchrow, Morris S., 21–22
Garden City, Long Island, 28–30
Gargano, Charles, 251
Garth, Dave, 297, 397, 400–401, 404
    break with RG and Lategano, 405, 409,
        411
    as campaign manager in 1993, 270–271,
        281
    and Cuomo gubernatorial endorsement
        of 1994, 298, 302
    fusion ticket in 1993 campaign, 273–275
    and RG link to Cuomo, 279
Gay Men's Health Crisis, 176, 198
Gays
    and education relative to, 368
    and RG's 1989 campaign, 198–199
    and RG's administration, 369
    St. Patrick's Day Parade, 245–246
Geist, Bill, 365
Gelman, Mitch, 281
George magazine, 412
Gialoreta, Gina, 25, 27, 55, 62
Gibson, Jim, 101–102
Gibson Dunn law firm, 449, 450
Gifford, Bernard, 370
Gigante, Mario, 149
Gigante, Vincent "the Chin," 149–150, 155
Gilbert, David Mack, 184
Giller, Ron, 405–406
Gillers, Stephen, 53
Gingrich, Newt, 305, 308, 311, 312
Giordano, George, 284
Girgenti, Richard, 275–277
Gist, Woodrow, 334–335
Giuliani, Andrew (son), 4, 189, 397, 414,
    440
    attendance at mass, 461
    birth of, 164
    and Goalie, 419
    golf, 422
    inaugural address, 397
    Yankees baseball games, 378–379, 413
Giuliani, Caroline (daughter), 4, 411, 461
    birth of, 207–208
    "Take Your Daughter to Work" day, 419
Giuliani, Cathy (cousin), 284, 456

Giuliani, Charles (paternal uncle), 18, 21, 44–45

Giuliani, Charles Jr. (cousin), 44

Giuliani, Debby (cousin), 44

Giuliani, Donna Hanover. *See* Hanover, Donna (second wife)

Giuliani, Evangelina (paternal grandmother), 17–18, 43

Giuliani, Evelyn (paternal aunt), 18, 45, 62

Giuliani, Harold (father), 13, 63–65
  aggressiveness of, 13, 14, 17
  as bartender at Vincent's Restaurant, 25–26, 31
  baseball, 23, 25–26
  childhood of, 13
  death of, 106–107
  job as groundskeeper at Lynbrook High School, 31–32
  and Judge MacMahon, 68
  as loan sharking collection agent, 26–27, 31, 46–47
  marriage to Helen D'Avanzo, 17
  move to Garden City, 28–29
  nervous breakdown of, 40–41
  as partner at Vincent's with Edward D'Avanzo, 47–48
  prostate cancer, 63, 65, 104
  relationship with Jack O'Leary, 37–41
  respect for work of, 319
  respect more important than love, 466–467
  and RG's *Meet the Press* statement regarding, 466–467
  robbery, trial, and imprisonment of, 14–17, 32, 106–107, 339
  teaching RG boxing, 20, 339

Giuliani, Helen D'Avanzo (mother), 13, 20–22, 61, 63–64
  appearance in commercial in 1993 campaign, 284
  childhood of, 13–14
  employment of, 32–33
  home at 444 East 86th Street, 241
  illness of 1989, 207–208
  marriage to Harold Giuliani, 17
  meeting with Alfonse D'Amato, 133–134
  move to Garden City, 28–30

and RG as U.S. Attorney for the Southern District of New York, 134

and RG's political affiliation, 103

and RG's relationship with Regina Peruggi, 44, 54, 57, 71–72, 83–84, 102, 143–144

Giuliani, Marie (paternal aunt), 18, 44

Giuliani, Olga. *See* D'Avanzo, Olga Giuliani

Giuliani, Regina Peruggi. *See* Peruggi, Regina (first wife)

Giuliani, Robert (cousin), 44

Giuliani, Rodolfo (paternal grandfather), 17–18, 31

Giuliani, Rudolph (paternal uncle), 21, 28, 44, 45, 145, 469(n2)

Giuliani, Rudolph Jr. (cousin), 44

Giuliani, Rudolph William Louis (Rudy)
  and Anderson Kill Olick & Oshinsky, 241–243
  announcement of separation from Donna Hanover, 439
  appreciation for John Fitzgerald Kennedy, 35–36, 44
  appreciation for Robert Kennedy, 51, 54–55
  as assistant U.S. Attorney for the Southern District of New York, 72–90
    change in view of humanity, 75
    and Leuci cases, 77–83
    and Podell case, 85–90
  as associate deputy attorney general, 1975–6, 91–95, 103–114
    and Frank Rizzo, 93–94
    Prospect House apartment lifestyle, 94–95
  as associate deputy attorney general, 1981–83, 103–133
    background check, 105–106
    and FBI's involvement in drug enforcement, 139
    and Haiti, 114–133
    and McDonnell Douglas case, 107–110
  childhood of
    baptism and religious upbringing, 22, 30
    baseball, 22–23, 28

birth, 20
and Bishop Loughlin Memorial High
    School, 33–37
boxing, 20
character of, 49
desire to become priest, 35
electoral politics, 35
and Garden City, 28–32
his telling of past history, 65–66
move to North Bellmore, 32
opera, 30–31, 35, 39
paper route, 30
relationship with Jack O'Leary, 39–40
and Sound Beach, 43–45
clerking for Judge MacMahon, 68–70
draft deferment of, 71
college years of
    and fraternity pledging, 50–51
    and Kathy Livermore, 44, 51–52, 146,
        189
    and Manhattan College, 48–51
    and New York University Law School,
        52–55
    opposition to Vietnam, 54, 70–71
    and Quadrangle magazine, 51
    and ROTC, 71
    and student political activities of,
        50–51
    support of Civil Rights, 54
    working at Vincent's for a day, 53
decision regarding New York Senate race
    of 1988, 165–166, 169, 172, 213, 396
family as policemen, 45, 61, 340, 469(n2)
home at 4 East 86th Street, 241
as mayor
    abortion, 306
    affirmative action, 325
    AIDS, 307
    and Anthony Baez case, 329–330
    benefit of doubt to police, 291
    building up of managers in police,
        fire, mayoral, and law departments,
        371
    campaign finance contribution
        irregularities, 452–453, 455–456
    circle of top aides, 296–297
    Civilian Complaint Review Board
        (CCRB), 333–334

claim to have ended welfare, 319
condemnation of methadone, 314
conflict of interest and corruption,
    445–457
crime, 244, 341–365
deconstruction of social service
    support systems, 307–311
and Diallo case, 330–331, 332
employment patronage, 446, 453–457
financial plan of 1995, 307–311
firing of press aides and control of
    media, 407–408
forcing Cortines out of office,
    367–368
homeless program, 295–296, 298
hotel tax reduction, 289, 298
inauguration, 397
initial severance program, 289–290,
    298–299
lack of minority leaders city
    government, 322–323
and Louima case, 328
Medicaid and Medicare, 295, 298, 308,
    318–319
and Newt Gingrich, 306–308
New Year's eve 2000, 1
and Patrick Dorismond, 336–340
personal relationship with Crew,
    378–380, 382, 467
political ethics of (political
    contributions, bribery, and
    patronage), 445–447
public assistance policy, 294–295,
    313–339
and pushing Bratton out, 346
refusal of permits to demonstrators,
    381
and relationship to and endorsement
    of Cuomo in 1994, 297–303, 309
relationship with blacks and
    minorities, 291–293, 325–327
relationship with family, 287–288,
    419
restriction of pornography, 9–10
salary of, 427
school system, 367–394
school vouchers, 371, 382–388, 393
tax cuts, 289

Times Square renewal, 6–10, 298
traveling in 1997–1998, 381
war against the poor, 307–312
welfare rolls slashing, 316–317,
    321–322
mayoral campaign of 1989
    abortion, 194, 195, 197–198
    after first five months through the
        primary, 201–219
    AIDS, 190
    announcement speech, 189–190
    death penalty, 192–193
    defeat of Lauder, 211
    first five months, 189–200
    gay rights, 198–199
    general election, 221–240
    homelessness, 189, 190–192, 193
    Liberal and Conservative Parties,
        194–197
    and Nazi (Berger) incident, 204–207
    and Noriega issue, 203–204
    plans to face Koch, 193–194, 221
    purported vote fraud, 259, 270
    race, 191, 225, 238–239
mayoral election campaign of 1993,
    265–288
    Crown Heights, 269, 275–277
    and D'Amato patrons, 255–256
    press style, 272
    racial issues, 265–267, 269–270
    running mates of, 273–275
    Staten Island, 275
    strategy for in face of history,
        265–267, 269
    vulnerability study commissioned for,
        71, 272, 283–284
mayoral campaign of 1997, 12, 417
    blacks, 327
    nonpartisanship, 459
opera love, 83, 85, 380
opposition to Vietnam war, 54, 70–71
and Patterson, Belknap & Webb, 64,
    95–101
    and Albert Terranova, 98–99
    and Aminex Resources Corp., 99–101
    and Elliot Cuker, 99
political movement to the right over the
    years, 103

political style of, 10–12
    arrogance, 43, 445
    as brash and self serving, 6, 9
    creation of his own life story, 466–467
    emergency mode, 296
    as gladiatorial, 153–154
    having it both ways, 248–250
    malleability, 310–311
    non-sharing of media time, 3, 344
    reinvention, 239
    strength of will, 11–12
    taking credit, 6–10, 148, 161, 319, 344,
        364
preparing for 1993 mayoral candidacy,
    241–263
    and endorsement of D'Amato,
        252–256
    and New York Police Department
        rally and riot of 1992, 259–263
    and Occhipinti affair, 256–259
    stand on Crown Heights, 247–248
presidential aspirations of, 3, 52, 381
promiscuity, 84, 283, 440–441, 442
prostate cancer, 435–436, 464, 466
real estate holdings and finances,
    424–425
religious practice of, 460–461, 463
Senate race with Hillary Clinton, 1, 3,
    339, 468
    affair with Nathan, 430–431
    decision to withdraw, 461–466
    and Lategano, 427, 462
    making peace with upstate interests,
        457–458
    religious issues, 4, 460–461
    reshaping himself as Republican,
        458–459
    use of race, 326
    withdrawal announcement, 465–466
as U.S. Attorney for the Southern
    District of New York, 1983–1989, 62,
    67, 134–190
    announcement of leaving the office,
        187
    and Bess Myerson case, 159–161, 183
    "Commission" case, 147, 150–156
    and contempt for public corruption,
        163

and drug enforcement, 139–142
and Ed Koch investigation, 175–189
insider trading prosecutions, 157–159,
  171–172
legacy of, 172–174
and media, 148–149
and New York Mafia, 146–156
Parking Violation Bureau (Friedman)
  case, 162–165
and Perlmutter case, 140–142
and philosophy on drugs, 141–142
possible mayoral interest, 186, 188
Social Security cases, 142–143
and Social Security disability cases,
  142
and Tony Lombardi, 182–183
undercover drug buy with D'Amato,
  148
Wedtech investigation, 166–170
white collar crime prosecution, 142,
  157–161
and White & Case, employment at,
  203–204, 241
  See also Hanover, Donna (second wife);
  Lategano, Cristyne; Peruggi, Regina
  (first wife)
Goalie (dog), 379, 403, 419
Godfather, The (motion picture), 155
Gold, Eugene, 57
Golden, Cherrie, 58
Goldstein, Leon, 370, 454
Goldstock, Ronald, 150, 154
Goldwater, Barry, 51
González, Elian, 2
Good Day New York (television show), 423
Goodman, Hazelle, 434
Good Morning America
  "Commission" indictment interview,
  152
  NYC as safest major city in US, 349
Goodrich, Solomon, 102
Goodwin, Michael, 215
Gore, Al and Tipper, 438
Gotti, John, 155, 156
Gould, Milton, 160
Graffiti, 365
Grant, Bob, 304, 326
Grath, David, 259

Gray, William, 94
Green, Mark, 12, 93, 284, 303, 334
Greenwald, Art, 111, 423
Gresser, Carol, 370, 373
Grievance Committee of the Association of
  the Bar of New York, 90
Grillo, Carl, 233
Grinker, Bill, 177
Gross, John, 84, 90, 241–242, 297, 453
  illegal contributions fine, 452
  and Pataki vs Cuomo endorsement, 300
Guzman, Pablo, 271

Haiti, 114–133
  adult program for and Regina Giuliani,
  101
  boat people, 110
  interdiction of refugees, 122–123
  treatment of returning refugees,
  119–121
Haitian-American Alliance, 338
Haitian community, animosity toward RG,
  338
Haitian Refugee Center, 114, 117
Hall, Clifford, 393
Hall, Harold, 14–15
Hall, James C., 95
Hall, Jim, 101–102, 234
Hamill, Peter, 247
Hammonds, Marva, 321
Hampton, Lionel, 245
Hanover, Donna (second wife), 4, 5,
  335–403, 412–417
  annulment of marriage to Stanley
  Hanover, 144
  appearance at Madison Avenue shopping
  fair, 417
  and Art Greenwald course, 423
  background of, 110–112
  beginning of relationship to RG,
  113–114
  control of the children, 419
  and Cristyne Lategano, 411, 412
  display of private life with RG in public,
  396
  finances of, 401, 423–426
  Food News & Views job, 282–283, 399,
  401–402, 423

and Fox Television, 282, 401, 420,
    423–424
heating up and cooling with RG in 1999,
    421–423
home at 444 East 86th Street, 241
and *House Beautiful* television series,
    423
influence on RG, 395–396
job at WPIX, 135, 208–210
and Judi Nathan, 439, 440, 464
legal separation announcement and
    being kept out of public life, 439, 462,
    464
and Libby Pataki, 427–428
life at Gracie Mansion, 398, 402–403
marriage ceremony with RG, 146
marriage difficulties with RG, 380,
    411
and Matilda Cuomo, 299–300
mayoral campaign of 1989, 190, 208,
    209, 395
mayoral campaign of 1993, 268–269,
    281–282, 286, 395
move to 86th Street apartment, 136
Parking Violations Bureau (Friedman)
    case, 164–165
and RG as U.S. Attorney for the
    Southern District of New York,
    133–134
and RG's cancer, 437–438
The Vagina Monologues performance,
    434, 438
vacations without RG, 288, 414
Hanover, Stanley, 111–112, 144
Harding, Ray (Liberal Party head), 194,
    195–197, 210, 214
    and Cuomo gubernatorial endorsement
        of 1994, 298, 301
    and Dinkins love letters, 232, 233
    election of 1993, 275
    employment as lobbyist, 447–448, 453,
        468
    passing of campaign garbage in 1989,
        225, 227
    and RG as mayor, 297
Harding, Robert, 447, 448
Harding, Russell, 447
Harris, Jeff, 60–61, 79, 96, 106–107, 112,
    134–135

as RG's deputy on Haiti, 114, 115, 118,
    120, 123–124, 126, 127
Harris, Joyce, 128
Hart, Gary, 188
Hatch, Orrin, 104
Hauer, Jerry, 3
Hawkins, Yusef, 199, 221, 223, 271, 328
Hayes, Bob, 191–192, 246, 314
Haygood, John, 260
Heiskell, Marian, 7
Helmsley, Leona, 1, 161, 450
Henry, Lloyd, 327
Herman, Arnold, 187
Hess, Michael, 337
Hession, Bernadette, 443
Hession, Noeline, 443
Hevesi, Alan, 12, 293, 348, 451, 453, 464
Hibey, Richard, 128
Hickey, Catherine, 383
Hill, Stanley, 294
Hirsch, Charles, 350
Hispanics
    being stopped by NYPD, 334
    Civilian Complain Review Board
        (CCRB), 333
    criticism of Dinkin's not hiring enough,
        249–250
    employment in city positions, 323, 324,
        325
    initial appointments of by RG in 1994,
        292
    and RG's 1989 election, 199, 230–231
    See also Race
Hobgood, Harlan, 127–128
Hoffenberg, Steve, 242–243
Hoffman, Steve, 53, 54
Hogan, Frank, 28
Holbrooke, Brad, 208–210, 283
Holtzman, Elizabeth, 133, 273
Holzmann, Larry, 127
Homeless, 189, 313–321
    election of 1989, 190–192, 211
    plan of late 1993, 246–247
Hooper, Michael, 129–130
Hoover, J. Edgar, 1
Hopkins, Mary Ann, 2
Horkovich, Bob, 243
Horowitz, Craig, 412–413
Horton, Ray, 244, 375

Hotel tax, 10–11
Howard, Elston, 379
Howe, Irving, 311
Hughes, Charlie, 325, 326, 373–375, 455
Hunter, Karen, 386
Hynes, Joe, 278, 332

Ickes, Howard, 237, 280
Immigration and Naturalization Service,
    116, 121, 125, 130, 132
I'm Not Done Yet (Koch), 179
Impelliteri, Vincent, 28, 270
Imus, Don, 304
Independent Budget Office, 313
Inner Circle revue and dinner, 415, 434,
    443
Innis, Roy, 262, 274
Inside Edition, 396
Insider trading prosecutions, 157–159,
    171–172
Institute for Puerto Rican Policy, 61, 249
International Lawyers Committee on
    Human Rights, 129
International Monetary Fund and aid to
    Haiti, 118
In the Name of the Law (Puccio), 81
Irish and amnesty for immigrants as issue
    in 1989 election, 239
Italian Charities of America, Inc., 35, 50
Italy, 19

Jackson, Jesse, 223
Jaffe, Joe, 80, 81, 87, 88–89
Javits, Jacob, 133
Jefferies, Boyd, 158
Jensen, D. Lowell, 108–109
Jewish Press, 276–277
Jews
    ad in Yiddish newspaper Algemeiner
        Journal, 223
    anti-Semitism of Manhattan College
        students, 49
    Crown Heights incident, 247–248
    and Garden City, 29
    and Jackie Mason, 224–225
    and Jitu Weusi, 225–226
    liaison to Orthodox Jewish community,
        292
    and North Bellmore, 32

voting polls relative to in 1989 election,
    207
Job Centers, 317, 318
John Birch Society, 51
Johnson, Dante, 333, 337
Johnson, Lyndon, 51, 466
Jones, Barbara, 148, 154
Jones, Glenda, 169
Jones, Lee, 175, 176, 179–180, 342
Jones, Michael, 332–333, 337
Jones, William, 267–268, 269
Julian, Mike, 359, 365
Juste, Jean, 114

Kalikow, Peter, 206, 233, 237
Kaplan, Bruce, 111
Kappner, Augusta, 102, 234–235
Karmon, Andrew, 335
Kasirer, Suri, 448–449, 453
Kauffman, Bill, 460
Keating, Kenneth, 51
Kefauver, Estes, 90
Kelling, George, 244, 345
Kelly, Clarence, 92
Kelly, Ray, 260, 352, 364
Kennedy, Jackie, 52
Kennedy, John Fitzgerald, 36, 52, 92, 132,
    145, 200
Kennedy, John F. Jr., 256
Kennedy, Robert, 51, 54, 200
Kennedy, Robert Jr., 458
Kerik, Bernie, 454
Kessner, Thomas, 327
Kieves, Larry, 184
King, Evelyn, 287
King, Larry, 94
Klein, George, 7, 210
Klein, Joe, 192
Knapp, Whitman, 163
Knapp Commission, 74–76, 77, 78, 261
Koch, Ed (NYC mayor, 1977–1989), 221,
    286
    and Bensonhurst murder of 1989,
        199–200
    comments about Jesse Jackson, 193
    and Cortines final interview, 369,
        375
    and Donald Manes, 161
    election in 1981, 266

endorsement of RG in 1993, 256,
    278–279
final break with RG, 454
homosexual investigation of, 175–188
1989 election, 71, 200, 239, 270
and Podell case, 86–87
relationship to blacks, 291–292, 327
renewal of Times Square, 7
stroke of 1987, 177–178, 179
switch to the right during Reagan years,
    311
and Yusef Hawkins murder, 328
Koeppel, William, 405, 450, 456
Kojak (television series), 76
Kramer, Ann, 243
Kramer, Barry, 49
Kramer, Larry, 175, 176, 179, 180, 181, 182,
    184, 185, 244
Kramer, Marcia, 175, 179, 382
Kreiger, Al, 70
Kuriansky, Ed, 457
Kurtz, Howard, 192
Kurzban, Ira, 131

Lachman, Abe, 297, 301
La Guardia, Fiorello, 12, 190, 239, 265, 311,
    327
Langelia, Gennaro "Gerry Lang," 150
Langhan, Joe, 282
Laroche, Victor, 120
La Rossa, James, 88, 89
Lategano, Cristyne, 5, 364, 385, 442, 450
    announcement of her former affair with
        RG, 439
    appointment as Convention & Visitors
        Bureau head, 426–427
    cooling of relationship to RG, 420–423
    and Crew's letter to the *Times*, 377
    denial of sexual relationship with RG,
        462
    as female press aide in 1993 election,
        272, 404–405
    financial benefits to, 409, 426
    marriage of in February, 2000, 427
    as press secretary, 405
    relationship with RG, 5, 380, 409–417
Lauder, Ronald (1989 mayoral primary
    opponent), 199, 201–203

debate with RG, 210
and defeat in 1989 election, 211
negative ads against RG, 203, 207, 212
Laurino, Maria, 145
L.A. Weekly and Koch article, 186, 188
Lawler, Andy, 185
Lawrence, David, 183, 184, 253, 256–257,
    279–281
Lazar, Michael, 162–163
Lazio, Rick, 462
Leach, Robin, 282
Lear, Norman, 142
Léger, Georges, 115, 116, 123, 125, 128
Leonetti, Philip, 155
Letterman, David, 397
Leuci, Bob, 60–61, 77–84, 125, 340
Levi, Carlo, 19
Levi, Edward, 91, 92
Levien, Doug, 57
Levine, Andrew, 351
Levine, Dennis, 157–158
Levine, Randy, 11, 170, 239, 297, 300–301,
    373, 392
    baseball-related employment after
        leaving RG, 451–452, 453
    and Cuker, 444
    traveling with RG, 420
Levitt, Lenny, 175, 179, 186, 225, 354
Levy, Harold, 393, 394
Lewittes, Joel, 100
Lewittes, Michael, 406, 409
Lhota, Joe, 3, 297
Liberal Party, 193–197, 300, 301–302, 448
Libert, Jack, 213–214, 215, 217–218, 253
Lindau, Alfred, 14
Lindenauer, Geoffrey, 162–163
Lindsay, John V. (NYC mayor, 1966–1973),
    60, 74, 239, 266
    comparison to RG, 200, 354
    race relations, 327
    support of by Liberal Party in 1965 and
        1969, 194, 265
    West End mistress of, 441
Lipp, Joan, 30
Little, Ed, 170–171, 216–217
Livermore, Kathy, 44, 51–52, 145, 189
Livoti, Anthony, 25, 35
Livoti, Frank, 329–330

LoCicero, John, 175
Lombardi, Tony, 178–189, 239, 253
    activity in 1989 mayoral campaign, 227,
        228–229
    attacks on D'Amato, 213–215
    continued contact with RG, 214–215
    election of 1993, 279
London, Herb, 201, 299, 304
London, Rusty Kent, 168
Long, Mike, 202–203, 254
Long Island Rail Road, 30, 36, 48
Los Angeles Times and Koch and RG, 256
Louima, Abner, 328
Lubavitcher Jews and Crown Heights
    incident, 247–248
Lubin, Michael, 107–110
Lumet, Sidney, 78, 415
Lynbrook Public High School, 31–32, 40,
    404
Lynch, Bill, 186, 193, 223–224, 225,
    227–228
    and Dinkins love letters, 231, 233
    election of 1993, 278
Lynn, Chris, 369
Lyon, Chris, 226, 232–233, 236–237

Mack, Fred, 256
Mack, Walter, 148
MacMahon, Lloyd F., 67–70, 73, 92
    and Aminex Resources Corp., 99–100
    and Nazi (Berger) incident, 205
    support for RG as associate deputy
        attorney general, 91
    wake for Harold Giuliani, 106
Mafia, "Commission" Case, 146, 150–156
Maldonado, Jose, 454
Malin, Joan, 295–296, 313, 315, 316
Maloney, Andy, 148–149, 155, 279
Maltese, Serph, 251
Mandelino, Elizabeth, 24, 55, 59
Mandelino, Michael, 59
Mandelino, Philomena, 23
Manes, Donald, 161–165, 450
Manhattan College, 40, 48–51
Manhattan Institute, 245
Man of Honor, A (Bonanno), 146, 150, 155
Maple, Jack, 343, 344, 347, 353, 405
Marchi, John, 318

Marcos, Imelda, 1, 161
Margiotta, Joe, 133, 137, 138
Margolick, David, 271
Marin, Frank, 196
Marino, Ralph, 278, 299
Mariotta, John, 166, 170
Mark Rich & Co., 142
Martin, John, 134, 137, 147, 154, 173
Martinez, Eddie, 177
Marymount Manhattan College, 102, 301,
    320, 419, 441
Mason, Jackie, 224–225
Mastro, Randy, 253
    as lobbyist, 449–450, 453, 468
    patronage charges against RG, 453
    as RG's chief of staff, 292, 296
Maximus, 451, 453
May, Willie, 245
McAvoy, Annemarie, 417
McAvoy, Jack, 178, 180
McCaffrey, Barry, 314
McCall, Carl, 326, 348
McCalla, Jocelyn, 338
McCarthy, Joseph, 149
McConnell, Robert, 105
McDonald, Edward A., 147
McDonnell Douglas case, 107–110
McFarlane, Rodger, 176, 244
McGuire, Jim, 215–220, 253
McGuire, Phil, 342
McKay, James, 167–169, 170
McKechnie, Diane McGrath, 454
McKenna, Chris, 53–54
McKinley, James, 341
McLaughlin, Marty, 233–234
McLean, Richard P., 40
McLoughlin, Frank, 358–359
McManus, Therese, 234
Mederis, "Wild Bill," 216
Meese, Edwin III, 1, 166, 167, 168, 170, 213
Meet the Press, 466–467
Mendelson, George, 107–110
Merli, Joe and Lina, 63–65, 326
Merli, John, 64
Messinger, Ruth, 326, 348, 366, 461
    American Jewish Congress luncheon,
        373
    and Crew, 388

education campaign ad, 376–377
Metropolitan Opera, 35, 125
Metropolitan Republican Club, 190
Metropolitan Transit Authority
crime strategies for, 345
and graffiti and scratchitti, 365
Michael Hayes (television series), 1
Michael's Restaurant, 400
Mika, Richie, 59
Milken, Lowell, 211, 212
Milken, Michael, 1, 171–172, 211, 212
Millard, Charles, 8
Miller, Fred, 358–359
Miller, John, 227, 343
feud with RG, 407–408
and Lategano, 405, 406–407, 409
Minnelli, Liza, 251
Mirra, Anthony, 70
Mitchell, Andrea, 463
Mitchell, John, 90
Model Cities Administration, 76–77
Modugno, Thomas, 461
Molinari, Guy, 11, 186, 231, 260, 269, 304, 451, 454
and Board of Education appointments, 368, 370
D'Amato's courting of in 1993, 251
endorsement of RG in 1989 mayoral election, 202
and Occhipinti case, 256–259
Molinaro, Jim, 251
Mollen, Milt, 276
Montuoro, Joseph, 401
Moore, Jackie, 235
Morales, Pedro, 76
Morgenthau, Robert, 74
Moriarty, James, 143
Morning, John, 326
Morra, Carmine, 59–60
Morvillo, Bob, 77, 78–79
Moss, Sarah and Jim, 84
Moynihan, Patrick (US Senator, 1977–2001), 135, 166, 185, 239, 277
decision to not run in 2000, 381, 458
Mr. Sorley's Old Ale House, 53
MTV and Times Square, 7
Mukasey, Mike, 82–83, 97, 239
Mulheren, John, 172
Mullen, Francis, 139

Municipal Assistance Corporation (MAC), 298–299, 300
Murder, 341–342, 350–355
Murdoch, Rupert, 272, 424
Murphy, Richard, 405
Myerson, Bess, 1, 159–160, 179, 183, 186, 187, 224

Nachman, Jerry, 204–205, 206, 214, 233–234, 237
Nader, Ralph, 93
Nagourney, Adam, 203, 236
Nard, Jack A., 104
Nathan, Bruce, 431
Nathan, Judith, 428–434, 436, 441, 468
appearance at emergency command center on Millenium eve, 4, 434
first Official Mayoral Date with RG, 440
and RG's possible Senate campaign, 464–465
Nathan, Richard, 175–188
National Coalition for Haitian Rights, 338
National Conference of Catholic Bishops, 200
National Law Journal
and RG's securities prosecutions, 172
and RG's use of office for political career, 148
National Motor Vehicle Title Information System, 357
National Stolen Auto Part Information System, 357
Nation of Islam, 290
Nazi (Berger) incident, 204–208
Nemeroff, Robert, 97
Ness, Eliot, 150
Neuberger, Fred, 166
New 42nd Street, 8
Newfield, Jack, 175, 179, 197, 236, 416, 459
Newsday, 271, 281, 297
crime rate, 354–355
and Dinkins contribution to Committee to Honor Black Heroes, 225
and Dinkins stock ownings, 237–238
and Donna Hanover, 396
and Marcos case, 161
questions submitted to candidates, 272
and RG's claim of dreaming up "Commission" case, 154

and RG's cutting of school budgets, 376
Wall Street Three, 159
Newsweek and Jackie Mason's racist
  comments about Dinkins, 224
New Victory Theater, 9
New Year's eve 2000 celebration, 1–5
New York City
  cleanliness of, 11
  plummeting of crime in, 2
  registration changes between
    1989–1993, 266
New York City Administration for
  Children's Services, 324
New York City Board of Education,
  289–290
  budget cuts, 309–310
  hiring of Crew, 367
New York City Campaign Finance Board,
  261–262, 445, 452
New York City Children's Court, 13
New York City Civilian Complaint Review
  Board (CCRB), 333
New York City Conflict of Interest Board,
  346–347
New York City Convention and Visitors
  Bureau, 5, 426, 442
New York City Cultural Affairs
  Commission, 160
New York City Department for the Aging,
  309, 324
New York City Department of Citywide
  Administrative Services (DCAS), 324
New York City Department of Homeless
  Services (DHC), 295–296
  cuts in budget of, 313–314
  cuts in Medicaid benefits, 318–319
  drug treatment programs, 314
  emergency shelter eligibility standards
    enforcement, 315–316
  food stamps, 318
  police sweeps of homeless, 315
  students, 318
  Work Employment Program, 319, 320,
    321
  workfare, 294, 316–317, 318
New York City Department of
  Investigations, 280, 405
New York City Equal Employment
  Practices Commission (EEPC), 325

New York City Film and Theatre Advisory
  Committee, 443
New York City Fire Department, 289–290,
  324
New York City Health & Hospitals
  Corporation (HHC), 180, 289–290,
  309
New York City Housing Authority, 323
New York City Housing Development
  Corporation (HDC), 448
New York City Human Resources
  Administration (HRA), 289–290,
  320–323, 324, 451, 453
New York City Human Rights
  Commission, 191
New York City Juvenile Justice, 322, 324
New York City Office of Collective
  Bargaining, 300
New York City Office of Emergency
  Management, 3
New York City Parking Violations Bureau
  (PVB), 162–163
New York City Planning Commission, 297
New York City Taxi & Limousine
  Commission, 324, 369, 454
New York City Trade Waste Commission,
  449
New York City Youth Corps, 191
New York City Youth Services, 309
New York Civil Liberties Union, 328, 334
New York magazine, 210, 369
  the death penalty, 192
  and Dinkins cable stock holdings, 238
  and Donna Hanover as RG's advisor,
    395
  and Horowitz article on Lategano,
    412–413
  "Only Good Thing" ad, 10
  and RG and Bratton's "ending of crime
    as we know it," 346
  and RG's taking credit, 161
New York Police Department
  and Abner Louima, 328
  and Alton Fitzgerald White, 5
  and Amadou Diallo, 328, 330–331, 332
  and Anthony Baez, 329–330
  appointment of Bill Bratton, 289
  benefit of doubt to police, 291
  black personnel, 323

Civilian Complaint Review Board
(CCRB), 333–334
Compstat meetings, 344, 347, 354
hiring of new recruits, 289
increase of size of, 342
narcotics undercover operations,
337–338
Nation of Islam incident of 1994,
290–291
Operation Juggernaut, 347
and Patrick Dorismond, 335–339
plans originating with the department
rather than mayor's office, 343
police corruption revelations begun in
1968, 74–77
police misconduct, 5, 328–339
police shooting statistics, 335
refusal to hold hearing on crime
statistics, 348
replacement of Bratton with Safir,
346–347
and RG's family's history of
involvement with, 45, 61, 469(n2)
school security, 369, 382
September 1992 rally and riot at City
Hall, 259–263
shooting of seventeen-year-old boy in
1994, 291
Special Investigating Unit (SIU), 78, 80
Street Crime Unit (SCU), 331–332
sweeps of homeless, 315
See also Crime; Crime rate statistics
New York Post
abortion in 1992, 197–198
and attack on Crew, 388
and Cindy Ng, 229
criticism of RG and Safir for releasing
confidential records of Dorismond,
336–337
and Dinkins love letters, 233–234
drafting Koch for governor in 1982, 342
Forum on AIDS, 175, 177
homeless plan of 1993, 247
and Jitu Weusi and anti-Semitism,
225–226
and Koch's purported homosexuality,
177
"low blows" in 1989 campaign, 235–236

and Nathan-RG affair, 437, 465
Nazi (Berger) story, 204–206, 208
and Patrick Dorismond, 339
and Phil Thompson scandal, 227
and RG's leaking of negative stories to,
388
and RG's relationship to family, 288
support of RG through 1993 campaign
and first term, 272
New York Public Interest Research Group,
457
New York State Organized Crime Task
Force, 150
New York Times
backing of Koch for mayor despite
homicide rate increases, 342
and Butterfield story on crime, 366
and Colombo investigation, 147, 151
conflict between RG and D'Amato in
1989, 211
and Crew threat to quit over vouchers,
386
crime rate stories, 341, 342, 343, 348,
360
criticism of RG's stiff campaign style in
1989, 210
and Cuker and RG, 447
and D'Amato staff using "fascist" slur to
advantage, 254
and Donna Hanover interviews, 414, 420
election of 1993, 249, 267, 271, 285, 286
and Haiti, 129–130
and Jackie Mason and 1989 campaign,
225
and Lategano's appointment as head of
CVB, 426
lobbying during RG's tenure, 449
and Molinari, 251, 252
negative stories passed by 1989 RG
campaign, 227
New Year's eve 2000 command center, 5
and Podell, 88
review of Donna Hanover's 1993
election ad, 268–269
and RG's assessment of problems facing
Southern District, 139
and RG's backing of Cuomo in 1994, 302
and RG's campaign against Cortines, 369

and RG's participation in 1992 NYPD
    riot, 261, 263
and RG's philosophical commitment
    relative to HRA, 322
and RG's replacement as U.S. Attorney
    General Southern District, 213
and RG's U.S. Attorney legacy, 173
savings and police force, 289
school system, 369, 377, 385, 387, 391,
    392, 393
Senate seat in 1988, 166, 186
Times Square, 7, 8, 9
and Washington being stopped by police,
    334
welfare and homeless cuts, 317
New York Times Magazine
    cutting welfare as social elixir, 317–318
    and Lategano criticisms, 422–423
    and RG and "Commission" case, 154
New York University Law School, 52–55
New York Yankees. See Yankees, New York
Ng, Cindy, 229, 230, 232
Nicholson, Joe, 175, 177, 178
Night Falls on Manhattan (motion
    picture), 415
Nightline and "Commission" indictment
    interview, 152
Nixon, Richard, 90
NJN television station, 401
Nofziger, Lyn, 166, 167
Noriega, Manuel, 203
Normal Heart, The (Kramer), 176
Novoa, Joe, 82
NYC 2000 apparatus, 5

Obermaier, Otto, 172, 211, 212, 218, 253,
    258, 279
O'Brien, Gerry, 255
O'Brien, John, 265, 285
Occhipinti, Joe, 256–259
O'Connor, Cardinal John, 188, 246, 382,
    437, 461
Office of Professional Responsibility, 104,
    109
    and Occhipinti affair, 257
O'Hare, Joseph, 452
O'Leary , Brother Jack, 31, 34, 37–41, 56,
    65–66, 144

O'Neill, Tip, 86
Operation Juggernaut, 347
Opportunity America, 451
Orena, Vic, 156
Ormento, John (Big John), 70
Ortado, Michael, 32
Ortaldo, Bartolo, 32
Owens, Major, 193

Pancio, Carmine, 69–70
Paoli, Lillian. See Barrios-Paoli, Lillian
Paper, The (motion picture), 399, 414
Papir, Manny, 410
Parental Choice Program, 384
Parking Violations Bureau (Friedman) case,
    162–165
Parsons, Dick, 400, 424
Parsons, Richard, 95, 103
Parver, Jane, 138
Pataki, George (NY Governor, 1995-), 9,
    278, 311, 438, 457
    budget cuts in 1995, 308–309
    campaign vs Cuomo and RG, 299, 300,
        301, 302, 304–305
    changes in homeless policy, 314, 315
    third term candidacy, 462
Pataki, Libby, 427–428, 438
Patronage, political, 446
Patterson, Belknap & Webb, 64, 95–101
PBA, 261–262, 290
Pedowitz, Larry, 140
People and Donna Hanover, 395
People v. Harold Giuliani indicted as
    Joseph Starrett, 14–17
People vs. Larry Flynt, The (motion
    picture), 414
Perl, William, 69
Perlmutter, Daniel, 140–141
Persico, Carmine "the Snake," 147–148,
    150, 154, 156
Peruggi, Regina (first wife), 44, 54, 57, 283,
    441
    annulment of marriage with RG,
        143–145
    Center for Continuing Education and
        Mental Health, 95
    CUNY's York College, 95
    formal ending of relationship, 114

Four Seasons authors' affair, 419
marriage and life with RG, 71–72
marriage troubles with RG, 84, 96,
    101–102
Marymount Manhattan College, 102,
    301, 320, 419, 441
move with RG to 83rd Street apartment,
    83
speaking of annulment in 1989 election,
    234, 235–236
Washington, D.C. Prospect House
    apartment living style, 94–95
Peruggi, Richard and Rita Marie, 44, 235
Peruggi, Salvatore, 44
Petrides, Mike, 368
Phillips, William, 75, 340
Phi Ro Pi fraternity, 51
Piccoli, Leonard, 453–454
Pinkett, Mary, 260
Placa, Alan, 35, 51, 398, 460
    annulment of marriage to Regina
        Peruggi, 143–144
Podell, Bertram, 85–90, 124, 164, 447
Podemo, Joseph, 16
Poitier, Sidney, 142
Police Benevolent Association, 257
Police Department. See New York Police
    Department
Polonetsky, Jules, 454, 459
Pope John Paul II and Haiti, 129
Pornography, restriction of, 9–10
Powell, Michael, 271
Power, Pasta, and Politics (D'Amato),
    213–214
Powers, Bill, 255, 300, 304
Powers, Kathleen, 373
Powers, Peter, 83, 145, 186, 299, 344, 397
    and Bishop Loughlin High School, 35
    and Cindy Ng, 229
    and Cuker, 444
    and Cuomo vs Pataki endorsement, 300
    and Dinkins love letters, 232, 235–236
    and Lategano, 404, 405, 409, 411, 412
    and Manhattan College, 50
    as mayoral aid, 297
    mayoral campaign of 1989, 210, 225
    mayoral campaign of 1993, 281
    return to private life, 442–443, 450, 451

and RG's early political aspirations, 135
and Sandra Feldman, 373
Preeg, Ernest, 116, 117, 118, 119, 122, 124,
    125, 128
Presidential Task Force on the
    Administration of Justice, 167
Pressman, Gabe, 192
Prince of the City (book), 78
Prince of the City (motion picture), 77–78,
    79, 82, 415
Prizzi's Honor (motion picture), 365
Project Read program, 376
Prosecutors, The (Stewart), 107, 135
Prostate cancer
    and Alan Hevesi and Joe Torre, 464, 466
    and Harold Giuliani, 63, 65, 104
    and RG, 435–436, 464, 466
Prudential and Times Square, 7–8
Public Integrity Division, 218
Puccio, Thomas, 80, 81, 137, 154, 163
Purdom, Todd, 268

Quadrangle (magazine), 51
Quality of life initiative by NYPD, 315
Quinn, John, 58

Race, 191, 291–293, 322–323, 325–327
    and Dyson's remarks in 1994, 293
    election of 1993, 265–267, 269, 270
    preparations for 1993 mayoral
        candidacy, 248, 249–250
    See also Blacks; Hispanics
Racketeer Influenced and Corrupt
    Organizations Act of 1970 (RICO),
    146, 154, 163
Radio Television News Directors'
    Association, 237
Ragtime (Broadway musical), 5
Rangel, Charlie, 326
Rastelli, Rusty, 151, 154
Ratner, Bruce, 8, 9
Rawlings baseball factory, 123–124
RCA Records and Times Square, 7
Reagan, Ronald, 63, 103, 213, 449, 459
    appointment as U.S. Attorney for the
        Southern District of New York, 135
    Cuban refugees, 132
    Haiti, 117–118

Regan, Ned, 300
Reiter, Fran, 196, 399, 426, 442, 448, 453
Rendell, Ed, 297, 308
Republican Party
  mayoral politics in New York City,
    265–266
  reshaping of himself for race with
    Clinton, 458–459
  and RG's affiliation with, 103
  and RG's circle of top aides, 296–297
  strength of in New York City in 1989,
    194
Resto, Steven, 330
Reynolds, James, 134
Rice, Norman, 308
Rickman, Herb, 183–184, 186
Rigas, Gregory, 455
Rizzo, Frank, 93–94
Rizzo, Judith, 367, 384, 390
Robbins, Tom, 175
Roberts, Sam, 263
Robinson, Jackie, 23, 325, 379, 422
Robinson, Sugar Ray, 27
Roche, Collen, 419
Rockefeller, Nelson, 145
Roditi, Doris, 351
Rodney, Vladimir, 338
Romano, Benito, 205, 211, 214, 217–218,
    253
Roosevelt, Franklin, 265
Rose, Alex, 193
Rose, Joe, 296, 406, 407, 409
Rosenbaum, Norman, 276
Rosenbaum, Yankel, 247, 268, 276, 332
Rosenberg espionage case, 69
Rosenblatt, Marty, 413
Rosner, Edmund, 78–79, 82
Rosner, John, 70
Ross, Barbara, 229
Rothenberg, David, 175
Rubenstein, Howard, 420, 437, 450–451
Rudin, Leo, 429
Rufino, Pat, 84, 235
Russell, Boyce, 60
Russert, Tim, 466
Russianoff, Gene, 452, 457

S & A Concrete, 152

Sabini, John, 72
Sadownick, Doug, 175
Safir, Adam, 421
Safir, Howard, 92, 346, 347, 419
  auto-theft decline, 356
  and Baez brutality case, 329–330
  Civilian Complaint Review Board
    (CCRB), 334
  and Diallo case, 331
  and Dorismond case, 336–337, 339
  narcotic undercover operations, 337–338
  "quality of life enforcement options"
    against homeless, 315
Sagor, Elliot, 78–79
Salerno, "Fat Tony," 1, 75, 151, 153–154,
    155
Sampson, Rana, 366
Sanders, Steve, 392
Sansaricq, Bernard, 123–124, 126, 338–339
Sansaricq, Gregory, 338
Sant, John, 107, 109
Sarant, George, 456
Saurino, Frances, 259
Savage, Richard, 332
Savarese, John, 140
Scalia, Antonin, 92
"Scans", Mickey, 46
Scarpa, Greg, 58
Schanberg, Sydney, 253, 369
Schermerhorn, Richard, 213
Schmitt, Edward, 15
Schmults, Edward, 104, 135
Schneider, George, 35, 36
Schonfeld, Reese, 282, 399–401
Schools Choice Scholarship Program, 384
School system, 367–394, 467
  budget cuts in, 376
  "Cool Schools" program, 399
  social promotions, 393–394
  test scores, 376, 382, 389, 394
  vouchers, 371, 382–388, 393
Schriefer, Russ, 207
Schulman, Claire, 386, 454
Schumer, Chuck, 4
Schwartz, Bart, 85, 140, 141
Schwartz, Bill, 163
Schwartz, Richard, 296, 322, 451
Schwartz, Tony, 169

Schwartzman, Paul, 36, 145, 249
Scoppetta, Nicholas, 78–79
Scuderi, Marie and Frank, 43, 45
Scuderi, Robert (cousin), 61
Securities and Exchange Commission, 157
Segarra, Ninfa, 292, 296, 322, 368
Seifman, David, 235–236, 435
Selig, Bud, 451
Senft, Michael, 142
Sentinel Government Securities, 142
Serafin, Kim, 412
Serpcio, Frank, 74
Sexton, Brendan, 2
Seymour, Whitney North, 73, 74, 75, 77
Shafran, Lester, 162–163
Shaheen, Mike, 109, 112
Shanley, Anthony, 36
Shapp, Milton, 93
Shargel, Gerald, 87, 88
Sharpton, Al, 199, 200, 226, 290–291, 326
Sheehy, Gail, 159
Sheer, Tom, 154
Sheindlin, Gerald, 329
Sherwin, James T., 172
Sidewalk cleanliness, 10
Siegel, Fred, 290
Siegel, Martin, 158, 159
Siegel, Norman, 328
Silver, Ron, 2
Silver, Sheldon, 393
Simon, Stanley, 163, 165, 166, 170
Simon's noodle house, 420
Sinatra, Frank, 251
Sing Sing Prison and Harold Giuliani,
    16–17
60 Minutes, 146
Slater, Donald, 48
Slotnik, Barry, 204, 206
Smith, Ada, 327
Smith, Kathleen, 112, 234
Smith, William French, 103–104, 116, 131,
    135, 139, 151–152, 449
Solerwitz, Jack, 218
Somma, Nicholas "Doc," 55, 56
Sound Beach, 43–45
Spellman, Eugene, 129–130
Spence, Harry, 375, 376, 390
Spielman, Valentine, 15

Spitzer, Eliot, 334
Sprizzo, John, 172
Squeegees, 2, 364–365
Stainback, Sheila, 209
Stanchi, Edward (cousin), 61
Stanchi, Florence, 60
Stanchi, Ralph Jr., 59–60, 61
Stanchi, Ralph Sr., 59, 60, 61
Stanchi, Vincenzo (maternal great
    grandfather), 18, 23
St. Anne's Catholic Elementary School, 30
Stapleton, Ruth, 414
Starr, Kenneth, 131
Starrett, Joseph. See Giuliani, Harold
Staten Island
    closing of landfill on, 11
    secession of issue in 1993, 251–252, 275
Staten Island Advance and Occhipinti case,
    257, 259
Stein, Andrew, 230, 251, 255
Steinbrenner, George, 450, 451
Steinfeld, Allan, 406
Steisel, Norman, 450
Stern, Henry, 185, 244, 296
Stern, Robert A.M., 7–8
Stewart, Charles, 150
Stewart, James, 107, 108
St. Francis of Assisi Catholic Elementary
    School, 22
Stish, Tom, 432
Stockton, Peter, 105
Stone, Oliver, 157
Stone, Roger, 193, 194
St. Patrick's Day Parade, 245–246
Straight, Candy, 401
Stutman, Robert, 148
Sullivan, Barry, 6
Sulzberger, Arthur Jr., 8
Sun Sentinel, 113
Supreme Court and Haitian detention
    camps, 131–132
Sutton, Percy, 279
Syzbala, Renee, 96, 97, 115, 116, 124, 126,
    133, 134

Tabor, Timothy, 158, 159
Tatum, Bill, 175, 179, 186
Taylor, Mary Gaye, 3

Teeter, Robert, 202
Teitelbaum, Bruce, 292, 409, 412, 448–449, 468
Tendy, William, 68, 70
Terranova, Albert, 98–99
Terwilliger, George, 258
Thaivu, Sam and Ellie, 124
Thompson, Bill, 371
Thompson, Phil, 227
Thompson, Robert, 68–69
Thornburgh, Richard, 94, 104–105, 211, 257
Tice, Jack, 461
Time magazine and Bratton cover, 346, 354
Times Square
    New Year's eve 2000, 1
    renewal of, 2, 6–10
    Robert Stern plan, 7–8
Times Square Business Improvement District (BID), 2, 8, 9, 10
Time Warner, 400, 424
Timoney, John, 343, 344, 346
Tishman Urban Development Corporation, 9
Today show, and RG's claim regarding graffiti, 365
Tontons Macoutes, 118, 123–124, 127
Torre, Joe, 466
Tortorello, Anthony, 58
Towers Financial, 242
Town & Country and interview with Donna Hanover, 403
Traub, Jim, 422
Travis, Jeremy, 366
Turnaround (Bratton), 343
Turner, Jason, 321, 322, 451
Turner, Shelton, 85, 86
TV Food Network (TVFN), 399–401, 425
Tyler, Harold "Ace," 91–92, 93, 94, 104
    and Donna Hanover, 135
    and Marcos case, 161
    and Myerson case, 159–161
    and Patterson, Belknap & Webb, 95–96, 100–101
    and Regina Giuliani, 95, 96
    and RG's family criminal history, 106
    and RG's political affiliations, 103
    and Tabor, Wigton, Freeman arrests, 159

United Federation of Teachers (UFT), 373, 375, 384
United Nations High Commissioner for Refugees and Haiti's treatment of returning refugees, 121
U.S. Conference of Mayors, 308
U.S. Marshals Service, 92
U.S. v. U.S. Telephone & Paul A. Brown, 74
Urban League's Student Transfer Education Program, 29
Urgenson, Larry, 253

Vacco, Dennis, 450
Vallone, Peter, 246, 293, 337, 348
Vanity Fair
    corruption by public officials, 163
    insider trading scandal, 159
    and Lategano-RG relationship, 380, 415–416, 440
Van Meter, Jonathan, 417
Velella, Guy, 202, 251, 255, 453
Velella, Vincent, 255
Viacom and Times Square, 7
Victory 93, 255, 305
Victory Theater, 8
Vidal, Raquel, 230, 231–232, 236–237, 238
Vidal, Sara, 230–231, 238
Vidicksis, Florence Stanchi, 61
Viguerie, Richard, 460
Village Gate, 224
Village Voice, 210
    and Dinkins cable stock issue, 237–238
    and Dinkins love letters, 234
    and Jackie Mason, 224
    and Koch and AIDS policy, 186–187, 188
    marriage to Regina, 145
    and Regina Peruggi speaking of annulment in 1989 election, 235–236
    and Velella family and Genovese family, 255
Vincent's Restaurant, 24, 25–27, 30, 31, 47, 48, 53
Visconti, Assunta (cousin), 21, 33, 55
Visconti, Fanny D'Avanzo (maternal aunt), 21, 32
Visconti, Frederick (cousin), 21
Visconti, John (Sylvester), 21, 32–33, 469(n4)

Voelker, Anthony, 359–360
Vogue and interview with Hanover, 417
Von Essen, Tom, 454

Wade, Richard, 448
Wagner, Mary, 104
Wagner, Robert, 270
Wagner, Robert Jr., 244, 286, 368
Waldman, Jay, 169
Walker, Jimmy, 265
Wallach, E. Robert, 167–168, 169–170, 172,
   212
Wall Street (motion picture), 157
Wall Street Journal
   insider trading cases, 172
   non-support of RG in 1989, 239
   and Patterson Belknap, 97
   and Podell bribery case, 86
Wall Street Three, 159
Walsh, Jim, 307
Washington, Rudy, 322, 334–335
Washington Post
   ad in Yiddish newspaper during 1989
      election, 223
   and McDonnell Douglas case, 108, 109
   and RG as coalition mayor, 306
   and RG's record on minorities, 326
Washington Times and Dinkins love
      letters, 236
Waste Management (WM), 449–450
Watergate, 92
Webster, William, 139, 151–152, 153
Wedtech Corporation, 166–171
Weiss, Baruch, 169
Weld, William T., 170, 245
Welfare recipients cuts, 2, 11, 316–317,
   321–322
Wells, Ted, 169
Wertheimer, Fred, 109
West, Togo, 92, 93
Westwind (Coast Guard cutter in Haiti),
   121–122, 124
Weusi, Jiti, 225–226
White & Case law firm, 203–204, 220, 241

White, Alton Fitzgerald, 5
White, Jimmy, 27, 90
White, Mary Jo, 329
"White collar crime committee," 93
Whitman, Christie, 401
Wigton, Richard, 158, 159
Williams, Treat, 79
Wilpon, Fred, 451
Wilson, Gary, 432–433
Wilson, Howard, 142, 457
Winick, Bruce, 132
WNYC radio station, 310
Wolf, Dan, 179, 184–185
Woodside, Queens, 72
Work Employment Program (WEP), 319,
   320, 321
Workfare, 316–317
World AIDS Day, 381
World Trade Center, 5
WPIX and accusations of bias over
      Hanover's employment there during
      1989 mayoral campaign, 208–209, 282

Yankees, New York, 22–23, 325, 379, 404
   and Harold Giuliani as fan, 25–26
   and Levine, 451
   and RG's watching of, 378, 413, 419
Yankee Stadium and plan to build new,
      305, 381–382, 450
Yglesias, Linda, 416
Young, Denny, 137, 148, 169, 220, 239, 241,
   259, 438, 468
   aide to RG as mayor, 297, 344
   and Judi Nathan, 433–434
   and Lategano, 406, 407
Young, Louisa, 433–434
Younger, Irving, 67

Zacharioudakis, Manos, 429–430, 431, 432,
   433, 435
Zinsmeister, Karl, 460
Zornow, David, 140, 163, 205
Zuckerman, Mort, 272, 452